1295 18.50

FAMILY INTERACTION

FAMILY INTERACTION

RALPH H. TURNER

UNIVERSITY OF CALIFORNIA, LOS ANGELES

JOHN WILEY & SONS, INC.

NEW YORK • LONDON • SYDNEY • TORONTO

10 9 8 7 6 5 4 3

Library of Congress Catalog Card Number: 71-118627

ISBN 0-471-89300-5

Printed in the United States of America

To Christine

and

Cheryl and Lowell

for their unflagging love

PREFACE

The approach and many of the ideas in this book evolved during a decade and a half of teaching a course in the sociology of the family. The book's content reflects greater interest in understanding the internal processes of individual families and less interest in comparing a prototypical middle-class American family with prototypes from other eras and other nations than many textbooks for such courses. The course I developed and now offer in this volume was thoroughly and even partisanly sociological, but I belong to a breed of sociologists to whom small groups and social individuals are figure and society is ground—the microsociologists, as Theodore Newcomb calls us.

The book offers what I hope is a fruitful way of examining family life. Empirical research dealing with the family supplies almost an embarassment of riches, and I have drawn on these studies extensively but selectively. There can be no other test of the value of an approach than its usefulness in illuminating existing research and informing new research. But the *approach* is paramount, and the book must be evaluated for its ideas more than for its summarization of empirical work.

Aside from the microsociological perspective, there are at least three features of my approach that may be unusual. First, before stressing the uniqueness of the family, I believe that we should exhaust the usefulness of viewing the family as governed by the same principles as other common social phenomena. The individual family unit is a species of the genus of the small group. Hence we should learn a great deal that is applicable to family life by reviewing what we know about small groups. I have not hesitated to look outside family sociology for theory and empirical findings regarding interaction in small groups when it seemed plausible that the principles might apply to family life.

Second, I have chosen to start by examining internal family processes in the abstract and then to look by stages at the surrounding society and its influence on the internal processes. Many writers prefer to start by talking about society as the setting in which family life occurs. It is my conviction that we can know what to look for in the larger setting only by understanding the working of internal family processes in the abstract—a view elaborated in Chapter 1. Because it is boring and difficult to communicate about processes like decision making and conflict in entirely abstract terms and because one should not make unreasonable demands for deferred gratification on the part of students who sign up for a course in the family, I have liberally illustrated the early part of the book with examples that show how family life is influenced from outside. It is not really until Part 3 that the theoretical focus is on the family as it reflects the larger social setting.

Finally, readers who look for the usual separate review of socialization theory and research will be distressed to find socialization materials scattered throughout the book. It is a central assumption of my approach that socialization is the residue of interaction and consequently that the best way to look at socialization is in connection with the study of interaction. The kinds of lasting effect that interaction has on individuals are reviewed in a preliminary chapter on socialization as one of the universal processes in any group (Chapter 8), and the consequences for family process of building self-conscious socializer and socializee roles into the family structure receive special treatment (Chapter 14) as one of the ways in which the functions society assigns to the family make it different from other groups. Elsewhere, aspects of socialization are taken up as part of the discussion of interaction in connection with roles, love, sex, participation in the kin group, and placement of the family in a social class system.

More ideas in this book were probably borrowed from Willard Waller than I have remembered to acknowledge. The psychosociological approaches of Joseph K. Folsom and Robert F. Winch have also given me inspiration, and I was fortunate to study the family under Bessie A. McClenahan, George B. Mangold, and Ernest W. Burgess. If my words are sometimes true to life, Christine, Cheryl, and Lowell are responsible. Many of my illustrations are taken from intimate student accounts of family conflict episodes. Among those who read portions of the manuscript and gave me the benefit of their criticism were Robert C. Angell, Tamar Becker, Charles Bowerman, Shelley Chandler, Oscar Grusky, Joan Moore, and Adam Pearce. Alan C. Kerckhoff and Sheldon Stryker read the entire manuscript with great care and perception, and several of their suggestions were followed in the final revision. My wife Christine helped at all stages in the work. The manuscript was typed by Anna Baca, Lois Bleier, Dione Hinger, Mary Schaeffer, and Sandra Westfall.

RALPH H. TURNER

Los Angeles, California
June, 1970

CONTENTS

Part 5   The Family in the Community

FAMILY INTERACTION

PART 1

THE IDEA OF FAMILY INTERACTION

CHAPTER 1

THE STUDY OF FAMILY INTERACTION

Of all social phenomena, the human family ranks near the top in the frequency and in the variety of perspectives with which it has been studied. The aims of investigators, their methods, and their conclusions vary so widely that any attempt to encompass the whole would produce little but a disjointed catalog. Hence any effort to examine the family as a social object must begin with a statement of the basis for selecting and organizing items from the total body of ideas and knowledge.

Initially we make a broad distinction between studying the family in its own right and introducing it into investigation in order to explain some other phenomenon. For example, there is conflicting evidence—or at least conflicting interpretation of evidence—concerning the relationship between divorce and delinquency. Public officials often lay the blame for delinquency on parental divorce. Refined statistical analyses that take account of such related factors as socioeconomic level suggest a less notable relationship.[1] Most investigations of this kind are guided more by an interest in accounting for delinquency than by an effort to clarify the character of family life. When other correlates of delinquency turn out to be more important, the investigator shifts his attention away from divorce in order to maximize his findings about delinquency.

The incidental scraps of knowledge about family life gleaned in this manner are often valuable to the student of the family. For example, Sampson, Messinger, and Towne, seeking to account for sustained improvement or relapse in released mental patients, found that intensive examination of family interaction was a necessary preliminary to satisfactory explanation.[2] Studies of this kind are among the most useful sources of data and ideas about family life, and we shall not hesitate to draw on them. But in offering an approach to the study of the family, we shall attempt to organize the questions we ask and the generalizations we

[1] Sophia M. Robison, *Juvenile Delinquency: Its Nature and Control*, Holt, New York, 1950, pp. 108–112.
[2] Harold Sampson, Sheldon L. Messinger, and Robert D. Towne, *Schizophrenic Women: Studies in Marital Crisis*, Atherton, New York, 1964.

advance about significant dimensions of family life rather than about the interesting aspects of society and the individual over which the family may have some influence.

The family is especially often examined as an avenue for the study of the individual. A prodigious amount has been written on the subject of the family and personal adjustment. Important though they are, questions of what the family has to do with development of intellectual capacities, creativeness, and motivation toward achievement again cannot provide a suitable basis for organizing theory and knowledge regarding the family. The family unit rather than its individual members is the focus of investigation.

The Focus of Analysis

The Family as Object. When it is an object for study in its own right, the family often means different things to different investigators. Three distinctions are of interest here. First, when speaking of the family, investigators sometimes refer to a culture pattern and sometimes to actual practice. When we are told that the American family is monogamous, relatively egalitarian, neolocal (the married couple set up their residence independently rather than living with either set of parents), or that absolute authority was vested in the head of the ancient Roman family, or that the mother was subordinated to her eldest son in the prewar Japanese family, the statements refer to patterns embodied in the culture. But actual family configurations are seldom precise replicas of culture patterns. There is always variation from family to family, and common practice in a society is often quite different from the recognized system of family life. Many of the early serious studies of the family, such as Westermark's classic *History of Human Marriage*,[3] were attempts to establish an evolutionary sequence. Invariably such studies focused on culture patterns and could pay only minimal attention to the way family life was actually lived. The pioneering attempt to relate family patterns to the mode of subsistence, by Hobhouse, Wheeler, and Ginsburg,[4] and the spate of recent studies depending on the data summarized for easy reference in the Human Resources Area Files,[5] are concerned more with the generally accepted idea of what the family should be like in a given society than with how the family works in practice.

[3] Edward A. Westermarck, *The History of Human Marriage*, MacMillan, London, 1891.
[4] Leonard T. Hobhouse, G. C. Wheeler, and Morris Ginsburg, *The Material Culture and Social Institutions of the Simpler People*, Chapman & Hall, London, 1930, pp. 142–227.
[5] For a convenient brief description of the Human Relations Area Files, see George P. Murdock, "Feasibility and Implementation of Comparative Community Research," *American Sociological Review*, 15: 713–720, December 1950.

By the family in this volume we shall mean actual social units rather than the idealized ones embodied in culture patterns. By family processes we shall mean repeatable sequences of events in actual families rather than those which are thought right or natural or which people believe to be generally practiced in a given group or society. The culture patterns are not to be ignored, because they are among the elements that shape practice. The fact, for example, that the family is supposed to be relatively egalitarian affects the strategy by which a wife dominates her husband and vice versa, even when it fails to limit unequal dominance. But family patterns constitute one among a set of conditions that determine the actual course of family life.

A second distinction is between the family in the *nuclear* sense or with reference to some larger kinship grouping. The nuclear family is a unit consisting of a man and woman united as husband and wife in socially recognized marriage and the natural and adopted children they have accepted as part of that unit.[6] The larger kinship groupings range from extended families—groups of systematically related nuclear units that carry on many of the standard aspects of family life collaboratively and take up more or less common residence—to clans and lineages, and the like. In choosing to focus on the former, we arbitrarily select the unit that is most fundamental in modern society. But we must not ignore the larger units, since the organization and conduct of the nuclear family is deeply affected by the kinship system it is enmeshed in. But we shall be interested in kinship, not as a phenomenon in its own right, but as one of the conditions that influence the nuclear family.

And third, we shall mean by the family the individual unit rather than any population of units in a given society or community or social class or ethnic group. We are more interested in the difference between two neighboring families, one of which is harmonious and the other highly conflictual, than in the fact that the rate of family conflict in this neighborhood is different from that in some other neighborhood. We must often rely on data that compare rates and typical family characteristics in different kinds of communities for ideas about individual family dynamics and for at least tenuous evidence bearing on hypotheses about individual families. Indeed, some of the most interesting hypotheses about differences among individual family units have grown out of efforts to explain group differences. It is merely important for our purposes not to lose sight of the objective, which is to explain differences among individual families.

[6] The definition is a free adaptation from the first component in the definition given by Ernest W. Burgess and Harvey J. Locke, *The Family: From Institution to Companionship*, American Book, New York, 1953, p. 7.

The Guiding Questions. Having established that we are interested in the actual individual nuclear family unit in its own right, we must still specify what we are most interested in predicting or explaining about the family. It would be a mistake to proceed as if the same formulation would do just as well to explain the size of the family and the feelings of members toward one another. Theories related to these two matters will, of course, have much in common. But the most productive strategy is to take a cluster of questions that are so closely interrelated that the same body of basic generalizations will supply answers to all.

Among the most important or interesting questions about the way the family functions as a social unit are three that seem closely interrelated.

First, to what extent does the family function in harmony or in conflict? Later we shall have to try to indicate what is meant by conflict with more precision, but for the moment we start from a common-sense query—why do the members of one family fight all the time and those of another seem to have easy and constructive relations in everything they do together?

Preliminary exploration of conflict and harmony suggests that it is difficult to separate the first question from the second, namely, to what extent is the family as a unit able to reach decisions and divide up the tasks involved in family activity? At first glance this may even seem to be the same question asked differently. Failure to reach group decisions and failure to play complementary parts in the family drama are often the cause or the expression of conflict. But further reflection shows that the questions are interrelated but not identical. Occasionally a family marked by incessant conflict turns out to be highly efficient in reaching agreement and getting family activities done. Often a family whose relationships are generally harmonious may nevertheless be incapable of reaching family decisions and getting on with family tasks.

Concern with conflict and harmony leads us also to a third question, which often seems to be the same question in still another form. How tightly or loosely bonded are the individuals who make up the family? Or how easily can the family unit be destroyed by being broken down into a set of component individuals? A high degree of conflict is often equated in our minds with nearness to breaking apart, and harmony with the presence of intense bonds. But further reflection again indicates that relationships with relatively little conflict are sometimes broken by divorce, by a child leaving the family, or by brother and sister going their totally separate ways, and that families with abundant conflict continue unbroken. Clearly there is a relationship, with the weakening of bonds being one of the usual consequences of heightened conflict. But in a more fundamental sense, there must be bonds to account for conflict. Otherwise, why would people stay together long enough to fight? Similarly, even ineffectual family decision making and division of labor presume some bondedness.

In one sense, then, the question of bondedness is the foundation question, underlying the others. Before we can say why persons fight one another, we must ask why they come together and stay together in the first place, rather than going their separate ways and ignoring one another. Before we can say why they fail to reach decisions, we must know why they need to reach group decisions at all.

The question regarding bondedness is also a different kind of question from the others. Conflict and decision making are activities that can be observed in the daily activities of the family, or reported from past activities, or generated in contrived situations. Bondedness is not an activity, but a potential, and therefore can only be inferred and not observed. The only direct empirical measure of bondedness would be modeled after a laboratory test for the tensile strength of a piece of metal. The metal is placed in a device that applies successively greater force until the exact amount necessary to pull it apart can be recorded. The nearest feasible approach to such a procedure is the observance of families that do and do not break under varying stresses in actual life situations. But we cannot directly observe the sequence of increasing and decreasing bondedness in a family.

If we are prepared to assume that bonding is a continuous process, however, so that the force required to break it into a set of separate individuals is higher one day and lower another, our central concern is with three continuous and highly interrelated processes. Together they include the most important aspects of what we usually mean by the functioning of a group. In technical sociological terms, they can be usefully treated as a system, in the sense that each process affects and is affected by the course of each of the other processes.

When we attempt to study these processes, it will be clear at once that the family consists of units within units. Bondedness, ease of decision making, and conflict all vary from pair to pair within the family and between and within alliances, such as children versus adults and men versus women. In some instances it is entirely reasonable to speak of these matters for the family as a whole; in other instances it is necessary to consider subunits. The most important pair for these purposes is the married couple, who normally exist as a unit before the children arrive and continue as a pair after they have left the intimate family circle.

Subsidiary Topics. Once the questions have been defined, it begins to be apparent just what things must be done in order to approach answers to the questions. First, if there are processes in the group, they take place through some medium. The medium through which conflict takes place has a good deal to do with the nature and limits of conflict. Just as one would not seriously attempt to study the more complex electrical processes without first finding out what was known about the character of electricity, so one can hardly speak intelligently of these family processes without first considering their medium.

Social interaction is the medium through which bonding, decision making, and conflict occur. In order to reach decisions, family members must interact in some manner. Neither harmony nor conflict can occur without interaction. But interaction is governed by its own set of rules, and its course is determined by a set of principles. These rules and principles establish the framework within which conflict and harmony, decision making and the division of labor, and bonding take place. Hence an understanding of interaction in the broader sense must preceed concern with our principal interests.

An investigation might be concerned simply with explaining momentary conflict and decision making. But it is difficult to think of the family in any important sense except as spanning a period of time. The most interesting thing about conflict is that it is sometimes progressive, sometimes endemic, and sometimes self-correcting. Bonding is interesting especially because the bonds that hold newlyweds together must be different from those which hold them together in their old age, and the intense bonds between parent and young child necessarily become weaker. A family decision reached easily but with private resentment sets the stage for a later decision to proceed less smoothly. The family is a group in motion, in which each event is less important for its immediate effects than for its contribution to cumulative developments.

If we think of the family as a succession of events, each of which can be assessed in terms of bonding, decision making, and conflict and each of which has a residual effect on the next episode, then we must consider how the residual effect occurs. If an episode is completed, the family members go their separate ways; but their next episode is different in consequence of the first, and the connection must be made through the attitudes of the members. The process by which episodes of interaction have cumulative effects on the attitudes of the interactants is called *socialization.*

Socialization is often viewed strictly as the relationship between experiences systematically repeated in infancy and childhood and the personality of the developing individual. But the difference is merely in the time span under consideration, and in the concern with relatively enduring or transitory attitudes. Each interaction episode has some socializing effect.

A final element is necessary to complete the approach, although its importance may be less clear until the main processes have been examined in some detail. If the processes we speak of fit together in some kind of system and if the interrelations of the processes maintain some stability over time, there is reason to search for a set of organizing principles. Is there a framework within which these processes can be examined together rather than separately? *Role theory* appears to offer the most promise for this purpose.

The main body of the book is devoted to these six topics, namely, interaction, bonding, decision making, conflict-harmony, socialization, and the family as an organization of roles.

The Substantive Approach

The Family as a Small Group. Three features of the substantive approach of the book require special note. First, it is possible to approach the family primarily from the point of view of its uniqueness as a social phenomenon or from the point of view of its identity with other phenomena. Many treatments of the family take the former course, beginning by stressing those features which make the family different and basing analysis largely on them. The sacredness with which the family is viewed and the emotion aroused in its defense combine to favor the uniqueness approach. This tendency was at one time so strong that the field of study known as *family sociology* came to be relatively detached from the main lines of sociological theory.

It cannot be sufficiently stressed just how contrary to scientific procedure and damaging to the study of the family such an approach is. One main objective of science is the parsimonious organization of knowledge. It begins by substituting generalization about classes of cases for repetitive statements about innumerable individual cases. It seeks further to discover the full range of types to which a given principle is applicable. An important scientific goal is approached whenever the investigator is able to explain a wide range of phenomena with a small number of principles. Every time a generalization can be formulated in such a way that it explains happenings in the family and other groups, progress has been made.

Since a great deal of study has been devoted to other types of small groups, both stable and transitory, within and outside larger organizations, it would be wasteful to overlook such generalizations as a ready source for principles that might apply to the family.

We proceed on the basis that what seems initially unique usually turns out, on careful observation, to have more in common with other phenomena than had been supposed. Studies of large organizations so divergent in purpose as a church, a business organization, an army, and a school have independently produced generalizations that turned out, on comparison, to be the same. The introduction of instant election forecasts by computer on the basis of early returns has shocked many persons into understanding that widely separated people from comparable social and economic categories react quite similarly to an election campaign. There is likewise justification for thinking that the family should have much in common with other types of small, stable groups.

Since World War II there has been a massive amount of experimental research using small groups. Many of the questions asked by researchers have not been particularly relevant to our interests in the family. All but a very few studies have dealt with ad hoc groups, whose members come together without prior acquaintance and leave before they have a chance to form durable patterns. The laboratory situations have generally been such as to prevent the full swing of conflict and harmony. And bondedness has been simple and unemotional, such as the requirement of submission to experimentation in connection with a college course of some kind. Nevertheless much that might apply to the family can be gleaned from some of these studies and from earlier field observation of small groups.

Recently there have been a few studies that tested standard small-group hypotheses, using conventional experimental techniques, on actual family groups. In a number of such instances the small-group hypotheses have not been confirmed.[7] Coalitions, for example, may not form according to prediction in the family.[8] But these studies, far from invalidating the approach that sees the family first as an instance of a small group, suggest two principles. First, many of the standard hypotheses in the small-group literature deal only with the emergence of structure in a group without prior organization. It would be implausible to expect that a group such as the family, with years of interaction during which an organization had been crystallized, would react as flexibly to a single experimental session as does an artificial group with no prior organization. But the same principles may have operated in the family initially, and they might operate if the experimental situation could be made powerful enough and repeated sufficiently often. It is worth noting that family small-group studies are generally negative in the failure of the experimental effect rather than positive in support of a different relationship.

Second, the uniqueness of the family in many instances is more correctly its commonality with a special class of small groups. For example, it may

[7] Morris Zelditch, Jr., points out some of the problems in methodology and conceptualization that make many findings of this kind indecisive. See "Family, Marriage and Kinship," in Robert E. L. Faris, (ed.), *Handbook of Modern Sociology*, Rand McNally, Chicago, 1964, pp. 699–707 *et passim*.

[8] Fred L. Strodtbeck, "The Family as a Three-person Group," *American Sociological Review*, 19: 23–29, February 1954.

have been the sentiment surrounding family life, or the clearly defined authority of the family, that explained the infrequency with which certain types of coalitions formed in family groups. If either of these explanations is valid, the apparent uniqueness of the family is translated into a characteristic shared by other small groups with common key features.

Our procedure, then, is to go as far as possible by assuming that the family behaves like any other stable small group. After the broadest base for generalization has been exhausted, we shall attempt to deal with apparent uniquenesses by treating the family as an example of a more restricted class of phenomena. For example, we shall ask what difference it makes to family processes that the family is a group characterized by intense societal regulation and governed by relationships of sentiment among its members, that it universally combines members of both sexes, and that it normally combines generations. In this way we hope to set aside the family mystique and discover, insofar as possible, whether what happens in the family happens predictably, because the family is an instance of a group with a specifiable set of characteristics.

Emphasis on Process. A second feature of our approach is an emphasis on process. Since words like "process," "dynamics," and "change" are positively valued, the pious assertion of interest in process is commonplace in sociology. But an adequate process approach has been notably difficult to develop and is in constant danger of degenerating into vague descriptive statements that are of little use. In the short range, a static approach is more productive of generalizations which can be subjected to test and whose conditions of applicability can be specified.

In the simplest terms, a process approach seeks to describe the sequence in which events occur, and a static approach aims to specify what condition will coexist with other known conditions. The relational approach produces generalizations such as the following: "Divorces were most likely to occur during the second or third year of marriage;"[9] "For any member of a small group [a family?], the higher his rank, the greater his conformity;"[10] "Persons with higher marital success scores tend to have a stronger desire for children, whether they have them or not, than those with lower marital success scores;"[11] "The development of a ritual by a family is an index of the common interest of its members in the family as a group."[12]

Statements of this kind are immediately interesting and useful, and the

[9] Paul C. Glick, *American Families,* Wiley, New York, 1957, p. 140.
[10] Terrence K. Hopkins, *The Exercise of Influence in Small Groups,* Bedminster, Totowa, N.D., 1964, p. 65.
[11] Ernest W. Burgess and Paul Wallin, *Engagement and Marriage,* Lippincott, Chicago, 1953, p. 722.
[12] James H. S. Bossard and Eleanor S. Boll, *The Sociology of Child Development,* Harper, New York, 1960, p. 296.

student of family life must constantly test his theories against them. But by themselves they tell us little about the individual case and usually suggest that the more interesting question is why the generalization should apply.

The idea of process is excellently summarized in Waller and Hill's discussion of a process they call *alienation*, the progressive sequence of events through which a married couple moves from initial solidarity to marital breakup:

> It rests upon crises after each of which the relationship is redefined upon a level of greater alienation and greater instability; these crises are interlarded, usually, with periodic reconciliations and periods in which the couple make a determined attempt to adjust to life with one another. Alienation is a summatory social process; like mating, it is a process in which each response leads to the next in line and the motive for each new step is furnished by the experiences of the process up to that point. . . . [13]

The disappointing feature of process formulations as they so often appear in sociological studies is their tendency to offer a sort of average set of stages, which are then of no more direct applicability to the individual case than the static generalizations we have discussed. Indeed, the reader is bound to be disappointed on reading further in Waller's examination of alienation to discover that he describes an almost invariant sequence that, once started, leads inevitably to the terminal point of divorce. The more interesting observation is how, in many instances, couples are able to progress—sometimes more often than once—through the prior stages of "disturbance of the affectional-sexual life of the pair," "mention of the possibility of divorce," "appearance of solidarity is broken,"[14] and then restore the working relationship between themselves. Waller's imputation of inevitability to the sequence incorporates the bias introduced by his having selected for study only those cases in which the process was carried to its completion.

The foregoing comments point to the crucial difference in objective underlying productive and sterile process formulations. The sterile formulations describe typical sequences. Because they are only typical, they have no special applicability to individual cases. They are like the description of steps in a terminal illness, which the physician can predict and recognize but about which he can do nothing.

A productive process formulation, on the other hand, is devised specifically to identify the *turning points*, where the process can go one way or another, and the *crucial events*, which determine for each turning point

---

[13] Willard Waller and Reuben Hill, *The Family: A Dynamic Interpretation*, Dryden, New York, 1951, p. 513. Quoted by permission of the publisher and Reuben Hill.
[14] *Ibid.*, p. 514.

the course that the process will take. It is attuned to a variety of outcomes rather than to a single outcome. It is like a description of steps in an illness that enables the physician to apply the right treatment at the right time and to alter the treatment as the illness progresses.

Used from this point of view, the process approach makes two ideas central to any analysis. First is the assumption that there is some leeway at each step in the process and that the specific alternative followed at one step has an effect on the next step. For example, an insulting remark by one family member may be ignored or returned in kind by another family member. The next step in the sequence, whether toward conflict or conciliation or discontinuance of the interaction, depends heavily on the nature of the response.

Second is the assumption that the effect of any given event or situation is different at different stages in the process. The gentle reply that stops the development toward conflict at the start may intensify anger when the conflict is fully developed and may again promote conciliation after the conflict has passed a point at which continuation is threatening. The presence of an outsider, witnessing the exchange, may inhibit the development of incipient conflict but intensify its development when the conflict has gone far enough so that his presence enhances commitment on the part of the interactors.

Closed System and External Influences. The third distinctive feature of our approach to the family is in some respects an extension of the process approach. It concerns the manner in which an investigator sets about dealing with the effect on family life of events and circumstances from outside the family. The family is subject to a wide range of external influences. Divorce rates rise during prosperity and decline during economic depression, and so do marriage rates.[15] An industrial way of life requires vastly different family patterns from a traditional agricultural economy. Community provisions for children and the elderly extensively alter the terms of interaction within the family.

Theories have been devised specifically around a relationship between family and society. Perhaps the best-known theory of this kind is that of family functions. As presented by Ogburn,[16] Zimmerman,[17] Burgess and Locke,[18] and many other sociologists and anthropologists, the tasks that are essential to the functioning of a society and the maintenance of its members are distributed among the institutions it comprises, including the

[15] Burgess and Locke, *op. cit.,* pp. 558–559.
[16] William F. Ogburn, "The Family and its Functions," in President's Research Committee on Social Trends, *Recent Social Trends in the United States,* McGraw-Hill, New York, 1933, pp. 661–708.
[17] Carle C. Zimmerman, *Family and Civilization,* Harper, New York, 1947.
[18] Burgess and Locke, *op. cit.,* pp. 462–470.

family. The enlargement of the functions of one institution reduces those of another. And any general change in the conditions that a society operates under affects the distribution of functions. Thus the family is under a strain to abandon functions adequately handled by other institutions, to take on functions to which it is suited and which are not otherwise served, and to adapt its pattern of organization to facilitate the performance of its functions.

The functional approach has been immensely useful, and we shall have occasion to consider it further in Chapter 11. But as a comprehensive approach it has certain limitations for our purposes. First, it is a theory regarding generalized patterns of family organization rather than the variation among individual families in a society. The separation of functions takes place among school, state, church, and the like, and families in general. Since all families in the community operate in the same institutional setting, the postulated tendency is to make them all alike. Second, its usefulness in accounting for the gross outlines of family life is not matched when we require a more detailed account of family life. Since there are normally a variety of ways in which any function can be served and since institutions may engage in contest over the disposition of particular functions, the functional approach must be supplemented by other theories if statements of any precision are to be made. And third, there are necessarily many features of family life shaped by external forces by way of other than functional principles. Functionalism might be one of several principles accounting for the impact of society on the family, but not the only one.

In contrast to theories that take the relationship between family and society as their point of departure, *closed-system*[19] theory begins with the internal dynamics of the family. In order to specify the probable effect of an external condition on any object, it is first necessary to have a description of the properties of the object. For example, to anticipate the effect of n degrees of external heat on a physical object, one must know its composition, size, density, shape, and exterior hue, among other properties. Only with such knowledge can one say whether it will shatter, melt, rise into the air, or "respond" in other ways. Under the closed-system approach the investigator attempts to establish insofar as possible the properties of the family as a system of processes, before attempting to generalize about the effects of various external variables on the family.

When simple physical objects are under investigation, the statement of

[19] The closed system has been carefully developed by Florian Znaniecki, although the approach followed here places more emphasis on the constructive combination of perspectives than Znaniecki's. See *The Method of Sociology*, Farrar and Rinehart, New York, 1934.

properties can be largely a catalog based on the behavior of similar objects in response to external conditions. To know that an object is made of glass enables us to draw on what is already known about the effects of heat on other glass objects.

In case of objects that have internal processes, such as an engine or a living plant, to describe the properties means principally to say how the internal processes operate. Any serious consideration of the effects of varying the fuel, the load, or the atmospheric conditions on the operation of an engine would scarcely be attempted without first understanding the general principles of the engine's operation. Similarly, serious consideration of the effects of transplantation, pruning, watering, and sheltering on a plant would be organized on the basis of an understanding of plant chemistry and function. One could simply accumulate a set of discrete observations about the response of the engine or plant to various external conditions, but they would remain an unintegrated catalog if there were not a conception of the internal processes.

For the family, this approach means that we attempt to make a statement that is at least complete in outline about the internal sequences and contingencies in decision making, conflict, and the like, before we examine the effect of such external conditions as the male occupational role, or placement of the family in a stratified society on the course of decision making or the frequency of conflict. We begin by examining the family in what must seem a highly artificial manner, as if it operated in a vacuum, ignoring its social setting. In fact, what we ignore is not the external influences but only their external significance.

The point can be clarified by returning to the example of an automobile engine. We know that its speed is increased by pressure on the accelerator; but it makes no difference who applies the pressure, or in what mood or social situation, or even whether the source of pressure is animate or inanimate. The engine is designed, with its controls, so as to respond specifically to depression of the accelerator. Identifying the specific causes that the system responds to is the crucial step toward dealing with external variables in a coherent and comprehensive manner.

The example tells us something further about the relationship between external influences and the operation of a system. Research might reveal, for example, considerable correlation between the driver's motives and the speed at which the automobile moved. In the absence of understanding regarding the mechanics of the engine, one might then infer a direct connection between the driver's motives and the speed of the engine. This is, of course, a classic example of magical thinking. Magical thinking stems from failure to recognize that external conditions become effective only when they are converted to the causes that the system responds to. Thus the driver's intention affects the speed of the engine only to the extent to which intention is translated into adjustments in pressure applied to the accelerator.

Here, then, is the difficulty with starting by examining the effect on the family of the business cycle, the mode of subsistence, or the legal structure governing marriage and divorce. The effects of these conditions on the family are not uniform. Stricter divorce laws strengthen one marriage and weaken another; economic depression enhances conflict in one family and harmony in another. Only when we understand in general terms what increases and reduces conflict are we in a position to find order rather than whimsy in the contradictory relationships between these external conditions and family process. Once we understand conflict process as a self-contained system, we are in a position to trace the translations of cause and effect that must occur between a drop in the business cycle and some modification in the harmony of life in a particular family.

Combining these three emphases, we shall attempt at first to make fairly general and abstract statements regarding the course of interaction within the family, but with a minimum of attention to what is distinctive about the family as distinguished from other small groups. But the ultimate purpose of this kind of analysis is to provide the basis for an orderly consideration of the effect of external influences on family life. Any system, such as the automobile engine, the internal processes of a living plant, and the family as an interactive system, is activated from outside. The purpose of understanding plant chemistry is to be able to understand and generalize about the effects of sunshine, rain, transplantation, and other external conditions on the internal processes. Apart from running their predetermined course when set in motion, the internal family processes depend on influences from outside for activation and direction. A new employment opportunity that is contingent on the family's moving to another community is the external circumstance that activates the patterned process of decision making in the family. A delinquency that brings public disgrace to the family triggers one of the characteristic conflict processes within the family.

Hence the abstract analysis of family processes will lead to a consideration of some of the more systematic external influences on the family and the respects in which the family differs from other enduring small groups. The uniqueness of the family and the specification of major external influences turn out to be two sides of the same task. The family is unique because of the societal regulation it operates under, because of the tasks assigned to it, and because of the socially expected terms of interaction—love, for example. In each instance specification of the uniqueness is at the same time a statement of external influence. The family is also unique because of its composition; but it is through the external roles of adult male, adult female, and child that many of the important societal influences are introduced into the family.

CHAPTER 2

THE PROCESS
OF INTERACTION

The objective of the present chapter is to supply a framework for analyzing brief episodes of interaction. As illustrations of what we shall attempt to explain, two brief accounts of minor family conflict follow. Our concern is not solely with conflict, but the elements of interaction often appear more clearly in conflict than elsewhere. Both reports are only as accurate as the memory of one participant, and the direct quotations should be regarded only as paraphrase. Since neither the events, nor the observation, nor the recording were controlled or subject to independent check, these reports cannot be regarded as data. They are offered here, as elsewhere in the text, solely as aids to exposition, as illustrations to give substance to the abstract principles that are discussed in detail.

CASE 1

The following episode is between a male college freshman and his parents, takes place in their home, at the dinner table, and is reported by the boy. The son customarily brings home morsels of information for the benefit of his modestly educated parents. At a previous meal he had tried to get his mother to buy margarine instead of butter, on the basis of what he had learned in a consumer-education unit at school. His mother was adamant, persisting in a folk belief that margarine was dangerous to health. The father had mentioned reading something recently on the subject and had suggested that the son was probably right. On the occasion of this episode margarine is being served for the first time.

MOTHER: Did you notice? We are having margarine today. How do you like it?
SON: Well, how did that happen?
MOTHER: Let me tell you what happened. I was in the grocery store today, and they were out of butter. I was looking at the margarine, and I remarked about my doubts to the grocer. Well, there was a very nice-looking woman standing behind me. She was nicely dressed and educated-looking. She spoke right up and told me that this belief of mine had been disproved and that margarine was just as healthful as butter. In fact, she said they were even using it in hospitals. So I bought the margarine.

The mother now looks plainly as if she expected approval for having done what the family wanted her to.

SON: (*in a scathing tone of voice*): Well, just who was this woman?

MOTHER: (*surprised and hurt*): Why, she was a very nice-looking woman. Why, I could tell by the way she spoke that she knew what she was talking about.

FATHER: (*trying not to be too provocative*): It's pretty hard to tell how much a person knows by her tone of voice.

SON: (*more scathingly than ever*): You mean that you believe just anything that some complete stranger tells you, just because she sounds emphatic enough?

MOTHER (*angrily*): Well, of course, I could tell she knew. She didn't have to say anything. She wouldn't have spoken if she didn't know anything.

SON: Well, our word doesn't mean a thing when we tell you real, proved facts that we get from good, reliable sources. But if you hear it from a stranger on the street, well, then you know it's so.

The family members finish dinner without speaking to one another and with averted eyes.

CASE 2

This episode is between a middle-aged husband and wife, with their daughter and her girl friend (both in college) present, at the dinner table in their home. The episode is reported by the friend, who is a house guest and is having her first meal with the family. On the day prior to the episode a friend of the family had suffered a heart attack and had been taken to a local hospital. The wife had received no news subsequent to the first report.

HUSBAND: John called me today and told me his wife had regained consciousness, but said she was paralyzed.

WIFE: What? Is she really paralyzed? How far paralyzed?

HUSBAND: Well, she can't talk but. . . .

WIFE: Then she's really in a bad way. Will she recover? How much does it cost for her care with a specialist and all?

HUSBAND: Well, it's. . . .

WIFE: Will she be in the hospital long? I hope she keeps getting better. Will she get any better, or is there a chance she'll die? Does the doctor know how much longer she will be paralyzed? How does she eat?

HUSBAND: She can't swallow, so they are feeding her intravenously, but. . . .

WIFE: How much longer will she be in this condition? Did the doctor say? Why can't she swallow?

HUSBAND (*quite angry by now*): For goodness sakes, stop it! Stop asking so many questions! I'm not going to answer them.

DAUGHTER (*laughing*): Golly, how can Dad possibly get a word in edgewise, Mom, if you just keep asking questions?

FRIEND (*laughing*): Please, I'll just die of curiosity if you don't tell us what happened.

The husband remains silent and just frowns at his wife for a few seconds. When he seems just about on the verge of losing his temper, he suddenly relaxes and smiles. The two girls burst out laughing, especially because of the husband's ridiculous appearance when he had been on the verge of losing his temper. The wife looks sheepish, then smiles at her husband and winks.

WIFE: I know, Daddy, I'm wrong when I talk so fast, and I'm sorry.

HUSBAND (*smiling*): O.K. But you do make me angry when you won't stop asking a string of questions until you've run out of breath. Why, I can't even say one word before you begin another series.

WIFE (*leaning over and giving her husband a little hug*): Yes, I know it is impolite and makes you angry, but I was so excited and wanted to know as quickly as possible about everything. I'm sorry, dear.

The conversation about the sick friend continues amicably.

The sequence of events in the family is a long chain of cause and effect, each link being one episode, such as those we have reported. Each episode takes some of its unique shape from the sequence of such events that has preceded it. And each episode leaves a residue in the attitudes and memories of the participants that will affect, in some degree, the tenor and direction of the next episode. If the members of a family are deeply attached to one another after years of interaction, it is because many such episodes have worked to reinforce or augment attitudes of affection among the members. If a family breaks up, it is after a chain of such events has accumulated attitudes of dislike or disinterest among the members.

In discussing the interaction process in the present chapter, we limit ourselves principally to the simple interaction between two persons. Extension of the approach to include several family members can best be made after the principles of pair interaction have been developed. The chapter begins with an outline of the communicative interaction process, followed by a discussion of the bases on which interpretations are assigned to one's own and another's communications. The conditions that give direction to interaction are explored in the rest of the chapter.

The Interaction Sequence

An interaction episode begins with a gesture made by one person.[1]

---

[1] This treatment of interaction owes most to the tradition of George H. Mead and Herbert Blumer. See Mead, *Mind, Self, and Society,* University of Chicago Press, Chicago, 1934; Blumer, *Symbolic Interactionism,* Prentice-Hall, Englewood Cliffs, N.J., 1969. More extended treatments of interaction from similar vantage points are found in Tamotsu Shibutani, *Society and Personality,* Prentice-Hall, Englewood Cliffs, N.J., 1961; and in George J. McCall and J. L. Simmons, *Identities and Interactions,* Free Press, New York, 1966.

Gesture is used here in the broad sense of any behavior that can be assigned some meaning by the actor or observer and ranges from anything as subtle as a body posture indicating fatigue to a carefully delivered lecture. The initiator of interaction has some interpretation of his gesture in mind and tests the gesture against the interpretation as he makes it. A father speaking to his child recognizes that his voice is harsher than he means it to be and softens his tone or adds some remarks to correct the false impression he started to give. When the gesture is finished, the initiator assumes a state of prepardedness, anticipating certain kinds of response from the person toward whom the gesture was directed. A woman complaining casually of a headache is unable to say exactly what response she expects from her husband. She is prepared for no response, for a slight expression of sympathy, or for an offer to do the evening dishes. But she is not prepared for an expression of pleasure over her misfortune, an outburst of anger, or a comment on the state of the federal debt.

Before we speak of the response of the second person to the initiator's gesture, we must introduce a convention that often lessens expositional confusion. Instead of using terms like the first and second person or initiator and responder, we speak of *ego* and *alter* as the two persons in the interaction. Which is designated ego and which alter is of no great consequence, except that we label as ego, when possible, the person from whose point of view we assign meanings to gestures, or the person who is the principal actor, or, lacking either of these differences, the initiator of interaction.

Alter (the second person) now receives ego's gesture, places his own interpretation on it, and responds on the basis of this interpretation. But there is not ordinarily a sharp separation between the interpretation and the gesture. The gesture as it is perceived and remembered is often distorted into greater conformity with the interpretation placed on it. Ego's perception and memory of his own gesture have similarly been distorted. Consequently the "facts" of the communication as each interactor remembers them justify his reactions more fully than an objective recording. Finally, in making his response gesture, alter has in mind an interpretation of his own gesture and is prepared for a certain range of response on the part of ego.

The foregoing simple sequence of gesture and response we call stage 1 of the interaction process. During this stage each person is acting without preconceptions derived from the current interaction sequence. At the close of this stage each has developed preconceptions. Each now anticipates and measures the gesture of the other against this anticipation or preparedness. In practice, stage 1 can exist only in degree, since the total absence of preconceptions is unimaginable.

Stage 2 we call the stage of testing and revision. Now ego not only receives and interprets alter's gesture but recognizes it as one he is prepared for or one that falls outside the anticipated range. But the state of preparedness precedes interpretation, and the gesture as seen and understood is shaped by ego's state of preparedness. The usual tendency is to place on the gesture some interpretation one is prepared for. If ego is fully prepared for a gesture of sympathy, he may miss the slight note of sarcasm in alter's response. If ego fully expects a slight from alter, even a sincere compliment is likely to sound sarcastic.

We speak of alter's gesture as *congruent* if ego recognizes it as a response he is prepared for. The subsequent course of the interaction depends on whether it is congruent or not. When the response is congruent, interaction continues in a preestablished direction.

When the response is *noncongruent*, however, there is an interruption of communication, and ego has to reconsider his next gestures. An expression of pain, for example, may call for no further discussion after the anticipated response of compassion. But when the interaction is not satisfactorily completed, because the response is one of amusement, ego is forced to reconsider and is likely to make a further gesture to bring the matter to a satisfactory conclusion. After possible reconsideration of the meaning of alter's gesture, three general courses of action are open to ego. He may abandon his effort to communicate, he may attempt to reassert his original intention, or he may disregard his first gesture and respond as if alter had initiated the interaction, thus following the latter's lead.

The remainder of interaction follows the second-stage pattern. The same variables are at work, except that with each successive gesture it is possible to reconsider any of the previous gestures. Either participant may then attempt to reassert or reformulate any in the sequence of his previous gestures, or he may reconsider the interpretation he has made of any in the sequence of the previous gestures made by the other. The interaction continues until both are satisfied or until one or both prefer to discontinue the interaction.

The cases at the beginning of the chapter both reveal the round of interpretation and response. In case 1 the mother found the son's response noncongruent. She attempted to reassert the intention of her original gesture. After failing in this effort, she preferred to abandon the interaction rather than accept the son's lead by turning to an exchange of insults. In case 2 the period during which the father was on the verge of placing one interpretation on his wife's gestures, only to relent and assign another, more favorable meaning, was plainly reported. The two girls, who were not part of the main exchange, supplied an interpretation while he was undecided, and they undoubtedly made it more difficult for him to interpret his wife's gestures as a personal affront and easier to interpret them as a humorous personal foible.

Bases of Gesture Interpretation

If each person's behavior during interaction depends on the interpretation he makes of his own and alter's gestures, then exploration of the sources of gesture interpretation is indispensible to understanding interaction. A gesture usually has a basis of standard meaning, like the dictionary definition of a word or the common understanding of a kiss as a gesture of affection. But the refined meanings that make the same words a joke in one situation and a threat in another are based on the social setting of the interaction. Parts 4 and 5 of this book are largely concerned with the way the variable setting of family life shapes the meaning that members place on one another's gestures, and the effects that these meanings then have on the patterns that interaction follows. Without attempting to anticipate the detailed discussion in these later chapters, we can point to some of the general sources of the meanings people use when they interpret gestures in family life.

Cultural Symbols. Most gesture interpretation starts from the culturally shared meanings within any society. But even these meanings vary according to region, social class, national background, broad religious groupings, age, and other units with distinctive subcultures. For example, kissing, necking, petting, and other forms of heterosexual play often convey different meanings with respect to seriousness of attachments and degree of affection in rural as compared with urban subcultures. Certain forms of ritualistic adolescent behavior appear to adults as concerted revolt against adult authority, but adolescents assign more moderate interpretations. In these instances miscommunication is likely to occur when a man and a woman from rural and city subcultures respectively meet and when an adult and an adolescent interact.

The correct interpretation of gestures ordinarily requires considerable experience of living among those who share the culture or subculture in question. This experience is necessary to recognize the conventional understanding as well as the literal meaning of gestures. Within American culture it is quite conventional to state things in grossly exaggerated and highly dramatized form. Through familiarity with conventional usage a member of American society learns to apply a *conventional discount* to literal meaning.

Dating and courtship incorporate many ritual forms that, taken literally, might be understood as conveying special attachments. As ritual forms, however, they are conventionally understood as mere forms of play. The male "line" incorporates flattery and exaggerated attention to the girl, and the girl expresses the expected amusement at her partner's jokes and indicates what a good time she has had on the date. So long as the two share an understanding concerning the appropriate conventional discount, no unwarranted conclusions will be drawn by either, and gestures that exceed conventional statements of affection are likely to be recognized as such. But a certain amount of experience in dating is necessary before these fine judgments can be made.

In the process of controlling their children, parents soon exhaust the power of words of moderation. Consequently, over a period of time they come to speak in exaggerated terms. The appropriate discount is made within the family, because both the parents and the children have learned what the relationship between literal and effective meaning is. The threat to "knock your block off" or the declaration "I wish I had never had you kids" is appropriately discounted, because experience has shown that neither expression is meant literally.

In-group Meanings. Every group of persons who share a series of experiences over a period of time and discuss their experiences among themselves acquires a fund of shared memories. These memories in their full detail are known and carry common connotations for members of the group but not for outsiders. Certain expressions or symbols trigger these memories and these expressions thus become the gestures that convey special in-group meanings.[2]

In one family an experience at the time of the daughter's second birthday supplied in-group meaning to a gesture. The daughter sat wide-eyed as the cake and candles came in and as her parents and older brother sang "Happy Birthday." Near the end of the song, when the daughter's name was sung, she reacted with surprise as if she knew for the first time that all the fuss was about her. As the song ended, she said delightedly, "Happy day-day me!" On the occasion of each birthday since that time someone has said, "Happy day-day" or "Happy day-day me," the others responding with smiles and gestures of warmth as the feelings aroused by the original incident are reawakened. The special meaning of the gesture "happy day-day" is shared only by members of the family, on the basis of the original unique common experience.

Image of the Gesturer. Communication between complete strangers is often a halting affair, because it is difficult to know how to interpret a person's gestures unless one knows something about him. Are certain re-

[2] In-group languages have been extensively discussed by sociologists. For an example from another kind of group, see Frederick Elkin, "The Soldier's Language," *American Journal of Sociology*, 51: 414–422, March 1946.

marks to be taken seriously or as subtle humor? In a friend, past experience tells us the kind of person he is, and the interpretation is easier. Gesture interpretation depends on our having some image of the other person. Once we feel that we have a person typed or are convinced that we know him as a person, we are likely to miss meanings that are not consistent with our image. Ego does not catch the joke made by his usually sober friend, and he laughs at serious remarks by his usually humorous alter.

After extended interaction, ego's image of alter is mainly a residue of interaction. Ego's image of alter is subject to testing, leading to either reinforcement or revision in stage 2 of the interaction process. Since the response that ego expects from alter reflects the image that ego has of him, the congruence or noncongruence of the response reinforces or challenges the image.

Extended examination of the interaction process in small incidents within the family was initially justified by suggesting that each such episode of interaction leaves a residue that shapes subsequent interaction. Among the most critical of these residues is the image that each is forming of the other. As each family member tests, revises, and stabilizes his image of every other family member during successive interactive episodes, the result is the cumulative formation of a set of images that each family member has of every other member. As these images develop, they control, in considerable degree, the interpretations that each places on the other's gesture and thus slant the meanings that are gleaned in family interaction. These images tend to force each new interaction episode into the same pattern as former episodes, so that as either harmony or conflict becomes chronic, group decision or indecision recurs.

The illustrative episodes at the beginning of the chapter show that the participants had well-formed images of each other before the episode began.

In case 1 the son probably would not have so readily interpreted his mother's acting on the advice of an outsider as an insult if he had not already built an image of her as insufficiently cognizant of his knowledge. The mother would hardly have failed to recognize that her actions reflected unfavorably on her son's judgment if she had not already formed an image of her son as cantankerous and unwilling to grant her due credit. Again the episode probably reinforced both sets of images.

Levels of Gesture Interpretation. One of the lines of gesture reinterpretation available when alter's gesture is noncongruent is to assign a hidden meaning to the gesture. A boy is hit by a ball during a little-league baseball game, and his solicitous father runs to ask if he is hurt. The father is prepared for some indication of whether he is hurt badly or slightly. But the son's nonchalant response that he is unhurt, with an effort to get up and walk to his position as if nothing had happened, is noncongruent. The father almost certainly then interprets the gesture as concealing the son's true feelings in front of his peers and suspects that he is actually in pain. Interpretation of this kind, in which the gesture is regarded as concealment or faulty representation of alter's actual feeling, can be called interpretation at the *empathic level*. In empathic interpretation ego ascribes an attitude or feeling to alter that is at variance with the *face-value* meaning of his gesture. Priscilla Mullens' famous though fictional query to John Alden, "Why don't you speak for yourself, John?" in Longfellow's poem, is a classic example of empathic interpretation. Although at face value Alden's gestures expressed only Myles Standish's feelings toward her, Priscilla read them as his own. An interpretation need not be correct to be empathic, and the feeling it ascribes to alter may be favorably or unfavorably viewed. It merely ascribes a disguised feeling to alter, but a feeling that alter is assumed to be fully aware of.

Besides face-value and empathic meanings, there is a third level that interpretation may take, which can be called *diagnostic*. A diagnostic interpretation infers something from the gesture about the state of alter which is at variance with the face meaning of the gesture and which alter is assumed to be unaware of. The classic diagnostic interpretation is that of the psychiatrist to whom the patient's gestures are believed to reveal attitudes in the patient that the latter is completely unaware of.

In the normal course of interaction interpretations are expected to be made at face value. Interpretations at other levels, and especially at the diagnostic level, are regarded as affronts to personal dignity. In the baseball illustration, the more the father rejects the son's denial of injury, the more the son is likely to insist on it. On the other hand, if the father appears to accept the son's gesture at face value but offers another reason for his coming out of the game for a few minutes, the son is morely likely to acquiesce. Both father and son are then interpreting each other's gesture empathically, but maintaining the appearance of face-value interpretation. The privilege of diagnostic interpretation is explicitly given to the psychiatrist by his patient, and is subject to being withdrawn. Parents usually claim the privilege of both empathic and diagnostic interpretation of their children's gestures, although the privilege is likely to be contested by the children unless used discretely. Relationships of intimacy, such as those between lovers and friends, carry with them license for a limited amount of mutual empathic interpretation. The wife expects her husband not to accept her assertion that she "feels fine" at face value but to recognize the signs of her true feelings.

Values in Interaction

Our analysis of meaning in simple interaction does not yet explain the *direction* that interaction takes. When alter interprets ego's gesture as an insult, which he sees as consistent with his image of ego, does he respond by entering into full-scale conflict or does he try to avoid it? In the most general terms, interaction is guided by the *values* of the participants and restricted by the *norms* they recognize. We speak first about values in family interaction and come back to norms later.

A value is a category of objects, tangible or intangible, toward which an individual reacts in a positive or negative rather than neutral manner. When the perceived meaning of alter's gestures appears to promote ego's positive values and depreciate his negative values, ego attempts to maintain the direction that interaction is already taking. When the perceived meanings depreciate ego's positive values and promote his negative values, he tries to change the course of interaction in favor of his value system. Value is a more general term than such concepts as need, drive, urge, impulse, and wish.[3] The latter are psychological concepts that might be used to explain why a person values certain objects. But for our purposes it is sufficient to know that certain values are held, without asking why.

Much interaction is casual, lacking any well-identified purpose. In casual interaction alter merely notes the value relevance of ego's gesture in the course of interpreting it and shapes his response accordingly. But in more seriously directed interaction, some value is elevated to the special guiding position of a goal for at least one of the participants. As soon as there is a goal, ego assigns meaning to alter's gestures principally in terms of their relevance to fostering or impairing the goal.

Task- and Identity-oriented Interaction. When interaction is directed, there is a further important distinction to be made. Some interaction is directed toward a goal which requires the collaboration of two or more persons, but in which the attitudes of the participants toward one another are means rather than ends in themselves. Family members work together to prepare a garden, to play a game of tennis, to plan and execute family finances, to discuss a controversial television program. Following Robert F. Bales, we call interaction, insofar as it is directed in this manner, *task-oriented*.[4] The task in such activities as watching a television program together need not be sharply focused, but it organizes the collaboration among the participants.

On other occasions interaction is primarily directed by each member's

---

[3] Dorothy D. Lee, "Are Basic Needs Ultimate?" *Journal of Abnormal and Social Psychology*, 43: 391–395, July 1948.

[4] Robert F. Bales, *Interaction Process Analysis: A Method for the Study of Small Groups*, Addison-Wesley, Cambridge, Mass., 1951.

concern about how the others feel toward him. Ego's chief goal is to affect the attitudes of alter toward ego. The task, if there is one, becomes secondary, and the relations between persons primary. The goal can be to foster friendly or hostile attitudes, to promote respect or fear or love. Interaction in which the task is secondary to the relations among persons has been called *social-emotional*.[5] But for the purposes of the ensuing analysis we use a slightly different distinction, contrasting *identity-oriented* to task-oriented behavior. The identity is the self of an individual. Identity interaction is more concerned with fostering the self than with the task toward which collaboration is ostensibly directed. The attitudes sought are those that support ego's self-conception.[6]

In practice, interaction does not separate neatly into these two kinds. Since the family consists of relations that are both comprehensive and intimate, every task is overlaid with identity implications. But because the family is also the medium through which major tasks of collaborative living are carried out, the relatively identity-oriented interaction of courtship must give way to a much more task-oriented interaction in marriage.

There are several differences between task and identity interaction. First, in task interaction, gesture interpretation is predominantly at the face-value level, each participant being primarily interested in what the other is trying to convey rather than in deeper interpretation. The empathic and diagnostic levels of interpretation become of great importance, however, when interaction is identity-oriented. The matter of predicting and anticipating the other's next moves becomes both more complex and more crucial, so that it is necessary to go beneath the surface.

Second, task interaction involves only minimal attention to assigning credit and blame for the course of events. But the identity interaction of lovers is largely taken up with exchanging credits. The idea of the identity or self is inseparable from credit and blame. We do not blame or credit an animal for his good or bad features, because we do not believe that he has a self. The identity is that which is creditable and blameworthy in the individual.

Third, in task interaction one's gestures are forms of communication. Although they are communication for a purpose, they still convey to the

---

[5] *Ibid.*
[6] The distinction does not correspond exactly with Bales' task versus social-emotional behavior. In groups such as the family there is much interpersonal coordination and control behavior that constitutes simply the central tasks of family interaction. Thus not all social-emotional behavior need be regarded as strictly identity-oriented. Furthermore, in labeling the behavior as we do, we seek to focus attention on the difference in the object of attention more than on the mode of expression. Whether it is "emotional" or not, we are concerned with the difference between action predominantly concerned with self-enhancement or self-protection and other forms of action.

receiver the same core meaning they do to the initiator. In identity inter-action the gesture is used to gain a certain kind of reaction from the other. Since the reaction of the other cannot be solicited simply on the basis of shared interest in a task, the gesture must be used with greater calculation. As a result there develops a wider discrepancy between the meanings attributed to the gesture by the gesturer and the receiver. The gesture, then, specifically communicates only a part of the meaning that the gesturer finds in it. Consequently, when interaction shifts from task to identity direction, the gesture ceases to be primarily a device for communication and becomes an *interpersonal technique*. It becomes a device used to create a desired kind of relationship between two persons, through ego's implant-ing in alter the desired person image of alter.

Finally, in task-directed interaction there is very little attention to one's own self-image—the kind of appearance one is making in the situation. In popular terminology one is not self-conscious. In identity interaction, how-ever, a major focus of attention is the self-image. Ego must attend con-tinuously to his self-image and certainly manipulates it to get the desired response from alter. This point is central to much of the analysis through-out the book and requires extended attention.

Self-image and Self-conception

The most important difference between task and identity interaction is the strong focus of attention on the self-image in the latter. By the self-image we mean the appearance one makes, either to ones self or others, in a particular situation. Preoccupation with self-image means that ego inter-prets alter's gestures primarily as they reveal alter's image of ego. Ego re-sponds on the basis of whether the image accords with his desires and uses interpersonal techniques to foster the desired self-image.

The self, or identity, is a kind of value but a special one. The self is an "object" that the individual tries to protect and advance. At its core the self appears to be an abstract idea or a mental construct, since it is not pos-sible to locate and identify any tangible referent for self. Empirically the self exists as an attribute of various more tangible objects, such as the body, the words one speaks, the music one plays, one's various creations. The self is that intangible object to which are attributed the various tan-gible and intangible objects designated as "my own." In spite of the in-tangibility, the self is ordinarily the most "real" object in the experience of each individual.

The self-image is something inferred in a situation. It may be inferred from the gestures of others one is interacting with, as the way one appears to them. It may be inferred from the imagined role of someone not present, as the way one would appear to a mother or father or priest. Or it may be the way one sees oneself in a situation. In every instance the self-image is evaluated as favorable or unfavorable to the self. It is the medium through which one judges that the course of interaction is fostering the identity or damaging it.

For any self-image to be evaluated, there must be some standard of comparison. One may be able to describe an ideal self vaguely, consisting of what he would like to be if he could live in a world where perfection was practical. For the ordinary mature individual, however, the ideal self recedes into the background of awareness and seldom comes into play as a vital standard to judge the self-image against. To be told that he is not likely to equal the current baseball home-run king or television quiz wizard may upset a young boy, but an older man is not likely to take such advice as an insult. Although such outstanding achievement might still be a fantasy ideal to the man, he is no longer likely to regard a less perfect image as deprecatory to himself. Clearly there is a more realistic criterion that the self-image is judged against than the fantasy ideal self in the normal adult.

The realistic criterion is designated the *self-conception*.[7] By the self-conception is meant the image that corresponds to what a person regards as really himself. Awareness of a self-conception is indicated by such remarks as "I don't know why I did it. I wasn't really myself at the time," or "I intend to prove to you that I am not really that kind of person but am a person you can respect in spite of my occasional delinquencies," or "Although I have moments of temper, I am fundamentally a very easy-going person."

The self-conception exists because of the assumption that a person can view some of his actions as more characteristically "himself" than others. Although not universally so, it is ordinarily the behavior in our "better" moments which corresponds to the self-conception. Like the ideal self the self-conception is somewhat more favorable than a statistical profile of a person's behavior. It is not an accurate reproduction but a photograph with the blemishes retouched.

The self-conception, unlike the ideal self, is firmly anchored to actual behavior. It depicts the possible rather than the ideal. It is the working standard or criterion for determining satisfaction or dissatisfaction with the self-image. When the image corresponds with the self-conception, there is general satisfaction. When the image appears superior to the self-concep-

---

[7] The treatment of self and self-conception owes most to the traditions of Charles H. Cooley and of Muzafer Sherif and Hadley Cantril. See Cooley, *Human Nature and the Social Order*, Scribner, New York, 1922; Sherif and Cantril, *The Psychology of Ego Involvements*, Wiley, New York, 1947. A fuller development of this view of the self-conception is found in "The Self-conception in Social Interaction," in Chad Gordon and Kenneth Gergen (eds.), *The Self in Social Interaction*, Wiley, New York, 1968, vol. I, pp. 93–106.

tion, there is likely to be elation. When it appears inferior, there is disappointment and an effort to restore the image to the level of self-conception. When interaction creates an image more favorable than the self-conception, the experience may be called self-enhancing. The opposite experience is self-disparaging.

In casual or task interaction the awareness of self is at a minimum. So long as the interaction is neither markedly self-enhancing or self-depreciating, it continues without important self-consciousness. But if the course of interaction appears to present a self-image widely discrepant from the self-conception, the immediate result is to heighten the awareness of self. The result is that gestures are then interpreted according to the self-image they convey and interaction is likely to shift to an identity orientation, the individual seeking to capitalize on his self-enhancement or repair his self-disparagement, as the case may be.

The self-image is brought into interaction when the gestures of the other are interpreted as characterizing or reflecting on the self. Such an interpretation is most certain to be made when the other specifically generalizes about the initiator in some form, such as "You are always so thoughtful" or "So you have forgotten again." Direct characterizations of one's important activities or belongings or creations are the same as characterizations of the self. Self-characterizations may occur indirectly when it appears that the gestures of the other assume an unfavorable image of self. When the response is noncongruent and the stage of testing and revision is underway, ego may discover that alter's gesture can be rendered comprehensible by attributing to alter a certain image of ego. Alter may seem to be drawing unfavorable conclusions about ego's motives or assigning ego exceptional credit.

The self-image also emerges in the role one discovers himself enacting in the interaction sequence. If one not accustomed to such a role discovers that he is playing the role of a leader, his orientation shifts in accordance with his novel self-image. A father whose self-conception is that of a mathematical wizard may be sensitized to an implied unfavorable self-image when he discovers the children going to their mother rather than to him with their mathematical questions. The self-conception conveys certain roles that an individual should play in the family or other group. When the roles actually played are different, the resulting self-image becomes a matter of attention and comparison with the self-conception.

Norms of Interaction

The most general source of direction in interaction comes from an individual's values. When interaction is directed, some values are elevated to the special position of goals while a subordinate set of values is viewed as means and conditions. When interaction is identity-oriented, a special kind of value, the self, is preponderant in directing interactve participation. Still a further kind of value, known as a norm, or rule, of interaction, also gives direction.

A norm is a rule, a statement that specified behavior must be carried out or avoided. The many norms that regulate family life rather closely in all its aspects and their variation from society to society will demand our attention from time to time. But our principal concern at the present is with one group of norms governing interaction by itself. If the interaction within the family is compared with a game that several players participate in, the interaction norms are the rules of the game.

Although most persons would have some difficulty in stating clearly even a small fraction of the rules that apply to interaction, the rules are nevertheless recognized and asserted when conditions demand. One person may refuse to answer the communication of another, asserting, "You have no right to speak to me that way" or "Mind your own business!" Ordinarily the rules remain in the background of the participants' awareness. Each of us is trained so that the rules are generally observed without conscious thought. But when a violation occurs, the rule is likely to be recognized, and the communication of the other refused.

Kinds of Interaction Norm. The norms governing interaction fall into three broad groups. First are the general norms of interaction, those which apply equally to all the participants and are widely accepted. Such a norm is the obligation of any individual who is addressed in the proper manner to respond to the communication of the other. Another such norm is the requirement, under most conditions, that each participant respond to the other's communications on the basis of a face-value interpretation. To read hidden meanings into another's words or to attempt to explain or diagnose them rather than answering them at the same level they were presented at is a violation of the accepted rules of interaction.

A second group of interaction norms governs the communication between persons in particular statuses. There are rules that govern what a man may say to a woman that do not apply to his conversations with other men. There are rules which limit what a child may say to an adult and which restrict the subjects that a parent should discuss with his child. Many of these rules are merely the application to particular statuses, such as parent and child, of the more general rules that govern relations between superiors and subordinates. A superior, for example, may challenge a subordinate to account for his behavior, but a subordinate may not make such a demand of a superior. The superior may offer unsolicited advice to the subordinate, but the latter may offer advice only when requested by the superior. Rules such as these apply within the family whenever the relationship between any two statuses is inequalitarian. In the patriarchal family they apply to husband-wife relations, and in family systems that assign superior standing by age they govern relations among siblings.

The final group of interaction norms includes those which develop within a group as a product of sustained interaction and apply only to the members of the group. These *in-group norms* are companion phenomena to the in-group meanings that arise from unique shared experience. Within a family some of the traditions that accumulate are converted to rules. "In our family we don't do it that way." Although rules of this kind are often formulated by parents to buttress their children against outside influence, they are not necessarily imposed merely in this direction. The children may generalize from customary behavior in the family and treat the custom as a rule, thereby making departure more difficult for the parents.

Reciprocity Principle. It is a fundamental characteristic of social norms of all kinds that they are bound up in a system of mutual obligation. Each participant in the social order has both obligations and privileges that are interdependent.[8] If it is one man's obligation to interpret another's gestures at face value, it becomes the latter's privilege to have his gestures interpreted in this manner. But more important still, one man's obligation to abide by the rules conveys a right to expect and insist that others also abide by the rules that apply to their positions. Conformity to interaction norms consequently makes sense and is largely assured by such incorporation of rules in a network of mutual obligations.

This underlying interdependency of norms gives rise to a general normative *principle of reciprocity*, which states that ego's obligations are conditional on alter's performance of his obligations toward ego. Ego is released from his obligation to abide by the rules in dealing with alter if alter has violated the rules in dealing with ego; ego is obligated to exceed what the rules would normally require of him if alter has exceeded his obligations in dealing with ego. These two sides of the reciprocity principle are also governed by a rule of quantitative equivalence. A small violation of rules by one participant justifies a small but not a large violation by the other. A large excess beyond one's obligation cannot be matched by a small excess in the other. Few people would openly advocate this kind of reciprocity as an admirable ethical system, but it is easily recognizable from the justifications that persons offer for their behavior in concrete situations.[9]

The negative side of the reciprocity principle can be illustrated in an imaginary husband-wife dispute. The rule that discussion should deal only

---

[8] Alvin Gouldner, "The Norm of Reciprocity: A Preliminary Statement," *American Sociological Review*, 25: 161–178, Apr. 1960.
[9] This extension of reciprocity in a working folk morality goes beyond the reciprocity principle as discussed by Gouldner.

with relevancies and only with current incidents is violated when some item of behavior from the past is mentioned. As soon as alter violates the rule by asking, "But remember the time when you . . .?" the reciprocity rule is invoked by ego to justify suspending the application of rules to his own remarks. "So long as you are bringing up the past, what about the time when you . . .?" Or the violation may be matched by suspension of some other rule, such as the rule to respond relevantly to the other's communication. Thus ego can say, "I refuse to discuss the matter with anyone who uses those tactics."

On the positive side, if alter overlooks an apparent slur, he thereby imposes an obligation on ego to overlook an insult by him. If one person makes conciliatory advances by offers of compromise or concession, an obligation is imposed on the other to match the first person's conciliation. Each member of a family who exceeds his obligations in carrying out family responsibilities places other family members in the position of owing him something.

Interaction Norms and the Identity. The usual operation of social norms presumes that they are so thoroughly incorporated into behavior as to require little conscious attention. Perceived violations bring them to the forefront of attention, both for the offended person and for the violator, who must defend or expiate his misbehavior. With sufficiently intense interest in the matter under discussion, the game being played, the job being done (strong task orientation), however, the participants are unlikely to notice rule violations or to allow interaction to be diverted by them. With an appropriate image of alter, ego may not even interpret his behavior as a norm violation.

Once attention is fastened on the normative aspects of interaction, however, the character of the exchange shifts. As we have indicated, the obligation of one person is the privilege of another. The obligation of the child to respect the parent is the privilege of the parent to be respected. Consequently norm violation has the quality of personal damage to another. The object that is damaged by violations of the rules of interaction is the self or identity. The self-conception of each person incorporates his generalized status as a person entitled to certain kinds of respect and consideration from others and his particular statuses with the special kinds of treatment he is thereby entitled to expect from persons occupying other particular statuses. When the rules of interaction are violated, the self-conception is not honored. The self-image in the situation falls short of the self-conception. Thus the immediate result of violation of the rules is to sensitize the affronted participant to his self-image, thus turning interaction away from tasks and toward an effort to restore an acceptable self-image.

Norms and Interpersonal Technique. Once interaction becomes preoccupied with self-image, it becomes, by definition, identity-oriented. Violation of the rules of interaction tends to divert interaction toward identity orientation. When such a transition occurs, the principal interpersonal techniques consist of making use of the rules of interaction to restore the favorable self-image. Once attention is called to the norm violation, not only the self-conception of the person affronted is threatened, but the self-conception of the violator also. The objectives of the person affronted are to reinstate the desired self-image by repeating the interaction sequence in correct form, or to elevate the self-image by securing debasement of the image of the other, or both. By conspicuously violating the norms himself or demanding an apology, the affronted person damages the self-image of the other in retaliation. The tactic of the norm violator is to deny that a norm violation occurred or to attempt to demonstrate that the other had first violated the rule and thereby released him from the corresponding obligation. The resulting interaction is only satisfactorily terminated by mutual acceptance of lowered situational self-images.

Because of the character of normative preoccupation as diverting interaction away from task orientations and because of the special advantage that accrues to the affronted person in being able to depart from the ordinary rules of interaction, the creation of situations in which alter will first violate the rules often becomes an interpersonal technique. Waller and Hill have referred to this type of interpersonal technique as the *manipulation of morality*.[10] The technique consists of manipulating situations so as to place the other at a moral disadvantage that can then be exploited.

The technique may consist simply of watching for any behavior by the other that can be construed as rule violation and then assuming the posture of affront, while calling the delinquency to the attention of the other. When one person raises his voice slightly, the other may interpret this as a violation of the rule of reasonableness and tolerance in the face of differences. By the aggrieved reproach "You don't need to shout at me" he places himself in the situation of moral advantage, implying his own right to depart from the rules.

The technique is often more highly developed as a stratagem for provoking the other into a norm violation that can then be exploited similarly. A husband who knows that his wife's breaking point comes a little before his own may cleverly maintain the semblance of tolerance and reasonableness, while taxing the patience of his wife until she loses her temper in the anticipated manner. As soon as this happens, he assumes his hurt posture and either terminates, with this advantage, a discussion that was otherwise running to his disadvantage or proceeds with the use of tactics that would

[10] Willard Waller and Reuben Hill, *The Family: A Dynamic Interpretation*, Dryden, New York, 1951, pp. 302–303.

have been regarded as unfair except for the wife's initial violation. A child likewise may learn that his parent becomes highly repentant after losing his temper and thus subtly provoke an angry parental outburst to gain some special concession that might otherwise be withheld.

The reciprocity principle also incorporates the idea that moral credit can be banked for withdrawal at a later time when it will be more useful. Although the norm against delving into the distant past in interaction limits the period for which moral credit may be saved, at least fairly substantial short-term savings are possible. The banking procedure may also be used as part of the interpersonal technique of manipulation of morality. By giving in rather conspicuously to another in a dispute, one may in a later disagreement cite one's own superior virtue as placing an obligation on the other to do his part in resolving differences this time. Or by pointedly doing somewhat more than one's proper share of work in the home, a family member can store up a bank account he can draw on to force a decision in his own direction or to escape some especially arduous task later. The role of martyr is a life plan built about the use of this technique in interpersonal relations.

Summary

Interaction consists of a sequence of gestures, each of which is interpreted as the basis for a response gesture. When ego gestures, he also interprets his gesture and prepares himself for a certain range of responses from alter. If alter's response gesture, as ego interprets it, is one he is prepared for, his reply is in line with his original gesture. If not, some further testing for a workable basis of interaction is necessary. Interpretations of gestures are based principally on culturally shared and in-group meanings, on images that ego has of alter, and on states of preparedness in ego. Each interactor tries to make gestures that will direct the course of interaction so as to foster the objects he values. In identity interaction the guiding value is the self-conception, and interaction is characterized by much attention to the interaction sequence itself, interpretation of gestures at the empathic and diagnostic levels, assignment of credit and blame, and gestures used as interpersonal techniques rather than for communication. Interaction is governed by a large number of norms that keep task interaction, in part, from becoming identity-oriented but precipitate identity interaction when they are violated. Because of the principle of reciprocity of normative obligation between interactants, norms can sometimes be manipulated.

The discussion in the present chapter dwells on the brief interaction sequence but also calls attention to the basis of more stable patterns of interaction. Each person tests and revises or reinforces his conception of alter and his self-conception with each episode. These self- and other-conceptions, in turn, influence the pattern of the next interaction episode. The result is that ultimately each interacting couple and group develop a pattern or a few patterns that give consistency and stability to their interaction.

Transition

Our chief interest in this book is the relatively more enduring patterns that individual episodes contribute to. In Part 2 we discuss a selected group of key processes that involve the more enduring pattern of family interaction. Chapters 3 and 4 deal with bonding, the formation of ties that bring and hold persons together in families, and with the change and weakening of these bonds. Chapters 5 and 6 deal with the central task process of decision making and with its by-product of dominance and subordination of individual family members. Chapter 7 examines the key identity processes of conflict and harmonization. And socialization is the subject of Chapter 8.

PART 2

THE BASIC GROUP PROCESSES

CHAPTER 3

BONDING: THE INDIVIDUAL AND THE FAMILY UNIT

In explaining the existence of any group, it is useful to think of *bonds* as bringing the members together, keeping them together, and causing them to interact within the group. A bond, or tie, exists when some *value* of the individual's—shared or unique—is felt to be fostered by association and interaction with some other person or group. One joins a club because he likes to associate with the members or because he and the members share a common interest in playing bridge or seeking enactment of tax-reducing legislation. Adults marry and remain married because in their experience the marital relationship offers the realization of ends they value. Ties between parents and children are the expression of benefits that each experiences from the parent-child association.

Group members may have a fairly clear notion of what brings them together, like the members of a committee with well-defined responsibilities. But many groups are established and sustained without the participants' ever having a clear understanding of the crucial bonds. Even groups with rather clear objectives normally develop an overlay of relatively unrecognized ties. Simmel has pointed out that the sheer enjoyment of sociability enters into almost every group, regardless of its formal purposes, and becomes one of the effective bonds.[1]

In the American family the ties are never fully explicit. The attraction between parent and child and among brothers and sisters is taken almost completely for granted or disguised by statements of socially approved sentiment. Popular advice on marriage maintains an uneasy balance between looking for the practical benefits of financial well-being, prestige, or marrying a good housekeeper and the dominating consideration of falling in love. Many resolve this dilemma by attempting to deny altogether that practical considerations matter. Thus fully half of some sixty college women refused indignantly, when interviewed, to answer the question

[1] Georg Simmel, "The Sociology of Sociability," translated by Everett C. Hughes, *American Journal of Sociology*, 55:254–261, November 1959.

"What kind of occupation would you most like to have in your future husband?" Their objection was that they would marry for love and not because of the man's occupation.[2]

Whether recognized or not, the nature of the ties in any group determines the nature of its dominant activities and the points of strength and weakness in the relationship. Just as we could not begin to study an organization sociologically without first attempting to identify its purposes, we must try to examine some of the major bonds in family life before proceeding to analyze the other processes that take place within it.

The Nature and Study of Bonds

Interdependence versus Harmony. A crucial distinction must be made between studying the nature and strength of the bonds that hold a relationship together and examining the processes of conflict and harmonization. If we speak of the presence of bonds that unite persons in a group as *bondedness* or *interdependence*, a high degree of interdependence does not necessarily signify a very *harmonious* relationship, nor does minimal interdependence indicate that conflict exists. Harmony and interdependence are related in a complex manner, but they are not identical properties.

Conflict does not take place unless there are bonds to keep the antagonistic individuals interacting. Cooley makes this observation in quite general terms:

> Opposition between one's self and some one else is also a very real thing; but this opposition, instead of coming from a separateness like that of material bodies, is, on the contrary, dependent upon a measure of community between one's self and the disturbing other, so that the hostility between one's self and a social person may always be described as hostile sympathy.[3]

In the absence of bonds of some kind neither of the potential antagonists cares sufficiently to make an issue of the matter with the other. Mere divergence of interest and opinion leads to *avoidance* rather than conflict, unless there is something to make the participants want to stay together to fight over their differences. A high degree of interdependence means that persons are forced to interact, regardless of whether the interaction is harmonious or conflictual. Indeed, we shall see later (Chapter 7) that it is precisely this coexistence of bondedness and opposition that underlies the most violent and volatile of family relationships. The opposite pole from harmony is conflict, but the opposite pole from interdependence is *indifference*.

[2] Ralph H. Turner, unpublished study.
[3] Charles H. Cooley, *Human Nature and the Social Order,* Scribner, New York, 1922, pp. 130–131. Quoted by permission of the publisher.

The Continuous Process of Bonding. It is customary among students of the family to investigate mate selection and the stability of established marital and family relationships as two separate topics. Differences between the bonds that bring about mate selection and those in established marriage might justify entirely separate treatment if bonds did not also undergo constant change throughout the duration of a marriage and of a parent-child relationship. Two simple illustrations of changing bonds in the family will suffice. A man and woman are mutually bonded by a common interest in intellectual matters. After children are added to the family, the wife is prevented from devoting the time necessary to maintain currency in intellectual matters and can no longer engage in discussion on the same level as her husband. One of the sources of solidarity is thereby weakened. The bond between parent and infant is often the complete dependence of the infant and the parent's sense of gratification in the infant's dependence and responsiveness. Physical and social maturation reduce and even eliminate the dependency, so that unless other bonds are present, the relationship moves in the direction of indifference.

Thus bonds are subject to continuous change, even in an established relationship. The change from courtship to marriage does not differ in principle from the shifts within established family relationships. Before considering the different relationships separately, we shall attempt to establish the common features of all the bonds that apply to different stages of the family experience.

Bonds and Selection. The examination of bonds includes two overlapping but partially distinct questions. First is what brings and holds people together in general. Queries as to why people are attracted to the marital status or why parents in general feel strong attachment to their children can be answered without reference to the specific mate or child. Second is the issue of who chooses whom and why. The question becomes why ego chooses a particular mate out of all the people in the world, why a parent feels a closer bond to one of his children than to the others.

Separating these two questions calls our attention to the fact that bonds vary in their *discrimination*. Some bonds unite one specific individual to another specific individual. Other bonds simply tie an individual to a certain kind of group without respect to who its specific members may be. The woman who recently secured her thirteenth divorce in the Los Angeles courts probably had effective ties to marriage as a relationship in general but only minimal ties of a discriminating kind. In examining bonds, it will be necessary to keep in mind a continuum from the kind of attachment in which no one else could take alter's place to a need that can be satisfied by almost anyone.

Field of Choice. Although bonds may be selective, the choice is always relative to an available range of alternatives. A person's choice is restricted by the extent of his social contacts and the people who will reciprocate his interest. Although it is probably less true today, the occupations of teacher and secretary traditionally have been contrasted for the range of choice they opened up to women. The woman teacher met relatively few men in her occupation, and they were chiefly principals and parents. The secretary, on the other hand, came in contact with many young men. A wide range of choice was possible for the secretary, but the teacher had to take what was available or go without.

Even with a wide range of contacts, a person's choice is effectively limited by the degree of his own attractiveness. The opportunity to cultivate values that require selective bonds depends on the availability of people who will reciprocate interest. The range of choice is limited in kind as well as in number. The kind of men a secretary meets will differ from those a librarian or a debutante or a factory worker meets.

The limitation in each person's field of choice has been studied in a number of researches dealing with *propinquity* in mate selection.[4] Propinquity means nearness or proximity. The hypothesis tested is that the likelihood of any two persons' marrying varies inversely with the distance apart they live. Findings have consistently supported the hypothesis, in spite of a popular belief that the distant and strange has a romantic attraction, lacking where familiarity has bred contempt. Propinquity in mate selection does not necessarily mean that those who live nearby are more attractive than those at a distance. We are simply more likely to meet and have sustained contact with persons nearby than with those at a distance.

A typical investigation into propinquity is that of Marvin R. Koller.[5] Koller selected samples of 1132 and 1200 marriages, respectively, from the official register of marriages in Columbus, Ohio, during 1938 and 1946. Residences of husband and wife at the time of filing were plotted on a city map, and the distance between them measured in standard city blocks of 1/8 mile. In order to determine whether residential propinquity was greater than would have occurred by chance, the investigator took a random sample of 100 men and 100 women who were not married to each other and made a similar analysis. Although one-fourth of the married pairs lived within about three blocks of each other, the equivalent figure for the control sample was 17 blocks. The median distance for the control sample was 29 blocks, compared with about 13 blocks for the married pairs.

[4] The pioneering study was by James H. S. Bossard, "Residential Propinquity as a Factor in Marriage Selection," *American Journal of Sociology*, 38:219–224, November, 1932.
[5] Marvin R. Koller, "Residential Propinquity of White Mates at Marriage in Relation to Age and Occupation of Males, Columbus, Ohio, 1938 and 1946," *American Sociological Review*, 13:613–616, October 1948.

Besides confirming the hypothesis of propinquity in mate selection, Koller's study shows that categories of persons differ in the degree that propinquity restricts the choice of mate (see Figure 1). If the data are interpreted as indicating field of choice, it appears that men who married between the ages of 24 and 27 chose from a wider field than those older or younger at time of marriage, and men in occupations with higher status (professional, managerial, clerical, and sales) likewise had a wider field than those in lower occupations. A wide field of choice enables men of optimal age and occupation to be more selective in their choice of mate than others can be.

A great deal of the effort devoted to refining the measurement and theory of residential propinquity in mate selection has been ably reviewed and criticized by Alvin Katz and Reuben Hill.[6] Residential segregation of ethnic groups and other populations that, for cultural reasons, tend to be endogamous complicates the picture, although nearness in space appears to be a correlate of mate selection even after statistical correction for segregation is made. Perhaps, as Katz and Hill suggest, the most adequate theory to encompass all the research findings is an adaptation of the theory of intervening opportunities, developed by Samuel Stouffer to describe migration patterns. In mate selection, as in migration, "the number of persons going a given distance is directly proportional to the number of opportunities at that distance and inversely proportional to the number of inter-

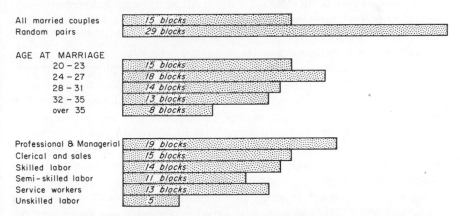

Figure 1.   Median city blocks between residences of husband and wife at marriage. (Adapted from Marvin R. Koller, "Residential Propinquity of White Mates at Marriage in Relation to Age and Occupation of Males, Columbus, Ohio; 1938 and 1946," *American Sociological Review*, 13:614–615, October 1948.)

[6] Alvin M. Katz and Reuben Hill, "Residential Propinquity and Marital Selection: A Review of Theory, Method, and Fact," *Marriage and Family Living*, 20:27–34, February 1958.

vening opportunities."[7] This means simply that the more attractive and eligible girls there are near at hand, the less likely a man is to go far afield to find himself a wife.

Our interest, however, is not in residential propinquity by itself, but in clarifying the distinction between field of choice and bonds. Mate selection depends on differential bonding between men and women who fall into each other's fields of choice. A theory of mate selection requires these two components. Specification of the field of choice depends on the marriage system. Under schemes of arranged marriage the field of choice is determined by the parent's social linkages rather than the young people's worlds. But in a system like our own, in which marriage normally develops from social contacts leading to dating and courtship, the field of choice is defined by three kinds of factors. First, the field of choice is limited to men and women who have an opportunity to meet one another. Here we must add to the obvious factor of physical distance the membership in mixed sex groups and patterns of movement, such as commuting between suburb and city center, that bypass intermediate areas.

Second, the field of choice is limited by the extent to which the situation in which people meet facilitates interaction on a personal rather than impersonal basis. For example, the development of personal relations is probably facilitated by interaction in a collaborative rather than an oppositional situation, in a social and recreational rather than a business setting, when people meet as peers rather than as superior-inferior, when the situation facilitates continued association rather than a single meeting. Under our norms of courtship the field of selection is broadened by participation in a setting, such as the school, where informal personal associations can be cultivated without commitments or implications of more serious relationship. Often the field of choice for middle-aged persons is restricted because of the tendency to define every informal association between unmarried men and women as a serious step in courtship.

Third, the field of choice is limited by social control that enforces the cultural norms regarding who should marry whom. For each person there is a field of *eligibles*. Summarizing the restrictions placed on mate choice in American society, Burchinal observes that endogamy is most generally enforced with respect to race, age, socioeconomic status, religion, and ethnic identity.[8] The pair's associates and family intervene to varying degrees to make courtship easier or more difficult according to how they judge the appropriateness of the match.

---

[7] Samuel A. Stouffer, "Intervening Opportunities: A Theory Relating Mobility and Distance," *American Sociological Review*, 5:846, December 1940, quoted in *Ibid.*, p. 32.
[8] Lee G. Burchinal, "The Premarital Dyad and Love Involvement," in Harold T. Christensen (ed.), *Handbook of Marriage and the Family*, Rand McNally, Chicago, 1964, p. 646. This chapter (pp. 623–674) presents an excellent survey and comprehensive bibliography of mate selection studies.

Two qualifications to our discussion of the field of eligibles are essential. First, the field is not a neatly bounded entity but a system of gradations. Among those who meet, circumstances conspire to make it easier or harder to develop personal rather than impersonal acquaintance and facilitate or impede thought of the possibility of marriage. Second, although we distinguish between the rules governing mate selection, which help define the field of choice, and the attractions or bonds that form between people, they are not altogether separate in practice. It is the nature of social control that rules and restrictions are often translated into values, so that they determine preferences spontaneously. Thus the eligible person is often also the one who seems naturally most attractive. We shall discuss this tendency at greater length in the subsequent chapters dealing with the sentiments of love.

Love and Family Bonds. The most obvious answer to the question of why people are attracted to each other and why they remain so is that they are in love. In one very real sense the answer may be correct and adequate, as should become clear later when love is examined at length. The answer, however, is not particularly helpful in explaining who will be attracted to whom or in distinguishing those whose bonds will become closer over the years from those who will drift apart. To explain attachment in terms of love is like saying that a child runs from a dog because of fear. Flight and fear are simply the action and feeling aspects of the same phenomenon, and nothing significant has been said until some explanation of the presence of fear is given. Similarly, love is the name of a feeling involving a strong attraction. The appropriate questions are why, when, and with whom people fall in love and what circumstances affect the durability of the love and attraction.

Provisionally we shall make the following assumptions about love, subject to revision based on the study of bonds and, later, of love as a cultural sentiment.

1. Love is a feeling or experience that reflects the presence of bonds between people more than it is a bond in itself.

2. Love endures or declines because the bonds between lovers remain effective or become ineffective rather than because of any inherent quality of the feeling of love itself.

Inferring Bonds. Since experiments with family solidarity are unethical and people's statements of what attracts them to the family are of limited validity, inferences concerning the nature of bonds in particular cases must always be provisional. Four kinds of evidence are often used to establish the nature of bonds.

First, observations of who associates with whom can be used, if there is some way to rule out limitations in the field of choice and if it is possible to compare situations in which the same people do and do not seek each other out.

Second, comparison of rates of marriage among different groups of people can sometimes be used. For example, the probability of marriage for a man or woman beyond the twenties is highest for divorcees, least for singles, and intermediate for widows (see Figure 2). But before we infer that divorcees are most attractive to the opposite sex, we must consider that a woman who has already delayed marriage beyond the usual age probably does not wish to marry or holds standards so high that they limit her field of choice. Higher marriage rates for men than women merely reflect their earlier mortality, giving the surviving men more choice than women.

Third, many of the correlates of success in marital-success studies can be regarded as indices of the kinds of bonds that hold marriages together. But the methods of these investigations do not distinguish accidental from essential correlates.

Fourth, studies of behavior when relationships are disturbed or broken often expose ties that are otherwise hidden. Bereavement studies have provided many clues to family bonds. The most valuable mine of clues concerning the nature of marital bonds is still the clinical study of ad-

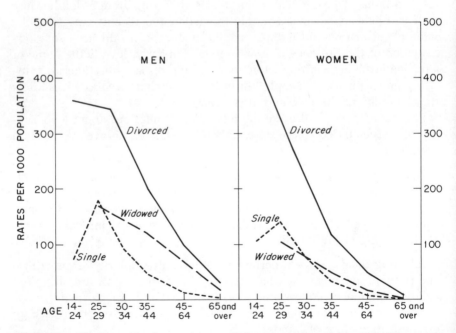

Figure 2.   Marriage rates by previous marital status. (Adapted from U.S. Department of Health, Education, and Welfare, *Vital Statistics of the United States, 1960*, vol. III, secs. 1, 2, and 7: *Marriages*, pp. 1–28.)

justment to the trauma of divorce, published by Willard Waller in 1930.[9]

Order of Presentation. Our discussion of particular bonds will be organized under three broad rubrics: first are those bonds which tie the individual to the family as a group or to marriage as a relationship, more than to specific persons; second are the more discriminating bonds that attract and tie to specific individuals; and third are the bonds which develop in the course of a relationship and which bind people as a by-product of their continuing interaction with one another. Finally we shall examine the relative vulnerability of different kinds of bonds and the conditions that make for stability or instability of attachments in the family.

Membership Gratifications as Bonds

It is probably safe to generalize that in most organizations the most effective bonds holding the members together are the gratifications that come from membership in the group as such, apart from ties among the individual members. Furthermore, there are probably only a very small number of groups in which there is no element of membership gratification contributing to the other bonds in solidifying the group. Even a pair of close pals gains some prestige simply from the fact that they are a group and share secrets unknown to outsiders.[10]

Two principal variables probably determine the relative importance of membership gratifications among the bonds that hold any group together. First, the larger the group, the more indispensable the part played by membership gratifications. A small group can be held together entirely by personal attachments. And a large group is usually held together in part by personal attachment within cliques. But the circumstances of size prevent solidarity on a group-wide basis organized about purely personal attachments. Thus loyalty to a nation, a church, a service club, a school, or a chamber of commerce tends to be loyalty first to the group.

The second variable is the extent to which the group is recognized, dealt with as a unit, and given some special standing and functions by the larger social unit within which it operates. When a small group of friends comes to be known in the neighborhood or community as "that set," they gain prestige from membership that becomes an added incentive for belonging. The more a group is thought to do important work and to convey prestige, the more membership in the group tends to become an end in itself.

The family in American society is not a large group, but it is recognized in the society, assigned what are regarded as very important tasks, such

[9] Willard Waller, *The Old Love and the New: Divorce and Readjustment,* Liveright, New York, 1930.
[10] See Georg Simmel's discussion of the fascination of secrecy in *The Sociology of Georg Simmel,* Kurt Wolff, ed. and trans., Free Press, New York, 1950, especially pp. 332–333.

as child rearing, and membership confers some distinct status. Thus, if our hypothesis is sound, there is reason to expect that membership gratification by itself plays an important part in the complex of family bonds.

Married Status as a Value. The married state is more highly regarded than the unmarried state, for persons of appropriate age. This is especially true in the case of women. There is, in fact, no altogether acceptable term in common use by which to speak of unmarried women without conveying an overtone of disrespect. For men the definition is more ambiguous. Although the older bachelor is generally depicted in a mildly unfavorable light, often humorously, the married man is also often pictured as having been trapped—caught in a moment of weakness by the ever-scheming female. By contrast the young man who is both attractive and able to remain single is something of a symbol of strength.[11]

The rewards attached to marital status by itself and the penalties of the unmarried status are of three kinds, which we shall discuss in order of increasing importance.

First is the prestige of being married. The marriage ceremony ritualizes a high regard for the wedded state. A parent can take pride in his children and their accomplishments. Even the fiscal credit rating of a person is likely to be higher simply because he is married.

Second is a moral or normative implication attached to marriage and nonmarriage. From time to time popular magazine articles discuss bachelorhood and spinsterhood with the theme that it is each person's duty to marry and that those who do not are shirkers. The bachelor, especially, and sometimes the spinster are described as willful, selfish persons, and marriage is glorified for its self-sacrifice.

Probably more telling for the mass of the population than either of the foregoing considerations is the implication of personal competence and normality associated with the married state and the suspicion that the unmarried may be disoriented, incompetent, maladjusted—in some sense personally inadequate. For the female in American society there is the implication of unattractiveness. The folk assumption is that every woman wishes marriage; nonmarriage then represents failure to achieve her wish. For the man there is likewise a reflection on his masculinity. If the man is not especially attractive, then his failure to marry is identified with weakness and possible impotence. If he is clearly attractive and holds out too long, the suspicion of homosexuality is often spread through gossip. The attractive man or woman with no discoverable personal deficiencies who fails to marry represents a continuing puzzle to those about him and is likely to be plagued constantly with questions or insinuations about why he or she has not married.

[11] See the discussion in Chapter 13.

In even more general form the implication of normality associated with marriage rests on linking the desire for marriage with maturity. Fundamentally the unmarried man or woman is likely to be depicted as immature, naive, unacquainted with life, indulging in childish habits. Marriage is regarded as the point at which the individual relinquishes the immature and irresponsible patterns of adolescence and becomes a more sober and responsible adult.

Marriage is usually seen as the normal accompaniment of maturity. But characteristics associated with a desirable state of some kind inevitably become translated into evidence of that state. Maturity and normality are not states that can be obviously and objectively identified. No person can observe his own behavior and say at a given moment, "I am now a mature individual." Consequently much importance comes to be attached to objectifiable criteria to prove one's maturity to himself and others.

The act of demonstrating overtly to oneself and others that one has achieved a given status is called *validation*. Marriage is one of the key devices, along with becoming financially self-sufficient, for validating personal adequacy, heterosexual normality, and personal maturity. Learning this connection explicitly or implicitly, most individuals expect to become married on reaching maturity. Turning the relationship around, they become anxious about their own adequacy, normality, and maturity when marriage is unduly delayed.

The most general reason why people marry is because, from early childhood, when they began to perceive the structure of their family of orientation, they have taken for granted that at the appropriate time they would embark on their own family life. The expectation, reinforced by implications of normality, morality, and prestige, is converted for the average person into a strong desire to become married. This desire is enacted in play by the child. As a deferred goal it is in the background of many of the maturing individual's activities. When the individual reaches an age at which it is important to regard himself as mature, the expectation becomes an active drive toward marriage that often overrides many of the discriminating tendencies that might otherwise be operative.

Individuals differ greatly in the extent to which the married status is an important means of self-validation. To many the connection is taken for granted but carries no great urgency. To others there is a vital and pressing need to be married in order to prove themselves. The degree to which the married status itself plays an important part in the bonds leading to marriage and holding a marriage together depends on two variables, namely (a) the extent to which the individual connects married status with self-validation and (b) the extent of insecurity or deficiency regarding self-validation.

Different people seek self-validation in different ways. To one person

self-validation lies in accomplishing something creative—scientific innovation, literary achievement, artistic accomplishment. To another the exercise of control over large groups of people is the means of proving himself
—in political leadership or by commanding a vast commercial enterprise.
The self-validation of being married, assuming an adult family role, receiving the love and respect of a parent from his children, must compete
with these other avenues. One woman may vest her identity predominantly in achievement in a profession or in receiving the adoration of the
masses, so that the bonds of the married and parental state are of small
importance. She will readily abandon a marriage that is inconvenient.
Another woman may vest her identity primarily in the marital and parental statuses and submit to great inconvenience and unpleasantness
rather than accept the implication that she has failed in this important
area of self-validation.

Whatever the extent to which self-validation is concentrated in the marital status, the individual's attitude may range from one of confident
assurance to one of urgency stemming from compelling anxiety. The individual who suffers no major discrepancy between self-image and self-
conception, who is generally satisfied with himself, is likely to exhibit the
former attitude. The person who is anxiously aware of serious self-defi-
ciencies is driven to prove in some tangible way as quickly as possible
that he really is adequate. Likewise, any threat to an existing marriage
arouses anxieties about personal adequacy that foster preservation of the
marriage at all costs.

Great anxieties about self-adequacy often lead to what may be called
panic marriage. The youth who proposes to the first girl who smiles at
him, the girl who becomes deeply involved with the first older boy who
expresses interest in her, each with a fear that there may be no other
chances if this one is passed up, usually reflect this kind of anxiety. Panic
marriage is undiscriminating with respect to mate. Several of the prediction researches have shown that marriage at a very young age has a
lower probability of success than later marriage.[12] Probably a disproportionate number of such very early marriages are panic marriages doubly
plagued by inadequate testing for compatibility and by the personal deficiencies of those involved.

When the self-validation of marriage is moral or religious, the same
principles apply, except that such imperatives have been imposed more
strongly on remaining married than on becoming married. The Christian
dictum "Whom therefore God hath joined together, let no man put
asunder" imposes an indiscriminate bond that operates regardless of the

[12] Earnest W. Burgess and Paul Wallin, *Engagement and Marriage*, Lippincott, Philadelphia, 1953, p. 521.

adequacy of the particular relationship between the individuals involved.

The entire discussion of membership gratifications to this point has dwelt on marriage, but similar principles apply in varying degrees to the bond holding parent to child, holding child to parent, and holding sibling to sibling. For the parent there is prestige in having children and in the respect the children show him. There is often a moral imperative to bear children and nearly always to be close to one's children. Except when disowning or disinheriting children is a socially sanctioned escape, the moral obligation that ties parent to child is, in western society, one of the most vitally supported of all social duties.

Bearing children serves as evidence of masculine and feminine adequacy, and the parent's relation to the child is a reflection on his maturity. The man who has an admiring son is the envy of other men. The woman whose children are affectionate toward her and confide in her enhances her own sense of personal worth and success. To the child there is likewise prestige, moral imperative, and personal adequacy implied in his relationships to parents and siblings.

Instrumental Gains. There is another kind of benefit gained from membership in any group, which is somewhat different from those we have thus far discussed. A status often carries with it certain instrumental benefits; that is, it facilitates the attainment of objectives that are not germane to the status or group membership itself. A lawyer who joins a church so as to make favorable contacts through which to enhance his legal practice is primarily concerned with the instrumental benefits of church membership. If a person marries or stays married or bears children or maintains good relations with a sibling because the relationship will be useful in some way, we may speak of an instrumental bond.

There are rights or privileges conferred on a person by virtue of the married status, and, conversely, the married individual is freed from certain obligations. Marriage in American society confers independence from adult supervision and releases one from many of the standard obligations toward his family of orientation. The extent to which the individual sees marriage as providing independence and the degree to which he experiences his relationship within the family of orientation as one of friction, restraint, or unwanted responsibility determines the likelihood of this kind of marriage.

Task Bonds

When people form a group, the most general reason they do so is in order to accomplish some end that no single person can achieve as well alone. Although we prefer emotionally to think of the family relationship entirely in terms of person orientation, the family in all societies carries out important tasks for its members which cannot be accomplished by the individual or which can be done better through the family union.

Integration on a task basis can be either *symbiotic* or *cooperative*. By symbiotic we refer to a relationship in which two or more persons have different individual goals, but by combining in a group, each can achieve his own goal better than he could alone. By cooperative we refer to a relationship in which people combine in a group because they share a common goal they can promote better together than apart.

The concept of symbiosis comes from biology, where such relations of mutual benefit have been observed extensively in the plant and animal world. The small birds who eat insects from the alligator's mouth, thus finding a source of food for themselves while relieving the alligator of an annoying pest, illustrate such a symbiotic relationship. In the strict sense such a relationship is symbiotic only if the participants are not consciously aware of the mutual dependence. Some truly symbiotic relationships exist in marriage, but many quasi-symbiotic forms of interdependence are found.

The most obvious of these task interdependencies is the division of function between breadwinner and housewife in the traditional American family pattern. But as this traditional specialization of tasks has been blunted, this kind of symbiotic bond has become a less compelling source of family union. If providing an income and maintaining a home constitute the most conspicuous symbiotic bond, raising children and improving their situation in life are among the most conspicuous of the cooperative bonds between husband and wife. The common desire for children creates a bond of special strength, because it is one of the very few activities that, in American society, cannot normally be satisfied in a different kind of union.

Because of the highly complex and varied character of sexual gratification, it plays quite varied parts in the total bond structure of different families. But the elemental need for sexual gratification should be viewed as a task bond, since a heterosexual relationship is preferred by most people, and gratification can initially be supplied as well by one cooperating individual as another. Sex operates as a family bond only to the extent that sexual satisfaction is easier to obtain or more acceptable or more gratifying when obtained with a marital partner than elsewhere. Without the mores circumscribing or prohibiting premarital and extramarital relations the sexual bond would be a much less effective source of family interdependence. Without the training that makes sexual release more gratifying in an intimate than in a casual relationship, the family bond would likewise be weaker. Whether sexual gratification is a cooperative or symbiotic task bond depends on the mutuality of sexual desire and gratification.

Our aim in discussing task bonding has not been to enumerate and weigh the importance of specific activities in uniting the several pairs that make up a family. Almost any activity which an individual enjoys or needs to engage in and which can be made more enjoyable or more effective by acting collaboratively with someone else is a potential source of either cooperative or symbiotic task bonding. Unlike a specialized organization, the family is the arena for a wide variety of activities and the setting for collaboration in diverse tasks. Hence the family is typically held together less by the prominence of a single shared activity than by the cumulative effect of a few major task interdependencies and a large number of minor collaborations.

Any theory of task bonding that is to be useful in understanding family interaction must explain how a lasting bond develops. If a bond is viewed as an aspect of a collaborative act in process, the bond should terminate when the act is completed. And we know this to be true for many of the collaborative acts we find ourselves involved in. But three circumstances combine to extend the bonding effect beyond the duration of the collaborative act and help determine whether the bonds persists or not.

1. Man is a future-oriented creature who is seldom concerned only with the action underway. He looks to the future, and if the activity is one he is likely to repeat on later occasions, the anticipation of collaborating again with the same person remains a bond between periods of activity. Tasks that by their nature are recurring and periodic are a source of bonding whenever the collaborative experience is successful.

2. An activity that brings two people together for a period of sustained interaction supplies an occasion out of which other bonds may develop. The interaction in one activity can permit the discovery of additional bases for collaboration that would otherwise have remained undiscovered. It may also result in occasional identity-oriented interaction, leading to the formation of the more personal kind of bond discussed in Chapter 4. If we think of latent bonds as existing wherever two people have common interests or skills that could be combined in effective collaboration, every individual has many latent bonds to almost every other individual. But only when the occasion brings them to interaction do these latent bonds become active. The importance of collaboration of any kind is that it sets in motion an interaction sequence that often translates latent bonds into active ones.

3. Finally, the experience of shared enjoyment seems to have a residual bonding effect that cannot be reduced to any other principle. Here we must distinguish between the strictly instrumental or work aspects of an activity and the feelings that arise because the activity means something more to the participants. The feeling of enjoyment can be derived from

the product of the activity: for example, pride in craftsmanship or ingenuity, and aesthetic enjoyment. Or enjoyment may come from the activity itself in the exhileration of confronting a challenge or pleasure in the setting in which the action is carried out. In either case, enjoyment is the "bonus" to activity. Enjoyable experiences tend to be relived in memory and to be the object of efforts to repeat if circumstances permit. Each time an enjoyable experience is relived in memory and each time the individual seeks to repeat the enjoyable experience, the bond is reawakened and reinforced.

Although the success and enjoyment of collaborative activity determine the potential for bonding that lasts beyond the duration of the activity, the field of choice continues to be a limiting circumstance. Thoroughly successful and enjoyable collaborations are most often not repeated because the partners have no further opportunity to collaborate. People who might have formed strong and lasting bonds are moved out of each other's fields of choice by the course of events.

Selectivity in Task Bonding

Although bonds derived from task interdependencies tie the individual to the group or relationship more than to a specific person in a great many instances, they do supply the basis for varying degrees of discrimination. Some pairings create more compatible task partnerships than others. Just as a man who establishes a business partnership is quite selective in whom he chooses as a partner, although he is primarily interested in the business rather than the man, so a woman desiring to bear and raise children finds some men more acceptable task partners than others. The most general observation of selective bonding that appears relevant to our discussion of task bonding is the tendency toward homogamy.

Homogamy. The question of whether likes or opposites attract is old. The first impression is that likenesses provide a readier fund of bonds than differences. Common goals, common means, and similar conceptions of family decision making should all contribute to task-based bonds. The division of function required to carry out many tasks, however, is aided by individual differences. Decision making runs into difficulty if all parties are either personally indecisive or given to very strong opinions. The family may be like a group of boys who all want to play baseball but none of whom will play any position but pitcher. Some kinds of differences undoubtedly facilitate the development of a role structure that is effective in getting jobs done.

In this connection it has often been stressed that cultural similarities are more conducive to mutual attraction and lasting bonds than are cultural dissimilarities. Similarities in education, socioeconomic class background, religious affiliation, and many other respects are cited. Each of these similarities means that the marriage partners will share a great many goals, making room for cooperative task integration. The similarities also mean that they will have been accustomed to many of the same procedures in making and effecting decisions. But they also probably mean that they will have learned much the same conceptions of what the proper differences among men, women, and children in the family decision-making process should be. The man and woman from a similar class and educational background will not necessarily have been trained to play the same roles. But they will have been trained to expect much the same roles of ego and alter in the family.

A great many empirical comparisons between the characteristics of husbands and wives have been reported in sociological literature.[13] The principle of *homogamy*—that people marry persons who are more like than unlike themselves—receives abundant support with respect to physical characteristics, attitudes, and social background. The most comprehensive investigation of homogamy was based on Burgess and Wallin's 1000 engaged couples. The study has the advantage that subjects were tested before they had the chance to become similar in attitudes by living together. Every one of 51 items dealing with social background and attitudes showed some degree of homogamy. The degree of homogamy varied greatly for different objects, as shown in Table 1. Religious and family

TABLE 1   HOMOGAMY IN SOCIAL CHARACTERISTICS AND ATTITUDES

Groups of Items	Number of Items	Mean Coefficient of Contingency
Religious affiliation and behavior	4	.54
Family background (socioeconomic, community, nativity characteristics, etc.)	6	.38
Courtship behavior	4	.33
Conceptions of marriage	17	.31
Extent and type of social participation	11	.24
Family relationships (family of orientation)	9	.12

SOURCE: Adapted from Ernest W. Burgess and Paul Wallin, "Homogamy in Social Characteristics," *American Journal of Sociology*, 49:124, September, 1943. The coefficient of contingency was separately computed for each item and averaged for each group. Because of a mathematical peculiarity of the coefficient and because there were only three or four possible responses to each item, a perfect correlation would have produced a coefficient somewhere between .82 and .87.

[13] Ernest W. Burgess and Paul Wallin, "Homogamy in Social Characteristics," *American Journal of Sociology*, 49:109–124, September 1943; Burgess and Wallin, "Homogamy in Personality Characteristics," *Journal of Abnormal and Social Psychology*, 39: 475–481, October 1944; Burgess and Wallin, *Engagement and Marriage*, pp. 208–213; Burchinal, *op. cit.*, pp. 645–658.

backgrounds are quite impressive bases for homogamy, but the similarities regarding relationships to the family of orientation and extent and kind of social participation are minimal.

Robert Winch has challenged all the evidence regarding homogamy of social characteristics.[14] He suggests that the evidence can be fully explained on the basis of propinquity. Boys and girls have more opportunities to meet others from similar social and religious backgrounds and to meet them under circumstances that are favorable to forming serious attachments. Many married couples originally met through social clubs, religious organizations, and school association, which all help bring together persons of similar background. Since propinquity applies not only to place of residence but also to social and religious background, the supposed evidence of homogamy may tell us nothing about who would prefer whom if people had equal opportunity to meet all kinds of people. Hence we must conclude that research has not yet been subtle enough and controls have been insufficient to distinguish between the bonding character of similarities in social background and attitude and the extent to which these similarities dictate fields of choice.

The observation of homogamy does not afford an explanation of bonding but offers empirical clues to the formulation of theories to predict and explain differential bonding. In this connection, observations of the circumstances under which homogamy does and does not prevail are the most useful form of evidence. Accordingly, a study by Kerckhoff and Davis is of particular interest.[15] Ninety-four college couples who were engaged, pinned, or seriously considering marriage filled out questionnaires in October 1959 and again the following May. In October the 188 students were asked to rank ten standards by which family success might be measured. The correlation between their rankings supplied the measure of value consensus for each couple. In May they were asked whether they were closer to being a permanent couple than they had been in October. Answers to this question supplied the dependent variable in the study. The predicted relationship between value consensus in October and progress toward permanence in May was statisically significant. Couples were then divided into those who had gone together for 18 months or more and those who had gone together for less than 18 months. Among the short-term couples, the predicted relationship was again found. But among the

[14] Robert F. Winch, *Mate Selection: A Study of Complementary Needs,* Harper & Row, New York, 1958.

[15] Alan C. Kerckhoff and Keith E. Davis, "Value Consensus and Need Complementarity in Mate Selection," *American Sociological Review,* 27:295–303, June 1962. The important findings regarding need complementarity, which are essential for adequate interpretation of this evidence, are reported in Chapter 4.

long-term couples, there was no longer a relationship large enough to meet the requirements of statistical significance.

If homogamy is strongest with respect to organizational affiliations that tend to determine fields of choice and if it is more characteristic of earlier than later stages of courtship, it may have less significance for the enduring bonds among family members than for initial associations and relatively transitory ties. Either personal ties determine deep and enduring relationships, or a more complex principle than similarity of attitude and affiliation is required to describe the operation of enduring task bonds.

Balance theory is one elaboration of the homogamy principle, developed by Fritz Heider[16] and Theodore Newcomb[17] and tested by Newcomb in a study of male university students in an experimental residence house. If one individual A is attracted to another B and if A discovers that B's attitude toward a third person or impersonal object or value X is dissimilar to his own, he experiences a strain. In order to reduce the strain, he must either change his own attitude, or attempt to change B's attitude, or discover that his attraction to B is less than he thought. This ABX or *balance theory* does not pretend to explain the origins of attraction between two people, but it does supply a basis for predictions regarding the persistence of bonds and rebonding. Moderately unbalanced systems are tolerated. But the strain of an unbalanced system is great when the attraction between A and B is intense and when the object X is important and has a common effect on A and B. Balance theory has obvious application in explaining the constantly changing intensity of bonds for each of the pairs of individuals making up a family.

Value and Role-compatibility Theories. A similar assumption of homogamy but a different emphasis regarding the dynamics underlying it are incorporated in what Robert Coombs calls a *value theory* of mate selection.[18] He uses a conception of value that is similar to the view presented in Chapter 2. Couples are mutually attracted because they share similar values, and presumably parent-child and sibling bonds vary likewise according to their similarity in values. It is not so much the pursuit of these values as goals of collaborative activity, however, that makes them relevant to bonding but their effect on the interpersonal relationships that are incident to association for any purpose whatever. Coombs believes that it is simply easier and more satisfying to do whatever you are doing in association with someone who shares your major values than it is with someone whose values diverge too much from your own:

[16] Fritz Heider, *The Psychology of Interpersonal Relations*, Wiley, New York, 1958.
[17] Theodore M. Newcomb, *The Acquaintance Process*, Holt, New York, 1961.
[18] Robert H. Coombs, "A Value Theory of Mate Selection," *Family Life Coordinator*, 10:51–54, July 1961.

Emotional satisfactions are attained in connection with values. When a value is directly attacked or is ignored under circumstances which normally call it to attention, those who hold the value are resentful. Because of this emotional aspect it seems reasonable to expect that persons will seek their informal social relations with those who uncritically accept their basic values and thus provide emotional security. Such compatible companions are most likely to be those who "feel" the same way about "important" things, i.e., those who possess similar values.[19]

Coombs's statement extends the relevance of homogamy to a broadly conceived collaborative relationship but offers no clue to the varying applicability of the homogamy principle to different kinds of values and to relationships of different duration. Bernard Murstein attempts to find the basis for bonds in collaborative activity without accepting either homogamy or heterogamy as generally applicable principles.[20] He proposes that role-compatibility theory explains the homogamy found in empirical investigation as indicating those respects in which likeness makes for compatibility. All persons have expectations regarding the roles they wish their partners to play, which reciprocate the roles they wish to play themselves. Although Murstein deals only with mate choice, the principle is equally applicable to the intensity of bonds in all family relationships. An older child has ideas about the roles he and his younger brother should play in interaction; a child quickly forms images of what mother-child interaction should be like. Bonds form when the role that alter plays agrees closely with the role that ego wishes alter to play and when alter's role facilitates ego's playing the role he wishes. A girl tends to "choose the spouse who is most likely to fulfill the key roles she has in mind for a husband and who will allow her to fulfill the important roles consonant with her conception of 'wife.' "[21]

In order to test this approach, Murstein had a modified Edwards Personal Preference Schedule filled out by both members of 99 couples who were engaged or going steady. He compared each individual's description of an ideal spouse with the self-description by his mate to secure a measure of role compatibility. In order to constitute a control group the investigator combined the men and women in pairs at random and made a similar comparison. He then found that both homogamy and role compatibility characterized the true pairs as compared with the random pairs. But role compatibility went further in accounting for the pairing of in-

[19] *Ibid.*, p. 51. Quoted by permission of the E. C. Brown Center for Family Studies and the author.
[20] Bernard I. Murstein, "Empirical Tests of Role, Complementary Needs, and Homogamy Theories of Marital Choice," *Journal of Marriage and Family*, 29:689–696, November 1967.
[21] *Ibid.*, p. 690.

dividuals than did homogamy, supporting the investigator's theoretical position. When each person's description of an ideal mate was compared with his description of his own mate, the association was even stronger, as would be expected. Murstein makes the following observation:

. . . some needs, such as "deference," "autonomy," and "abasement," do not fit either a homogamy, complementary needs, or role compatibility theory very well when the respective self-concepts or the role-compatibility inter-perception scores are involved. One possible explanation for this finding is that those needs are not directly translatable into roles desired for the self and for the fiancee. A man may want his wife to show deference to his parents but not to other disliked elders; he may want her to be autonomous at home when he is downtown in his office so that when the furnace stops she does not call him in a helpless manner. Yet, on another occasion, he may resent autonomous behavior on her part if he thinks they ought to go to a play and she insists on a concert.

What is suggested, therefore, is that couples do not choose each other by needs, but by roles.[22]

Mutual Gratification and Economy of Decision. At the risk of adding to the multiplicity of formulations in this area, we shall suggest two principles that, taken together, subsume much of what we have already observed about interpersonal selectivity in the formulation and maintenance of task bonds. Whether the various interests of family members and potential family members link them together strongly or not depends on whether their respective goals are such that they can be attained more effectively in collaboration than separately and whether the nature of the relationship between the two individuals is such that they can collaborate and make decisions with a minimum of delay and friction. We shall call these principles *mutual gratification* and *economy of decision*, respectively.

The principle of mutual gratification holds that the strength of the task-based bonds in any family is a function of the ratio of activities that serve the members' mutual ends to the activities that serve the ends of only some of the members. In each instance the reference to activities is the number of activities multiplied by the importance of the ends being served. A single highly important unifying goal offsets several minor divisive ones. The mathematical form of this statement is altogether hypothetical. There is no evidence bearing directly on a formulation of this character. The approximately mathematical statement is useful, however, in sharpening the hypothesized logic of task bonds and stating the principle in a manner that will ultimately permit testing.

Converted into common sense, the formula means that compromises

[22] *Ibid.*, p. 695. Quoted by permission of The National Council on Family Relations and the author.

offset the positive gratifications of a relationship. To the extent that members seek the same or mutually supporting ends, there will be strong bonds among them. But to the extent that the ends they seek are unrelated or actually impede each other's goals, the bonds will be weakened.

In the statement of this principle we attempt to allow for both cooperative and symbiotic collaboration. Common values are undoubtedly the most prevalent and important source of mutual gratification in collaborative task activity. But it is a mistake to overlook the extent to which stable relationships in marriage or between parent and child arise out of the manner in which people with different values serve their respective ends through a collaborative relationship.

The second principle takes cognizance of the fact that collaboration is more than the parallel pursuit of common ends. No matter how similar their goals, two persons may have difficulty sustaining a working relationship. But if they cannot work together or if the attempt to work together generates a great deal of friction or consumes inordinate amounts of time, either their goals will not be reached or the cost of reaching them will outweigh the benefit of attaining them. If two persons cannot reach decisions about the means to their shared ends and the respective roles they should play in pursuing these ends, the latent task bonds between them can never be activated into effective bonds. Hence we speak of an economy-of-decision principle, that the more easily two people can reach decisions, the greater the opportunity to form bonds on the basis of cooperative or symbiotic collaboration.

The strength of task-based bonds in any family is a function of the ease with which decisions can be reached, and the ease of decision making comes about from one of two conditions. Either the individuals have the same ideas about the means for accomplishing given ends, or there is an effective decision-making relationship between them. A couple may agree on the ends they wish but have difficulty in coming to agreement on how to go about gaining these ends. A bond of unity about a shared interest in raising children may be weakened if the parents have been trained to rather different ways of caring for children. Those who naturally go about things in much the same way have a great advantage in this respect.

No matter how much convergence of methods there may be, a great many decisions must be made in instances when the members would proceed in different ways or when no one has a ready-made procedure. Such formal procedures as majority vote are often inapplicable in the family because many decisions must be made by only two persons. Unequal authority is one system that facilitates decision making. Regardless of the extent of agreement on ends, a family may fail altogether to attain the goals they seek if they are caught up in a pattern of indecisiveness or if every decision requires an excessive amount of interaction.

In Chapter 4 we shall suggest that some evidence used to support the complementary-needs theory of mate selection can be interpreted as well or better as an indication of the working of this economy-of-decision principle. Generally speaking, unequal authority is the most widely used device for simplifying decision making. Organizations and groups regularly and willingly designate individuals, give them authority to make decisions, and agree to abide by these decisions for periods of time. A common response to the indecisiveness of the committee of peers is to propose such a delegation of authority. Investigations that show bonding between the relatively dominant and the relatively submissive, or the initiators and the followers, suggest the situation in which decision making is simplified, so that the pair can get on with the activities that bring them the realization of their values and personal enjoyment.

CHAPTER 4

PERSON BONDS AND VULNERABILITY

Pressures toward social participation through the family unit and the practical advantages of collaboration with other family members create a reservoir of relatively impersonal family bonds. The principles of mutual gratification and economy of decision make some pairs more bondable as siblings, spouses, or parent and child than others. Although it will be long before sufficiently crucial hypotheses are tested to disentangle the many hypothetical kinds of bonds, contemporary folklore places greater emphasis on another kind of bond, linking family members as persons.

Two ideas—the linking of selves or identities and zero substitutability—underly the concept of person bonding. Person bonds are realized through the identity-oriented aspects of social interaction rather than through task accomplishments. Identity gratifications that come from affiliation with alter bind ego to alter. Both task rewards and identity gratifications may spring from the same interaction, but there is no necessary perfect correlation. Successful collaboration between husband and wife in the task of establishing a high standard of living may nevertheless fail to produce gratifications for each in the personal association between them.

Although we think of the identity as unique to the individual, identities do fall into types, with the result that identity bonds do not necessarily eliminate substitutability altogether. It is still possible to gain similar identity gratification from a class of alters and not just from a single individual. It is more the myth of the self than the reality that equates identity bonding with zero substitutability. Indeed, substitutability is probably reduced to zero only when bonds apply to the continuation or development of a relationship that is already in process. Only the uniqueness of an interaction pattern already established between two persons supplies the basis for a bond that cannot be as adequately satisfied by someone other than the existing partner.

In light of this distinction, we shall examine bonds in two categories. First are the bonds that depend on identity rather than task aspects of interaction, that bind because they reinforce or improve the self-conceptions of the partners. Second are the bonds that develop in connection with the ongoing interaction between persons who have already been brought together because of some other bond. The first we shall designate as *identity bonds.* The second, because they grow with interaction, we shall call *crescive bonds.*

Identity Bonds

Identity gratification is gained whenever ego is made aware of a self-image that reinforces a favorable aspect of the self-conception or tends to improve the self-conception without imposing new and anxiety-producing demands on the individual. An identity bond is established whenever the identity gratification is perceived to come from association or interaction with some other person.

There are two principal ways in which the association of one person with another can generate an identity bond. When a relationship of *identification* exists, ego assimilates into his own self-conception the qualities he perceives in alter's identity. When the effect is to enhance his own self-conception, ego experiences a bond to alter. Under this form of bonding the manner in which alter acts toward ego is less important than the existence of a situation that permits identification and a conception of alter such as to enhance ego's self-conception when the identities are merged. Without respect to the alter conception, the nature of alter's *response* to ego may enhance ego's self-conception. Alter may treat ego with deference or with evident trust or with warm appreciation or in other ways that convey a very favorable image of ego. The experience of being treated in this manner supplies motive force for continuing or repeating the interaction.

Before examining these two forms of identity bond in greater detail, we should call attention to the interrelatedness between the two kinds of bonds. Although there are marked differences between relationships of identification and response, it is difficult to maintain either relationship within the family without an element of the other. If there is no favorable response from alter, ego finds it difficult to maintain identification for an extended period. The identification of a younger sibling with an older one is an almost universal bond. Only occasional favorable response from the elder is needed to keep it alive. But even in this relationship a persistent ignoring or disparaging treatment from the elder eventually undermines identification. Similarly, the value of most responses to ego is affected by the alter conception that ego holds. To be treated with affection or respect by a person of admirable qualities means more than to be treated in this way by a person of inferior qualities. Hence some gain from identification is an important adjunct to most response bonds.

Mutual bonding does not necessarily mean that each person is tied to the other by the same kind of bond. The bond in one direction may be more heavily weighted with task elements and be reciprocated by a bond that relies more on identity gratifications. A fairly common kind of reciprocity occurs when identification and response bonds are paired. In any relationship of inequality, identification is more common from the subordinate to the superordinate member, and identity-enhancing response is more frequent in the opposite direction. Hence identification often plays a larger part in the wife's attachment to her husband and response in the husband's attachment to his wife. Similarly the small child gains by identification with his parent and the younger sibling by identification with the older. The small child or younger sibling reciprocates by expressing admiration and granting indulgence toward the parent or elder sibling, thereby establishing the basis for a parent-to-child or elder-to-younger response bond.

Bonds of Identification. If we use "identification" in the least complicated sense,[1] as an attitude in which a person experiences what happens to another person as if it had happened to himself, then identification is at the heart of the family relationship. Each member experiences pride in the accomplishments of the others and suffers humiliation in their embarrassments. The parent who swells with pride when his child performs before the Parent Teachers Association or who feels as if everyone were laughing at him when his child forgets his lines in the school play is reflecting this identification.

The sources of identification are both internal and external. The latter come from the simple tendency to observe and think of people in groupings rather than as separate individuals. We tend to think of members of any foreign nation together rather than as distinct individuals, blaming each for what we dislike about the nation as a whole. If a member of some church becomes involved in public scandal, we are inclined to treat it as bringing discredit on the entire congregation. If a man achieves some unusual success, those who are known as his close friends reap some of the glory because, in the eyes of outsiders, they are identified with him. The folk practice of treating family members as a unit is even more marked than in the case of other groups. There is less escape from shared disgrace and a more certain gain from shared renown.

Because each of us has learned to take this attitude toward others in groups and because others constantly respond to us according to our group memberships, we adopt the corresponding attitude toward ourselves in relation to our groups. We often take responsibility for the acts of others within our group, and we accept credit for their accomplishments. Thus

---

[1] Robert F. Winch develops a more complex conception of identification in relation to the family and examines other established conceptions. See *Identification and its Family Determinants: Exposition of Theory and Results of Pilot Studies*, Bobbs-Merrill, Indianapolis, 1962.

the external source of identification, in the attitudes of outsiders toward us, is unwittingly incorporated into our own attitude toward ourselves.

The internal source of identification is more difficult to specify, and its explanation is subject to more controversy. But there are clearly situations that are conducive to identification, some of which are ephemeral and some of which outlast the situation. Such identifications may be quite diffuse and applicable to almost anyone if the situation is right. Members of an audience feel indignant when one of their members questions a favored speaker in an unfair manner, taking the attack on the speaker personally. A moment later they may find themselves identifying with the questioner when the speaker goes too far in humiliating the questioner by exposing his error for all to see. The presence of some other bond seems to facilitate the experience of identification in an appropriate situation. A small child may cry when a brother or sister is punished or hold his breath when the vaccination needle is injected into his mother's arm.

It is not necessary for our purposes to explain the psychological mechanisms underlying the internal sources of identification. Whether it represents an elementary libidinal mechanism, as viewed by psychoanalysis,[2] or a basic aspect of what Charles H. Cooley calls "sympathy,"[3] or whether it is derived solely from internalization of the attitudes of others as discussed under external sources, it becomes a pervasive aspect of attachments. Once established, the connection can operate either positively or negatively. The potential benefits from being identified with a certain person supply much of the dynamism of attachment. And the personal gains or losses from identification tie individuals closer together or force them into conflict.

The lasting consequence of identification is some modification in the self-conception. By virtue of being associated with some individual, one's own identity takes on characteristics from the identity of the other. To the extent to which the identity is thereby enhanced, a bond is formed. A consideration of identification as a family bond, then, requires examination of some of the ways in which linkage within the family enhances self-image in the short range and the self-conception in the long range.

Prestige is the most obvious aspect of the self-image affected in identification. Its importance is openly acknowledged in the adolescent term "rating."[4] A boy is known by the kind of girl he can "rate." The reflected gains from being associated with a glamorous girl, an athletic champion, a popular figure, or a person of wealth are too well known to require elaboration. Although we do not have specific evidence on the matter, it is a

[2] Sigmund Freud, *New Introductory Lectures on Psychoanalysis,* Norton, New York, 1933.
[3] Charles H. Cooley, *Human Nature and the Social Order,* Charles Scribner, New York, 1902.
[4] Willard Waller, "The Rating and Dating Complex," *American Sociological Review,* 2:727–734, October 1937.

plausible hypothesis that women whose husbands are successful in business or a profession necessarily acquire a higher opinion of themselves than wives of less successful men.

Identification may also be connected with one's ideals, moral and otherwise. One is attracted to a person who seems to have qualities of character he wished that he had but in which he feels deficient. Through identification he shares the sense of being personally more adequate in these areas.

Theodore Reik, developing a common theme from psychoanalysis, attributes falling in love to a panicked effort to escape from the discrepancies between the perceived self and the ideal self through identification.[5] Through the training that a child receives from early childhood onward he acquires a superego that sets up unattainable standards of excellence and moral perfection. Against this set of standards the individual accumulates a fund of dissatisfaction with himself. From the strict moral code he cannot fully comply with he develops a pervasive sense of guilt. The sense of personal inadequacy and diffuse guilt becomes unbearable, so that he forms a strong identification with another person who appears perfect in these respects.

Unfortunately there are no perfect people, or at least there are not enough to take care of the imperfect people who need to form such identifications. Consequently the imperativeness of the need leads to a fantasy solution. The individual attributes to some other person a degree of perfection quite unrelated to his objective characteristics and forms the identification. He idealizes his partner in order that through identification he may acquire a new and perfect self-image.

Although Reik discusses the mechanism with respect to mate love, it applies equally to all the attachments within the family. The developing conscience of the child and his idealization of the parent go hand in hand. Discovery of but a minor defect in the parent is intensely distressing because of the identification. The parent, in turn, is attached to the child in part because of the child's promise of becoming something better than the parent. Many of the stresses in parent-child relations that seem to a disinterested observer to have no reasonable basis spring from the parent's distress in having to accept the image of the child as subject to all the same deficiencies as himself.

Although the stress on this aspect of identification process stems from psychoanalytically oriented thinking, the descriptive outlines of the process do not require a psychoanalytic explanation. Reik's observations con-

---

[5] Theodore Reik, *A Psychologist Looks at Love*, Farrar, Straus & Giroux, New York, 1944. Comparing the married and unmarried members of 59 matched pairs of women college graduates, Floyd M. Martinson found greater ego deficiency as measured by standard personality tests on the part of the married women. See "Ego Deficiency as a Factor in Marriage," *American Sociological Review*, 20:161–164, April 1955.

tribute to the understanding of family process and family bonds and can be interpreted through any one of several alternative psychological theories.

Identification, Aspiration, and Comparison. Insofar as identification plays a part, there is a tendency for potential mates to fall along a continuum from most to least desirable. Because each person's self-conception is unique, the scale from most to least desirable is not the same for everyone. But since the criteria for assigning prestige and moral excellence are preponderantly similar among persons raised in a common culture, the scales of desirability are also very largely shared.

If only the mechanism of identification were at work, a kind of free-for-all would take place, in which everyone competed for the most desirable mates and the least desirable wound up reluctantly having to accept partners as undesirable as themselves. The overwhelming majority would either not marry or consider their marriage close to failure from the very start.

It is well known, however, that whenever objects are ranked in value on some kind of scale, the majority of people nevertheless do not strive for the best. Rather, each person settles roughly on some level he aspires to, and for the majority this level is not the highest. In fantasy the individual may still aspire to the top, but in practice his sights are lower. There is a body of research and theory dealing with level of aspiration and intended to uncover the determinants of each person's aspiration level.[6] On the basis of laboratory experiments it has been amply demonstrated that in general an individual lowers his aspirations after a series of failures at any task and raises them after successes. To a considerable extent each person's prior experiences of success and failure in his relations with the opposite sex should help to determine how high he sets his goals in mate selection.

If we go beyond the laboratory evidence, we can view successes and failures as modifying or reinforcing the self-conception. One sets a level of aspiration tentatively in tasks he has had no prior experience in by generalizing from other experiences that are somehow related. The level of aspiration is thus determined generally by the self-conception. Apart from fantasy, those who have a higher estimate of their own qualities are more likely to strive to find a mate with higher qualities of excellence. Since people probably have some tendency to overestimate themselves, this principle does not preclude their striving for someone a little better with whom they can identify to their own advantage. As pointed out in Chapter 2, the

[6] For a classic statement of level of aspiration theory, see Kurt Lewin, Tamara Dembo, Leon Festinger, and Pauline S. Sears, "Level of Aspiration," in J. McV. Hunt (ed.), *Personality and the Behavior Disorders*, Ronald, New York, 1944, vol. I, pp. 333–378. For a statement concerning more recent research, see John W. Atkinson, *An Introduction to Motivation*, Van Nostrand, Princeton, N.J., 1964.

self-conception develops out of the discrepancies between a set of ideals and the self-image, as the latter appears in situation after situation. In most people the pull of the ideal self makes the self-conception a description of the individual in his best moments rather than in his average performance. But the recurring experience with self-images prevents the self-conception from becoming entirely divorced from the attainable. The self-conception sets the level of attainment which the individual regards as success and to which he normally aspires. Identification accordingly ties ego to alter if alter's qualities appear to match ego's self-conception.

Another consideration limits level of aspiration in marital selection and prevents most people from seeking an identification bond with the "most perfect mate." In close and continued interaction any gross differences in valued characteristics necessarily set in motion a tendency to compare one's self with the other. Comparison and identification are in a sense opposite relationships but are bound to coexist in a close and continued relationship. Constant association with an obviously superior person serves by contrast as a constant reminder of one's own deficiencies. The repeated arousal of the feelings of one's own personal inadequacy or diffuse guilt by contrast to the other's perfection is an unpleasant experience and makes the relationship uncomfortable. A man who admires a girl who is much more intelligent than himself nevertheless risks being constantly shown up for his own limited intelligence. Consequently the tendency to form a bond of identification with such a girl is offset by the discomfort experienced in association wth her. The self-conception operates in this second manner as a limiting force on the tendency to establish identifications with persons whose characteristics are much superior to one's own.

Parenthetically it is worth noting that fantasy is not subject to this latter limitation. Hence hero worship takes the place of some of the unattainable identifications in real life.

Invidious comparison does not apply to those areas in which the definitions of sex roles assign a given value more to one sex than to the other. A girl who earns only a small income as a salesclerk need not feel uncomfortable in association with a wealthy business executive, since a woman's prestige does not depend on her earnings in the same manner as a man's does. A man who holds the view that high moral standards apply more to women than to men can benefit from identifying with a morally exceptional woman without feeling the intense discomfort of invidious comparison. If he accepts the moral ideal equally for himself, however, the discomfort of unfavorable comparison occurs. Similarly, age differences can remove this limitation to identification in case of parent-child relations and older-younger sibling relations.

Although the most common effect of the identification bond is to favor attachments with persons who are relatively high, or at least as high or a little higher than ego, in some consensual prestige hierarchy, there are important exceptions to this rule. These exceptions occur when something in the life history of ego has led him to develop a somewhat idiosyncratic prestige hierarchy. If ego is sufficiently isolated from others so that he is unaware of their evaluations or if he has built up defenses that nullify or even reverse the effect of judgment by his parents and others who would normally be close to him, identification can lead to "marrying down."

Just such a pattern of rebellious marriage is described by Linton Freeman among a small group of University of Hawaii students.[7] He selected eight interethnically married students and fourteen others who dated exclusively outside their own ethnic group. They were interviewed extensively over a six-month period, and the features common to them all were extracted to form a general characterization. Although relations among ethnic and racial groups in Hawaii are notably harmonious and intergroup marriages are both legal and socially tolerated, each major group still has strong norms against such marriages. Consequently, marriage and serious dating are overwhelmingly within the white, the Chinese, the Japanese, and other major groups.

Freeman found that each of these twenty-two students reported becoming seriously alienated from his own ethnic group well before the age of dating. Each had developed feelings of rejection in connection with childhood social relationships in his own ethnic group. In the schools they attended social life was largely organized about ethnic identity, and so all these students generalized their feelings and felt resentful against all members of their own ethnic group.

Thus, an individual's ethnic group became identified as an agent of frustration and was negatively evaluated on that basis. It became important to escape identity with the group. Often there was a conscious desire to get away from the group and from the things which symbolized it. Deviant behavior of some sort was the universal response . . . a self-perpetuating cycle was built up in which deviation intensified rejection and rejection enhanced deviation.[8]

After rejecting his own group, the individual developed an interest in another group rejected by his own. Identification with the new group and acceptance of its values provided a new sense of superiority and a basis for explaining rejection by his own group. The new ethnic group was really superior, and it was because at heart he was really one of them that his own group could not accept him. Dating exclusively within the new ethnic group then became part of the process of confirming identification with that group. Members of the new group were often idealized, and the idealization applied in full force to datable members of the opposite sex. Since

[7] Linton Freeman, "Homogamy in Interethnic Mate Selection," *Sociology and Social Research*, 39:369–377, July 1955.
[8] *Ibid.*, p. 372. Quoted by permission of the Editor and the author.

members of the new group who were available for dating were themselves rebels of the same sort, these relationships were often stormy. Sometimes the individual went through a series of love affairs with different representatives of the same group, each time seeking to consolidate the same kind of personal identification.

It is important in making use of Freeman's findings to recognize that they apply to only an unknown fraction of interracial and interethnic marriages. Only eight of his subjects were married, and there is no doubt a large amount of casual interethnic dating that was systematically excluded from study by the criterion of exclusively interethnic dating. The Hawaiian situation is distinctive in at least two important ways: there is a large field of eligibles within each ethnic group, so that interethnic dating is not forced on people; and well organized ethnic communities have facilitated the clear formulation and enforcement of norms governing interethnic relationships. Within such a setting, and undoubtedly in many mainland community settings, rejection of one's own ethnic or racial group—what Kurt Lewin called self-hatred in his examination of Jewish attitudes[9]—facilitates the establishment of a strong identification bond as a basis for marriage outside one's original membership group.

Response Bonds. The identification bond can be called a kind of identity bond, because it depends for its effectiveness on the support and enhancement of ego's identity through his association with alter. There is another major way in which the identity can be fostered in the family relationship. This is through the manner in which alter responds to ego as a person. Alter's responses to ego can evoke in ego the kind of self-image that is favorable to his self-conception, in which case further interaction with alter is rewarding apart from any tasks that are accomplished. Whenever a child shows admiration toward his parent or spontaneously gives affection, the gratification that the parent feels activates a response bond. When a girl acts toward a boy as if she preferred his company over that of all other boys, she supports his identity and creates a tie to herself. When a husband evinces sensitivity to his wife's state of health, his responsiveness is a source of bonding for his wife.

One aspect of the response bonds is the general sensitivity, concern, and responsiveness of one person to another. The identity is supported in any relationship in which one's communications are readily understood and appreciated. The identity is supported when the pattern of response supports one's own feelings. When ego's enthusiasms arouse enthusiasm in alter, when his resentments arouse resentments, the gratifying experience of supportive response establishes a bond. People are tied together by common symbols that convey meanings between them more fully than they do

[9] Kurt Lewin, *Resolving Social Conflicts*, Harper & Row, New York, 1948, pp. 186–200.

with others. Shared enthusiasms, fears, and ambitions tie people together because they can express them with the assurance that they are understood and that their communications are sympathetically received.

This general sensitivity and responsiveness is partly a quality of the individual and partly of the fit between the interacting people. It is also partially a by-product of the presence of other bonds. It is recognized in folk thinking when the boy-who-meets-girl comments, "We just seem to talk the same language," or, "We are soul mates." The sensitivity can also be in part a consequence of novelty, its extreme manifestations declining with familarity.

A second aspect of response bonds is the reinforcement of ego's distinctive self-conception by the way in which alter responds to him. People differ widely in the kinds of response they find rewarding. One person gets satisfaction from being pitied; a bond is established to anyone who responds with the appropriate pity. Another takes pleasure in rivalry and banter. Still another likes to have people treat him as a pillar of strength. Some of these responses are rewarding because they validate the cultural roles that have been made part of the self-conception. The girl who acknowledges in her response the policeman's courage, the lawyer's acuity, or the author's creativity reinforces the identity of each.

Other rewarding responses seem to be more securely anchored to the person and less to the cultural role and are often thought to be rooted in personality needs. By analogy to needs for food and air it is assumed that personalities require certain kinds of responses from others if they are to remain healthy. The individual is seldom explicitly aware of the nature of his personality needs, but a sense of pleasure suffuses any relationship in which they are gratified. The relative importance of the many personality needs varies among individuals, so that the kind of response that establishes a bond for one individual need not do so for another. Robert Winch has made the interplay of personality needs between ego and alter the basis for a major theory and an important study in mate selection, which merits careful review.[10]

Complementary Needs or Homogamy. The question of whether bonds are more effective among those who are alike or different arose in connection with cultural characteristics. The evidence favored *homogamy*, or the tendency for ego to select a mate who is similar to himself. The question arises again with respect to the personality characteristics involved in response relationships. On the one hand, it can be argued that response is more easily attained when people have similar personalities, since each is then able to understand and detect the moods and the meanings in the

---

[10] Robert F. Winch, *Mate-selection: A Study of Complementary Needs*, Harper & Row, New York, 1958.

other's communications more readily. On the other hand, it often takes opposite personalities to satisfy each other's needs. For example, if an individual requires a great deal of personal support and reassurance in a relationship, another person of the same sort would be least able to give it to him.

Ernest Burgess and Paul Wallin, as part of their follow-up study of 1000 engaged couples, tested the homogamy hypothesis for personality characteristics.[11] The engaged couples answered 42 questions from the Thurstone Neurotic Inventory and made self-ratings on 23 selected personality traits. On 41 of the 42 inventory items the similarity of engaged pairs is greater than would be expected if couples had combined at random, and for 14 items the finding is significant at the 1 percent level. Correlations between fiancé and fiancée scores on eight composite inventory measures (depression, social introversion, inferiority, etc.) ranged from .11 to .20. These are low correlations, but all exceed the 1 percent significance level. Twenty-one of the 23 self-ratings show greater similarity than would be expected, and nine of these are statistically significant. Burgess and Wallin's investigation of socioeconomically upper-level engaged couples thus shows relatively little relationship between the personality characteristics of the mates, but also shows that whatever small relationship is present is in the direction of homogamy rather than heterogamy.

A considerable number of subsequent empirical investigations has been addressed to the questions of homogamy and complementary attributes in the personalities of mates. Few of these studies have produced clear-cut findings in support of either positive hypothesis, although the measures of personality are often of doubtful validity and negative findings may not be fully creditable; for example, in a study of newlyweds and engaged couples in Sweden, Jan Trost found homogamy in social characteristics but not in personality characteristics. When the subjects reported their estimates of the mate's personality, however, it became evident that they perceived themselves as significantly alike in personality.[12] In the United States, J. Richard Udry followed up 150 college engaged couples for three to five and one-half years. Comparing those who married with those who broke their engagements, he found no difference in the degree of personality similarity, nor in the degree to which individuals perceived their mates as being similar to themselves.[13]

[11] Ernest W. Burgess and Paul Wallin, "Homogamy in Personality Characteristics," *Journal of Abnormal and Social Psychology*, 39:475–481, October 1944; and *Engagement and Marriage*, Lippincott, Philadelphia, 1953, pp. 208–213.
[12] Jan Trost, "Some Data on Mate Selection: Homogamy and Perceived Homogamy," *Journal of Marriage and Family*, 29:739–755, November 1967.
[13] J. Richard Udry, "Personality Match and Interpersonal Perception as Predictors of Marriage," *Journal of Marriage and Family*, 29:722–725, November 1967.

Posing the issue as homogamy versus heterogamy of personality has undoubtedly established a useful starting point for exploratory research but hardly incorporates any of the promising theoretical leads to the nature of bonding. The postulation of specific kinds of pairing of bonds, such as task-person bonding or identification-response bonding, leads to hypotheses that specific configurations of personal characteristics appear in combination rather than to expectations of any generalized similarity or difference.

The most serious effort to test the hypothesis of systematic differences in personality between mates is the work of Robert Winch.[14] Winch does not propose that opposites attract in general but that people with certain kinds of personality differences naturally respond in ways that satisfy each other's personality needs and consequently form strong mutual response bonds. A person with a strong need "to give sympathy and aid to a weak, helpless, ill, or dejected person or animal" (nurturance) and another person with a strong need "to be helped by a sympathetic person; to be nursed, loved, protected, indulged" (succorance) are said to have *complementary needs* because each naturally wants to act toward the other as the other wants to be treated. Winch hypothesized that wherever love plays a large part in mate selection, complementary needs are the governing principle in selective mating.

Confronted with the choice of using data such as the Burgess-Wallin questionnaires on a large number of subjects or securing intensive data on a few married couples, Winch chose the latter alternative. Twenty-five young middle-class married couples were individually given a two- to three-hour "need interview," a case history interview, and a Thematic Apperception Test. Each individual was then rated on twelve personality needs and three general traits, each of which was further subdivided according to principles that need not concern us here. Winch first hypothesized that husband and wife ratings on the 15 variables and their subtypes would be negative, calling this *type I complementariness*. He further hypothesized that certain combinations of needs and traits would be complementary (*type II complementariness*). By logical analysis he identified all the pairs that should complement each other and hypothesized that high-score combinations would occur more often on these pairs than on others. Including both types of complementariness and taking account of the fact that not all types of needs and traits were represented in all their variations in his sample of 50 men and women, he tested 388 possible relationships. Since 256 of these were in the hypothesized direction, he concluded that the complementary-need hypothesis had received substantial support. Because the many variables are not truly independent in the statistical

[14] Winch, *op. cit.*

sense, it is doubtful that a test of significance can legitimately be applied to the general finding. But the result is nevertheless impressive.

Just as we worried about whether social homogamy findings might merely be measuring propinquity rather than preference, we must ask whether complementary-needs theory is the best explanation for Winch's findings. Examination of Table 2 shows that some of the complementary

TABLE 2   TEST OF COMPLEMENTARY NEEDS

Needs in Complementarity	Number of interspousal correlations			
	Number of Permutations		Total in Hypothesized Direction Whether Significant or not	Significant in Hypothesized Direction at One-Sided 5% Level
	Total	Tested		
Type I Complementariness				
$H:r<0$				
Needs:				
Abasement	16	4	4	3
Achievement	4	2	2	
Approach	4	2		
Autonomy	16	4	2	
Deference	16	4	3	2
Dominance	16	4	4	
Hostility	16	4	3	
Nurturance	16	4	3	
Recognition	16	4	4	
Status aspiration	1	1		
Status striving	1	1	1	
Succorance	16	4	4	2
Traits:				
Anxiety	4	2	1	
Emotionality	4	2	2	1
Vicariousness	4	2	2	
Subtotal for Type I	150	44	35	8
Type II Complementariness				
$H:r>0$				
Two needs:				
Abasement-Autonomy	32	24	23	3
Abasement-Dominance	32	16	14	12

(Continued)

TABLE 2   TEST OF COMPLEMENTARY NEEDS (*Continued*)

	Number of interspousal correlations			
Needs in Complementarity	Number of Permutations		Total in Hypothesized Direction Whether Significant or not	Significant in Hypothesized Direction at One-Sided 5% Level
	Total	Tested		
Abasement-Hostility	32	24	22	8
Abasement-Nurturance	32	24	5	
Abasement-Recognition	32	16	7	
Achievement-Deference	16	8	6	2
Achievement-Dominance	16	8	2	
Achievement-Recognition	16	8	4	1
Achievement– Status aspiration	4	4		
Autonomy-Deference	32	24	19	2
Autonomy-Hostility	32	16	9	1
Deference-Dominance	32	32	32	20
Deference-Hostility	32	8	7	3
Deference-Nurturance	32	24	5	
Deference-Recognition	32	24	9	2
Dominance-Succorance	32	24	17	2
Nurturance-Succorance	32	24	20	2
Status aspiration– Status striving	2	2		
Two traits:				
Anxiety-emotionality	8	8	2	1
One need and one trait:				
Achievement– Vicariousness	8	4	4	
Dominance– Vicariousness	16	4	4	2
Nurturance-Anxiety	16	12	6	1
Recognition– Vicariousness	16	4	2	
Status striving– Vicariousness	4	2	2	1
Subtotal for Type II	538	344	221	63
Total for both types	688	388	256	71

SOURCE: Adapted from Robert F. Winch, *Mate-selection*, Harper, New York, 1958, pp. 113–114, by permission of the author.

relationships supplied much more of the support for the overall conclusion than others. Only three of the 24 instances of type II complementariness supply 40 out of 63 significant confirmations. The three are deference-dominance, abasement-dominance, and abasement-hostility. These three pairs are very similar in describing a relationship in which one partner is probably quite subordinated to the other. It is strange that the complementary-need hypothesis should only work impressively in such instances. If the bond being measured is a complementary response relationship, it should be just as strong in combinations that do not revolve about dominance and submission. On the basis of a cluster analysis Winch notes that a general dimension he calls *assertive* versus *receptive* personality characteristics accounts for the principal findings of complementariness.

We are reminded of the principle that affects the strength of task bonds, namely, *economy of decision making*. The problem of reaching pair decisions is great when either two highly assertive persons or two highly receptive persons are together. A well-accepted relationship of inequality, however, simplifies decision making. In the former instances there is little opportunity to discover and develop task bonds. In the latter instances the potential task bonds have a maximum chance of reaching fruition. Perhaps, then, Winch has discovered the importance of a workable decision-making relationship in the formation of task bonds rather than a general principle governing the formation of response bonds. We cannot say, on the basis of present knowledge, which interpretation is preferable. We must be content to recognize that our ideas still outrun our knowledge by many lengths.

Two other studies offer possible clues to the place of person bonds and especially of the response bonds assigned central importance in the theory of complementary needs. Jerold Heiss observed 54 unmarried college couples in laboratory discussion sessions, employing Bales's interaction measures. The general prediction that men would exhibit more task-oriented actions and that women would exhibit more positive (social-emotional) reactions was weakly confirmed for the 54 couples. The expectation of more negative reactions by men than women was not confirmed. When the pairs were divided into three groups, however, consisting of 24 casually dating couples, 10 seriously dating couples, and 24 couples who regarded themselves as seriously committed and expecting to marry, there were differences between the casual daters and the committed group, with serious dates falling between or resembling the casual group. The traditional sex-linked differences in task and positive reactions were clear for the casual daters but blunted for the committed daters. Heiss proposes that greater intimacy and familiarity bring a decline of "posing" by those women who do not privately believe in the traditional role for women. Women play the part expected of them in casual relations, for fear of being excluded from the dating market, but drop the facade as the relationship becomes more serious.[15]

If the change suggested by Heiss actually occurs, it is possible that complementary needs become relevant to bonding only after the relationship has been established on the basis of other bonds. Either group membership, task bonds, or identification bonds, or bonds based on ritualized response predominate in early encounters. Only as ritual wears thin can response bonds that reflect more intimate and unique modes of response become factors in the bonding process.

In the longitudinal study mentioned earlier, Kerckhoff and Davis found value consensus to be of lesser importance in relation to progress toward permanence among couples whose relationship was of long standing compared with those of shorter duration. Also included in the investigation were measures of three kinds of need complementarity. Three pairs of five-item scales were used, measuring inclusion, control, and affection. One scale measured the desire to have others act so as to "include" the subject, and the paired scale measured the desire to act so as to "include" others. There was a similar pairing of receptive and active stances with respect to control and affection. Need complementarity was measured by the fit between how ego wishes to be treated and how alter wishes to act. When couples are divided into short-term and long-term groupings, the following findings emerge:

For the short-term couples there is no hint of a relationship between complementarity and progress toward permanence. But for the long-term couples the relationship is significant at the .02 level in the inclusion area and at the .05 level in the control area. In the affection area the direction of the relationship is the same, but it is not statistically significant.[16]

The findings here are quite consistent with the inference drawn from Heiss's data, that response bonds based on personal dispositions to act become a significant basis for bonding only after a relationship has progressed beyond the first stage of association. Two further observations about the Kerckhoff-Davis data are in order. First, we do not know if it matters whether the man or the woman is high on the exercise of control compared with the acceptance of control. The same must be said for inclusion and affection. Hence, the relationship of these findings to the acceptance or rejection of cultural sex roles is not clarified. Second, we do not know whether an individual can be high on both the active and receptive scales

[15] Jerold S. Heiss, "Degree of Intimacy and Male-Female Interaction," *Sociometry,* 25: 197–208, June 1962.

[16] Alan C. Kerckhoff and Keith E. Davis, "Value Consensus and Need Complementarity in Mate Selection," *American Sociological Review,* 27:300, June 1962. Quoted by permission of the American Sociological Association and the authors.

of the same need. Thus we do not know to what extent need complementarity as measured here indicates the matching of opposite personalities.

Both the Heiss and the Kerckhoff-Davis studies point our attention toward those bonds which develop once a relationship is already established and suggest the transition to our next topic.

Crescive Bonds

The attachment between newlyweds seems intense; the feeling of a mother for a newborn child is deep. Apart from difficulties arising from other sources, the loss of the mate or the child at this time can be handled with less personal readjustment than after several years of involvement. Over and beyond the bonds that are initially present, new bonds emerge and old bonds become intensified when people have been closely involved with one another over a period of time. And these bonds, more than any others, link unique individuals. The bonds of identification and response we have spoken of link individuals because of certain key shared or complementary qualities, but there are always potentially other individuals whose qualities would supply equally gratifying response. But the bonds that develop as a residue of interaction link uniquely irreplaceable individuals. Because these bonds are not present at first and develop only gradually we have called them *crescive*. The development of such bonds between husband and wife is ultimately the source of assured persistence and stability in the marital relationship. Their emergence between parent and child is the basis for the continuing relationship after the dependency bond has been dissolved.

The emergence of these bonds is neither entirely automatic nor inevitable. Characteristics of the initial bonds and the situation within which the relationship exists affect their appearance or nonappearance. The roles that the participants follow in relation to one another facilitate or limit their growth. In subsequent discussion of factors favoring or opposing stability in family relations we shall examine the determinants of crescive bonds. For the present, however, we shall merely describe some principal forms of such bonds.

Investment in Incomplete Action. It is characteristic of human behavior that it is organized into social acts that have a beginning, a series of steps toward completion, and a denouement. So long as the act is incomplete there is some tension, some preoccupation, that makes it difficult to accept interruption or termination before the act is completed.[17] If one sets out to plant a garden but manages only to dig up the soil, the incomplete act re-

[17] George H. Mead, *The Philosophy of the Act*, University of Chicago Press, Chicago, 1938; Ellsworth Faris, *The Nature of Human Nature*, Harper & Row, New York, 1937, pp. 144–154.

mains in his mind for days or weeks. The press brings us occasional stories of someone who set out to be an artist in his youth, was forced to set the goal aside in order to make a living, and then achieved artistic success after retirement. For an incomplete act to lie dormant so long is perhaps unusual, but over a shorter time span acts that are begun, and especially acts in which considerable thought and eneregy have been invested, exercise pressure toward completion.

When the acts that are incomplete involve the collaboration of others, they create bonds. Ego needs alter in order to finish tasks and identity sequences that are unfinished or unsatisfactorily terminated. The incomplete action may be no more than an argument that did not eventuate satisfactorily. Ego may seek out alter in order to finish the argument more satisfactorily on a later occasion. In Dumas' classic novel *The Count of Monte Cristo* the "count" is led to resume interaction with his oppressors after many years in order to bring an act of revenge to a satisfactory conclusion.

Family life is full of plans for the immediate and distant future. A vacation is planned, a home improvement is considered, education of the children must be anticipated, plans for next year when there will be more free time are constantly offered. The plans sometimes become so numerous and pervasive as to be oppressive, family members protesting that they would like for once to live in the present. Plans arise out of the alternatives to simple decisions. In deciding to visit Yosemite Valley rather than the Grand Canyon on this year's vacation, the family is likely to agree that some other year they would also like to see the Grand Canyon. The result is that at any moment family life is a tangled skein of unfinished actions that all tend to bring the members back together.

In bereavement there is sometimes an almost compulsive effort to complete some of the activities that were planned with the deceased member. The wife may feel herself driven to take the trip that she and her husband had often spoke about together. When the bereaved person does something that had figured in earlier family planning, he finds himself constantly reminded of the deceased. These responses help to highlight the operation of the bond created by investment in incomplete action.

Shared Experience and We Feeling. There is always a bond between those who have shared an experience that made some indelible impression in memory. Men who were in the same military engagement are drawn together to discuss it, although they may not have known each other at the time. The experiences that family members undergo together build on the initial bond of common interests.

Against the background of common experience there is almost inevitably some development in the direction of common attitudes. Shared attitudes and shared experiences help to make the family members think in terms of "we" instead of "I" and "you." Supplementing these internal sources of we feeling are the external pressures we discussed in connection with identification. A period of being treated by outsiders as a unit commits the members to retaining the unity. Outsiders force on the member the tendency to think of himself in connection with the others rather than in isolation.

The shared-experience bond is more subtle and permeative than the simple acquisition of similar memories of past events. Any significant event is first experienced tentatively, and the firm characterization that comes to be lodged in memory is produced through the process of communicating about the event. When people share an experience, they talk about it and observe each other's reactions to the event, putting forth their tentative definitions and seeking a credible version of the event that can be confirmed by the others. In this way the sharing of experience, accompanied by the collaborative efforts to define and interpret the event, tend toward the creation of a shared account of the event. Thus as two or more persons have a succession of shared experiences, they develop a wider and more firmly rooted common conception of reality, a conception that sets them apart from others who have not been part of the same experience circle. As the shared reality becomes more firmly differentiated from the realities of outsiders, the members need each other more and more for the confirmation of their views of events.[18]

Family members not only share many experiences directly, they participate in one another's experiences indirectly by discussion while the event-defining process is still taking place. As Berger and Kellner have pointed out, partners in marriage become each other's validators of experience, with the result that successive conversations create between them a common view of reality into which to fit new experiences as they occur.[19] The same thing happens in each of the other family relationships, except that there is a preestablished version that one imposes on the other when the child takes over a parental view of reality or a younger sibling adopts the world of his older brother or sister:

Each partner ongoingly contributes his conceptions of reality, which are then "talked through," usually not once but many times, and in the process become objectivated by the conversational apparatus. The longer this conversation goes on, the more massively real do the objectivations become to the partners. In

[18] See Maurice Halbwachs, *La Mémoire Collective*, Presses Universitaires de France, Paris, 1950, esp. pp. 1–34.
[19] Peter Berger and Hansfried Kellner, "Marriage and the Construction of Reality," *Diogenes*, 46:1–24, Summer 1964.

the marital conversation a world is not only built, but it is also kept in a state of repair and ongoingly refurnished.[20]

Since the definiteness and dependability attributed to one's conception of reality depends on the effectiveness with which a common reality is affirmed between an individual and his most intimate associates, the bonding implications become clear. "Both world and self thus take on a firmer, more reliable character for both partners."[21] Continuing the conversations contributes stability to the individual's world of reality, reinforcing the foundation on which decisive action depends. The need to continue the reality-producing conversations that usually find their most effective locus in the family constitutes one of the most durable crescive bonds for the married couple and often brings a child back to interact with his parents or a sibling after most other bonds are no longer in effect.

Interlocking Roles. In any group there is some initial adjustment as the members work out their respective roles for the accomplishment of group tasks. Similarly in the family, as a matrix for getting essential business done, a division of tasks takes place. As a result, each of the family members relinquishes some tasks he could very well perform, because they are assigned to another member. The children fail to develop certain skills because these are adequately handled by someone else in the family. The result is to make each member more dependent on the others than he would have been had he never participated in the family group. A wife, for example, who gives up her employment after marriage is normally at a disadvantage in attempting to return to work several years later. A man who once cooked for himself may lose his skill after a period of allowing the wife to cook. A child depends on a parent to make certain kinds of decisions for him merely because he has never had practice in making them himself.

The interdependence of family members becomes a good deal more subtle than the examples cited above. A child becomes dependent on a sibling to goad him into action. A wife who constantly makes suggestions finds it difficult to act on them without her husband at hand to express approval. In some relationships the wife is unable to act on her ideas until her husband has expressed his doubts and thus goads her into proving her idea. Without the other to play his role many of the simplest tasks become difficult to carry through. Again the evidence from bereaved persons is relevant. Often the bereaved is unable to carry out simple tasks or make simple decisions without the spouse to play out his role in the process.

[20] *Ibid.*, p. 13. Quoted by permission of the International Council for Philosophy and Humanistic Studies, Unesco, Paris, and the authors.
[21] *Ibid.*, p. 14.

Responsibility. The consequence of interlocking roles is dependence of one on the other. The obverse of this growing interdependence is a sense of the consequence to the other if the relationship is broken. When a person is concerned about the consequences of his actions, we speak of his sense of responsibility. With increasing interdependence in the family the sense of responsibility for the welfare of family members becomes an increasing bond.

As early as during engagement one party may be reluctant to sever a relationship because of the hurt that will be done to the other party. The bond of responsibility moderates divisive tendencies between parent and child. From the birth of the child this applies to the parent's attitude, and it begins to characterize the child's attitude as he matures sufficiently to understand potential consequences and accept responsibility for his actions.

Although the sense of responsibility can often be countered by placing blame on the other, it cannot so easily be deflected when some of the parties affected are innocently involved. A married couple may restrain divisive tendencies because of their concern over the upset to their own parents. Many marriages are believed to have been held together because of the sense of responsibility that the parents feel for their children.

Although there are undoubtedly some instances in which marriages are held together merely because of responsibility for children, there are undoubtedly also many in which parents feel this to be the case but in which there are other bonds at work of which they are unaware. Attempts have been made to estimate the probable extent of this mechanism from various reports of children and childlessness in relation to divorce. These reports have been consistent over several decades in showing a higher percentage of childlessness among the divorced than among the non-divorced couples.[22] There are two immediate problems in accepting these findings, however. Since divorces are more likely to take place early rather than late in a marriage, a disproportion of divorced couples may have begun divorce proceedings before they would have borne children in normal course. Until it is possible to equate the divorced and nondivorced by duration of marriage, which has not been fully done, the figures cannot readily be interpreted.

The second problem of interpretation has to do with cause and effect. Even if the correlation of divorce with childlessness withstood the treatment just suggested, it would still be possible that the presence of the children itself was not the factor keeping the marriage together. The kind of people who wish to have children may be also the kind who are more likely to find gratifications in marriage and build effective bonds.

[22] Paul H. Jacobson, *American Marriage and Divorce,* Rinehart, New York, 1959, pp. 129–135.

In the latter connection the early Burgess-Cottrell marriage prediction study explored the hypothesis that the desire for children rather than the presence of children was the variable crucially related to marital adjustment.[23] Both the presence of children and the desire for children were positively related to marital adjustment. When the two items were combined, however, the desire for children was clearly more important. And when those who desired children and those who did not were examined separately, in each instance the presence of children was not significantly related to adjustment, and the apparent trend was in the reverse direction. Adjustment is not the same as strength of bond; maladjustment in marriage can coexist with strong bonds, as we have indicated. And the reactions of the sample may well reflect the fact that they had mostly been married only a few years when the frustrations of children were still quite obvious and those without children had not yet given up hope. Subject to these qualifications, the Burgess-Cottrell evidence suggests that the presence of children may not be the effective bond.

More recent evidence has even called into question the basic relationship between divorce and childlessness. Eleanor Bernert has noted that according to 1950 census information an even larger proportion of divorced families had one or more children under eighteen years of age than of unbroken families. Contrasting these findings with earlier evidence, she states, "Though the data are not strictly comparable they do suggest that the role of children as restraints upon family disruption has been somewhat weakened."[24]

Whether the sense of responsibility is an effective bond or merely a rationalization for less apparent bonds, it varies greatly in the feeling tone associated with it. The sense of responsibility can be a detached, cold sense of obligation, a conviction of stern duty or a contract that must be met. At the opposite pole the sense of responsibility is submerged in a sense of sympathetic involvement with others. The latter applies to people who are deeply moved by witnessing or anticipating any hurt to another. When responsibility takes the first form, the sense of responsibility may be an unpleasant experience, so that only what psychiatrists might call very compulsive or rigid persons would be guided by it over the long run. The sympathetic kind of responsibility, however, does not evoke the same ambivalence and provides a less complicated bond.

Adjusted Communication and Response Patterns. Most communication is hedged about by a certain amount of reserve—some concern about how freely one ought to speak on certain subjects, how best to state the matter

[23] Ernest W. Burgess and Leonard S. Cottrell, Jr., *Predicting Success or Failure in Marriage*, Prentice-Hall, Englewood Cliffs, N.J., 1939, pp. 258–261.
[24] Eleanor H. Bernert, *America's Children*, Wiley, New York, 1958, p. 37.

to avoid misunderstanding, or what kind of reaction to anticipate from the other person. In any relationship continued over a period of time there develop some areas of sufficiently mutual understanding that people come to speak about them without reserve. But ordinarily such penetration of reserve is segmental; that is, it applies to a segment of one's life and not to the whole. When communication shifts away from the area of special mutuality, the reserve returns and communication takes on a less spontaneous and expressive quality.

There is immense gratification in any relationship marked by a minimum of reserve, so that people can abandon their ordinary defenses. Even in the absence of any strong instrumental or identification gain there is a tie to any person with whom one can relax normal barriers. Often in the business world a one-sided relationship of this kind develops in which a trusted subordinate becomes a confidant. One expresses antagonisms or fears within the hearing of the confidant that could not be mentioned to others. He may even propose plans of action to the confidant, not in order to have the confidant's evaluation, but merely to hear and evalute his own plan against a sympathetic sounding board.

The family is the kind of group that is especially conducive to the elimination of reserve. Given a minimally harmonious relation, the freedom from restraint develops in many areas of interaction and not merely segmentally.

One of the developments favoring relaxation of the inhibitions to expression is the stabilization of self- and other conceptions. The more firmly implanted the conception each has of the other, the less impact any single episode has on those conceptions. One remark or action out of character may lead a casual acquaintance to form an entirely erroneous impression of the actor. An expression of greed by a usually generous man may surprise his wife but it is not likely to shatter her conception of him unless, as we shall mention later, there are special reasons why she should be receptive to such a revision. Since family interaction is not limited to one sphere of interest, the stabilization of conceptions applies to much more nearly the whole range of one's activities, and the range of unhampered expression is equally wide.

A considerable measure of ordinary behavior is ceremonial, playing up to a role as a necessary prelude or accompaniment to the real thing. In this category fall the polite modes of address and the preliminaries that have to be carried through before people can get down to business. Such behavior is part of maintaining a ceremonial image that in many situations is more important than the functional image. To a doctor, for example, the bedside manner (the ceremonial image) is sometimes more important in determining his professional success than his medical skills. The maintenance of such an image clearly prevents free and relaxed expression. In a close and continuing relationship, the ceremonial image is usually shattered. The transition, as the ceremonial curtain is drawn away, may be traumatic. But once it is accomplished, there is a relaxation not otherwise possible. Just as there is often a sense of intense relief when a once-guarded secret is out, so elimination of the necessity to maintain the ceremonial image establishes a bond between those involved.

A further development that permits freer expression is learning to interpret and cope with the response of the other. A child can tell a parent something he knows will make the parent angry, because he has learned to take the parent's anger in stride. The anger of the school teacher or other adult may be greatly feared, but the child has learned that the more familiar anger of the parent does not last indefinitely and can be weathered. He may also have learned the interpersonal techniques that dispel or mitigate the anger. Having frequently experienced the full range of responses that alter uses, ego finds less uncertainty to fear and may act spontaneously, with minimal thought to the consequence.

Reinforcing these spontaneous processes are two important institutional characteristics of the family. One is the relaxation of many of the symbolic devices by which people keep their distance socially from others. Dropping the conventions about clothing is only the most notable of these. The other characteristic is the wall of privacy that applies to the intimate affairs of family life. Privacy is the reciprocal of intimacy; barriers can be dropped if privacy is assured. In spite of the delight people feel over a little juicy gossip, friends and acquaintances are themselves embarrassed when a family member reveals too intimate matters concerning family life and often try to stop the individual from making further public revelations.

The result of these processes can be seen in the quite contrasting personalities that people sometimes display within the family and outside. The youth who is an athletic symbol of strength in his school may whine to his parents. The great man does not often behave as a great man toward his wife. And the poised PTA president may lose her temper with her children. In all these instances the shared freedom to yield to impulses forbidden outside the family is a bond that develops if conditions are favorable in the family.

Vulnerability of Bonds

After an enumeration and examination of varied kinds of bonds that tie together husband and wife, parent and child, or brothers and sisters, we come back to the question of permanence. The apparent intensity of feeling connected with the attachment between two people at any moment in time seems a poor clue to the probable continuance of the attachment. One of the principal problems of both theoretical and practical interest in family study is to identify those relationships which are likely to persist and those which are not. The problem breaks down into two related questions: which kinds of bonds are intrinsically more durable and which are temporary; and what conditions favor continuance and strengthening of bonds and what conditions tend to weaken them?

To denote this problem we shall borrow an apt term from the pioneering investigation of family stability and instability by Robert C. Angell.[25] Comparing families in some of which interpersonal relationships deteriorated as a consequence of reduction in income during the economic depression of the late 1920s and the 1930s, Angell described the organization of some families as *vulnerable* and the organization of others as *invulnerable*. He introduced these terms because loss of income clearly had no automatic effect on family relations. The families in which interpersonal relations were most disturbed were not necessarily those which suffered greatest financial privation. Rather, some families were organized in such a way and the interpersonal relations before the depression were of such a nature that they were not damaged by the adjustments that had to be made to severe loss of income. Other families were so organized that interpersonal relations quickly deteriorated when economic privation set in. Thus Angell classified them as vulnerable or invulnerable in the face of financial privation.

In borrowing Angell's terminology we shall make two alterations, neither of which does violence to his meaning. First, we shall extend the terms to apply to any kind of exigency, including altered life situation and time. And second, for the present we shall limit its application to the bonds that hold the family together. Thus we shall speak of bonds that are subject to weakening over time or under altered circumstances of life as vulnerable and those which are relatively impervious to time and change as invulnerable. Since relationships are ordinarily maintained by several bonds rather than a single tie, we shall also speak of a relationship as vulnerable or invulnerable, depending on the net effect of the various bonds.

Two generalizations are immediately suggested from the foregoing discussion. First, the greater the number and diversity of bonds holding a relationship together, the greater its invulnerability. Any particular exigency may weaken some bonds, but the presence of a number and variety of bonds makes it unlikely that all the bonds will be vulnerable to the same kind of crisis. Many of the observed correlations between predictive factors and measures of marital success can be plausibly construed as indicating that several rather than merely a few bonds exist between the

[25] Robert C. Angell, *The Family Encounters the Depression*, Scribner, New York, 1936, pp. 16–17, *et passim*.

couple at the time of marriage. For example, marriages on very short acquaintance, whose prognostication of success is relatively low, are especially likely to be based on only one or two bonds rather than several. Parental approval for a marriage, which is also positively correlated with success, may well indicate that bonds of a different kind than those which the young couple recognize are also present.

The second generalization is that the more extensive the development of crescive bonds in a relationship, the more invulnerable it becomes. Since crescive bonds are those which lock interacting individuals in a continuing relationship, they serve in a way that no other bonds do to make each person indispensable to the other. Crescive bonds eliminate the substitutability of persons in a relationship and are therefore less vulnerable than most other kinds of bonds.

Before pursuing the general question of vulnerable and invulnerable relationships further, we shall examine some of the bonds that are vulnerable to specific kinds of exigencies. After this discussion we shall return to the more general question of vulnerable and invulnerable relationships.

Bonds of Variable Strength. Some bonds are intrinsically temporary in nature, arising out of a passing situation. Two Americans meeting in a foreign country are drawn together because of common background but may have nothing in common when among other Americans. A boy and girl joining a group in which all the other couples are already paired are brought together by the situation and may have no other tie. A man who has suffered a severe blow to his self-esteem may be greatly attracted to a woman who expresses interest in him, because her interest in him helps to rebuild his self-esteem. After the effects of the trauma are past, the tie evaporates. Bonds of this sort are *situational*. They arise out of some specific situation, and their life is limited to the continuance of the situation.

Bonds may also be specific to stages of individual development. The infant requires a parent to tend to his physical wants; as he becomes an adult, this dependency vanishes. The young man starting in business who depends on a great deal of assistance from his wife is able to replace her help with a paid staff as he becomes successful. Our requirements and sources of gratification continue to change throughout life: what a woman wants in a husband at age twenty-five and at age fifty-five are different. Bonds reflecting the gratifications of a specific stage in development are vulnerable in the normal maturation process. Viewed in relation to the problems of education, these normal changes have been called developmental tasks.[26]

The preceding discussion has concerned bonds based on wants or needs

[26] For a discussion of developmental tasks and family life, see Evelyn M. Duvall, *Family Development*, Lippincott, Philadelphia, 1957, pp. 95–120, *et passim*.

that can dissipate. But a need that is more or less enduring only functions as a bond when it can be satisfied. Any bond, then, is vulnerable to alterations in the conditions that made gratification through the family possible.

Many obvious examples could be cited. The man who is attracted to a glamorous woman by a bond of identification ceases to gain from identification when she loses her glamor and with it the prestige that he is able to share. The girl who is attracted to a man who is very popular in adolescent circles ceases to gain by identification when their married life separates them from the adolescent arena of the husband's popularity. The bond between a man and woman whose attraction for each other rests on their mutual interest in art and music becomes inactive when the husband's work and the wife's domestic responsibilities monopolize their time.

Whether a bond of identification is vulnerable in this manner depends on the extent or depth of the identification. Identification always means experiencing some of the feelings that one would if he were in the other's position. But it also involves a further emotion as a reaction to these feelings. A woman whose husband makes an embarrassing mistake in public feels first the embarrassment that comes from being identified with him. But then she feels either annoyance at him for having placed her in so embarrassing a position or some further feeling appropriate to his point of view, such as anger toward the person who embarrassed him or sympathy toward the husband in his state of shame. In the first instance the identification is partial. There is identification to the point of experiencing the embarrassment of the husband's mistake. But at this point the self is sharply dissociated from the other (the husband), and the subsequent feeling is a reaction to the husband. In the second instance the wife not only feels the embarrassment as she would in the husband's position, but she follows it up with reactions taken from the husband's standpoint. The identification, then, continues through both phases.

To the extent to which identification remains partial, all bonds dependent on identification are vulnerable to changes that eliminate the gain from identification. To the extent to which identification is complete, however, succeeding identificatory experiences build up a fund of common memories, a habituation to we feeling, and interlocking habit systems. Thus crescive bonds cumulate from the identification process and the outcome is a bond that is no longer vulnerable to removal of the initial basis for identificatory gain.

Instrumental and task-orientation bonds are also subject to termination. In American society a frequently shared task orientation in the family is the maintenance and betterment of standard of living. The task involves earning, often including supplementary earning by others than the breadwinner. It involves economy and care in consumption to gain the most from income. And it may incorporate a do-it-yourself motif to escape the costs of labor. To the extent to which such a task orientation becomes an important bond the relationship is vulnerable to events that lessen the family's ability to maintain such a standard.

R. C. Angell, in the investigation already mentioned, found that strong commitment to maintaining a certain standard of living was more likely to characterize those families which subsequently experienced deteriorated relationships during the Depression than those which maintained their stability.[27] It may seem obvious in retrospect that loss of income weakens most those families who gained the greatest part of their strength from achieving a certain level of income. A large proportion of all the crises that upset the ordinary routines of family life, however, affect the standard of living at least indirectly. Earl Koos, in his study of the problems encountered by tenement families, indicates that the financial strain imposed by a death in the family is sometimes more disrupting than the emotional impact of the death itself.[28] In his study of family adjustment to the wartime absence of the husband, Reuben Hill found that placing a very high value on maintaining a given standard of living was associated with poorer adjustment.[29] To the extent, then, to which many of the crises of family life in our society have effects on the family standard of living, a bond of common orientation toward maintaining or bettering living standards is vulnerable to a wide range of exigencies.

Vulnerable and Invulnerable Relationships. The thesis of the preceding discussion might be summarized as follows: To determine the kinds of exigencies that any family is vulnerable to, it is necessary to identify the kinds of bonds that hold the family together. Having dwelt on the variation in sources of vulnerability, we are now prepared to return to the matter of generalized vulnerability. To what extent are there variables that affect the family not so much by making it differentially sensitive to different sources of disruption as by making it generally subject or resistant to weakening bonds?

One of the most important variables affecting the vulnerability of the whole relationship is whether the ties linking individuals to the family are regarded as *sacred* or *contractual*.[30] A contractual relationship is one into which people enter on the basis of an understood group of mutual obligations. The important feature of the contractual obligation is its reciprocal character. When one party fails to perform his obligations, the

---

[27] Angel, *op. cit.*, pp. 50–54, 258–264.
[28] Earl L. Koos, *Families in Trouble*, King's Crown, New York, 1946, pp. 64ff.
[29] Reuben L. Hill, *Families Under Stress*, Harper & Row, New York, 1949.
[30] For a classic discussion of the idea of contract, see Henry S. Maine, *Ancient Law*, Oxford University Press, London, 1959.

other is released from his. Dissolution of the contract is reasonable redress.

In a sacred relationship, however, familial obligations are not merely responsibilities to the other present members of the family. They are obligations to God, or to ancestors, or to an abstract principle. The misbehavior of other members of the family does not relieve ego of these sacred obligations. The bond is not contingent on variations in the behavior of other members. In our own society we usually view the bond of parent to child in this manner, refusing to grant the parent the right to disown a minor child. Similarly, but with a little more contractual leeway we regard the bond of child to parent and between siblings as sacred obligations.

At the start of Chapter 3 it was remarked that choices and satisfactions are relative to the range of available alternatives. Any change in the available range of alternatives or in the individual's perception of the alternatives affects the stability of certain kinds of bonds. In the ordinary course of urban life in the United States a married person encounters potential alternatives to his own spouse throughout life. Occasional reports of individuals with excessive divorce records probably indicate such a process of reacting to slight disappointments by looking for new alternatives.

Ordinarily the network of bonds prevents a married person from regularly viewing each new acquaintance as a potential alternative to the present spouse. There are, however, certain circumstances that drastically enlarge the range of potential alternatives and thus render some of the bonds of task orientation, identification, and response ineffectual. Either a change of situation to one in which many more alternatives abound or an elevated self-conception that makes a larger range of potential mates seem attainable weakens some bonds. The first kind of change is illustrated in case of the country boy who marries "the girl next door" and then discovers for the first time by moving to the city that there are many other girls than those he already knows. The second is illustrated by a man who achieves considerable success from an inauspicious beginning. Married when his self-esteem was low, he becomes progressively dissatisfied with his wife as his evaluation of himself improves.

Such alterations of self-conception are not uncommon, especially among men. In American society the criteria of sexual attractiveness are different at different age periods. Hence the man of some brilliance, destined to achieve business or professional prominence and material comfort, may as an adolescent have a limited conception of his marital desirability because of the prevalence of athletic standards at that age. Long-continued schooling that prevents a man from proving himself by acquiring financial independence likewise leads him to conceive of himself poorly in the marriage competition. Success, increasing his social desirability and his self-confidence, opens new possibilities to him.

It is possible that one of Alfred Kinsey's observations concerning sex behavior among American males illustrates this kind of vulnerability.[31] Because of the many unknowns in the composition of his sample and in the meaning of responses to his questions, the findings cannot be accepted with confidence. They are, however, still a valuable source of hypotheses. Kinsey referred to all the ways a person achieves sexual orgasm as "total sexual outlet." For the married male this can include marital intercourse, extramarital intercourse, masturbation, nocturnal emissions, homosexual relations, and relations with animals. He attempted to determine the percentage of each individual's total outlet that was supplied by each kind of activity. The percentages could then be compared by age and educational level. Such comparisons rest on the assumption that equivalent samples of men were secured in each age bracket and each educational grouping. Because of Kinsey's sampling methods, the assumption is doubtful, especially in case of age, but we have no basis for knowing in which direction the subsample differences would have affected the findings. With these qualifications in mind, we can look at Figure 3, in which only marital and extramarital outlets have been recorded. Among men of low educational attainment the extent of extramarital relations declines with age and that of marital relations increases with age. Among men of high

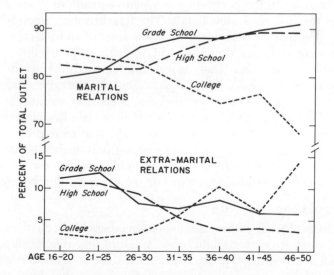

Figure 3.   Age trend of marital and extramarital relations for men by educational attainment. (Adapted from Alfred C. Kinsey, Wardell B. Pomeroy, and Clyde E. Martin, *Sexual Behavior in the Human Male,* Saunders, Philadelphia, 1948, p. 382.)

[31] Alfred C. Kinsey, Wardell B. Pomeroy, and Clyde E. Martin, *Sexual Behavior in the Human Male,* Saunders, Philadelphia, 1948, pp. 382–384.

educational level approximately the opposite trend is shown. Educational level can serve as an approximate index of socioeconomic success, and extramarital relations as a negative index of the bond of loyalty to the wife. Apparently the bonds of loyalty to the wife more often become weaker with age among the socioeconomically successful men than among the less successful. If this interpretation is just, it may be that alternatives increase for the more successful and contract for the less successful with increasing age. Perhaps also the increased sense of personal worth that accompanies the successes of educated men makes some of them disappointed in the wives they married when they were just starting out in life.

There is also a kind of vulnerability to newly sensed alternatives that characterizes the family relationship that has settled down to a sort of deadly routine, with only task orientations and interlocking roles to hold it together. The absence of response bonds and identifications makes the relationship colorless, with its continuance simply the line of least resistance. In folk terminology the wife complains that her husband simply takes her for granted. Earl Koos pointed out some rather extreme cases of this kind to which he applied the term *narcotization*.[32] These were families in which the dull unenthusiastic routine continued unaffected by the usual crises of tenement life. The families had been desensitized to such an extent that they responded to neither opportunity nor difficulty.

An awakening to the possibility of a more exciting or richer life is the condition that weakens such bonds. The folk literature depicts the husband too preoccupied with his work to be responsive to his wife and the wife too busy with her domestic and parental responsibilities to think much about her situation. Then as the children reach the age of full-time school or when they leave home as young adults, the wife suddenly confronts an emptiness. As she searches for something to fill her life, she becomes, for the first time, fully aware of how little her husband means to her. The folk stories then feature her sudden attraction to a more exciting kind of man, leading at least temporarily to unfaithfulness toward her husband. How frequent is such a pattern in reality we do not know, although its frequent enactment in fantasy has been documented.

Summary of Chapters 3 and 4

The characteristics of any group—its members, the activities they engage in, what strengthens and what weakens the relationship, the organization of roles, the foci of conflict, and the resources that generate a positive sense of value—all depend on the bonds that hold the group together. Bonds vary among members and they change as conditions change. Bonding always occurs in relation to alternative affiliations, within

[32] Koos, *op. cit.*, pp. 48–50.

a more or less limited field of choice. Husband, wife, and children are in part tied to the family itself as a way of life and in part to one another as unique individuals. In addition to bonds that are present at the initiation of any relationship there are crescive bonds, which link people in closer and unique interdependence as a result of continued interaction. Whether a relationship such as marriage or brother-sister loyalty persists for a long time depends on whether crescive bonds arise to strengthen the initial ties and whether the major bonds are vulnerable or invulnerable in the circumstances under which the family lives.

Several issues of interest arise in connection with the study of bonds. One concerns the relative strength of ties between those who are similar and those who are dissimilar in cultural characteristics and personality. The preponderance of evidence favors the former (the homogamy principle), although there is some partially convincing evidence to support the theory of complementary needs. Certain special kinds of personality differences probably supply more effective bonds than do simple likenesses, especially after the initial stages of the relationship.

Collaboration in task behavior is an important source of bonding, because successful collaboration leads to the anticipation of future collaboration, because collaboration creates the setting in which other bonds can be activated, and because of the residual bonding effect of shared enjoyment. Bonds form selectively in the cource of task activity according to two principles, namely, mutual gratification and economy of decision. The strength of the task-based bonds in any family relationship is a function of the ratio of activities that serve the members' mutual ends to the activities that serve the ends of only some of the members. The more easily two or more persons can reach decisions, whether because of the fit of their personalities or the organization of their relationship for decision making, the greater the probability that bonds will form on the basis of whatever potentially gratifying activity they attempt.

Person bonds, as distinct from task bonds, are primarily of two kinds. Identification with another person who exhibits admirable or desired personal qualities and accomplishments is an important source of bonding, especially in tying a person of lower status to one of higher status. Response bonds develop when alter's reactions to ego evoke in ego the kind of self-image he seeks to establish. A reciprocity of identification bonding in one direction and response bonding in the other is a frequent pattern in child-parent and wife-husband relations.

Under favorable circumstances bonds that were not involved in bringing people together will develop in the course of interaction. Foremost among these crescive bonds are the investment that people make in incomplete action, when that action requires continuing collaboration with the same partner; shared experience leading to shared definitions of reality that can only be verified and revived through interaction with the person who shares that conception of reality; interlocking roles, the phenomenon whereby each party's adjustments to the other eventually make him dependent on the role played by the other in playing out his own roles; the sense of responsibility for the welfare of the other; and the adjustment of communication and response that allows relaxation of inhibitions and escape from the preliminary negotiation and testing that impedes much normal interaction.

The vulnerability of a relationship is an inverse function of the number, diversity, and strength of bonds and especially of the crescive bonds that link individual to unique individual more than most other bonds. Each kind of bond has its special vulnerability. Many bonds are intrinsically situational and hence are vulnerable to a changed situation. Bonds are vulnerable to dissipation of the wants or needs that the relationship satisfies, to change in the relationship so that it can no longer satisfy the crucial wants, and to newly sensed alternatives.

DECISION-MAKING PROCESS

There are two major sets of processes relating to the conduct of group activity that correspond to the task orientations and the identity orientations, respectively. Central to the accomplishment of group tasks is *decision making*. Central to the relationship among identities are *conflict* and *harmonization*. Chapter 5 examines the decision-making processes and Chapter 6 the principal by-product of decision making in the form of dominance patterns. Chapter 7 is devoted to conflict and harmonization. These processes are never separate in real life, and we shall have to take note of the effects of harmony and conflict on decision making and of patterns of decision making on harmonization and conflict as we proceed.

We shall begin this chapter by discussing the nature of group decision making, stressing the separate elements of *assent* and *commitment,* and then distinguishing between consensual, accommodative, and de facto decisions. Next we shall examine paths toward agreement in the family, considering first the generally applicable sequence from orientation to evaluation and finally to control, and then looking separately at the process of achieving consensus and at the bargaining and coercion through which accommodations are reached. Obstacles to agreement will receive special treatment. And finally we shall look at family decision making as problem solving.

The Nature of Group Decision Making

By group decision making we mean a process directed toward unambivalent group assent and commitment to a course of action or inaction. Since decisions that seem final at one time are often reconsidered later, we must think of decision making, like bonding, as a continuous process. The ideas of assent and commitment serve to distinguish group decision from the decision and action of an individual member. Assent may be active in the form of declaration by each member that he supports the decision. Or it may be passive, members merely bypassing the opportunity to challenge a decision made for them by some of the members.

Commitment refers to the irrevocability of assent. When an individual makes a decision, he is committed to it by his action or inaction, regardless of how he may regret the decision later. But in a group the action stemming from a decision may actually be carried out by some rather than all of the members, and those who do not act may later try to disidentify themselves from the decision. Even persons who actually participate in the execution of action may attempt to disidentify themselves from the decision by some tactic, such as charging other members with keeping relevant information from them or placing irrelevant pressures on them in the course of decision making. In such situations there is danger that the decisions will be viewed as the decisions of some individuals in the group rather than of the group, in which case commitment is lost.

Kinds of Decision Making. Decision making differs according to the character of assent and commitment. The ideal image of decision making is one in which the initial differences of viewpoint are eliminated through discussion until there is eventual agreement. Some family members decide that the suggestions of others are better than their own, or some new suggestion arises during the discussion that all recognize as best. The result is a decision to which all give equal assent and all feel equally committed without private reservation or personal resentment. Since all are equally identified with the decision, there are no left-overs from the discussion to be finished when the next discussion comes up. A decision of this kind is known as *consensus*. It is not so frequent in the family as romance would have it.

More common is the kind of decision in which some members give assent in order to allow a decision to be reached and not because they are privately convinced that the decision in question is best. Such a decision is not consensus but *accommodation;* agreement is achieved by the adjustment of some or all of the members to the irreconcilability of their views. The accommodation may be achieved amiably or with bitterness; assent may be a response to coercion or a voluntary concession; the form of accommodation may be compromise in which each gives up as much as the other or a sacrificial act in which some yield and others have their way. An accommodation is always an agreement to disagree, to adopt a common decision in the face of recognized and unreconciled private desires.

Two important differences in the aftermath of accommodation compared with consensus will concern us from time to time. First is the character of commitment to the decision. In both instances the members are committed by the fact that they assent publicly. Commitment, however, is unconditional when there is consensus, but it is often felt to be conditional when an accommodation has taken place. Because ego makes concessions in the interest of agreement with alters in the group, the alters incur a debt to ego. The debt is sometimes explicit, as in an open compromise. Each person's commitment is then conditional on the others' compliance with the terms of compromise. More often the debt is implicit. Without explicit consideration, no two persons assess the degree of sacrifice involved in assent equally. The child who passes up an opportunity to play with a friend because his mother wants him to accompany her shopping feels that his mother is indebted to him. The degree of felt indebtedness depends on how badly he wished to play with the friend on that occasion, something that only he can evaluate. When the child demands that the trip be cut short on the grounds that he did not really want to go in the first place (denying commitment), he appears to his mother to be reneging on a decision to which he gave assent and accepted commitment. In a sense, then, an accommodative decision is seldom a thoroughly completed act but is always subject to the possibility that it will be reopened in the midst of some later action.

The second important difference lies in the implications of the two courses of decision for the identities of the participants. An accommodative decision usually accords more with the wishes of some members than of others. The result of such differentiation is that persons most closely identified as individuals with the group decision come to be defined as *dominant*. Because all eventually accept the decision as their own in consensus, there is less awareness of winners and losers. But it is possible to speak of accommodative decision making as the specific process through which dominant and submissive positions in the group are established. Even in a quantitatively perfect compromise, the individual who proposes the compromise that is finally adopted gains points thereby.

If one reflects on his own family experience, he can hardly avoid noting that these two forms of decision making fail to encompass many of the decisions by which family routine is kept in operation. Many discussions finish inconclusively and are then decided by events. An argument about which motion picture to attend may be decided by the failure to reach agreement until it is too late to attend any. Indecision about what to have for dinner leaves a decision that affects the whole family in the hands of the wife when she goes shopping. Such decisions sometimes follow ineffectual discussions and sometimes occur in the absence of any group consideration of the question at all. What all such events have in common is that agreement is by the absence of dissent rather than by active assent, and, more important, commitment is by the course of events rather than by acceptance. Such decisions are made in fact rather than in words but in a context of events such that members of the group find themselves committed. Consequently we borrow a term from law to designate these as de facto decisions.

An instructive account of de facto decisions is supplied in an analysis of lower-class Puerto Rican families by Joseph Stycos, Kurt Back, and Reuben Hill.[1] Their problem was to ascertain why so many of the parents failed to use contraceptive devices to control the size of their families. It was determined that knowledge of these techniques was widespread and that individually both husbands and wives would have preferred small families. The answer they secured was that certain cultural obstacles prevented husband and wife from discussing the topic of contraception with each other, with the result that the effective decision on family size was de facto rather than accommodation or consensus. The authors propose that lack of communication regarding family limitation had the following consequences:

1. A tendency for each spouse to assume that the other does not care how many children he or she has.

2. A failure to share knowledge of birth-control methods.

3. A tendency not to adopt birth-control methods, and, if adopted, to practice them somewhat ineffectively.

The lack of communication on family planning would seem to be the consequence of at least two cultural factors.

1. Female modesty inculcated early in childhood makes many women reluctant to bring up such matters; and leads males to conclude that such matters are not for discussion with their wives.

2. Male dominance leads some husbands to believe that the sphere of family planning is their prerogative alone, and makes wives reluctant to initiate conversation or action. Moreover, there is some evidence suggesting that when conversation does occur it tends to be one-sided; i.e., the male talking, the female listening.[2]

Obstacles to communication and inconclusive discussion have both cultural and individual bases. A boy may confide in his sister regarding a girl friend when he hesitates to tell his parents. In general, the more precarious are personal identities within the family, the more obstacles there will be to communication (as we have noted in connection with bonds) and the more frequent will be de facto decisions. Previous experience of conflict and inconclusive discussion with a member or over a specific problem engenders unwillingness to enter into new discussion. The mere pace of life renders

[1] J. Mayone Stycos, Kurt Back, and Reuben Hill, "Problems of Communication between Husband and Wife on Matters Relating to Family Limitation," *Human Relations*, 9(2): 207–215, 1956.

[2] Ibid., pp. 213–214. Quoted by permission of the Tavistock Institute of Human Relations and the authors.

discussion of all issues impracticable, leaving many decisions to the group-committing actions of single individuals or of events.

De facto decisions contribute to patterns of domination if events repeatedly force the group to acknowledge the decision of one member as theirs. There is always some ambiguity about the character of commitment in these decisions, which leaves them as potentially unfinished business.

Paths toward Agreement

The success of a family group in reaching decisions is not merely a function of its members' individual decision-making abilities. People who make individual decisions easily and without crippling second thoughts are often unable to make decisions together. The attainment of mutual assent and commitment is central to both consensual and accommodative decision making. In some respects the process leading to assent and commitment is similar and in some respects dissimilar in the two kinds of decision making. We shall first consider what may be a common pattern and then look separately at the two kinds of agreement.

Phases in Group Decision Making. What may be a generally applicable sequence was uncovered in a series of laboratory studies of contrived small groups. Groups were assigned problems to solve and were observed according to the Bales system.[3] A classification consisting of twelve categories is used to identify each act made by a member of the group. Observers who are trained in the use of the scheme keep a complete record of each action as the group activity progresses. Afterwards it is possible to compare the relative frequency of each of the twelve kinds of action for individuals, for groups, and for different stages in the group's interaction. In collaboration with Fred Strodtbeck, Bales used the reports on 22 such sessions to test a hypothesis of successive phases in group problem solving.[4] The hypothesis holds, first, that there are three phases of preoccupation with the problem itself. The first is a phase of *orientation*, of identifying the problem. As the initial problems of orientation begin to be resolved there is an increase in activities of a second kind, known as *evaluation*. These are questions and statements of appraisal, weighing the merits of various courses of action. When sufficient evaluation work has been done so that the problem becomes increasingly one of getting the group to agree on one of the possible solutions, the third, or *control*, phase ensues. During this phase

[3] Robert F. Bales, *Interaction Process Analysis: A Method for the Study of Small Groups*, Addison-Wesley, Reading, Mass., 1951. For a brief recent review of the method and its later applications see Bales, "Interaction Process Analysis," *International Encyclopedia of the Social Sciences*, 1968, vol. 7, pp. 465–471.
[4] Bales and Fred L. Strodtbeck, "Phases in Group Problem Solving," *Journal of Abnormal and Social Psychology*, 46:485–495, October 1951.

there is heightened pressure to secure agreement, which necessarily means applying pressure to dissident members.

Paralleling these problem phases there is also a sequence in the identity relations among members. As the discussion proceeds, some members are placed in disadvantageous positions by having their suggestions criticized or being subjected to group pressures toward conformity or by finding the discussion increasingly monopolized by others. As a consequence interpersonal tensions grow, being aggravated by evaluative activities and especially augmented by control activities. The result hypothesized is a steady increase in both negative and positive reactions in the interpersonal or social-emotional area. The negative reactions reflect the tensions directly, and the positive reactions are the counterefforts to maintain solidarity and harmony in the group.

The percentage summary in Figure 4, based on dividing each of the 22 sessions into three equal phases, shows that the hypotheses all receive support. Two facts about the data should be noted. First, the hypotheses hold as relative differences in rates rather than absolute differences; that is, there are fewer control acts than either evaluation or orientation during all

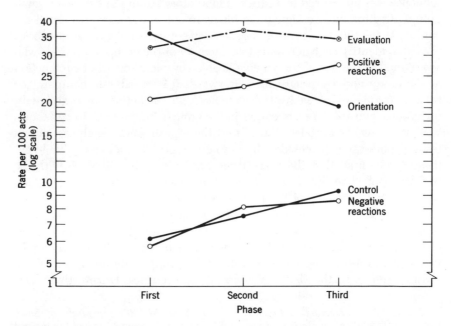

Figure 4. Relative frequency of acts by kind and phase, based on 22 sessions. (Adapted from Robert F. Bales and Fred L. Strodtbeck, "Phases in Group Problem Solving," *Journal of Abnormal and Social Psychology*, 46:488, October 1951.)

phases of interaction, but control acts increase steadily throughout the sequence. Second, the differences between phases are not very large, although they are as impressive as the results that sociological investigation is usually able to secure. Whenever differences are both relative and small, there is always a possibility that the findings might be better explained by some other hypothesis that has not come to our attention at the present.

None of the groups included in this investigation was a family unit, and Bales and Strodtbeck designate a set of conditions that make the formula in its entirety inapplicable to the usual family decision-making episode. Among these conditions are primary preoccupation with a fairly specific problem of group planning and decision which can be made on the basis of facts but which is not open and shut; absence of large status differences among members; and absence of a customary pattern for decision making. The steps that Bales and Strodtbeck describe are very likely part of family decision making, but parts of each sequence have usually been resolved before the specific episode occurs. It is useful to think of an ideal sequence modified by the experience of previous interaction and the specific organization of the family unit. In the case of recurring family issues, for example, orientation and evaluation have been largely completed in the past, so that control becomes disproportionately important, with its attendant identity overtones. Here may be one simple explanation for the troublesome observation that people often appear to be less reasonable in the family than they are with strangers and acquaintances.

Values in Consensus. If a decision is to be reached by consensus after initial disagreement, some members of the family must come to feel that the decision corresponds with their own values in the course of the decision process. If we rule out an actual change in values as normally occuring too slowly to modify the outcome of specific group decisions, there remain three important ways such a change can come about. First, a new proposal may be introduced subsequent to the initial disagreement, a proposal that accords with a value shared by all members of the group. When family members are divided over expenditure of family income, one member suddenly remembers something that all had earlier agreed they wanted to buy the first time a little extra money was available. Second, a course of action that some members evaluate unfavorably in light of one value may be reappraised when a different value is brought to bear on it. A youth who is reluctant about the family's spending the summer away from home may be favorably disposed when the presence of others of his own age at their summer destination is called to his attention. Third, some members' images of the disputed course of action may be altered so that they are now positive rather than negative with respect to their values. A reluctant member discovers that the neighborhood to which the family is considering moving is not so unattractive as she thought at first.

Back of consensus, then, there are always some shared values or a felicitous combination of values such that two people desire the same thing for different reasons. The wider the range of common values held by members of a group, the more frequent are consensual decisions. Likewise the wider the range of common perceptions of situations, the more frequent are consensual decisions.

Consensus is actively pursued and does not usually just happen. Hence whatever enables members to induce agreement in others must be included among the conditions facilitating consensus. The greater the degree to which members understand the values of other family members, the greater the likelihood they will be able to link proposals convincingly to values that are important to other family members. The active and passive principles are complementary. Consensus becomes automatic when the value commonality is sufficient. But consensus can also be attained through the active efforts of members toward agreement in the absence of many common values if some members have sufficient understanding of others' values so that they can indicate appropriate relationships.

When these observations are related to the differences between consensual and accommodative decisions, another kind of generalization is possible. The more extensive the common values of family members or the more extensive the understanding that members have of one anothers' values, the less often will decision making contribute to unequal domination in the family, the less often will commitment to group decisions be conditional or ambiguous.

It is often supposed that more of the decisions are consensual in relationships of long duration than in newer associations. Parent and child or husband and wife come to know each other better and to share more of the same values. Thus according to the hypotheses we have suggested, there should be more basis for consensus. Other considerations must be noted, however. The constantly changing world of experience for the growing child, taking him increasingly out of the family world, probably fosters neither mutual understanding nor adherence to common values. For husband and wife there are also somewhat separate worlds, sometimes more divergent after the husband is fully launched in his career and the wife in child rearing than during the more fully shared world of dating and school. Furthermore, the very acceptance of accommodation as a modus vivendi for family life reduces some of the initial incentive toward intimate understanding and uniformly shared values. Hence it is by no means obvious that consensual decisions become more frequent as the family relationship endures.

Some evidence bearing on this question was sought by Udry, Nelson, and Nelson, who attempted to test the following nine hypotheses:[5]

(1) The longer a pair has been married, the more the members will agree with one another. (2) The more frequent the interaction, the greater the agreement. (3) The longer a pair has been married, the more the members will understand one another. (4) The more frequent the interaction, the more the understanding. (5) The more democratic the relationship, the greater the agreement. (6) The greater the agreement, the greater the understanding of the couple for one another. (7) The more democratic the relationship, the greater the understanding for one another. (8) The accuracy of perception of mates improves with time. (9) Perceived agreement declines over time in marriage.

Except for the last, each of these hypotheses bears on the conditions we believe related to consensual decision making.

Unfortunately, in testing the hypotheses, these investigators were able to use only 34 college-student couples, married from one to ten years. As the tool for assessing agreement they adapted the Allport-Vernon-Lindsey Study of Values, a notably abstract instrument whose indices usually achieve only indifferent effectiveness as predictors of behavior in commonplace situations. With these caveats, the procedure and findings are worth reporting. Each individual filled out the values schedule *a* privately for himself, then *b* as he believed his spouse would fill it out, then *c* as he believed his spouse would expect him to fill it out. Finally husband and wife were brought together and asked to agree on *d* a common set of answers for the two of them. By comparing the various pairs of answers the investigators secured an *agreement* score (similarity of husband and wife answers under condition *a*), an understanding score (comparing ego's *b* responses with alter's *a* responses), and a measure of *perceived agreement* (comparing *a* and *c* responses by the same person). Comparison of *a* scores with *d* scores supplied a measure of how equally or unequally each partner contributed to the pair answers. A set of intercorrelations was computed among the variables of agreement, understanding, perceived agreement, equality of influence, hours per week spent together, and years married. Except for a substantial relationship between actual and perceived agreement, none of the relationships was either large or statistically significant. Thus the authors are forced to conclude that none of the initial hypotheses are supported by the data.

In light of the small number of cases, the excessive homogeneity of the sample, and the irrelevance of the value instrument to the day-by-day con-

[5] J. Richard Udry, Harold A. Nelson, and Ruth Nelson, "An Empirical Investigation of Some Widely Held Beliefs about Marital Interaction," *Marriage and Family Living*, 23:388–390, November 1961. Quoted by permission of the National Council on Family Relations and the authors.

cerns of family life, these negative findings are not to be taken at face value, and the nonsignificant relationships are worth noting. Nonsignificant correlations of .15 were found between agreement and years married, between relative equality in decision making and years married, and between agreement and relative equality in decision making. Hence it may be premature to abandon the general hypothesis that consensual decisions become more frequent as the duration of marriage increases.

Coercion and Bargaining. Accommodative decisions are made somewhere on a continuum from coercion to bargaining.[6] It is hard to make an absolute distinction between these two processes, since coercion can readily be conceived as bargaining with a negative value; that is, the good that one receives by accommodation is the avoidance of some penalty that the other is in a position to administer. Also, there is often uncertainty in bargaining concerning whether the coercive potential of one member may not make a lower price seem adequate for the product being exchanged. Nevertheless, there are differences of degree in the attitudes of participants toward their commitment and in the relationships under which the two forms of accommodation take place. Ideally bargaining leads to willing agreement, to which each is committed because of the benefits he gains from agreement. Coercion means unwilling agreement, to which commitment is assured only by the continuance of coercive power. Coercion can only take place in a relationship of inequality whether enduring or situational. The relation of parent to child, or stronger to weaker sibling who has grasped a precious belonging of the other and threatens to break it, are typical instances. Bargaining proceeds most easily in a situation of equality but often occurs when interactional norms or group bonds prevent the individual with superior power from using it coercively. The mother who has been taught that she should not force obedience on her children must strive for consensus or fall back upon bargaining.

Bargaining may seem like a cruel word to apply to the deliberations of members in the intimate family relationship. But bargaining is simply a general term for any interaction in which the concessions that one member makes to another are expected to be reciprocated in some manner, so that over the long run the sacrifices of each will balance out. The nearest pheno-

---

[6] Family decision making was examined as a bargaining process by Clifford Kirkpatrick, in *The Family as Process and Institution*, Ronald, New York, 1955, pp. 294–295, *et passim*. The bargaining approach has been generalized as exchange theory, applied to simple interpersonal relations by George Homans in *Social Behavior: Its Elementary Forms*, Harcourt, Brace & World, New York, 1961. A brilliant and comprehensive elaboration of exchange theory is found in Peter Blau, *Exchange and Power in Social Life*, Wiley, New York, 1964; and a briefer summary by Blau in "Interaction: Social Exchange," *International Encyclopedia of the Social Sciences*, 1968, vol. 7, pp. 452–458.

menon to economic bargaining, in which the exchange is either simultaneous or ensured by the force of law, is the explicit compromise.

Empirical research on bargaining in social interaction suggests that bargaining is normally tempered by a concern with equity. In several studies the subjects have been unwilling to exploit advantageous bargaining positions to the full. Rather than taking all they can under the rules of the game, they try to distribute winnings with consideration for the losers. Summarizing a body of research, Ward Edwards comments as follows:

The main finding from these studies of multiperson games seems to be that people import into bargaining situations a strong desire for equity. Equity seeking is promoted by effective and free communication and seriously hindered, or even prevented, by severely restricted communication. Equity seeking produces results in conflict with those implied by game theory and similar theories about rapacious economic men. . . .[7]

There may be more than charitable and fellow feeling to account for this finding. At least two features of bargaining work against driving the hardest bargain possible when continuing relationships with the same person are anticipated. For one thing, being generous at the bargaining table is a way of establishing the expectation of generous treatment at some later time when the current winner may be the loser. For another, as Blau points out, a bargaining relationship rests on trust.[8] Without legal contracts or exchange of tangible goods, there is no way to guarantee that a bargain will be kept. Being a little generous is a way of inviting and offering trust and thus assuring the other that the relationship can proceed with confidence.

Whenever a relationship is regarded as in any way personal, the bargaining must be understood but not expressed. To specify the price expected for kindness done to a friend makes the kindness meaningless.[9] This general observation is even more true of affectional relations in the family, although quite explicit bargaining is often practiced within each of the family pairs when the practical exigencies of child rearing, division of household chores, distribution of money allowances for various purposes, and other family tasks are at stake. In other respects bargaining in the family is implicit, quantitatively approximate, and based on the general confidence of members in the fairness of the others. The family member who accedes to something that another strongly desires often does so with no thought of return. It is only when several unilateral concessions have been made in succession or when the other is unwilling to reciprocate at

[7] Edwards, "Behavioral Decision Theory," *Annual Review of Psychology*, 12:492–493, 1961. Quoted by permission of Annual Reviews, Inc., and the author.
[8] *Exchange and Power in Social Life*, pp. 91–97.
[9] *Ibid.*, p. 93; see also Ralph H. Turner, "The Navy Disbursing Officer as a Bureaucrat," *American Sociological Review*, 12:346, June 1947.

some later occasion that a sense of injustice finds expression in the explicit language of bargaining.

A questionnaire study of 800 students in a college introductory sociology course illustrates the rejection of explicit bargaining in at least one kind of family situation, even when the respondents believe that an effective bargain could be struck. Marwell and Schmitt presented four kinds of situation—job, family, sales, and roommate—in which the principal actor was not doing so well as he could. Several courses of action for bringing the actor into line were proposed for each situation, and the students indicated which courses would be effective, in their opinion, and whether the person with bargaining power in the situation would or would not use each technique. In general the students endorsed the use of those techniques which they also said would probably be effective. The notable exception to this generalization fell in the area of family relations. The situation described a teen-age son who was getting bad grades in school. Many students felt that promising to increase his allowance if he devoted more time to studying would be effective but also indicated that the technique should not be used.[10] A plausible explanation for the finding is that students objected to the explicit bargaining involved in the promise of increased allowance in exchange for more serious study as a violation of their conception of the proper nature of family relations.

The ease and expeditiousness with which accommodative decisions take place, then, depend on the degree of imbalance in coercive power among family members or the degree of faith that each has in the ultimate balancing out of the bargaining process. The latter especially is part of the image that each member has of the others, subject to reinforcement or modification with each experience of implicit bargaining.

Coercion especially, and bargaining to a lesser degree, are further affected by the formation of coalitions. One of the commonest forms of coercive coalition is the pressure that a majority imposes on the lone individual or minority who refuse to give their assent to the course of action favored by the majority. Once a clear trend is apparent in decision making, the individuals who do not conform are increasingly perceived as obstructionists. According to the reciprocity principle, once they are so defined, obstructionists are by definition not adhering to the norm of helping the group reach a decision, and the majority then feel justified in disregarding the normal rules against applying coercion. If mother and the children have agreed upon a weekend family activity, the tendency to apply majority coercion to the reluctant father mounts. Such coercion is probably an appreciable factor in bringing decisions to completion.

[10] Gerald Marwell and David R. Schmitt, "Attitudes toward Parental Use of Promised Rewards to Control Adolescent Behavior," *Journal of Marriage and Family*, 29:500–504, August 1967.

The relative frequency of bargaining as contrasted with coercive decisions in the family is governed by several principles. The relative frequency of bargaining decisions is greater when (a) there is relatively little inequality between family members, (b) there are norms against the use of coercion, (c) there is faith in the future reciprocation by other family members, and (d) there is a norm against defining the dissident individual as an obstructionist. The speed with which agreement is reached probably varies roughly from the coercive decision, which is quickest, to the implicit bargain, to the slowest, which is the explicit bargan.

Obstacles to Agreement

Agreements are reached in any group chiefly because the members want to agree so that they can get on with the objectives they are associated in the group for. Accordingly it is the bonds holding the group together that provide the ultimate incentive for reaching agreements. The stronger and more varied the bonds, the greater the incentive to reach a decision. But different kinds of bonds have varying effects. One probable difference is a tendency for identity bonds to apply an unselective pressure and to favor consensus or implicit bargaining. Since the interpersonal relationship is the center of attention in the operation of identity bonds, the nature of the problem at hand is not so important as the achievement of agreement on all matters. The explicit recognition of bargaining introduces an impersonal and conditional element to the relationship that threatens the interrelation of identities. Task bonds, in contrast, act as selective incentives. The bond of financial enterprise creates an incentive to reach agreement on financial matters but not necessarily on recreational or child-raising matters. Furthermore, there is no inconsistency between explicit bargaining and a relationship for the pursuit of recognized objectives. Consequently, the tendency to reach agreements in any specific aspect of family life will be a function, first, of the presence and strength of a bond related to that area and, second, of the strength of identity bonds in the family relationship.

Opposing the incentives and pressures toward reaching agreements, there are also obstacles that make members of the family reluctant to give assent to a reasonable proposal or even to press for family adoption of their own proposals. The first obstacle is the implicit bargaining. For the individual who has made the suggestion that might, with a little urging, be accepted as the group decision, the problem is what other members will feel he owes them in return for their assent. Consider the following example of a dating couple. The boy's suggestion regarding a place to go on the date has been followed for three successive weeks. On the fourth weekend the girl is likely to feel that she now has a strong moral right to dictate the weekend activity, regardless of the relative merits of her suggestion and his. On the basis of this experience the boy may attempt to avoid controlling successive decisions, especially on matters that are not terribly important to him, so as not to put himself at a disadvantage when a big decision looms. The girl, having learned to exploit such bargaining advantages, may be equally unwilling to control the decision. The result may be a recurrent jockeying, especially on minor decisions, in which each tries to get the other to say what should be done. Occasionally individuals develop this bargaining approach to interpersonal relations to the extent that the receipt of any kind of favor from another is experienced as threatening. The mother who forces her children to return any gifts given them by outsiders supplies a gross instance. More subtle is the parent who responds to proffered help from spouse or child by rigging the situation so that the helper is really more trouble than help and then disavowing any debt to the helper with the slogan, "If you want something done right, you have to do it yourself."

If bargaining is defined broadly enough, it can encompass all the obstacles that we shall mention. But for our purposes it is still useful to enumerate separately two of the by-products of unequal participation in the decision-making process.

The first of these by-products, with which we shall deal at greater length in Chapter 6, is dominance-submission. According to the logic of bargaining, there are advantages to occasional submission. On the other hand, we have already noted the emergence of patterned relationships out of any succession of interaction episodes. In accepting submission, ego runs the risk that a precedent will form and he will be carving out a subordinate role for himself in the family. Such a role is disadvantageous both from the standpoint of being able to satisfy his own wishes in the family and from the standpoint of the kind of identity established. The fear of falling into such a role is then met by resistence to good suggestions, delaying tactics by which the individual lessens his apparent degree of submission, or the insistence on minor modifications and compromises, so that the other is never unqualifiedly identified with the decision.

The other by-product is the assignment of responsibility and credit. Dominance and submission are the immediate identity consequence of concluding any decision by accommodation. But credit and responsibility are the later consequences after there has been an opportunity to evaluate the decision. If the idea that was adopted turns out to have been good, the person most closely identified with the decision can take credit. His respect in the family and sometimes outside the family is strengthened, and his suggestions will be given more weight within the family subsequently. If the idea turns out to have been bad, then to have been most closely associated with the decision means that responsibility must be accepted, and the consequences of credit all operate in reverse. If the parent follows the child's suggestion on one occasion with unfortunate results, the parent is quite likely to use the failure as a sufficient justification for giving less hearing to the child's suggestion in the future.

In consequence of the foregoing an individual may seek to gain credit for what he anticipates will be a good decision by prolonging discussion and may wait for someone else to take the initiative in a decision that cannot promise much. If one member becomes the persistent and vigorous advocate of a suggestion, the originator of the suggestion may be forgotten and the credit transferred. A contest for credit delays decisions and often provokes new differences to be resolved. Decisions are impeded by jockeying to avoid responsibility for a decision by such tactics as being very "democratic" or pointing out the drawbacks to one's own suggestion, so that someone else has to make the strong assertion in its favor.

The conditions facilitating and blocking decision making may be broadly summarized by saying that they are of two kinds. First, there are the similarities and differences of preference among the family members, including the interest in accomplishing objectives that are shared or require the collaboration of other family members. Second, there is the nature of the identity relationships among the members and the apparent implications of the decision and of the way it was reached for future identity relations in the family. The former are more easily made explicit and dealt with by discussion because of the ready segmentation of task bonds; that is, people can admit their differences of preference in one area without threatening the bond that arises out of common task interests in another. The latter, however, are not easily dealt with explicitly except in their positive aspects. One may give as his reason for agreeing with another that he loves her, but it will be more difficult to acknowledge that there are respects in which what enhances her identity damages his. Identity bonds are not so readily segmented, and admission of an area of identity incompatibility threatens all identity bonds. Consequently decision-making patterns in any family normally develop by taking identity relations into account without explicitly recognizing them. They are dealt with explicitly only to the extent that conflict or harmonization takes the place of decision making; this is the subject of Chapter 7.

Family Decision Making as Problem Solving

If decision making begins with a problem, the outcome sought is solution of the problem. When a decision is reached, the decision can be evaluated according to how adequate a solution it affords to the problem. There have been important studies of the effectiveness with which family units are able to cope with major crises, such as unemployment of the breadwinner, wartime separation because of military duty, disruptions occasioned by natural disasters, and bereavement.[11] But relatively little is known about the adequacy of solutions to the steady flow of small problems that require constant mobilization of family decision making. Research on group problem solving in other contexts, principally laboratory groups and business organizations, suggest some determinants of problem-solving effectiveness that may be applicable to the family.

Determinants of Problem-solving Effectiveness. Several laboratory investigations have been directed to the problem of whether individuals or groups are more effective and more efficient problem solvers. As might be guessed, results seem to vary according to the kind of task, and it is impossible to give a generally applicable answer. For many simple problems the group does no better than an individual. In all cases when it is possible for solitary individuals to solve the problem, the group is less efficient than the individual as measured by the number of man-hours required for a solution. In those instances when the group finds a better solution than any individual alone, the reason seems to be that members of the group ask more questions and thereby secure more information than any single individual would do. The group can therefore command a more comprehensive picture of the alternatives from which the best solution must be chosen.[12] Thus an important determinant in the effectiveness of family problem solving is the extent to which members contribute a range of alternatives wider than one individual could have supplied.

Studies of problem solving in organizations have impressed investigators with the narrow range of alternatives usually presented for consideration. Most problems have been confronted before or are fairly similar to previously encountered problems, and the previous solutions are advanced. Other solutions offered are chiefly small variations from the customary solution.[13] Informal experience sugests that a similarly limited range of suggestions is also common in the family and that neither parents nor children ordinarily venture far from familiar solutions to their problems.

As Hoffman, Harding, and Maier have observed, there are often more viewpoints available in a group than are actually expressed. The presence of a highly dominant figure seems, according to experimental findings, to inhibit the expression of alternatives at variance with his own preferred solution. Through an experiment in a work group situation Hoffman et al. were able to show, however, steps that increased the subordinates' resist-

[11] See Reuben Hill and Donald A. Hansen, "Families under Stress," in Harold T. Christensen (ed.), *Handbook of Marriage and the Family*, Rand McNally, Chicago, 1964, pp. 782–822.

[12] Carl P. Duncan, *op. cit.*, esp. pp. 417–419.

[13] Julian Feldman and Herschel E. Kanter, "Organizational Decision Making," in James G. March (ed.), *Handbook of Organizations*, Rand McNally, Chicago, 1965, esp. pp. 620–623.

ance to the superior and generated some initial conflict, leading to an increase in the frequency of high-quality solutions to a problem.[14] For the family, the unequal-authority situation applies to parent-child decision making and sometimes to husband-wife decisions. By analogy to the experiment, the extreme importance that some family decisions hold for a member ensures that in many instances a wide range of alternatives is presented.

The alternatives presented can be no better than the resources commanded by individual family members. But the diversity introduced into the family by the combination of two kinship lines and diverse age and sex subcultures favors the presentation of multiple alternatives for many problems. Thus we hypothesize that a range of alternatives will be presented in the course of problem solving in those families in which (a) members have divergent backgrounds or extrafamilial reference groups and (b) authority is not used to suppress the presentation of alternatives by members of less authority, in those situations in which (c) a new solution is important to one or more members who do not hold primary authority.

The presentation of alternatives offers no assurance that each will gain a serious hearing and fair appraisal. A second factor in problem solving is the quality of attention and selection among alternatives. Suggestions made by a child are often received with a friendly pat on the head and given no serious thought. The ideology of the generation gap supplies a ready-made basis for youthful disregard of parental suggestions about many spheres of life. These are merely two instances of the censoring effect of ego and alter conceptions on the communication of suggested solutions to problems in the family. In general, serious consideration of alternatives presented by all family members is limited by the development of a set of ego and alter conceptions that either sharply distinguish the degree of competence assigned to each member or assign members mutually exclusive competencies. Thus if the father is viewed or views himself as omnipotent relative to other family members, he is less likely to take their suggestions seriously, and the quality of family solutions will be poorer. If the mother has sole competence in kitchen matters and the father in garden affairs, neither is likely to give adequate thought to the range of suggestions that might be forthcoming from other family members.

The problems with which the family deals are not those for which there are certain best solutions. There is generally no way to be sure whether the favored solution will turn out to be best or not. A third factor in problem-solving adequacy is therefore an optimal willingness by the group to

[14] Richard Hoffman, Ernest Harburg, and Norman R. F. Maier, "Differences and Disagreement as Factors in Creative Group Problem Solving," *Journal of Abnormal and Social Psychology*, 64:206–214, March 1962.

take risks. Without some willingness to accept risks, there is no option but to follow the traditional solutions. With excessive risk taking family life becomes a gamble in which the odds are against winning.

It has often been supposed that decisions made by groups are likely to be more conservative than those made by individuals. There are some plausible reasons why risk taking should be inhibited in the group. The responsibility involved in a decision affecting others may lead to a sobered perspective. Also, the individual who persuades others in a group to join him in a risky decision must face the blame if the decision turns out unhappily. On the other hand, the willingness to take risks is undoubtedly greater when the individual is assured of social support and when his social position is secure. The latter conditions should apply to a strongly bonded family unit, when relationships within the family are well defined and harmonious. Furthermore, when the family structure is not rigidly fixed, the proposal of unusual courses of action may be a way of striking for leadership. Hence some group decisions and especially family decisions may incline toward risk taking more strongly than individual decisions.

Although there is no research specifically bearing on this question in the family, Wallach, Kogan, and Bem have studied a simple form of risk taking among college students. Groups of six students—fourteen all-male groups and fourteen all-female groups—made choices between safe and risky but potentially more rewarding alternatives in twelve situations. Subjects first filled out the choice questionnaires individually, then discussed each situation so as to arrive at unanimous group decision, and finally recorded their reconsidered individual choices privately after the group discussion. There were further steps and groups in the experiment that need not concern us here. The results show a significant shift in the direction of riskier decisions when group decisions are compared with the initial private choices. The effect remains in the private choices recorded after the groups were disbanded.[15]

Whether a test situation such as this one indicates a genuine inclination to take risks is problematic, since the subjects did not themselves undertake any risk or stand any chance of benefitting. But the findings do help to discredit any a priori assumption of group conservatism.

Decisions Concerning Common and Individual Activity. Undoubtedly problem solving differs according to the kind of problem confronting a group. Kinds of problems important to the family are suggested by the discussion of bonding and will be indicated in subsequent chapters dealing with some of the more distinctive features of the family as a small group.

[15] Michael A. Wallach, Nathan Kogan, and Daryl J. Bem, "Group Influence on Individual Risk Taking," *Journal of Abnormal and Social Psychology*, 65:75–86, August 1962.

Within the family, however, there are clearly two broad kinds of problems to be solved by group decision, suggesting rather different implications for the process. One set of problems concerns those activities in which family members participate in common or in collaboration, such as taking a summer vacation or maintaining a common household. These problems involve the interrelated phases of choosing what is to be done and working out the division of labor to accomplish the family task. The other set of problems concerns the individual actions of family members, actions that nevertheless fall under family control and require adjustments in the behavior of others.

The problems of common and collaborative activity are those with which students of group problem solving have generally been concerned. But the family is in large measure the staging ground, the coordinating agency, and the regulating center for a wide range of individual activity. Scheduling meals, vacations, use of automobiles, entertainment for friends of various family members are constant problems in the family. The system of obligations that family members hold toward one another, and the specific responsibility of parents to regulate the behavior of children mean constant adjudication and interpretation of the acceptable limits of individual behavior.

The juxtaposition of these two kinds of problems gives rise to what Hess and Handel have designated as one of the five essential processes of the family, namely, establishing a pattern of separateness and connectedness.[16] More than most other groups, the family is the focus of mutually adjusted individual activity. By its nature it fosters individuality and is often the most fertile ground for the expression of individual uniquenesses. More than other groups, the family is expected to know its members as individuals, and members are supposed to foster one another's uniquenesses. Yet the members are highly interdependent. The very pursuit of individuality is made possible in part by the willingness of family members to adjust to one another. Furthermore there is a foundation of common and collaborative activity without which the family does not exist. There are no clear prescriptions for determining the proper mix between activities which are shared and those which are enjoyed separately. Sometimes the findings from prediction studies, such as the higher success scores when the married couple take their vacations together rather than separately,[17] have elicited the generalization that a preponderance of common rather than

[16] Robert D. Hess and Gerald Handel, *Family Worlds: A Psychosocial Approach to Family Life*, University of Chicago Press, Chicago, 1950.
[17] See Kirkpatrick, *op. cit.*, p. 353, on community of interest and marital adjustment; Harvey J. Locke, *Predicting Adjustment in Marriage*, Holt, New York, 1951, pp. 252–253.

separate activities facilitates marital satisfaction. This seems to be much more a problem, however, that must be worked out uniquely for each family. In their case studies Hess and Handel review a wide range of relatively effective adjustments, from the family in which there is a strong penchant for doing everything as a group to the loosely knit family in which members largely go their separate ways.

Criteria of Problem Solving. The classic situations in which problem solving has been studied are those in which there is some objective criterion by which to distinguish between a good and a poor solution. Group production and competitive success provide criteria for evaluating work groups. In some family activities there are objective criteria, as when the family falls increasingly in debt or when the children become delinquents, but in most respects this is not so. There can be no clear criteria when family members do not explicitly set major goals for family life. If one family fails to rise socially while another family does so, it is likely that members of the first family are uncertain just how important family social standing is to them. Even when a family is clear about one or two major goals, there are usually no objective measures available. If family members wish to be happy together, how is their success to be judged? In the absence of production and profit measures for family life, problem solving can usually be judged only subjectively or normatively. Either the members' feelings about the family experience or conformity to mores and folkways serve as criteria. It is possible to study the recognition and attack on specific problems in families. But in crucial respects the quality of problem solving in different families cannot be compared except in terms of the extent to which members of society judge the family's influence on the community to be constructive.[18]

[18] See the discussion of difficulties in arriving at a defensible criterion of marital success in the design of prediction studies in Ernest W. Burgess and Paul Wallin, *Engagement and Marriage*, Lippincott, Philadelphia, 1953, pp. 470–506. A more recent review of criteria of marital success, though more limited to an operational perspective, is found in Charles E. Bowerman, "Prediction Studies," in Christensen, *op. cit.*, esp. pp. 237–245.

CHAPTER 6

DETERMINANTS
OF DOMINANCE

Preestablished patterns of dominance help determine the outcome of every decision and the division of labor through which it is implemented, but episodes of decision making are the medium through which patterns of dominance are created. In discussing the variables that determine who will control the outcome of any accommodative decision, we are explaining the emergence of patterns in which some members of a family get in the habit of waiting for another's view before taking a position strongly.

Dominance is a common-sense idea which does not correspond exactly to any empirically specifiable phenomenon and which can be broken down into several equally imprecise elements on further examination. The idea of dominance is deceptively simple: the dominant person runs the show, and the submissive member always gives in. There are few families or other groups, however, in which any person always gets his way. The best that we can do is to place the family members at various points along a continuum from dominance to submission. But in order to do so, we must somehow measure decisions so that we do not count winning an unimportant decision equally with winning an important one. Clearly any such operation must be somewhat arbitrary and imprecise.

In any concrete case when we try to decide who is dominant we are likely to look for several different indices. First, we note whose suggestion is most clearly reflected in the group decision. This is the procedure followed by Fred Strodtbeck in his "method of revealed differences."[1] Husband and wife pairs are given a problem and asked to arrive at a common solution they can both accept. But after they have considered the problem individually and before they have begun their discussion, they privately record the solutions they prefer. Dominance is then defined according to whose private solution becomes the accepted pair solution.

This conception of dominance creates little difficulty in the pair relationship. But in triads and larger groups there is often an individual whose

[1] Fred L. Strodtbeck, "Husband-wife Interaction over Revealed Differences," *American Sociological Review*, 16:468–473, August 1951.

forte is not in making good suggestions but who is nevertheless able to determine more often than others which suggestion will be adopted.

Respect or prestige is another component in the complex of dominance. Respect is normally accorded the individual who dominates, and the respected person is more likely to have a good hearing and consequently to have an opportunity to persuade others. But the respected person is sometimes treated ritually, his views heard politely but dismissed as irrelevant. Such is often the position of the grandparent, or of the parent when he communicates with a group of his child's peers.

There are other distinctions that can be made, such as between initiators and followers and between actual and potential dominance. But for our purposes dominance will refer to control of the outcome of group decisions. A family member is dominant to the degree to which the fact that he favors a given solution increases the chances of the solution's being adopted as the family decision. The true measure of such dominance requires an experimental situation in which it is possible to arrange that an individual will change his preference while the decision is in process. Such a step would ensure that the connection between his preference and the group's adoption of his solution is a reflection of his power and not fortuitous. But in practice various observational approximations are usually required in the study of actual families.

Authority

Among the determinants of dominance in this sense, the most basic can be called *authority*. Authority refers to a belief in the propriety of one person's exercising more dominance than another, a belief shared by members of the family. Authority may derive from some earlier decision of the group, such as the election of officers or the agreement to allocate responsibilities. It may derive from the action of a larger body whose right is respected, as when the father's authority is justified on the grounds that the state through its laws holds him responsible for the behavior of his children. Or it may be a matter of traditional belief whose origin is unknown to the believers. The last is the usual basis for the authority of parents over children, the authority of the adult male over the adult female, and sometimes the authority of the eldest child over the younger children.

The key to the operation of authority is mutual belief. The parent must take it for granted that he ought to have final say over matters involving himself and the children in order that he will assert his authority when necessary. The children must believe that they ought to submit to the parent's will when the parent is insistent, although the parent's coercive power is ineffectual. The belief in authority is characteristically buttressed by an *ideology*—a set of beliefs about the nature of things that supplies a rationale for the required behavior. The traditionally superior authority of men over women was supported by a set of beliefs regarding intellectual and temperamental differences between the sexes that convinced both men and women of the latter's inferiority in practical and intellectual matters. Authority of parent over child is based on an ideology regarding the nature of maturity and the consequences of maturation that is not subjected to empirical test and undobutedly exaggerates the differences of competence and judgment between adult and child.

Frequently authority is attributed to the possession of coercive power rather than to belief in its legitimacy. Authority often develops historically out of coercive power. In the contemporary situation authority is usually supported by coercive power. Parents can administer physical punishment to their children, restrict their freedom, withhold their allowance. Where the male authority is strong, men can similarly coerce their wives. But the change in women's and children's status in the western world has shown us that it was the belief in the right of persons with authority to use coercive power that gave husbands and parents the power. The husband could punish his wife by withholding her allowance for domestic expenses only because she believed that he had a right to control finances. Most parents can restrict their children's freedom effectively only when the children believe in parental authority. Authority, then, is mutual belief in the right of unequal domination with the supplemental right to enforce domination when necessary by coercive methods, supported by a justifying ideology.

Since authority is a set of beliefs and attitudes transcending the individual episode, it provides a basis for predicting dominance in the individual situation. Over the long range authority is affected by events both within and without the family. The successful execution of family activities in violation of authority undermines it; successful assertion of authority reinforces it. But authority such as that of the parents over the children or the authority of the eldest son under a system of primogeniture is not determined primarily in the individual family. Later we shall speak about the impact of the larger cultural and social structure on the family. For the present we can note that authority in the family is firmly anchored outside the individual family, so that the course of interaction in the family usually leads only to variations in the established authority pattern rather than complete transformations.

Organization Fostering Dominance

It is commonplace that authority may reside in one person but effective power in another. Although authority is the underlying variable in family dominance because it comes from outside, there is far from a perfect correspondence between authority and dominance. Such observations as this in the study of large-scale social organizations—the business corporation, military establishment, or government bureau, for example—have led to a distinction between formal and informal organization.[2] The formal organization is described by the organization chart, which designates department heads, assistants, and other levels of authority. But persons intimately familiar with the corporation or bureau often know an individual who wields more influence in his department than the department head. The informal organization refers to the unofficial distribution of actual power. If functionaries are asked who is in charge in a department, they reply with the formal organization. If a knowledgeable functionary is asked how one gets something done in the department, he answers by naming people high in the informal organization. Similarly, the question "Who is head of the household?" is answered with reference to authority or formal organization. But there may also be an informal organization that is partially at variance with authority. The wife may actually dominate a family in which the father is acknowledged head. Or the actual power of husband and wife may be quite unequal in a family that is explicitly egalitarian.

Authority is only completely translated into domination when the group in which it is exercised is organized so as to support it. There are two important respects in which the organization of the family for decision making has the effect of differentiating its members with respect to dominance, regardless of the authority patterns. Authority patterns are reinforced or contradicted, depending on how these features of organization relate to the locus of authority. The two aspects of organization are the communication network through which decisions are reached and the differential control of means by which decisions are carried out.

Communication Networks. Studies of both small and large groups have shown that communication is seldom of equal intensity within each pair of individuals in any group. A group is sometimes broken into small cliques within which there is much communication but between which there is little. Husband and wife may communicate more often, more intimately, and about a wider range of subjects than either does with the children; and the children may similarly constitute a clique. Age and sex identifications affect rates and kinds of communication, as do many idiosyncratic features of the relationship. Consequently, although true cliques do not develop in a five-person family group, the intensity of communication within each of the ten pairs of individuals is unlikely to be equal.

[2] The term "informal organization" has been replaced by several more precise terms with the advance of research in large-scale organization. Similarly, in family study the reference to informal organization merely points to the operation of several organizing principles not explicitly provided for in a model of formal family authority.

Attendant on such unequal communication is the emergence of intermediaries in communication. If a group has two cliques, one or two members of each clique are likely to become the intermediaries through whom the two cliques communicate. If any decisions that require the assent and commitment of the entire group are to be made, these individuals are crucial to the attainment of decision.

The relative frequencies of communication between pairs of members in the group and the differentiation of members into some who communicate directly, some who communicate only indirectly through others, and some who serve as the intermediaries for communication between others is known as the communication network of the group. There is a special area of small-group research concerned with identifying the kinds and components of communication networks and the properties of each.[3] The properties of networks are studied in the laboratory by artificially forcing members to follow specified lines of communication. For example, an intercom unit is installed from office A to office B and another from B to C, so that B can communicate directly with either A or C but A and C can communicate only by asking B to relay a message. We are not yet prepared to apply all the findings from such research to the family, but one idea is of considerable importance.

The individual who serves as an intermediary in communications between others but who can communicate without an intermediary himself is said to hold a central position in the communication network. Complicated communication networks introduce some positions that are intermediary for several pairs of members and other positions that are intermediary for a few. Furthermore, communication networks are themselves usually matters of degree, A sometimes communicating directly with C but more often communicating by way of B. Hence we must compare members of the group according to their degree of *centrality* in the communication network. The more pairs who communicate through ego, the larger the proportion of their communications that occur through ego, and the larger the proportion of group members with whom ego communicates directly, the greater the centrality of ego in the communication network.

The importance of the concept of centrality for our purposes lies in its correlation with dominance. The greater the centrality of the member, the greater his dominance. The correlation arises out of two kinds of

[3] Some of the many studies of communication networks have been summarized by Josephine Klein, in *The Study of Groups*, Routledge, London, 1956; and by Murray Glanzer and R. Glasner, "Techniques for the Study of Group Structure and Behavior: II, Empirical Studies of the Effects of Structure in Small Groups," *Psychological Bulletin*, 58:1–27, 1961. For evidence specifically dealing with centrality and influence, see Terence K. Hopkins, *The Exercise of Influence in Small Groups*, Bedminster, Totowa, N.J., 1964, pp. 74–76.

advantage that the high-centrality member has in controlling the outcome of the decision-making process. First, because he communicates directly with more people, he is in a better position to know the attitudes and opinions of most of the members of the group. As we indicated in the discussion of consensual decision making, such knowledge makes it possible to appeal to values that are important to the individual in winning his consent to the decision. Second, as an intermediary he is able to censor and modify the communications to suit his purposes as he relays them. Such censorship and alteration are likely to be done naively rather than conspiratorially in the family. But nevertheless, the way the mother relays the children's request for a beach trip to the father is bound to strengthen or weaken the request according to her own inclination.

A common form of communication network in the family takes roughly the form of the capital letter Y. As diagrammed in Figure 5, the network involves the father, the mother, and two children. The width of the connecting lines indicates the relative frequency of communication between each pair of members. The heaviest communication is between the father and the mother and between the children. The next heaviest lines are between the mother and each of the children. The children and the father

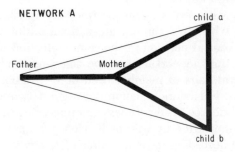

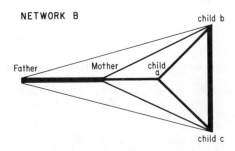

Figure 5.   Two family communication networks.

communicate least because of the physical separation during most of the children's waking hours and because of a minimum of common experiences and concerns. If we assume that many decisions with which the father is concerned require the assent of the children and vice versa, it is clear that there has to be a great deal of communication that depends on the mother as an intermediary. Hence the mother has the highest degree of centrality. According to the hypothesis we have discussed, she is able to exercise considerable domination within the family, in spite of mutual recognition of the father's superior authority. Indeed, there is a paradox here, since one of the factors contributing to the mother's centrality is the father's authority. The greater the father's authority, the less the children are likely to make requests directly to him. An interesting speculation, empirically untested, is the hypothesis that the more unequal the authority of the father in the family, the more powerful the offsetting dominance arising out of the centrality of the mother.

We have also diagrammed a slightly more complex network that is common in the American family. The mother is still most central, but one child now occupies a position of lesser centrality as a frequent intermediary between the mother and the other children. The larger the family, the more likely such positions of secondary centrality are to arise. Sometimes the eldest child, sometimes the youngest child in his special role as family pet, sometimes the child whose attitudes fall between those of parents and children, and sometimes a child cast in the role by events or the suitability of his own personality becomes the children's emissary and the mother's contact man. His dominance is enhanced in consequence.

In practice, such networks become immensely complicated. For one thing, the condition of mutuality is seldom so perfectly met as we have assumed. The mother may give instructions for one child to pass on to the others, but the children may initiate all their communications to the mother directly. Furthermore, communication networks may be different for different areas of concern. One network is followed in matters of proper behavior, establishment of family rules, and related topics, but quite a different network is followed when the question is how to spend a free weekend. The result of this segmentation is different patterns of dominance for different areas of family decision making.

Control over Implementation. The second aspect of family organization that affects domination in the decision-making process is the individual's position in relation to control of the means of carrying out the decision. Assent without commitment, we have noted, does not complete the group decision. The ultimate commitment is based on somebody's carrying out the decision. When not all members have equal control of the means of carrying out the decision, the enthusiastic assent of some becomes more important than the assent of others. A family decision on what to have for dinner is worth no more than the compliance of the person who shops and the person who cooks. A family decision on finances depends on those who spend the family income. A family decision that one of the children should go to college is no better than the efforts which the child makes to meet college entrance requirements.

Some years ago Ernest Burgess and Harvey Locke described the suburban American family as *matricentric*.[4] They carefully avoided calling it matriarchal, which would have meant that the mother held more authority than the father. But in calling it matricentric, they indicated that in fact the mother was firmly in control, largely because the father's life as a commuter isolated him from the details of the family enterprise. In thus characterizing the family, Burgess and Locke were adumbrating both the notion of power deriving from communication centrality and power from the fact that the mother is actually the one who must carry out the decisions.

Resources and Interpersonal Technique

Authority and the communication and action organization of the family are primarily attributes of the family group and serve to distribute the dominance of individuals within the group. From the individual point of view, each person also has certain *resources* that contribute to his ability to wield greater or lesser dominance over others. Investigations of power in small groups frequently begin with experimental distribution and redistribution of these resources among the members.[5] For our purposes the resources that enhance a member's dominance can be divided into the values he controls and the interpersonal techniques he has mastered.

An enumeration of resources would simply be a listing of the things that people value, insofar as one person can limit or facilitate another person's access to these values. Like the bases for attraction between people, the bases for dominance are diverse and often idiosyncratic. The significance of some specific kinds of resources to different aspects and stages of family life will be explored in subsequent chapters, as shifting patterns

---

[4] Ernest W. Burgess and Harvey J. Locke, *The Family: From Institution to Championship*, American Book, New York, 1945, pp. 131–134.

[5] For reviews of research dealing with power and influence in groups, see Paul F. Secord and Carl W. Backman, *Social Psychology*, McGraw-Hill, New York, 1964, pp. 273–293; Dorwin Cartwright, "Influence, Leadership, Control," in James G. March (ed.), *Handbook of Organizations*, Rand McNally, Chicago, 1965, pp. 1–47. Resources are central to the theory of marital power tested by Robert O. Blood, Jr., and Donald M. Wolfe, in *Husbands and Wives: The Dynamics of Married Living*, Free Press, New York, 1960, esp. pp. 44–46.

of dominance come under review. Interpersonal techniques are also varied, and individuals differ greatly in their skills. It is not uncommon to find one family member who has few of the objective resources that ordinarily facilitate dominance actually controlling much of family life through his masterful use of a broad repertoire of interpersonal techniques. In general terms, the effective use of interpersonal techniques depends on having an adequate repertoire of techniques and understanding situations and persons sufficiently well so that the appropriate techniques are selected for use in each situation.

But people often do not use the techniques they have at their disposal, or they use them rather ineffectually. Afterwards they find it difficult to understand why they did not say what they had on the tip of their tongue, why they did not take advantage of the known weaknesses of the others, why they did not use appeals that had been effective previously, or why they presented their position in such an unconvincing manner. Using a metaphor from the sport of boxing, we say that a person sometimes pulls his punches. Rather than landing blows with the full force he is capable of, the boxer fights indecisively. Similarly, in discussion ego fails to exploit an argument, a point of strength, to the extent that is possible and lets the advantage fall to alter, whose position is intrinsically weaker. Whatever leads a person to pull his punches during the family decision-making process contributes to domination by the other person.

Self-confidence. Authority is again the most frequent explanation for a person's using the interpersonal techniques he knows to the full or hesitating and using them weakly. But the effectiveness of authority is partially a consequence of another pervasive variable, which is the degree of self-confidence each feels vis-à-vis the other. In his classic study of a young men's gang in a Boston slum, William F. Whyte was able to show that even a member's skill at bowling was affected by his position and social acceptance in the gang.[6] As his position declined, he lost self-confidence in relation to other members, and he was unable to marshall all the skill at his disposal when playing with them.

The self-confidence we speak of is a product of the self-image and other images of the interactors. It reflects the cumulation from previous interaction and the placement in the situation of the moment. Just as a winning athletic team may consistently lose to a particular team that is generally inferior to it, the relations between one pair in the family may have developed so as to reverse their general pattern of family dominance.

Importance of the Issue. A second variable affecting the extent to which

[6] William F. Whyte, *Street Corner Society*, University of Chicago Press, Chicago, 1955.

members use the techniques at their disposal is the importance to them of the issue at hand. The more important the outcome on a given matter, the more an individual works at gaining a decision acceptable to him. The member to whom an issue is unimportant may settle for any decision to gain peace and quiet.

Norms Regulating Interpersonal Technique. A third variable is the set of norms that designate the techniques that are permissible in particular kinds of relationships. Many if not most such norms are supportive of authority. Such are the rules that allow an adult to use a wider range of techniques than a child when they interact. But there are other rules, such as those which relate to the tradition of chivalry in the United States. Although the traditional conception stresses male authority, it softens the impact of authority by proscribing some techniques more severely for men than for women. The display of anger and indignation and the use of insults are less condemned in the woman than the man when they interact with one another. The display of hurt and the appeal to weakness are available to the woman but not to the man. Even the woman's right to change her mind is acknowledged in the folk ideology, allowing her to be less constrained by requirements of consistency than the man. The same restrictions do not apply when each is interacting with another of the same sex. Hence the man may be thoroughly ruthless in his dealings with men but only moderately effective in the same kind of decision making with women.

Here again there may be a paradox based on compensating processes. The more the man's authority is respected, the more he is likely to feel bound by the norms of chivalry in our western culture. Intimacy, familiarity, and informality in a relationship, however, tend to undermine both authority and norms that apply differently to the parties to interaction. Hence the greater intimacy in the family that has developed during the last century or two has weakened one advantage for each of the sexes.

The impact of sex-differential norms of this kind is most dramatic in the relations among young children. When a boy and girl play together, there is a much greater chance that the boy will wind up getting into trouble than the girl. If there is a dipsute settled in the boy's favor by physical coercion, the boy is likely to be in trouble with his parents for hitting a girl. If the girl wins the physical exchange, the boy is likely to get little comfort and to suffer a great deal of ridicule for having been beaten by a girl. If the girl uses the tactic of crying or otherwise playing on her weakness, she is likely to receive outside help. If the boy does similarly, he is

---

[7] Margaret Mead has explored these ambiguities in childhood sex roles in American culture in some depth. See *And Keep Your Powder Dry*, Morrow, New York, 1965, esp. pp. 80–114.

branded a sissy.[7] We do not know to what degree these mechanisms help to account for the stronger and longer development of girl avoidance in boys than of boy avoidance in girls prior to adolescence.

Aversion to Conflict. A fourth variable affecting the use of interpersonal techniques is the willingness of the individual to provoke anger and engage in conflict in conjunction with decision making. People interpret expressions of anger quite differently and hold different degrees of aversion to open conflict. Those who fear conflict and regard the expression of anger as a serious breach in any relationship are constantly under constraint not to use interpersonal techniques that might push the other too far. Those who are not disturbed by conflict and who regard expressions of anger as events of only passing significance are free from such restraints and have considerable advantage when interacting with the former kind of person.

The concern with conflict and anger may be a matter of norms, or it may be a personalized pattern of gesture interpretation reflecting anxieties and past experiences with conflict. Norms of humanitarianism, love, and nonviolence act against the individual's dominance and place the individual governed by them at a disadvantage in relation to persons not so governed. If, as Karen Horney suggested, one effect of the competitiveness of modern society is to make people exceptionally anxious lest they make any enemies, then in relations with individuals from other cultures such persons would be at a disadvantage.[8]

Less Interest. A final variable is the concern with the relationship itself —the strength and nature of the bonds. Edward A. Ross and, later, Willard Waller have enunciated the *principle of less interest,* that in any pair relation the person who cares less whether the relationship continues is in an advantageous position for domination.[9] He is freer to use techniques without thought to the risk involved. The member who is more concerned about the relationship then finds himself minimizing his efforts to gain the group decision in his concern to maintain the relationship itself.

The principle has its most direct application to courtship when the attachments are unequal. A boy who is deeply attached to a girl who regards him as only one of many equally desirable dates will quickly find himself making concessions to the girl's every whim in order to ensure another date. The girl meanwhile can assert her wishes with no great concern for the consequences, since alienation of the boy means little to her.

Ordinarily the bonds in a family relationship are varied and strong enough so that the concern with persistence of the relationship itself is

[8] Karen Horney, *The Neurotic Personality of Our Time,* Norton, New York, 1937.
[9] Willard Waller and Reuben Hill, *The Family: A Dynamic Interpretation,* 1951, pp. 190–192.

not uppermost. The concern is often uppermost in the relationship between adults and their elderly parents or between adult siblings, when the mutual ties are minimal and one-sided bondings develop. Bonds not only require continuance of a relationship, however, but maintenance of the kind of relationship in which the bonds in question are satisfied. The principle of less interest can then be extended to the difference in the degree to which members are concerned with the quality of their relationship. If ego depends on the relationship for more important and more numerous gratifications than alter, ego will be the more reluctant to use interpersonal techniques that might make the relationship less harmonious. When alter has many alternative sources of gratification outside the family, he can allow the family relationship to proceed less satisfactorily if this is the consequence of having his own way.

The normal relationship of parent and child illustrates this principle and also shows the change that occurs as the individual's social status changes. Although there is normally a powerful bond between parent and child that neither would seriously risk breaking, there is a difference in the extent to which each depends on the relationship for his major gratifications. The child depends on the parent for nearly everything he wants, so that any disturbance in the relationship between them is highly threatening. To the parent, on the other hand, the child is one of several sources of gratification. If the relationship is temporarily impaired, it is a less serious matter. Hence the parent has the advantage of less interest, facilitating his dominance over the child.

As the child grows, however, the exclusiveness of the child's dependence on the parent for important gratifications declines. Meanwhile, the dependence of the parent does not lessen and may even become greater because of the favorable evaluation of youth and unfavorable view of aging in American society. Hence the less interest differential shifts until eventually it works to the advantage of the child in dominating the parent. Such shifts from a favorable to an unfavorable position relative to domination are not ordinarily understood by the principals in the drama and are likely to be the source of much anxiety and resentment.

Coalitions

The discussion of decision making and dominance to this point has proceeded as if each member of the family interacted individually in relation to the other members. Often, however, this is not the case. Before the matter of a son's allowance is opened for discussion with him, the father and mother are likely to have discussed the matter and agreed on a sum, so that they can present a united front. Children often join forces to evade or directly oppose the rules that a parent seeks to impose. The mother and daughter may ally themselves against using Saturday for the masculine interest of attending a baseball game. In each of these instances the simple process of decision making is complicated and patterns of domination modified by the formation of coalitions.

Coalitions resemble other elements of decision making in contributing to the outcome of the process, and in turning into more stable alliances that persist after the episode is past. A coalition or alliance is a subgroup within the larger group held together by bonds that are additional to or more intense than those of the whole group. All the same principles of bonding that apply to the family as a whole apply to pairs and larger subgroups within the family. Common interests, identity bonds, and all the crescive bonds operate to bring some members closer than others. Members who are thus bonded are likely, in the absence of countervailing tendencies, to act as coalitions in a decision episode. Acting as a coalition, members are able to pool their individual assets so as to increase their chances of dominance.

The most general cause of coalitions is thus the differential strength of bonds creating enduring subgroups within the family. Coalitions also arise in any decision-making episode in connection with the effort to secure a favorable decision. Their specificity to the episode in process is underlined in the definition suggested by William Gamson: "Coalitions are temporary, means-oriented alliances among individuals or groups which differ in goals. There is generally little value consensus in a coalition and the stability of a coalition requires *tacit neutrality* of the coalition on matters which go beyond the immediate prerogatives."[10] Because members of a coalition are not agreed on other matters, the coalition lasts only so long as the interaction is restricted to the issue they have joined forces on.

Hypotheses regarding which participants will form coalitions with which others in the course of any specified contest have been formulated from game theory and other theoretical vantage points, and some have been tested in laboratory situations. Fred Strodtbeck compared the laboratory behavior of three-person family groups with that reported by Theodore Mills involving nonfamily groups.[11] He found that in the family groups the tendency to break up into a pair (coalition) and a third man was less notable and that the effect of disagreement in the most influential

[10] William A. Gamson, "A Theory of Coalition Formation," *American Sociological Review*, 26:374, June 1961.
[11] Fred L. Strodtbeck, "The Family as a Three-person Group," *American Sociological Review*, 19:23–29, February 1954.

pair on stability of position in the group was less. These findings may reflect the only partial applicability of standard coalition theories to a group with the pervasive bonds of the family.

Formation of Coalitions. Without attempting to do more than sample coalition theory, we shall suggest applications of the simple principle that each person seeks the cheapest coalition that enables him to win.[12] If we assume that all members of the family have slightly different views on a matter that must be decided, one way a decision can be achieved is by a coalition of members working out their own agreement and then presenting a united front to the entire family. But there are three costs to the coalition member. First, he must concede something to the coalition. Second, he must abandon his freedom to take any individual position and to pursue it with his own strategy. Third, he incurs an indebtedness to any other members of the coalition who make greater concessions than he to the coalition. To minimize the first cost, he attempts to ally with someone whose views are minimally different from his own or who can be prevailed on to adopt his position. To minimize the second cost, he prefers a coalition within which his own power is relatively high—a coalition he can dominate rather than one in which he will be dominated. Only the individual who stands little chance of gaining any consideration at all on his own is ready to enter into a coalition with a person much more powerful than himself. To minimize the third cost, he prefers a coalition within which mutual benefits are fairly equal, so that he incurs no obligation for the future.

The foregoing principles must be further qualified by noting that the cost that the family member is willing to pay depends on how important it is that he win the decision or have his views significantly registered in it. The family differs from the simple game situation in two important respects here. First, all members are seldom equally concerned about the outcome of a particular decision. And second, the family is governed by a moral order that imposes obligations that all members be considered and that implicit bargaining take place over a period of time. Many decision-making episodes are efforts to gain agreement on some matter that can be resolved by simple authority or coercion if agreement is not otherwise reached. And because of implicit bargaining a member may prefer to concede a decision to others in confidence that he will receive compensating consideration on a later occasion, rather than enter into a coalition at the present.

Under as complex conditions as these it is difficult to predict coalitions

---

[12] See Gamson, *op. cit.*, pp. 373–382; Theodore Caplow, "A Theory of Coalitions in the Triad," *American Sociological Review*, 21:489–493, August 1956. Caplow, *Two Aganist One: Coalitions in Triads*, Prentice-Hall, Englewood Cliffs, N.J., 1968.

except when one of the three principles seems so important as to lessen the importance of the others. But we can describe some frequent kinds of family coalitions and note how the principles apply.

1. The coalition of a majority to force agreement by a dissenter has already been described. Here the cost is minimal, because there is already agreement and all coalition members become equal as members of the majority. With agreement in sight, it is important to complete the process and get on with the activity itself.

2. Children frequently form coalitions against a parent. In this case the common interest is crucial, and whether an effective coalition emerges is likely to depend on neither member's using the coalition to strengthen his individual position with the parent at the expense of the other and on the softness of the parent's position. The characteristic behavior of children is some alternation between competing for the parent's favor and forming coalitions for their mutual benefit. In most instances the actual power of the parent exceeds that of the children in coalition. According to coalition theory, no coalition is formed between the pair in a triad unless their combined strength exceeds that of the third person, since they still cannot win. But since assent is valued because of the very nature of the family, the parent allows the formation of a coalition between the children by not making use of all his power.

3. Mother-child coalitions are especially frequent in patriarchal families, where the father's power is greater than the mother's. In return for supporting the mother the child expects special treatment from her.

4. A child often attempts to form a coalition with one of the parents, paying with special services and affection for the extra support that he receives for his desires.

5. Father-mother coalitions are formed to combat quasi-coalitions between a child and persons outside the family. The child often claims the existence of a coalition between himself and his peers or his teachers or his scoutmaster or other persons outside the family who support his course of action. Unlike the situation in a true coalition, the validity of this claim cannot usually be tested easily, but the parents form a coalition because their positions are mutually threatened.

6. Father-mother coalitions are often formed to forestall the development of child-parent coalitions. Advice to parents often stresses the danger that a child will play one parent against the other in order to win his way. The remedy is for parents to present a united front to the children, that is, to form their own coalition.

Dissolution of Coalitions. Once formed, coalitions are notoriously unstable, and there may be a succession of tentative coalitions in the course of an interaction episode. Some of the relevant conditions under which coalitions break down are the following.

1. Coalitions tend to disband when it develops that their combined strength is insufficient to alter the course of the decision.

2. A corollary to the first proposition is the tendency for a coalition to disband when it provokes the formation of a countercoalition that makes the members' position weaker or no stronger than before. The principal dangers of the children's coalition are that they provoke the parent into using his full power, or that they provoke a countercoalition between the parents or the parent and another child.

3. Coalitions tend to disband when the role of one of the members within the coalition becomes unacceptable. Typically the member finds himself increasingly dominated within the coalition or finds that the other member is speaking for the coalition without first consulting him.

4. Coalitions tend to disband when members of the coalition use tactics that are not acceptable to all. Such tactics either violate the norms of interaction as one or more members understand them or threaten to impair the bonds in the larger family relationship. Characteristically one member of the coalition goes too far, alienating others in the coalition who do not wish to be identified with such tactics. The mother may withdraw from the coalition with the father when the latter's discipline over the children becomes too severe. The younger child withdraws from the coalition when the older child's open opposition to the parent reaches a degree that threatens to impair the parent-child relationship.

Standard coalition theory makes the simple assumption that the game is won by possession of a certain number of resources and that the resources of a coalition are equal to the sum of the resources of its members. Family battles are won more by moral suasion, and it is difficult to place a measurement on each member's resources, that is, power. It also seems unlikely that in such interaction the persuasive power of a coalition is equal to the sum of the power of its members. Some of the norms of interaction even operate to make certain coalitions stronger than the sum of the power of their members. Rules of fair play, for example, make a coalition of underdogs stronger than the sum of their individual members. Any time a coalition of all the children against the parents is brought to public view, the parents are placed at a great disadvantage.

Recurring coalitions bringing the same individuals together are a source of more permanent alliances as crescive bonds develop between them or as the family power structure creates an enduring task bond. The power differentiation of members as part of the decision-making process is one element contributing toward bonds of different intensity between different family pairs.

Summary of Chapters 5 and 6

Decision making is the core of the task-oriented processes of family life and can be defined as a process directed toward securing unambivalent group assent and commitment to a course of action or inaction. Family decisions are of three kinds. Consensual decisions are those in which commitment is complete, because all believe that the best decision was reached. The more common accommodative decision, in which individuals assent to a proposal they do not privately regard as best, leads to conditional commitment. Family members may reopen an issue or repudiate commitment if they feel that other parties to the agreement have not kept their part of the compromise. Accommodative decisions also contribute to patterns of dominance and subordination to a greater degree than consensual decisions. Many family decisions are de facto, forced on the family by events in the absence of discussion or following fruitless debate.

Bales and Strodtbeck outline a small-group decision-making sequence that is partially applicable to the family. Periods of orientation, evaluation, and control follow in sequence, with an accompanying increase in interpersonal tensions with counterefforts to protect group solidarity. Decision by consensus depends on common values or sufficient understanding of others' values so that effective persuasion is possible. Accommodative decisions take place by varying degrees of coercion or bargaining. Family bargaining is usually implicit, only approximately quantitative, and based on confidence in the long-range fairness of other family members. The ease and expeditiousness of accommodative decision making depends on a high degree of coercive imbalance or on faith in the long-term balancing of concessions and gains and on the strength of bonds that supply the incentive for reaching group decisions. The chief obstacles to agreement apart from incompatible individual preferences are jockeying for a favorable future bargaining position, efforts to maintain a favorable position relative to dominance and submission, and attempts to escape responsibility for precarious decisions and gain credit for promising ones.

Whether the decisions reached in a family lead to effective solutions of their problems depends on how diversified a set of alternatives the family structure allows them to consider. There is no convincing reason to believe that family groups are consistently more cautious than individuals in making decisions. Since family problem solving concerns both group problems and problems of individual members, effective problem solving requires that each family develop a pattern that combines connectedness and separateness among its members.

The fundamental determinant of family dominance is authority, or the belief in the propriety of unequal dominance. To be effective the belief must be mutual and must be supported by an appropriate ideology with external support. Much of the coercive power in the family exists only be-

cause of belief in the authority of the individual who coerces. Patterns of
authority-based dominance are undermined or reinforced by the social
organization of the family. Unequal rates of communication between different pairs of family members lead to networks in which some members
communicate by way of intermediaries rather than directly. Centrality in
the network facilitates dominance. The organization of the family also
gives members unequal control over the means for carrying out family
decisions. Those who control the means are in a position favoring dominance. Authority is further undermined or reinforced by the ability and
willingness of members to use the interpersonal techniques at their disposal effectively. Maximum use of techniques or an opposite tendency to
pull one's punches is affected by ego's self-confidence vis-à-vis alter, importance of the issue, norms regulating the use of certain techniques in
certain relationships, and attitudes toward conflict. The most interesting
determinant of effective use of interpersonal techniques is the principle
of less interest, that the person who has less to lose from a deteriorating
relationship is in a position facilitating dominance.

In the course of decision making family members often form coalitions
(temporary alliances) to offset the dominance of one or more other members. Coalitions may be less common in the family than in other small
groups because of the importance of identity bonds, and standard principles governing coalitions must be qualified because individuals in the
family often have much more power than they actually use unless provoked. Nevertheless, coalitions commonly arise in the family among the
majority who seek assent from a dissenting member, between children
against their parents, between mother and child against a dominant father,
and between parents against their children and their peers. According to
coalition theory any individual prefers a coalition in which the other members' views differ little from his own, in which his dominance is relatively
high, and in which benefits are mutual so that he incurs no long-term indebtedness. Coalitions dissolve when they are ineffectual(especially when
they arouse a strong countercoalition), when the individual finds his own
position in the coalition unfavorable, and when the coalition uses tactics
unacceptable to all its members.

CHAPTER 7

CONFLICT AND HARMONY

Decision making and conflict-harmony are respectively the key task-oriented and identity-oriented processes in the small group. All task-oriented activity depends on the decision-making process. All identity-oriented activity depends on conflict-harmony. As he takes account of his relations with others as persons in the group, ego discovers that his own self-image can be fostered only at the expense of alter's, or he discovers that the two identities are mutually supportive. In the former instance the process is conflict; in the latter it is harmony. Conflict is like a child's seesaw, with the identities of ego and alter on the two ends. Whenever one identity is enhanced, the other is damaged; whatever lowers one identity raises the other.

Social conflict, as we use the term, must not be confused with psychological conflict, defined as "a situation in which a person is motivated to engage in two or more mutually exclusive activities."[1] Social and psychological conflict may or may not be found together: there is no necessary correspondence between the two ideas. Social conflict does not include all the forms of opposition that emerge "whenever two or more persons (or groups) seek to possess the same object, occupy the same space or the same exclusive position, play incompatible roles, maintain incompatible goals, or undertake mutually incompatible means for achieving their purposes."[2] Rather, as Lewis Coser states, "Social conflict may be defined as a struggle over values or claims to status, power, and scarce resources, in which the claims of the conflicting parties are not only to gain the desired values but also to neutralize, injure, or eliminate their rivals."[3] We stress the concluding phrase of the definition, that an autonomous goal of injuring the opponent is the distinguishing mark of conflict.

In discussion over differences of opinion or interest each participant's investment in his own suggestions remains subordinated to the task-

[1] Edward J. Murray, "Conflict: Psychological Aspects," *International Encyclopedia of the Social Sciences*, 1968, vol. 3, p. 220.
[2] Robert C. North, "Conflict: Political Aspects," *ibid.*, vol. 3, p. 226.
[3] Lewis A. Coser, "Conflict: Social Aspects," *ibid.*, vol. 3, p. 232.

oriented purpose of achieving a decision that all can agree to. In conflict, by contrast, disagreement can be satisfactorily resolved only by what each participant perceives as the forced imposition of one viewpoint on the others. *Competition* is striving for scarce goals and does not become conflict so long as each competitor is chiefly concerned with his own success and the losses suffered by others are incidental.[4] *Rivalry*, which suffuses sports and such interpersonal play as banter, is like conflict in the preoccupation with defeating the rival. But in rivalry the contest is enjoyed primarily for its own sake and losing does not eliminate the enjoyment. Rivalry differs from conflict in (a) placing greater value on the contest than on the outcome and (b) being governed by norms that protect the participants' identities from serious hurt. The intensity of conflict is also normally limited by a set of rules,[5] but considerable injury to the combatants' identities is allowed before the boundaries are reached.

As we noted in Chapter 3, neither conflict nor harmony can exist without bonds. Potential oppositions simply dissolve as indifferences when there are no bonds. This observation has been extended by Georg Simmel, who proposes that conflict may actually be a source of bonds between the conflicting parties[6] and that "the closer the relationship the more intense the conflict."[7] It is true that any sustained interaction may produce crescive bonds, and interlocking roles are a frequent product of conflict. But such interdependencies are not specific to conflict and probably develop more rapidly and firmly in harmonious interaction than in conflict. Similarly, illustrations of family members fighting over matters that seem unimportant to outsiders are easy to find, but as a general principle requiring that every close relationship be marked by the magnification of small difficulties into constant and intense conflict Simmel's second principle is transparently ridiculous. The most important effect of conflict is not to establish bonds but to erode existing ones. And the most important effect of intense bonds is not to heighten conflict but to provide incentives and means to avoid and conciliate it. Muzafer Sherif's classic experiment in which, the pervasive conflict between two groups in a boy's camp was changed to harmonious cooperation by the introduction of a "superordinate goal" that required their collaboration[8] documents the latter observation.

[4] Robert E. Park and Ernest W. Burgess, *Introduction to the Science of Sociology*, 2d ed., University of Chicago Press, Chicago, 1924, pp. 574–579.
[5] See Lewis A. Coser, *The Functions of Social Conflict*, Free Press, New York, 1956, esp. pp. 121–128.
[6] *Ibid.*, pp. 121–138.
[7] *Ibid.*, pp. 67–72.
[8] Muzafer Sherif, O. J. Harvey, B. Jack White, William R. Hood, and Carolyn W. Sherif, *Intergroup Conflict and Cooperation; The Robbers Cave Experiment*, University of Oklahoma Press, Norman, 1961.

Main Questions. Several questions demand extended treatment in an analysis of conflict. First, we must determine the nature of the immediate circumstances under which conflict develops. Second, we shall examine the nature of conflict itself as a process, its characteristic strategy and tactics and its sequences. Next we must explore the aftermath of conflict. Of special interest are those instances in which the effect of conflict is cumulative and the end product is severance of bonds and those instances in which there is an aftermath of reconciliation and harmonization. Finally, the general causes of conflict and harmony will be explored at a level removed from the actual interaction sequence, as we attempt to specify the general kinds of circumstances conducive respectively to conflict and harmony.

Conflict as Process: Initiation of Conflict

Sometimes conflict develops out of differences in attitude or behavior between persons who are interacting. Such instances point to the question "What determines whether differences will become conflict or not?" In other cases conflict appears in the absence of differences, or differences develop out of conflict rather than preceding it. Such instances call for a broader answer than that supplied by preexisting differences.

In dealing with the important questions about conflict, it will be useful to employ a skeletal set of stages applicable to most conflict in a relationship such as the family—held together too intensely for annoyances to be forgotten or for the relationship to be severed at the first sign of distress. The sequence consists of the following five stages:

1. Gesture exchange transforming interaction into conflict;
2. Period of conflict—the exchange of symbolic blows;
3a. Accommodation—the cessation of overt conflict, or
3b. Conciliation—activation of the counterprocess of harmony;
4. Reassessment—typically a period following the end or interruption of overt conflict during which the participants reenact the conflict in imagination;
5. Aftermath—subsequent reactivation of conflict, avoidance, or conciliation, based on the results of the reassessment stage.

The most general statement of the immediate cause of conflict (stage 1) is contained in the definition of conflict itself. If conflict is a relationship in which the participants are attempting to improve or protect their own self-images by damaging the identities of the others, the immediate cause must lie in circumstances leading ego to perceive the identity of alter as a threat to his own identity. In response to such a perception ego issues a gesture that disparages alter's identity. If alter replies by attacking ego's identity, or responds defensively so as to require that ego apologize or withdraw his gesture (which he can seldom do without some damage to his identity), the conflict is then fully initiated.

A simple illustration of interaction between a mother and a six-year-old daughter will clarify the process. The daughter shows a picture she has just drawn to her mother, and the following dialogue ensues:

DAUGHTER: How do you like my picture, Mother?

MOTHER: That's very nice. Keep on like that and before long you will be drawing beautiful pictures.

DAUGHTER: Aw, you never like anything I do.

MOTHER: Oh, quit complaining! That's all you do: complain, complain, complain.

The mother may be assumed to have intended a compliment to the child but has made her comment with an adult's standard of artistic excellence in mind. The child, on the other hand, notes only that by implication the mother has said that her picture is not beautiful, that it will still take time before she really draws well. The daughter feels her self-image disparaged by the mother's remark and seeks to protect her own identity by disparaging her mother's. Her response is, therefore, the initiation of conflict by issuing a gesture that is a direct attack on the other's identity. The mother, having understood her own remark as a compliment, retaliates by characterizing the daughter in a disparaging manner. With such a reply the initiation of conflict is now complete.

Stage 1, then, consists in the most rudimentary manner of a gesture exchange in which one participant acts as if the participants' identities were linked negatively and the other accepts the assumption as a basis for his response. In order to predict when such a transformation will occur, we shall assume that interaction most frequently proceeds with a task orientation, concern over the participants' identities being subordinated until the participants are sensitized to identities in a negative manner. Alternatively, positively toned identity interaction can switch to a negative course.

The identity always has a dual aspect, as actor and as person observed. It is through these two aspects that sensitization takes place.

1. When action is blocked and the identity of the other is viewed as the obstacle, the identity relationship begins to take precedence over the task relationship.

2. When ego perceives an unfavorable self-image in a situation and ascribes it to the peculiar relationship of ego and alter, a similar sensitization takes place. Whether the sensitization leads to conflict or to harmony—an effort to bring the identities back to a reinforcing relationship—depends on the incentive to avoid conflict, which will be discussed further in relation to conciliation.

Blocked Decision Making. Goal behavior is frequently blocked, momentarily or for a longer time, in an interactive situation. For conflict to ensue, the blockage must be coupled with a view of the other's identity as responsible. When one person asserts and the other disagrees, the problem is not necessarily identities. Only when ego attributes the disagreement to the kind of person he pictures alter as being does the disagreement have conflict potential. Ego relates the disagreement to other aspects of alter's behavior or to his prior conception of alter and interprets the disagreement in a personal context. For this reason conflict can sometimes develop more quickly among persons well acquainted with each other than among strangers, who have no crystallized conceptions of each other (unless occupational, racial, or other stereotypes are applicable).

Conflict based on blocked behavior arises out of the course of decision making, which may be unsatisfactory in at least three different ways. First, the repeated failure of family members to arrive at group decisions is conducive to such a definition. The individual normally feels that he could easily reach a decision for himself and attributes the indecision to others in the group. The sophisticated view that attributes collective indecision to the relationship itself rather than to the indecisiveness, stubbornness, or unreasonableness of individuals is rare. A succession of indecisive episodes contributes cumulatively to a set of images that prepares members to view the other as person as the obstacle and thus initiate conflict. The variables we have already mentioned that determine whether decisions will be reached or not constitute one step in the causal chain leading to conflict. The presence of a family organization that poses recurring obstacles to decision making is an enduring factor in conflict.

Second, rejection of the legitimacy of a group decision (commitment), arising from different views of the rules governing decision making or different interpretations of their application to the present situation, leads to the perception that identities are in opposition. The husband's view that the decision about where to go on vacation is his prerogative may not be shared by his wife; the child's view that a group decision is as committing to the parent as to him may be denied by the parent.

Third, unfavorable decisions attributed to coercion bring identities into opposition. When coercion is an aspect of what is respected as legitimate authority, the conflict potential is minimal. It is likely to take the form of the minor conflict exemplified in the delight children take when they can expose a parent in a mistake or misdeed. But the sense of being forced to acquiesce in a decision without being able to establish a fair bargain places the individual in the position of seeing the other in opposition as person.

These three by-products of family decision making are frequent avenues to conflict. Their antitheses can be applied to harmony. Harmony in the family is a function of (a) a value consensus or a family organization facilitating the expeditious achievement of family decisions, (b) agreement on the norms of decision making and their application, and (c) achievement of agreement by respected authority and satisfactory bargaining.

In addition to the problems of group decision making, there are abundant opportunities for one person's behavior to block the goals of another, but these lead to conflict only when alter's behavior can be perceived as illegitimate—a violation of interactive norms. In addition to the wide range of specific norms that may be violated, there are two broad norms of recurring importance. These are the norms of precedent and bargaining. Because of the interdependence of persons in close and continuing interaction, each person begins to plan his behavior on the basis of the consistencies in the other's. As Waller and Hill have pointed out, the wife who regularly gets dinner at the same hour because her husband has always come home at the same time feels that he has no right to come home later without telling her.[9] Bargaining justice is generally supposed to regulate the extent to which each person in a relationship yields his own objectives for the sake of another's. When the distribution of sacrifice is felt to be inequitable, conflict potential is increased. Equitability is not identical with equality, of course. In a given family it may be thought equitable that the child should get to do what he wants less often than the parents do.[10]

Unsatisfactory Self-image. Emergence of an unacceptable self-image attributed to the identity of the other can occur in several ways. The most obvious is when one of the participants explicitly labels the other unfavorably or when he implies an unfavorable label. In the episode of the mother and her daughter's picture, the mother implied what the daughter regarded as an unfavorable image. Because the girl's perception had been favorable and because of previous experiences in which the daughter felt that the mother could not see her good accomplishments, the unfavorable depiction was attributed to the mother as person. Maneuvering to shift responsibility or claim credit is a common source of unfavorable images, placing identities in an inverse relationship.

A second major way in which self-images lead to conflict is through a course of interaction in which alter's behavior casts ego in an unfavorable role. This happens commonly in connection with recurring dominance pat-

[9] Willard Waller and Reuben Hill, *The Family: A Dynamic Interpretation*, Dryden Press, New York, 1951.
[10] See discussions of distributive justice in George C. Homans, *Social Behavior: Its Elementary Forms*, Harcourt, Brace & World, New York, 1961; and Peter M. Blau, "Justice in Social Exchange," *Sociological Inquiry*, 34:193–206, Spring 1964.

terns and in connection with a division of labor that is unfavorable to the self-conception. The wife proceeds to diagnose mechanical failure in the automobile with such effectiveness that the husband finds himself in the position of being her assistant mechanic—a role that threatens his masculine self-conception. It becomes almost indispensable that he discredit her mechanical competence at some point, so that he can regain the role that supports his self-conception. The assumption of initiative or even offering assistance can often be interpreted as implying the other's incompetence. The more one's competence in any area has been called into question, the more he is likely to make such interpretations. Both the child and the elderly person are likely to make such interpretations of efforts to help them in normal tasks.

What constitutes an unfavorable self-image is often contingent on the audience. A boy who suffers no self-disparagement when he washes dishes within the privacy of his home may experience severe embarrassment when forced by his mother to do so in the presence of one of his peers.

The unfavorable role situation frequently comes from the deterioration of rivalry. There is a fine line of distinction between rivalry and conflict that can easily be crossed. Play among children shows a constant alternation, with a period of rivalry interrupted by a brief conflict exchange, followed by a return to the game and continuing interruptions. Rivalry occurs not only in sports but as good-natured banter in which people trade friendly insults or as one-upmanship. The right to enter into such bantering relationships is normally contingent on a certain degree of intimacy, and the banter itself is often a way of symbolizing to each other that the degree of intimacy is great. But the fact that each is being disparaged, although with the understanding that remarks are not to be taken at face value and that at all times someone is winning and someone losing creates a precarious situation. The precariousness of the relationship is probably the reason it serves so admirably to demonstrate the intimacy and intensity of bonds between persons, since a similar exchange between persons less intimately bonded would clearly be conflict. There is the danger that the "insults" will be taken at face value, that a suspicion may creep in that they are actually meant as insults in spite of their coloring as rivalry.

There are two norms which keep rivalry from becoming conflict and whose violation is typically the occasion for conflict. One is the rule that in rivalry the contestants avoid each others' sensitive zones. Sportsmanship in a game requires that one contestant not take advantage of another's size or physical deformity. Sportsmanship in banter requires that banter not be concerned with any matter the other is not able to laugh about. Banterers learn to watch the reactions of others and withdraw from any subject that begins to arouse resentment. The other rule is to be a good winner. The victor by convention makes some indication of how well the loser played or attributes his victory to luck or experience, so as to protect the other's identity. When, however, the victor makes a great deal of his victory, rubbing in the defeat to the loser, he oversteps the bounds of rivalry and involves the identity of his opponent. By teasing his sister for her inability to reply to his bantering insult, the boy converts rivalry into conflict.

Identification is another mechanism through which one individual may be the agent for damaging another's self-image. It is paradoxical that one of the sources of bondedness in the family also creates a source of conflict not present in more casual relationships. We recall that identification refers to the character of a relationship in which one member experiences what happens to another as if it had happened to him. The social institution of the family identifies family members in the eyes of outsiders, and the intimacy and continuity of interaction create spontaneous identification. The consequence of identification is to unify family members in many situations—whenever one is hurt, abused, or unjustly treated by an outsider. But through identification each member can bring embarrassment or disgrace on other members. The teen-ager whose father casually walks out in front of the house in his bathrobe and slippers feels himself humiliated as the object of neighborhood ridicule. The girl feels her own good reputation and dignity threatened when her brother is in trouble with the law.

The specific importance of identification in such cases is made apparent by the difference in the way an individual reacts to the same behavior when identification is not involved. A woman who joins in the hearty enjoyment of a risqué joke told by someone else's husband at a party suddenly feels humiliation and anger when her husband tells one of the same kind. A boy associates easily with an acquaintance who regularly makes a fool of himself but suffers acute discomfort when his brother does similarly.

Evelyn Duvall presents an instructive example of how such identification can cause parent-child conflict, in the following excerpt from an interview with a Midwestern mother:[11]

A few weeks ago a mother asked if I would let S_____ come up to her house and play with her little girl P_____. I let S_____ go up to the house and she seemed to have had a good time. She didn't repeat her visit and the mother didn't repeat her invitation. I didn't wonder about this at all. Then the other day I was at a luncheon which P_____'s mother attended and we were at the same

[11] Evelyn M. Duvall, "Conceptions of Parenthood," *American Journal of Sociology*, 52:200–201, November 1946. Quoted by permission of the University of Chicago Press and the author.

table of bridge. She embarrassed me terribly. She asked me, "Who is S_____'s boy friend?" I explained that S_____ didn't have a special boy friend; that all the little boys around the neighborhood she called boy friend. I asked her why she asked. "Well, S_____ paraded in front of P_____ like this [and Mrs. G. jiggled her shoulders and squirmed her hips] and said to her, 'P_____, do you know what my boy friend calls me? Son of a b_____.' " If there had been a hole around I would have fallen through. What a *time* to tell me! I'm ashamed to let S_____ play with P_____. Imagine what her mother thinks! She must think we use that language around here. I put pepper on S_____'s tongue.

This manner of inducing conflict most frequently involves an outside audience in whose eyes the action is judged and whose unfavorable reaction extends to all members of the group. Individual relationships differ greatly in the degree of identification, and whole family systems differ in this respect. Families in America today probably exhibit less than the western family of previous centuries. Husband or wife may sometimes join the crowd in laughing at a spouse's ineptitude, or a child at his parent's pecularity. A strong emphasis on privacy, on limiting what is revealed to outsiders, is probably a protective accompaniment to a strong emphasis on identification. The greater the degree of identification, the potentially more damaging to the family is any intimate self-revelation by a family member. The exceptionally free attitude toward public self-revelation associated with the popular vogue of psychiatry in American society today is probably made possible by the severe limitation of identification, which involves conversely a high degree of individualization of the family.

In episodes such as we have been discussing there are two different points of reference, leading to different responses. The individual who has been hurt by identification (ego) cannot disparage alter in front of the audience, because he only suffers more damage to his own identity. He is likely to apologize for alter, to minimize the seriousness of alter's mistake, or attempt to withdraw from the situation. But in the private relation to alter, when separated from the audience, ego may either continue to act supportively or attack alter for the hurt he has brought to ego, as the mother did in the account just presented. In the former instance there is an intensification of harmony; in the latter instance conflict ensues.

Which direction will be taken is often difficult to predict, and there is often dramatic oscillation between the poles of conflict and deep sympathy and defense in such situations of identification damage before an audience. At least three variables probably affect the outcome in the individual case. First, there is undoubtedly a difference in the character of identification bonds. If identification is limited to experiencing the reactions of outsiders—the most superficial form—ego is almost certain to experience alter's identity as the source of threat to his own. But identification is usually more complete than this in a family relationship, involving an empathic relationship. When the latter exists, there is considerable pressure toward harmony rather than conflict. The presence of the more superficial form of identification in the family is often a reaction to a succession of experiences of damage from identification, so that the empathic aspect has been eroded. Perhaps only after repeated embarrassment from the square behavior of his parents does the teen-ager learn not to empathize. Similarly, husband-wife relationships of this sort prevail in areas of repeated embarrassment.

A second variable determining individual outcomes is the attitude toward the group thought to be making the unfavorable evaluation. If the group is not one that is respected or whose good will is sought, the tendency is for ego to adopt the standpoint of alter, rejecting the unfriendly reaction. If the group is positively valued, like the mother's bridge group or the teen-ager's peer group, the tendency is to take the standpoint of the group toward alter, leading to conflict.

Finally, the outcome depends on ego's evaluation of the behavior itself. If he shares the standards by which the behavior was unfavorably evaluated, he is more likely to assign responsibility to alter for the damage to his own identity. If he does not share the standards, he is less likely to attribute the damage to alter but to take alter's standpoint in attributing it to the group.

With this last point we call attention to the fact that a family member may experience a damaged identity through identification with the behavior of another without an audience. Whatever characteristics are important in the individual's self-conception are expected in persons identified with him, unless specifically excluded by definitions of age, sex, and other roles. Failure of a family member to come up to moral standards or standards of competence or physical fitness that are important to one member are experienced as threats to the identity of the latter. In the initial adjustments of a newly married couple such problems of identification may extend to such minor matters as how one brushes his teeth, small deviations in clothing style, and peculiarities of appetite. Because of identification, members of a family quarrel about matters that cause no dissent among acquaintances.

Conflict Strategy and Termination

The Strategy of Conflict: Stage 2. The classic studies of conflict deal with such phenomena as warfare in which each contestant seeks to kill or disable large numbers of the opposition. The objective of most conflict in the family is limited by the norms proscribing serious hurt and by the bonds, which usually survive many conflict episodes. The mere effort to control the other's behavior or to gain an advantage does not constitute conflict. The key objective of the typical family conflict is the simultaneous damage to the other's identity while protecting or enhancing one's own. We must remember that conflict takes place on the premise that ego's identity will suffer unless alter's identity is damaged. Father's self-esteem is in a precarious state until he can deflate mother's self-image. In the illustration of the mother and daughter, the mother must admit to some unfairness or defect of judgment if the damage to her daughter's identity is to be repaired.

The identity is always appraised through the eyes of some audience. A boxer must convince only the judges and spectators that he has fought better; the opinion of his opponent is unimportant. But family conflicts usually concern identity relationships within the family and are not directly governed by outsiders. Hence, the objective of family conflict is to damage the identity of alter in alter's eyes. If alter fails to recognize that he has suffered a damaging slight, the blow has not struck. The most satisfactory outcome for conflict from the point of view of the contestants is that alter openly admits to self-disparagement and relates it to some superior quality of ego. Hence, an important element of family conflict strategy is to put the other in a position in which his discomfiture is plain to himself and his opponents. The parent demands a degrading confession from the child. The wife places her husband in the position that he cannot avoid openly admitting his social *faux pas* to her.

Much if not most conflict is merged with an effort to coerce or outbargain the other in the course of accommodative decision making. When decision-making episodes become conflict, giving assent to a course of action sought by the other acquires the meaning of self-depreciation. All the tactics for dominating a decision-making sequence then come into play as conflict tactics. But because the issue under dispute is no longer of paramount concern in its own right, a special conflict strategy is made available. The substantive issue of decision making can change in the course of conflict, but the identity implications of winning are transferred to each new issue in turn. Hence an effective strategy is to divert the battle from an issue with respect to which ego's position is weak to one with respect to which ego's position is strong. A physically weaker child can defeat a physically stronger child in conflict if he can divert the exchange away from monopolization of a favored toy to the exchange of ridicule over failings in school. Perhaps one of the most striking characteristics of conflict protocols is the successive changes in the topic of debate, as if by free association. But these changes are more correctly identified as evidence that combatants are using the strategy of attempting to focus the conflict on an issue that gives them an advantage.

Accompanying offensive strategy there is always defensive strategy, which centers about protecting one's own identity. A frequent by-product of attacks on another's identity is stimultaneous injury to one's own identity. Such injury often occurs when the attack can be construed as a violation of the norms of interaction, so that the attacker acquires the image of an antisocial person. Hence, a major part of conflict strategy is to clothe one's attack on the other in a manner that enlists the support of the rules. One such procedure is to make attacks under the guise of justice and righteousness. To this end the assumption of an attitude of indigation is common. Attacks may be clothed as legitimate retaliatory punishment—something the other person has coming to him, something he deserves, something he has been asking for. The parent strategy in conflict with a child is commonly to clothe his attack as a justified effort to reform the child. The child must recognize the error of his ways and acknowledge it before the parent in a humiliating manner. A major aspect of family conflict of all kinds, then, is attempting to make one's attacks from a morally protected vantage point.

Simulated conciliation is another tactic by which the attacker may protect his position. By hurting the other person while seeming to take the initiative in moderating the conflict, he shifts the responsibility for continuing conflict to the other. The blow that would otherwise be unfair is less vulnerable when it places alter in the position of having to choose to disregard the conciliatory gesture in order to reply adequately to the injury.

The consequence of any blow is to place its deliverer in a protected or exposed position for the anticipated blow in return. Conflict strategy involves the effort to attack the other in such a way as to remain in a good defensive position. A good defensive position is one that makes it difficult for the other to retaliate in a telling manner. Maneuvers to legitimize one's attack, such as we have just discussed, serve this purpose. Two other common tactics deserve note.

An ambiguous gesture is a device that allows the combatant to charge misinterpretation if alter is able to retaliate effectively. If the husband, for example, offers a disparaging remark as a statement about women in general, he places himself in the advantageous position that he can deny that he meant to refer to his wife if she is able to respond in kind. Furthermore, having chosen an unfavorable interpretation of a remark that need not have been so interpreted puts her in a disadvantageous position. A common form of ambiguity between husbands and wives is clothing attack as good-natured banter, a form of rivalry, which calls on the other to take the insult in good spirit as a joke.

Another tactic of this kind is to make an attack before an audience in such a way that it is not recognized by the audience but is recognized by the person to whom it is directed. The recipient then confronts the norm against revealing conflict before outsiders and may be inhibited from replying at the time. Children often learn that they can say things they know annoy their parents with assurance that the parents do not respond before outsiders. The wife may take advantage of the norm that parents should not argue in the hearing of their children to criticize her husband, assured that he is unlikely to retaliate. If he does retaliate at the time, he is in the disadvantageous position of having violated the norm, and if he retaliates later when they are alone, he is in the weakened position of holding a grudge or bringing up something from the past.

It should be clear that the kind of tactics we have discussed apply to a special kind of conflict situation but one that is typically that of the family. It is a situation in which the participants are bonded so that their identities are linked to their performance of the obligations in the relationship. In a nonfamily relationship with few bonds or in the latter stages of alienation in which most of the family bonds have been severed, the manipulation of normative relationships within the group becomes less important, and the manipulation is increasingly related to an external audience.

Conflict Resolution: Stage 3. Just as there is frequently confusion between conflict and discussion as processes, so there is often confusion between the manner in which conflict is resolved and the process of reaching agreement in discussion. It is this confusion which leads to statements about the value of family conflict in clearing the air or undue emphasis on the potentially integrative consequences of conflict. The difference between the procedures for coping with disagreement as a problem in decision making and the nature of conflict resolution is the most important implication of the restricted definition of conflict we have used. The essence of conflict is most clearly revealed in an examination of the conditions and process of conflict resolution.

Agreement in a decision-making situation normally requires that one or more of the disagreeing persons discover merit in the other's assertions. After an initial stage of asserting individual positions, discussion moves toward agreement and resolution as the discussants give cumulatively greater credence to other assertions and proposals than their own.

But the nature of conflict is different. The most salient remarks made in the course of conflict do not contribute positively toward any resolution of the conflict. The assertions during conflict are in one form or another insults and accusations. The more seriously the insults are taken, and the more certain each becomes that the other truly means what he is saying, the more difficult becomes the resumption of normal interaction. The proposals advanced are conflict tactics, and serious acceptance of these proposals would involve self-debasement that undermines much of the identity bonding. The gestures made in the course of conflict serve to define and reinforce the inverse relationship that has been established between the identities of the combatants. The more seriously each takes the remarks of the other, and the more their meaning is given full credence, the more firmly entrenched is the conflict principle that whatever improves alter's self-image demeans ego's self-image. If agreement in discussion is made possible when the discussants begin to take each other's remarks seriously, resolution of conflict is only possible when the combatants cease to take their own remarks and those of the others seriously.

The interruption or resolution of conflict is not set in motion because one sees the merit of the other's observations. A withdrawal from conflict occurs (a) to avoid further hurt from the other, (b) to avoid escalating the hurt to alter, (c) to protect bonds from damage, (d) because ego damages his own self-image by engaging in conflict, or from some combination of these four aims. Conflict is always a risky matter, since retaliation can be anticipated. If the strategy of conflict is to attack without being exposed to counterattack, it is part of strategy to attempt accommodation when the danger of hurt from counterattack exceeds what is to be gained from attack. An insult or an accusation may be let pass without answer, rather than risk provoking still another insult in reply. Obversely, as conflict escalates, ego realizes that his next blow will do increasing hurt to alter. It may only be possible to retaliate for alter's last attack by opening up an old and extremely painful wound. But ego's own norms of behavior, or his fundamental human sensitivity, or his underlying concern for the welfare of alter makes him unwilling to increase the hurt to alter to this extent. Accordingly he interrupts the conflict by failing to retaliate or by doing so lamely.

When conflict threatens the values whose attainment is sought in the relationship, winning the conflict becomes excessively costly. To the extent to which there is awareness of the bonds, conflict is discontinued when the bonds are threatened. The task bond of playing a game is often so intense in children's play that recurrent episodes of conflict are interrupted and left unresolved in order that the participants can get on with the game. Parents frequently allow a child to get away with an unjust and unkind remark, rather than risk provoking the child to assert even greater independence.

Finally, the use of insults and trickery and the aim of doing hurt to another are often inconsistent with the self-conception of a humane person. As the conflict proceeds and escalates, ego sees a progressively less acceptable self-image coming into sharp focus.

Interruption of the conflict sequence may take the form of either accommodation or conciliation. Accommodation means initially a cessation of overt conflict without resolution of the underlying conflict relationship. There is either a de facto or a more or less explicit agreement to discontinue further attacks for the present.

Conciliation is a set of gestures that constitute an offer both to discontinue further attacks and to discount prior gestures by both parties. The conciliator cannot merely offer an end to further conflictual gestures, since this alone does not alter the negative relationship between identities built up in the course of conflict. He admits that what he said in the heat of conflict was exaggerated or totally unwarranted. Because he was suffering indigestion and consequently was in a bad humor or because matters at the office had made him unduly tense, he said things he did not really mean. Such are culturally standard gestures of conciliation in American culture, constituting an implied offer to discontinue further attacks and discount prior gestures, conditional on a similar disaffirmation on the part of the other.

The reinterpretation of prior gestures as banter is one of the most effective techniques of conciliation. It serves to discount the conflictual gestures without placing the conciliator in the position of admitting lack of judgment or restraint. If the other does not reciprocate, the conciliator is not placed in the disadvantageous position of having admitted that he did not always mean what he said. And it makes it equally easy for the opponent to accept the new basis for discounting gestures without self-humiliation.

Conflict is normally not an enjoyable experience. Although the intense feeling of the moment may overcome its unpleasant features, the aftermath is likely to be a lingering sense of hurt for each of the participants and awkwardness in resuming interaction. The memory of past conflicts colors the current reaction with the result that each impulse to conflicting behavior is likely to arouse some dread of the consequences of conflict. The character of this dread and its relations to the bonds depends somewhat on whether the bonds are task-oriented or identity-oriented.

When task bonds predominate, the important consequence of conflict is to impede the decision-making process, disrupting work toward the objective at hand. The greater, then, the value attached to the task, the greater the reluctance to allow its disruption by conflict. Although a strong task bond intensifies the conflict potential of some difficulties, it also supplies a greater motive to avoid conflict behavior and to get interaction back on a strictly task-oriented basis. A strong task bond creates a strong motive for accommodation, for adjusting to differences, allowing differences to go unsettled on the basis of some working concession or compromise or simple avoidance. Since the principal interest is in completion of the task, the participant prefers to allow some slight to his self-esteem to go uncorrected rather than divert further energies from the task. Or he makes an apology or accepts a compromise that does not adequately establish his own identity in order to get interaction back to the task orientation.

When identity bonds predominate, conflict is more than a distraction; it directly threatens the bonds themselves and the relations between the two identities that are the core of the identity bonds. Although the same tendency toward accommodation is present, certain kinds of identity bonds require more than accommodation. To the extent to which the bond depends for its value on the image that alter holds of ego, accommodation is insufficient and a degree of harmonization is called for. The distinction can be illustrated by the comparison between an identification bond and response bond. An individual can continue to gain prestige by being associated with a prestigeful person although considerable strain exists between them. Consequently an accommodation that leaves the conflict-facilitating condition unchanged but prevents it from erupting in overt conflict is often likely to suffice. Strains in identity relations, however, prevent intimate responses from taking place. A mere accommodation, therefore, impairs the response relationship and destroys some of the value that comes to the participants. Hence the strongest tendencies to conciliate and harmonize identities in the face of high conflict potential probably occur when response bonds play a major part in the relationship.

Testing and Commitment. The occurrence of occasional conflict can be expected in any relationship. Hence it may be less important to understand the onset and course of specific episodes of conflict than their aftermath. Some conflict is chronic, recurring from time to time without notable alteration or deterioration of the relationship. Some conflict is episodic, coming in waves, alternated by periods of serenity. And some conflict is cumulative, each episode building on the former episodes toward a progressive deterioration. Our most important problem is to learn how to tell which of these courses will be followed.

In the ideal set of stages we have outlined conflict proceeds to the point where it is excessively threatening and is then interrupted by some technique of accommodation. Following the cessation of actual conflict, the participants have an opportunity to reconsider and restructure the entire sequence. Their behavior subsequently reflects this restructuring. Reconsideration can take place most readily and fully when the overt conflict itself is recessed, although such reconsideration also takes place during the conflict. Hence the final stages may be concurrent with the stages of overt conflict and accommodation. Man never ceases completely to observe and appraise his own behavior and the course of events in which he is involved.

Two features of the conflict process are most relevant to the latter stages but characterize the entire sequence to a degree. These aspects are *commitment* and *testing*.

All interaction incorporates some commitment, based on the fact that an individual utters a gesture in the presence of a hearer and must in some sense recant if he later wishes to be freed from it. There is further commitment in all interaction, because alter determines his response on the basis of ego's gesture. To attempt to withdraw the initial gesture then forces a reassessment of the gesture exchanges that followed it. The commitment is more serious in conflict than in most kinds of interaction, because the sacred ground of the identity is more directly implicated and because each has made himself an object of attack by the other through his gestures. One may relatively easily withdraw a proposal to visit a certain restaurant, and the change may be attributed to impulse or faulty remembrance of the quality of food served there. But one cannot so easily dispose of an attack on the self-image of another. One does not attack others without reason. Hence there is always suspicion that the disavowed gesture was really meant after all or that the gesturer suffered some personal deficiency. Furthermore, the gesture has probably provoked retaliatory attack on ego's identity, and to withdraw the initial gesture does not automatically heal the wound from the retaliatory gesture. There is, then, a marked tendency for conflict to be committing to the participants, both because of the seriousness of the gestures issued and because of the reciprocal character of antagonism and response.

If the foregoing were the entire story, conflict would always be cumulative, leading inevitably to destruction of the relationship. But conflict also incorporates a process of testing. The conflict gestures that ego makes are continuously tested for their effects in the four respects that relate to conflict interruption. First, they are tested by the extent and effectiveness of the retaliation they bring. During the reassessment stage the individual may decide to attempt to avoid reactivation of the conflict in order to avoid further damage to his own identity. During overt conflict he may decide to seek an accommodation to prevent more harm being done. It is useful to speak of this kind of conflict resolution as a *power accommodation*, because it is based on fear of the other's power. Except for recessing the conflict so that constructive relations may take place, power accommodation itself is not a step in the direction of harmony. Weakness on the part of the other is a sufficient change in the power situation to permit reactivation of such a conflict.

Second and third, the conflict gestures are tested by the damage they seem to be doing to the bonds and to the still-valued alter. If there is an important respect in which conflict can lead to discovery and an eventually more harmonious relationship, it is that people discover how much a relationship means to them when it is threatened by conflict.

Fourth, the conflict gestures are tested reflexively for their effect on the gesturer's self-image. Because of the norms he honors, the individual feels guilty about the attacks he has made or uncertan about his own fairness and integrity. In the last three kinds of testing the normal result is more than a power accommodation; it is a genuine conciliation with steps toward harmonization to offset the conflict.

Reevaluation and Aftermath: Stages 4 and 5. The idea of a reevaluation stage rests on the theory of the act as a goal-directed sequence of behavior that normally continues until completed in some manner, as discussed in Chapter 4.

Initially the act of conflict requires that alter's identity be damaged and that alter be forced to accept the damage, while ego's identity remains unbesmirched. In the usual accommodation the act is not completed. Alter has parried the blows so that convincing damage was not done or has penetrated ego's defenses so as to do harm to ego. Whether the end is achieved on a note of power accommodation or active conciliation, the failure to complete the original goal remains.

The fundamental tendency during the reevaluation stage is to reenact the course of the conflict imaginatively, but with modifications to make it come out better. Sometimes the reenactment is done by way of a verbal account to a third party, the account incorporating improvements on the actual events. The other's blows are more effectively parried and ego's blows are more vital in the retelling. Children go through this stage quite naïvely, using their parents, siblings, and peers as their audience. This fundamental tendency, reinforced by the commitment that has occurred, makes the reassessment stage a rehearsal for the next round of conflict. The insult is perfected so as to strike home more effectively next time; the defense is replanned. After such preparation the individual often seeks a pretext to reopen the old conflict, confident that he will come out better the next time.

The testing we have spoken of, however, is also intensified during the reassessment stage. How the initial act may be superseded by one directed toward a new goal of harmonization is illustrated in the following episode:

My fifth-grade daughter frequently brought her school spelling list to me to review with her before her test at school. Words were first assigned on Monday, the children were supposed to study all week, and on Friday they were tested. On some previous occasions my daughter had delayed studying seriously until the last moment. One Friday morning she brought me the list, just as I was getting ready to leave for work. Pressed for time, I asked in annoyance why she hadn't asked me the evening before. Then I started reviewing her, only to find that she didn't know about half of the words. With each word she missed I became more annoyed, and finally angrily told her I had to leave, that there was no use in further review because she hadn't studied, and generally berated her for neglecting her study. I left her in tears. On the way to work I found myself going over and over the event, becoming progressively more upset over my behavior. I found myself trying out ways in which I could have handled the situation without provoking her tears. At work I hunted about for some token to bring home to her. When I returned home I brought her an art eraser, and carefully avoided any query about her spelling test. I made a mental note to ask her next Tuesday to help her on that week's spelling.

In this account the strained relationship between father and daughter was a threat to the gratifications that the father received from his daughter's dependency and responsiveness and reflected unfavorably on the father's self-conception of control and reasonableness. The unsatisfactory outcome of the act led to the father's preoccupation with the event, and each imaginative reenactment brought out more painfully the unsatisfactory aspects. Eventually, the goals of repairing the relationship and reestablishing his own self-respect superseded the original goal of conflict, leading to an aftermath of active conciliation. If the original conflict purpose is altered in this fashion, reevaluation becomes a rehearsal for future conciliation.

Chronic and Cumulative Conflict

Conflict in a family relationship becomes chronic or cumulative when there are continuing conflict-provoking situations in the organization of the family. Whether the conflict is chronic or cumulative depends on whether major family bonds are vulnerable to the recurrent conflict or not.

Personality Sources of Recurrent Conflict. In any relationship there are occasions when members see each other as obstacles to achievement of individual ends or group purposes and when one person's behavior casts the other in an unacceptable role. For conflict to recur, either chronically or cumulatively, the organization of the family must be such that the same obstacles to decision making or similar identity problems recur each time interaction over certain subjects takes place. Explanations for such lasting features of organization are usually found either in the personalities of family members or in the nature of the social organization of the family itself.

Personality explanations are of two kinds. They attribute recurring conflict either to the presence of one or more members whose personalities consistently interfere with the achievement of decisions or threaten the identities of others, or they find explanation in the incompatibility of family members. The vast majority of research dealing with marital conflict has approached the problem from the former standpoint, seeking to distinguish the kinds of persons who are good marital risks from those who are poor risks.

The Maladjusted Personality. The most common presupposition of psychiatric and adjustment psychology investigations of marital conflict is that the individual who has difficulty in other interpersonal relations is also likely to have difficulty in marital relations and other family relations. Accordingly personalities are classified as maladjusted, neurotic, irrational, immature, emotionally deficient, and the like, and it is hypothesized that such attributes bode ill for family relations. A volume devoted to the psychological analysis of family life would find an endless list of personality traits that have been said to be related to adjustment in marriage. For our purposes, it is sufficient to review a few of the approaches of this kind.

Neurosis as an obstacle to marital harmony is the central assumption in psychiatric study. This viewpoint is the basis for a volume edited by Victor W. Eisenstein, in which he refers to the strategy of the psychiatrist as "exposing the neurotic components in the constant interplay of mutual hostility, i.e., in the compulsion to repeat forgotten infantile situations in the current relationship."[12] The neurotic is a person whose behavior in crucial situations is governed by goals and meanings of which he is unaware and which constantly block the achievement of objectives he consciously pursues. Thus, although he believes he wishes to reach agreement with other family members, he unconsciously fears agreement and accordingly acts so as to prevent agreement whenever it is in sight. Or he may suppose he wishes to enhance the self-image of his partner, although unconsciously fearing the good repute of the other as a threat to his own identity.

Investigators have attempted to test the hypothesis that neurosis or personal maladjustment is negatively associated with marital success. An early study of this kind was conducted by the psychologist L. L. Terman.[13] A schedule containing items to measure marital happiness and items from the Bernreuter Personality Inventory and the Strong Interest Test was filled out by 792 married couples. The happiness schedule was an adaptation of the Burgess-Cottrell marital adjustment measure, supplying separate scores for husbands and wives. The Bernreuter Inventory is a standard instrument for personality assessment, supplying a total adjustment score and several special scores based on endorsement of statements believed to be symptomatic of neurosis or maladjustment. Terman found little overall correlation between total adjustment scores and marital happiness scores, al-

[12] Victor W. Eisenstein (ed.), *Neurotic Interaction in Marriage*, Basic Books, New York, 1956, p. ix.
[13] Lewis M. Terman, *Psychological Factors in Marital Happiness*, McGraw-Hill, New York, 1938, pp. 366, *et passim*.

though a great many individual items were associated with happiness scores.

In a later study Robert Winch related adjustment in engagement to scores on the Thurstone Neurotic Inventory among 42 couples. He found that a high neurotic score for either male or female was unfavorable for adjustment and that a high score for both was even more unfavorable.[14]

Unadjusted Life Patterns. Somewhat similar to the idea of neurosis, but of sociologically greater relevance is Harriet Mowrer's attribution of domestic discord to the "unadjusted life pattern" of one of the partners. Her analysis, too, stems from clinical evidence:[15]

The life pattern may be said to be *unadjusted* when the individual's conception of himself and his role in society is of such a nature that it interferes with, rather than facilitates, his adaptation to social requirements. . . . Thus the individual's conception of his role becomes so highly individualized that he finds it difficult either to accept the social definitions of that group in which he desires status or to find a group which will treat him more favorably for any length of time.

The simplest form of unadjusted life pattern that Mowrer describes is the *escape response pattern*, in which mechanisms such as illness or alcoholism are used to escape the responsibilities imposed by the marital role. But more interesting to the sociologist are the patterns that reflect "the presence within the individual himself of two or more equally persistent roles." In the cases cited the individual had experienced a strict upbringing as a child but at adolescence had come strongly under the influence of a libertine group and wholeheartedly adopted their way of life. The earlier life pattern, however, remained latent, to reassert itself later, with the result that the individual carried about two contradictory life patterns. In the unadjusted life pattern that Mowrer calls *conflicting roles*, the individual vacillated between patterns. For a time he abandons his libertine ways in disgust, determined to be a fully respectable member of society. But the thrills of the libertine role are not forgotten, and as respectability becomes more and more frustrating, he breaks away and returns to the libertine life. But after a time the libertine life begins to seem shallow, and he experiences guilt until he returns again to the conventional life. Whichever way of life he follows, he cannot help criticizing it from the standpoint of his other life way. When he enters marriage, the lack of consistent values and a consistent self-conception make the establishment of any satisfactory system of decision making, division of labor, and self-other conceptions im-

---

[14] Robert W. Winch, *The Relation between the Neurotic Tendency and the Adjustment in Engagement*, unpublished master's thesis, University of Chicago, 1942.
[15] Harriet R. Mowrer, *Personality Adjustment and Domestic Discord*, American Book, New York, 1935, pp. 44–45. Quoted by permission of the author.

possible. A third pattern called *dual roles* is similar, except that the individual has learned to partition his life in such a manner that he can enjoy both roles without either interfering with the other. He may have a wife in one town and a mistress in the other. But the comprehensive character of family life makes such partitioning difficult to maintain, and once it is breached, the same difficulties disturb the family functioning.

Deficient Empathic Ability. A third conception of personality types ill-suited to family life centers specifically on the individual's ability to relate himself to others, stressing *empathic* or *role-taking ability*. Harrison Gough has proposed a conception of psychopathy as a condition in which the individual is unable to perceive correctly the manner in which others see and interpret his behavior.[16] Behavior he believes should bring him favorable reactions actually alienates others from him. In the interaction process outlined in Chapter 2 such an individual is one whose interpretation of his own and others' gestures is so consistently and widely at variance with the interpretations that others are making that agreements cannot be reached and identities are constantly being unwittingly damaged.

Nelson Foote and Leonard Cottrell have expanded this conception to a more inclusive attribute which they call interpersonal competence and which they suggest as a fruitful key to family research.[17] Although not formally defined, interpersonal competence corresponds roughly to "skill in controlling the outcome of episodes of interaction." The parts that constitute interpersonal competence are (a) health, (b) intelligence, (c) empathy, (d) autonomy, (e) judgment, and (f) creativity. Foote and Cottrell propose that these characteristics in combination facilitate effective family operation in a democratic society.

Predisposing Factors. The foregoing three approaches have in common that they propose that recurrent conflict-precipitating behavior in the family is only an extension of similar behavior in other group contexts. The further possibility that there are personal attributes which do not impede relations in other groups but which do in the family must also be noted. Marital-success-prediction studies have generally produced a list of predisposing factors that are actuarially shown to make the individual a good or a poor marriage risk. In a comprehensive review of such studies, Clifford Kirkpatrick has listed the following most fully substantiated premarital predictors of marital success:[18]

[16] Harrison G. Gough, "A Sociological Theory of Psychopathy," *American Journal of Sociology,* 53:359–366, March 1948.
[17] Nelson N. Foote and Leonard S. Cottrell, Jr., *Identity and Interpersonal Competence: A New Direction in Family Research,* University of Chicago Press, Chicago, 1955, pp. 36–60.
[18] Clifford Kirkpatrick, *The Family: As Process and Institution,* Ronald, New York, 1963, p. 389. Quoted by permission of the publisher and the author.

Happiness of parents' marriage
Adequate length of acquaintance, courtship, and engagement
Adequate sex information in childhood
Personal happiness in childhood
Approval of the marriage by parents and others
Engagement adjustment and normal motivation toward marriage
Ethnic and religious similarity
Higher social and educational status
Mature and similar chronological age
Harmonious affection with parents during childhood

It will be noted that these are mostly facts in the past history of the individual. They are significant, perhaps as experiences that have left a residue in the individual personality, perhaps as indices of personality attributes. In either instance they distinguish persons who are likely to precipitate conflict or harmony recurrently by their behavior, although the nature of the connection is not indicated.

Personalities Congenial to Family Life. Others have offered hypotheses more directly connected with the family processes themselves. Judson Landis, for example, has asserted that the determination to make a success of marriage is an attitude essential to success.[19] Robert Winch proposes that a high degree of personal self-sufficiency precludes the formation of bonds but the moderately dependent person is better suited to family life.[20] Implicit in much of William I. Thomas' writing is the assumption that the Philistine—the conventional, conforming, uncreative person—finds marriage more congenial than the Bohemian—the iconoclastic seeker after novelty.[21] Harvey Locke has interpreted a group of items in his interview comparison between divorced and happily married couples as indicating five general personality characteristics that are favorable to marital adjustment.[22] The five are as follows:

Directorial ability, as measured by self and mate ratings on acceptance of responsibility, strictness in dealing with children, leadership, ability to make decisions readily, determination, and not being easily influenced by others.

Adaptability, as measured by self and mate ratings on "giving in" in arguments, not being dominating, slowness in getting angry, and quickness in getting over anger.

[19] Judson T. Landis and Mary G. Landis, *Building a Successful Marriage*, Prentice-Hall, Englewood Cliffs, N.J., 1958, pp. 5, 6.
[20] Robert W. Winch, *The Modern Family*, Henry, New York, 1952, pp. 392 ff.
[21] *Social Behavior and Personality: Contributions of W. I. Thomas to Theory and Social Research*, Edmund H. Volkart (ed.), Social Science Research Council, New York, 1951, pp. 125 ff, *et passim*.
[22] Harvey J. Locke, *Predicting Adjustment in Marriage: A Comparison of a Divorced and a Happily Married Group*, Holt, New York, 1951, pp. 171–244. Adapted by permission of the publisher and the author.

Affectionateness, as measured by self and mate ratings on affectionateness and demonstration of affection.

Sociability, as measured by self and mate ratings on making friends easily, enjoyment in belonging to organizations, moderate concern with what people say and think, a sense of humor, and by reported number of friends for self and mate before and after marriage.

Conventionality, as measured by reported church membership and attendance and by sacred rather than secular marriage ceremony.

With regard to evidence of this kind, two major questions are inescapable. First, to what extent would respondents who were sensitized to the fact that they were discussing an unsuccessful relationship be consequently inclined to rate both themselves and their mates low in retrospect? The fact, noted by Locke, that ratings of spouse were more diagnostic than ratings of self, lends support to the suspicion that systematic bias was at work. Second, to what degree were the personal characteristics affected by the malfunctioning relationship, affectionateness being impeded by ill-feeling, directorial ability frustrated by family disorganization, and adaptability hindered by the failure of implicit bargaining?

Incompatibility. The idea of incompatibility concerns the fit between two personalities, irrespective of their individual adequacy in other relationships. Two people who are both good marriage risks individually may have characteristics that make it difficult for them to arrive at decisions, carry out joint activity, and support each other's identities. Conversely, it is possible that persons with individually low marriage-risk ratings might fit together so well as to offset their disadvantages.

Compatibility is an exceptionally difficult idea to test empirically and is generally applied ex post facto to explain marital conflicts on an ad hoc basis. Our earlier discussion of the causes of conflict suggests a general formula consisting of two pairs of variables to predict the extent to which conflict is recurrent in a family. First is the extent of differences in goals and means that are relevant to the collaborative aspects of family life, multiplied by the obstacles to easy assent and commitment in family decision making. Thus personalities may be incompatible either because of the extent of family-relevant differences or because they cannot fit into a smoothly operating decision process. If only one of the two variables is low, compatibility is not substantially reduced. Second is the extent to which identities are problematic in the relationship, multiplied by the extent to which identities are crucial in the bonding of the relationship. These are the variables which determine whether differences and decision-making problems are quickly converted into conflict or not. Identities are problematic when self- and other conceptions have not yet been stabilized in a relationship and when each person's self-conception is such as to challenge in some way that of the other. In order to spell out the meaning of incompatibility in personality terms, we need research to catalog these relatively unworkable combinations of self-conceptions.

Organizational Sources of Recurrent Conflict. The obverse of personality explanations for recurrent conflict is explanation on the basis of the nature of family organization itself. These explanations may be further divided into two kinds. First, the tasks assigned to the family, the values that people seek to realize through family life, may be sources of recurrent conflict. Many writers have asserted that too much is expected of the modern American family, more than it can reasonably be expected to supply. Conflict accordingly develops, because the standards of identity support and agreement are unrealistic. When organization incorporates incompatible objectives, activities in one area cannot be pursued without blocking those in another.

Second, the system of decision making and division of labor may be a constant source of conflict. Organizational "experts" are hired by business and government to make their organization function more efficiently, without necessarily introducing changes in personnel. A reassignment of responsibilities in the family can sometimes cause it to operate more smoothly. The institution of the formal family conference may end indecision. A greater delegation of decision-making responsibility may smooth out family operations. A clearer definition of responsibilities so as to lessen overlap and uncertainty may facilitate harmony.

Organizational sources of family conflict have been treated thus briefly, because they will be brought into focus again in Chapter 9, dealing with the family as a system of roles.

The question is sometimes raised as to which explanation is more important, personality or organization, for recurring conflict. The query is a pseudo-question, because it presumes that the two kinds of explanation are independent. Either kind of explanation, if carried far enough, subsumes the other. Whenever we say that a kind of personality cannot function in the family, we must take for granted the organization of the average family. With sufficient modification of family organization we could undoubtedly devise a relationship in which any personality could function. Whenever we say that an organization creates recurrent conflict, we must assume average personalities. A personality with much greater than average adaptability could undoubtedly function without inducing conflict in an organization that does not work for most people. In choosing, as we shall in this book, to stress the organizational side, we do not deny the value of explanation from a personality base.

Cumulative Conflict. Whether recurrent conflict is chronic or cumulative depends on whether the major family bonds are vulnerable to the conflict that takes place. We return, then, to the interrelation of bonds and conflict-harmony. Since bonds are the principal force supplying an incentive to conciliation, cumulative conflict reflects the absence of sufficient bonds to cause conciliation between conflict episodes. Recurrent conflict affects the strength of bonds in two ways. Some kinds of bonds are vulnerable to conflict. And conflict impedes the development of most kinds of crescive bonds.

Bonds are vulnerable in three ways: through the disappearance of the desire or value on which the bond is based, through the elimination of gratification, and through the reevaluation of alternatives. The second and third ways concern us. Activity bonds are vulnerable to failures of decision making that prevent the attainment of the gratification on which the bonds are based. Economic bonds, for example, are vulnerable to inability to reach decisions on financial matters. Recreational bonds are vulnerable to inability to reach decisions in these matters. Disillusioned married people frequently look back wistfully at the earlier uncomplicated years when they enjoyed doing a number of things together they now find it too troublesome to reach agreement on.

Response bonds are directly vulnerable to conflict itself, since conflict sets identities in opposition. Identification bonds, on the other hand, need not suffer loss from the mere fact of abundant conflict and often remain as the source of periodic conciliation. Similarly, the bonds that tie individuals to the family by itself—the belief in the inviolability of family ties or the assets of marriage as a status—are not necessarily affected.

Although the direct destruction of bonding gratifications by conflict is quite selective, the reevaluation of alternatives is a more generalized form of vulnerability. The strength of every bond is a function not only of the gratification received but also of the unavailability of gratification from alternative sources. The appraisal of alternative sources of satisfaction is strongly affected by the frustrations and gratifications incident to attainment of the main gratification. Although a woman may continue to receive the same identification benefits from her marriage in spite of much conflict, the discomfort of frequent conflict makes the alternative sources of prestige seem more attractive than before. Although the clash of identities may not interfere with the economic bond, the husband continuing to be as good a provider and the wife as effective a budgeter as ever, the recurrence of disturbing conflict makes each more sensitive to the possibility of working out a satisfactory livelihood without the other.

Alternatives are always partial unknowns. An alternative that is readily available, such as a second suitor to an engaged girl or enlistment in the army as an escape from the family for a seventeen-year-old boy, supplies gratification of unknown degree. When no alternative is immediately available, as in case of the boy who leaves home without a job prospect or the mother who divorces her husband without clear prospect of family support, there is added the risk that no gratification will be found. But prospects that the available alternative will be gratifying look brighter and the risk of no gratification is made to appear less serious when conflict accompanying the relationship encumbers current gratification with much discomfort.

Because many of the early bonds in family life are transitory, it is essential that new bonds emerge to take their place. But the emergence of crescive bonds can be impeded by recurrent conflict. A good deal of conflict can be compatible with the formation of crescive bonds. Family members may develop interlocking roles in conflict, so that one is dependent on the other's stubbornness to save him from taking responsibility for unpleasant decisions or even on the other's hatefulness to reassure him of his own personal virtue by contrast. Common experiences may provide a fund of shared enthusiasm strong enough to break the circle of recurrent conflict. Even adjusted communication and response can develop. The boy whose mother constantly berates him may become so accustomed to her bitter tongue that it has little effect, so that he may continue to find her a useful confidante in spite of the predictable diatribes that ensue. Chronic conflict may coexist with the development of crescive bonds.

Growth of these crescive bonds, however, usually presumes an initial period relatively free of conflict during which their growth is well started. Mother and son may have had a much more harmonious relationship during his earlier years, so that he adjusted gradually to her negativeness as he approached adolescence. Husband and wife typically pass through extended courtship and honeymoon periods during which such bonds are started. In the absence of such an initial period of harmony the adjusted communication is impeded, interlocking roles of a satisfactory kind are improbable, the failure to reach decisions and carry them out prevents the accumulation of a fund of shared positive experiences, and collaborative plans are not developed. Likewise, sufficiently intense conflict at any stage can prevent the further development of any such bonds.

Because the typical family in our society is held together by a diversity of bonds, chronic conflict is probably more frequent than cumulative conflict. Chronic conflict sometimes follows a cyclical course, developing cumulatively until the danger to crucial bonds is exposed, whereupon there ensues a period of active conciliation. Or individuals may alternate as conciliators, conflict at one stage being more threatening to parent than child and later more threatening to child than parent.

Summary

Conflict is different from mere disagreement, competition, rivalry, and other forms of opposition, because it includes the aim of hurting the other person. Conflict is based on an opposition between identities, such that whatever enhances the identity of one combatant damages the other's, and damaging alter's identity becomes a way in which ego can enhance his own identity. There is no simple relationship between the intensity of bonds and the intensity of conflict, except that conflict cannot take place without sufficient bondedness to prevent the dissipation of opposition into indifference.

Conflict occurs when the negative implications of a relationship for the participants' identities take precedence over the task aspects of their interaction. This occurs most frequently in the family when (a) action is blocked and the identity of the other is viewed as the obstacle, and (b) ego perceives an unfavorable self-image in a situation and ascribes it to the peculiar relationship of ego and alter. Blocked action is attributed to identities, following repeated failure to reach group decisions, when members view the rules governing decision making differently, when unfavorable decisions are reached by coercion, and when illegitimate actions by alter block ego's goals. An unfavorable self-image is ascribed to alter when alter directly characterizes ego unfavorably, when alter's behavior casts ego in an unacceptable role, when rivalry deteriorates, and through identification under certain circumstances.

The strategy of family conflict revolves about simultaneously inflicting damage on the other's identity while protecting or enhancing one's own. Because there is often no audience and little tangible injury to be done each other, offensive strategy in the family emphasizes forcing the other to admit self-disparagement. Defensive strategy includes disguising attacks as indignation or as conciliation, using ambiguous gestures, and using private barbs in front of outsiders. Resolution of conflict is different from resolution of disagreement: disagreement is resolved by each party's taking the remarks of the other seriously; conflict requires that each discount the insults and accusations made by the other. Conciliation is an offer both to discontinue further attacks and to discount prior gestures by both parties. Conflict typically reaches a point where it threatens the well-being of either participant or the bonds they value, followed either by conciliation or more often by accommodation. After accommodation there is a stage of reassessment, during which commitment pushes the family member toward reopening the conflict later, but a process of testing his private feelings determines whether commitment or conciliation will prevail. Usually during imaginative reenactment of the conflict the tendency toward conciliation is dominant.

Conflict becomes chronic when enduring personality characteristics of members or patterns of family organization are such as to provoke conflict. Neurosis, unadjusted life patterns, and deficient role-taking capacity are personality characteristics conducive to chronic conflict. Less is known about what combinations of personality characteristics make for chronic conflict because of incompatibility. Organizational sources of chronic conflict are treated in Chapter 9. Conflict becomes cumulative when family bonds are vulnerable to conflict, especially through the reevaluation of alternatives.

CHAPTER 8

SOCIALIZATION

Socialization is the process of interaction viewed as the medium through which individuals learn to cope with society. The process takes place most dramatically in infancy and childhood, when the existence and nature of society are first being learned and when effective and ineffective techniques for dealing with society are first being distinguished. But the process occurs throughout life, and adults as well as children are constantly modifying their conceptions of society and their adaptations to it. Socialization is an aspect of interaction in all groups; but the continuity, intensity, and priority of family life make it the most crucial locus of socialization.

Socialization and Conformity. A large part of socialization is learning conformity. The child must learn to speak a standard language rather than one of his own invention; he must learn to accept routines, clothes, authority, moral codes, and innumerable restrictions of impulse. The effectiveness of this process is shown by the amazing uniformity of prejudice and opinion among adults from the same segments of society, a uniformity they seldom recognize.

But it is a mistake to equate socialization with conformization. Socialization is a broader process that also creates diversity. The first component of socialization has to be gaining an impression of the social order. And in most respects simple conformity is the easiest, although often not the most rewarding, way of coping with the social order. But the individual who masters the system of rules and their enforcement so as to become adept at evading them need not be regarded as less socialized than the conformist. The employee of a business concern who learns the social organization and then seeks to alter it in order to improve its functioning is no less socialized than the more conforming bureaucrat.

Socialization is sometimes used popularly to mean becoming altruistic or learning to see the other person's point of view. As sociologists use the term, no such meaning is implied. In order to work out relationships with alters who constitute society, ego must understand their point of view in some degree and must bear them in mind when acting himself. To this extent there is a common element in the sociological and popular concep-

164

tions. But taking account of the other's point of view in this sense does not necessarily imply an altruistic attitude.

Socialization as the Residual of Interaction. Socialization is not a different process but merely a different aspect of the interaction process we have concerned ourselves with already. Each interaction episode leaves its residual in the conceptions of self and other. The formation, modification, reinforcement, and elaboration of these conceptions is the essence of the socialization process. The interest in socialization is distinctive only in concentrating on the generalization and persistence of these residuals.

Residual self- and other conceptions are applied to relationships outside the family. In his relations with the mother and sister within the family the boy acquires conceptions of girls and women and of himself in relation to them. From the experience of care or neglect within the family during infancy the child learns a generalized self-other relationship that colors his approach to persons he will meet later. The memory of an experience outside the family is assigned new meaning after being introduced into family interaction by being recounted to a parent or sibling.

Socialization is concerned with the persistence of the learning attendant on interaction. At one time considerable emphasis was placed on locating single crucial episodes, usually called traumatic experiences, that would account for lasting attitudes. But recent emphases have been on recurrent and consistent socializing experiences as the sources of lasting self-other conceptions. Some experiences leave deeper imprints than others, but the reinforcing effect of repeated verification of preestablished conceptions through interaction is probably the most important factor in persistence.

Deliberate and Inadvertant Socialization. Socialization is carried on deliberately and with an elaborate strategy by parents and teachers, by "enlightened" adolescents toward their parents, sometimes by older siblings, and often by one spouse toward another. But socialization cannot be limited to its deliberate form. First, every act of deliberate socialization has its unintended effects. The mother who attempts to train her child to be neat and orderly may, by the kind of reciprocity she establishes with the child, actually teach him that it is a good thing to stay clear of mother when she is on a rampage. Or the father who attempts to teach his child never to keep something that belongs to another person may actually be teaching him that it is discreet to conceal what he wants to keep. Besides such reverse effects as these, there are also incidental by-products to every socializing exchange.

Second, socialization takes place in the course of interaction that is not guided by any intention to socialize. James Bossard has pointed to a variety of ways a guest in the home is a socializing influence on the children, quite without recognizing the part he is playing.[1] From a very early age peers socialize one another without intention or thought to what they are doing.

Deliberate socialization is a form of task interaction involving strategies by the agent in dealing with the outside group and the socializee, and responses and strategies on the part of the socializee. In Chapter 14 we shall review the peculiar twists given to interaction when it is centered on socialization. But the actual learning and shaping of personality that takes place is a cumulative response to the more comprehensive set of relationships within the family. The specific mechanisms of learning are the province of psychological study. But the broad patterns of learning, which differ according to the character of the family and the socializee's position in it, concern us. We must keep in mind that, although the most dramatic evidences of socialization apply to children, all members of any group undergo some continuous socialization as a by-product of every interaction experience.

Conveyance of Family Culture

The simplest conception of the kind of learning that takes place in the family, and one that adequately describes a great deal of evidence, is the conveyance of culture. Culture in this simple sense is treated as the shared ways of acting characteristic of a society. Since the family gives its own special slant to these ways, omits some, and adds others, we can speak in a more limited sense of family culture. The emphasis here is on a uniformization process, the impact of socialization being measured by the extent to which family members come to exhibit the same patterns of behavior and attitudes.

The range and amount of evidence showing resemblances of opinion and attitude between parents and children is overwhelming. No single variable approaches the political affiliation of parents as a predictor of political affiliation of the adult.[2] Boys from similar socioeconomic backgrounds, with similar measured intelligence, and subject to similar school influences are shown to differ in their desire to attend college largely according to the value that their parents place on college.[3]

Typical of many investigations is the finding regarding voting behavior

---

[1] James H. S. Bossard and Eleanor S. Boll, *The Sociology of Child Development*, Harper & Row, New York, 1960, pp. 158–182.
[2] See Scott Greer and Peter Orleans, "Political Sociology," in Robert E. L. Faris (ed.), *Handbook of Modern Sociology*, Rand McNally, Chicago, 1964, pp. 813–814.
[3] Joseph A. Kahl, "Educational and Occupational Aspirations of 'Comman Man' Boys," *Harvard Educational Review*, 23:186–203, Summer 1953, David J. Bordua, "Educational Aspirations and Parental Stress on College," *Social Forces*, 38:262–269, March 1960.

in Elmira, New York, in the 1948 presidential election.[4] A sample of 500 voters for the two major parties supplied information on the usual political inclinations of their fathers. As Figure 6 reveals, the majority (72 percent) of voters conformed to the paternal pattern. Conformity was a little stronger among the younger voters, but the relationship remained in spite of age. Since socioeconomic status is so important a determinant of voting behavior and since there is a correlation between the socioeconomic status of parent and child, the authors repeated the analysis with status held constant. Voting behavior continued to show a close relationship to paternal politics even within socioeconomically homogeneous groups.

There is considerable anecdotal evidence that husband and wife also undergo an inadvertant mutual socialization toward uniformity. It is more difficult to establish such a principle empirically, however, because husbands and wives are self-selected according to a good many prior similarities at the time of marriage. One piece of research produces specifically

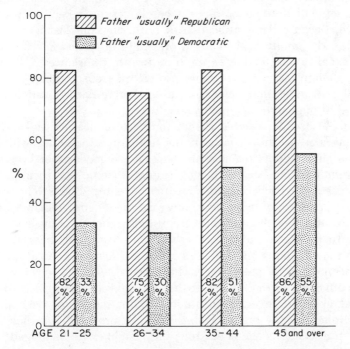

Figure 6. Percentage voting Republican according to father's politics, Elmira, 1948. (Adapted from Bernard R. Berelson, Paul F. Lazarsfeld, and William N. McPhee, *Voting*, University of Chicago Press, Chicago, 1954, p. 89.)

[4] Bernard R. Berelson, Paul F. Lazarsfeld, and William N. McPhee, *Voting*, University of Chicago Press, Chicago, 1954, pp. 88–91.

negative findings regarding the hypothesized tendency for husband-wife similarity in values to increase with greater marriage duration.[5]

Early treatments of culture conveyance leaned heavily on imitation for an explanation. Imitation still figures in thinking about the process, with stress on the importance of parents and elder siblings as behavior models. But at least three concepts suggest more elaborate processes by which the conveyance takes place.

Canalization. First, in the psychological process of canalization an individual learns to seek gratifications for a physiological need in certain ways and to reject other physiologically adequate means of gratification.[6] Although the need for food itself is not created by the family, the family inculcates an elaborate set of attitudes by establishing a uniform set of social conditions under which food gratification is usually secured and systematically providing only certain foods and not others. The child may learn to have difficulty enjoying or even eating food from a dirty table, without previously saying grace, in the presence of an enemy, when the dessert is served before the entrée, or when fingers must be used instead of silverware. Because the gratification of most physiological needs is first provided in the family in the context of family ritual and in deference to existing canalizations, extensive uniformities are transmitted. The sexual function, though maturing later and proscribed from gratification within the family of orientation, undergoes as elaborate a canalization as any other need through more symbolic procedures.

Coping. A second principle is that the patterns learned in the family are retained because they constitute the techniques for coping with situations. The child adopts the parents' language behavior, not because he prefers to imitate, but because he gets results when he uses their language that he does not get when he uses his own invented sounds. The parents' and siblings' patterns of behavior supply ready-made strategies for handling a variety of situations that the child is constantly encountering. The special influence that a slightly older sibling seems to have probably reflects the fact that the situations with which he has just learned to deal are those newly encountered by the younger child. Social techniques owe much of their effectiveness to the mere fact that the relevant others regard them as natural, appropriate, or legitimate in the situation. When the child uses the techniques already prevalent in the family, provided that they do not seriously transcend his age or sex role, they are likely to be judged appropriate and hence to have some effectiveness.

---

[5] J. Richard Udry, Harold A. Nelson, and Ruth Nelson, "An Empirical Investigation of Some Widely Held Beliefs about Marital Interaction," *Marriage and Family Living*, 23:388–390, November 1961.

[6] Gardner Murphy, *Personality*, Harper & Row, New York, 1947, pp. 161 ff.

The best verified predictor of marital success, as variously measured, is the reported happiness of the marriages of the couple's parents.[7] The correlation seems to apply although children of unhappy marriages often resolve that their own marriages will not be like their parents'. There are many possible explanations for such a correlation, but one makes use of the notion of technique. In the family of orientation children learn a repertoire of social techniques for dealing with minor and major crises of interpersonal relations. Children learn what to do when insulted, when slighted, when unable to control a group decision, or when someone else shows indications of unfavorable self-image. Where conflict has been prevalent and cumulative between the parents, it is likely to have extended to the children, and the children are likely to have learned the same kinds of techniques that promoted parental conflict. When similar crises are encountered in the family of procreation, the conflict-precipitating repertoire of techniques is the most natural set of responses.

Identification. The concept of identification suggests a third feature of the conveyance of family culture. Under identification as we are using the term one individual experiences events happening to another as if they were happening to him. One person sees events as if he were in another's shoes. Hence he also frames a response in imagination and sometimes overtly as if he were in the other's position. Where there is continuing identification, an individual develops a set of responses to events that reflect the position of the person with whom he identifies as much as his own position. There is likely, then, to be much similarity in their characteristic modes of behavior. The correspondence is not perfect, because the process is not imitation. But considerable uniformization occurs because of the adoption of a common perspective in the assessment of situations.

Although identification of this kind provides a less exact copy than sheer imitation, it may nevertheless create a less easily eradicated similarity. If a child has simply learned a pattern by imitating his mother, he can easily imitate some other person and shed the old pattern for a new one. People who have conceived of no other pattern than the one they have been following sometimes change fairly easily when exposed to a new set of patterns. But if a child, because of identification, has adopted the mother's vantage point as the perspective from which he sees and understands situations, he will have developed an integrated set of patterns that support one another and are not vulnerable to the mere presence of a new example. Radical change will require a new identification and the repudiation of the old perspective.

Because of this relationship it has been suggested by some that the

[7] Ernest W. Burgess and Paul Wallin, *Engagement and Marriage*, Lippincott, Philadelphia, 1953, pp. 513–515.

conscience cannot develop without a deep and intimate identification between the child and some adult.[8] A conscience is said to exist when the individual is committed to certain standards of behavior that are strongly resistant to change, when the individual continues to control his own behavior in much the way that his mentor would have done even when there is no one present to disapprove or punish, and when violation of a norm provokes feelings of guilt that are not unlike the disapproval experienced earlier from the mentor. Patterns may be diligently followed in the absence of conscience but are readily altered to fit a group in which different norms prevail. Certain rigidities may develop because of anxieties surrounding rules. But the conscience as a self-assured commitment to a complex of norms and values with the characteristics we have noted may develop only out of a social system engendering intense identification of socializee with agent. The western small-family system may be the ideal setting. Under a large-family system it is likely that only a few of the children would be able to form such identifications, perhaps accounting for the frequency of black sheep in respectable families.

Reactions to Frustration and Gratification

There is a danger when socialization is treated as the conveyance of culture that the individual organism is viewed as a neutral receptor for whatever culture dictates. The opposite approach to socialization is made when the learning environment is treated primarily as the source of frustration and gratification of impulses, drives, or needs arising out of the nature of the organism. Culture from this point of view is primarily a set of rules that limit the satisfactions available to the individual, and socialization consists of learning the reactions brought on by frustration. Freud's assertion that "civilization *is* suppression," and his massive prescription for society's ills by lessening restraints, express this view.[9] This approach also takes more account of social organization than the conveyance approach. The sources of frustration and gratification may lie in the organization of the group fully as much as in the culture. As Freudians have pointed out, the presence of a sibling in the family is a potential source of frustration for any gratifications from parents.

[8] See Eleanor E. Maccoby, "The Development of Moral Values and Behavior in Childhood," in John Clausen et al, *Socialization and Society*, Little, Brown, Boston, 1968, pp. 229 ff.

[9] Sigmund Freud, *Modern Sexual Morality and Modern Nervousness*, Eugenics Publishing Co., New York, 1931; *Civilization and its Discontents*, trans. Joan Riviere, Hogarth, London, 1930. A more sociological scheme for incorporating aspects of this approach into family study is offered by Murray A. Straus, in "Power and Support Structure of the Family in Relation to Socialization," *Journal of Marriage and Family*, 26:318–326, August 1964.

This approach is also more amenable to explaining diversities that develop among siblings in the same family than culture conveyance. Many investigations have sought differences between children according to order of birth or number of siblings. The only child has been pictured as thrown disproportionately into interaction with his parents, many of his childish interests being frustrated and the development of older interests being encouraged, with the result that he is likely to be precocious and a leader but unpopular with his peers.[10] The eldest child is likely to receive exceptional gratification during infancy because of his monopoly of parental attention, and special advantages throughout life if he is regarded as the family heir. He is thought, however, to suffer especially poignant frustration when the birth of a second child suddenly shatters his monopoly of his parents' love. The second child gets the elder's cast off toys and outgrown clothes and is expected to match any standard of achievement set by the elder. Although the achievements of eldest children gain them listing in *Who's Who* and similar compilations more often than their proportion in the population, middle children have been said to produce more than their share of "restless neurotics." The youngest child is often indulged past the age when other children are forced to abandon infantile satisfaction.[11]

In fact evidence regarding systematic personality differences according to birth order is relatively indecisive and contradictory, taken all together. It would be dangerous to treat any of the hypotheses of unequal frustration according to family position as more than interesting ideas, at the present time. Some of the hypothesized principles may be correct, but the complexity of socialization relations and processes in the family makes them often difficult to demonstrate. Probably the best-supported hypothesis holds that the more exclusive parental attention given initially to the eldest child heightens his reliance on social support. In the face of frustration, he is more likely than other children to seek social affiliation and is consequently especially susceptible to the influence of others.[12]

A movement in child rearing immediately following World War II placed great stress on gratifying infantile impulses and avoiding frustration, so as to supply a basic sense of security. Security is simply gratification projected into the future. A person is secure if he has no anxieties and preoccupations that color his approach to related situations throughout life. Psychoanalytic theory has held that there are stages of development that must follow one another, and if the individual is prevented from

[10] Bossard and Boll, *op. cit.*, pp. 94–97.
[11] *Ibid.*, pp. 100–107.
[12] Stanley Schachter, *The Psychology of Affiliation: Experimental Studies of the Sources of Gregariousness*, Stanford University Press, Stanford, Calif., 1959, pp. 42–52.

securing gratification appropriate to one stage, the development cannot proceed normally. His development is said to be fixated. Frustration at one level of development also causes the individual to try for satisfactions appropriate to an earlier level, or to regress.

There are alternative psychological explanations for many of the apparent socialization consequences of frustration. Empirical efforts to link personality characteristics to specific infantile experiences, such as feeding or toilet-training regimens, have been generally but not entirely unsuccessful.[13] Regardless of the specific psychological theory that eventually turns out to be most adequate, a broad guide is supplied by the sociological theory of the act.[14] Commencement of an act sets in motion a tension that tends to keep the act going or reactivate it after interruption until a satisfactory completion is achieved. An unsatisfactory termination or interruption close to success heightens tension most. Hence, when a child is stopped just as he is about to enjoy the fruits of his effort, the tension to try again later is great, or when his efforts end unhappily in punishment the impulsion to redo the act so as to make it come out right the next time is strong. If there have been frequent unhappy experiences before, however, each effort is hedged about by a fear of failure or punishment, and the result is a mixture of drive and anxiety. A succession of such experiences builds cumulatively, creating preoccupations that carry over into other situations and anxieties that recur whenever the same kind of situation is encountered. The anxieties are incorporated into the images of the principals with which each relevant situation is entered. All acts are not necessarily completed, and it is doubtful that the persistence of the tension to complete an act is sufficient in an infant for lasting preoccupations to develop, although learning to anticipate situations begins early. Recurring frustrated acts, however, probably have more lasting effects as the child reaches an age when acts are no longer easily diverted.

The institutional arrangement whereby frustration and gratification are vested in the same persons is important to the socialization process. Because the parents are such important sources of both experiences, the attitude developed toward them is ambivalent. The ambivalence robs

[13] William H. Sewell, "Infant Training and the Personality of the Child," *American Journal of Sociology*, 58:150–159, Summer 1952; Harold Orlansky, "Infant Care and Personality," *Psychological Bulletin*, 46:1–48, January 1949. For some positive evidence, see Frieda Goldman-Eisler, "Breastfeeding and Character Formation," in Clyde Kluckhohn, Henry A. Murray, and David M. Schneider (eds.), *Personality*, Knopf, New York, 1953, pp. 146–184.

[14] Ellsworth Faris, *The Nature of Human Nature*, McGraw-Hill, New York, 1937; George H. Mead, *The Philosophy of the Act*, University of Chicago Press, Chicago, 1938.

behavior of its spontaneity and renders behavior somewhat fortuitous, even for the actor himself.[15]

Social Framework of Frustration. An oversimplified conception that treats the organism as the source of desire and family and society as the sources of frustration has sometimes been followed. But the involvement of society and its agency, the family, is more complex. First, the impulses that are socially frustrated may themselves be social products. The family inculcates values in its members and may in turn frustrate them. Such thoroughly social values as honesty or the acquisition of wealth are as subject to social frustration as physiological drives. The frustration occurs because the family or society does not supply the opportunity to gratify the impulse or because contradictory values are also promoted. The family may promote the value of wealth and luxury in the child while living in poverty. Or the family may be the source of values of both the shrewd businessman and fair play, so that the individual encounters situations in which he must violate one of his values to follow another. The degree of restraint or seeming deprivation that people can undergo without experiencing frustration is phenomenal when society supplies no stimulation to a contradictory course of action.

Second, what constitutes gratification and frustration is relative, subject to social definition. The family helps create expected levels of consumption and achievement, and frustration is relative to these. The gratification of hunger, bodily discomfort from heat and cold, and sex desire are likewise judged quite differently according to the manner in which people have been taught to define their need levels.

Finally, deprivation is socially defined and mechanisms are socially provided for dealing with it. Courage in the face of danger, perseverance in a difficult task are clearly forms of deprivation not experienced as frustration so long as they are appropriately defined socially. Let them be redefined as foolhardiness and exploitation, and the identical forms of deprivation become frustrating. Meeting a socially approved test of some kind is normally experienced as gratifying rather than frustrating. The family plays an important part in defining a minor physical hurt as frustrating or as an opportunity for a test of endurance, in defining military service as annoyance or patriotic opportunity, and similar contingencies. Mechanisms for coping with frustration after it is experienced are likewise learned in the family, such as face-saving gestures, translation of misfortune into humor, or prayer. The socialization consequences of frustration are largely mitigated where techniques of this sort are learned.

[15] Sylvia Brody, *Patterns of Mothering*, International Universities Press, New York, 1956, pp. 73–109.

A portion of socialization is the conveyance of family culture, but another is the experience of gratification and frustration. Socialization consists as much of learning what to experience as frustration and learning relatively frustratable values as of reacting to frustration itself. The hypothesized effects of cumulative experiences of frustration in socialization are of two general kinds. One is the creation of preoccupations and anxieties that depress levels of aspiration and weaken resoluteness of action, lead to compulsive action, and combinations of these. The other is the shaping of the images of broad categories of people, so that subsequent interactions are slanted in advance.

Adaptation Milieu

There is more to the individual's relationship with his social environment than merely experiencing gratification or frustration and learning a set of reactions. The individual actively enters into the environment, learning ways to take advantage of it, to exercise control of it. Behavior that starts as a mere reaction to frustration or gratification turns out to afford the individual some mastery over his environment and hence is adopted as a recurring tactic of adaptation. Socially effective techniques other than those conveyed as culture are discovered and learned.

The adaptive learning approach places even more emphasis on social organization than the preceding view, since every social relationship becomes a milieu in which socialization consists of discovering the most rewarding system of adaptation. The social environment is conceived not primarily as a set of barriers but as a set of opportunities or challenges. The adaptation approach also facilitates the understanding of socialization to diversity as well as uniformity. The situation that each child in the family must master is different because it reflects the advantages and disadvantages of his own position and includes in the environment all his siblings.

Adaptive learning begins in the earliest experiences of the infant. The temper tantrum that originates as an expression of discomfort and tension can bring special solicitude from the parents. If it does, it is adaptive for the infant and is likely to be retained as an interpersonal technique. When parents are greatly concerned that the child eats regularly and that he does not experience physical discomfort, they often inadvertantly make the refusal to eat or the waking and crying pattern adaptive to the individual. The child then learns to refuse food when he is not sated or to cry during the night for the sake of the extra attention and favors he receives.[16]

---

[16] Lester W. Sontag, "Some Psychosomatic Aspects of Childhood," *The Nervous Child*, 5:296–304, 1946.

The adaptive learning of more enduring social significance takes place when the child begins to interact as a person. The youngest child may learn that displays of weakness bring quick assistance from his older siblings who enjoy tending him, but the older child cannot get results with such a tactic. A child may learn that a show of affection toward his parents usually softens their anger when he has violated a family rule. In a family in which overt conflict is feared, one child may discover that if he asserts himself loudly and angrily his parents often give him what he wants rather than allow an unpleasant scene to develop. Learned in the family, these techniques are then tested outside the family and, given moderate success, become generalized techniques for coping with interpersonal situations.

The adaptive framework allows special leeway for the hypothesis of an alternation of generations with respect to personality characteristics. There has been much popular speculation to the effect that the hard-working, resourceful self-made man provides everything for his son, who learns a passive, irresponsible pattern of adaptation, squandering his wealth. If the son is successful enough at squandering his wealth, his son in turn finds initiative and effort more adaptive than passive receptiveness, recapitulating the personality configuration of his grandfather. Although matters seldom proceed so simply and regularly in real life, Percival M. Symonds has presented some suggestive evidence in support of an alternation-of-generations hypothesis.[17] In response to an appeal to former students now working professionally with children, twenty-eight sets of comparisons, each between a child whose parents were dominating, strict, and punitive and one whose parents were submissive to the child were received. Each cooperating investigator was asked to make extensive, descriptive accounts of the behavior of an appropriate pair of children, including a report of a visit in the home, and to complete a behavior check list for each child. The number of cases is small, the selection of cases fortuitous and subject to unknown biases, and the observation procedures of the separate investigators unsupervised. Hence, conclusions can best be described as suggestive. With these qualifications, we quote from the study:

The results may be summarized by saying that children of dominating parents are better socialized and have more acceptable behavior than children of submissive parents. They show the results of training in their behavior. They are more interested in and have a better attitude toward work at school. On the other hand, they tend to be more sensitive, self-conscious, submissive, shy, retir-

[17] Percival M. Symonds, *The Psychology of Parent-Child Relationships*, Appleton-Century-Crofts, New York, 1939, pp. 104–140.

ing, seclusive, and to have greater difficulty in self-expression than children who are given more freedom. Children of dominating parents conform more closely to the mores of the group in which they are reared.

Children of submissive parents, on the other hand, are disobedient and irresponsible. In school they tend to be disorderly and classroom nuisances; they lack interest or capacity for sustained attention. They do not possess the regular orderly habits of the well-supervised child and are more inclined to be tardy and lazy. On the other hand, they are forward, and can express themselves effectively. They tend to defy authority, to be stubborn, and unmanageable. . . .[18]

Differences such as these are easily interpretable in part as the consequences of adaptive learning. Children in the two kinds of situations have learned what techniques enable them to get the most out of the family relationship. Outside the home they carry with them the same general approach to the mastery of situations they learned in relation to their parents.

Development of Meanings

Each of the foregoing relationships correctly describes some phases of the complex process of learning in the family. But each deals directly with the kind of responses that the individual learns to make to a situation. In the earlier discussion of interaction process (Chapter 2) we noted that interpretation intervenes between the situation and the response gesture. The structure of the situation is not intrinsic; it must be supplied through interpretation by the actor. In the discussion of socialization as learning in response to frustration we found it necessary to dwell on the fact that what is and is not frustrating is a function of the preparation that the actor brings to the experience. Seeing or hearing and interpreting are not ordinarily sharply separated, so that for the actor the interpretation he places on the experience is the fact he responds to. An even more fundamental kind of learning than adopting culture patterns as behavior guides, establishing reactions to frustration, and developing adaptions to situations is the acquisition of an interpretative framework through which events are experienced in preparation for the appropriate responses.

Culture as Interpretative Framework. Culture consists of a system of categories into which objects and experiences can be placed. The categories are linked in a system of meaningful relationships, so that the individual gains a feeling of understanding the object that has been classified. In addition to the objects in the physical world, these categories apply to people and their attributes, providing the individual with a framework through which to define his own feelings and actions as well as to impute attitudes to others. The categories include the values through which be-

[18] *Ibid.*, p. 118. Quoted by permission of the publisher.

havior is appraised as good or bad, the criteria by which it is adjudged rational or irrational, the motives by which the behavior of self and others is explained and predicted, and the sentiments by which subjective sensations are identified and the linkage between subjective states and overt behavior established.

The family is foremost in presenting this interpretative framework to the child by a combination of making symbolic indications and establishing a matrix of interaction such that the individual can only predict and exercise control over the behavior of others by organizing his own experience in accordance with the framework. By naming objects, motives, feelings, and values, the family members indicate the categories of experience to the children. By engaging in conversation in which the symbols are used instead of actual objects, their indications assign the categories a reality independent of the phenomena themselves. At the same time, the behavior of older family members is so completely linked to the interpretative framework that the child can adequately prepare himself for parental responses only by learning and adopting the same framework, by learning to make basically the same interpretations of events and gestures that others in the family are making. Hence an adaptive mechanism works to facilitate the incorporation of the cultural framework into the child's perspective.

Values are indicated by labeling events and behavior and exhibiting a comprehensive pattern of response. The child's naïve defense of his sister against an older child is labeled courage, and evidences of approval are heaped on him. A friend's drawing is called beautiful or creative, or some product of hammer and saw is described as ingenious. The loss of money is labeled wasteful; lying late in bed is labeled lazy. The child learns gradually to incorporate such value judgments as a part of his experience of others and of himself.

Motives. The child also finds himself in a situation in which every socially consequential action is assumed to have a motive that accounts for it.[19] If no socially comprehensible motive can be assigned, the actor must be out of his mind. Designation of an acceptable motive is treated as explaining the behavior. The motive assigned to the behavior normally has the same kind of positive or negative evaluation as the behavior itself. But under some circumstances the assignment of a good motive for a bad action can deflect disapproval, and the assignment of an evil motive for a good action can take away credit for the act. Motives, then, are more

[19] The discussion of motives reflects the thinking of Charles Blondel, in *The Troubled Conscience and the Insane Mind*, Trench, Trubner, London, 1928; Kenneth Burke, *Permanence and Change: An Anatomy of Purpose*, Bobbs-Merrill, Indianapolis, 1965; Hans Gerth and C. Wright Mills, *Character and Social Structure: The Psychology of Social Institutions*, Harcourt, Brace & World, New York, 1953, pp. 112–129.

powerful weapons than actions in manipulating social approval and disapproval.

The relationship of motives to control is illustrated by the manner in which the child is first given the idea of motive. Questions of motive are not raised in the ordinary course of behavior but only when unexpected and disturbing behavior occur. When the child misbehaves, he is asked, "Why did you do that?" or told why he did it. Designation of a motive that is convincing to the parent is necessary to bring interaction to a conclusion. Occasionally a good motive works and removes all disapproval. But usually a bad motive, followed by the appropriate evidence of remorse, is required. Acceptance of the bad motive does not necessarily avert punishment, but it brings matters to an end and permits the resumption of other interaction. Once the idea of motive is grasped in crude form, the child demands to know the motives for all kinds of behavior by others and sometimes even by himself. As he learns to identify his own impulses according to the repertoire of motives he has been supplied with, he gains a basis for making self-conscious direction of his own behavior.

Each family imparts its own repertoire of motives and its own degree of leeway in assigning motives to behavior. From his distinctive vantage point, each member of the family learns a somewhat different system of motives.

Sentiments. Sentiments are socially distinguished kinds of feeling. Each has its socially learned forms of overt expression and its socially recognized place in interaction. Sentiments such as mother love, mate love, indignation, pity, sympathy, resentment, jealousy, shame, guilt, pride, and aesthetic feeling must be learned. They have emotion at their base but are socially organized and evaluated systems of response. Anger and fear, as simple emotions, are socially neutral. But the sentiments such as indignation and temper are sharply differentiated socially. Sentiments have a common base of human responsiveness that probably depends on rather intimate interaction for its original evocation.[20] But their organization into socially meaningful units means that exactly the same set of sentiments is not found in all societies and the character of the sentiments varies among individuals according to the circumstances of their socialization.

C. H. Cooley argued that the intimate primary-group kind of interaction is the precondition to the development of the underlying element of human responsiveness to other human beings in such forms as tenderness and pride.[21] Children raised in large institutions without the oppor-

---

[20] See Gordon W. Allport, *Personality and Social Encounter*, Beacon Press, Boston, 1960, esp. pp. 199 ff.; and *Becoming: Basic Considerations for a Psychology of Personality*, Yale University Press, New Haven, Conn., 1955, pp. 31–35.
[21] Charles H. Cooley, *Human Nature and the Social Order*, Scribner, New York, 1902.

tunity to experience intimate primary-group interaction would be expected to lack something in the warmth and intensity of response to people. Anger and fear, which by themselves are simple emotions rather than social sentiments, would not necessarily be lacking. But the relations among people would be more impassive than for the child raised in the primary group.

The organization of social responsiveness and feeling into specific sentiments incorporating appropriate behavior proceeds in much the same way as the designation of motives.[22] Indeed, sentiments are one kind of recognized motivation that the individual may claim. The child must learn to discover and identify a complex of subjective sensations as the appropriate reaction to a situation that finds him in a specified relationship with others. When he has been frustrated and his frustration can be attributed to violation of norms by another person, he learns to identify the sensations he is feeling as indignation. When he feels a subjective disturbance over misfortune experienced by a person socially less powerful than himself, he learns to call this compassion. In both cases the reaction is identified as socially approved, and the sentiment as such could not be experienced until the individual had learned the norms applicable to the situation. When he identifies the feeling as indignation or compassion, the child must learn that there is a somewhat distinctive tone of voice that must be assumed in each case if others are to accept the child's conception of his own sentiment. Likewise, some kind of action appropriate to the indignation or compassion is required. Once learned, the connections are automatic, so that the tone of voice is used without thought and the pressure to act indignantly or compassionately is internal in the same way as the pressure to complete any act. The nature of social sentiments will be discussed further in Chapters 10 and 13, dealing with love.

Symbols. Through all these forms of socially established meanings there runs the concretizing and legitimatizing function of symbols. Symbolic designations—principally language—are used to communicate about the intrinsically private sense of value, motive, and sentiment. Without symbols it is inconceivable that values, motive, and sentiment could exist. Symbols not only make these meanings possible; they limit or facilitate the kinds of meanings that can be experienced. Basil Bernstein has distinguished between a *public* language and a *formal* language, suggesting that the two systems of symbolism offer different possibilities for abstract thought.[23] A public language is "descriptive, tangible, concrete, visual, and of a low order of generality" and is capable of communicating only diffuse

[22] Charles Blondel, *Introduction à la Psychologie Collective*, Colin, Paris, 1952.
[23] Basil Bernstein, "Some Sociological Determinants of Perception," *British Journal of Sociology*, 9:159–174, June 1958.

and crudely differentiated feelings. Because of its crude and imprecise character, a public language is an impediment to abstract thought and intelligence. A formal language makes use of "subtle arrangements of words and connections between sentences" to convey fine differences of feeling. Mastery of such a language prepares the individual to make abstract relationships among objects the basis for thought. Because only public language is normally learned in the working-class home, the child has difficulty with complex symbolic tasks at school and scores poorly on intelligence tests. The middle-class child, who is more likely to have learned a formal language, appears to have higher intelligence when tested on his ability to handle abstractions.

It is now possible to clarify the initial assertion that socialization is simply the process of cumulative development of self- and other conceptions, which is the normal by-product of every interaction episode. Objects become meaningful when their nature implies the kind of action that people take toward them. The framework of meaning learned through the socialization process consists of ways of seeing objects from the standpoint of various kinds of actors. The framework of meanings is thus acquired in the course of forming images of self and others.

A further development of the theory of socialization to cultural meanings and particularly of the manner in which the process can lend to diversity as well as uniformity will be made in connection with the discussion of roles in Chapter 9.

Summary

Socialization is social interaction examined as the process by which a person learns a working relationship with the social order. Although learning to conform is the most conspicuous and simplest aspect of socialization, it is only one of the forms of relationship that the individual learns. Because of the priority and continuity of family experience, the family is generally regarded as the major locus of socialization.

The substance, as distinct from the process, of socialization consists of four kinds of learning. First, socialization is the conveyance of family culture. Conveyance is more complicated than simple imitation of the behavior of models, since it includes canalization, transmission of social and material techniques, and identification. Second, socialization consists of learned responses to the frustrations and gratifications of various impulses. Again, socialization to frustration is not merely a response to societal norms and conditions that interfere with physiological needs. Many of the impulses that are frustrated are themselves social products, and socially induced impulses often collide. Society, through the family, teaches the individual what events are to be experienced as frustrating and provides the means for handling frustrations of various sorts. Third, socialization consists of learning effective adaptations to the situations in which the socializee often finds himself. Finally, socialization is the acquisition of an interpretative framework that determines the meanings people assign to experience. Included are values, motives, and sentiments, and the medium through which meanings are transmitted is the symbol. The meanings of objects inhere in the actions people take toward them. The framework of meanings is acquired (the core of socialization) through the process of seeing objects from the standpoint of the various kinds of actors in the individual's range of experience, among which the family members are first and most continuous in their significance.

Transition

We have stated some principles governing operation of the four processes that are central to our interest in family interaction. Although our illustrations are mostly from family life, we have tried to identify principles of bonding, decision making, conflict-harmonization, and socialization that should apply to a variety of groups, of which the family is but a special case. We are approaching the point where our main concern is to identify the peculiarities of the family that give these processes distinctive patterns, unlike the patterns found in other groups.

If distinctive meanings are attached to gestures in families as compared with other groups, it must be because families bear a somewhat unique relationship to society. If family bonds are vulnerable to different exigencies than the bonds in other groups or if distinctive devices for conciliating conflict prevail in families, the explanation should be sought in the distinctive ways in which family and society interact. Hence we look for principles that describe the ways in which society imposes a distinctive pattern of organization on family life and through which the social setting contributes meanings to gestures and influences the course of family processes on a day-to-day basis.

Two general tendencies supply the key to much of the remaining analysis in this book. First is the tendency for any lasting group to develop a structure of *roles*. Roles bring the various family processes into a comprehensive organization. Through the principles of *functionality* and *viability*, family role structure is shaped by the tasks assigned or left to the family by society and by the roles that family members play outside the family. Second is the tendency for a lasting group to develop a distinctive tone or quality that pervades all interaction within it and thus to affect every process and the meaning of every gesture. The family is nearly unique among groups in the expectation that members act toward one another with exceptional responsibility and yet that all such responsible behavior occurs with complete spontaneity. This union of responsibility and spontaneity is accomplished through the social sentiment of love.

Part 3 of this book explores the organization of family life into roles and the nature and effects of the distinctive tone of family interaction embodied in the sentiments of love.

ROLES AND SENTIMENT

CHAPTER 9

THE FAMILY AS A SYSTEM OF ROLES

In our search for underlying patterns that will help us understand the family group we observed that a process of bonding sorts individuals into groups; that interactions become shaped into episodes of making and executing family decisions and of engaging in conflict or harmonization; and that successive episodes of interaction have cumulative effects on the way family members approach subsequent interaction that we call socialization. All these processes are further organized into a somewhat recurrent drama in which family members develop and play identifiable roles. The tasks and identities of family life are divided up and grouped into roles, and each family member is cast in a particular set of roles. Each family member then depends on the others playing their roles to make it possible for him to play his role, or else he must induce others to change their roles so that he can change his.

The first essential in the idea of role is that the various activities that can take place in a group are clustered, and once a member establishes a particular cluster of activities as his, he is supposed to stay with his own cluster and not dabble in the activities of another role. The mother role clusters the activities of cooking, housekeeping, and attention to the child's physical needs, and it is thought natural and consistent for whoever does one of these tasks to do all of them. This principle applies not only to the roles associated with well-defined status in the family—mother, father, oldest child, grandmother, for example—but also to the informal and often more identity-laden roles described by Benne and Sheats, such as *encourager, harmonizer, compromiser, aggressor, blocker, recognition seeker*, and others.[1]

A second essential principle of role theory is that, once a system of roles is developed, family processes proceed haltingly unless the members play their respective roles. If ego cultivates the role of mediator in family conflict, others are likely to become less restrained in their tendency to insti-

---

[1] Kenneth D. Benne and Paul Sheats, "Functional Roles of Group Members," *Journal of Social Issues*, 4:41–49, Spring 1948.

gate conflict, depending on ego to mediate and restore harmony. Once such dependence is established, family conflicts go unresolved unless ego plays his role. Reciprocally, ego's influence and standing in the family may depend heavily on his skills as mediator, and his position diminishes when others cease to play their antagonist roles. A chronic dissenter in the family may constantly force others to consider alternative ways of handling family tasks and prod them into making decisions instead of letting events take their course. A family that has come to depend on the dissenter suddenly collapses into indecisiveness and de facto decisions become the rule when ego discontinues his dissent.

A third essential principle of role theory is that ego takes the role of alter in order to determine what role to play himself and how to play it. *Role taking* means placing oneself imaginatively in alter's position in order to assign a role to him. Ego's image of alter is formed by identifying his characteristic roles, and the interpretation of his gestures depends on identifying the role that alter is playing. Because of role taking there is a dynamic tension between stability and repetition on the one hand and innovation and change on the other. It is easiest for ego to play out the standard role of parent, daughter, and the like, and the habitual interpersonal roles he has been cast in. But the more clearly he understands alter's role, the stronger the tendency to innovate in order to cope more effectively with alter's behavior than his customary role enables him to. A mother is frequently torn between acting the way she understands a mother is supposed to act and trying something quite different when her efforts with her child seem ineffectual. We shall stress this coexistence of continuous change and resistance to change in family role structure throughout our subsequent analysis.

In applying role theory to family interaction, we shall first examine role differentiation and allocation, the fundamental processes of organizing activity into separate roles and assigning roles to individuals. Then we shall look at some of the peculiarities of stabilized role systems, such as abound in families. Next we shall consider how role change can take place in the family, and we shall conclude by noting how role systems organize the socialization process.

Role Differentiation and Allocation

Research with small groups has abundantly demonstrated that, when people engage in collaborative activity for several sessions, a role structure develops spontaneously. The two processes in the development of role structure are *differentiation* and *allocation*. Differentiation is the grouping of activities into what are regarded as consistent packages, so that whoever does *a* also does *b* and *c* but does not do *e*, *f*, and *g*. Allocation is casting—assigning particular individuals to play particular roles.

The family does not, of course, form spontaneously. The basic role differentiations are culturally predefined, into what husbands do, what wives do, what male children do, and so forth. But choices are still available among alternative kinds of parent and child roles, and the skeletal roles are subject to elaboration and modification. Furthermore, much of the content of the culturally standard role differentiations embodies patterns that would develop spontaneously in the kind of family situation people encounter at a given time and place, even in the absence of culturally predefined roles. The emergence of recurrent forms of role differentiation in groups, irrespective of the kinds of members who compose them, reflects two general principles. One is each member's search for a *viable* position, and the other is the *functional* requirements of the group.

A viable position is one from which the individual can develop a strategy of action and establish an identity in the group. The term itself has been popularized in game theory, where a viable position is one that allows the individual to remain in the game. It is not necessarily a winning or altogether satisfactory position, but it is one from which the individual can avoid being forced out of the game.

The functional principle rests on the simple observation that not all imaginable combinations of roles work and that some combinations work better than others. If a workable role differentiation is not attained, the group falls apart, or it fails to accomplish its aims.

Viable Roles. One of the simplest contexts in which to understand the construction of a viable role is in relation to a well-established concentration of dominance in the family. Very unequal dominance represents a potential threat to other family members, who may have difficulty maintaining self-esteem and be unable to satisfy their interests. Responses to dominance consist either of developing some strategy to offset the dominance partially or of cultivating a special pattern of satisfactions that can be best realized in a situation of subordination.

A common device to offset domination in part is to develop one or more special spheres of family life in which the otherwise subordinated person exercises complete control. In the traditional patriarchal American family the wife characteristically made the kitchen her special province and, although submitting to her husband in most matters, contrived to convince her husband that only a woman knew what to do in the kitchen. The low prestige of kitchen competence made his invasion of her special province unlikely. But to protect her province more fully, she found it necessary to maintain an air of mystery about the kitchen, to prepare the kitchen with booby traps against occasional invasion by the male, and to inculcate in her sons a profound conviction of their own incompetence in the kitchen.

Mystery is commonly maintained by the use of jargon and by insisting that personalized judgment and experience rather than a standard formula is the only way a result can be attained. The special language of cooking is akin to the secret passwords of children and the jargon of adolescents in supplying an air of mystery to commonplace transactions. In each instance a subordinated group is attempting to carve out its private sphere of activity in which it is free from surveillance. The insistence that a good cook judges how much of each ingredient to use by feel rather than using standard measures serves the same end.

The booby traps are strategems to complicate the task of the male who sets foot in the kitchen and again are like the conspiracies by which adolescents manage to make adults who try to invade the adolescent world look like fools. A private system for keeping supplies, often in unlabeled containers, serves in this respect. If it can also be arranged that a male leaves sufficient confusion after being in the kitchen so that the preparation of his next few meals is impared, the woman's province is protected.

Folk literature has often helped to convey the conviction of male domestic incompetence. A Mother's Day seldom passes without comic strips taking up the traditional plot in which father and son try to get breakfast in bed for mother, with such awful results that they eventually let her prepare an edible meal and clean up the mess they have created. The socialization process within the family proceeds by selective interpretation. When a daughter drops a dish, she must be more careful in the future. When a son drops a dish, it is only to be expected when a man comes into the kitchen.

With the shifting dominance situation in the family, it is sometimes the husband who looks for an area of masculine competency from which he can exclude women. Children form secret clubs that on examination lack the sinister nature that parents sometimes ascribe to them.

Invasion of these private spheres threatens the working role structure of the family and may even threaten the dominance of the invader by leaving the subordinate no option but frontal challenge. In the many American families in which the wife's insulation from the world outside the immediate neighborhood ensures her ultimate subordination within the family, the sharing of domestic chores by her husband is more of a threat to her viable position than a relief from drudgery. The wife who insists on preparing meals when she is ill rather than letting her husband do so may be driven by an important consideration beyond simple duty.

A second stratagem to offset one-sided dominance is the cultivation of understanding of the dominant person. A subordinated person may learn to make the best of his situation and to win frequent concessions by learning to detect the moods of the dominant person and to identify the kinds of appeal he is least able to resist. There is an elaborate folklore among employees about the most favorable circumstances for approaching their employers to ask for a raise in pay or a day off. Secretaries are thought to learn to read their employers' minds. Under systems of slavery the slave owners are usually insensitive to the attitudes of their slaves, frequently holding totally false images with utter confidence. Among the slaves, however, there normally develops a considerable lore about each master, and sometimes great sensitivity to the subtle gestures of the master. In each of these instances the one-sided sensitivity and understanding are a consequence of the differential adaptive utility of such understanding. The master gives orders that must be obeyed. If his dominance is sure enough, he need pay little attention to the attitudes of his subordinates. To the subordinates who can only seek willing compliance with their requests, however, every bit of understanding of their superior increases their chances of planning an effective strategy. Because it is adaptive, such differential learning is likely to be a normal aspect of the socialization to a dominance-submission relationship.

There has long been a belief in a special faculty called women's intuition. Although the belief is undoubtedly largely a myth that helps buttress the traditional male-female role differentiation, a plausible case can be made that it has a partial foundation in fact. Under the long-standing subordination of women to men, learning to detect and interpret the subtle gestures of the opposite sex accurately has been more adaptive for the woman than for the man. Such learning comes partly from individual discovery during the socialization process, partly from the accumulation of a woman's repertoire of folk techniques for understanding and dealing with men, and partly from the selective direction of attention during interaction. This explanation offers no support for such mystical aspects of women's intuition as a supposed ability to anticipate events. Furthermore, it makes women's intuition specifically the consequence of their subordination, leading to the prediction that most of it will have disappeared in American society during the last two generations of equalization between the sexes. Finally, the hypothesis is complicated in practice by the situation in which a mother and son form a coalition against a very dominant father, so that the son learns the sensitivity both directly from his adaptive situation and through communication from his mother.

Roslind Dymond has made a study of empathic ability of group members, comparing the performance of men and women.[2] Empathy was de-

[2] Roslind F. Dymond, "A Scale for the Measurement of Empathic Ability," *Journal of Consulting Psychology*, 13:127–133, April 1949. There are important difficulties with this method of measuring empathic ability, some of which relate to specific theoretical meanings assigned to empathy and some of which involve statistical artifacts in the measurement process. For our use of the concept, and with the emphasis on change among the same group of individuals, most of these difficulties are of minor relevance. See Lee J. Cronbach, "Processes Affecting Scores on 'Understanding of Others' and 'Assumed Similarity,'" *Psychological Bulletin*, 52:177–193, May 1955.

fined as "the imaginative transposing of oneself into the thinking, feeling and acting of another and so structuring the world as he does." The instrument for measuring this ability consisted of four sets of five-point ratings, each using the same six personal traits. Each group member first (a) rated himself on each of the six traits, then (b) rated each other member of the group, (c) rated each other member as he thought he would rate himself, and (d) rated himself as he thought each member would rate him. Comparisons between ego's judgment of how alter rates himself and alter's own self-rating and between ego's judgment of how alter rates ego and alter's own rating of ego supply a measure of error that serves as a negative index of empathic ability. Twenty-nine female and twenty-four male members of a social psychology class were divided into ten groups that met once a week to discuss and plan a class project. The rating test was administered after the third meeting and again six weeks later. Each student's deviation score was computed as the total number of points he was in error in his ratings for all the members of his group. The mean deviation scores are shown in Table 3. On the first test there was no difference between the sexes. But after the groups had met several times, the women students were able to improve their empathic ability significantly, but the men were not. The improvement is not large or impressive, but it is consistent with the hypothesis that women are better able than men to detect and interpret the gestures that indicate an individual's attitudes toward himself and others after a period of acquaintance.

Both of these strategies contribute to a differentiated but interdependent system of roles, combining activity and identity orientation in each role. There are also other modes of adaptation that do not counter the dominance but sieze on possible advantages of subordination. One common adaptation of this kind is the role of the irresponsible critic. An advantage shared by the political party that is out of power and all subordinated

TABLE 3   EMPATHIC ABILITY OF MEN AND WOMEN

| | Mean Deviation Score | |
Trial	Males	Females
First	52.1	51.4
Second	50.9	45.6

SOURCE: Adapted from Roslind Dymond, *op. cit.*, p. 130, by permission of the American Psychological Association.

groups is that they escape responsibility for the whole group's errors. Similarly, if the husband dominates family decision making on financial matters, he must also be prepared to accept responsibility for financial crises in the family. Freed from such responsibility the wife and children can indulge themselves in several ways. First, they can propose unreasonable schemes and plead for unreasonable expenditures in confidence that the responsible person will make the considered decision. Second, they can criticise the dominant person freely. If the dominant person's decisions are wise, the subordinate person has lost nothing. But whenever the decisions turn out to have been wrong, the subordinate is in the position to point out how much better his judgment was. The traditional nagging wife often makes use of this strategem through her constant criticism. Her role would quickly lose its viability if the husband began to act on her suggestions and challenges. The "wise" person who remains untroubled by crises while constantly calling attention to just how badly things are being handled is employing a similar device. The person rendered impotent by subordination can devise a role in which he exploits the twin privileges of uninhibited symbolic expression of his impulses and the cultivation of the Monday-morning quarterback's sense of superior judgment.

A variation on the same principle is the cultivation of moral perfection. Few if any are able to meet the complex demands of life in modern society without compromising the ethical ideals from their religion or humanistic philosophy. The monastery is an institutional arrangement to permit selected individuals to attain a higher degree of moral perfection than would be possible if they were forced to cope with the world in the normal manner. In American family life women were traditionally the guardians of moral idealism and responsible for inculcation of religious ideals in the children. The eighteenth-century novel *Pamela: or Virtue Rewarded*, by Samuel Richardson, depicts in prototype the theme that pure virtue is the only proper course of action for a woman in distress.

Still another adaptation to dominance is the strategy of weakness demanding protection. The tradition of chivalry perpetuates a whole set of protective measures owed the weaker sex by the male in return for the unquestioned acknowledgment of his dominance. Children often learn to cultivate this device, displaying a weakness and need for nurturance within the home that is quite in contrast to their ability to handle themselves among their peers.

A final adaptation is to become the mediator who softens the impact of the dominant individual on other members of the group. Where the father is a disciplinarian, the mother may carve out a gratifying role by supplying the salve after a whipping, sneaking food to the child after he has been sent to bed without dinner, and serving as the confidante to whom the children can say freely the things that would get them into trouble with father. This comforting or nurturant role has marked rewards in relations with the other subordinate members of the groups and can be exercised most readily by a person who does not actually control group decisions.

Dominance is a major axis about which viable roles are differentiated, but it is not the only one. Another is the protection of a common value. There is often some ambivalence toward even the values that are most important to an individual. The result is that under appropriate circumstances one can be either the advocate or the challenger of the same value. If he finds the value under attack and in apparent danger, he is roused to its defense. When the value is being securely advocated and he can be confident that the value will withstand the attack, he is likely to become the challenger if there are no social penalties attached to this part. In established relationships some polarization into advocate and challenger roles regarding major shared values is a common development. This is one of the frequent by-products of deliberate socialization. Because the parents adopt unqualified advocacy of the values in question, the only role that offers any unique or creative opportunity or provides any basis for interaction other than playing yes man is the challenger role. The child may be adopting the value in spite of his family role. Both parents and children are often surprised at the extent to which the children in other situations become ardent advocates of the values they have regularly challenged within the family. On the other hand, the response to the challenger role is often to become a stronger advocate than one's convictions warrant. The person allocated the advocate role finds himself setting standards he would not otherwise have done. Children who regarded their parents as prudes are sometimes surprised in later life to find out how their parents behave when freed from the socialization responsibility.

Functional Role Differentiation. Functional role differentiation includes the division of labor that is specific to the activities of the group in question and division according to the universal requirements of decision making and decision execution, conflict control, and bonding that apply to all groups. The socialization function of the family requires a differentiation into agent and socializee roles that is not required in a different kind of group. The procreation function requires some differentiation between husband and wife that allows the wife to concentrate her attention on the infant during crucial intervals.

The division of labor between husband and wife has differed greatly from time to time and from society to society. Sometimes it is clear that the division of labor has been adapted to the activities pursued in the family;

for example, the requirements of American frontier family life modified the northwest European division of labor, because women had to become adept at some of the traditional masculine skills if the family was to survive. On the other hand any close correspondence between dominant family functions and patterns of role differentiation between husband and wife has not been demonstrated by cross-cultural or intracultural research.

Bales and associates have hypothesized the necessity for two kinds of leadership in groups, one concentrating on the task or problem at hand and the other on the problem of relations among the members of the group. As we have already noted, in the process of reaching and carrying out group decisions, there are likely to be threats to the identities of group members. Such threats create a danger that task behavior will be diverted to conflict, with the result that decisions are not completed. Hence the specifically task-oriented interaction must be accompanied by an identity-oriented process of conciliation. Group members are likely to feel ambivalent toward their task leader. Disproportionate responsibility for the choice between acceptable and unacceptable ideas and for the allocation of desirable and undersirable roles in the division of labor is assigned to the task leader. Furthermore, his superior power and superior knowledge are potentially threatening to the identities of group members. Consequently, although he is respected and admired, relations with him must be somewhat guarded, somewhat lacking in ease and intimacy. He cannot then effectively mediate the tensions that arise between identities. Another person who is less involved in task leadership is in a better position to resolve identity problems among the members. He can joke so as to lessen the seriousness of the entire matter, and he can offer supportive remarks to bolster threatened identities.

The principle here is twofold. First, if a group is to function effectively, there are two different areas in which leadership must be supplied. Second, the nature of the two areas is such that each kind of leadership is more effective if it is specialized rather than concentrated in a single individual.

Bales and Slater report research designed to test this hypothesis.[3] Sixteen groups of three to six paid Harvard undergraduate males were assembled, and each was observed in a small group laboratory for four sessions. Groups were made up of strangers and were required to reach a group decision regarding a hypothetical administrative problem. Their interaction was observed and recorded in the manner described for the Bales-Strodtbeck study of phases in group problem solving (see Chapter

[3] Robert F. Bales and Philip E. Slater, "Role Differentiation in Small Decision-making Groups," in Talcott Parsons and R. F. Bales, *Family: Socialization and Interaction Process*, Free Press, New York, 1955, pp. 259 ff.

5), and members were ranked by their frequencies of talking and receiving communications. After each session the subjects were asked to rank the members of the group according to (a) who contributed the best ideas for solving the problem, (b) who did the most to guide the discussion and keep it moving effectively, and (c) how well you personally like each of the members. An effort was then made to determine which of these rankings were more closely associated with the others (see Table 4). The evidence is rather clear that talking, receiving, supplying ideas, and guiding discussion are interrelated, but being liked is less closely related to the other variables. Some support is thus supplied for the hypothesis of a specialization between task leadership and leadership in the area of personal feelings.

Bales and Slater then eliminated sessions in which ties for top rank occurred on either the ideas or liking ranking and those in which the best liked was highest on either ideas or guidance. From the remaining 23 sessions a comparison of the behavior of the two kinds of specialists can be made. Table 5 has been reproduced from their report. It should be remembered that categories 1 to 3 and 10 to 12 reflect social-emotional orientations and categories 4 to 9 reflect task orientations. The authors summarize the table as follows:

Note that the man in the top Idea position is higher in giving suggestions and opinions whereas the man in the top Liked position is higher in giving and receiving solidarity and tension release. The Idea man seems to receive more agreement. The Liked man, perhaps somewhat paradoxically, shows more negative reactions although he does not receive significantly more. The Liked man also may be slightly higher than the Idea man in asking for opinion and suggestion. These differences may perhaps be best summarized by saying that the Idea man shows a concentration of activity in the task area, whereas the Liked man shows

TABLE 4   TASK AND SOCIAL-EMOTIONAL LEADERSHIP

Number of sessions out of a possible 56 in which a given person holds top position in one and only one rank order out of five possible rank orders.

Talking	6.0
Receiving	6.5
Ideas	7.0
Guidance	8.1
Liking	22.8
Total	50.4

SOURCE: Adapted from Bales and Slater, op. cit., p. 278, by permission of the publisher and the authors.

TABLE 5   COMPOSITE PROFILES OF 23 TOP MEN ON IDEA RANKING AND 23 TOP MEN ON LIKE RANKING FOR THE SAME SESSIONS

Interaction Category	Initiated		Received	
	Idea Men	Liked Men	Idea Men	Liked Men
1. Shows solidarity	4.19	4.79	2.90	3.68
2. Shows tension release	5.97	7.71	8.40	10.38
3. Shows agreement	14.60	14.97	22.92	17.88
4. Gives suggestion	8.66	5.68	6.14	6.36
5. Gives opinion	31.30	27.20	26.28	28.86
6. Gives orientation	17.90	17.91	15.24	13.73
7. Asks orientation	3.66	3.43	2.78	3.01
8. Asks opinion	2.39	2.73	2.00	1.98
9. Asks suggestion	.98	1.58	.72	.33
10. Shows disagreement	7.31	8.43	9.5	10.21
11. Shows tension increase	1.97	3.67	1.30	1.37
12. Shows antagonism	1.07	1.90	1.74	2.21

SOURCE: Taken from Bales and Slater, *op. cit.*, p. 279, by permission of the publisher and the authors.

a concentration in the socio-emotional types of activity, both positive and negative.[4]

Morris Zelditch, Jr., has explored the applicability of the same hypothesis of role differentiation to the family by a comparison of customary patterns in 56 culturally distinct societies. Drawing on the theoretical formulations of Parsons and associates, he labels the two roles *instrumental leadership*, referring to task emphasis, and *expressive leadership*, emphasizing identity relations. The principal criteria for classifying cases on the basis of ethnographic reports were set down as follows:[5]

Ego is the instrumental leader if:
Ego is boss-manager of the farm; leader of the hunt, etc. Ego is the final court of appeals, final judge and executor of punishment, discipline, and control over the children of the family.
or if:
Alter shows respect to ego; the relations of ego and alter are constrained, reserved; alter on occasions indicates hostility toward ego.

[4] *Ibid.*, p. 280, by permission of the publisher and the authors.
[5] Morris Zelditch, Jr., "Role Differentiation in the Nuclear Family: A Comparative Study," in Parsons and Bales, *op. cit.*, pp. 307–351; criteria adapted from pp. 318–320, by permission of the publisher and the author.

or if:

>Ego's siblings are equated in status and role with ego, and play an instrumental role with respect to ego's children; e.g., father's sister is treated with respect, and is called "female-father."

Ego is the expressive leader if:

>Ego is the mediator, conciliator, of the family; ego soothes over disputes, resolves hostilities in the family. Ego is affectionate, solicitous, warm, emotional to the children of the family; ego is the "comforter", the "consoler", is relatively indulgent, relatively unpunishing.

or if:

>Alter is at ease in ego's presence, emotionally attached to ego, is close and warm in relation to ego.

or if:

>Ego's siblings are equated in status and role with ego and play an expressive role with respect to ego's children; e.g., mother's sister is terminologically a "mother" and is warm, indulgent, close. Or mother's brother is termed "male-mother" and is warm, indulgent, etc.

Testing the hypothesis that the two forms of leadership are differentiated, Zelditch found 46 cases of differentiation as opposed to 10 in which such differentiation was lacking. He notes further that some of the 10 cases may not be truly negative on more careful examination. But adhering conservatively to the gross findings, we must conclude that there is strong support for the hypothesis of a general tendency to differentiate adult family roles between task and identity emphasis, although family systems may, in a minority of cases, be able to work out a different principle of roles that operates effectively.

A somewhat different kind of functional differentiation into roles is suggested in a study of secondary-school students by Matilda White Riley and Richard Cohn.[6] As we suggested in the earlier discussion of decision making, every group must have mechanisms for ensuring sufficient member conformity so that group decisions can be carried out. The principal mechanisms are approval of conformity and disapproval of deviance. Bonds between pairs in the group are threatened, however, when disapproval and approval are applied indiscriminately. Furthermore, it is known that attachments between persons prevent their seeing each other's faults fully. Riley and Cohn suggest that any individual receives approval when he conforms, from one group of associates, and disapproval when he deviates, from a different set. In this way he is subject to both positive and negative group controls, but the positive and negative control functions are differentiated. Whether it would be an appropriate extension of this reasoning to propose that a group such as the family differentiates member

[6] Matilda White Riley and Richard Cohn, "Control Networks in Informal Groups," *Sociometry*, 21:30–49, March 1958.

roles according to their positive or negative control activities, or whether each member exercises positive control over some and negative controls over others, is not clearly indicated. The data of the investigation cover only part of the general hypothesis, showing that the same student has relatively conforming traits attributed to him by his friends and nonconforming traits attributed to him by those who dislike him. It seems probable, however, that so important a function as ensuring commitment to group decisions supplies a basis in some manner for division among family roles.

Allocation of Roles. The question of who gets which role is partly independent of the question of what differentiation into roles occurs and partly interrelated. The two general principles at work are the fit of the role to the person and the relative dominance that determines access to roles on the basis of desirability. Whenever alternative role differentiations can be made to work in a group, the jockeying to fit persons to roles can determine which system of roles emerges.

When the choice is among roles that are of equal prestige and general desirability, the possession of different kinds of skills and congeniality between role and person prevail. Zelditch, in the study already mentioned, found that in 48 of the 50 societies the wife's role was the relatively more expressive. Apparently there is at work a consistent principle of allocation in most societies. Probably bearing and suckling the child places the mother in a more favorable position for performing the expressive role, and the restrictive periods brought on by pregnancy and suckling are obstacles to consistent enactment of the instrumental role.

Roles, however, are seldom of equal advantage and prestige. Division of labor normally works so as to enable the enactors of some roles to command greater reward than others. In modern society, for example, occupational roles are so organized that the manipulation of symbols brings larger rewards than the manipulation of concrete objects, the producer of a product more than its inventor, the administrator more than the technical expert. Given the unequal rewards attached to different roles, allocation involves a struggle in which the most desirable roles go to those who are able to dominate, in accordance with the principles cited in Chapter 6.

Role Systems in the Family Group

Role Systems in Groups. A role can be a part in the larger society, played by many individuals, such as the female role, the aged role, the hero role. But since members of a sustained group, such as the family, interact repeatedly, roles with a broad cultural reference tend to be replaced by comprehensive roles comprising the parts that each member regularly plays in the family. This tendency represents the preponderance of the interactional anchorage over the cultural role-playing anchorage, and the outcome is the adjusted communication and response discussed in Chapter 4. When it is observed that a great scientist is never a genius to his wife, a glamor girl almost inevitably is someone quite different to her husband, and the scholarship student is primarily the girl who fails to make her bed but is appreciative of her mother's cooking, the predominance of the intrafamily role is indicated.

The tendency to develop unique family roles is enhanced by a privacy barrier that insulates family interaction from the outside world. In occupations in which occupational effectiveness is contingent on maintaining a special image of the person, such as school teaching, it is often considered wise to ensure the insulation by living in a different neighborhood from one's clients. In contemporary urban families it is often a strain to have guests in the home, even when they are well liked. In front of outsiders the tendency to perform according to cultural role prescriptions is enhanced, and the unique family roles are held in abeyance. The result is that interaction is awkward, decisions must be reached by unpracticed procedures, and surface interpretations of gestures must be maintained in contradiction to mutual understanding. The insulation between family and outside is never complete, the self-conception penetrating the barriers if nothing else does. Hence the unique roles must have moderate compatibility with the members' cultural roles, a point we shall expand subsequently in discussing the actor in relation to his roles.

The unique system of roles determines the way the essential business of family life is carried on. In one family the roles are interrelated, so that decisions are made and activities carried out with a minimum of sentiment. In another the process of decision making requires expressions of affection for each to play his role. In still another, roles are so organized that expressions of anger are a necessary way of indicating that a decision is seriously desired, so that chronic conflict is built in as a phase of group decision making. The organization of roles can make explicit bargaining a necessary step in each transaction. It can place each member constantly on guard lest the other encroach on his prerogatives. Such differences in the manner in which the day-to-day interaction is carried out have sometimes been called differences in texture, some textures being smooth and some rough, some interesting and some uninteresting.[7]

The principle that interlocking roles become the only way in which the business of the group can be transacted without major reorganization

[7] For a study emphasizing the unique role structure in five families that were studied in depth, *see* Robert D. Hess and Gerald Handel, *Family Worlds*, University of Chicago Press, Chicago, 1959.

has given rise to the interesting hypothesis of *role appropriation*.[8] The hypothesis proceeds from a general assumption that there is a tendency for established roles in a group to perpetuate themselves irrespective of personnel changes. This is readily observable when a family takes in a new member, expecting him to fill the gap left by a recently lost member. In somewhat modified form it is apparent when the occupant of a less essential role changes his behavior to enact a more important role when the latter is lost to the family. Such changes occur when the father or mother dies and one of the children then abandons his child role to fill the parental one. The specific hypothesis is that the same role is not enacted by two members, so that if one member preempts another's role, the latter changes his behavior.

An interesting application of this hypothesis is to be found in a study of the child and his family in reaction to disaster. The problem was to determine from interviews with children and family members how the children were affected by a tornado that did a great deal of destruction in Vicksburg, Mississippi. Although there was frequently increased dependence on parents for reassurance and demand for attention and affection, there were some instances of reversed roles between parent and child. In these families the mother went to pieces, demanded attention and special consideration from those about her, including the children, and failed entirely to play the reassuring comforting role of the culturally standard mother. In these families the children did not show the same deterioration as the mother, but actually assumed to varying degrees the dependable, reassuring, comforting role normally expected of her. The authors of the study note that typically not more than one member of the family adopted so highly dependent a role and that others rose to the occasion in compensating degree.

Hypotheses that assign such extrapersonal reality to roles need to be treated with reasonable skepticism, as the authors of this study do. But when it is understood that the unique system of roles within the family has become the medium through which family life is transacted, it does not strain the sociologist's credulity too far to propose that members, who are well familiar with one another's roles through role taking, should automatically cover for one another when one fails to carry out his role. What we are not yet in a position to say, however, is what the conditions are that determine whether such covering takes place or not.

Normative Component of Roles. Under some circumstances some of the

[8] Stewart E. Perry, Earle Silber, and Donald Bloch, *The Child and His Family in Disaster*, National Academy of Sciences—National Research Council, Washington, 1956, pp. 34–35.

role conceptions that group members hold become norms. They become more than neutral anticipations that behavior follows a certain course; they become feelings that other members ought to behave in the anticipated manner. The two principal sources of such normative conceptions are the linkage of roles to culturally identified statuses and the implicit or explicit bargaining among group members for the allocation of roles. The former include the many familiar propositions about how a teacher, doctor, or minister should behave, the obligations of married status or of parenthood, and the duties of children toward their elders. The latter two are based on the reciprocity principle (Chapter 2) and justify the imposition of a set of obligations on one member of the group by acknowledging his right to demand that others in the group fulfill obligations toward him.

The bargaining principle underlies and justifies the normative aspects of roles attached to formal statuses, although the underlying bargain is seldom brought to light unless the norms are questioned. In the traditional marriage arrangement, the wife gives up the right to earn her own living, and in return she is entitled to alimony in case of divorce. The wife's obligation to forego financial independence is justified by the right to demand continued support from her husband. In the traditional family it is the child's obligation to obey his parents, but the obligation is justified by his parents' duty to set an exemplary standard of conduct for him. It is this principle which has led Clifford Kirkpatrick to speak of roles as collections of obligations and rights that must somehow be balanced in the minds of the participants if the roles are to be conscientiously followed.[9]

Working out the details of the unique family roles incorporates continual bargaining. Washing the dishes is traded for a period of television monopoly. A child's chore, such as mowing the lawn, is traded for the free control of his spending money. Each complete role and each task that can be incorporated in a unique role involves certain advantages or disadvantages. By allowing alter to play a role that is advantageous in some respects, ego feels entitled in the name of justice to incorporate some offsetting advantages in his own role.

The existence of such normative role conceptions, whether arising from the bargains made in the family or from outside notions of what the roles of husband and wife, mother and child, uncle or grandparent should be, introduces two kinds of complication into the family functioning. First, the unique family role evolved by a member may fall short of the normative conception or may exceed it. Second, the normative role conceptions of family members may differ or correspond. The first can be called *role adequacy*; the second, *role consensus* or *dissensus*.

[9] Clifford Kirkpatrick, "The Measurement of Ethical Consistency in Marriage," *International Journal of Ethics*, 46:444–460, July 1936.

During any interaction episode the role behavior may deviate from the characteristic role of the family member and in doing so may be adequate or inadequate with respect to the normative role conception. But we are concerned here with the relatively enduring patterns of interaction. The role inadequacy of the husband in the American family today is quite general, as reflected in the uniform theme of such family comic strips as "Blondie," "Dotty," and "The Berries." Both husband and wife admire the "strong" husband, the man who runs his family and is a pillar of strength in time of crisis. But few husbands are able to incorporate these qualities in the working roles in the family.

Role inadequacy is one of the prime conditions underlying chronic conflict in the family. It must be recalled that various kinds of disruption in the normal transaction of family business may or may not induce conflict, depending on whether the disruptions are attributed to the identity of one of the members. If the image that ego has of alter is one of high role adequacy, it is unlikely that the source of disruption is located in alter's identity. An established conception of role inadequacy, however, provides a ready explanation for any disruption. Hence every disruption is likely to start a conflict episode, with chronic conflict resulting.

A conception of exceptional role adequacy, on the other hand, does not necessarily set the stage for an intensified harmonization, because role phenomena can never be understood apart from the interplay between roles. An exceptional role adequacy not balanced by equally exceptional role adequacy on the part of the other becomes a threat to the latter's identity in two ways. First, ego's identity is made to appear all the more inadequate because of the constant example of alter's identity. Second, alter's over-compliance with his obligations makes ego morally indebted to alter, according to the reciprocity principle. In either case the effect is to establish a relationship between the two identities such that whatever enhances alter's identity damages ego's, and whatever damages alter's identity enhances ego's, which is the essence of conflict. Harmonization, then, is probably facilitated by a fairly high and balanced degree of role adequacy between family members.

Role dissensus is likewise a major condition provocative of chronic conflict. Role dissensus means that members are using different criteria in the judgment of adequacy, so that no system of working role relationships can actually satisfy the sense of justice of all the members. For this reason it is a plausible (but unsupported) hypothesis that role dissensus is more likely than low role adequacy to bring about cumulative conflict. A working set of patterns through which family business can be transacted in spite of chronic conflict can be evolved when members share the same standards for judging each other's adequacy. By accepting the same depressed evaluation of his identity that others hold, the inadequate member may adopt an appropriate pattern for himself. Others then may incorporate in their own roles some of the advantages they are entitled to in light of the first member's inadequacy, and an effective division of tasks and organization for decision making can result. But role dissensus forestalls this kind of adjustment.

An investigation by Alver Jacobson affords a possible empirical test of the correlation between role dissensus and cumulative conflict.[10] Jacobson interviewed a sample of divorced and married couples, presenting them with sets of statements designed to contrast a fairly comprehensive traditional conception of husband and wife roles with a modern conception. The divorced couples showed more indication that they were following contradictory sets of rules than the married couples.

Many studies of small groups and large-scale organizations have dealt with role consensus as a variable in group functioning. Generally such studies warrant the conclusion that task aspects of the group proceed more effectively and efficiently when role consensus exists. Decisions can be reached more easily, an effective division of labor can be developed, and members are more effective in carrying out the tasks assigned them when there is mutual agreement on what is each member's proper responsibility. In addition such studies show that members regard each other more favorably when role consensus is high.[11] To the extent to which the family situation is analogous, these studies suggest that role dissensus facilitates chronic and cumulative conflict both by the relationship established between identities and the obstacles it poses to satisfactory completion of activity objectives.

Kirkpatrick has called attention to a special form of role dissensus that characterizes the relations between the sexes in American society.[12] He proposes that there are three culturally acknowledged roles for the married woman. The *wife-and-mother* follows the traditional pattern of keeping the house, raising the children, and ministering tenderly to her husband. The *companion* serves principally as an aid in her husband's occupation, through being a gracious hostess and maintaining a glamorous and poised bearing. Housekeeping and care of children must be delegated to servants, so that the companion can perform her role properly. The

---

[10] Alver H. Jacobson, "Conflict of Attitudes toward the Roles of the Husband and Wife in Marriage," *American Sociological Review*, 17:146–150, April 1952.
[11] *See* Bertram H. Raven and Jan Rietsema, "The Effects of Varied Clarity of Group Goal and Group Path upon the Individual and His Relation to the Group," *Human Relations*, 10(1):29–44, 1957; Bernard Berelson and Gary A. Steiner, *Human Behavior: An Inventory of Scientific Findings*, Harcourt, Brace & World, New York, 1964, p. 353.
[12] Kirkpatrick, *loc. cit.*

partner has her own career and income, so that husband and wife roles are parallel. Household tasks, care of children, and the like, are no more the wife's than the husband's responsibility.

Each of these roles includes certain privileges not incorporated in the others, and each privilege is balanced by an appropriate responsibility; for example, the first two roles obligate the wife to be financially dependent and consequently carry with them the right to alimony in case of divorce. Since the third role imposes no such obligation, it is only fair that the wife should forego the right to alimony. In the second role the wife is obligated to remain attractive, relaxed, and gracious, in return for which she is entitled to freedom from housekeeping and child care. In choosing among roles of this sort, however, the connections between rights and duties are not always kept in mind. Hence women are likely to conceive of their role so as to include rights from more than one role but duties from only one, and men conceive the women's role as including duties from more than one role but rights from only one. Each sex forms a conception that places the balance of rights and duties in its own favor.

To test his hypothesis, Kirkpatrick used an inventory of role conceptions, consisting of statements of rights and duties of married women, drawing on each of the three roles just described. The inventory was administered to 161 men and 241 women students at the University of Minnesota, and to 152 of their fathers and 165 of their mothers. After the inventory was filled out, statements of privilege representing different roles were paired for analysis; for example, the following two statements were paired as indicating the privileges of companion and wife-and-mother roles, respectively:

The "clinging-vine" wife is justified provided she clings sweetly enough to please her husband.
Women should demand money for household and personal expenses as a right rather than as a gift.

Five such pairs combining partner and wife-and-mother roles, five combining companion and partner roles, and two combining companion and wife-and-mother roles were identified. The number of men and the number of women who endorsed both items were recorded for each pair. Statements of obligation were paired in the same way and the frequencies of double endorsement recorded. The hypothesis requires that men should endorse pairs of obligations more often than pairs of privileges and that women should endorse pairs of privileges more often than pairs of obligations.

The findings are summarized in Table 6. The hypothesis is consistently supported. Furthermore, the same pattern applies to both generations, supplying no justification for the view that the alternative roles are now coming to be better understood and accepted than they were in an earlier generation.

Role Change and Instability

Although stability to the point of keeping the family enacting even a rather inefficient system of roles is the notable consequence of the interlocking nature of roles, change does occur. In order to understand the dynamic of change in roles that have already become stabilized, it is useful to divide the sources of stability into value and sentiment on the one hand and the working system of reciprocities on the other. Value and sentiment have to do with the members' attitudes toward the role reciprocities they are involved in. A perfectly integrated system of roles would be one in which the two sources supported each other, that is, a system of viable positions that reinforce one another while getting the family work accomplished and making the members of the family feel that the roles are what they should be. We may speak of roles in *stable equilibrium* when this is the case, since a small change either in the working reciprocity system or in sentiment and value is not enough to neutralize the equilibration process. A minor or temporary disaffection, such as a child's doubt that his parents' privileges or their demands on him are just, is not enough

TABLE 6 ENDORSEMENT OF PRIVILEGES OR OBLIGATIONS OF TWO MARRIED WOMAN ROLES

Average Percentage Endorsing Both Role Combinations	Male Students	Female Students	Fathers	Mothers
Partner, wife-and-mother:				
Privileges (5 pairs)	15.2	20.4	19.9	25.7
Obligations (10 pairs)	23.6	10.6	27.0	16.1
Companion, partner:				
Privileges (5 pairs)	23.1	29.6	18.8	26.7
Obligations (8 pairs)	20.0	9.0	23.0	13.2
Companion, wife-and-mother:				
Privileges (2 pairs)	42.5	44.9	32.6	45.5
Obligations (3 pairs)	12.0	8.0	12.9	9.7

SOURCE: Adapted from Kirkpatrick, *op. cit.*, pp. 450–458, by permission of the University of Chicago Press and the author.

to offset the equilibrating influence of the interdependence of their roles. And if the latter is profound enough, it withstands even a marked and sustained disaffection. Likewise, a strong enough feeling that the roles are as they should be overcomes the erosion of role interdependence.

Role change is most likely to take place when precipitating conditions operate on a role system that is in a state of *unstable equilibrium*. Unstable equilibrium exists when either sentiment or reciprocity alone is maintaining the system. A condition that disturbs the remaining source of stability is then likely to instigate a general alteration in the role system. If only sentiment is maintaining the role system, any basis for doubt about its rightness quickly brings change. If reciprocity is maintaining the system without support of sentiment, any disruption of reciprocity brings change.

Studies of the effect of crises, such as economic depression, war, disaster, and death, on family life have generally shown that the state of the family prior to the crisis determined its susceptibility to the impact of crisis. Most of these studies have been concerned with the bonding aspect of family process and their findings are interpretable as indicating the vulnerability of family bonds (see Chapter 4). But one study of role change brought about by the husband's unemployment during the depression of the 1930s illustrates well the difference between stable and unstable equilibrium.

Mirra Komarovsky reports interviews with the husband, wife, and one child in each of 58 families in the winter of 1935 and 1936.[13] All were native-born, white, urban, Protestant, families in which the husband had been unemployed for a year or more and had formerly been the family's sole provider. In each of these cases we can safely assume that the role reciprocity system between the husband and other family members had been severely distrubed by the elimination of his breadwinner function. Komarovsky sought to determine whether the husband experienced a loss of dominance in consequence. If we look on dominance as an aspect of the total role relationship, we may interpret it as an index of change or persistence of the role system in which the husband was involved. After the elimination of one case in which evidence was indecisive, only thirteen cases revealed a loss of dominance. The cases were further classified according to the pre-unemployment basis for the husband's authority. Dominance based on love or traditional belief in the husband's authority was called *primary*. This category corresponds closely with support of a system of roles by sentiment and value. When coercion or economic dependence was the basis for the husband's authority, the term *instrumental* was used. Although instrumental dominance is a little less comprehensive

[13] Mirra Komarovsky, *The Unemployed Man and His Family*, Dryden, New York, 1940.

than our conception of role reciprocities, it will serve as an index for present purposes. In Table 7 we are able to compare the persistence of the husband's dominance under the two conditions and also in cases in which it combined both sources.

It is probably safe to assume that in most instances that Komarovsky reports as primary, there was also a working reciprocity. Komarovsky made no effort to distinguish cases in which a working reciprocity was lacking. If such an assumption is justified, the instrumental cases represent one kind of unstable equilibrium and the primary cases mostly a stable equilibrium, with role change accordingly.

Four major conditions can operate to bring about a general change in the system of role relationships. These conditions readily induce change when the equilibrium is already unstable. They further translate a stable equilibrium into an unstable one. If they are initially strong enough or sustained and cumulative in character, they nulify even a stable equilibrium.

The first condition is any set of circumstances that affects the strength of the family bonds or the place of these bonds in the values of its members. The importance of family life to a member determines the amount of energy and resourcefulness he devotes to establishing the role relationship he desires. A common family pattern is characterized neither by chronic conflict nor by a vital harmonization—a kind of dead level of interaction. This condition comes about from a minimal investment in the family. A change in the opportunities for gratification elsewhere or a change in the need for family kinds of gratifications, such as accompanies stages in the life cycle, increases or lessens the individual's investment in the family and thus upsets the working equilibrium, moving the family toward or away from this perfunctory level of interaction.

The second condition is a change in a member's adequacy of role per-

TABLE 7   EFFECT OF UNEMPLOYMENT ON HUSBAND'S DOMINANCE

Basis of Dominance	Loss of Dominance	No Loss of Dominance
Primary	2	33
Mixed	3	8
Instrumental	8	4
Total	13	45

SOURCE: Adapted from Mirra Komarovsky, *op. cit.*, p. 54, by permission of the author.

formance. Either an improved or a lessened adequacy alters the reciprocities. The normal progression of the life cycle inevitably brings such change,
technological change or coaching and assistance in role performance have
an effect, and changes in the environment, such as the crises of war, depression, and natural disaster, may help or hinder role performance. Komarovsky's study and others show that economic depression, by imparing
the husband's ability to perform the breadwinner portion of his role,
changes the system of family reciprocities.

Another study somewhat in the Komarovsky tradition calls attention to
some peculiarities of the way in which a short-term change in role adequacy makes lasting changes. Earl L. Koos interviewed members of 62
tenement-district families in New York City recurrently over a two-year
period to determine the kinds of serious family troubles they encountered,
consequences for family organization, and efforts at solution. One of the accompaniments of crises or threatened crises he noted was a change in *role
evaluation*. A change in role evaluation is not an objective change in role
adequacy but a change in the evaluation that other family members make
of ego's role adequacy. To the members of the family, ego appears to be
performing more adequately, whether in fact he is or is not. *Role devaluation* occurred when ego was held responsible by the members for the
crisis or for dealing with it ineffectually. Thus role inadequacy in one
aspect of role performance led to devaluation of the unchanged performance in other aspects of the role.

In one illustrative instance the foreign-born father had refused to allow
the daughter, who was sick with pneumonia, to be taken to the hospital
until her condition had become unnecessarily critical. The role devaluation that accompanied the resentment of other family members is reflected
in the husband's remarks some time after his daughter's recovery:[14]

> I don't know how to make of it. I earn the same money I did before, I provide
> the goods for my family just the same, but they don't like it now the way they
> did. We're always poor, but they don't complain. Now, because they're mad
> with me about Agnes and the hospital, and don't pay no attention to what I say,
> now they don't like what I earn. I don't understand—I earn the same. But before,
> they're satisfied; now, they raise hell and tell me I'm a poor no-good-for-nothing.
> Now I catch hell both ways—no boss, no good for keeping the family.

In another family the re-evaluation was upward. The husband, whose
dominance in the family was slight, surprised everyone by solving a serious
problem of debt. The result was a lasting change in others' attitudes towards him, reflected in the wife's statement eleven months later:[15]

---

[14] Earl L. Koos, *Families in Trouble*, King's Crown, New York, 1946, p. 103. Quoted
by permission of Columbia University Press.
[15] *Ibid.*, p. 97, by permission of Columbia University Press.

The Mister [she had always referred to him prior to the trouble as John, or more frequently as "he"] did something to all of us when he fixed that mess. He's never been the same since; it seems to me he's a bigger man. I don't know what to make of the change. Why, Jack and I think he's a much more important man than we did before. He's somebody *to lean on* now!

The reevaluation in this instance undoubtedly persisted, because the initially changed response of wife and child evoked a more assertive and competent role from the husband, which in turn justified and reinforced the changed role on the part of mother and son.

A third kind of change is an alteration in the compatibility of the different tasks in the family, making for a regrouping of activities into a new role differentiation. Social and technological change has had notable long-range effects of this character. For example, the traditional role of the child combined a fairly extensive set of household tasks with socializee responsibilities. But progressive changes in the time and effort demanded by public education have forced most of the household tasks to be dropped. The traditional role of wife and mother centered on household tasks and household-centered productive activities. Factory production stripped the wife of much of her economically productive activities, technological advances cut the time and energy required by housekeeping, and public education freed her from much custodial and socializing responsibility for her children. As a consequence a new role that combined wife-mother responsibilities with gainful employment outside the home became practicable.

Finally, insofar as role differentiation is the division of labor through which family activities are consummated, a change in the activities that the family serves threatens the equilibrium. The source of change is a complement to the first, since it concerns not the strength and importance of the bonds but the actual family activities they involve. The mere completion of tasks or the life-cycle changes in tasks may have this effect. Much of the standard differentiation between husband and wife roles is functional to their socialization task and ceases to have any reciprocity support when the children have grown up and left home. In a sense society delegates tasks to the family. A family that carries the responsibility of maintaining law and order for its members and physical protection from outsiders requires a different role differentiation from one that depends on the state to care for these matters.

The effect of a state of unstable equilibrium, or any of the causes of change we have mentioned, on the actor is to induce an experience of role strain.[16] The actor feels himself unjustly under pressure to play a role he

---

[16] William J. Goode, "A Theory of Role Strain," *American Sociological Review*, 25: 483–496, August 1960.

does not believe in or feels unequal to the demands of the role. That aspect of the pressure to change the system of roles which concerns the actor's attempt to find a viable role is largely an attempt to alleviate role strain.

The commonest kind of role strain is the experience of being unable to perform a role adequately because of conflicting demands of other roles. The career, various community roles, and roles in churches and voluntary organizations compete with family roles for the time and energy of the individual. Or they make inconsistent demands on the individual. The wife's profession, for example, may require habits of dispatch and impersonal efficiency that are inconsistent with the patience and tenderness demanded in her wife-and-mother role.

Socialization to Roles

The many disparate processes and reactions that make up socialization can be given some organization by viewing socialization as the learning of roles through role taking and role playing. The child begins learning isolated responses to isolated gestures by the standard elementary psychological processes. But his own behavior begins to take on the character of role playing when he begins to see the behavior of alter as a role and to interpret specific gestures in this context. The roles of important alters are learned in large part by playing at them, that is, by playing mother or daddy or policemen in play with other children. By thus confronting in play a wide range of situations from the standpoint of the part he is playing, the child expands his conception of the role of alter as a basis for interpreting alter's behavior in the real situation.

Learning Role Systems. Our understanding of socialization is enhanced by noting the principle that a role is always a way of coping with some other role. Roles are therefore never learned singly, but always in pairs or larger systems. The role of the relevant other must be learned in order to learn the role one is playing. The child learns the parent role in the process of working out his own role. The male learns the female role in the process of working out the male role.

The role that is learned is neither complete nor exactly as understood by alter. Many facets of alter's role do not come into the interaction between ego and alter and remain unknown or misunderstood by ego. The aspects directly involved in the interaction may be given a different organization by alter than by ego. It is merely sufficient that ego should have developed a conception of alter's role that works in the sense of enabling ego to make satisfactory preparation for alter's gestures and to envision appropriate responses to situations he has not seen alter face. The important point is that ego has learned two roles in their relation to each other.

With this principle of system role learning in mind we can suggest that the principle of adaptive learning illustrated from Symond's research (see Chapter 8) is incomplete as it stands. When a person learns a pair or system of roles, which of them he enacts in any situation depends on the way he assesses the roles of relevant others in the situation. The child who learns to be extremely submissive in his relation to a tyrannical parent does not merely learn to be a submissive person. Rather, when he senses the weakness of a smaller child he may simply adopt the tyrannical role he has learned as the basis for his submissive family role. Learning a pair of roles means that a person is potentially capable of enacting either of the pair. The identification of the role of alter is tentative, so that the child may revise his conception and adopt the complementary role if he discovers that the second child will not adopt the submissive role. This is the basis for the principle of role appropriation. When a group of people have learned a common system of roles, ego may respond with alter's usual role when some crisis leads alter to adopt ego's usual role.

What a person learns through acquiring pairs of roles is a way of conceiving situations. He populates a particular group or situation with certain kinds of roles in interaction with one another. A child raised in a highly authoritarian family does not so much learn either the authoritarian role or the submissive role for himself as he learns to define a wide variety of situations as consisting of one person exercising a domineering role and the others a completely submissive role. The more stable difference is not between the person who learns a submissive role and one who learns a domineering role but between the person whose experience has taught him to populate situations with interacting domination-submission roles and the person who conceives situations as made up of roles differentiated primarily on dimensions other than dominance-submission. Such role-system conceptions are the framework that supplies interpretations for the gestures of self and other and assessments of the probable effectiveness of various interpersonal techniques.

Self-conception. Fundamentally, roles are learned as parts, and the good actor can play several. They are like maneuvers in a game, the actor adopting a different set of maneuvers according to which ones most effectively counter those of others. But in many areas the normal adult does not so easily enact either of a pair of roles. One role in each pair or system comes to be easier for him—more natural and more characteristically his. The self-conception is the organization of those roles he feels at home in. The self-conception is the anchorage that limits the socialized individual's ability to adopt socially opposite roles easily as maneuvers in response to whatever roles are present in the situation. The self-conception is the major limitation on the principle of role appropriation.

The self-conception, as we indicated in Chapter 2, grows out of experience with the interplay of ideal and attainment. The individual incorporates in his self-conception roles which experience has taught him can be performed with sufficient adequacy so that role strain is minimized but which are rewarding enough so that he is motivated to try to perform them. Roles are ranked according to prestige and worth, partially on the group's consensual scale and partly by their relation to the idiosyncratic values of the individual. The individual who experiences too much role strain as leader may find the role of leader's henchman a more viable one for him and yet more rewarding than being a mere member. At the same time, a dimension of self-esteem in the self-conception reflects the individual's valuation of his own identity role and identity-role adequacy.

Successful enactment of a role requires practice. The child of a domineering parent who is able to force the other children in the neighborhood to play the same submissive role to him that he plays at home gets abundant experience in the domineering role. From such success he may be able to incorporate in his self-conception the role of dominance that his parents have taught him to value highly, although he has never been able to play it in relation to them. Another child in the same family situation may, because of age or physical weakness or the nature of supervised activity, never be able to practice the domineering role. When the occasional opportunity presents itself, role strain is so great that he incorporates into his self-conception the submissive role. The general principles governing the allocation of roles both within the family and outside thus determine whether the individual gets the experience of successfully playing a role that makes it possible to bring it to his self-conception.

Learning Prototype Role Differentiations. Of the role differentiations that the individual learns to make, some are of more pervasive significance to his ability to orient himself socially than others. Talcott Parsons has proposed that the child typically learns the differentiations that are indispensible for his participation in society in a predetermined series of steps.[17] At each stage his social world is organized into a number of role pairs. The transition comes when the stable state is disturbed, and in the process of learning to cope with his initially chaotic situation he learns to bifurcate his system of roles on one new dimension.

The child's first social relationship is oral dependency on the mother. In this stage there is a fusion of the self with the mother and other relevant social objects. A system of behavior is learned that does not differentiate kinds of active social roles. The crises that come with attempts to institute some discipline over the child disrupt the relationship, and the new

---

[17] Talcott Parsons, "Family Structure and the Socialization of the Child," in Parsons and Bales, *op. cit.*, pp. 35–151.

equilibrium is one in which the child differentiates the roles of himself and his mother. In the process he has learned to recognize his first role differentiation, which is based on the unequal relationship between the powerful and the weak. He has also learned how to cope with this kind of relationship. As his relationship extends more fully to other members, he encounters his next crisis, during which he must learn to differentiate the roles of his father and his mother vis-à-vis himself. He has previously interacted with his father but not on the basis of a role systematically differentiated from that of his mother. With this transition he learns to differentiate roles that are instrumental from ones that are expressive. He continues to make the earlier differentiation on the basis of power, but he now subdivides on the two dimensions rather than one.

The next transition carries him into a differentiated set of relationships with persons outside the family, chiefly the school and peer group. In the process of learning the difference between relating himself to a family member and to his peer group or school he learns the next broad kind of role differentiation. His role relationship with family members is *particularistic*, in the sense that it is the unique relationship of one person to another. Relationships with outsiders are *universalistic*, in the sense that people are not unique individuals but examples of categories of people. Role relationships are on the basis of general rules applicable to all members of the category, ego adopting one role in relation to a peer and a different role in dealing with a teacher, simply because they are peer and teacher respectively rather than because of any personal relationship with them as individuals. Thereafter the child is able to distinguish those relationships whose requirements are uniquely personal from those which are general.

Finally, the last steps toward adulthood teach the child to differentiate between ascribed and achieved statuses and their accompanying roles. Statuses within the family and to a considerable degree even in the lower grades of school and the peer group are based simply on one's being born in a particular family and neighborhood and being of a particular age group rather than being earned. These statuses must be distinguished from the rights and duties that go with such achieved statuses as school valedictorian, class president, all-city football team member. When the individual has learned to make the sixteen-fold differentiation of kinds of roles using these four key distinctions, he is then prepared to approach roles in specialized kinds of situations in a manner appropriate to adult society.

Parsons proposes that these steps correspond to the steps in psychosexual development outlined by Freud but that the role differentiation framework affords a social rather than physiological explanation for the progression. The one-role stage is oral dominance, followed by the anal and oedipal stages, with Freud's latency and mature heterosexuality stages corresponding to the last two.

Roles as the Substance of Meaning. Socialization has been discussed as the development of meanings that supply the basis for interpreting experiences. Meanings are conveyed partially through language and other symbols, but symbols must be related to experience if they are to have any content. The most general way symbols are given meaning is by attaching them to specific kinds of role relationships. The command "You must clean up your room" conveys only the notion of obligation learned through experience with the parent's ability to enforce obligation. Because each parent who says, "You must," establishes a somewhat different role relationship with his children, the specific meaning of the command is different from child to child. To one child the command signalizes the start of a bargaining exchange, in which the child seeks to exact the maximum promised reward for compliance. To another child the term signalizes imminent danger from the anger of the parent. To still another it is the gesture that informs him that he has now got the better of the parent. Symbols are used as a phase of a role exchange; the meaning they acquire reflects their place in that role exchange.

The Swiss psychologist Jean Piaget has shown how children at different stages of maturation may impart altogether different working meanings to the same set of rules or moral inmperatives.[18] He further proposes that the differences in meaning are a product of the kind of social relationship in which the rules are being learned and used. Younger children discussed the rules of the game of marbles as a set of absolutes not to be challenged or modified to suit the occasion. A rule required no justification; the fact that it was the rule was enough to demand conformity. This kind of understanding of rules Piaget called the morality of *constraint*. Older children regarded rules as conventions that the group agreed on so that they could play the game. So long as the group agreed, it was acceptable to change the rules. This attitude was labeled the morality of *cooperation*.

Piaget then urged that the child's conception of the rules reflected his relationship with the rule giver. To younger children the rule giver was a parent whose unequal dominance was translated into the absolute character of the rules. To older children the rule giver was the peer group, in which decisions were reached on the basis of relatively equalitarian exchange. The character of the rules derived from the nature of the child's relationship to his peers. Piaget then suggested that a morality of cooperation might be learned earlier when the parent-child relationship was

[18] Jean Piaget, *The Moral Judgment of the Child*, Harcourt, Brace & World, New York, 1932.

less authoritarian, when the parent encouraged the child to engage in a reciprocal decision-making exchange in order to come up with a set of rules for behavior.

Summary

Role theory supplies a comprehensive pattern for bringing the processes of bonding, decision making, conflict-harmonization, and socialization into closer interrelationship and for understanding the effect of the society on the working of these processes within the family. A role is the behavior characteristic of a kind of actor, and the behavior of individuals is interpreted against the roles they are assigned to. A role is always a comprehensive way of interacting with one or a set of relevant other roles and cannot be understood apart from this relationship. There is always an interplay between the improvization that results from role taking and the uniformization that comes from playing a role according to prescription.

Within the family there is a differentiation into roles and an allocation of roles among the members that are primarily determined by cultural definition. Cultural role conceptions are least subject to modification by informal family processes when they are integrated into a system of value, sentiment, and belief, when society exercises surveillance and support, when the conceptions are held unanimously within the society, and when they are comprehensive. The informal processes determining the pattern of role differentiation center on each member's effort to attain a viable position in the scheme of interaction and the functional requirements of family operation. Members attempt to work out viable roles in relation to a highly dominant other by developing their own spheres of exclusive control within the family, by cultivating understanding of the dominant person (which may partially explain the supposed women's intuition), by maximizing the advantages of irresponsibility, by cultivating moral perfection, by claiming the protection due weakness, and by fashioning a mediator role between the dominator and other dominated family members. Differentiation also often develops between the advocate and the challenger of shared values. Attempts to account for variations in family role differentiation between societies according to dominant family function have had only limited success. There is considerable support, however, for the hypothesis that some differentiation between the major instrumental role and the major expressive role in the family is a universal functional requirement. Informal allocation of roles is determined by the fit of the role to the person and by dominance in gaining the more desirable roles.

Within the family there is a tendency for unique family roles to displace cultural roles to some degree. There is also a tendency for the role structure to become stabilized to such a degree that a change in personnel does not change the roles. There may even be a principle of role appropriation, that when alter preempts ego's role in a particular situation, ego then plays alter's usual role rather than his own. Roles acquire normative components because of their linkage to culturally defined statuses and because of the bargaining involved in their allocation. Bargaining over rights and duties is governed by the conception of justice implicit in the reciprocity principle. Because of the normative component, the individual family member is judged according to his role adequacy, the extent to which he performs as a father, wife, child, or grandparent should. Role inadequacy is a prime cause of chronic conflict, because it is the basis for involving the identity of the person with low role adequacy whenever difficulties arise in decision making or execution. Role dissensus is also a major source of chronic conflict, because it means that family members are operating under different sets of rules.

An integrated system of roles is held together by reciprocity, consisting of mutual viability and functional effectiveness, and by sentiment, the feeling that the roles are right and gratifying. When either of the kinds of support is weakened, the roles are unlikely to change immediately, but the result is an unstable equilibrium in which even small damage to the remaining support causes a change in the system of roles. Typical conditions inducing such change are an alteration in family bonds, a change in role adequacy, an alteration in compatibility of different tasks in the family, and a change in the kinds of activities with which the family is concerned. Unstable equilibrium induces a condition of role strain in individual members of the family, making them feel either under unjust pressure to play roles they do not believe in or unequal to the demands of the role.

Socialization is the process of acquiring a repertoire of roles through which to act and to orient oneself to others. Roles are never learned singly but always as pairs or sets of interacting roles. Because the individual learns the role of alter while playing his own role, he is able to play the role of alter when others in the situation are playing his usual role. Over a period of time, however, the self-conception incorporates certain roles and denies others, so that the individual is no longer able to play effectively all the roles he can take. Parsons has proposed a fundamental system of role differentiation by successive divisions into new pairs, brought on by the use of discipline by the mother, the differentiation between mother and father, differentiation between family roles and external roles, and finally the distinction between ascribed and achieved statuses. It is the system of roles, primarily within the family, that supplies the meaning for the symbols whose acquisition is central to socialization.

CHAPTER 10

OBLIGATION AND LOVE: THE TONE OF FAMILY INTERACTION

Interaction in one group is distinguished from interaction in another by the tone or quality of the interaction. The distinguishing tone of any "standard" group in society is transmitted in the cultural conception of the group and maintained in the relationships between the group and the larger society. The tone, in turn, gives both direction and limitation to the operation of the interaction processes we have been examining.

The distinctive tone of family interaction reflects the combination of what superficially seem to be two contradictory elements. On the one hand, family relationships are pervasively *responsible* relations. Society has surrounded the family system with constraints, so that decisions to establish, terminate, or alter family units radically are not made casually. Decisions regarding family participation are weighted with long-lasting and far-reaching consequences. On the other hand, family relationships are governed by a principle of *spontaneity*, that people establish and terminate family relationships primarily because they wish to, and that relationships among family members are governed by the members' feelings toward one another. Love is the justification for marriage and is the socially recognized explanation for the accommodations that members make to one another and even for the exercise of authority within the family.

In this chapter we shall first review some of the functions that make the family important to society and then discuss regulation and support of family life by the community. We shall then explore the meaning of love as a social sentiment—a cultural device that has the effect of harnessing emotion so as to create spontaneity in conformity to social norms and values. Next we shall note the obstacles to giving and receiving love that arise in social interaction. We conclude by considering what difference it makes for decision making, conflict, and other family processes that family relationships are characterized by love.

Social Functions of the Family

Responsibility originates in the fact that actions have consequences. When particular patterns or roles have fairly consistent consequences that give support to the culturally established round of life in a society, we call these consequences *social functions*. The recognized functions of the family are the justification for the elaborate set of regulations and supporting coercions in which the family is embedded.

It has often been suggested that the stability of the family is a product of the functions it performs. Those functions which involve recognized gratifications to individuals become bonds between family members. Those functions recognized as valuable or essential to the welfare of society—care and education of children, for example—are implemented by close societal regulation of family life. The stability of family life is enhanced by more intense bondedness and closer regulation when the functions performed by the family are many and varied.

Declining Functions. The careful examination of changing family functions in modern society by Ogburn has been the basis for most subsequent statements.[1] Because of the wide range and importance of family functions a century or so ago it was hardly possible for an individual to enjoy full membership in society and take care of his basic needs for living except through membership in a family unit. Since that time, "there have been two noteworthy changes: (a) a transfer of functions away from the family; and (b) an independent growth of functions outside the family."[2] *Economic* functions of the family, especially those having to do with production, have been transferred to the factory and other settings outside family life. "Those services that require a large capital outlay, that are cheaper outside the home, or that are performed infrequently in the home tend to be the first to go."[3] Although it is hardly now indispensable, the family remains important as a unit of economic consumption, to the extent that Friedan could plausibly charge commercial advertisers with promoting a special conception of family life and the wife role as a means of ensuring high levels of material consumption.[4] *Combat* functions, common in earlier periods and vestigial in feuds between clans, have been almost entirely transferred from the family to the modern state. *Protective* functions, involving security in old age and personal crisis and

---

[1] William F. Ogburn, "The Family and Its Functions," in President's Research Committee on Social Trends, *Recent Social Trends in the United States*, McGraw-Hill, New York, 1933, pp. 661–708.
[2] William F. Ogburn and Meyer F. Nimkoff, *Technology and the Changing Family*, Houghton Hifflin, Boston, 1955, p. 142.
[3] *Ibid.*, p. 130.
[4] Betty Friedan, *The Feminine Mystique*, Dell, New York, 1963, pp. 195–223.

defense of life, limb, and property, have been transferred to government, private charities, and financial organizations such as insurance companies. *Governmental* functions include the general control and discipline of members. The "governing authority of the male head and of parents is much curtailed;"[5] the governing of children remains but is extensively shared with outside agencies, such as the school and municipality. *Religious* functions have declined because of the general secularization of society, and educational functions have been transferred in large part to the schools.

The *recreational* function elicits a more qualified judgment. Ogburn originally noted evidence that such forms of recreation as taking family walks might be more common among city families than in rural areas.[6] If present rural patterns are representative of a way of life that was prevalent when the United States was predominantly rural, such comparisons might indicate persistence of recreational functions. Ogburn and Nimkoff offer a later assessment of this and other evidence: "We conclude, therefore, that in modern cities the function of family provision of recreation has lessened somewhat but that during the last few decades there has been a revival of some home recreations due largely to electrical inventions. . . ."[7]

Changing Functions. Burgess and Locke, building on Ogburn's argument, found evidence of a change, rather than merely a decline, in family functions. A function of *companionship,* involving the unity that "develops out of mutual affection and intimate association of husband and wife and parents and children,"[8] is said to have become more important at the same time that traditional functions declined. The destruction of the traditional neighborhood and the heightened ephemerality and impersonality of the urban way of life have transferred the demand for intimate and durable interpersonal relationships increasingly onto the family. Along with this change has gone not simply a weakening of control in the family but a shift in the character of control. Although the evolution is far from completed, "the family in historical times has been in transition from an institution with family behavior controlled by the mores, public opinion, and law, to a companionship with family behavior arising from the mutual affection and consensus of its members."[9]

These and other functional analyses depend on the assumption that changes external to the family lead to changes in (a) the needs of society and its members that must be satisfied, whether in or out of the family

[5] Ogburn and Nimkoff, *op. cit.,* p. 135.
[6] Ogburn, *op. cit.,* pp. 675–676.
[7] Ogburn and Nimkoff, *op. cit.,* p. 132.
[8] Ernest W. Burgess and Harvey J. Locke, *The Family: From Institution to Companionship,* 2d ed., American Book, Boston, 1953, p. 23.
[9] *Ibid.,* p. 23.

and (b) the means for their satisfaction. The rise of new educational and economic needs that can be more effectively gratified outside the family shifts the balance from the family toward other institutions; the rise of new socialization needs, because of psychiatric conceptions of personality formation, may shift the balance toward the family. The family is to be regarded as one medium among many in the society through which the essential and desirable ends of life are sought. Over the long range, there is a continuous redistribution of activities between the family and other agencies.

Continuing Functions. In these classical functional analyses, disproportionate attention was focused on functions that made the family indispensable. A search for functions of this character may have been illusory, since the amply demonstrated adaptability of mankind suggests that no institution is totally indispensable. But if we consider only functions that are in fact generally gratified through the family, although they might just as well be gratified in other ways, there is still a great deal of responsibility heaped on family life today. We shall list several functions that are generally recognized and expected to be accomplished through the family and therefore supply the basis for public control over family life.

It is firmly expected that the family will be an *economic* unit, holding and transmitting property, distributing income, maintaining a common household through which consumption is organized and carried out, and engaging in secondary forms of production. In spite of all the well-documented changes, the household as an economic unit still supplies the framework in which family life is built and the context in which other functions must be accomplished. The most fully elaborated regulations over family life have to do with property disposition. Problems of income and property disposition loom large in family readjustment to divorce and bereavement. Some arrangement for economic self-sufficiency is still one of the most generally recognized conditions for entry into marriage.

Second, the family is expected to perform an *individual-care* function. One of the problems in a group of any size, and more especially in a large organization, a community, or a society, is that of ensuring that each member's welfare is the specific responsibility of one or more other members. When this is not accomplished, individuals get lost and forgotten, the missing are not noticed until too late, the sick and injured are not cared for early enough to be cured. This is the problem for which buddy systems are established in youth camps. If no child is allowed to go swimming except with a buddy, each child is responsible for knowing at all times the exact whereabouts of his buddy, thus assuring that a drowning child is not overlooked until too late.

Unlike most groups, in which members are replaceable and each is responsible more for the group objectives than for individual members, the family is a unit within which each member is uniquely irreplaceable. The school teacher reports one child absent but need not concern himself with where the child is until the absence has continued several days; family members are expected to be concerned about a few minutes of unexplained absence. The school principal may write off the juvenile delinquent as one failure more than balanced by the school's many successes; the delinquent's family is supposed to continue to be concerned about his unique fate.

The familiarity with routine and mood and subtle gestures facilitated by the interdependence and intimacy of family life contribute to the performance of this function. Because they know one another's habits of promptness, family members know whether to be alarmed over a minute, an hour, or a day's tardiness. Intimate familiarity enables them to detect illness or preoccupation on the basis of the minor changes in appearance or disposition unnoticed or unassessable by others.

Societal pressures support this function. Parents are taken publicly to account for not knowing the whereabouts of their children when the latter get into trouble. Damaging delay in calling a doctor means questioning of family members regarding their attention to the unfortunate member.

Third, the family is supposed to serve a *custodial* function. If individual care is directed toward keeping the individual effective, custody refers to protecting society from potentially disruptive behavior by individuals. The child who has not learned responsibility, the defective adult who is an embarrassment and disrupter of groups, and the elderly person who is not able to recognize his own limitations are to be contained by the family members.

Except for restricting the child, many custodial responsibilities are being shifted from the family. But the transfer of responsibility is made very difficult. Often the indignity of legal action is required, as in legal commitment to an institution. Just as there is a ritual of assigning and accepting responsibility in the marriage ceremony, there are rituals supposed to expunge the responsibility. But it is doubtful that such rituals are well enough established in American society to be effective in dissolving the sentiments of responsibility in the individuals involved.

Fourth, the family remains a unit of social and *community participation and placement*. A child has very little social identification without his parents, and most social group participation by children presumes active support by the parents. The married couple is the unit of participation in much of adult social life. Universities relax their impersonal entry standards to grant priorities to relatives of alumni; recruitment into many occupations is largely through family connection. And although the state may treat the individual adult as a citizen, the social class system, which operates informally to maintain a social order in which the fictions of the state can be applied, takes the family rather than individual as its unit.

Fifth, the family is expected to supply much or all of the *allowable sex relations* for its members. In its prohibition or serious disapproval of extramarital relations and in its attitudes ranging from total disapproval to approval under circumstances of discretion for premarital relations American society has much in common with other societies. Whatever the uncertainty and disagreement over the restrictions that should be imposed on sexual gratification, sex relations within the family are restricted to the marital pair, and sexual cooperation within the marital relation is obligatory.

Sixth, the *procreation* function is the exclusive province of the family. Whatever permissiveness there may be regarding sex relations, bearing and bringing up children is a family activity. Suggestions that in American society, as in many peasant societies throughout the world, pregnancy following premarital sex relations is solved by precipitate marriage, indicates the force of the norm limiting procreation to the family.

Seventh, the *socialization* function still centers on the family. Ogburn proposed that the decline of other functions was leaving "personality functions" as pivotal to the family in modern society.[10] Training to experience the fundamental human sentiments and motives, to adopt an appropriately positive attitude toward the rules of society, and to use the vastly complex communication system incorporated in language are all largely left to the family.

Regulation and Support

The nature of regulation, from law to the informality of gossip, need hardly be mentioned. Society hardly separates spheres of nonconformity from spheres of conformity in the assessment of an individual. Accordingly, one who seriously violates the regulations of family life is likely to find association in his conventional social milieu difficult. Waller spoke of a "divorce prejudice,"[11] as a pervasive set of unfavorable attitudes, ranging from personal distance to lowered bank credit ratings, that dogs the divorcee. Similar prejudice applies to other aspects of family failure.

On the other hand, conspicuous success in family life creates an a priori qualification for many desired positions and presumption against suspicion of evil-doing in other areas.

The controls over family life are augmented by the tendency to assign credit and responsibility collectively in the family. Although the divorce court maintains the legal fiction of an innocent party, the unformalized

[10] Ogburn, *op. cit.*, p. 661.
[11] Willard Waller, *The Old Love and the New*, Liveright, New York, 1930.

social sanctions tend to be registered against all members of a deserter's family; the sexual indiscretions of any member tend to reflect against all members of the family.

Control through Agents. Two features of the regulation imposed by society to ensure that family life serves the accepted functions deserve to be stressed. First, in holding specific family members primarily responsible for ensuring the performance of certain functions, some unit of the larger society makes the family member its *agent*. The concept of agent is important in examining the effect of society on family process and will be developed extensively in connection with subsequent discussion of deliberate socialization. An agent is an intermediary who exercises some authority in one relationship because of authority exercised over him in the other relationship. Almost inevitably an agent sees his relationship to those whom he tries to influence differently from the way they see it. He may not be free to act as he chooses and may not be fully convinced of the value of the objective he is pursuing. But those whom he is influencing seldom see beyond the immediate relationship of direction and authority to the agent's own ultimate source of direction and authority.

The designation of a family head and the authority vested in him must be understood in relation to the concept of agent. Zimmerman has called attention to the fallacious picture of absolute paternal authority often applied to highly patriarchal family systems.[12] The power of life and death over family members, the power of disinheriting a child or divorcing a wife, suggest vast power located in a single individual. But the power is also simultaneously an obligation. In the event that a member dishonors the community, the family head is under obligation as the community's agent to have the member killed. Folk tales in such patriarchal societies abound with sensitive tales of the husband who is forced by higher duty to divorce the wife he adores or to exile the child he loves. The near sacrificing of his son Isaac by Abraham illustrates well that his apparent absolute authority was only that of agent for the ultimately powerful Jehovah.[13]

Family as Pawn. The other feature of family regulation that deserves special attention is the tendency for the family to become a *pawn* in struggles between other units of society. The historical picture of the last 1,000 years is especially clear regarding the effect of struggles for power between church and state on the regulation of family life. The entrenched power of the medieval church saw marriage as exclusively a divine institution, governed only by the laws of the church. The emerging power of modern states saw regulation of the family taken more and more out of the hands of the church and placed under the state. The present accom-

[12] Carle C. Zimmerman, *Family and Civilization*, Harper & Row, New York, 1947.
[13] Genesis 22.

modation, in which the ascendancy of the state is accomplished but the usefulness and quasi-independence of the church acknowledged, is reflected in the secular regulation and registration of marriage, birth, and divorce, combined with the option of civil or religious marriage ceremony.

Family regulation likewise becomes a pawn in struggles between competing schemes of education. The ascendance of secular public education in the United States means that families wishing another form of education must support two systems of schools. It means, too, that family routines must be accommodated to the schedule of schooling and that parents are held responsible for assuring that children acquire the specified education.

The family inevitably becomes a pawn in any revolutionary struggle. Because the family usually transmits traditional values and outlooks from father to son and existing inequalities of opportunity and possession, efforts to transfer power away from the family and to the revolutionary state are standard parts of the effort to implement revolution. The example of Soviet Russia is instructive. Following the revolution there was an extended period of weakening family bonds and controls over its members, so as to interrupt the continuity of traditional society and culture. Once the continuity was sufficiently broken, efforts were then made to reinstate a srengthened family system, through which the revolutionary doctrine, now become conservative ideology, might be effectively perpetuated.[14] Some of the same revolutionary fervor went into creation of the Israeli kibbutz. And from the more radical elements in the American progressive-education movement came an effort to neutralize family influences on the child by extending the school day and pushing the school life back into infancy.

The system of regulation over the family that prevails in American society is not, then, the simple product of rational or intuitive consideration of family requirements and functions. The shape given to the family by the functions assigned to it, or assumed by the mass of families, is modified by demands made on the family as a pawn of institutional struggles. These outlines must then be further reshaped so as to allow for family group function and the establishment of viable member roles.

Social Support. The social pressures by which the external regulation of family life is accomplished are, at least in middle-class circles, predominantly positive and implicit. Negative pressures are sporadic, in response to apparent deviations; support for the family ideal is a continuous form of pressure. Positive pressure in its most general form consists of concerted patterns of acting as if each family were actually performing its appointed functions and adhering to the accepted rules.

[14] Alex Inkeles, "Family and Church in the Post-war USSR," *The Annals of the American Academy of Political and Social Science*, 263:33–44, May 1949.

Waller and Hill speak of "pair expectations of success" and "public support for the married dyad" as important bases for marriage solidarity:

In reasonably sophisticated circles, people usually see the importance of the appearance of solidarity and address themselves consciously to the task of building and upholding a fiction of solidarity even if the reality does not exist. When such a facade is erected to disguise the true state of a marriage, members of the outer group recognize, perhaps, that the picture does not conform to reality, but they attempt to give no sign of such recognition.[15]

The public not only expects the married pair to succeed, thereby providing a looking-glass self which supports the front of solidarity which the pair builds up, but it provides a kind of insulation of privacy within which the workings of the pair can operate without public scrutiny. The sanctity of the home is but a sentimentalizing of the public support given to the pair as a closed system.[16]

These processes apply to the entire family system and not merely to marriage. Outsiders act as if all were well within the family. If they over-hear a family quarrel, they try not to let the family know, or they discount the harsh words as reflecting no deep antagonisms. If one family member vents his discontent to an outsider who knows the family, the outsider is embarrassed and usually resists the communication. If the parents are feared to be shirking their socialization and custodial responsibilities toward a child, the first response is to act even more strongly as if the parents were assuming their responsibilities.

By playing their parts in this manner, the outsiders create a reciprocity in which it is hard for the family members not to play the conforming part. Playing the part in relation to the outside world does not ensure conformity within; but it affords support for conformist tendencies already present. And the simultaneous working of these processes on many families creates the general illusion of a higher community-wide standard of approximation to the ideal than exists in reality. The illusion buttresses the expectation of fulfillment of family obligations and ideals.

Love as a Social Sentiment

Although every interaction has components of feeling, the family is distinctive in the part played by organized sentiments called love. In folk thinking about the family, love is a sufficient explanation for many of the crucial events and relationships. Falling in love explains marriage; maternal love explains the great sacrifice of a mother for her child; filial love explains a son's life-long effort to redeem his father's reputation; fraternal love explains the mutual support of adult brothers and sisters in the face of adversity. The experience of love in an appropriate relationship re-

[15] Willard Waller and Reuben Hill, *The Family: A Dynamic Interpretation*, Dryden, New York, 1951, p. 323.
[16] *Ibid.*, p. 324.

quires no explanation; it is only the absence of love that indicates that something is amiss. Folk thinking ordinarily locates the something amiss in the moral order. Evil people are unable to love truly.

More searching consideration indicates that love is complicated, diverse, and far from automatic in its incidence or in its effect on behavior. Furthermore, the presence of love may be as much consequence as cause of a relationship. People are often troubled by inability to feel the love they should toward a parent or sibling or child. The fact that normal behavior in the family is supposed to be an expression of love and that there are specialized forms of love to fit each kind of institutionalized relationship within the family suggests that love is both shaped by the family system and a variable in its operation.

We can best begin by exploring what the various sentiments that pass under the name of love have in common. Mate love has been more extensively studied than other forms, and investigators often use it as the prototype in thinking about other types of love. Since consummation by sexual union is a prominent feature of mate love and is amenable to psychophysiological study because of its easily identified bodily processes, such an approach often leads the investigator to search for a sexual basis for all types of love. By starting with the common features of all familial love, however, we should be in a better position to determine later just what sex contributes that is distinctive to mate love.

Sentiment and Emotion. A distinction must be made from the start between sentiment and emotion. An emotion is a pervasive agitated physiological state known to the individual by massive visceral and kinesthetic sensation and to others by overt behavior indicative of the tension. If the emotion is identified by the individual experiencing it, the tendency is toward some behavior that will relieve the tension. Emotion is thus rooted in physiology, its dynamics are relatively independent of culture, and its basic forms are given in the nature of the human organism rather than learned.

A sentiment, on the other hand, is a socially defined complex of feeling that indicates a characteristic relationship to a social object and is accompanied by tendencies to behave in the socially appropriate manner. It incorporates emotion but does not correspond exactly to any emotion.[17]

As an illustration, the emotion of rage or anger can be compared with

[17] A concept of sentiment as a more socialized phenomenon than emotion was developed by Shand and by MacDougall. The present conception owes much to Blondel and carries somewhat further the logic of Kirkpatrick's component-package formulation of love. See Alexander F. Shand, *The Foundations of Character*, Macmillan, London, 1914; William McDougall, *An Introduction to Social Psychology*, Methuen, London, 1908; Charles Blondel, *Introduction à la Psychologie Collective*, Librairie Armand Colin, Paris, 1952; Clifford Kirkpatrick, *The Family as Process and Institution*, Ronald, New York, 1955, pp. 271–276.

the sentiment of indignation. The infant registers a state of arousal that the observer identifies as rage, especially if the observer can connect the state to some frustration. But indignation comes only after the child has learned the social concept of justice and therefore is able to experience anger under the special circumstance of being the victim of someone's deliberate injustice. As a learned phenomenon, a sentiment, such as indignation or any form of love, has cultural modes of expression. In order to be indignant, one must learn how to appear outraged, to maintain a stance and tone of voice that distinguish the manifestation from another less socially acceptable sentiment often called temper. One must have mastered the cultural sense of equivalence sufficiently to know what kind of demands on the other to make in the name of indignation. And one must learn to experience indignation rather than temper or simple rage.

Because the sentiment is learned, it is an ideal pattern and therefore is often not fully exemplified in the behavior of individuals. The nature of an emotion is established by direct observation of individuals in states of emotion, under conditions that allow the emotion to be manifested without inhibition. But the observations of what people do under the influence of a sentiment must be corrected by reference to the conceptions they share regarding the sentiment. It is well known that many people who try to be indignant wind up looking foolish rather than impressive. Similarly, love is often described as an ideal which few attain but which many attempt with poor success. We are not suggesting that the learned sentiment does not usually arise spontaneously but merely that like all learning the acquisition of sentiments is necessarily imperfect. Popular ideology has it that loving is doing what comes naturally but also admits how badly the first few attempts are likely to succeed. Hence there is the folk notion of the great lover, who serves as a model after whom people may pattern their own efforts.

Because they are learned and because they pertain to relationships that are socially meaningful in a particular society, both the nature and the repertoire of sentiments vary from culture to culture. We expect to find an emotion such as rage in all people in all societies; indignation probably requires a special kind of culture. It is clear that the manner of expressing love is culturally relative. But in addition, the very existence of some of the forms of love we recognize is probably peculiar to a few cultures like our own.

Physiological and Cultural Levels in Sentiment. In an oversimplified manner it is possible to speak of two levels in any sentiment, the psychophysiological and the sociocultural. In common sense, the psychophysiological level is the more "real" of the two, and the sociocultural is simply a natural expression of the more fundamental level. Thus one is thought to feel indignant, in some visceral sense, and it is then only natural to express the feeling. From this popular view, the specifications for genuine love presented by Paul, which presume that the individual can cultivate the indicated feelings within himself,[18] appear beautiful but ineffectual. The commonest treatment of sentiments in contemporary behavioral science accepts the underlying assumptions of more recent folk conceptions but gives them sophisticated treatment. Physiological experiences are thought to initiate, provide the motive power, and give the dominating direction to the sentiment and its behavior.

These views can be simply contrasted to the conception of sentiment underlying the present treatment. Under the foregoing views the sociocultural level of sentiment has the function of servicing the psychophysiological. The dynamic consideration is visceral imbalance and the restoration of the steady state; the sociocultural realm adds to the disturbance, places obstacles and limitations on release of tension, but must ultimately supply the avenues for release. Under the contrasting view man is seen as a social being, existing as man only through relations with other social beings. Sentiments are fundamentally crucial forms of relationships among people. The fundamental social fact is the exchange of meanings among people. But in order that these meanings have a quality of spontaneity, the psychophysiological level in this sense has the function of servicing the sociocultural.

A further contrast lies in the treatment of homogeneity and heterogeneity at the two levels. The orthodox view regards the psychophysiological level of a sentiment as homogeneous and the sociocultural as heterogeneous. Thus there is an effort to find the uniform physiological and psychological states and processes that underly the varied forms in which love is expressed. The contrasting view holds that the homogeneity lies in the kinds of relationships that people establish under the governance of what they conceive as the experience of love but that for different people and at different times the physiological and psychological accompaniments of the sentiment are quite different.

There is also an important temporal distinction between sentiment and simple emotion that relates to the homogeneity issue. It is the nature of emotion that it is of limited duration; a sentiment, on the other hand, can be enduring. The organism cannot tolerate the uninterrupted state of crisis that constitutes emotion. Anger, sexual arousal, and similar states are episodic. But one may remain indignant and continue to feel love between moments of intensified emotion. If the sentiment persists while psychophysiological states vary, it is difficult to account for the sentiment on the basis of a particular psychophysiological state.

[18] I Corinthians 13.

It would be a mistake to go to the extreme of insisting on a homogeneity of sentiment at the sociocultural level without any effect from the psychophysiological heterogeneity. A sentiment is a feeling about a relationship which is identified in culturally shared terms, which leads the individual to engage in forms of interaction that implement the sentiment as the culture defines it, and which is verified in the individual by certain internal sensations that he has come to recognize and accept as indicators. The sentiment takes on slightly varied forms in each individual who learns and manifests it. In common with any phenomenon rooted in the mastery of a cultural pattern, the sentiment varies according to the completeness with which it is learned, exposure to subcultures, and the system of social relations within which it is learned.

Love as a Cultural Pattern. If the distinctive homogeneity and dynamics of love are not to be found in the physiological sources of feeling but in a set of culturally identified and distinguished patterns, fruitful analysis must proceed from examination of the cultural patterns. We shall attempt to describe love in terms that have applicability to all its recognized family forms, from mate love to filial love and fraternal love. As a cultural phenomenon, love is not the same in all cultures and has even changed substantially in recent centuries. The pattern described, then, will be one that is apparent in the public beliefs of the dominant American middle class. After a description of the pattern, it will be possible to consider again the problem that love is considered a feeling and must therefore have some physiological source of sensation as a component.

Love, in all the forms found in the family, implies first of all an attraction between people. If this were the whole story, we could simply refer back to the discussion of bonds and dismiss love from further consideration. But all attractions are not love. Love is an attraction experienced in a particular manner and leading to behavior of specified kinds. Hence we must first examine the distinctive characteristics of an attraction that lead us to regard it as love.

1. Love as a form of attraction is assumed to be *enduring*. Variations in the surge of sensation and enthusiasm are recognized, with moments of intense feeling between mother and son or brother and sister, separated by periods of indifference and hostility. But love is assumed to be present underneath these variations, latent but ready for instant manifestation. The brother who insults and abuses his sister in moments of rage is supposed to be ready to feel compassion and remorse in an instant if he "really" hurts her and to find himself instantly coming to her defense when outsiders join in the attack against her.

As we shall note later when speaking of romantic love, not all the relationships to which the term love has been applied are supposed to be enduring. But to the extent that the sentiment of love has been assimilated to the family, so that family relationships supply the prototype for love, there is a tendency to distinguish casual attractions from love. The distinction is prospective, in the sense that once a feeling is identified as love the expectation is established in the lover and in others that the relationship will endure. Such a prospective orientation establishes a framework of meaning within which particular events and feelings can be interpreted.

The distinction is also retrospective, in the sense that particular attachments can be reinterpreted on the basis of their duration. A feeling experienced as love while it occurred can be discounted as not having been love if the bonds do not persist or if the feeling cannot be maintained or reawakened from time to time.

2. The love relationship is *pervasive* rather than segmental. Love is distinguished from those attractions between people which relate just to special interests they share and which operate only while they are engaged in a particular kind of activity together. It is not wholly set aside in work relationships and is affronted by efforts to exclude alter from certain aspects of ego's life.

3. The love relationship is *intimate*. Intimacy refers to the invasion of the usual boundaries set in interaction and exposure of the self in respects normally concealed. A brother and sister may confide in each other about their romantic lives and about troubles they have got into. When a husband keeps the nature of his office worries from his wife, she can legitimately wonder about his love for her.

4. The obverse of intimacy is trust. Only in a *trusting* relationship can one expose himself. By indulging in intimacy, one runs the risk of looking ridiculous or of revealing weaknesses that can be used to advantage in bargaining or conflict. Trust is the conviction that alter will not take advantage of the opportunities in this fashion.

5. The lover is *altruistic* toward the loved one. He is constantly aware of the interests and desires of alter and gains personal pleasure from being able to contribute toward their gratification. Self-sacrifice has long been the cornerstone of concepts of love. The self-interest component in many forms of attachment between people is freely recognized. But the most convincing evidence of love is to be found in a relationship demanding the greatest disregard of self-interest.

6. Partner to altruism is the *compassionate* attitude of the lover. One of the classic exemplars of folk wisdom, King Solomon, used compassion as the criterion of mother love. The true mother preferred to give up the child rather than see it divided between the two rival claimants. Adolescent love is often detected by the failure of a member of one sex group to

join in the enjoyment over some misfortune that has befallen a representative of the other sex.

7. If members of a group are altruistic and compassionate in their attitudes toward one another, it follows that decision making among them should be *consensual*. If there are differences that require compromises and concessions to reach decisions, altruism means that the concessions should be made without reservation, and compassion prevents the outcomes from being a basis for assuming dominance. Love, except in some of its romantic forms, does not seem to require a complete sharing and unanimity of desires as the basis for consensus. The son who sets aside his educational ambitions to support the family and the daughter who withdraws from the marriage market to care for an invalided mother serve as examples of love, because they accept without reservation or bitterness a family arrangement that requires the sacrifice of their individualistic aims.

8. Love is a *responsive* relationship. Interaction with the other is intrinsically enjoyable. Response bonds are assigned particular saliency in love relationships. Love is perfectly commensurate with separation, so much that the persistence of attachment during absence is often viewed as a test of the genuineness of love. But there is always a longing to interact and a search for opportunities to restore communication.

9. Love is an *admiring* relationship. "Love is blind" conveys the expectation that the lover distorts the good qualities of the loved one in the favorable direction. Admiration implies an identification bond, as do compassion and altruism.

10. Love is *spontaneous*. The spontaneity is marked by its uncontrollable rise, which is often characterized in folk tales by its manifestation in the face of a determination not to love. Spontaneity is also indicated by the uncontrollable inner sensations that accompany it and bring it on. Love is sharply distinguished in the cultural repertory (but not in practice) from that performance of obligations in the family which comes about because of belief in the rules or from a sense of personal honor.

11. Finally, love of the right kind in a family relationship is regarded with moral approbation and is obligatory in at least a minimum degree. As a *valued* complex of feeling and behavior, love turns our attention back to the regulation and control of family life.

Socialization to Love. The pattern is taught by example and by admonition. Children's stories convey ideas of sibling love, filial love, and other forms, with both positive and negative examples. Adults and other children point out inconsistencies in the child's behavior. An inconsistency is the coupling of behavior that corresponds to the sentiment with behavior that contradicts it. From the cultural standpoint, the child who seeks the company of a friend but is unwilling to share his toys is inconsistent. Gradually the child comes to structure his world in the framework that his culture provides, whether by eschewing parts of the complex lest they bring the rest with them or by developing the whole complex.

Children are also taught by direction and example that love in its appropriate form is natural to associations between appropriate people. As learning proceeds, interaction gets structured into acceptance of the sentiment as a whole in an appropriate relationship or massive resistance to the whole complex. As boys and girls reach the age at which love can be expected between them, there is often an initial drawing away, a rejection of otherwise normal compassion and tenderness, lest the whole sentiment be implied by the part. The relations between siblings often swing between extremes as the sentiment is accepted or rejected in the whole.

The relationship between the attitudinal and behavior aspects of the love sentiment and the bonds creating and maintaining the attraction between members can best be described as reciprocal. As the patterns are learned, the sensing of bonds between appropriate persons tends to evoke the relevant pattern. When a shared experience, an externally indicated identification, or formation of a coalition against other family members sets up a bond between siblings, their cultural learning tends to evoke the sentiment complex as a total patern. When an adolescent boy and girl experience a bond, they perceive the interdependence as love and tend spontaneously to experience the total sentiment.

On the other hand, in an appropriate setting the receipt of evidence of love is a gratifying experience and hence likely to invite at least partial reciprocation. When this occurs, the love behavior sets in motion a bonding process that can then provide the basis for fuller manifestation of the love sentiment.

Any specific form of love does not necessarily imply any specific set of bonds. We have noted that the conception of love calls for person-to-person bonds, with response bonds having particular saliency. But saliency and effectiveness are not the same thing. It is the genius of love sentiments that they channel attachments based on the most diverse kinds of bonds into a relatively common complex of behavior, which, if it is successful, facilitates the diversification of bonds and the growth of crescive bonds.

The sensations taken to indicate a sentiment undoubtedly come in part from recognized and unrecognized desires in specific relationships. Adolescent love without a sexual component would certainly be a rather different experience. But a great deal of what is called feeling is probably merely spontaneous anticipation, the imagination of the full enactment and reciprocation of the behavior indicated by the sentiment. There is probably a real set of sensations attached to the sentiment that come from muscular and visceral preparations for the indicated action and from the tensions aroused because of the uncertain outcome of interaction. For example, the tenderness and compassion of love imply a nonrigid body position, relaxed from the postures of serious task behavior, a tendency to reach out and make bodily contact, placing the arms about the other, and similar expressions. The mass of kinesthetic sensation tells the individual the positions his body is in, when he chooses to attend. Because love implies certain muscular states, it also involves a distinctive complex of kinesthetic sensation associated with these muscular states. Likewise, the vulnerable position in which the individual who expresses love places himself in case his intimate revelations are not reciprocated or his altruism is used as a basis for the establishment of dominance ensures an element of anxiety. The anxiety, like the muscle sensations, is probably not sensed as an independently identifiable experience but merged into a total feeling identified as love.

Each form of love leads to somewhat different behavior, although all have in some degree the common core we have described. Common sense assumes that the feeling toward the person impels him toward one or another kind of behavior. But man is poor at recognizing specific components from the complex of internal sensations reaching him. He often cannot recognize mild hunger unless it occurs at the appropriate hour, and fatigue is likely to be misperceived unless it is preceded by exertions normally thought sufficient to produce fatigue. The awakening of a bond points toward the kind of behavior that is appropriate in a positive relationship between people representing the roles at issue. Anticipation of behavior sets in motion anticipatory muscular and visceral readjustments that convey the sensation of something happening. It is perhaps enough that some kind of massive sensation is experienced, apart from its specific physiology. The learned linkage of the appropriate kind of love and love behavior to each specific form of relationship is so strong as to impose meaning on the sensations, unless their specific character is especially dominant.

Love as Social Control. The lack of fundamental contradiction between the spontaneous and responsible character of family relations is indicated when love is seen as a form of social control. Attractions and repulsions between people are, in their relatively unsocialized forms, sporadic and changeable and too unpredictable to form the basis for the more serious tasks of life, at least as they have been traditionally organized in our society. The sentiments of love contribute toward the ordering and stabilizing of attachments. In a sense the internalization of the sentiment supplies a continuous bond, not of sufficient strength to maintain a relationship alone, but such as to carry the relationship along between periods when the crucial bonds are in operation. Learning the love sentiments is part of learning the norms of stable and enduring ties that are parts of the family system.

In one sense the love sentiments create in people the need for a sort of comprehensive and intensive group matrix to serve as a base from which to venture into the community. It is important to make this observation, because there are other ways of regularizing and stabilizing ties, as in the work world. Even family life can be organized as a considerably less intense set of relationships, as we shall observe in examining the extended family system, with much less reliance on and demand for the kind of sentiment recognized as love in our society.

If love sentiments are vehicles of social control through regularizing attachments between certain socially relevant categories of people, they also protect identities by disguising a variety of bonds under a cover of socially acceptable and personally complimentary meaning. For a mother to recognize that her attachment to her son is partially a transfer of identification bonds from her husband, as the years have transformed the latter into a relatively ordinary and undistinguished individual, would hardly facilitate relationships in the family. But to feel mother love welling up within her is both highly acceptable and admirable. Recognition that his sister's attachment to him is partially compounded of the fact that she can deal directly and directively with him in the way her sex role prevents her from doing with boys outside the family would probably lead a brother to place a barrier between them. But sisterly love is understandable and complimentary so long as it is displayed without public embarrassment.

Finally, love sentiments impel and direct behavior in the manner prescribed for family relationships. The feeling aspect of the sentiment demands action; the ritual aspect indicates the appropriate action. Mate love helps make a man want to work hard at his employment and invest the proceeds in a suitable home for his family. There is nothing intrinsic about the sex-laden attachment of a man to a woman that makes so indirect an expression automatic or natural, apart from cultural learning. But the framework of meaning in which the man places his own impulses leads him to desire ardently to realize his love through actions of this kind.

Obstacles to Love

Any cultural pattern is learned in a system of social relationships, and full internalization, so that the pattern becomes a spontaneous and complete form of behavior, depends on a favorable set of social relationships. Similarly, the expression of a sentiment, once it is learned or while it is being learned, is facilitated or impeded by the social relationship it is to be practiced in. There are people who are difficult to love, in spite of bonds and appropriate statuses, because the responses they make do not support love. Anticipation or fear of inappropriate responses impedes the expression of love, and contradictory definitions of the meanings of situations and actions block the expression of the sentiment. If we remember that socialization is merely the name of a cumulative residue of images and interpretations from a series of interaction experiences, examination of attitudes that impede spontaneous and complete expression of love in culturally appropriate situations supplies clues to both the course of love in particular relationships and the more generalized ability to love as a product of socialization.

Betrayal of Intimacy. Intimacy and compassion-altruism are crucial aspects of loving for present consideration, because they depend on appropriate responses in a relatively short range of time. Admission of alter to intimacy and altruistic behavior are impeded by an attitude of defensiveness, a *fear of betrayal.* The fear of betrayal is evoked in a particular relationship by several kinds of response on the part of alter to prior intimate revelations and altruistic actions. These are responses that weaken the trust that is the essential complement to these kinds of action.

The initiation of intimacy by ego is an invitation to alter to substitute empathic interpretation of ego's gestures for the conventional face-value interpretations. In some circumstances it constitutes license for a certain amount of diagnostic interpretation. By withdrawing the conventional barriers, ego allows alter to look behind the manifest aspects of ego's gestures; by offering clues to the concealed meanings of his behavior in the form of relatively exclusive tips, ego in some degree obligates alter to use the cues and look behind the normal facade. But ego runs a double danger in doing so. On the one hand he is affronted if alter fails to accept the invitation to make empathic interpretation. Disturbances in family relationships are especially likely to be attributed to *insensitivity.* Insensitivity often refers to the failure to use empathic interpretation where the relationship calls for it—the persistence of face-value interpretations; for example, the mother is hurt if the family members accept her protestations of good spirits at face value and fail to detect the malaise beneath.

On the other hand, once the door has been opened to empathic and diagnostic levels of interpretation, they can be used in nonlove contexts. In a decision-making situation mediated by bargaining, knowledge of otherwise hidden weaknesses, of ulterior purposes, of ambivalent attitudes and desires supplies a potential weapon. Where intimate knowledge is unequal, there is considerable bargaining advantage. But even when there have been intimate revelations on both sides, the selective use of empathic or diagnostic interpretations can be an effective tactic. Extensive mutual use of empathic and diagnostic interpretation in a bargaining relationship almost certainly transmutes the interaction into conflict because of the identity threats. When alter is more concerned with reaching a decision or ego's identity is less vulnerable in the situation, the mere suggestion of empathic or diagnostic interpretation by ego can provoke concessions from alter to forestall complete diversion of the relationship into conflict, with the resulting failure to gain any agreement to the point at issue.

When a person has experienced tactical disadvantage or identity hurt through either failure to use the clues and invitation to empathic interpretation or the carry-over of license to inappropriate situations, he is defensive about entering further intimacy. The girl who confides a failing in her brother, to have him use it against her in their next dispute, will require greater impulsion next time to offer a confidence. The husband who confides his fears of an unfavorable outcome to a current business dealing in his wife, only to have her throw it back at him in a later dispute over the time he is spending away from home on his work, will be more resistive against later attempts by his wife to read his true feelings.

Intimacy can be violated in another way by carrying the privileged image outside the closed circle. Part of the trust implied by intimacy is the maintenance of privacy. Without privacy, the revelations become simply another part of the public image of the individual. If alter reveals intimacies to others, ego loses control of his own public image to this extent and also finds his identity treated without respect to the sacredness implied in selective intimacy.

Violations of privacy are especially likely to occur when intimate knowledge is prestigeful and when the group is one in which the norm against such revelations is not salient. Thus a child breaks privacy in revelations about his parent to other children, about his opposite-sex sibling in his own sex group, and about an older or younger sibling in his own age group. These are also relationships in which alter and his associates are far removed from the kind of experience that makes it easy for them to identify fully with ego in the sacredness he attaches to the privileged information and in which the nature of the group is such that the knowledge is not intrinsically hurtful. Parents are especially likely to regale other adults with accounts of the cute things done and said by their children. The child's perspective and the adult's on these matters are quite different. Discovery of the privacy violation makes the child more reserved in his subsequent relationship with the parent.

In addition to these innocent violations of privacy there are instances in which the privacy barrier is broken in order to form a coalition against the other. Formation of coalitions is an ordinary aspect of much decision making. But a coalition with an outsider undermines the value of the insider relationship and treats the tender of intimacy as a pawn rather than a sacred action.

The precarious inner self of intimacy can also be damaged by clumsy handling. Ego may offer a revelation for alter to accept without extended comment. Alter may mistake the intent and pick up the revelation and make it an issue of discussion. The child may long to confess a misdeed to his parent, wishing only to have the parent know. The matter may be still too sensitive for the child to bear open discussion. If the parent indicates simple acceptance and appreciation of the nature of the communication as an offer of intimacy and avoids further discussion, the child is encouraged to tender intimacies in the future. But if the parent insists on a painful discussion of the matter, the child is likely to be more defensive in the future.

Finally, fear of betrayal of intimacy results from alter's misconstrual of the cues into an unacceptable image of ego. Especially common sources of such fears are the naïve oversimplifications—the stereotyping—of images. Each person's image of himself is usually that of a complicated person, too subtle to be fitted easily into the common brackets. Too ready indication of full understanding or formulation of simple images leads ego to draw back from full intimacy. Initially, efforts are often made to indicate the uniqueness and complexity of self, especially when bonds of a substantial character unite persons. A woman tries to convince her husband that her feelings about the household are not merely those of the typical housewife and the child to convince the parent that his wild ambitions are not simply typical childhood dreams. But failure of these efforts can lead only to defensive behavior that mutes the expression of love.

To recapitulate, intimate revelation places ego in a precarious situation. His identity can be damaged by any of a variety of inappropriate responses, ranging from innocent misinterpretations to calculating abuse. Although we have not outlined them, many similarly damaging responses to altruism are possible, for altruism likewise places the individual in a precarious situation that requires a reciprocal and protective response from the other. Damage to the identity following tentative offers of intimacy or altruistic advances lead to defensiveness against further betrayal.

Extensive experiences of this character during socialization to the love sentiment render the individual unable to play the part of lover except in a highly guarded way. Love is attempted without intimacy or with token intimacy. Accordingly the rituals of love are not given substance by the behaviors that make love genuine. Or love becomes disproportionately a possessive relationship, when altruism fails to balance off the desire to possess the other. Since the ideas of intimacy and altruism must certainly be learned with the total complex, ritual substitutions for free intimacy and altruism become parts of the practice of love. But without the real forms of behavior, the ritual practice of love becomes a betrayal to the partner, who is similarly forced to withdraw to escape identity damage and bargaining disadvantage.

The inhibition of these features of love from fear of betrayal may be general, leading to a pervasive inability to enter into a love relationship, or specific to a relationship with particular people, or restricted to a moment and situation. Every act of love is tentative in the sense that it invites the appropriate response, may be followed by intensified efforts to establish the desired relations, but eventually is withdrawn if the proper reciprocation cannot be attained. In every pair relationship within the family there are episodes of frustrated love offers, reciprocation being prevented by preoccupations and moods and situations of the moment. Against the continuing relationship an occasional experience of this kind may count as little. But a consistent experience leads to readjustment of self-other images so as to remove love from the conception of this relationship. Consistent experiences of this kind during childhood, in a range of family relationships, lead to so generalized a defensiveness that entry into a spontaneous love relationship with anyone is impossible.

Attempts to establish relationships may still appear, especially at the age when courtship is the normal behavior or when comfort and response are especially needed. Although the individual overcomes his defensiveness to the extent of a genuine invitation to intimacy or a genuinely altruistic act, his anxieties are likely to frustrate his effort. The advances are likely to be unnatural and clumsy because of inexperience and anxiety, so that they are misunderstood. And they are likely to be accompanied by an anxious demand for evidence of appropriate reciprocation. The result is a demandingness that destroys the chance of spontaneity in alter's behavior, and a hypersensitiveness to possible indications that trust is being violated that leads to withdrawal before the effort has been adequately tested.

Preoccupation with Assigning Responsibility. The ability to respond to alter with compassion is another crucial component of love that is sensitive to the manner in which ego has learned to perceive situations. Compassion requires an unguarded personal identification with the other. In this respect the foregoing discussion of fear of betrayal applies. One way to make a person look foolish is to simulate injury, evoke his compassion, and suddenly reveal the dissimulation in the presence of an audience.

The ability to offer spontaneous compassion is also often a casualty of social-control processes. Control over relationships in accordance with the regulations of society rests on several mechanisms. We have noted that love, by impelling and guiding behavior in approved directions, is one mechanism. The ultimate inclination of society and its agents to use coercive force is another. Love is considered the preferable motive and is supposed to be salient in family relationships. Between these two extremes lies the assignment of personal responsibility. If rules have been violated or harm done, specific culprits must be identified. Sometimes mere identification of the culprit is enough to bring about control, but in any case assignment of responsibility is a necessary prelude to the use of punishment and coercion.

There is an inherent conflict between compassion and the assignment of responsibility. If responsibility is to be assigned objectively, personal feelings must be held in abeyance lest the judgment be distorted. In such case compassion becomes a halting and artificial response.

But even when the conception of assigning responsibility objectively does not prevail, the opposition remains for two reasons. First, along with responsibility goes the concern for punishment to the culprit. Preoccupation with responsibility means that punishment must be meted. Any suspicion that the injured person was in some respect responsible for his misfortune transforms his hurt into merited punishment. Second, emphasis on responsibility means that ego must ensure first that no responsibility is placed on him. It becomes so important at the moment to assure others that "I didn't do it" that compassionate concerns must take second place.

The former situation is especially likely to be found in people who have responsibility for the behavior of others. Parents come to anticipate the misfortunes that befall their children and try to warn and train them to avoid them. When the misfortune occurs, their efforts to forestall the event have failed. Often the parent can only blurt out, "Why didn't you watch what you were doing?" when persons outside the family and free of personal responsibility are responding with compassion.

The second situation is especially frequent when ego and alter are both under direction and judgment from a person in authority. A child is often too anxious lest blame be cast on him to be able to experience compassion. Children whose parents demand that every misfortune be followed by an accounting fail to learn compassion and are accordingly unable to play the part in love relationships adequately.

There is an inherent dilemma here, that the family is a closely regulated unit, that members of the family have heavy personal and collective responsibilities imposed on them, and that a major task of the family is to inculcate observance of a wide range of society's rules; at the same time family relations are supposed to be characterized by compassion, and the ability to feel compassion is an essential element in being able to give love. The key to the dilemma appears to lie in tolerance for considerable latitude with respect to the rules and acceptance of societal aims as values more than as norms. Whether mastery of rules is taken as a positive aim—pride in accomplishment—or whether rules are unwelcome restraints is largely a matter of how they are presented in the family situation. Latitude for deviations from rules is facilitated by family privacy, limited age expectations, and freedom from complete identification of family members with one another by the community.

Bargaining Attitudes. Impediments to love are also found in the ability to receive and accept love. For the most part the same fears of betrayal and preoccupation with assignments of responsibility impede the acceptance of love. But special note should also be taken of the impediment of a bargaining preoccupation. We have noted earlier that a gift or a kindness is turned into a point gained over the receiver—a coup—when the relationship is defined as bargaining. The approach to interpersonal relations from the standpoint of bargaining is the product of experiences in which earlier favors are subsequently cited as the justification for demands on the recipient. The parent is often tempted to remind the child of his unequal contribution to the family in order to secure his compliance to a demand. Children's birthday parties in which efforts are made to adjust the value of the gift given to the gift received are learning experiences with respect to the barter element in gift exchange.

As in other respects, single experiences are seldom crucial, and the preponderance of relationships in which bargaining is not important permits the acceptance of favors without reserve and anxiety. Even failure of parents in most instances to implement occasional threats to withdraw favors to their children in the face of noncompliance probably keeps preoccupation with bargaining at a minimal level.

But when prior experience with the same person or generalized interpersonal experience leads the individual to perceive the relationship as one of bargaining, altruistic behavior by alter arouses anxieties in ego and leads to mechanisms that prohibit his unqualified acceptance of the behavior as a tender of love. The offer may be refused—the gift is too much, the help is not really needed, alter's time is too valuable to waste in helping ego. The offer may be reinterpreted so as to deny its altruistic character—ego accepts alter's offer to go out of his way, because he realizes that alter really wants an excuse to get away from his other obligations. Or there may be a scramble for quick reciprocation before alter has a chance to exploit the advantage created by his altruism. Whatever the mechanism, alter's advances are not accepted as love by ego, and further advances are discouraged.

In general terms, then, the ability to implement the culturally learned sentiment of love in interpersonal relations depends on a socialization experience and an interpersonal relationship in which identities are treated with discretion—as sacred objects; in which adherence to rules is not a focus of major preoccupation and anxiety; and in which attention to bargaining has played a secondary part, applying only to special kinds of situations rather than to the normal routine. At the same time, loving depends on mastery of an elaborate set of norms and interpretations of behavior and their internalization as a framework within which interpersonal relations are experienced.

Love and Family Interaction

Many effects of the presence of love sentiments on the processes of interaction in the family have been suggested in the course of discussing the nature of love and its obstacles. The most general effect of love is to define the valued and acceptable terms of family relationships. By defining certain kinds of bonds as the essence of family relationships and others as subordinate or even irrelevant, society requires in effect that both the implementation and the dissolution of the less relevant bonds be translated into the functioning of response bonds and the more personal forms of identification bonds. Improved economic functioning is only reluctantly recognized as a basis for closer bondedness, and economic deterioration must be translated into failures in response and identification to justify weakening the relationship. By setting consensual decision making as the norm, the love sentiments render openly accommodative decisions somewhat unstable and make them a basis for devaluation of the relationship. "There is something wrong with us" if every decision requires compromise and the close accounting for prior decision outcomes. And the love sentiments both intensify the motivation to avoid conflict and the reassessments required in the wake of conflict episodes.

Love and Decision Making. Love brings family behavior more firmly under the control of agencies outside the family. Because love is verified by the evaluation of the community, love is demonstrated by conformity to community demands. The school official, the youth leader, the church official urge that parental support and participation in their programs are a necessary proof of the parent's love for his child. The sentiment of love is like a relay device that steps up the intensity of the community demands on the family. A man owes it to his family to get along at work; a child owes it to his parents to do well at school. Failure to submit to direction in either sphere creates the suspicion that family love is lacking.

Love augments the demands that family members can make on one another. A simple decision-making situation is converted into a test of love when one member says, "Do it my way this time just because I ask you." Acceptance of the love sentiments adds an element to that testing which is a normal part of every interactive episode. At base there is general testing to establish the meanings of gestures, with accompanying preparation for changed lines of action in the event of noncongruence. But insofar as being loved is a valued state in family relations and is over the long run a condition to giving love freely, there is an undercurrent of testing the love of the other. Because love is supposed to be pervasive, it can provide the basis for diversionary interpretations during interaction centering on almost any object.

The idealistic and moral flavor of love can become a cover for the use of love as a control device in family interaction. Love is said to be a force for good, and in some circles it used to be common to hear of a woman marrying a disreputable man in order to reform him. Manipulation and coercion that would be disparaged in overt form can sometimes be condoned in this kind of disguise.

In a more general way, the giving of love can be a tactic facilitating control in decision-making interaction. The fawning wife of an earlier era turned aside her husband's anger and gained concessions by her offers of love. A child often learns similarly to play on the parent's softness. A child's kiss or hug has won many a family contest.

Love and Conflict Resolution. Love supplies incentive for the avoidance and resolution of conflict, over and beyond the incentives derived from the bonds underlying the relationship, and contributes distinctive patterns of conciliation. The incentive is both positive and negative. The desire to avoid conflict, empathic interpretations of alter's gestures that facilitate early recognition of potentially identity-damaging situations, and the admiring relationship all act positively in this direction. Negatively, a love relationship augments the potential identity damage from conflict. Conflict almost surely means some violation of trust, with the use of intimate knowledge to hurt the other. The intimate and potentially damaging knowledge that each has of the other is greater because of the love, and the threat to the relationship of trust must be added to the other dangers from conflict. Insistence on finding the explicit justification and pivot of the relationship in response bonds and certain kinds of identification bonds—an essential part of love—places emphasis on just those bonds which are most vulnerable to conflict. As a consequence, conflicts between persons who see their relationship as love tend to be terminated and conciliated quickly, and elaborate avoidances and conciliatory procedures are usually developed to forestall the materialization of incipient conflict.

In a relationship heretofore defined as love, the reassertion of love constitutes a distinctly effective device for conciliation. Because of the permanence and nonsegmental character of love, participants must accept that in a crucial test the union of love is more important and more powerful than the division over particular issues. The injection of a declaration of love or a reminder of love in the course of conflict is a way of discount-

ing the current identity problem or the identity-damaging conflict gestures. It says to alter that the gestures were not really meant—the essential
step in conflict conciliation. Apart from love, the usual manner of making
such admissions involves self-humiliation, because of the admissions of
fault and error. Ordinary conciliation is an even more difficult step, because the conciliatory gesture is too easily interpreted as a sign of weakness, to be met by a demand for more complete surrender as a condition
for restored harmony. But when love has been the mutually accepted
term of relationship, the reassertion of love in a situation of stress is a
highly valued step. In a sense, this is what love is for—to carry people
through the most difficult moments. Unless alter is prepared to reject
the entire love character of the relationship, he is under great pressure to
acknowledge the merit of ego's action and respond with his own declaration of love or other conciliatory steps. But alter's response is made
easier, because he too can escape the denigration of acknowledging his
own faulty gestures by responding with a declaration of love.

It should not be assumed that the immediate consequence of such an
expression or exchange of love reassurance is to dispel the angry emotion
generated in the course of conflict. If feelings change in an inkling, it is
probably because the threat to the bonds or the sense of personal fault
in the developing conflict is sufficiently intense to arouse strong anxieties.
Such anxieties are most likely to be aroused early in a relationship, as in
courtship or the initial adjustment period of marriage, when the bonds
have not been sufficiently tested for durability or when one party senses
a weakening of bonds, as in the parent who sees his child's growing self-
sufficiency. Normally feelings persist for a time and subside more gradually. But this is the distinctiveness of human behavior, that symbolic
reorientations can precede and evoke changes of feeling.

An esoteric by-product of the place of love as a conciliatory device is
the folk sentimentalization of the lovers' quarrel, primarily in the mate
and courtship relationships but occasionally in other family pairs. The
speed and effectiveness of reconciliation from conflict is in some sense a
proof of love. The qualities of love are tested under stress, and the sudden
turning away is hardly possible apart from the power of love. Furthermore, the problem with any sentiment, such as love, which is supposed to
be continuous, is to find within oneself the deep feelings that give it reality
and vitality. The relatively sudden transition from conflict to the exchange
of love expressions supplies some of the emotional turmoil that can make
love more than a platonic relationship. Thus the lover's quarrel is often
thought to be good and even essential. And persons anxious to prove to
themselves that their relationship is truly love provoke a play of conflict
over trivial issues in order to enact the conciliation through love.

Because of the persistence of feelings of resentment and anger under the cover of love declarations, this pattern is not likely to persist once sufficient conflict experience has lessened the anxiety provocation of ordinary conflict. Indeed, its use without full and prompt dissipation of conflictual feelings can lead to doubts concerning the reality of love and almost surely leaves a residual of sensitive areas that will be provocative of negative identity orientations in the future.

Summary

The general tone or quality of interaction in the family is distinguished from other groups by the combination of what superficially seem to be two contradictory elements. Family relationships are pervasively responsible relationships, which means that they are subject to intense social regulations; yet they are supposed to be marked by the spontaneity of love. The family is closely regulated, because it performs important functions for the community. Although some of its traditional functions have become less important in recent years, the family is still a crucial economic unit, is nearly the only group in which care for the irreplaceable individual is paramount, provides custodial services and forms a unit for community participation and placement, is the setting for most allowable sex relations, is the only wholly acceptable locus for procreation, and is the primary agency for socialization. Community control over family life creates the role of agent, one who exercises authority in the family because of authority that is exercised over him in some outside relationship and makes the family a pawn in institutional power struggles. But community control of family life is more positive than negative, through social support and expectations of family success.

Love, far from being a naïve impulse or emotion, translates social regulation of the family into spontaneous individual desire, as a social sentiment. A sentiment is a feeling about a relationship which is identified in culturally shared terms, which leads the individual to engage in forms of interaction that implement the sentiment as the culture defines it, and which is verified in the individual by certain internal sensations that he has come to recognize and accept as indicators. A sentiment exhibits more homogeneity at the sociocultural level than at the psychophysiological level and has an enduring quality that emotion lacks.

All kinds of family love—marital, paternal, filial, and sibling—have certain basic characteristics in American middle-class culture. Love is (a) enduring, (b) pervasive, (c) intimate, (d) trusting, (e) altruistic, (f) compassionate, (g) consensual, (h) responsive, (i) admiring, (j) spontaneous, and (k) valued. The cultural patterns of love are taught by admonition and example and require that the learner become familiar with the appropriate behavior and the situations to which it is applicable and learn to identify certain internal sensations as indications of love. The apparent contradiction of control and spontaneity in the family is clarified when love sentiments are understood as mechanisms for social control by which interpersonal attractions and repulsions are stabilized, modified so as to favor family life, and given a socially valued meaning even when based on diverse and sometimes discreditable bonds.

Mastering the cultural forms of love does not guarantee the ability to give and receive love effectively. The ability to love depends also on a socializing experience and a current interpersonal relationship in which identities are treated with discretion as sacred objects, adherence to rules is not a focus of major preoccupation and anxiety, and explicit bargaining is only a minor theme.

The fact that family relationships are characterized by love has notable effects on all the family processes and especially on bonding, decision making, and conflict. Other bonds must be subordinated to response bonds and the more personal forms of identity bonds in the minds of family members. Love supplies a vehicle through which outside agencies can make demands on family members and a tactic that can be used by members in their efforts to control family decisions. Most important, love greatly enhances the repertoire of devices for effecting conciliation in case of conflict. The sentiment of love is like a highly complex mechanism. On the one hand it contributes to the bondedness of the family, evens out some of the ups and downs, and gives a spontaneity and identity-enhancing tone to many of the obligatory routines of family life. But like any complex mechanism it has a vast and varied potential for malfunctioning. And in case of serious malfunction, it can multiply other difficulties in family interaction.

Transition

The role structure in any group and the functions assigned to it are inextricably tied up with the group's composition. If family processes and the meanings of gestures follow unique courses, the most obvious place to look for explanations is in the unique composition of the family. No other small social unit consists of male and female and at least one member who is a generation younger. Hence all family interaction is shaped by the peculiarities of interaction between sexes and age groups. Whatever influences shape male and female roles in the society at large affect the nature of family roles, and whatever characteristics the society gives to age roles are a constraint on family organization. The assignment of certain functions to the family goes along with its peculiar composition. Thus the organization of the family unit about a male and female adult and the function of supplying sexual relations go together, and the combination of adult and child and the socialization function are inseparable.

Part 4 examines the distinctive characteristics of family interaction that result from the unique composition of the family and these two associated functions.

FAMILY COMPOSITION:
SEX AND AGE

CHAPTER 11

SEX ROLES:
INSTITUTIONAL
ANCHORAGES

Compared with other small groups, the family is distinctive in being organized about a male and female head. Three chapters are devoted to exploring the effects of this unique composition on family processes and family roles. The present chapter asks how institutional anchorages of male and female roles affect family organization. Chapter 12 asks a similar question about the personality or style aspects of male and female roles. Chapter 13 asks how the social function of providing for sexual gratification affects family processes.

Family Role Priority. There are two ways in which the relationship between societal and familial sex roles can be approached. It can be assumed that the peculiar character of interaction in the family leads to a sex-role differentiation especially attuned to the unique conditions and requirements of life in the family and that this role differentiation is generalized and carried over into spheres of life outside the family. Or by contrast it can be assumed that there is a pervasive system of sex-role differentiation in the society that tends to be carried into the family as into other settings.

Two instances of research using the former assumption make the issues clearer. In the jury system of justice, a collection of untrained and typical citizens are supposed, under the constraints and direction of court procedure, to engage in rational discussion and reach just decisions. Part of rational discussion is participation without respect to differences in social position, so that the outcome is not foreordained by the status of the jury. Strodtbeck and Mann sought to determine whether this assumption was valid with respect to sex composition.[1]

Twelve juries of twelve persons each were assembled on the basis of names drawn by lot from the regular jury pools of the Chicago and St. Louis courts. Each jury listened to the recording of an automobile negli-

---

[1] Fred L. Strodtbeck and Richard D. Mann, "Sex Role Differentiation in Jury Deliberations," *Sociometry*, 19:3–11, March 1956.

gence case and was then instructed to discuss the case, under supervision of a court bailiff, and return a verdict. The discussion was tape-recorded, and subsequently all acts were classified in the twelve categories of the Bales system.[2] The results for the 127 jurors who initiated five or more acts each are reported in Table 8. The twelve categories have been collapsed into four main groups for simplicity's sake, and it is the comparison between positive reactions (social-emotional) and attempted answers (task) we are interested in. Because there is a relationship between rate of participation in the discussion and kind of action, Strodtbeck and Mann report the rates separately for the more and less active participants. The differences are clear and consistent, with females making a larger share of positive reactions and males a larger share of attempted answers. The authors conclude that the finding "strongly confirms the hypothesis that there is a continuance in jury deliberations of sex role specialization observed in adult family behavior."[3] They note further that "a task emphasis tends to be selected by men and a social-emotional emphasis by women."[4]

The findings are not compelling, however, with respect to the first conclusion, and the second conclusion is correct only in a limited sense. The sex difference in emphasis is relative; both men and women emphasize primarily the task behavior demanded by the situation, and both men and women contribute to interpersonal harmony by occasional supportive

TABLE 8   SEX DIFFERENCES IN JURY BEHAVIOR

	Percentage Distribution of Acts			
	Male		Female	
Type of Act	Inactive	Active	Inactive	Active
Positive reactions	13	11	27	25
Attempted answers	71	71	60	55
Questions	6	8	7	8
Negative reactions	10	10	6	12
Total	100	100	100	100
Total acts	1,486	12,413	648	3,093
Number of jurors	41	45	23	18

SOURCE: Adapted from Fred L. Strodtbeck and Richard D. Mann, "Sex Role Differentiation in Jury Deliberations," *Sociometry*, 19:7, March, 1956, by permission of the American Sociological Association and the authors.

[2] The Bales system was discussed in Chapters 5 and 9.
[3] Strodtbeck and Mann, *op. cit.*, p. 8.
[4] *Ibid.*, p. 11.

behavior. The conclusion that family roles have carried over into jury behavior is no better supported than the alternative interpretation that societal sex roles are so pervasive that they cannot be easily dismissed in any special setting. The question still to be answered is whether the differentiation is more intense in the family than in the jury and whether the family is the source of differentiation.

The position is presented even more sharply in the work of Parsons and of Zelditch, already cited.[5] Parsons explains the development of the idea:

In the course of Bales's early studies of the structure of small task-oriented groups certain striking analogies to the structure of the nuclear family emerged. This gave us the idea that the parents tend to constitute a "leadership coalition" in the family, and that the members of this coalition perform roles differentiated from each other in the same fundamental way as in the dual leadership of the small group; namely, in terms of the greater "instrumental" specialization of the "idea" man, analogous to the husband-father, and the greater "expressive" specialization of the "best liked" man, analogous to the wife-mother.[6]

In more concrete terms, Zelditch argues the position:

Why after all, are *two* parents necessary? For one thing, to be a stable focus of integration, the integrative-expressive "leader" can't be off on adaptive-instrumental errands all the time. For another, a stable, secure attitude of members depends, it can be assumed, on a *clear* structure being given to the situation so that an *uncertain* responsibility for emotional warmth, for instance, raises significant problems for the stability of the system. And an uncertain managerial responsibility, an unclear definition of authority for decisions and for getting things done, is also clearly a threat to the stability of the system.[7]

Dedifferentation of Family Roles. The preceding investigators form their conclusions by reasoning from what they see to be essential to family life. But a more empirical approach has been used by certain other investigators, with different conclusions. Robert Leik expressed doubt that a sharp differentiation into instrumental and expressive roles was feasible in the daily intimacy of a family, supposing that role differentiation was demanded more by the responsibilities women and men are called on to perform outside the setting of immediate family interaction than within it. A laboratory experiment was devised in which three persons were given the problem of discussing a specified issue of relevance to family life and reaching consensus. Nine family groups consisting of father, mother, and college daughter were recruited as subjects. Each

[5] Talcott Parsons and Robert F. Bales, *Family: Socialization and Interaction Process,* Free Press, New York, 1955.
[6] *Ibid.,* p. vii.
[7] *Ibid.,* p. 312.

person participated in three discussion sessions, each on a different topic, once with two other persons from his own age-and-sex group, once in a family group made up of strangers (a father, a mother, and a daughter), and once in his own family group. It is the comparison between the latter two experimental settings that is of interest. If the distinction between instrumental and expressive roles originates in the family and is carried over into other settings, differentiation of behavior should be clearer in family groups than in familylike stranger groups.[8]

Observers behind one-way screens classified behavior in a modified version of the Bales categories, and the investigator computed task rates and emotion rates for each of the subjects in the two experimental conditions. The results are summarized in Table 9. The task rate was the proportion of all task behavior in the session initiated by the person in question, divided by the proportion of all behavior in the session initiated by the person in question, and multiplied by 100. The emotion rate was the proportion of all positive emotional behavior in the session initiated by the person in question, divided by the same rate as before, and multiplied by 100. Rather than reporting rates in detail the author has simply divided cases according to whether the rate was above 100 or not. In order to simplify the table, we report only the number of persons with rates above 100 (the number not above 100 is always the difference between the number above 100 and nine, which is the total number of persons in each family-role category).

The findings are opposite to those expected in case the family role differentiation were primary and support Leik's assumption that sex roles

TABLE 9   ARTIFICIAL AND FAMILY GROUPS

| | Number of Sessions (N = 9) | | | |
| | Artificial Groups | | Family Groups | |
Family Member	Task Rate >100	Emotional Rate >100	Task Rate >100	Emotional Rate >100
Father	6	1	6	1
Mother	3	7	5	5
Daughter	3	7	1	7

SOURCE: Adapted from Robert K. Leik, "Instrumentality and Emotionality in Family Interaction," *Sociometry*, 26:140, June, 1963, by permission of the American Sociological Association and the author.

[8] Robert K. Leik, "Instrumentality and Emotionality in Family Interaction," *Sociometry*, 26:131–145, June 1963.

are less clearly differentiated within the family than without. The men behave much the same in the artificial and family groups, assuming a relative task emphasis. The behavior of the adult women, however, is less clearly differentiated according to the traditional sex role within the family group than it is outside. Daughters' roles are even more consistently differentiated within the family, but the combination age-sex role distinction probably confuses the issue here. The author summarizes these findings as follows:

It appears that mothers and daughters play comparable roles with strangers. But when interaction takes place within the family, mothers "take over" a greater share of the task area, with a somewhat lessened (but still important) emotional emphasis. Concomitantly, daughters "back out" of the task sphere even more than they did in role playing sessions. . . .[9]

A similar issue underlies the comparison of family group behavior in the home and in the laboratory. The normal family mode of interaction should be more directly displayed in the familiar home surroundings than in the strange and unhomelike setting of the laboratory. John F. O'Rourke observed the decision-making behavior of 24 three-member family groups in both home and laboratory.[10] He found that "the positivity of fathers and children decreased as they moved from home to laboratory while that of mothers increased."[11] Thus male-female specialization in relation to expressive behavior was less in the more familiar and appropriate home surroundings than it was in the laboratory situation.

A further kind of evidence bears on this question. The argument for the primacy of role differentiation in the family rests on the conviction that the family works better with such differentiation than without it. A study of 96 married couples in urban Illinois by Farber confirms the findings of several other investigators, that high marital integration scores are positively associated with the placement of high evaluation on social-emotional aspects of family life by the husband.[12] The serious problems in using self-rating scales for marital adjustment are not to be overlooked, but insofar as the findings are to be taken seriously, they suggest that marriage works better if masculine specialization is moderated when applied to marital interaction.

Theoretical Basis. The expectation that role differentiation by sex is less clear within the family than out of it stems from the small size of the nuclear family and its intimate, sentimental character. From a functional

[9] Ibid., pp. 140–141.
[10] John F. O'Rourke, "Field and Laboratory: The Decision-making Behavior of Family Groups in Two Experimental Conditions," Sociometry, 26:422–435, December 1963.
[11] Ibid., p. 434.
[12] Bernard Farber, "An Index of Marital Integration," Sociometry, 20:117–134, June 1957.

point of view, too polarized and unvarying a pattern for role differentiation and allocation makes for inflexibility in a self-contained group that is very small. In an office with only one official and one secretary the official has to answer the telephone from time to time, and the secretary has to make a higher level decision occasionally when the official is unavailable. The same is true of the family. With only one man and one woman, illnesses, the irregular tempo of work, and the varying availability of members make occasional disregard of standard role differentiation essential if the tasks of the family life are to be completed. As soon as the family becomes larger, however, and the adult female role is shared with a grandparent or a daughter approaching maturity, it becomes easier to adjust the tasks between the women and thus maintain the inviolability of the sex-role differentiation.

Our logic suggests the principle that there is a diminishing relationship between size of family group and the possibility of maintaining rigid sex-role differentiations, with the increase from one to two persons capable of playing a particular role making the greatest difference, succeeding additions making smaller increments toward role differentiation, until a point is reached at which the addition of members ceases to make any difference. When external pressures to maintain rigid sex-role differentiations are great, the family group must be opened by bringing in outsiders as needed to share the male and female roles in emergencies. Wealthy families are often able to employ servants in order to maintain the classic sex roles. The neighborhood group often serves in this manner in peasant and working-class families, the mutual-aid pattern operating within sex groups rather than by family units. Women of the neighborhood assist one another in women's tasks and the men in men's tasks. Since the privacy principle is violated by these forms of aid, the following hypotheses are suggested: The small family governed by a strong privacy principle is characterized by an internal sex-role differentiation that is less rigid and polarized than characterizes its members outside the family; whenever strong role differentiation is maintained—by strong traditional beliefs, and the like—in a small family that adheres to the privacy principle, there is a reduction in task effectiveness and a tension toward violating the privacy principle, and these strains are likely to play an important part in the pattern of chronic and cumulative conflict in the family.

It is worth noting that Zelditch's observation, that the American pattern of family sex-role differentiation is more flexible than that which he found in most societies, is to be expected on the basis of the small size, the privacy emphasis, and the love sentiment in the American family.[13]

The organization of the family around sentiment likewise makes a rigid sex-role differentiation unworkable. It is the nature of love that it demands

---

[13] Parsons and Bales, *op. cit.*, p. 312.

reciprocation of sentiment in some form. Even giving-receiving relationships require some form of sentiment development in each role.

Male Occupational Role

The critical anchorage of the characteristic male role is to his occupation or career. In American society it is well-nigh impossible to be a man without having an occupation, and how much of a man and what kind of a man one is are to be measured largely by the nature of the occupation and the success with which it is pursued. Numerous studies have shown that most men believe that they would work even if it were not economically necessary. Commenting in connection with one such study, which reports on a national sample of 401 employed men, Morse and Weiss offer a general statement of the place of work:

To the typical man in a middle class occupation, working means having a purpose, gaining a sense of accomplishment, expressing himself. He feels that not working would leave him aimless and without opportunities to contribute. To the typical man in a working class occupation working means having something to do. He feels that not working would leave him no adequate outlet for physical activity; he would just be sitting or lying around. To the typical farmer, just as to the typical individual in a working class occupation, working means keeping busy, keeping occupied. But work has a much more pervasive importance for the farmer. The boundaries between work and home life are not as sharp for him, and life without work is apt to be difficult to consider.[14]

It may not be too great an exaggeration to say that the adult male role consists of pursuit of an occupation, participation in activities contributory to successful pursuit of an occupation, and indulgence in activities contingent on adequate pursuit of his occupation. Other major institutional anchorages for the adult male role tend to be overshadowed by the occupational base. A man is already adjudged a useful citizen if he is succeeding at a respected occupation, and the full participation in the community as a respected and influential citizen is usually conditioned on an adequate degree of occupational success. Similarly, a man is adjudged prima facie to have performed a major share of his responsibilities as husband and father just by virtue of having a good record in the world of work, and it is only with great effort that we are able to think of a man as a good husband and father unless he takes his work responsibilities seriously.

Four features of the occupational articulation of the male role will be examined, because they affect the terms of a man's relationship with his wife and his participation in the family.

Occupation and Identity. First, a man's occupation *identifies* him.

[14] Nancy C. Morse and Robert S. Weiss, "The Function and Meaning of Work and the Job," *American Sociological Review*, 20:198, April 1955. Quoted by permission of the American Sociological Association.

Modes of address, deference, and topics of conservation are varied according to the occupation of the man being addressed. Privileges in the community are accorded and responsibilities imposed on the basis of occupation. For example, Wardwell and Wood remark that certain forms of extra-professional service are expected of a lawyer and not necessarily of persons in other occupations.[15] He is expected to be available as a public servant, "available for various kinds of non-political leadership, particularly where a community service or philanthropic purpose is involved," and to assume responsibility for "law-related activities, such as legal-aid societies and lawyer-reference plans."[16] Although lawyers by no means universally adhere to these expectations, their performance validates the respect normally accorded the lawyer.

There is a distinction in the manner in which a man identifies and is identified with his occupation. He may take a relatively casual attitude toward his work, saying characteristically, "It's a job." Or he may view it as a *vocation*. Edward Gross explains:

> The term "vocation" means literally a "calling" and as such refers to occupational situations in which the person's work is felt to be his whole life. He identifies with his work as a burden and feels an obligation to try to be especially good or proficient.[17]

Most workers fall somewhere between the extremes of a vocational and a casual attitude, with a wide range of individual variation. To the extent to which the casual attitude prevails, masculine identity depends more on the fact of being employed and on the instrumental benefits in money, power, prestige, and perquisites than on the instrinsic nature of the occupation and progress in the particular occupation. The vocational attitude means that the individual is committed to progress in his chosen occupation, rating such progress ahead of the instrumental benefits that might accrue from a strategic change of occupations. Perhaps the sense of vocation is highest in the ministry, and we find it difficult to think of a minister who turns his administrative skills to good account by accepting a higher-paying executive position in industry, although we find little difficulty in understanding the motives of a semiskilled worker who changes industry or goes into a different line of work when he can improve himself by doing so. The professional engineer with the strongest vocational commitment is prevented from accepting advancement to a higher-paying position in industrial administration; the university professor with the greatest voca-

[15] Walter I. Wardwell and Arthur L. Wood, "The Extra-professional Role of the Lawyer," *American Journal of Sociology*, 61:304–307, January 1956.
[16] *Ibid.*, pp. 305–306.
[17] Edward Gross, *Work and Society*, Crowell, New York, 1958, p. 202.

tional commitment is deterred from abandoning his scholarship and teaching to enter the societally more prestigious academic administration.

Occupation and Time Orientation. Somewhat related to the identification aspect of work role is its function in giving a time orientation to life. The individual's values, his interpretations, and the direction of his social participation may reflect an orientation strictly to the present, toward the future, or toward the past. The past orientation is likely only in cases of relative failure and with the approach of old age. But present and future perspectives are in part linked to whether work life has the character of a *career* or not. Wilensky defines a career as

. . . a succession of related jobs, arranged in a hierarchy of prestige, through which persons move in an ordered (more-or-less predictable) sequence. Corollaries are that the job pattern is instituted (socially recognized and sanctioned within some social unit) and persists (the system is maintained over more than one generation of recruits).[18]

When a person follows a career, the prestige and other rewards from the job he holds at the moment are of less concern than the career line to which the job contributes. The medical interne may live less well than an automobile assembly-line worker, but his life is geared to the future rather than to the present. Without a future orientation, the identity of the apprentice, the clerk who is learning the business, the junior officer in a military organization, the graduate student in a university, would suffer. But he is assisted in this orientation, because others treat him accordingly. He is enabled to make long-range plans because lending agencies take account of his anticipated career line.

Occupation and Preeminent Demands. Third, work life makes demands on time and energy that are granted legitimate priority over demands from other institutional spheres. That a man's job requires him to work late or to be out of town on a business trip is sufficient excuse for declining or canceling almost any other form of engagement. Job transfer or an opportunity to better himself professionally is sufficient justification for leaving friends, disrupting children's schooling, and abandoning community responsibilities to move the household to another community. The schedule determined by work determines the life schedule and the schedule into which other relationships must fit. The work schedule may relent occasionally to take account of illness or exceptional demands of sentiment, but ordinarily all other aspects of the life schedule must accommodate to the work schedule, even to the extent of the number of days that one may be ill.

[18] Harold L. Wilensky, "Orderly Careers and Social Participation: The Impact of Work History on Social Integration in the Middle Mass," *American Sociological Review*, 26:525, August 1961.

Occupation and Instrumentality. Finally, the instrumental benefits from work life, in money, prestige, perquisites, and skills and influence that are transferable to other than work situations, determine the kind of life that a man can lead. Not only is the socioeconomic level dependent on proceeds of the work life, but the general style of relations with others is influenced by skills and characteristic work relations. The craftsman's immediately useful skills provide a basis for neighborhood mutual aid, which the white collar worker may lack. The man whose occupation rests on the direction and manipulation of people is likely to find it easiest to participate in the community on the same basis.

Male Occupational Roles and Family Interaction

Each of these features of the work role has a series of consequences for the marital relationship. The character of the occupation and the extent of occupational success determine at once the degree to which an identification bond can constitute an important element of coherency in the relationship. But an effective identification bond requires certain kinds of relationships between husband and wife and sets the stage for certain sources of family disharmony not found in the absence of a bond identifying the wife with her husband's occupation.

Differences in Vocational Perspective. Discrepancies in the degree to which the husband's occupation is viewed as vocation or job are common in the marital relationship. Whether the vocational outlook is a sense of mission, pride in the possession of a craftsman's unique skill, or simply the pride of employment in one kind of industry to the disparagement of other industries, it limits the freedom of the individual to follow a strategy in work life that brings maximum instrumental benefits to the family. Although the fiancée or wife may adopt some of the inflated evaluation and positiveness toward the occupation that her husband exhibits, she does not come to her identification by the process of choice, nor does she experience the commitment of activity progressively focused on the occupation. Hence, in choices that pit vocational values against instrumental considerations, she is less likely than her husband to regard the occupation as a sacred object and is at least more likely to treat its values as discussable.

When a discrepancy in perspective of this kind is openly recognized in the family, the husband's vocational commitment becomes a high-cost item in family bargaining, weakening his decision-making positon. A hypothetical but not uncommon example will illustrate the situation. A highly skilled cabinetmaker, because of commitment and pride in craftsmanship, resists the opportunity to take more remunerative and dependable employment in the mass production of cheap furniture. If his wife has come to share his attitudes of craftsmanship, the sacrifice of income for integrity is a consensual decision, leaving no residue of imbalance between husband and wife. In addition, the shared commitment to an unpopular value contributes to the emergence of a crescive bond between them. But if the wife regards her husband's attitude as mere pigheadedness or thinks him old-fashioned, she feels free to exact concessions in exchange for indulging him. Since there are pervasive norms that equate good husband with good provider, she holds her husband responsible, and the issue becomes oriented to identities, with conflict ensuing. The husband can likewise find normative support for his position. In such a setting the prediction is for lessened dominance by the husband, decisions of accommodation followed by the loser's waiting for a more favorable bargaining situation to withdraw commitment to the preceding decision, and chronic conflict, becoming cumulative if vital alternatives are present.

The very issue of vocational versus instrumental orientation creates a stressful situation when the husband has doubts of his own regarding the wisdom of his vocational commitment. Studies of professional careers suggest that there is a common stage of disillusionment, during which the practitioner wonders whether it is all worth it and cannot repress the suspicion that his work is as much a racket as a service.[19] The presence of such ambivalence makes the pressure from the wife especially stressful. Whichever way an ambivalent man turns, he cannot escape self-recrimination for not having gone in the other direction. If he moves away from the vocational perspective, knowing that he is compromising with his wife's position, he cannot avoid feeling that she is in some sense responsible for his defection from a higher ideal.

When the wife shares her husband's vocational perspective and identifies through his occupation, she may still not see the issues that confront him and affect the family in the same manner as he, because she has an external reference group and he a reference group internal to the occupation to define the vocational goals. From the point of view of the community, prominence in applications of knowledge represents the highest attainment for the scientist and authorship of a best seller for the writer. But within the scientific fraternity the most publicized applications are often thought to be uncreative, and among writers the compromise of literary excellence necessary in popular writing is known only too well. The isolation of the wife from the inner circles of the vocation may prevent her from recognizing her husband's vocational commitment for what it is.

[19] Charlotte Buhler identifies a stage of career reassessment in the mid-forties. "The Curve of Life as Studied in Biographies," *Journal of Applied Psychology*, 19:405–409, 1935.

Finally, identification, as we have observed in the general consideration of conflict, is a potent source of conflict when it remains at an objective level. If it is to be transformed into a deeper form of identification,
there must be some manner in which the wife can involve herself in the
production of the prestige of the vocation. In some instances the wife
becomes full partner with the husband, a pattern that is common in the
small family business establishment or family farm. But ordinarily such
partnership does not fit the nature of the work arrangements in modern
society. There are three common patterns incorporated into the wife's role
when she builds a role anchored to the husband's by identification. First,
she may *interpret* her husband's role, drawing on an inside knowledge to
explain and forecast the husband's behavior. Newsmen attempt to exploit
this pattern to get inside and advance tips regarding decisions by men in
public office. The possibility of building this pattern satisfactorily into a
wife role depends on a considerable degree of public interest in the occupation and on comprehension of the occupation by the wife. In highly
technical fields the wife is seldom able to play this part effectively because
of her own ignorance; and effectiveness depends in any case on existence
of the kind of relationship in which the husband confides a great deal
about his occupational life to his wife. In short, unless other patterns (to
be mentioned) are available to her, the wife's identification with her
husband's vocational perspective is limited and constitutes as much a
source of conflict as of interdependence, unless the response bond is such
that the husband seeks to confide in her, and public interest and her own
technical command of the occupation are such that she can play the part
of interpreter of his occupation.

Some occupations are so arranged that the wife can *support* or *extend*
her husband's role. Vocational support often involves the wife as reception-
ist for her young professional husband, although continuation of such a
role beyond the first few years except on a substitute basis tends to imply
insufficient professional success and, reflecting on the husband, negate the
reward to be gained from identification. In vocations marked by a sense
of mission, such as the ministry, welfare agency administrator, or progressive labor union leader,[20] it is expected that the wife will play a support role. But the commonest form of support, which is also consistent with
relatively high status occupations, is that of social secretary and hostess.
As business corporations attempt to develop a vocational ideology among
business executives, many also expect the wife to apply this kind of supporting part.[21]

[20] Alvin W. Gouldner, "Attitudes of 'Progressive' Trade-union Leaders," *American
Journal of Sociology*, 52:389–392, March 1947.
[21] William H. Whyte, Jr., "The Wives of Management," *Fortune*, 44:86ff., Oct. 1951.

The wife role built about support of her husband's vocational role is viable when the nature of the occupation is such that support in a manner consistent with the family station is possible and to the degree that problems in the realm of decision making and dominance can be minimized. If the wife plays the support part effectively, she is granted, and may claim, increasing credit for the occupational success of her husband. A development of this kind enhances her claim to play a significant part in decision making relative to the vocation. If the initial family role structure was built about her subordination in the vocational sphere, as the idea of support implies, the result is an unstable role structure that produces a succession of reluctant accommodations in decision making and leads to a mutual sense of injustice and conflict.

There is less danger of power struggle when the wife role achieves identification with the husband's vocation through extending it. The wife of a businessman or professional often plays a part in the distinctly feminine spheres of community life, such as charity, welfare, and good causes, as the wife of a man in a respected vocation. Voluntary service roles in a church and the Parent-Teacher Association are available for credit at less exalted socioeconomic levels. This kind of wife role redounds to the credit of the husband through a reciprocal identification, but with the same danger that is inherent in any relationship of identification—that if it is played badly, it becomes an embarrassment.

When neither of these patterns is available or adequate, we encounter a problem somewhat similar to that of the wife with a more vocational perspective than her husband. Frustrated in her efforts to realize more than a superficial identification, she seeks to create a viable role in which the gratifications of vocational success are found independently of the husband's occupation. She may do this by creating her own independent world of achievement, through taking up a vocation of her own or by converting a hobby into the psychological equivalent of a vocation. The latter involves treating the hobby as obligatory and elevated, marked by concern lest the woman not be given the opportunity to make her contribution. Or she may accomplish an adjustment through working to imbue a vital sense of vocation in her children.

Both of these adjustments mean a special form of family role structure. Independent achievement can seldom be attained without some lessening of task bonds, since the wife cannot continue to adjust her schedule fully to the exigencies of the husband's work schedule. And the pattern in which the mother inculcates vocational values she fails to discover in her husband is likely to impede the development of identification bonds holding children to their father.

Career and Family Relations. As the time orientation of the occupation governs the life plan of the individual, so it sets a time orientation for the family. A career calls for long-range family planning, supplies a continuity and predictability that fit members for the disciplined regularity of organized community life, and accustoms members to perceiving present events and opportunities in relation to more lasting considerations.

That conventional community life is facilitated by, or at least is particularly consistent with, an orderly career, is suggested by Wilensky. Among 678 white male workers from the "middle mass" of occupations, Wilensky found

Men who have predictable careers for at least a fifth of their worklives belong to more organizations, attend more meetings, and average more hours in organizational activity. Their attachments to the local community are also stronger—indicated by support of local schools and, to a lesser extent, by contributions to church and charity.

In both formal and informal contacts, the men of orderly career, more than their colleagues of chaos, are exposed to a great variety of people: the fellow-members they see in clubs and organizations represent many social and economic levels; frequently-seen relatives and close friends are more scattered in space both social and geographical, cutting across neighborhoods, workplaces, occupations, or income brackets. Finally, the total participation pattern of the orderly is more coherent: close friends tend to form a circle and they overlap work contacts. (The data do not support the view that best friends share voluntary association memberships.) There is some indication that these friendships, anchored in workplace, forming a leisure-time clique, may also be longer-lasting.[22]

Correlations of this kind do not tell us what is cause and effect, and there is undoubtedly much overlap between Wilensky's "orderly career" and the vocational emphasis we have spoken of. But it seems eminently likely that those bonds which depend to some degree on community support and community participation are more easily realized when the husband follows a career.

Husband-wife discrepancies between job and career perspective have many of the same effects as vocation perspective discrepancy. But career-perspective discrepancies have a disturbing effect on task bonds not usually noted in the other instance. Each kind of career has its special requirements for adjustment of current economic life to the anticipated career line. Any career requires some short-range deferments and immediately unsatisfactory living arrangements for the sake of future benefit. If the wife does not share the husband's career perspective, family life is likely to be disorganized at the task level.

[22] Wilensky, *op. cit.*, p. 535. Quoted by permission of the American Sociological Association and the author.

Work Priority and Family Dominance. The priority of work schedules exercises the most tangible influence over family life, since it is normally expected that (a) family roles and schedules will be developed after the work schedule is known, so as to fit with it; (b) family life will be organized to support the husband's work participation (the family accepts and adjusts to the husband's fatigue after work, but the employer expects to receive the worker in top working condition); and (c) family organization is expected to be sufficiently flexible so that it can be adjusted without prior notice to temporary or lasting changes in work schedule. The immediate effect is felt in family decision making and patterns of dominance.

Determination of family decisions by outside events introduces an area of de facto decision making into the family. But the de facto decisions come by way of the husband, so that from the internal perspective of the family, there is automatic dominance by the husband in many decisions. From the family perspective, the wife must cancel engagements, alter meal schedules, and make other adjustments at the husband's word, whenever that word is backed up by reference to demands of work. To the degree to which some discretion is imputed to the husband in the acceptance of work demands, there is room for limited bargaining, and the decisions within the family take on some characteristics of an accommodation. In this situation the family becomes even more sensitive to the position of dominance of the husband.

An important general principle and clarification of the basis for dominance are indicated in this observation. The husband is able to commit the family to a de facto decision or to impose a decision to which other family members must make accommodation, because he is accorded the authority to dictate such decisions. Authority resides in acceptance by the family of the principle that exigencies of work life take priority and that the worker is the legitimate conveyor and interpreter of these demands. The basis for authority, then, is the imposition of demands from outside the group by way of a legitimate agent of the outside unit who is also a member of the group. Most of what we know as authority is of this character.

The authority of the husband to direct certain family decisions is therefore much more than simply adherence to a traditional belief in male authority but a product of the institutionalized subordination of family to economic life. And the latter subordination is more than merely a matter of tradition; it rests on the fact that the irreducible base of family life as we know it is economic. Without the removal of this economic base, as by some hypothetical universal family pension scheme, it is difficult to see how being a breadwinner can fail to carry authority in the family. The problems of effective and efficient coordination of the activities of many workers and the requirements of flexible economic organization render the adjustment of work schedules to individual family schedules impossibly complex.

It is the nature of dominance on such grounds as these that it is perceived differently by the parties involved. Wife and children see the relationship from the internal family group perspective, that their wishes, arguments, and plans are conditional on announcements from the husband. From their point of view the husband's position is one of power. To the extent to which bargaining enters, there is likely to be a feeling that the breadwinner has already had his own way a good deal and it is only justice for him to make concessions to family members in realms of decision not depending on the work life. To the extent that he is thought to have some discretion in the work realm, which is especially the case when his work is such that he sets his own schedule, the way is open for charging personal responsibility for decisions that frustrate other family members, leading to conflict.

But the breadwinner's point of view is different, because he sees matters from the perspective of the work setting. From this perspective his position is not one of authority but of subordination in a highly authoritarian and demanding organization. He is unlikely to perceive his situation in family decision making as one of power and discretion. Unless he is able to keep the perspectives of family and work sharply separated in his own mind, which requires unusual sophistication, he sees each instance in which he and the family must accommodate to work demands as a concession on his part. In subsequent bargaining within the family it entitles him to make compensating demands. Hence his conception of the bargaining balance and his assessment of justice and injustice in family decisions are likely to be grossly at odds with those of his wife and children.

This discrepancy is characteristic of any situation in which a member of a group exercises authority as agent of another group and has equal application to the parent function, as we shall observe subsequently (see Chapter 14). When it prevails, family relations are likely to exhibit several characteristics. First, decision making is slow and frictional, not only because of explicit bargaining, but also because the terms of bargaining are understood differently by the bargainers. Second, the mutual sense of injustice from contrasting evaluation of the rules ensures chronic conflict. Third, an enduring situation of this kind lessens the viability of roles on one or both sides, so that offsetting role adjustments are sought.

Adjustive role patterns for the wife and children make use of mechanisms such as those suggested in the general discussion of the family as a system of roles (see Chapter 9). But for the breadwinner, whose position from the internal perspective is one of dominance, applicable mechanisms are different. On the one hand the husband may accept the definition of his position as dominance, promote the ideology of male dominance and of family indebtedness to him for his labors and sacrifices on their behalf, and cultivate enjoyment of domination as an end in itself. Ever greater demands on the family to adjust their schedules to the husband's work and justification by denial of intrinsic satisfaction in work—"it is all for the wife and children"—implement the role. On the other hand the husl nd may withdraw as much as practicable from family participation, so that he participates in and is affected by fewer of the decisions other than those he is able to control.

The discrepancy in perspective we have outlined is less likely to occur when the wife shares a strong vocational commitment with the husband or when the results of family concessions to work schedules are translated into concrete and immediate instrumental benefits to the family. The first alternative is only possible when the husband first has a strong vocational perspective with which his wife can identify. A supervening vocational perspective transforms the relevant family decisions into consensus and thus nullifies their implications for family dominance. When work-schedule adjustments are transferable into overtime pay or extra fees in the short term or as contributions toward career development when the family shares the future orientation, they again are likely to be supported by family consensus and cease to imply dominance.

A further source of role strain and role instability exists when work-schedule adjustments are perceived as husband dominance in a family that holds an egalitarian ideology. Adherence to any ideology sensitizes one to see all deviations; an egalitarian ideology enhances the tendency for marital adjustment to the husband's work schedule to be perceived as male dominance, augmenting problems of decision making and the sense of injustice. But when the husband shares the egalitarian ideology, he is confronted with ambivalence about his own role. On the one hand he perceives his position as agent rather than imposer of authority, but on the other hand he recognizes the contradiction between his situation and the egalitarian ideal. Ambivalence of this kind weakens the husband's family bargaining position and strengthens the wife's dominance and, if it leads to irresolute acceptance of work demands, may impair work success. But impairment of work success lessens the possibility of escaping the problem through the wife's identification with a vocation or acceptance of rescheduling because of immediate monetary reward.

Male Occupation and Traditional Wife Role. The entire discussion of the effects of anchorage of the male role in the world of work on family role structure points up the character of the traditional conception of the wife role. The traditional wife seeks to make the home a place of recuperation from the strains of work, prides herself on her flexibility and resourcefulness in making adjustments in family schedules to sudden work demands, and identifies with her husband's occupation as a vocation and accepts it as a career. Although contemporary ideologies have tended to disparage the formulation of women's role in this manner, social structure has not lessened the actual dependence of family life on the breadwinner's efforts nor the priority assigned work demands in the male role. Heightened emphases on achievement and secular success have possibly strengthened the legitimacy of demands that family schedules be adapted to work demands. The achievement and success emphases perhaps facilitate vocational or career identifications with the breadwinner and adjustments for the sake of tangible reward. To the extent to which the husband is successful in his work life, this development makes the traditionally adjustive role of the wife a viable one.

The viability of the traditional wife role, however, tends to be contingent on a degree of the husband's occupational success which cannot be attained in many instances and which cannot be maintained in the majority of occupations in which a peak is followed by a period of decline for ten to thirty years before a standard retirement age is reached. The result is typically role strain for the wife and an unstable marital role structure.

In spite of these considerations the traditional husband-wife roles may still offer the most generally functional pattern of family organization in those occupations in which irregular and unpredictable work demands play the greatest part. Whyte has observed that executives in large corporations are generally convinced that the traditional wife is best for the rising corporation official.[23] And Straus found that among resettled farm families in the Columbia Basin, the more objectively successful in economic terms were more likely to include wives who conceived of their roles in traditional terms.[24]

Perhaps a viable egalitarian wife role that is not productive of impaired decision making and chronic conflict centered on problems of dominance is only possible when the husband and wife hold equally demanding work roles. But the problems of implementing such a pattern require separate consideration.

Woman's Role as Male Complement

The traditional woman's role in western society has been defined as a complement to the male role, its content determined by which tasks were not assumed by men and its standing subordinate. The unique capacity of

[23] William H. Whyte, Jr., "The Corporation and the Wife," *Fortune*, 44:109ff., Nov. 1951.
[24] Murray A. Straus, "The Role of the Wife in the Settlement of the Columbia Basin Project," *Marriage and Family Living*, 20:59–64, February 1958.

women to bear and nurse children might have led to a matriarchy, as it tends to do when the husband's position as society's agent in the family is insufficiently implemented. But the evaluation of family roles reflected the content and standing of male-female roles in the large clan and community units.

The past century has seen increasing opportunities for women to fashion roles on the basis of independent activities outside the family. But out of these developments there has not yet emerged anything in the nature of a clear-cut and normative woman's role. Motherhood as an anchorage within the family has been glorified, but it remains, as historically it always has been, a part-time activity and becomes more and more a temporary diversion during the total life cycle. The question of woman's role and its impact on the development of a family role structure must therefore be approached from the point of view of changes and alternative partial patterns.

In a general way the alternatives start from two foundations. Either the woman's role continues to be defined as some form of effective complement to the male role, whose inflexible core is accepted as a given; or the effort is to create a wholly independent role, resolving relationships to the male role by making adjustments in peripheral aspects of the female role.

Customary systems of role differentiation have histories. Developing under one set of conditions, they tend to persist in emasculated form after many changes have occurred. They persist because of the ideologies that grew up as their justification and because they supply the only ready guides to relatively predictable interaction.

Conditions Underlying the Traditional Role. The traditional breadwinner-housewife role differentiation between husband and wife grew up under conditions that were radically different from those which prevail today, in several important respects. First, economic production centered to a great extent about the home, and the family was primarily a cooperative productive enterprise. There was no clear separation between husband as producer and wife as consumption manager but a division of labor with respect to responsibilities in production. Smuts's observation that on a typical Kansas farm of the nineteenth century, "the work of women provided almost all that was necessary for keeping house, feeding, clothing, and otherwise sustaining the family,"[25] was also considerably true of nonfarm families in the towns. Vegetable gardening, tending poultry and livestock, canning, baking, spinning cloth, and manufacturing garments were among women's standard tasks.

The husband's part of the productive activity differed from the wife's

[25] Robert W. Smuts, *Women and Work in America,* Columbia University Press, New York, p. 8.

in ways that became more significant when production left the home. Men's work was differentiated into separate occupations, but all women's work was much the same, except insofar as wealth made domestic help in the home possible. Although men's work, like women's, centered on the home, it was the man's work that was the chief link to the outside world. As the center of production moved out, the husband became increasingly the agent of productive enterprise, and adjustment of family life to his schedules, which in turn were imposed on him from outside, became more important. Finally, man's productive work had always been more episodic and seasonal and women's work more continuous. The unpredictable and irregular character of demands of warfare and protection on men's time required that indispensable daily maintenance activities rest with women.

Second, money income was a minor part of the economic foundation of family life. With the essentials of food, clothing, and shelter produced in the home or secured locally through barter, the family standard of living was often as much or more a reflection of the wife's productive effectiveness as of the husband's. As the standard of living became increasingly a reflection of money income, with production and hence the source of income primarily from outside the home, the traditional housewife role made increasingly less contribution to the family standard of living.

Third, the family was large, and either the kin group or the neighborhood formed a cooperative unit with respect to many household tasks. The consequence of women's periodic incapacity, during key times of pregnancy, for the continuity of household productive activities was relatively minor when tasks were shared by two or more women. With today's isolated nuclear family, pregnancy is a more serious disruption to even the much more restricted productive activities of the housewife and more likely to require that the husband take over some of these activities for the interval.

Fourth, there was relatively little preoccupation with achievement of a particular class standing. On the frontier there were no clear class divisions to worry about, and in the more established areas there was little expectation that people would change class positions during their lifetimes. Class divisions revolve heavily about occupations, but standing within classes or in a setting that is relatively free of sharp class distinction can be greatly affected by the products and way of life in the household. So long, then, as the principal achievable distinctions were within classes, the work of the wife might be even as important as the husband's in determining family standing in the community. But as class ascent became increasingly important as the measure of success in modern urban society, the contribution that could be made to family standing by the traditional housewife's role became less and less.

Finally, the traditional role differentiation developed prior to the acceptance of the concept of an educated citizenry. Formal education hardly existed, except as preparation for certain professions, such as the ministry. Education was strictly vocational and normally took place as an aspect of apprenticeship or other arrangement for induction into certain employment. Girls learned what they needed to know in the same way as boys, through induction into their future adult work. But as education began to be divorced from preparation for specific occupations and was increasingly justified on the basis of the requirement of an educated citizenry, the denial of generalized formal education to women became more difficult to defend. The discrepancy between the interests and vistas derived from formal education and the limitations of the home has become vast. The limited scope of household activities and the absence of adult interaction are felt as stultifying. And the lack of alternative kinds of careers comparable with the wide range of occupational selection that is supposedly open to men runs contrary to the range of perspectives opened up through education.

Perpetuation of the traditional housewife role under contemporary conditions has made the wife, in spite of egalitarian ideology, at times a menial, at times an expensive luxury to her husband, her own identity within the community almost wholly swallowed up in her husband's and deprived of the basis for conceiving homemaking as a vocation and career. The result has been a rash of effort either to add content to the shell of the traditional housewife role or to adapt the family role structure to the assumption by the wife of a full work role, indistinguishable from that of the man. From the functional standpoint the problem has been to make the wife role into a more significant contribution to family welfare; from the viability standpoint the effort has been to reestablish bases for self-respect and independent power in the wife role.

Contemporary Wife Roles. Kirkpatrick described three roles that are available to the wife in American society. The *partner* role is one of complete equality with the male, the wife having her career in the same sense that the husband has his, and each contributing to the family standard of living. The *companion* role finds the wife cultivating social graces, personal attractiveness, and personal and sexual responsiveness to her husband, so that she may serve as hostess to his friends and relaxer and refresher to him. The *wife and mother* role concentrates on domestic and child-rearing duties, elaborated from the skeleton of the traditional wife role. The *companion* and the *wife and mother* roles are developments from the traditional role.[26]

[26] Clifford Kirkpatrick, "The Measurement of Ethical Inconsistency in Marriage," *International Journal of Ethics*, 46:444–460, July 1936.

More recently Parsons has suggested four roles from which the wife may choose. The *housewife* corresponds to *wife and mother*. The *glamor* role is very similar to Kirkpatrick's *companion*, emphasizing, as Kirkpatrick does, the necessity for cultivating attractiveness. *Careerist* is similar to *partner*. But the fourth, or *common humanistic* role, is one in which the wife finds a substitute for a vocation in community welfare activities, the pursuit of creative and artistic aspirations, and the pursuit of serious educational and political efforts.[27] Thus there are three elaborations of the traditional housewife role, without assumption of an occupation.

Homemaker Role. The new housewife role has been elaborated by turning consumption into a major enterprise, by raising standards of house-keeping, and by converting the custody and socialization of children from a sideline into a technical and full-time vocation. In keeping with its re-furbished character, it is best known as the *homemaker* role. The special character of the formal socialization role will be examined in a later chapter. But the technical expertize of modern motherhood gives the wife a realm of authority to which the husband who lacks such expertness must subordinate himself. Furthermore, it makes the wife an agent of outside institutions, in which name she can require that the family adjust to her schedule, in somewhat the same manner as the husband calls on his work schedule. To the extent to which the community holds a belief in the efficacy of socialization activities, motherhood is evaluated externally in terms of product in much the same way as an economically productive role is judged.

The new role brings marked change in family dominance and decision making. Stress on socialization makes attention to children's needs central and hence raises their position of dominance. Attention to the husband's wants must often take second place to the children's, for his personality is already fixed and cannot be twisted by frustration, as the child's can. The traditional ritual of establishing tranquility in the family just before the husband's return from work is often replaced by the frantic hour, during which the wife's patience after hours of being adaptable and reasonable gives out at the same time that she must hurry to get dinner. Thus it is ironic that the effective dominance of the husband in the home suffers most of all in just those home situations in which the effort is specifically to adhere most closely to the traditional role division.

The development of family organization about socialization is temporary. Growth of the children takes away the wife's vocation and much of the basis for her offsetting dominance vis-à-vis her husband. It is at this stage that women often attempt a belated change to one of the other roles.

---

[27] Talcott Parsons, *Essays in Sociological Theory*, Free Press, New York, 1954, pp. 89–103.

The homemaker role can mean an effectively working relationship with the husband to the extent to which he shares the value placed on socialization and to the degree that his own extrafamilial life and his personality are such that he is not excessively dependent on his wife for intimate response and support. Conflict is likely to revolve about the discrepancy between adherence to a traditional ideology of husband-wife relationships and the effective existence of a rather divergent pattern of dominance.

Companion Role. The *companion* role goes back to a traditional leisure-class wife role. With her husband's standing largely determined by social manipulations and herself freed from most domestic duties by paid domestic help, the wife becomes a valued display piece and an envied hostess for her husband. Freedom from many traditional domestic activities and extension of considerable affluence to much of the society have made some degree of performance of this role a possibility for many women. The essential subordination to her husband and dependence on him are retained, because her status is largely dependent on pleasing him. Except in the minority of instances in which the wife can continue until late in life to make a significant contribution to her husband's occupational success, and especially when her appeal is grounded on youthful glamor and sex appeal, the role becomes less viable with age.

The companion role demands, to a maximum, the external form of love but tends to elicit a decision-making pattern of bargaining. Because her appeal to her husband depends considerably on her appeal to other men, the companion walks a tightrope above infidelity. The role invites conflict over violations of fidelity and charges of exploitation in bargaining. Perhaps the role is most workable when there is acceptance of a contractual rather than sentimental basis for the relationship and when the wife has her own financial resources to protect her independence and continuing bargaining position.

A partial companion role is incorporated in the roles of many wives today as a secondary feature in one of the other standard roles. The expectation that such a pattern of glamor should accompany the new traditional housewife role is common. In some respects this combination makes a gratifying role for the woman, and it offers the husband something in exchange for his subordination to the requirements of child rearing. It also provides the wife an adult-world status. But the combination is probably too demanding for all but a few to achieve, and the risk is that, in trying for both, the wife may fail in both. In addition, both are roles that tend to weaken with the onset of middle age.

Humanistic Role. The common *humanistic* role is much like the career role, except that it is effectively available to fewer women and often fails to bring external validation of the worth of the activity. Except for Parent-

Teacher Association and other opportunities that are open primarily in connection with one's own children, most opportunities to develop a serious enterprise of this kind outside voluntary church work are limited to women with considerable education and talent. Furthermore, except when these activities are such that the wife can be the family's agent in her work, the enterprise is purely an individual and selfish pursuit, so far as the family is concerned. The husband may be pursuing his own interests and ends through his occupation, but he is also contributing income to the family. The wife, on the other hand, may be a drain on family resources. For both of these reasons, the common humanistic role tends to be an alternative to the companion role. Likewise it is really viable only for families in relatively comfortable circumstances.

This role, however, is less susceptible to damage with age and is more amenable to the development of mutual identification bonds. When the latter is the case, it facilitates a relatively egalitarian relationship in which a more spontaneous kind of love and less direct bargaining are necessary to achieve decisions.

In other respects many of the consequences are similar to those of the occupational roles for women and need not be reviewed separately.

Occupation as Anchorage for Woman's Role

Career with or without Marriage. As production moved out of the home and the family standard of living became almost exclusively dependent on money income—and earlier in families of such wealth that wives were freed from domestic productive activity—working for money, especially when work took place outside the home, came to be viewed as inconsistent with normal marriage. Hence the choice confronting women seemed to be between career and marriage. Even while undertaking a scholarly examination of the rise in the employment of married women, which she looked on with open favor, Breckenridge in 1933 implicitly acknowledged the separation:

There have been and still are four ways in which women obtain a living: (1) in the traditional relationship of marriage, which still implies an obligation on the part of the husband to provide those things suitable to the standard of life in which he places a woman and in return for which there is still the obligation to give marital companionship and to perform domestic services; (2) in the less frequent support of single women by relatives; (3) in the increasing legitimate employment for wages; and finally (4) in prostitution.[28]

Not only did this redefinition of the traditional role create a relatively

[28] S. P. Breckinridge, "The Activities of Women outside the Home," in President's Research Committee on Social Trends, *Recent Social Trends in the United States,* McGraw-Hill, New York, 1933, p. 709. Quoted by permission of the publisher.

impotent and unimaginative role for women; it also deprived the family unit of an important component of production. For a large share of the population a satisfactory standard of living was not and is not attainable without the productive activity of two persons. While a few middle-class women were dramatically denying the traditional role by pursuing serious vocations in the name of women's rights, masses of working-class and lower-middle-class wives and mothers were accepting mere jobs in factories in order simply to bring the family to the subsistence level. Thus significant inroads against the new homemaker role came, from the very start, in the functional impossibility of building families on the production of a single breadwinner. Even today the rate of married women's working continues to be negatively related to the husband's income and regularity of employment.[29]

If the nonproductive wife role was always a luxury, sustained with difficulty in most families because of the power of traditional beliefs, the popular pressure for women to choose between marriage and career has now largely disappeared. Myrdal and Klein declare the new situation, from the point of view of upper-middle-class women, with the flamboyance of the early suffragettes:

Those pioneering days are now over. With them has gone the need for women to make a fatal decision between irreconcilable alternatives. The Gordian knot of a seemingly insoluble feminine dilemma has been cut. The technical and social developments of the last few decades have given women the opportunity to combine and to integrate their two interests in Home and Work—if we may thus, in short, characterise the two spheres of interest. No longer need women forego the pleasures of one sphere in order to enjoy the satisfactions of the other.[30]

That girls now see the choice as between homemaking alone and a combination of homemaking and career is demonstrated by the responses of 1,437 high school senior women from a representative group of high schools in Los Angeles to the set question, "Do you expect to: Have a life-time career? (3.6%); Be a homemaker? (48.4%); Both have a life-time career and be a homemaker? (47.9%)."[31]

The new combination role is without well-established models and traditional prescriptions. But the degree of modification required in family organization can be inferred from several sources.

Values Sought through Wife's Occupation. Initially it is important to

[29] Hazel Kyrk, *The Family in the American Economy*, University of Chicago Press, Chicago, 1953, pp. 66–67.
[30] Alva Myrdal and Viola Klein, *Women's Two Roles: Home and Work*, Routledge, London, 1968, p. xvi. Quoted by permission of the publisher and authors.
[31] Ralph H. Turner, "Some Aspects of Women's Ambition," *American Journal of Sociology*, 70: 280, November 1964.

identify the values that are most important in the selection of this role. Attitudes of persons after they have tried the role reflect experience and may be quite different from the expectations with which the role is first attempted. But the initial values direct the efforts to shape the role and determine the sources of gratification and disappointment in early stages.

In the aforementioned study of high school seniors in Los Angeles, an effort was made to assess these values indirectly, so as not to have to rely simply on what women gave as their expectations and reasons for choosing careers. A most obvious explanation for women's decision to have a serious occupation is the desire for a higher material standard of living than could be attained solely on the basis of her husband's work. A comparison of the expected material level of living, however, between girls who chose to combine career with homemaking and girls who chose only homemaking showed no average difference. When groups were equated for the minimum occupational level they could be satisfied with in their husbands, there was still no difference.[32]

A further step was taken by examining the intercorrelations of the various measures of ambition. By using these measures to show which kinds of ambition had most in common and which had least in common, it was possible to make further inferences about the nature of women's ambition. In Table 10 we report the intercorrelations separately for career choosers and non-career choosers and a comparable analysis for the male classmates of these women in Table 11. In each instance the forms of ambition are arranged so that those having most in common are adjacent and those having least in common are most distant.

The absence of correlation between the level of women's own occupational ambition and their level of material expectation gives further confirmation that careers are not sought at this stage for their material reward.

The similar arrangement of variables in each of the three groups facilitates analysis. For both career-choosers and non-career choosers, material aspirations are most closely identified with the level of occupation they are prepared to accept in a husband. This relationship is matched by the observation that the man's own material aspiration is most closely tied to his own occupational aspiration. On the other hand, the woman's educational intentions are quite separate from her material goals. For career choosers they are highly related to the occupation named; for noncareer choosers they appear to stand apart.

Two inferences are at once suggested from these correlations. First, ambition is much more of a homogeneous whole for men than for women. Whatever makes for high ambition in one direction is likely to make for

[32] *Ibid.*, pp. 280–281.

TABLE 10   RANK CORRELATIONS AMONG SIX TYPES OF AMBITION, FOR WOMEN

Type of Ambition	Material	Minimum Husband Occupation	Minimum Husband Education	Own Education	Own Career	Preferred Husband Occupation
			Women Planning To Have Careers			
Material (N=546)		0.41	0.39	0.17	0.08	0.08
Minimum husband occupation (N=546)	0.41		.51	.29	.27	.21
Minimum husband education (N=546)	.39	.51		.43	.33	.22
Own education (N=546)	.17	.29	.43		.65	.22
Own career (N=484)	.08	.27	.33	.65		0.20
Preferred husband occupation (N=339)	0.08	0.21	0.22	0.22	0.20	
			Women Not Planning To Have Careers			
Material (N=563)		0.42	0.46	0.22		0.27
Minimum husband occupation (N=563)	0.42		.49	.33		.33
Minimum husband education (N=563)	.46	.49		.47		.42
Own education (N=563)	.22	.33	.47			0.30
Preferred husband occupation (N=374)	0.27	0.33	0.42	0.30		

SOURCE: *American Journal of Sociology,* 70: 278, November, 1964.

high ambition in another, and the pursuit of vocation and career does not stand apart from the pursuit of material comfort. For women, on the other hand, there are major forms of ambition totally unrelated to each other. Second, the separation of kinds of ambition applies to goals sought through the husband in marriage and goals sought independently of the husband. In picking a career, the girls are not seeking more of the same values they hope to attain through the efforts of their husbands but a different set of values.

The nature of the underlying kinds of ambition is suggested by com-

TABLE 11   RANK CORRELATIONS AMONG FOUR TYPES OF AMBITION, FOR MEN*

Type of Ambition	Material	Occupation	Education	Eminence
Material		0.42	0.48	0.35
Occupation	0.42		.72	.55
Education	.48	.72		0.66
Eminence	0.35	0.55	0.66	

*All correlations based on 1000 cases.
SOURCE: *American Journal of Sociology*, 70: 279, November 1964.

parison with the data for males. Men were asked when they would consider themselves successful enough so that they might relax and stop trying so hard to get ahead. Answers were in terms of continuing struggle for eminence within their chosen field of endeavor. It was this eminence measure which assumed the position in the arrangement of ambitions for males that was taken by the women's career aspirations. The contrast between this form of ambition and material ambition at the other pole suggests a distinction between interest in the extrinsic and intrinsic aspects of work. Material level of living is, par excellence, an extrinsic aspect incidental to the enjoyment and interest in the work activity itself and quite distinct from commitment and identification with the occupation. At the other pole is choice of occupation because of interest in the work and ends of the occupation. In men these two poles are not wholly separated, and higher ambition is likely to mean higher goals with respect to both extrinsic and intrinsic rewards. In present terminology, high material ambition and looking on one's occupation as vocation and career tend to go together. But women, before marriage, cannot foresee sufficient intrinsic satisfaction vicariously through identification with the husband's occupation. After marriage the part of *interpreter, supporter,* or *extender* of the husband's vocation may help but probably cannot normally equal the husband's active preoccupation. The women's educational ambitions express this value placed on the intrinsic satisfactions of accomplishment and work, and career aspirations are their prime vehicle.

If this analysis is correct, the demands a woman makes on her own occupational life are intense. It is clear that she seeks a vocation and not merely a job. But most men are apparently unable to find in their work a true vocation and ultimately settle down to more of a job orientation than a vocation orientation. The considerable merging of intrinsic and extrinsic ambitions permits continued commitment to the occupation and readjustment of expectations in terms of actual rewards. If women are no more successful than men in finding true vocations, they lack the same recourse as men. Instead of replacing the traditional role with a wholly new one, these girls have grafted the occupational role onto the traditional role, apportioning the extrinsic values to the traditional role and the intrinsic rewards to the occupational role. Hence disappointment in finding true vocational commitment destroys the basis for occupational ambition, which can then be restored only by reassessing and borrowing from the gratifications sought through the husband.

Role Adjustments to Vocation. We shall return to the problem of frustrated vocational orientation, but we turn for the present to the character of the role adjustments to be made in a family in which the wife pursues a full vocation and career.

Initially the marital roles and other dependent roles must effect a reconciliation between the preeminent scheduling demands of two occupations. If the wife role is traditionally the vehicle by which the family is kept flexible so as to adjust to the legitimate claims of the work world, the presence of two serious occupations means two sets of inflexible demands on scheduling and sometimes on place of residence. When the occupations are such that workers can dictate their own schedules in whole or part, one or both may still make the necessary adjustments. The author and the artist, for example, can often adjust; and if the adjustable occupation is the wife's, family life may be fitted into the traditional mold with a minimum of change.

But for most occupations, a new, looser, and less demanding relationship must be worked out if each partner is to continue to treat his occupation as vocation and career. Until a greater degree of separateness is achieved, the opposing inflexible occupational demands on scheduling must provoke contests of dominance. The normal priority of occupational social obligations over purely personal social activities must mean the occasional opposition between social obligations from his and her occupations. Occasional sacrifice of devotion to occupational success in adjustments to the other's schedule supplies a potent source for feelings of injustice, attributable to the identity of the other and hence a focal point of conflict.

The cost of developing the looser family structure that minimizes problems of dominance and sense of injustice is reduction of the potency of many of the traditional task bonds. One adaptation is then a role structure that is more loosely bonded but in balancing fashion is less demanding. A less intense pattern of love, with more acceptance of intimacy and other characteristic family satisfactions outside the family, may produce a functionally effective relationship for the purposes of its members, with viable roles for each. A contrasting adaptation is probably what Burgess and Locke had in mind when they spoke of the coming companionship family,[33] a relationship in which relatively weak task bonds are compensated for by intensified identity bonds. Although this pattern is often an ideal among persons who do not wish to sacrifice their independence but who at the same time long for a refuge from the loneliness and social insecurity of modern urban life, it is questionable whether it offers a workable relationship. Companionship and social response seem to be attainable to only a limited degree by direct pursuit, coming more often as by-products of the joint pursuit of mutually satisfying activities.

A further disposition must be made of the domestic tasks. There is little incentive except altruism or moralistic egalitarianism (either of which may be reinforced and expressed in the love sentiment) for the husband to take on these chores. His work already accords with the accepted definition of full time, and he sees little direct gain to himself in exchange for adding to his own burden. For the wife to assume the entire burden in addition to her occupation is to produce even greater overload. Whichever solution is followed means some physical exhaustion, with its impairing effects on both task and identity interaction. It also means a potential source of injustice arising from the different standards that husband and wife use in evaluating their respective family contributions. The husband who willingly takes on a share of the domestic duties is likely to feel that, in doing so, he is going beyond his duty and thus is entitled to be much appreciated for indulging his wife. From her point of view there is no indebtedness, since his adjustments are only what a working wife has a right to expect.

The conception of identity bonds incorporated in the traditional husband-wife relationship sees the wife tied to the husband through identification and the husband tied to his wife by a response bond. This pairing of response and identification bonds is consistent with an inequalitarian relationship and intense mutual attraction, conceived as love. A more mutual form of bonding is necessary in the case of dual careers but must be found without full community support. The community usually supports the wife's acquisition of prestige through her husband's accomplishments and is prepared to strengthen her satisfaction by labeling her as the power behind the throne. Any such conception in reverse is slightly humorous, and evidence of a wife's substantial achievements is likely to provoke competitive comparison more than the award of identificatory prestige to the husband. In short, the bonds in this kind of family arrangement must depend on personal desire with reduced community support.

Erosion of the Career Orientation. Finally we return to the problem

[33] Ernest W. Burgess and Harvey J. Locke, *The Family from Institution to Companionship*, American Book, New York, 1953.

of sustaining the wife's career determination within the setting of the family. Regardless of disappointment over intrinsic rewards from his work, the man's dedication to his job is maintained by the extrinsic rewards and by the absence of any viable alternatives. Opportunities may turn a job into a career, and persistence at work may reawaken vocational orientations from time to time. But failure of intrinsic gratification leaves women little to offset the difficulties of accommodating family life to the future orientation of career and the sacredness of vocation. With nothing to coerce the wife into continued career efforts and an alternative role awaiting her, she often slips back toward a more traditional role, assigning her job a secondary and less exalted position.

One result is what Gross suggests has come to be a fifth role for the married women:

. . . being assumed by an increasing number of women: the housewife who works but continues to regard her role as wife and mother as her major one. She is able to accomplish this by *limiting* herself to a distinct set of occupations (which may, however, change over time) rather than to try to enter full scale into direct competition with men, for the latter would force her to give her primary attention to her job rather than to her family.[34]

The relaxation of career dedication often takes place during educational preparation for the chosen occupation and helps to contribute to lower rates of completion of higher education by women, after an elementary and secondary school record which is superior to boys'.[35] Interruption of education means that many women enter occupations which convey less elevated standing in the community than they gain from their husband's positions.

Disappearance of the early career motivation is widely noted by students of occupational life. Smuts observes that "Most of today's working wives show no strong internal commitment to work . . . they work mainly in order to earn money they don't absolutely have to have."[36] Kyrk assesses the bases for women's work in the following terms:

[34] Gross, *op. cit.*, p. 162. Quoted by permission of the publisher.
[35] On superior secondary-school performance of girls, see G. R. Johnson, "Girls Lead in Progress Through School," *American School Board Journal*, 65:25–26, 1937, and Robert S. Carter, "How Invalid Are Marks Assigned by Teachers," *Journal of Educational Psychology*, 43:218–228, April 1952. Only 38 percent of degree-credit enrollments in United States institutions of higher learning in the fall of 1962 were women, compared with 51 percent of high school graduates for 1961–62 (see U.S. Office of Education, *Digest of Educational Statistics*, 1963, pp. 41, 58). Sixty-two percent of girls who were graduated from Los Angeles high schools in 1963, compared with 70 percent of boys, were attending college or junior college in the fall of the year (see *After High School*, City School Districts, Evaluation and Research Section, Los Angeles, 1964, p. 4).
[36] Smuts, *op. cit.*, p. 148.

There are undoubtedly some married women employed for other than economic reasons. The push in their case is their dislike of housework; the pull, the attractions other than financial of the work itself, the belief that their social usefulness is thereby enhanced, their desire to utilize special skills, experience, and competence. Any survey of the employments in which married women are found will convince one that this group is relatively small. For most there is also some degree of economic pressure—pressure which in some cases overrides their own preferences.[37]

In contrast to the steadiness of a career, women's work patterns are discontinuous with age, in a pattern which suggests that they are accommodated to the demands of the housewife role and are affected by the adequacy of the extrinsic monetary returns from the husband's occupational efforts:

The wife earns rather frequently, we might conjecture, early in the marriage before there are children. When all the children are under six, in nine-tenths of the families the husband is the only earner. As the children enter school, the wife earns more frequently, until about a fourth of the wives are earning when all are of school age. But, as the children leave school and join the father in the labor force, the frequency of her earning diminishes. In only a sixth of the families with another earner besides the husband was she working in April, 1947. After the children leave home and household duties diminish, the wife may again supplement the husband's earnings until her increasing age operates as a deterrent.[38]

Whether the work becomes a part-time vocation without career implications or a job performed strictly for financial gain probably depends on the family need for supplementary income as well as the extent of intrinsic gratification in work and its amenability to part-time pursuit. But in either case the organization of the family resumes the basic pattern of traditional role differentiation. It becomes a more adequate task unit because of the wife's income contribution. Role expectations are reduced to a more attainable level, because the wife, like the husband, gains some of her satisfactions outside the family. At the same time, it is subject to disruptions, because the wife's schedule can no longer be totally accommodated to the husband and children.

It is appropriate to conclude the discussion with a brief note of one piece of research that suggests the possible complexity of the effects of woman's work on the family authority structure. Blood and Hamblin set out to test the basic hypothesis that the husband-dominated family becomes more equalitarian as a result of the wife's employment outside the home. Questionnaires were administered in 60 marriages with the wife working full time and 60 marriages in which the wife was a full-time housewife, all in

[37] Kyrk, *op. cit.*, p. 72. Quoted by permission of the publisher.
[38] *Ibid.*, p. 66. Quoted by permission of the publisher.

the state of Michigan. On the basis of a scale measuring equalitarian versus authoritarian expectations in the family, it was hypothesized that husbands and wives in families where the wife was employed would hold more equalitarian attitudes than their counterparts. The hypothesis was confirmed for the women, but the men in the two situations did not differ in their attitudes. On the basis of a check list detailing areas of family decision making, it was hypothesized that working wives would have a larger percentage of areas in which their suggestions were adopted than the housewives. But there was actually no difference here. Based on still another check list, it was hypothesized that husbands of working wives would do a larger share of housework than husbands of housewives. This hypothesis was confirmed. Interpreting these mixed findings the authors conclude:

> This controlled comparison of marriages involving working wives with those in which the wife does not work suggests that her employment tends to result in a more equalitarian ideology for the wife but that she does not use her greater control over economic resources to bargain with her husband. Rather the husbands and wives studied appear typically to make their important decisions on a give and take basis and to arrange the division of labor in the home on the basis of the relative availability of the two partners to perform the necessary household tasks.[39]

Although these main conclusions need not be contested, they do play down the potentially discordant aspect of the relationship. If the career woman's husband performs a greater share of housework without either adopting a more egalitarian conception of marriage or granting the wife a greater weight in family decision making, an unstable role situation is suggested in which interactive role adaptations by the husband are not yet supported by a corresponding adjustment in his sense of what constitutes a valued role division. And if the wife holds more equalitarian values without corresponding changes in the husband's values, there appears to be scope for role dissensus.

Summary

Many investigators assume that the requirements of family life are the source of male-female role differentiation. But studies showing that people adhere more closely to their proper sex roles outside the family circle than within suggest that sex-role differentiation has its roots in community life. The small size of the contemporary nuclear family and the emphasis on sentiment work against strict sex-role differentiation within the private boundaries of the family unit.

[39] Robert O. Blood, Jr., and Robert L. Hamblin, "The Effect of the Wife's Employment on the Family Power Structure," *Social Forces*, 36:352, May 1958.

The male role is firmly anchored to occupational life. Occupation is crucial for the male identity, especially when occupation is viewed as a vocation rather than merely a job. Occupations supply distinctive time orientations to male life, make preeminent demands on their time and activity, and supply or deny the instrumentalities for many of the other roles they wish to play. The male occupational role is central in determining the possibility and character of the wife's identification bond to her husband. With the husband's occupation an omnipresent fact of married life, an important complication to decision making and contributor to conflict is the tendency for a wife to view her husband's occupation in more instrumental and less vocational terms than he. The identification bond is strengthened when the wife can serve as interpreter, supporter, and extender for her husband's occupational role. Because the husband must adjust to the demands of his occupation and the family in turn must accommodate to his demands on behalf of his occupational obligations, the husband appears to dominate his wife and children. But as an agent of the economic institutions, he perceives himself as controlled rather than controlling. Only the traditional wife roles are adapted to the preeminence of male occupational roles: more egalitarian wife roles require a husband role whose demands are less inflexible.

The traditional woman's role has been defined as a complement to the male role. Conditions to which this role was formerly adaptive have changed radically, and alternative roles have appeared, but none is yet complete and fully sanctioned normatively. The newer homemaker role caters less to the husband, and companion and humanistic roles are also widely followed. Increasingly women seek to combine homemaking with an occupational role for themselves. Some evidence suggests that women tend to bifurcate their ambitions, looking to a husband's occupation to supply such extrinsic values as material well-being and looking toward their own education and career for intrinsic satisfactions. Marriages in which both husband and wife have serious occupational roles must accommodate the often incompatible demands from the two occupations, sometimes by accepting a looser marital relationship. Mutual identity bonds become a possibility when the community supports them. The result of strains in combining home and work roles is often erosion of the woman's vocational interest and commitment to a part-time activity without career significance.

CHAPTER 12

SEX ROLES:
MEN AND WOMEN

It is abundantly apparent that the traditional organization of marital roles has been extensively shaped by the anchorage of the male role to gainful employment outside the home and of the female role to domestic and supportive activities; that historic changes and individual deviations in male and female role anchorages create an unstable equilibrium in the traditional marital roles; and that the relative importance and vulnerability of particular bonds, the pattern and ease of decision making, and the areas of conflict precipitation are altered when the traditional role anchorages are modified. But males and females are also "people," whose roles are more generalized than the specific institutional settings they are anchored to. Recognition of a comprehensive male role implies the existence of a characteristic male (or masculine) *style of behavior*, different from the feminine style. It also implies specific kinds and sources of role strain. Family interaction must take account of these differences in style and of the major role strains its members experience.

Investigators in all spheres of behavior and attitude, when they use male and female subjects, generally find that sex differences are as important or more important than the relationships they set out to isolate.[1] Nevertheless, after a comprehensive effort to characterize woman's nature, Klein observes, "An attempt to draw up a table of feminine traits, and to list the respective authors' agreement or disagreement on each point must fail because there is hardly any common basis to the different views."[2] It should be added that even consistently found sex differences are of fairly slight magnitude, and there is always much overlap between male and female distributions on any characteristic. With these qualifications, there are a few main differences between male and female styles that have received repeated confirmation in empirical research.

[1] For example, see Earl R. Carlson and Rae Carlson, "Male and Female Subjects in Personality Research," *Journal of Abnormal and Social Psychology*, 61:482–483, February 1960.
[2] Viola Klein, *The Feminine Character: History of an Ideology*, Kegan Paul, London, 1946, p. 164.

Whether women feel any more emotion and sentiment than men or not, the masculine pattern is to control emotion and minimize its spontaneous expression and the feminine pattern is to allow spontaneous and open expression (except perhaps in relation to aggression or hostility). A difference in masculine objectivity and feminine subjectivity has been documented in studies of values, of approaches to the analysis of situations, of ways of interpreting moral codes, and of religiosity. Masculine aggressiveness and exploitativeness show up even in preschool children, but women appear to be more accommodative and more concerned with facilitating social relationships. A masculine pattern of activeness and mastery contrasts with a more passive, accepting style for women. Similarly, conformist tendencies appear stronger in women; men are more likely to challenge conformist demands.

Patterns of Interaction

If the foregoing characteristics describe somewhat distinctive styles of interpersonal orientation and behavior, the question is whether in combination they describe a determinate pattern of interaction that can supply a basis around which the system of family roles emerges. Some such assumption underlies the Parsons-Zelditch view of a role differentiation between instrumental and expressive functions. Clearly the traits reviewed fit into this kind of characterization; but it still remains to be specified just what interaction is like when it occurs between personalities specialized in this manner.

Interdependence by specialization. Collaboration in a stable relationship can be on the basis of common attitudes and goals or on the basis of specialized but interdependent skills and interests. This is the distinction that Durkheim dubbed mechanical and organic solidarity. Although it does not preclude mechanical solidarity as well, the finding of personalities polarized on important socially relevant characteristics points toward the interdependence of specialization. The bonds in the relationships between men and women should rest to a considerable degree on the need of the unaggressive and conservative woman for the aggression and initiative and daring of the man, and the need of the man for the acceptance and tenderness and noncompetitiveness of the woman, and on the greater effectiveness of a social unit that combines these divergent skills than on one that has only one set.

Polarized characteristics suggest a pattern of decision making that assigns spheres of determination to husband and wife, so that decisions are easily reached without contest and the decision making process is not provocative of conflict except when one person invades the other's sphere. An obvious example is the division between concern turned outward from the marital unit and concern turned inward toward the sustenance of the unit. Aggressiveness and impersonality are traits that are likely to be of more use in dealing with the world outside the married pair; sentiment and social accommodativeness are qualities that facilitate the personal relationship.

But this kind of interpersonal specialization seems applicable more to the irresponsible interaction of dating and courtship than to the practice of marital relations. It fails to provide for the inventiveness, the readiness to change, the logic and calculation, all of which appear on the surface to be as necessary for effective handling of the domestic economic tasks and the management of family consumption as for the husband's activities. The assumption that polarization of personalities in this manner facilitates marital interaction is countered by Locke's finding that the wife's possession of executive ability increases the likelihood that a marriage will fall in the happily married rather than the divorced category.[3] If this kind of personality specialization describes a workable and satisfying interaction pattern it must apply principally to the few leisure-class marriages in which the wife is freed from domestic responsibilities altogether.

Stabilizing Role. A feature of this personality differentiation is the division into agitating and stabilizing roles. Aggressiveness, daring, initiative, and even impersonal logic set in motion courses of action that bring about changes and, because consequences are unpredictable, risk. The complementary characteristics ascribed to women can supply a stable base, conserving the old to permit safe retreat in case the new does not work and providing escape from the stark logical implications of personal failures through defining events on the basis of sentiment and personalities.

Koos observed that among his sample of tenement families the wife's role sometimes had a steadying effect during the economic crises that beset them:

There appeared to be real value to the family in having the mother in this sheltered position, in that it provided the other members of the family with one person to whom they could turn for anchorage. Mr. Berger stated this fact in these words:

"Mother [the wife] is really a god-send when we get into a jamb. She isn't out the way we are; the girl and I work and have to face the problem of trying to get along in our jobs and support the family and all. But Mother can stay at home and be sort of steady, and we can turn to her when things are pretty tough outside and know that she isn't so bothered by these things outside."[4]

[3] Harvey J. Locke, *Predicting Adjustment in Marriage: A Comparison of a Divorced and a Happily Married Group*, Holt, New York, 1951, pp. 175–192.
[4] Earl L. Koos, *Families in Trouble*, King's Crown, New York, 1946, pp. 98–99. Quoted by permission of Columbia University Press.

But this steadying effect may require more emotional control than expression, and the example does not fit the conception of masculine imperturbability. It may work in the illustration only because of the extent of institutional shielding of the wife. It is likely that the gain from feminine acquiescence is offset by emotionality, so that in the balance, personality polarization makes no contribution to this stabilization of the pair relationship.

Identification-Response Bonding. The personality patterns do suggest the reciprocity in which the female is bonded to the male by identification and the male to the female by response gratification. Creativeness, aggressiveness in socially admirable causes, initiative, and emotional control in difficult situations together suggest an image with which a person having less of these qualities might gain vicarious personal gratification and social prestige through identification. Reciprocal identification might attach to the tenderness and sensitivity that the man sees as lacking in himself, and undoubtedly such identification does occur. On the other hand, the feminine tenderness, the ability to react on the basis of personal attachment without attention to successes and failures, a readiness to acquiesce, and a show of admiration resulting from identification with her husband's manly qualities together supply the basis for highly gratifying personal response. The masculine qualities that create an object for identification do not, however, facilitate gratifying interpersonal response toward the female. Some writers, in their readiness to discover a natural reciprocity have ascribed a masochistic turn to women. Delight in being treated violently by an overpowering male is commonly attributed to women in the stories that appear in men's magazines. But even in this haven of wishful imagery for would-be masculine men, the violence may give way to tenderness once the female has submitted. Although valid cases of feminine masochism of this kind have been adduced, resentment and fear of masculine roughness and insensitivity are probably much more prevalent.

Thus, although personality polarization is suited to an identification-response binding, the resulting relationship is not wholly viable. Provided that the male finds objects for identification outside the family, which are readily available to most men in the hierarchical worlds of industry and the nation, the marital relationship can supply a gratifying complement to the work world. But if masculine qualities impair the ability of the male to supply response gratifications to his wife, the marital relationship deprives her of those satisfactions which are most peculiarly limited to the family in modern society.

The reciprocity in the modern sentiment of love is to some degree in opposition to a relationship of this kind. Giving love means placing oneself in jeopardy through trust in the sensitiveness and fidelity of the other; the female, then, runs the greater risk in love, from the identity point of view. The sentiment also points toward the love relationship as the valued and appropriate source of response gratifications, and the necessity to gain major response elswhere is interpretable as a deficiency in love. If masculine traits are partially incompatible with giving love freely, this personality polarization and the attendant identification-response bonding may have been better suited to a family system in which love played a less important part and in which family organization did not impair the development of intensive relationships of mutual response among women.

Communication Barriers. Any relationship built on specialization rather than commonality encounters problems of communication in decision making. When the specialization is in the realm of personality, communication barriers arise from the inability of each to place himself in the other's position and take his role penetratingly. The male finds difficulty in sensing the depth of a woman's distress over matters of sentiment or her concern with avoiding issues that may break out in stimulating and sometimes hostile controversy. The wife can only with difficulty understand the difficulties that her husband creates for himself by insisting on abandoning a successful routine to try a novel procedure, by resisting authority when his own interests are placed at stake by his resistance. Communication blockages impair the development of full intimacy demanded by the sentiment of love. They also impede decision making regarding those matters which cannot simply be resolved by assignment to one or the other's sphere of proper dominance.

The Problem of Organic Solidarity. Finally, there is a question regarding the suitability of organic solidarity as the basis for a relationship that is (a) nonsegmental and (b) deeply identity-involved. The most congenial pattern for a relationship built about strong specialization of tasks founded on personal differences is either a contractual or a hierarchical relationship. Under changing circumstances the burdens and rewards from each specialty change and are thrown out of balance. Under a contractual relationship the individual can bargain for readjustment in the division of tasks or reallocation to other roles. Because the relationship claims only a part of himself, he can discount the communication blockages, the unsuccessful bargaining. Specialized tasks inevitably carry differences in value and place the individual differently with respect to the power at his command. In this realm there is probably no such thing as a comprehensive specialization without inequality.

When contract does not supply the participant with bargaining strength, the mutual acceptance of hierarchy seems necessary to make the situationally subordinate roles viable. The acceptance of inferior status and formation of an identification bond on these terms reconciles the imbalance.

Indeed, our search for a pattern for stable interaction between the sexes on the basis of their behavioral styles points finally toward a relationship of inequality. The masculine qualities of emotional control and rationality, aggressiveness, activity, and nonconformity are those which find most congenial expression in a role of dominance; feminine emotionality, concern with social accommodation, receptiveness, and acquiescence are patterns of subordination. These differences appear to have less to do with facilitating any specific division of labor or any particular system of mutual personal satisfaction than with preparing for a relationship of inequality. The general problems of communication that arise with collaboration by specialization can be bypassed in part by acceptance of unequal authority, and the response deficiency of the female in the identification-response bonding pattern is made more tolerable.

The significance of male-female differences in style points so importantly toward dominance-submission that we shall return to the question after a brief consideration of the total family context and societal context for the sex differences.

Sex Specialization and Parenthood. If the sex difference in styles does not constitute a simple mode of interaction between the sexes, except through male dominance and female subordination, it has relevance to the family relationship when children are included. The feminine qualities seem better adapted to the sensitive and patient care of children and the cultivation of the children's sensitivity and tenderness. Some degree of polarization between the parents in authority versus tenderness, daring innovation versus the reassurance of the familiar, and the like, may dramatize to the child the nature of these choices which will confront him in many situations. The mother's influence can moderate without diluting the lessons of logic and impersonality brought by the father.

The difficulty with this and other formulations of the parental sex specialization is that the contemporary family organization is often not amenable to such a division of function. The scheduled absence of the father from home makes the part of disciplinarian difficult to sustain and unrewarding to him. As a result, the entire range of paternal and maternal function falls to the mothers, including those aspects in which her emotionality makes her relatively unsuited. Although the common interest in the child adds a bond to the husband-wife relationship, it does not resolve any of the problems of communication and inequality between the sexes. It may, for brief periods, supply the wife with the response that she fails to receive from her husband, but in the years of infancy the child's response to the mother is too simple and egocentric to be complete, and in adolescence the assertions of independence stifle the child's response. And by diverting the response of the mother from the husband to the child, it may weaken the identification-response reciprocity for the husband.

In short, although there is an obvious sense in which the configuration of feminine personality traits is adapted for the specialized function of motherhood, this specialization does not lessen the general observation that, for marital relations, the polarization of personalities probably does not contribute toward a viable system of roles except on the basis of female subordination.

Personality Specialization and Dominance. We return, then, to the issue of marital dominance. For a stable role equilibrium, the organizational circumstances and the values that apply to the roles must be supportive. At present, the relatively egalitarian values are associated with personality polarizations and institutional anchorage of the male role in his occupation, both of which contribute to subordination of the female. A situation of role disequilibrium not quickly righted by role change or alteration of the situation then becomes a source of difficulties in decision making and of recurrent conflict. So it is that problems of dominance arise early in the marital relationship.

The dominance problem is conventionalized in general sex rivalry. Boys versus girls is a popular way of organizing friendly contests from childhood into old age. In some groups the period of early youth is one of single-sex groups that require intense loyalty, demanding that members of the opposite sex be treated only as objects of exploitation. In joking patterns regarding courtship, outsiders define the process as one of mutual jockeying so as to enter marriage with an initial advantage in domination. These definitions are so insistent that on demand the courting couple stage an act of good-hearted rivalry as a necessary reassurance to spectators that their interest in marriage is serious.

Where personality differences are conducive to inequality but egalitarian values render such relationships unstable, modern chivalry supplies one mode of adjustment. Originally chivalry referred to the whole system and code of knighthood, one element of which was the knight's romanticization of service to his ladylove. In knightly practice the service was translated into license for sexual promiscuity and later refined to a system whereby the knight's affections were concentrated on a mistress. Because dealings with the mistress were outside the marital relationship, and thus freed from the task responsibilities of household maintenance, and were a segmental aspect of life for each, the identification-response pattern could be followed freely. But here the subordination of the mistress was mitigated by the knight's obligation to service and the elaborate code of courtesies and protections due her.

As knighthood died out, this aspect of chivalry persisted and was transformed, in those classes with sufficient leisure and economic surplus to permit the indulgence of such a luxury. The code of chivalry became a set of protective rituals practiced in public dealings with any woman of suitable class, justified on the grounds of her weakness and merited on the basis of her willing subordination.

That chivalric courtesy was owed the woman only when she accepted the dominance of her master as exemplified in Shakespeare's play *The Taming of the Shrew*. In this folktale of chivalry, the hero approaches his unsubmissive ladylove in much the fashion that a cowhand approaches a wild horse that must be broken so that it becomes a useful steed. Once the former shrew has proved her submission by sincerely agreeing to everything her lover says, even when it is palpably silly, she then becomes the object of chivalrous treatment.

Chivalry in its later forms serves both to offset unequal dominance and to supply some of the deficiency in response for the women. Kirkpatrick refers to contemporary remnants of chivalry when he says, "In many relationships between men and women the paradox of strength through weakness stands revealed."[5] Weakness of emotional control and greater emotional sensitivity demand protectiveness; receptivity to influence and incompetence at impersonal bargaining invoke the rules against taking unfair advantage of the weak. In *The Wayward Bus*, Steinbeck describes a middle-class woman who is certain that people always go out of their way to do special favors if only one asks nicely enough. And her belief proves true in practice, although each favor is given with secret cursing and resentment against her unfair use of feminine prerogative.[6]

The chivalric code provides a kind of ritualized response that can be potentially gratifying to the woman. It is incorporated into the male line in dating and courtship. In the segmented dealings of courtship, as in the paramour relationship, the avoidance of familiarity and comprehensive intimacy, and protection from dilution in mundane utilitarian relationships, allows such ritual response to be effective. But it is doubtful that it can continue to supply sustained response gratification in marriage.

It is worth noting that the norm of chivalry may still govern the public relationships of middle-class men and women in limited respects. In spite of the consistent finding that women more often make conforming judg-

---

[5] Clifford Kirkpatrick, *The Family: As Institution and Process*, Ronald, New York, 1955, p. 158.
[6] John Steinbeck, *The Wayward Bus*, Viking, New York, 1947.

ments than men in the Asch kind of experiment, several investigators have found that mixing the sex of subjects makes a difference. Luchins and Luchins found that males would conform more often to the erroneous judgments of females than of males.[7] And in two sets of experiments, other investigators found that men conformed more often in mixed-sex groups than they did in all-male groups.[8] These results may stem directly from chivalric concerns or merely from the distracting effect of the presence of women. But the situation for the male is one he often encounters, with the vestiges of both chivalry and sex rivalry at work. If he is right and the woman wrong, his victory is weakened by the norm of chivalry. But if she is right and he is wrong, there are added to his defeat the humiliation of being shown up by the weaker sex and the moral disapprobation of having contended against the woman. To vote with the girls and thus risk only a shared defeat is the safer course.

Individuals and Sex Roles

If our examinations have led us to the conclusion that observed sex differences are more a reflection of a past system of masculine dominance, as softened by chivalric codes in leisure-class settings, than a plan for contemporary marital interaction, we must consider how sharp and immutable these differences are. One possibility is that a traditional polarization tends to be self-perpetuating because of the pattern of differentiation about responsible and irresponsible roles in connection with shared values;[9] for example, the preemptive assignment of rationality to the male role permits the female to escape the constraints of logic, although in her very irrationality she depends on the male to give the necessary support to rationality. Likewise the secure assumption that the woman will display tenderness and sensitivity on appropriate occasions frees the man from responsibility in this area. Woman's acceptance of responsibility for protecting conventional values and morals frees the man to challenge and stretch the rules. If this kind of interpretation is sound, the polarization of personal styles does not express polarized values, nor need it penetrate very deeply.

We must also ask to what extent men and women are actually pressed into the molds we have described. It is important to observe that in all

---

[7] Abraham S. Luchins and Edith H. Luchins, "On Conformity with True and False Communications," *Journal of Social Psychology*, 42:283–303, November 1955.
[8] Read D. Tuddenham, Philip MacBride, and Victor Zahn, "The Influence of Sex Composition of a Group upon Yielding to a Distorted Norm," *Journal of Psychology*, 46: 243–251, October 1948; Harold T. Reitan and Marvin E. Shaw, "Group Membership, Sex-composition of the Group, and Conformity Behavior," *Journal of Social Psychology*, 64:45–51, October 1964.
[9] See Chap. 9.

relevant studies the differences between the sexes were small, and the overlap was great. In still other studies the conventional sex differences failed to appear altogether. Any pattern of random pairing for marriage would produce only a small majority of pairs in which the male differed from the female in the standard manner. Even if the characteristic sex differences conveyed a pattern for interaction, the specialization would be so slight in many cases as to be relatively inconsequential in relation to other role determinants. And so many cases would incorporate personality reversals, that in only a small minority of all marriages would the polarization be both in the correct direction and sharp enough to create a normative pattern of interaction independently of the constraints of institutional arrangements.

Sex-style Conceptions and Role Strain. Out of the institutional anchorages and sex styles in behavior there develop conceptions of the essential qualities of each sex. There may be one or more conceptions of a single sex, and there may be wide disagreement or uncertainty about the content. But the ideas of masculinity and femininity are nevertheless distilled and become valued patterns against which the individual identity is to be characterized and evaluated. As individuals vary in their attainment of a gratifying standard of masculinity or femininity and in their ability to develop and maintain a sex identity through the institutional anchorages available to them, there will be either great or little role strain, with varying consequences for participation in family life.

Major sources of role strain can be briefly recapitulated:

1. Inability or fear of inability to perform a role adequately is the simplest source of strain. It occurs under either of two main conditions. (a) Inappropriate role allocation, when roles are ascribed or the individual is prevented from changing roles because of commitment, means that the aptitudes of the individual do not suit the role. Whenever, as with sex roles, a relatively uniform role is ascribed arbitrarily to a set of people with highly varied potentialities, there is some role strain. And the intensity and frequency of the strain is greater when the role is least variant and most imperative. (b) Role demands that are excessive or inconsistent likewise ensure inadequate performance and resulting strain.

2. Failure of reciprocation is a second main source of role strain. Here the individual performs his role adequately, but the reciprocating role that gives it meaning and supplies the cues for its continuance is not evoked. The situation is one of disorganization—failure of the interactive aspect of a role system. Roles occur in systems, but each role is shaped partially by an independent set of determinants and partially by system interaction. Disorganization of this kind arises when the impact of the

former determinants is excessive in relation to the latter. In the instance of sex roles, this source of strain comes when external circumstances change the activities of women or the requirements placed upon men more rapidly than their patterns of interaction can undergo adaptation.

3. Failure of role performance to produce a sense of worth and accomplishment—divorcement of the behavioral pattern in a role from any sense of value—is a final important source of role strain. What attaches a secure sense of value to a particular line of activity is one of the least well-answered questions in behavioral studies. Perhaps the most satisfactory answer available at present is its integration into a mutually reinforcing set of behavior patterns that are geared to a mutually supportive system of values. From this vantage point there are two important circumstances that have sometimes led to a loss of the sense of value in performance of sex roles. One is the contradiction among roles played by a single individual. If a man's occupational role and the standards of masculinity of his male role are in contradiction, the sense of value in one or both roles must be undermined. The other circumstance is the necessary adaptation of a role to a changed situation, without accompanying changes in the system of values. As we observed in Chapter 11, much of the change in women's roles during the last century has been of this character, and the nature and prevalence of feminine role strain reflects this happening.

Sex role strain may be produced within or without the family, but it becomes important to know whether the family is seen to intensify the strain or relieve it. An important element in traditional family organization was the assumption that family life provides a man with a haven from that form of role strain which came from the high performance demands of his occupation. The idea that a woman finds her feminine fulfillment in motherhood is similar. In both instances role strain that has its origin outside family life and is relieved within the family becomes a bond. The effectiveness of the bond depends on the adequacy with which the family organization provides for these forms of gratification and also continuing activity of the external sources of role strain.

But role strain may also be produced or enhanced by the family. If an egalitarian family organization threatens the husband's conception of masculinity or the humdrum and labor of housework negates the wife's conception of femininity, family interaction is almost certain to be marked by chronic conflict.

The most general impact of role strain on an individual, at least until demoralization causes a full abandonment of the role, is to enhance the saliency of the role in all his interaction and to render its patterns more prescriptive and invariant. Some suggestive evidence of this kind of response is afforded by a questionnaire study of masculine-feminine attitudes. Three experimental scales were devised. An *obvious scale* was made up of items to which men and women reply differently, expressing differences that are popularly known. A *stereotype scale* was made up of items which people generally believed should distinguish the sexes but which in fact do not. A *subtle scale* was compounded of items that show sex differences of which people are generally unaware. The obvious scale does not figure in the present context. But the subtle and stereotype scales showed substantial negative intercorrelations for both men and women subjects.[10] Many speculative interpretations of this finding are possible. But one plausible judgment would be that those who fit less well into their ascribed sex roles, as indicated by their scores on the subtle scale, suffer role strain, to which they react by adhering more narrowly to the stereotypic features of the role.

If the sex role is especially salient to the individual and if he defines it very prescriptively and narrowly, the process of developing a unique system of roles within the family to fit the special circumstances of the family and the peculiar temperaments and interests of its members is impaired. Family interaction corresponds more closely with stereotypic male-female interaction than would otherwise be the case. Furthermore, the saliency of the sex role means that the individual interprets a wide range of situations and behaviors primarily on the basis of what they mean for the support or impairment of his sex-role identity. Decision making concerning family activities proceeds smoothly only when adequate steps are taken to see that solutions to problems and procedures for reaching agreement do not offer potential threat to the precarious sex identity. And the potential clash of sex identities is likely to be the most poignant source of family or marital conflict.

The individual who experiences role strain reacts in various ways to the strain. When the role strain is intense, the mechanisms by which relief from the strain is sought become insistent. If the strain is continued, they become established behavior patterns in the individual. These patterns become an additional element expressed in family interaction.

Because of the importance attached to sex roles and sex identities in our society, sex-role strain is both common and important in its effects on family life. Certain forms of masculine and feminine role strain merit more extended treatment.

Strains of Masculinity

Although the status of male is ascribed, in the strict sense that the individual has no choice over the assignment of his sex identification, there is

[10] Robert C. Nichols, "Subtle, Obvious, and Stereotype Measures of Masculinity-Feminity," *Educational and Psychological Measurement*, 22:449–461, Fall, 1962.

still a strong demand on every male to prove himself a man. In one sense there is a distinction between being male and being masculine. The former is ascribed; the latter is achieved. Many of the privileges accorded the male depend on demonstration of masculinity. But even when male privileges are accorded to the individual simply on the basis of his ascribed status, they are judged to be unmerited, and the decision that the male should have them is the product of reluctant accommodation rather than consensus.

Failure to back up his claim to male prerogatives with demonstration of masculinity not only undermines the man's bargaining position; it damages his identity—his self-respect and the respect accorded him by others. It is important to observe that in American society there are no institutional protections for masculine dignity, as there are for feminine self-respect. Masculinity can be called into question at any time, especially before full adulthood is reached, by placing the male in a position in which his failure to take effective action is a reflection on his masculinity. Because of the difference in institutional supports and in the cultural definitions of the two roles, a woman is more likely to lose feminine self-respect by action than by inaction, but a man more often loses masculine self-respect by inaction or insufficient or ineffective action.

The lesson that a man can have little self-respect without masculine self-respect is taught early and continually in the life of a boy. Parents and teachers use challenges to his masculinity as a technique to control disturbing evidences of childhood weakness and to protect themselves against the overdemanding requirements of sympathy. Other children quickly learn that the disrupting effect of sympathy on their play activities can be forestalled by discounting as feminine the claim that a boy might otherwise make for compassion. The boy who chatters too much in class is threatened with being seated among the girls. Femininity is the pervasive threat behind inadequate performance in a wide range of activities.

Demonstrating Masculinity. The ways of proving masculinity fall on a continuum from achievement in a distinctly male task to the adoption of a pattern of behavior that embodies masculine traits divorced from significant accomplishment. Successful pursuit of a man's occupation is the form of accomplishment that integrates masculinity into the social structure. Successful craftsmanship, business success, and professional accomplishments convey a manly stature and alleviate much of the need to offer further proof. In contrast to this performance in a stable role in society is the demonstration of masculinity through deeds of prowess. The heroic rescue at great personal risk, the performance of a feat requiring exceptional strength or endurance, the confident mastery of a situation that has left others panicked: such are the dramatic folk conceptions of masculinity. Although folk tales have such masculine heroes springing unpredictably to meet great crises, modern society institutionalizes provisions for feats of this character in the military and athletic establishments. Although most great military reputations today may be achieved through effective office work rather than direct combat, there is still a readiness to ascribe a distinctive and more vital quality to military than to civilian achievement. The amount of energy devoted to the discovery and promotion of athletic heroes suggests that some vicarious gains in masculine self-respect are available to ordinary men and boys through identification with the modern gladiators.

In the absence of either validating occupational success or demonstration of heroic qualities, a man can claim the privileges of manhood by acting like a man. Unlike heroic accomplishment, which at least need not be repeated every day, or occupational success, which has some continuity through institutional supports, the enactment of manly qualities must be continuous to be effective. Emotional control and impassivity, with resistance to human claims for sensitivity and tenderness, must be observed in all relevant situations. Aggressiveness, resistance to conformity and concession, deviance and unconventionality as ends in themselves must be exhibited with consistency. The masculine affectations are a regular attribute of boyhood in America and are often continued into adulthood. Because they constitute a manner rather than an accomplishment, they are vulnerable to challenge. The swagger is a promise of aggression and becomes an empty affectation when the bluff is effectively called. Hence a constant anxiety accompanies this manner of supporting masculinity. Either there is a touchiness—a hyperreadiness to translate the manner into action lest it be mistaken for bluff—or the bluff is exaggerated just in order to forestall a test.

Obstacles to Masculine Self-respect. Although American society makes the proof of masculinity quite crucial to self-respect in the male, it does not make provision for easy and dependable demonstration. As a consequence, deficiency in masculine self-respect is widespread. Several kinds of problems complicate the ordinary male's effort to establish his masculine self-respect.

First, it has often been noted that the boy is characteristically separated from his father and that, when he does see him, it is on occasions when his father is not engaged in behavior that is especially significant for his masculine identity. Thus the boy typically lacks an adequate role model whose successful approach to the requirements of masculinity he can observe and emulate easily.[11] Sociologists have observed that traditional

---

[11] Talcott Parsons, "The Social Structure of the Family," in Ruth N. Anshen (ed.), *The Family: Its Function and Destiny*, Harper & Row, New York, 1959, pp. 256–260.

farm life or the arrangement of the craftsman with his home workshop permitted the boy to see and understand his father's work and to begin early to acquire some of his skills through helping and copying. Similarly the girl can observe and work with her mother in domestic tasks in the ordinary household where the wife plays the full housewife role. Even when efforts are made to acquaint the boy with his father's work, the nature and importance of much of the work in modern society cannot readily be grasped by a child.

If direct emulation of the father is not available as the basis for learning how to play the masculine part, it is largely left to formalized instruction, the mass media, and peers. The mass media tend to exaggerate and sensationalize masculinity, dealing in heroic images and caricatures. Reliance on guidance from peers, who all share the absense of appropriate adult male models, merely compounds the problem. Formalized instruction suffers the artificiality and situational inappropriateness characteristic of most formalized cultural transmission.

Even when a clear model of masculine achievement can be located, the second problem emerges. Masculinity through socially integrated achievement is unavailable to many men and is not attainable for most men until well past the start of maturity. Feats of heroism and physical superiority are possible for only a few and then only when a crisis situation affords the opportunity. Institutional athletic prowess moves the boy into higher levels of competition in which recognition goes to fewer and fewer. Thus the high school star becomes a run-of-the-mill college athlete, and the college star is merely one of the team in professional athletics. Few validating occupations today are available before adulthood, and secure indications of success are frequently not forthcoming until a decade or two of occupational membership.

There is a discontinuity between boyhood and adulthood both in the opportunity for establishing masculinity and in the means available. Perhaps those who are most successful in masculine validation as boys make their achievements in athletics but then find their masculine attainments fading in significance as they reach maturity. For most boys the principal means is to ape the caricatured masculine behavioral styles. Depending as they must on peer-group response to their behavior, the validation is often whimsical and fragile.

The problem is further complicated by a third consideration, revolving about the nature of the masculine relationship with women. Traditional masculinity rested on male superiority and dominance over women. Modern egalitarian values can be accepted with generosity when masculine dignity is already securely anchored in accomplishment of some kind. But egalitarianism is a threat when masculinity lacks a firm base. Among boys, academic accomplishment cannot serve to validate masculinity, because school is viewed as a woman's province. Not only are women in command; the tasks are of a kind that can be performed as well or better by girls.

The communication of masculinity standards is further confused by the feminine control of boyhood, since women's conceptions of manly characteristics do not always correspond with the male version. A questionnaire study of university students in California brings out this discrepancy. One hundred unmarried male students and 100 unmarried female students filled out an adjective check list according to the kind of person they would ideally like to be, then according to their ideal for the opposite sex, and finally according to what ego believed was the opposite sex's ideal for ego's sex group. Using only words that had been identified as favorably regarded features of masculine and feminine stereotypes, the investigators found a discrepancy between men's self-ideal and the male ideal held by women. Although men predictably endorsed a greater number of masculine than feminine words in describing the self-ideal, women used approximately equal numbers of masculine and feminine words to describe the ideal male. Women wanted men to have all the masculine qualities that men wanted for themselves but also wanted them to have most of the desirable feminine features such as gentleness, sentimentality, and soft-heartedness. This discrepancy was not unnoticed by men, who correctly described the women's male ideal as about equally made up of masculine and feminine traits.[12]

Fourth, masculine validation is further confounded by myths of sex-specialized competencies. Traditionally the belief in masculine superiority has rested on the conviction that only men had the natural aptitude to perform the more prestigeful tasks in society. Women's inferior role was rendered viable in part by acknowledging that she too had aptitudes for certain tasks that men could not perform, although less important and prestigeful work. The beliefs were institutionally self-fulfilling, women being systematically denied the opportunity to learn to perform masculine tasks and confronted with inordinate obstacles when they had acquired the skills.

Traditional segregated schooling and special curricula for boys and girls helped keep these myths alive. In keeping the myths alive, they supplied a minimum basis for the security of masculine dignity. Institutional arrangements saved the boy from having to put his masculinity fully to the test. Freedom for girls to learn all skills and compete with boys in their own sphere makes the myths untenable. As long as being masculine remains a

[12] John P. McKee and Alex C. Sherriffs, "Men's and Women's Beliefs, Ideals, and Self-concepts," *American Journal of Sociology*, 64:356–363, January 1959.

salient component of self-respect and so long as it implies superiority over women male self-respect is constantly threatened by the prospect of a capable woman or a talented girl.

It is, of course, not inherently necessary that masculinity should be so salient a part of a man's self-respect. Nor is it inherently necessary that male self-respect be tied to male domination. But our traditional culture has made it so, and an interdependent set of institutional arrangements offers resistance to change. Yet compared with many other countries, masculine self-respect in the United States has taken considerable strides away from dependence on feminine subordination and inferiority.

Reactions to Strain. In response to the role strain that most men experience in youth and many continue to experience in adulthood, certain characteristic mechanisms have developed. Each is a caricature of behavior traditionally associated with the male role, an exaggeration of masculine behavior detached from any goals integrated into the social organization.

First is cultivation of the independent, nonconforming, aggressive features of the male style into a way of life. In positions of authority, such as in military command or supervisory posts in industry, it finds expression in arbitrary rulings and the studied use of coercion before it is shown to be needed. In many youths it finds expression in delinquency and deviancy. In still larger numbers it leads to a general disruptiveness and disorderliness on group occasions of all kinds.

A moderated form of this mechanism is the practice of male self-assurance and decision. It would be a confession of weakness to admit to lack of a definitely formed opinion on a matter relevant to male concerns or to change one's opinion in the face of convincing arguments by another. Hence there is often a characteristic male dogmatism and inflexibility in discussion. Frequently male strategy in discussion is to try to formulate a simple but comprehensive statement put forward as ending the need for further discussion. In schools a boy's commitment to holding and retaining an opinion is often an obstacle to learning in the complex areas where issues are not easily defined in black and white terms.

A second mechanism is the degrading of feminine activity and the cultivation of incompetency in feminine spheres. It is an anomaly found in many areas, that when people cannot prove themselves by what they can do, they fall back on the assertion of what they cannot do. The studied disinterest in music and art, the effortful singing out of tune, inability to read a recipe or sew on a button, and the eschewing of any reading matter that makes claim to literary qualities are among the common forms of this pattern.

Conventional behavior is downgraded in many spheres that are significant for later accomplishment. The definition of school conformity and school recognition as feminine probably contributes to the deficient performance of many boys in their elementary and secondary school work. It is interesting to note that the onset of underachievement may be different for boys than for girls. Underachievers are students whose school performance falls greatly below the level indicated by a measure of intelligence or aptitude. One investigator, studying a group of underachievers, found that the girls had begun to show a record of underachievement after the sixth grade, perhaps as they began to encounter adolescent problems. Underachievement in boys, however, began much earlier, with the first grade.[13] The latter suggests an enduring problem, such as an incompatibility between school achievement and self-respect.

The foregoing mechanism, added to the tendency to view relationships between the sexes in competitive terms, leads to a third pattern, the exploitation-avoidance attitude toward women. If his masculine identity is precarious, the boy is sensitized to the dominance aspects of any dealings with women. With such an approach, he is threatened by casual relationships in which there is no obvious dominance and is on guard lest they take a sudden turn to his disadvantage. The only way to escape this danger is to begin jockeying for control from the start. If the girl can be successfully exploited, there is a basis for reassurance regarding his masculinity.

The general experience of the boy has been that in free interaction the girl is often likely to gain the upper hand. In many dealings there is less risk to the girl, because her defeat or submission can be cast as an admirable indication of her femininity. Consequently, she has a wider latitude in the use of interpersonal strategies. Furthermore, operating under a system interpreted and enforced by women, the girl has advantages under the rules. As a result, boys often try to avoid dealings with girls except when the situation is such that they have a good chance of successful exploitation.

This exploitation-avoidance pattern makes any relationship of mutuality between the sexes impossible. It means that in conventionally regulated mixed gatherings there is a prompt tendency for such men to retreat from what they define as the feminine world.

The treatment of masculinity in popular men's and women's magazines may be indicative of this pattern. One investigator compared twenty-four short stories featuring an unmarried male protagonist in a popular woman's magazine with twenty-four from a popular men's magazine. He attempted to determine for each story what characteristics were presented as indicating the masculinity of the protagonist. In the women's magazine mascu-

---

[13] Merville C. Shaw and John T. McCuen, "The Onset of Academic Underachievement in Bright Children," *Journal of Educational Psychology*, 51:103–109, June 1960.

linity was conveyed largely by physical characteristics such as stature, broad shoulders, and muscular strength. In the men's magazine a much more important part was played by evidence of violence, dominance, and exploitation in dealings with women. Deliberately disregarding a woman's wishes, taking from her by coercion what she might willingly have given without force, treating her insultingly and insensitively appear frequently in these wish dreams for would-be masculine men.[14]

Role Strain and Marital Relations. Many implications of male sex-role strain for marital relations are at once apparent. In general terms the nature of marriage as patterned interaction between male and female is such as to make the sex roles and any adjustive mechanisms particularly salient; the tendency to interpret husband-wife interaction as an enactment of the male-female system poses an obstacle to the free development of unique family roles; and the mechanisms adopted in response to masculine role strain impose specific constraints on the mode of interaction to be worked out in marriage.

First, enthusiastic acceptance of marriage as a mutual good is inconsistent with the patterns we have described. Unless a man gains wealth through marriage, so that he can continue the attitude of successful exploitation, marriage is a form of surrender. Marriage means the acceptance of domestication, granting a woman legitimate claims on oneself, giving up much personal freedom and unaccountability. Courtship is conceived as a game in which the male tries to gain favors without incurring responsibilities while the girl tries to get the boy into a situation that allows her to trap him in marriage. The romantic setting that softens the boy's masculine toughness or pregnancy, which brings a moral or legal claim upon him, is seen as feminine tactics of entrapment. Whyte describes how the slum-dwelling corner boy broke off steady dating relationships when he discovered himself beginning to feel tender toward the girl, lest he weakened and it was too late to retain his independence.[15]

In the small study of magazine short stories, the masculine resistance to marriage is well reflected. The outcome of most of the stories in the women's magazine sees the protagonist bachelor duly married. In most of the man's magazine stories he gets what he wants and stays unmarried to the end.[16]

A frequent expression of masculine role strain is the *domination-absence pattern* in marriage. The husband asserts his domination whenever he is present and then absents himself at times when he might not be able to

---

[14] James L. Bull, "Masculinity Patterns in American Society," unpublished master's report in sociology, University of California, Los Angeles, 1959.
[15] William F. Whyte, *Street Corner Society*, University of Chicago Press, Chicago, 1943.
[16] Bull, *op. cit.*

maintain control. His effective domination is punctuated by a contrived unpredictability. By being late for dinner on frequent occasions, he notifies his wife that he has accepted no obligation to conform to her schedule. By absenting himself physically, or socially by sleeping and absorbing himself in television or book, he frees himself from give-and-take relationships.

The domination-absence pattern is fully practiced in many working-class homes in America and across a wide spectrum of classes in the Latin nations. But in more moderate form it also enters into the role patterning of more typically middle-class homes. The strain of a day's work is a legitimate claim for insulation from involvement in domestic problems within the traditional family system. The preemptive claims of the work schedule permit the manipulation of a little unpredictability to the husband's advantage. The myth of specialized spheres of competency permits the husband to make dogma in masculine areas while disdaining any knowledge in more domestic questions on which his wife can put opinions forward. To the degree to which masculine role strain remains a lingering factor in the husband's makeup, there is a tendency to use the dominance-absence pattern in these disguised and softened forms.

Inflexibility of sex specialization is another consequence of male role strain for marital and family relations. When the myth of sex specialization is accepted, role strain makes either female assistance in masculine affairs or male assistance in women's tasks threatening to masculine self-respect. As we noted earlier, such inflexibility places a severe strain on the task functioning of the small family unit, in light of the uneven pressure from time to time on male and female tasks.

A further consequence is the resistance of intimacy, with the resulting impairment of the love sentiment. In a relationship that is a constant potential threat to his male identity, it is hardly possible for the man to drop his guard fully and place his identity at the mercy of his wife. In relation to our earlier discussion of obstacles to giving love freely, we should add that masculine role strain is a major source of difficulty.

The threat of female domination brings out some of the same role adaptations in the male as discussed earlier (see Chapter 9) as general reactions to domination. In particular, intimacy is resisted through the preservation of spheres of life about which the wife is not allowed to know. These spheres are often shared with other men, and the premarital attitudes of sex competition and sex exploitation reasserted with more or less success in the one-sex group.

Finally, all these developments point toward the potential clash of identities. Attempts by the wife to bring about a more conventional middle-class pattern of roles is bound to heighten the sense of opposing identities and hence of conflict in such relationships. Identity clashes can only be minimized—if serious masculine role strain is in effect—by the acceptance of a loosely bonded relationship, making minimal demands on intimacy and granting maximum freedom from conventional marital restraint to the husband.

Role Strain in the Life Cycle. There are two points in the marital career when masculine role strain is likely to be at its height. Marriage takes place for most men at a time when their masculinity is still precarious. A man still in school has yet to try himself on the job. A man in the first years in a career has yet to foresee the course of his career clearly. Because marriage comes when this masculine uncertainty is vital, the newlywed husband is likely to exhibit some of the patterns we have described. He may assert his opinions dogmatically, make apparently pointless demands for compliance on his wife, be threatened by indications that she thinks for herself on some matters, and defensively preserve areas of privacy and unaccountability from her scrutiny. If the initial consequences of these mechanisms are not too disruptive, the years often bring a lessening of their use as the husband begins to achieve security in his occupation and assurance regarding his reasonable masculinity.

Masculine role strain is also a phenomenon of old age. The masculine behavioral style is also the style of youth, incorporating activity and daring and aggressiveness. Physical prowess declines; proficiency and income in many occupations become less. Lipman finds in a study of the elderly that the roles of male and female become less distinguishable with old age.[17] Whether the result is the reemergence of any of the earlier defensive patterns must be determined by study of marital-role reorganization in old age. But it seems likely that there are changes in bonds and decision making that reflect either the effort to reassert or ultimately surrender claims to self-respect on the basis of masculinity.

Strains of Femininity

The problem of the woman's role, her self-respect and her dignity, has been the subject of far greater explicit discussion than the man's. This disproportionate attention has probably not stemmed from any greater difficulty in finding self-respect and a viable way of life for women than men. Indeed the wreckage from failure in masculine achievement is much more dramatic in the plight of unattached older men, alcoholism, suicide, crime, and general demoralization than any evidence of the costs of feminine failures. But the greater attention focused on the problem of the woman's role probably results from four considerations. First, the admission of

[17] Aaron Lipman, "Role Conceptions and Morale in Couples in Retirement," *Journal of Gerontology*, 16:267–271, July 1961.

failure and disorientation is more easily reconciled with the traditional conception of woman's role as the weaker and more sensitive sex than it is with the male role. Thus a greater willingness to subject her problems to airing and to resort to counselors and psychiatrists has combined with a greater freedom from obligations that would preclude her devoting the time to analysis. Second, the problems of the male role have been extensively examined in other connections. Theories of crime are very largely formulations of strains and reactions in the male role, although not so specifically labeled. Likewise, researches into the strains in occupational roles are primarily treatments of the male role under a different label. Eliminate the implicit fact that the worker is a breadwinner with both short-range and long-range responsibilities to his family that can only be met through coping acceptably with the world of work, and the entire character of occupational life changes. Third, the nature of the masculine problem is simpler, if not more soluble, because it is a matter of reaching and retaining relatively unachievable but fairly well-defined goals, but the woman's problem is one of choice among alternatives and creation of a well-enough defined role to supply a guide and standard for personal evaluation. And finally, it has been the female role that has undergone dramatic change during the last centuries, changes in the male role being principally adaptive to changes initiated in the female role and readjustment of a traditional work role to suit the new context of employment.

Problem of Choice. Students of the feminine role have long seen the problem as one of making a choice of life-long significance, each alternative requiring the certain sacrifice of one set of gratifications in exchange for the uncertain attainment of another set. Margaret Mead early attributed the onset of adolescent stress and strain in girls to confrontation with this among other choices and noted the absence of any comparable difficulties in Samoa, where girls eased, on maturity, into the only adult role available to them.[18]

Two investigators explored the problem of choice among college girls in the United States, with similar objective results but rather different interpretations of the imponderables. Komarovsky interviewed girls in an eastern women's college, to find a high rate of uncertainty concerning their futures. Whether college would lead them to marriage or career, and what kind of life would ensue, were undecided for many.[19] Wallin replicated the study in a western coeducational university, with the same results.[20]

[18] Margaret Mead, *Coming of Age in Samoa*, Morrow, New York, 1928.
[19] Mirra Komarovsky, "Cultural Contradictions and Sex Roles," *American Journal of Sociology*, 52:184–192, November 1946.
[20] Paul Wallin, "Cultural Contradictions and Sex Roles: A Repeat Study," *American Sociological Review*, 15:288–293, April 1950.

Komarovsky sensed a great deal of anxiety over the choice among the girls she studied and saw it as an immediate and continuing source for a great deal of personal disturbance. Wallin, on the other hand, found his subjects approaching the uncertain future with less anxiety and more confidence that a worthwhile pattern would be found.

Why the investigators' impressions should have been different can only be a subject for guessing. But one possible explanation points to a variable that may be crucial in augmenting that form of role strain which derives from problems of choice. The girls in the eastern school were relatively isolated from casual relationships with eligible men, and statistics of the time showed an exceptionally low rate of marriage for graduates from such schools. Although these low rates might partially express the deliberate decision to eschew marriage, the widespread belief that men preferred wives less educated than themselves and the regional excess of women in the population contributed to the suspicion that the rates were not entirely the women's choice. Hence, underlying the whole question of choice lay the anxiety that there might be no real choice. By contrast, the women in Wallin's sample found themselves a small minority in an overwhelmingly male student body, a situation guaranteed to build confidence in the prospects of marriage.

Impotence and choice are both circumstances to which the individual can make adjustment singly, but in combination they create a problem of marked intensity. The traditional role for most women represented self-determination within the very narrow confines of the fate accorded her through marriage and the fortunes of her husband. Choice can be difficult but is common to many human situations. But the suspicion that events may impose one outcome undermines the value of the fated choice and augments the risk in taking the opposite choice. Even today the suspicion often lingers that a woman chooses an occupational career as insurance against spinsterhood and only becomes committed to her choice when she fails to receive suitable offers of marriage. Whether this is generally true or not is of little importance; the belief contributes to devaluation of the occupational choice and introduces ambivalence in what might otherwise be clear-cut preference. On the other hand, unqualified commitment to the homemaking role weakens a girl's position in the marriage market, since she must adjust her standards to suit the range of men likely to offer her a proposal.

This kind of difficulty does not end with the choice. Normal occupational disappointments reactivate the latent disparagement of the occupational choice. "Was this what I really wanted in the first place?" And the suspicion that fear of spinsterhood forced her to lower her "price" may plague the woman who marries in lieu of a career. To the extent to which these processes are applicable, we hypothesize that feminine role strain is least when major choices are made with a conviction that the choice is not determined by events outside the chooser's control.

Woman's Role as Marginality. Writers have sometimes equated modern woman with the sociological conception of a marginal man, devised especially to describe minority ethnic groups.[21] The marginal man is caught up in a choice situation he is unable to resolve. He belongs to an ethnic group with minority status but early in life aspires to membership in the higher-status majority group. As he makes his way into the dominant group, he learns their culture, a way of life that seems more sophisticated and more advanced than the parochialism of his own group. As he adopts the new culture and associates with its members, he comes to identify himself with this group. Then he experiences rebuffs, until he makes the traumatic discovery that the majority group regards him as an outsider and erects an inflexible barrier against his acceptance into intimate group circles. The result is a precipitate return to his original group and a period of overcommitment to its values. He cannot now escape the widening effect of immersion in the second culture and a continuing dissatisfaction with the limited horizons of the minority way of life. At the same time, he is now able to look at the majority culture critically. The result is that he finds himself poised between two ways of life, seeing both through a jaundiced eye, and unable to be fully satisfied with either full immersion in the minority group or peripheral status in the majority group.[22]

The recent history of feminine ideology recapitulates a pattern of this kind. The suffragette movement of the nineteenth and early twentieth centuries was concerned with gaining access to the world of men with their superior privileges. The traditional woman's role was regarded as parochial, limiting personal development, and symbolic of a degrading acceptance of personal inferiority. Any distinction between men and women implied unwanted inferiority, and even the special legal protections given women because of childbearing were to be wiped out under a proposed Constitutional amendment. Great gains toward equality were made during this period, but only modest inroads were made into traditionally male occupations. Then there followed a period during which a feminine mystique, as it was labelled by Betty Friedan, came to dominate the mass media and direct the work of counsellors.[23] The mystique elaborates the view that woman's essential nature is such that she can only find personal fulfillment through woman's traditional role, in child bearing, domesticity,

[21] Klein, *op cit.*, pp. 171–175.
[22] Everett Stonequist, *The Marginal Man: A Study in Personality and Culture Conflict*, Schribner, New York, 1937.
[23] Betty Friedan, *The Feminine Mystique*, Norton, New York, 1963.

and loving support of her husband. She must eschew the career and all
competition with men, give full reign to her natural talents in emotional
sensitivity, and play the receptive rather than assertive part that is congenial to her nature.

Friedan's book, with its massive reception, marks an attack on this
second stage, gives impetus to the growing effort to combine the traditional
and career roles, but fails to show how the hazards of the combination can
be escaped. Thus the career that is not really a career, because it must be
set aside for child bearing or to foster the husband's career, and housework
that must be done in what might otherwise be leisure hours suggest the
suspension of the marginal man between two worlds, in neither of which
he can participate unreservedly enough to gain a genuine sense of self-
respect.

Universal Femininity. With the decline of the antifeminist attitude of
the extreme suffragettes and the growing tolerance toward alternative roles
for women, there also seems to have been developing a somewhat new conception of feminity that is supposed to be manifested in whichever institutional role woman selects. Traditionally there was some contradiction between doing woman's work and being feminine. The paragons of femininity
whose delicate whiteness of skin was extolled by the romantic poets were
an altogether different set of people from the exemplars of motherhood
glorified in other poetry. Likewise, the serious pursuit of an occupational
career was, in the nineteenth and early twentieth centuries, often thought
to entail a rejection of femininity. Perhaps the women who selected this
course did not so often make that assumption. But the world in which they
followed their careers was pervaded by the belief to such a degree that the
appearance of femininity impaired occupational success. People often
found it difficult to place their professional confidence in the doctor or
teacher whose attractiveness as a woman was too apparent, and the business woman's dealings with men required unmistakable evidence that her
aims were strictly business.

The appearance of a universal feminine pattern, expected of housewife
and career woman alike and extended throughout most of the class system,
is a novel phenomenon. There have been universally admired images before, such as the saintly virgin of Catholicism; but for most people an
image of this kind was to be worshipped for its unattainability rather than
emulated widely. Pictures and popular essays about mother now feature
young and attractive women; the prototypical housewife works in her
mechanized kitchen in fashionable attire. Increasingly it is the lack of
feminine appeal that casts doubt on the competence of the professional
woman. The expansion of clerical occupations in the labor force, with their
clean surroundings and protection from physical labor, made the combina-

tion of work and femininity easier for large numbers of women. The compatibility of femininity with even a laborer's work was given popular sanction in the World War II folk figure of Rosy the Riveter.

Although the image has already acquired a normative character, conveying strong pressure on all women to conform in much the same way that masculinity is demanded of all men, its focal features seem to have been derived from Kirkpatrick's leisure-class companion role, which in turn grew out of the extramarital mistress role. Current developments require that Kirkpatrick's and Parsons' statements be revised to show that the companion or glamor role has become less and less a distinct and comprehensive role that a woman may choose or reject and increasingly the common ingredient in whatever role she chooses. In a vital sense, then, the common standard set before all women today is to play the part of leisure-class mistress or wife, not as a full-time preoccupation, but as an adjunct to either the housewife role or the career-and-housewife role.

In one respect the universal feminine component lessens the strain-inducing features of the choice before women and reduces the applicability of the marginal-man concept. Whether the woman chooses to be homemaker alone or to combine it with a career becomes less important for her self-respect as a woman. In either case her self-respect as a woman often depends more on the attainment of the commonly applicable image than on the cleanliness of her home, the qualities of her children, or her occupational success. Although nonmarriage becomes less tenable, the two major roles draw closer together and the sacrifice of alternative satisfactions in either choice less complete.

But in other respects the universal femininity introduces further sources of role strain. First, like any uniform ideal, the new femininity becomes a Procrustean bed into which normal human variability cannot be fitted without mutilation. The basic pattern of glamor is one that in past eras has been demanded of only a tiny fraction of all women. Undoubtedly the changes in economic and social life and advances in the medical arts have made the standard much more widely attainable than in the past. To the woman who finds the pattern personally uncongenial, neither sincere devotion to the domestic life nor dedicated pursuit of a profession frees her from appraisal on the basis of the feminine universals. If a man passes safely through the boyhood period when physical prowess plays so compelling a part, he may achieve occupational success in many ways and with varied aptitudes and temperaments, but his occupational success validates his masculinity. But the universal femininity is like the masculinity of childhood and youth—a pattern based on exemplification of a style of behavior rather than a product. Hence it offers less scope for individual variation.

Second, as a combination role, the new femininity is particularly demanding. With few exceptions the woman must divide her attention between occupation and femininity or between homemaking and femininity. Although the man's success at his occupation is often accepted as evidence of his being a good husband and father or at least serves as a socially acceptable excuse for considerable neglect of family life, feminine exemplification is less widely accepted in this manner for women.

Third, the universal femininity is as yet ill-defined. The importance of a woman's being feminine is more uniformly accepted than the standards by which her attainment of femininity should be judged. The feminine mystique of which Friedan writes is probably only one among competing interpretations of the new femininity, a version unduly shaped by conservative family ideals from European sources. This version centers on the sexual responsiveness of a traditional mistress in combination with the domestic exclusiveness of the traditional wife and mother and a total subordination to the male. Such a pattern clearly bears no sensible relationship to the historical developments in western culture. Perhaps it is the temporary product of a retreat from the extremes of suffragette antifeminism and the wish dream of influential males who have not yet resolved their own masculinity problems sufficiently to accept women in a relationship of equality.

The woman who seeks to define the feminine ideal also sees conspicuously displayed the ideal of the woman who dominates and manipulates men through her very femininity. The art of molding a man into a figure who looks and thinks of himself as the epitome of power and independence, whose every word and action can be controlled by his wife, receives much attention. Sexual attractiveness as a source of power competes with the notion of sexual surrender. In the face of such contradictory interpretations of femininity, it must be rare that a woman can be satisfied that she has achieved the ideal.

Fourth, whatever its varied applicability, the new universal femininity with its insistence on glamor is an attribute of youth. As middle age is approached, its only future lies in enhanced artificiality and more precarious ruses. The result must be an anxiety for early self-realization and a turning away from stabilizing orientations toward the future.

Fifth, even when femininity is conceived as a source of power, the pattern returns women to their earlier position of dependence on masculine acceptance and approval for their self-respect. The ultimate test of femininity remains the effectiveness of its appeal to men. Even when this appeal is used to manipulate, the very relationship, when sustained, subordinates the manipulator.

Finally, like the aberrant forms of masculinity, the new femininity is a matter of behavioral style rather than demonstrable achievement. Divorced from product, it lacks intrinsic worth, and the belief in its value must be maintained by mutual assurance and by playing the part so hard that there is no time to question its merit. Seldom can women escape doubts regarding its worth. The problem described in Chapter 11, that intrinsic satisfactions are divorced from extrinsic goals in the institutional role of women, must therefore be enhanced by the new femininity.

Momism. Consequences of feminine role strain for family relations are quite apparent and need little elaboration in general. The marginality of the woman's position makes for ambivalence toward the family. Bonds are intensified by the problems of feminine fulfillment, but the ambivalence makes for heightened readiness to see identity clashes. Strategies of decision making are shaped by both the wife's and the husband's conception of universal femininity.

One expression of feminine role strain has attracted considerable discussion, since Phillip Wylie wrote in scathing terms about mom in a popular tirade against modern social life.[24] A configuration known as *momism* has been described and interpreted variously but generally suggests a pattern of response to the residual ambivalence of choosing the housewife role and the consequences of unsuccessful incorporation of the pattern of universal femininity into the role.

Erik Erikson has presented one of the most succinct yet comprehensive summaries of what various writers include in the ideal-typical mom syndrome. He warns us that no woman is likely to show all the symptoms, although taken together they form a consistent pattern. "Mom" is a series of contradictions between her role as moral arbiter and her personal vanity and emotional infantility; her demands for respect from the children and her inability to accept blame when she is wrong; her maintenance of an arbitrary gap between adult and child statuses and failure to play an exemplary role that might justify the separation; her repressive attitudes toward sexual interests by her husband and children and her own efforts to combat aging by cultivating an artificial sexual attractiveness; her advocacy of self-restraint and her own obesity from overeating; her demands for toughness in her children and her personal hypochondriasis; and her partisan advocacy of traditional values and her own pathological fear of aging.[25]

This is a picture that suggests the response to a sense of impotence and purposelessness in one's role. Since convictions regarding values and the sense of power depend ultimately upon group definition and support, the attempt to maintain a tight control over those about oneself is a common

[24] Phillip Wylie, *Generation of Vipers*, Farrar, Strauss & Giroux, New York, 1942.
[25] Erik H. Erikson, *Childhood and Society*, Norton, New York, 1953, pp. 249–250.

way of seeking escape from these twin evils. With the future offering no promise of a better role, a vigorous reassertion of traditional values is a way of trying to recover a sense of worth in an archaic role. The role adaptation to subordination, in which women have cultivated the image of moral purity as a contrast to the moral compromises that the practical exigencies of man's role force on him, is twisted into a preoccupation with maintaining the morals of the children, devaluing the husband, and repudiating any suggestion of imperfection in herself.

Self-control and self-direction depend on a sense of value about one's role and a feeling of personal self-assurance. With these essentials lacking, the role strain destroys self-control. The sense of personal inadequacy makes any self-criticism intolerably painful, but without self-examination and self-criticism there can be no self-direction.

Although this configuration was described a generation ago, the signs of the new universal femininity are apparent in the preoccupation with sexual attraction and the phobia of aging. Here, too, the prospect is bleak and is met by frantic rituals that incorporate the desperate hope that youth and femininity might be attained in defiance of the normal physiological life cycle.

Probably such extremes of feminine role strain are rare. But with a full-fledged mom at the focus of family interaction, there is likely to be a pattern of dependency without the spontaneous aspect of sentiment to undergird it. Children either rebel or become dependent on the pervasive direction of their behavior by mom. The husband either withdraws increasingly from family life or submits as the hen-pecked husband. Here, too, spontaneous sentiment is eroded. And instead of the emergence of a firm role structure through which family members carry on essential family activities, there is a pattern by which personal direction from mom is necessary for the coordination of family behavior in any task.

Summary

Widely observed differences in the personal styles of men and women are often believed to be especially conducive to stable bonding and effective working relationships in the married pair. If women are less aggressive and daring than men, however, this difference does not facilitate their new role as family managers. If these same qualities contribute to a stabilizing role, women's greater emotionality detracts from such a role. If male and female personalities are conducive to a pattern of identification-response bonding, the wife is deprived of the gentle response she needs as much or more than her husband. The personality differences present barriers to intimate understanding and communication. Even for parenthood the traditional sex differences in personality are of little use today, because the mother must play the parts of both father and mother much of the time. In sum, the traditional personality differences between men and women are not conducive to a highly stable and mutually gratifying relationship and are no longer suited to any workable division of labor in marriage. Their only clear utility would be to facilitate a relationship of inequality. The vestiges of inegalitarian relationships embedded in traditional male and female personality styles bring with them pervasive sex rivalry and both harmonizing and exploitative use of the remnants of chivalry.

Personal sex-style differences are often superficial, reflecting role polarization rather than deep value commitments, and both males and females experience role strain because of the poor fit between individual predispositions and standard sex styles. When the family organization affords a haven from role strains experienced in other settings, an important bond is supplied. But the tendency for people to react to role strain by playing even more stereotypic roles in the family lessens the flexibility required for creation of an optimal role structure within the family.

Although the status of male is ascribed, masculinity must be achieved in the face of constant attacks on male self-respect. The principal methods for demonstrating masculinity are success in a masculine occupation; feats of prowess and daring, with the latter partially institutionalized through athletic competition; and the continuous display of manly behavior, such as the swagger and aggressive affectations. Proof of masculinity is difficult for most males because of the lack of intimate contact with an adequate role model, because occupational validation comes late in life and demonstrations of prowess are short-lived and possible for few, because of female dominance over boys and the identification of school as a sphere of feminine accomplishment, and because myths of sex-specialized competencies persist without institutional protection. Response to the typical role strains of youth include cultivating the independent, nonconforming, aggressive features of the male style; taking pride in remaining incompetent in feminine activities, often including schoolwork; and adopting an exploitation-avoidance mode of interaction with women. When these mechanisms are used, a man cannot accept marriage enthusiastically as a mutual good, he is likely to practice a domination-absence pattern in relation to other family members, he is often inflexible about sex specialization, he resists intimacy, and identity clashes with his wife are endemic. Masculine role strain is probably most intense about the time that marriages are established and in old age.

Although masculine role strain centers on achievement, feminine role strain centers on choice. Alternating fashions of feminism and suffragism suggest that women share essential characteristics of the marginal man. In recent years the traditional choice between feminine and nonfeminine roles has given way to a universal femininity—the feminine manner as a required adjunct to whatever roles a woman chooses. But the universal femininity brings new sources of role strain: a uniform style is once again imposed on all women, the new pattern is exceptionally demanding, the pattern is ill-defined, the attribute of glamor is easily attainable only for the young, a new dependency is created, and as a style rather than an achievement the pattern lacks intrinsic worth. One common expression of feminine role strain is momism.

CHAPTER 13

MATE LOVE AND
SEXUAL BEHAVIOR

In searching for determinants of the course that family processes will take, we have proceeded from the more general influences to the more specific. We have attempted to examine love as an attribute of many relationships in order not to fall into the error of ascribing an unwarranted distinctiveness to its most dramatic form, mate love. We have looked for influences on marital relationships that stem from men's and women's involvement in the economic foundation of society, from generalized differences in behavioral styles, whether learned or innate, and from the efforts of men and women to establish their personal self-respect through the framework of the sex roles. Thus consideration of the more specific fact that sexual behavior is distinctively and crucially a focus of marital relationships has been deferred.

Love and sexual behavior have not always been closely identified, but in the recent past this linkage has been important in family interaction. The linkage contributes a distinctive tone to mate love, but it also gives a special character to sexual behavior. The meanings attached to sexual behavior have been grossly different in different times and settings and continue to vary widely within our own society. Hence any consideration of the consequences of mate love and sexual behavior for the processes of family interaction requires examination of these different meanings.

Distinctiveness of Mate Love

Love Preceding Institutionalized Relationship. The involvement with sexual behavior is not the only feature that sets mate love apart from other forms of love. Equally distinctive in the western pattern is the fact that, although other approved forms of love are supposed to grow out of an already established and approved family relationship, mate love is supposed to develop before a family relationship exists and to serve as a basis for entering into such a relationship. In many times and places mate love has been less distinguished from other forms of love in this respect. Mace's eloquent and comprehensive description of the differences between oriental

314

and western conceptions of marriage places considerable emphasis here.[1] The westerner finds strange the oriental assumption that love will develop between husband and wife after marriage, although he is not unwilling to assume with equal confidence that mutual love develops spontaneously out of the right kind of parent-child relationship.

This peculiarity of modern mate love has several important consequences. First, it leads to severe ambivalence toward the initial development of mate love, in contrast to the unqualified approval of parental, filial, and fraternal love in their early and continued manifestations. In the latter instances the bond already exists in an approved institutional arrangement, and the addition of love is simply reinforcement of an approved bond and the shaping of an already sanctioned relationship into closer conformity with the social ideal. But mate love can be attached to a socially and personally inappropriate individual, leading to the formation of disapproved bonds.[2] Much of the parental anxiety about romantic love has nothing to do with the feelings or manifestations of love but expresses anxiety over the choice of partner in establishing a family. In many instances the lover's own ambivalence toward the sentiment does not vanish wholly at the instant of marriage but recurs from time to time.

Because it leads to the start of a new and initially unsupported relationship, mate love is also characterized by greater excitement and volatility than other forms of family love. The risk that intimacy will not be reciprocated, that trust will be violated, is somewhat offset in the already institutionalized family relationship where social norms and sometimes family authority support the love giver. But until there has been a binding acceptance of mutual obligation—formerly in betrothal or engagement, today seldom until marriage—each gesture initiating love incurs the risk of nonreciprocation. Hence the initiating gesture is often accompanied by considerable anxiety. When the response is favorable, the intensified release of anxiety gives rise to excitement.

A third consequence of the association of courting love with the establishment of a new relationship is its susceptibility to becoming a carrier for all sorts of dissatisfactions with existing personal relationships. The high ideal of love can be counterposed to the dissatisfaction with school or home or work as a strong claim to escape the unpleasant conditions through love. But when love incorporates this element, there are likely

[1] David R. Mace and Vera Mace, *Marriage: East and West*, Doubleday, Garden City, N.Y., 1960.
[2] In his interesting discussion of the universal occurrence of love, William J. Goode emphasizes the unpredictable rise of attachments not envisaged in the normal social order. See "The Theoretical Importance of Love," *American Sociological Review*, 24: 38–47, February 1959.

to be intensified efforts to control and manipulate the other in the name of love. If earlier dissatisfactions recur in relations with the beloved, no response is more natural.

Finally, because mate love supplies the continuity between courtship and marriage, there must be a discontinuity in the pattern of love. The love that leads to marriage and the love of husband and wife are supposed to be the same thing. But in marriage love is to be given free expression, and in courtship it is not usually regarded as genuine unless hedged about by control and discretion.

In sum, mate love is made more tumultuous and beset with more potential inner blockages than other forms of love, simply because it precedes and leads to a formally sanctioned relationship rather than developing out of one. Such a distinction between mate love and other forms of love is not so likely to appear when a system of arranged marriage prevails. Although it means an addition to unpredictability and risk in the marriage relationship, it also helps to make mate love by itself a delightful experience, even apart from the sexual anticipation and gratification to which it eventually leads.

Permanence of Love. There is another and closely related difference from other forms of love. In the modern conventional view, all love is thought to be naturally enduring, although unnatural events may destroy it. Because mate love is viewed as the basis and justification for marriage, it becomes especially important that a conviction of permanence be maintained. If love is thought to be capable of vanishing or shifting to a different object as unpredictably as it first arose, it becomes impossible to couple a belief in the permanence of marriage with the view that marriage should be founded on love. The sentiment of mate love has incorporated within the supporting belief system certain mechanisms that protect the conviction of permanence of love.

The first exigency that threatens permanence is the lessening of the anxious-excited component of love, a drawing back from the total intimacy often demanded at first toward a viable balance between intimacy and distance, and subordination of love to a place in the family routine—generally to the imperious demands of occupational life and child care. In face of the common fear that love has weakened, the married couple can draw on the conception of transformation of an immature, adolescent, romantic love into a mature but more vital form. With the aid of this cultural tool, the less volatile interdependence that comes from the crescive bonds can supply the basis for belief in the continuity of love.

The more disruptive exigency is the loss of attraction during courtship, especially through transfer to someone else. After serious and sincere protestations of love, the individual is distressed to discover that his own feelings have changed utterly. He must surely give up his belief in the permanence of love, except that the culture supplies him with the conception of a form of pseudo-love, easily mistaken for the real thing. The concept of *infatuation* is one that can only be applied retrospectively: if love does not last, one concludes that it must not have been love but infatuation. The myth requires that there be signs by which one can tell whether his feeling is love or infatuation at the time if he is only willing to search himself. Marriage manuals sometimes offer the young reader a set of cues. If he cannot recognize them at the time, he will surely be able to recall them afterwards, as proof that true love has not yet come his way.

Romantic Love. The term *romantic love* is often applied to the form of mate love most extensively featured by the media of mass communication and to varying degrees reflected in courtship behavior and marriage. Romantic love is chiefly an intensified expression of general love, with its demands for intimacy and the attributes that arise from the special characteristics of contemporary mate love. In particular romantic love exaggerates (a) the dependence on excitement and feelings of agitation and euphoria as indicators of love, (b) idealization of the mate and the perfectibility of the relationship, (c) the superiority of the moral claim of romantic love over any conflicting claims on the individual, and (d) reliance on love apart from rational decision and planning to ensure a successful marriage.[3]

Romantic love in western society has a history that began outside marriage and in relations of short duration or in worship of the unattainable. In this respect it represented the divorcement of love from the social responsibilities imposed in the normal family relationship. Romantic love in this tradition offered escape—gratification without acceptance of the usual obligations.

At the same time, there is an uncertain line between escape and hope, and romantic attitudes in general express a hope of improvement and a belief in human perfectibility. Romantic love came onto the western scene as an aspect of upper-class life at the time when the Crusades brought extensive contact with the unfamiliar and a loosening of the rigidities of medieval life. It has become an aspect of the life of the masses only very recently, as the fruits of the industrial revolution have been made generally available throughout the population. In each instance there was wide-

---

[3] A somewhat caricatured but extensive account of romantic love is to be found in Denis de Rougement, *Love in the Western World*, Harcourt, Brace & World, New York, 1940.

spread contact with the unfamiliar, which could be more readily idealized than the familiar, and a growing awareness of the possibilities of human improvement, which contributed to ideas of perfectibility. Two people who had known each other too briefly to have developed an inflexible mode of interaction assumed great risk in marriage but, just because of their flexibility, might be led by their ideals to form a better relationship than otherwise. Each person's treatment of the other as better than the person his behavior revealed might set up a role reciprocity through which the behavior of each might actually be improved.

The assumption of human improvability became the central element of romantic love as it underwent the historical assimilation into conventional family life. In this respect it was not only compatible with the religious ideal; it merged with it and helped to vitalize it. In this transition the marital ideal of permanence became a theme of romantic love, and the desire to assume the responsibilities of marriage was accepted as the natural expression of the sentiment. In conventionalized romantic love the escape element remains in subdued form, in the conviction that the task elements of the marriage will work out if the identity relations are right.

Still, the sentiment of romantic love is more congenial to a marriage relationship in which the wife plays the companion role rather than the occupational career and housewife roles. Thus it may contribute to dissatisfaction with both major wife roles and reinforce the emphasis on universal femininity. With romantic love dominating courtship, premarital interaction becomes the rehearsal for a pattern of family life that is not practicable except for a very few people.

Romantic love as an explicit pattern elevates the mutual response bond to dominant importance. But in practice the lack of intimate familiarity between the lovers, the unrealistic images of each other that impede initial growth of adjusted communication and response bonds, and the focus of interaction on the ritual and hence culturally standard aspects of love making prevent the response bond from supplying the selective element in the initial choice of a courtship partner.

Thus the absorption of romantic love into modern premarital patterns creates a discrepancy between the effective selective bonds and those which are explicitly idealized in love. Because of the emphasis on response, the prestige from identification is often mistaken for personal response and the ritual of courtship taken as a more fundamental kind of response than it actually is. The confusion between identification and response is probably an element in the feelings of shallowness and superficiality in relationships, the disappointment sometimes expressed at never really knowing one's mate.

The Meanings of Sexual Behavior

In all societies sexual behavior bears a special relationship to family life and, within the family, to the marital pair. But the relationship of sexual behavior to the family is not the same everywhere, and its effects on family and marriage are not uniform. Sex is invariably a heavily regulated form of activity, but regulated in widely different ways. The variations in regulation result from different meanings attached to sexual behavior. The differences in meaning affect family processes both indirectly through the resultant regulations and directly through the relationship of sex to bonding and the organization of roles.

Physiological Meanings. Sexual behavior has two elemental meanings, based on its immediate and long-range biological consequences. In the short-range it constitutes pleasurable stimulation, accumulating tension, and gratifying release. In the normal male the sequence occurs involuntarily if release is not voluntarily sought, so that the awareness of desire and relief is almost inescapable. Women, on the other hand, must learn to recognize the nature of the tension and the means for its release, and some apparently never do so. The intensity of release is heightened when genital stimulation is supplemented by more comprehensive bodily stimulation, and this may be especially important in the female. Because of awareness of the process, males normally seek means of securing relief without waiting for painfully delayed automatic release, unless specifically taught not to do so. Women are probably more dependent on actual experience or social teaching to seek sexual stimulation and release. The physiological sequence by itself need not lead to heterosexual intercourse, and it may well be only the union of physiological with social exchange that makes heterosexual experience more gratifying and more natural for most human beings than homosexual or other means of securing release. Thus the very channeling of sexual behavior into heterosexual intercourse already represents the addition of a social meaning to the simple physiological experience.

In the long-range, sexual behavior means reproduction. Here the connection must be learned. It was once common to speak of sexual desire as the expression of an instinct for reproduction or maintenance of the species. Such a designation is nonsensical, since neither the sexual impulse nor its gratification bears any connection with the desire for reproduction. It is not impossible that some societies have existed without knowledge of the connection between intercourse and reproduction, but there is a disposition to suppose that in apparent instances of this kind there may have been strong ritual concealment of what was actually known.

Because of the consequence of sexual intercourse in bringing new life into existence, it is inconceivable that any society would have regarded sex as a simple physiological need to be indulged impulsively for personal gratification. Perhaps the most important observation for the impact of sex on love and family life is that there are several social meanings of sex which are prevalent in our contemporary society and which are not wholly compatible with one another.

Sacred Meanings. It is hardly surprising that a sacred or magical significance should be attached to an act that produces life and that its regulation should be thought the proper sphere of religious leaders. It is the nature of the sacred that there must be taboos to protect it from profanation. The national flag, as a sacred national symbol, is protected by rules governing the way it is flown, the uses it may be put to, the forms of respect to be shown it, and even the manner of its disposition when worn out. Sexual intercourse with an improper partner or on an improper occasion becomes similarly an evil of concern to all when sacred meanings prevail.

The currently most important sacred signification is the Roman Catholic view that holds that sex is sacred and inherently good. But its sacredness lies in its being the specific means of reproduction. Whenever, then, sexual intercourse takes place in a manner calculated to frustrate the sacred purpose of reproduction, the sacred act is profaned. To attempt to secure the pleasure of sexual behavior while thwarting the sacred purpose is therefore sinful.[4]

But mixed in Judeo-Christian religious tradition has been the view of sex as either evil in itself or a lesser good than abstinence. When an act is so narrowly regulated as to be good under only limited circumstances, there is a tendency to take the next step and view it as sinful in all human uses. In the extreme, religious doctrine may declare that "we are all conceived in sin," and the fact that good can come from evil serves as an indication of the wonder of God's work. In the sacred context, sex also is viewed in relation to the ascetic ideal. Here the attention is not focused on the reproductive function but on the tension-release sequence. When it is held that development of our spiritual capacities requires utmost subordination of our bodily desires, fasting, physical discomfort, and sexual restraint or abstinence become positive values. Often ascetic codes take the form that abstinence is necessary for spiritual leaders and that restraint is required of the ordinary person. Sexual gratification within the marriage relationship becomes a necessary concession to man's ordinary weakness to save him from the much greater evil of sexual indulgence outside marriage.

Secular Meanings. The present century has seen abundant illustrations

[4] John L. Thomas, *The American Catholic Family*, Prentice-Hall, Englewood Cliffs, N.J., 1956, pp. 45–66.

of efforts and tendencies to define sex behavior on the basis of its reproductive consequences, but in a secular rather than sacred context. An aspect of pre-World War II nationalism was often a concern with boosting the birthrate in the interests of national expansion and power. Rewards and recognition for child bearing, as in Hitler's Germany, symbolized this meaning. Postwar developments have seen increasing preoccupation with limiting the birthrate.

There is little indication at present that either kind of secular definition can become sufficiently effective on a widespread basis to alter sexual behavior substantially, apart from tangible rewards and punishments. Sufficient preoccupation with the reproductive consequences to ensure consistent use of contraceptives seems to require a life geared to high material consumption, so that the birth of a child substantially affects the level at which people live.[5] But even when this is found, the gratifications of the act itself often lead to lapses of attention to the reproductive meaning, leading to unplanned pregnancies.

Serious Interpersonal Meanings. Meanings of sex based primarily on the relationship between the partners divide into those which imply a serious relationship and those which accept sexual intercourse as a casual matter. Serious interpersonal meanings differ greatly according to whether the relationship is one of mutuality or one in which the gratification and the desire are primarily on one side. In the latter instance, sex takes on the character of *property*, with one man owning the right of sexual access to one or more women. Under such an arrangement the man is free to dispose of the woman's sexual favors, although she may neither offer them to men of her choice nor refuse them when he chooses. There is but a fine line of distinction between such a straightforward treatment of sex as commercial property and patterns of marriage under which the wife, but only the wife, must be virginal at marriage and must limit her favors to her husband in marriage. Folk rituals in which the husband looks for bleeding as proof of his wife's virginity on the marriage night are still practiced. The idea that in extramarital sex relations it is the woman's husband who is the offended party is still strong in many quarters. The wife who would protect her husband's social esteem practices elaborate ritual avoidances regarding her association with other men, so as to make plain to all that there could have been no chance for improper relations. Although extramarital conquests may supply a claim to prestige in the male group, it would be the height of disloyalty to a friend to make advances toward his wife.

If we turn to mutuality, the sheer property and possession meaning of

[5] Alfred Sauvy, *Fertility and Survival: Population Problems from Malthus to Mao Tse-Tung*, Chatto and Windus, London, 1961.

sex gives way to *intimacy*. The latter meaning is so firmly entrenched in some circles that the more general term, intimacy, is often taken as a euphemism for sexual intercourse. This meaning of sex, like all the others, is learned. If intimacy is a penetration beyond the public layers of the self to the most private and most sensitive core, it means that the sex act as a physiological experience is subordinated to its personal and social meaning. The sex act becomes a symbolic exchange in which the experience of closeness, the euphoria of mutual abandonment of all "front" and concealment, is paramount, and the physiological release serves to make the symbolic meanings dramatic.

The intimacy meaning probably makes sexual intercourse a more vitally and comprehensively bonding experience than any of the other meanings. As a step in conciliation of conflict, sex acquires an effectiveness that cannot be attained through other meanings. But it also makes sexual gratification a more precarious matter, more dependent on day-to-day variations in the identity relations of the pair. Sex as property has value even when not used, and the gratification received in sexual intercourse makes no great demands on the rest of the relationship. The meanings that refer beyond the relationship to a sacred or secular context likewise make limited demands on the interpersonal relationship within which sex takes place. But the need for physiological gratification continues in periods when there is a loss of desire for the vital intimacy experience. The result is either abstinence and accumulating physiological tension or an unsatisfying sexual experience that moves toward the meaning of exploitation or property.

Casual Interpersonal Meanings. The omnipresent tension between the acceptance of responsibility and the desire for enjoyment freed from responsibility, between constraining one's impulses to fit the social order and allowing them imagined full range, is clearly reflected in the universal coexistence of committing and casual meanings for sex. The independent and continuous nature of the physiological need is not the only pressure toward understanding sexual intercourse as a casual exchange. The social value of novelty seems inescapable. The exotic person so intensely sought as a sexual partner can lose appeal with familiarity, and the individual can easily learn to find the major social gratification of the sex act in the experience of novelty with constantly changing partners. The sex act can be perceived as conquest, a simple extension of the rating-dating pattern in which sexual consummation is necessary for prestige. Thus the casual attitude toward sex can rest on as fully social a set of meanings as the more serious attitudes.

When mutuality prevails, sex becomes a form of *play* or a simple business transaction. When the relationship is not mutual, sex becomes *exploi-*

tation. In practice these meanings are heavily mixed. The casual affair, devoid of commercial aspects, is made suddenly unequal if the girl becomes pregnant. The risk that the woman must nearly always take so exceeds the male risk when long-term commitments are avoided that the exploitation interpretation is always close at hand. When strong norms against exploitation prevail, the onset of pregnancy is often a basis for reassessing the casual meaning of the sex act and assigning it, retrospectively, a more serious meaning. The forced marriage, when not simply a temporary expedient for legitimization of the child, often rests on considerable redefinition of the meaning of an initially casual act.

The undercurrent of exploitative connotations to sex is very strong in modern society. The overwhelming symbolization of exploitation through sexual terms in profanity is undoubtedly a highly effective mechanism for socializing youth to this kind of meaning. Yet it conveys an image of the sex relationship that is opposite to intimacy. If sex is exploitation, a man can attain full gratification in sex only with a woman toward whom he has no feelings of respect. His gratification is maximal when she acquires some commitment to him without his having any toward her. From her point of view, uncoerced submission requires acceptance of subordination.

Contradictory Meanings. With this range of meanings all found in modern society, it is frequent that sexual advances outside marriage and sexual relations within marriage involve partners who are applying discrepant meanings to the exchange. There is a systematic difference in prevalent meanings for men and women, a difference that is consistent with the masculine and feminine styles we have already viewed. The greater preoccupation of women with sentiment and their greater concern with harmonious interpersonal relations fit with a stronger tendency toward viewing sex as intimacy, and their greater interest in religion inclines them more frequently toward the sacred view of sex in both its negative and positive aspects. In men, the casual view finds much more support.

These differences in meaning are often understood by the persons in the relationship, in which case there is a preliminary period of bargaining during which each attempts to impose his own meaning on the exchange. Out of such bargaining emerge various tactics. The girl insists on entertainment and displays of affection as a prelude to sexual intercourse. The boy, accepting the terms, redefines them. Instead of stressing the affection and intimacy of the tête-à-tête, he defines the preliminary on the basis of its dollar cost as an openly disguised commercial transaction that is as devoid of intimate commitment as relations with a prostitute. Cultivation of a technique or line—a skilled and practiced approach that by its perfection must obviously have been used on many women—is designed to sweep the woman off of her feet without commitment. The woman counters by attempting to elicit assurances that this time the man has weakened, that he has been overtaken by genuine feelings in spite of himself. Men's magazines frequently feature a mixture of violent disregard for the woman's sensitivities, reaching outright aggression, with courtship and sexual consummation. The hostile element helps to nullify implications of intimacy that the woman might otherwise draw.

In this kind of relationship it is the man who pushes toward consummation and the woman who holds back. The longer the preliminary and the more extended the sexual foreplay, the greater the implication of commitment. The pattern is extended among those groups to whom courtship is a rivalry in which the male attempts to gain sexual gratification and conquest while remaining single and the girl seeks to attract the sexual attentions of a desirable partner and lure a proposal of marriage from him as a condition to granting sexual intercourse.[6]

The pattern may have a considerably more general effect on the nature of social exchanges between men and women because of the potential sexual meanings of any dealings between the sexes. Margaret Mead suggests that a general pattern so pervades relationships that it shapes even the play of a father with his preadolescent daughter. The little girl, she observes, "learns from her father the only game he knows how to play with women, the game in which he teasingly asks and she teasingly refuses."[7]

Although unrecognized differences of meaning set the stage for misunderstanding and exploitation, ambivalent meanings in the same individual frequently prevent a straightforward relationship on a single basis. Whyte's corner boys recognized the danger that repeated intercourse with the same girl sometimes leads to a shift in the boy's attitude toward acceptance of intimacy and commitment.[8] When intimacy declines in a continuing relationship, definitions of property rights often become more salient. Sometimes the feeling about the act changes during its course, a feeling of commitment and intimacy during the period of physiological arousal being followed by a more casual attitude as release is attained. The frequent discontinuity between premarital and marital definitions of sex is unlikely to be bridged without residues of the earlier casual attitude recurring in married life.

It is appropriate to summarize this discussion by observing that the effects of sex relations depend on the meanings that people learn to attach

---

[6] Arnold W. Green, "The 'Cult of Personality' and Sexual Relations," *Psychiatry*, 4: 344–48, August 1941.
[7] Margaret Mead, *Male and Female*, Morrow, New York, 1949, p. 276.
[8] William F. Whyte, "A Slum Sex Code," *American Journal of Sociology*, 49:24–31, July 1943.

to sex and not upon any natural or innate significance. Even within the confines of modern society several meanings are available and in contention.

The Regulation of Sex

The publication of the first Kinsey volume on the sexual behavior of men in the United States led to a great outcry.[9] Most of it was either in defense or attack on the mores, laws, and religious codes applied to sex behavior. The volume had clearly been written with just this kind of use in mind, since it dwelt largely on the frequencies with which approved and disapproved forms of behavior were reported.

In Kinsey's own interpretations of his findings, and in much of the discussion that followed, the axiom that regulation proceeds from meaning was overlooked. Codes of all kinds serve primarily to preserve the socially approved meanings from dilution and to protect valued persons and objects from harm when recognized meanings govern behavior. If sex is a sacred object, it follows inevitably that there must be a religious code to protect it from profanation. If sex means intimacy, the mores must incorporate disapproval of relationships of a casual kind or affect a compartmentalization of sexual activity that minimizes confusion between intimate and casual meanings. If sex is property, there must be laws to protect ownership and civil procedures for securing redress in case property rights are violated.

But there is also an interaction between meaning and regulation, so that regulations instituted to protect one meaning often contribute to the growth of another. One such instance is the constant reinforcement of sin and exploitation as meanings in connection with efforts to protect the view of sex as a sacred good. The sacred view requires particularly that the indulgence of sex desire be deferred until the individual is prepared to assume the responsibilities that stem from it, which normally means within marriage. But marriage must be delayed well beyond sexual maturity because of its socioeconomic ramifications. Socialization to the sacred meaning thus requires that the individual learn to defer gratification for a few years for the sake of the greater value to be realized in marriage. But several developments occur in the process. First, it is a generally applicable principle that important means acquire semiautonomous value as ends when they are pursued seriously for an extended period of time. Deferment of sexual gratification as a means tends to acquire an independent value in asceticism. Sexual gratification under any circumstances becomes at least a lesser good than abstinence, and overindulgence be-

[9] Alfred C. Kinsey, Wardell B. Pomeroy, and Clyde E. Martin, *Sexual Behavior in the Human Male*, Saunders, Philadelphia, 1948.

comes a profanation even in marriage. Second, teaching deferment of gratification is not easy, and the realistic parent knows that many pupils need stronger and more immediate motivations for avoiding sex gratification. A common approach is to seize on the special vulnerability of the girl to the consequence of sex. She can be taught to see sex as a form of exploitation, to regard all sexual approaches to her as efforts to get something for nothing. Girls are regaled with stories of men who have taken unfair advantage of unsuspecting women. The upshot of these procedures is to encourage the growth of ambivalent meanings about sex.

Code, Behavior, and Guilt. If the strictest of the standard codes—the complete limitation of sex to marriage—is taken as the point of reference, both widespread violation and extensive conformity can be observed in such statistics as are available. Only a minority of men, but a somewhat greater proportion of women, live their lives out without an experience of premarital or extramarital relations. On the other hand, conformity is indicated by the small proportion who indulge freely in extramarital relations or in unrestrained and promiscuous premarital relations. Unfortunately, Kinsey's work bypassed the matter of alternative codes and treated all behavior that deviated from the strictest of codes as nonconformity. Serious efforts have been made more recently to assess the codes separately so as to provide an adequate base against which to judge conformity.[10]

From both the Kinsey kinds of surveys of sex behavior and the case studies by clinicians has come a general conclusion that the prevalent sex codes demand more restraint than most people can achieve. In one example, Christensen and Carpenter report questionnaire findings from samples of students in the United States and Denmark. In both countries men more often approved of premarital coitus than women and more often reported having premarital experience. In the two American samples, one from a Mormon area (Utah) and one from the Midwest, reported behavior was in excess of approval. With codes stricter than behavior the authors infer that a substantial number of the Americans must feel some guilt over their sex lives. By contrast, the Danish sample expressed approval for more premarital behavior than was actually reported.[11]

The Danish findings suggest a pattern that is also undoubtedly present among some American groups and leave a question as to why the dis-

---

[10] Ira L. Reiss, *Premarital Sexual Standards in America: A Sociological Investigation of the Relative Social and Cultural Integration of American Sexual Standards*, Free Press, New York, 1960.

[11] Harold T. Christensen and George R. Carpenter, "Value-behavior Discrepancies Regarding Premarital Coitus in Three Western Cultures," *American Sociological Review*, 27:66–74, February 1962.

crepancy should exist. Unless limited opportunity is a sufficient explanation, there may be effective inhibitions that exceed the limitations imposed by the avowed code. In such a situation both behavior and avowal constitute ranges of the code.

Another kind of discrepancy has been brought out by Ehrmann. Questionnaires were administered to 990 college students in marriage and family courses. Respondents reported what for them would be an acceptable degree of intimacy in relations with an acquaintance, a friend, and a lover. The three queries were then repeated, but on the basis of what is acceptable on the part of another member of the peer group. The results for men were complicated and difficult to interpret. But for women there was a consistently higher proportion approving sex relations in each category by a peer than by oneself.[12] Girls imposed a much stricter code on their own behavior than they did on others.

A similar finding was secured in a slightly different way from another but smaller university sample. A hypothetical situation in which a young person engages in an episode of sexual intercourse on a casual and promiscuous basis was described in questionnaire. The subject was then asked to imagine himself as the young person and write freely how he would feel and what he would do afterwards. The same instructions were repeated with a friend rather than self as principal, the order of presentation being alternated on different questionnaires. Although most of the students anticipated personal feelings of self-disgust and guilt in the first instance, often stating that it would be difficult to be around their friends with this deed on their minds, most students also felt that they would be no less friendly and apply no sanctions after hearing of the episode when the friend was the offender. They often explain that sexual standards are a private matter: since no one but the participants are hurt, it is no one else's business. By contrast, when the procedure was repeated using a sizable theft of money instead of the sex experience, students generally felt that their friendship would be lessened or social pressures applied to right the offender's behavior. Here was not a matter of private morality but a public evil.[13]

If we return to the earlier observation that students reported premarital behavior they did not approve of, we must ask whether the private code or the peer code is meant. If students were reporting the former, their behavior might still have been within the limits that their peers were setting for one another.

Although regret over premarital incidents is often reported, profound

[12] Winston Ehrmann, *Premarital Dating Behavior*, Holt, New York, 1959, pp. 175–179.
[13] Ralph H. Turner, "Moral Judgment: A Study in Roles," *American Sociological Review*, 17:70–77, January 1952.

and disturbing guilt does not seem common.[14] Partly this is because most of the violators are probably less intensely committed to the code at the time. But the pathological instances of guilt are often found in individuals who have not overtly violated the code but who feel anxious and guilty over desires they cannot eliminate. "But I say to you that every one who looks at a woman lustfully has already committed adultery with her in his heart,"[15] supplies ideological justification for experiencing guilt in the absence of overt offense and for interpreting the anxiety as guilt. To the extent to which such a pattern is found among the conforming population, complications from guilt are underestimated by merely noting discrepancies between code and behavior.

The foregoing considerations combine to require a complex notion of regulation and conformity. They suggest that the codes are neither unidimensional nor unambiguous and that guilt bears no one-to-one relationship with code-behavioral discrepancy. And they also suggest an idea we have encountered in the examination of role change, the presence of norms that lack the effective support of value and ideology. Under mutually supporting values and norms, conformity is largely spontaneous and does not become a matter from which the individual draws credit to be used later in marital bargaining. Likewise, violation is an uncomplicated matter giving rise to regret and guilt, which can then be expiated, recompensed, or lived down, according to the procedures made available in the culture. But when norms lack the firm backing of values, conformity can create regret—self-depreciation over one's inability to overcome irrational inhibitions. And the working off of guilt based on either uncontrollable desire or behavioral violation is made more difficult by the recurring feeling that perhaps there is really nothing to feel guilty over. The clash between determining not to feel guilty and accepting guilt so as to dispose of it creates a situation of continuing and disturbing tension that is likely to be disturbing to the course of intimate personal relations with the opposite sex, both within and outside marriage and whether or not specifically sexual relations are involved.

Double and Single Standards. The common impression that either codes or behavior have become laxer in recent decades is difficult to confirm or refute with satisfactory evidence. There are reasons to suppose that the sex behavior of males in the last century was not dramatically different from the present, at least in the frequency of premarital behavior. Kinsey compares the rates for the older and younger generation males in his sample and finds no great difference.[16] Scattered bits of historical evidence suggest that a great deal was concealed beneath the stern cover

[14] Kinsey et al., *op. cit.*, 1948, p. 562.
[15] Matthew 5:28.
[16] Kinsey et al., *op. cit.*, 1948, p. 397.

of puritan public utterances in earlier American life. The specific instance of the church in Groton in which confession of premarital relations was made a matter of secret church record prior to the marriage ceremony indicates that perhaps as many as 50 percent of couples had something to confess.[17] By no means all or even a majority of the people belonged to the puritan camp, and much of the vigor of puritan preaching may have been a reaction against the actual state of affairs. The accounts of the custom of bundling, and later of frontier life, do not suggest a society with puritan morals in firm control.[18]

But fairly convincing evidence is at hand to show that premarital sexual intercourse has become more common among women, although such indications as we have still suggest—at least until the 1960's—that the majority of women remain virgins until marriage.[19] It is this trend which calls attention to the difference between a *double standard* and a *single standard*. The usual form of double standard is permissiveness and often active advocacy of premarital experience for men combined with a strict taboo that requires virginity of women until marriage. The husband's sophistication and command of the situation are supposed to facilitate a strong identification bond from his more naïve and innocent partner.[20] For such a system to work, there must be clear separation between two kinds of women: those who will eventually be wives and those who are available to satisfy premarital sexual demands. In order to protect the local men's long-term interests as far as possible, the code incorporates a strong taboo against experience with a virginal woman and against relations with women of the ingroup, from whom marriage partners are supposed to be chosen. As a consequence, men seek sex relations with girls from outgroups whose men are often equally bent on protecting their women. This element often plays a part in the local gang warfare in American communities among populations of Latin extraction.

A double standard of this sort rests on the coexistence of two meanings of sexual intercourse. Sex may have either a casual or a committing meaning, but not both at the same time, and situations must be so sharply defined that the meanings are effectively compartmentalized. The favored casual meaning is exploitation, sex being a form of conquest that redounds to the credit of the male but not of the female. This meaning is linked with a conception of masculinity in which successful exploitation is a primary means of demonstrating manliness. The commercial meaning is also recog-

---

[17] Arthur W. Calhoun, *A Social History of the American Family from Colonial Times to the Present*, A. H. Clark, Glendale, Calif., 1917–1919, vol. I, pp. 132–133 ff.
[18] *Ibid.*, vol. I, pp. 129–132; vol. II, pp. 149–170.
[19] Lewis M. Terman, *Psychological Factors in Marital Happiness*, McGraw-Hill, New York, 1938, pp. 321–322.
[20] A classic description of the detailed operation of a double standard was made by William F. Whyte, *loc. cit.*

nized, but only when the preferred exploitative means of securing sex is unavailable. The committing meaning of sex is property, the sexual favor of the wife being a property held exclusively for the husband. Toward his own property or what may some day become the property of his friends or himself the man practices a protective attitude.

It is clear that a code and a set of meanings such as this could not exist except on a secure foundation of female subordination to the male. The decline of the double standard and its replacement with a more uniform standard for men and women seem to have been an inevitable adjustment to the general equalization of privilege and responsibility between the sexes.

For interaction between the sexes it is important to note that femininity under the double standard is not established by playing the role that is complementary to the pattern by which a male establishes his masculinity. If the male establishes his manliness by sexual exploitation, the woman loses rather than gains in femininity by allowing herself to be exploited. The woman protects her femininity only by exacting the protective rather than exploitative attitude from a man.

A by-product of the double standard is some confusion regarding the sexual relationship in marriage. The two kinds of women under this system exhibit very different attitudes toward sex. Having once become known as nonvirgins, women have nothing more to lose by learning to enjoy the sexual experience. Hence the girls who are favored for promiscuous relations often express active sexual desire and responsiveness. The virgin, however, inhibits desire and is unlikely to be fully responsive in her initial experience. There are two consequences. First, sexual relations with his wife are likely to be less satisfying to the man than many of the experiences he has had with other women. Second, if his wife develops responsiveness and passion, her response signals the casual meanings he knows from premarital and extramarital affairs. A man under the double standard is often caught in the trap that he can respect his wife only when she is not fully responsive in sex relations.

Absolute and Graded Standards. If much of what has been termed a relaxation of sex codes is actually the necessary readjustment as single standards replace double standards, another element in the apparent trend may be abandonment of the absolute character of sexual codes. By an absolute code we mean one under which people are dichotomized into conformers and nonconformers, rather than arrayed along a continuum of nonconformity.[21] In many respects traditional American sex codes make

---

[21] The distinction between absolute and graded standards was developed by the author in Leonard Broom and Philip Selznick, *Sociology: A Text with Adapted Readings*, Harper & Row, New York, 1955, pp. 378–380.

no allowance for differences in seriousness of premarital and extramarital sex violations or for the frequency of violation or the degree of temptation under which the transgression occurred. The concept of virginity does not allow degrees, and grouping all individuals into the virgin-nonvirgin dichotomy throws together the individual with only a single experience and the individual with abundant and undiscriminating experience. The absolute standard has been applied more consistently to women than to men, both in premarital and extramarital sex, even in groups among whom the single standard is given nominal acceptance.

A graded rather than absolute standard is applied in many other realms of behavior governed by the mores. One could not regard the mores regarding theft and other violations of property rights as weak or permissive, but both popular ethics and the law incorporate elaborate gradations of judgment toward acts of thieving and toward the thief. We hesitate to label first offenders as thieves or to invoke the law against theft of objects of small value.

Many items of informal evidence suggest that the absolute standard in sex is being supplanted by a graded standard, even when premarital chastity is still held as a serious goal and high ideal. Promiscuity is a more serious offense than selective premarital experience; the single experience is to be forgiven; the slip that occurred when the individual was immature and impressionable is not taken as an indication of later mature character.

Sex and Intimacy. A third trend is partially concealed and partially revealed beneath the statistics of sex behavior. This is a shift toward a code under which the desirability and acceptability of sexual intercourse is determined by the degree to which it takes place in a relationship of tender feeling and intimacy.

The commonest form of this trend preserves the ideal of a union among sex, love, and marriage, while finding little or no fault with sexual intercourse between couples who are in love and sincerely intend marriage and only a little more fault in nonpromiscuous and affectionate relationships before marriage. The decline of prostitution and the increase of premarital experience among respectable girls suggests this pattern. And scattered indications are that the higher rates of premarital relations do not mark a proportionately greater promiscuity but that a large proportion of the girls limit their attentions to one man.[22] According to this trend, the code becomes a vehicle for the enforcement of a single meaning of sex, serious rather than casual, based on the relationship between the participants rather than any larger or secular context, and mutual rather than unequal. Whether this code then restricts the ultimate expression of love through

[22] Terman, *loc. cit.*

sexual intercourse to marriage depends on how fully the sentiment of love is assimilated to the family system.

The "new morality" popularized in the 1960's calls for reversal of the trend toward identifying sexual intercourse with intimacy, assigning it the casual but mutual meaning of play. The time of this writing is too early to ascertain whether a major segment of the population will adopt this reinterpretation. Some slight evidence of lessened concern over premarital experiences that do not lead to marriage might be consistent with such a trend.[23]

Mate Love and Marriage

Many efforts have been made to discover a simple relationship between sexual behavior and general adjustment in marriage. Aside from the extreme sexual determinists, many investigators, such as Dickinson and Beam, have concluded from case studies that apprehension and failure of gratification in sexual relations with her husband must almost inevitably color attitudes in other relationships with the husband and inhibit the relaxation of interpersonal barriers essential to intimacy.[24]

The views of Burgess and Wallin are typical of many sociologists. They suggest three generalizations. First, the relationship between sexual adjustment and other aspects of marital adjustment is reciprocal. Second, sexual adjustment in marriage is more effect than cause of general marriage adjustment. Since the sexual relationship is only one feature of a complex and comprehensive relationship, there is more scope for sexual adjustment to be facilitated or damaged by the total marriage pattern than for the reverse effect to occur. Third, the importance of sexual adjustment as a cause of general marital adjustment is proportional to the importance that the partners attach to sexual adjustment.

In their study of young married couples, Burgess and Wallin examine the interrelationship between questionnaire measures of sexual adjustment in marriage and general marital happiness. As indicated in Table 12, there is considerable relationship, but cases of wide divergence between the two kinds of adjustment are not exceptional. They do observe, however, that the relationship follows a rather different pattern for men and women. The combination of low marital happiness with high sexual adjustment is more frequent among men than women, but the combination of high marital-success scores with low sexual adjustment is more common among women. Burgess and Wallin interpret this finding as a difference in the

[23] Ira L. Reiss, "Premarital Sex as Deviant Behavior: An Application of Current Approaches to Deviance," *American Sociological Review*, 35:78–87, Feb. 1970.
[24] Robert L. Dickinson and Lura Beam, *A Thousand Marriages: A Medical Study of Sex Adjustment*, Williams & Wilkins, Baltimore, 1931.

TABLE 12   SEX ADJUSTMENT IN RELATION TO MARITAL HAPPINESS

| | Happiness scores (%) | | | | | |
| | Low | | Medium | | High | |
Sex scores	Husbands	Wives	Husbands	Wives	Husbands	Wives
High	11.2	25.2	22.0	40.8	36.4	58.5
Medium	26.0	47.0	40.5	43.8	41.6	30.3
Low	62.7	27.8	37.5	15.4	22.1	11.2
Total	99.9	100.0	100.0	100.0	100.1	100.0
No. of cases	(169)	(151)	(200)	(201)	(231)	(277)

SOURCE: Adapted from Ernest W. Burgess and Paul Wallin, *Engagement and Marriage*, Lippincott, Chicago, 1953, p. 692, by permission of the publisher.

expectations men and women bring to marriage. Because of the meanings that girls have been taught to attach to sex, they often expect rather little sexual gratification. As a consequence they are more easily satisfied in the sexual sphere than in other realms and accordingly rate their sexual adjustment more highly. Men, on the other hand, are likely to expect a great deal from sex in marriage and are therefore more likely to be disappointed with sexual adjustment in spite of satisfaction with other areas.[25]

Burgess and Wallin's data and their theorizing point to the necessity for taking the divergent meanings of sex into account in assessing its relationship to marriage. Their data do not help in assessing causality, but they do make clear that it is sometimes possible to compartmentalize sexual relations from the rest of the marriage to a considerable degree.

Perhaps the most hotly contested issue toward which research has been directed is the relationship of premarital sexual relations to marital adjustment. Here we find Kinsey and others arguing the advantages of premarital experience, with marriage prediction studies yielding modest but not altogether consistent negative associations between premarital experience and marital adjustment. The difference in findings that depends on the variables used is well illustrated in the Burgess-Wallin study. When the frequency with which the wife has orgasm in marriage is taken as the measure of sexual adjustment, the husband's premarital experience bears no relationship, but premarital experience by the wife shows a positive relationship. As Table 13 indicates, premarital relations exclusively with the future husband do not differ importantly from premarital chastity, but it is more diverse sexual experience that is associated with more frequent orgasm in marriage.[26]

[25] Ernest W. Burgess and Paul Wallin, *Engagement and Marriage*, Lippincott, Philadelphia, 1953, pp. 676–680, 689–695.
[26] *Ibid.*, pp. 362–363.

TABLE 13 WIFE'S PREMARITAL INTERCOURSE AND ORGASM IN MAR-
RIAGE

Wife's Orgasm Frequency	Wife's Premarital Sex Experience (%)		
	None	Husband only	Husband and Other Men
Never or sometimes	29.3	25.0	17.6
Usually	50.3	51.4	47.1
Always	20.4	23.5	35.3
Total	100.0	99.9	100.0
No. of cases	(334)	(204)	(68)

SOURCE: Adapted from Ernest W. Burgess and Paul Wallin, *Engagement and Marriage*, p. 363, by permission of the publisher. The category of women whose premarital experience was limited to men other than their future husbands is omitted from the classification because there were so few cases in this category.

When rating scales of sexual adjustment and general marital adjustment are used, however, results are different. Relationships between premarital sexual experience and the sexual adjustment scale are so confused that it would be difficult to conclude either a positive or a negative relationship.[27] Thus when a more socially significant criterion than the simple physiological response is used, the relationship vanishes. When a marital rather than sexual adjustment measure is used, the results are again unclear, but there is a modest preponderance of evidence toward association of premarital experience with low marital adjustment.[28]

Two important observations must be drawn from this and similar evidence. First, the aim of discovering clear and simple relationships between sex as a physiological experience and marital processes is illusory. The results to the present would not justify further research of this character that did not make a serious effort to sort out meanings of sex as a basis for seeking relationships. Second, none of these findings clarifies causal relationships. The sexual vigor that produces frequent orgasm in marriage may lower the girl's resistance to premarital experience. The acceptance of conventional values that favors positive evaluation of marital adjustment may also enhance resistance to premarital experience.

One instance of resourceful analysis of the limited kind of data generally available, which incorporates some effort to acknowledge the differential effects of divergent meanings of sex, is worthy of brief review. Hamblin and Blood carried out a reanalysis of Kinsey's data to see whether it was possible to select among the alternative explanations that have been offered to account for the finding that premarital sexual experience is

[27] *Ibid.*, pp. 363–367.
[28] *Ibid.*, pp. 367–371.

associated positively with the wife's orgasm adequacy, at least during the first year of marriage.[29]

One plausible explanation is that the earlier a girl starts coital experience, the more responsive she is, because there are fewer inhibitions to overcome. Kinsey's data show that women who married at under 21 years of age and women who married at from 21 to 25 years have had the same average amount of premarital experience, but the latter started their experience later than the former. Consequently age at marriage can serve as au approximate index of age of first coital experience, and the later-married group should have lower orgasm rates than the early-married group. In fact this is not so, and the opposite may be the case. Hence this explanation is contradicted by the data.

A second explanation, that practice makes perfect, would require that women who married early should have higher orgasm rates than women of the same present age who married later. When women 24 years old from the two groups are compared, again the predicted difference is not found and there may be a relationship in the opposite direction.

A third explanation attributes the low orgasm rates to moral and religious scruples. If this explanation were correct, a comparison of the devout and the inactive within major religious groupings should reveal lower orgasm rates for the more devout women. When the appropriate tabulations are made (see Table 14), there is an interesting divergence

TABLE 14   FIRST-YEAR MARITAL ORGASM RATES OF DEVOUT AND IN-ACTIVE PROTESTANTS AND CATHOLICS

Percentage of Marital Coitus With Orgasm	Protestants		Catholics	
	Devout	Inactive	Devout	Inactive
None	27	26	32	22
1–29	10	12	18	7
30–59	13	10	13	11
60–89	10	13	5	14
90–100	40	39	32	46
Total	100	100	100	100
No. of Cases	(430)	(564)	(112)	(88)

SOURCE: From Robert L. Hamblin and Robert O. Blood, Jr., "Premarital Experience and the Wife's Sexual Adjustment," *Social Problems*, 4:128, 1956; based on data from Alfred C. Kinsey, Wardell B. Pomeroy, Clyde E. Martin, and Paul H. Gebhard, *Sexual Behavior in the Human Female*, Saunders, Philadelphia, 1953, p. 404. For devout versus inactive Protestants: Marshall's $C=.23$, $P>.40$. For devout versus inactive Catholics: $C=2.89$, $P<.005$.

[29] Robert L. Hamblin and Robert O. Blood, Jr., "Premarital Experience and the Wife's Sexual Adjustment," *Social Problems*, 4:122–130, October 1966.

in the findings. The predicted relationship holds for Catholics but not for Protestants. But since Protestant morality condemns premarital relations as consistently as Catholic morality, moral scruples and guilt do not afford a plausible explanation for the results. Hamblin and Blood suggest two explanations. First, the meanings attached to the Catholic interpretation of the premarital code may lead to a view of sex as sinful by itself, but "devout Protestant females apparently develop scruples against premarital coitus *per se* but feel that sexual pleasure in marriage is not only legitimate but desirable."[30] Second, the Catholic attitude toward the use of contraceptives in marriage, in the face of widespread desire to limit childbirth, leads to fear of unwanted pregnancy when contraceptives are not used and guilt when they are, both of which make sexual intercourse a less satisfying experience.

Hamblin and Blood cautiously point out the limitations of the variables they were able to manipulate. But their reanalysis of Kinsey's own data discredits the most common interpretations of the relationship between premarital and marital sexual experience. And in keeping with the general argument of our discussion, it lends force to the position that the effect of a code that restricts or encourages indulgence in any specific kind of sexual behavior depends on the meanings attached to the behavior and its prohibition or encouragement.

Sex and Love in Marriage Process

Interrelations. Sex, love, and marriage must be thought of as three systems, each with its separate dynamics but applying often enough to the same behavior so that each is an element in the dynamics of the other two. The various tasks of married life, its regulation by society, and the consequences that stem from the organized interrelationship between the family and the rest of the community have a patterning effect in spite of the vagaries of love and sex behavior. The physiological periodicity and urgency of sexual need continues irrespective of love and marriage. And the sensation and attraction of love are independently determined by the sources of cultural learning and interpersonal bonding. The fact that the family as a system must take account in some way of the quasi-independent dynamics of sex and mate love contributes profoundly to the distinctiveness of family process compared with interaction in other small groups. And the many patterns for interrelationship among the three systems cause variability among processes in differently constituted families.

When systems are interrelated, they can be both supportive and disruptive at the same time. Minimization of disruption and maximization

---

[30] *Ibid.*, p. 128.

of support are commonly achieved by arranging the systems in a hierarchy of importance and by interpreting them as relatively close or separate.

Separation of Sex and Marriage. If the systems are viewed as separate, ranking can be minimal. In western societies separation ordinarily means a generally promiscuous system in which sex has little impact as bond or source of conflict in marriage. The system of courtly love in which each man might have both wife and mistress and each woman both husband and lover approximates this kind of separation. Love is divided into two kinds, one attached to marriage and stressing responsibility and the other attached to sex and stressing impulse. But this system was workable only for a privileged class who could afford the costs and the time, whose women could maintain the necessary personal attractiveness, and with adequate provision for the children born outside the marital union. Under situations more typical for the bulk of families, so great a separation is hardly feasible.

A separation of this kind has often been the goal of utopians. The temporal variations in the three systems cause adjustment difficulties when they are closely associated. The demands of sex tend toward a more or less regular cyclical pattern. The dynamic of sex by itself is such that the high peak of desire and gratification is followed immediately by a low point, with absence of desire. Consequently, when sex operates as a relatively unsocialized system, a period of most intense bonding is followed quickly by a period of minimal bonding. The dynamic of marriage consists of continuous responsibility, calling for unfluctuating bonds. The periodicity of sexual bonding in relation to the continuous character of family responsibility is the potential source of disruption that utopians sometimes seek to escape through institutionalized separation. The solution commonly is to remove most of the important functions that require stable bonds from the family and allow the primarily sex- and companionship-based marriage to be broken at will.

Perhaps the nearest approach to separation in a working family system has been that of the Trobriand Islanders, as described by Malinowski.[31] Here what Americans know as the paternal functions are divided between two individuals, and each man performs each set in relationship with a different woman. It is the incorporation of the arrangement within the extended family system that brings it under control and makes it generally workable in a way that the romantic-mistress system is not. The husband-wife relationship is the locus of sexual desire and gratification and of child bearing. The mother-father-child relationship is, then, one of intimacy, warmth, and spontaneity, relatively unencumbered with societal respon-

[31] Bronislaw Malinowski, *Sex and Repression in Savage Society*, Kegan Paul, Trench, Trubner, London, 1927.

sibilities. The mother's brother assumes responsibility for the education of the child and the economic and social requirements of his sister. Those functions which have to do with family maintenance and with responsibilities imposed by society are in the hands of the mother's brother. An implacable taboo against sexual interest between brothers and sisters symbolizes the complete separation of the sexual system from the impersonal responsibility elements of marriage. The confusion that arises from the necessity to maintain two separate meanings for sex—for child bearing in marriage and as play in the mistress relation—is avoided under the Trobriand system, because child bearing and sexual play are relegated to the same relationship. But it is clear, too, that such an arrangement can operate only under a stably matrilocal family arrangement, with the nuclear family firmly subordinated to the extended family.

Subordination of Marriage. The subordination of love and marriage to sex, which permits a casual meaning to be attached to sex, exists as a temporary stage in the life cycle or as a deviant pattern in modern societies. A major change in social organization, especially the stripping away of the parent-child relationship, would be necessary before such a pattern could become the norm. If the systems are viewed as closely interrelated, sexual compatibility becomes the principal bond in marriage, with declining sexual gratification and recognition of alternative opportunities for sexual gratification the principal sources of vulnerability.

Elevation of love to the position of dominance, with both sex and marriage subordinated, is the ideal of pure romantic love. In practice no such arrangement operates for long, since it takes the most unstable of the three systems and makes the others dependent on it. In practice, what must happen is that love is actually subordinated to the dynamics of either sex or marriage, operating as a disguise to conceal the source of the dynamics from the parties involved.

Marital Dominance and Bonds. The most generally workable patterns appear to have exalted marriage to the position of dominance, sometimes with the systems held in close relationship and sometimes with considerable separation. The fundamental difference between closeness and separation under marital dominance is that the former is a solution that maximizes the bonding power of sex in support of the marriage relationship and the latter minimizes the disruptive impact of sex through regulation.

The latter arrangements revolve about the definition of sex as property and sacred definitions that rely heavily on the concept of sin. The potentially disruptive effect of sexual periodicity on stable family interaction is reduced by training in the control and redefinition of sexual desire. When the suppression of desire for sex is complete, as it often has been in women, but not in men, the potential disruption is handled by introducing a concept of duty. Satisfying her husband's reasonable sex desires then becomes a bond, although normally only for the man, either because it is prohibited outside marriage or because it is so much more accessible within marriage.

A sexual bond of this kind is chiefly vulnerable to the discovery of outside alternatives for sexual gratification. The very separation of sex from the tender sentiments of love and from meanings of intimacy minimizes any advantage that the wife may have as a sexual partner, except for availability, and maximizes vulnerability from alternatives. The nearly universal accompaniment of this kind of arrangement is the development of a different set of meanings for sex outside marriage, which further augments the vulnerability. The casual meaning of sex before marriage and potentially outside marriage permits a freer enlargement of the experience with more cultivation of passion. Consequently the gratification intrinsic to sexual intercourse is likely to have been greater in nonmarital unions than within marriage. As a consequence, the sexual bond in marriage tends to be highly vulnerable and unstable, except among disadvantaged groups and unattractive men.

When sex and love are subordinated to marrige but the three are held to be closely intertwined, sex becomes a powerful bond, more because of what it symbolizes than because of the simple physical gratification. Sexual relations come to embody the sense of a highly distinctive and personal union between the marital partners. The symbolism may revolve about the sacred character of the union, sexual intercourse like a sacrament incorporating in one vital experience the sacredness of the whole marital relationship. Or, in keeping with apparent trends, sexual intercourse may be the tangible experience of intimacy, of the dramatic removal of all the physical and psychological barriers by means of which people are kept at a distance from each other. Sex is felt as an expression of love; but because it is not the whole of love, it is like a periodic reaffirmation of love and its satiation is not felt as a loss of love. It is the broadly extended meaning of love through which the bonding effect of the sexual experience is extended in time so as not to decline with satiation.

The bonding effect of this closeness of the three systems is reflected in its contribution toward a positive interpersonal incentive to marriage. Although the task aspects of the established family organization do play a large part as bonds in the continuing family relationship, they often have little potency as incentives for entering marriage in contemporary American society. Disproportionate importance is therefore attached to identity bonds. Love is the most comprehensive embodiment of identity bonds into a complex sentiment. When love is assimilated to the marriage system and reinforced by the harnessing of sexual desire, its bonding support of marriage is strong.

In a society oriented toward achievement and competition, the majority of men and women could hardly be regarded as highly desirable marriage partners by objective criteria. When marriages are based on task considerations and identity relations minimized, the individual can rationally accept his own limited bargaining power in marriage in the same way he accepts his modest occupational attainments. But when identity considerations are paramount, bonding becomes a problem. Here romantic love, assimilated to the marriage system, is a means to the establishment of some identity bonds and creation of a favorable guise for others. The idealization of the partner under romantic love creates the basis for an identification bond, and the removal of barriers through intimacy establishes a response bond. That sex is restricted to love and marriage, or at least that sex is a richer experience in love and love is only adequately fulfilled in marriage, minimizes the comparison of one sexual partner with another. In this respect sexual union is taken out of the arena of invidious comparison, and the experience with the spouse is a more unqualified bonding experience than it could otherwise be.

Marriage Dominance: Decision Making and Conflict. Decision making regarding sexual behavior, both within and outside marriage, poses many questions of interest, even apart from the effect of sex on general decision making in marriage and in the family. Fundamentally, different meanings of sex make for either de facto, coercive, bargaining, or consensual decisions. When sex is viewed as property or as exploitation, decisions are likely to be coercive. When sex is understood as intimacy and for some kinds of positive sacred meaning, there is a mutuality that makes many of the decisions consensual. In other circumstances the decision is a product of bargaining, usually the wife exacting promises and favors before accepting the relationship. De facto decisions enter, as we illustrated earlier, not so much into the sexual relationship as into planning regarding birth control. Here the presence of inhibitions against discussion leads to de facto decision.[32]

The effect of sex on the decision-making and conflict processes depends at first on the nature of sexual decision making. Accommodative decisions in one realm always leave a residue that affects bargaining or coercion in another. An unfavorable bargain in the sexual realm means stiffer bargaining in some other realm. The ease and outcome of decisions over family finances, child rearing, and the like, are thus subject to intermittent varia-

[32] See Chap. 5.

tion on the basis of the course of sexual relations. Conflict arises when bargaining runs against the rules. Because rules of sexual bargaining are not generally given public and respectable recognition, there is latitude for widely different conceptions of the rules—a situation with high conflict potential. How much withholding of sex by the wife takes place before she has violated her absolute duty as wife or before the husband is justified in seeking gratification outside marriage? What constitute reasonable sexual demands by the husband, and what constitute unusual and therefore high-cost bargaining demands? What other decision areas are immune against bargaining carry-over from the sexual sphere?

Although bargaining and its by-products may precipitate conflict, the separation of sex from love and marriage means that the consequences of disruptions in sexual gratification are more easily segmentalized when the desire for sex demands it, so as to produce only limited conflict. In contrast, when sex is the fundamental expression of love and the tangible expression of intimacy, continued failure to achieve satisfactory sexual experience threatens the underlying identity relationship. Contemporary preoccupation with the attainment of orgasm by women probably expresses both egalitarian concern and the view of sex as intimacy. Likewise, extramarital sex experience is likely to shake confidence in the trust and love between the marriage pair in a more irreconcilable manner than under other patterns.

Similarly, the sexual relationship is vulnerable to difficulties that originate in other areas of the marital relationship. During a state of conflict the participants can carry on normal interaction in some areas. The more intense the conflict, the wider the range of activities that are disturbed. The areas with least implications of intimacy are the last to be disrupted by conflict from another aspect of the relationship. If sex relations are simply need and duty for husband and wife, respectively, they can continue in the face of some conflict, in the same manner that the wife can still cook dinner and the husband carry groceries in from the car. The same observation applies when quite casual meanings are involved. But under the close union of sex, love, and marriage, sexual intercourse becomes the most intimate phase of interaction and is affected by relatively small conflicts over almost any issue in family life. Couples who hold to this pattern report that in any extended period of conflict sexual relations become the first casualty and are often the last activities in which normal interaction is resumed with the restoration of harmony.

Here, perhaps, there is a critical degree of potential conflict in a nonsexual area below which the close union of the three systems (a) reinforces the sense of positive identity relations and thereby resists translation of disagreement into conflict and (b) provides the incentive to prevent conflict from enlarging and to bring about early reconciliation; and above which sexual relations are disturbed, with the result that the seriousness and the pervasiveness of the effects of the conflict are augmented beyond what they would otherwise be. Once the critical point is passed, the all-or-none principle mentioned in the early discussion of conflict comes into play.[33] Either the threat to what is most valuable in the whole relationship becomes so great that there is a dramatic effort at conciliation, with sudden generosity in discounting previous conflict-provoking gestures, or all the more intimate aspects of the relationship are suspended. Because of this tendency for sex to be implicated, the attachment of intimate significance to sex and its subordination to both marriage and love tend to produce the all-or-none pattern regarding conflict.

In brief, then, the marriage can be a relatively low-keyed or high-keyed relationship. The attachment of meanings of intimacy and, in some forms, sacredness contributes to the latter, as does the close union of marriage, love, and sex, hierarchized in that order. High keying means more intense bonding, a deeper experience of gratification when all goes reasonably well, greater incentive to keep all phases of the relationship going well, but more serious disruption when these efforts fail. The difference between high- and low-keyed relationships is not one of stability but of the different sources and patterns of conflict and the difference in the character of gratifications found in each.

Summary

Mate love exhibits the same characteristics as most other forms of love, but more intensely. In addition, it has unique characteristics, because in western society it is supposed to develop spontaneously before the relationship it expresses has been institutionalized and because of special problems in maintaining the belief in its inherent permanence. The cultural pattern of romantic love pervades contemporary marriage, emphasizing mutual response bonds. The nature of sexual experience depends on the learned social meanings of sex, which in turn depend on the relationship of sex to marriage and love. The most prevalent current meanings of sex are the sacred meaning, the nonmutual view of sex as the use of property, the mutual view of sex as intimacy, and the views of sex as a casual relationship either of play or of exploitation. The coexistence of contradictory meanings of sexual experience complicates mate love and marriage. Because of the various meanings, there are also diverse codes regulating sex that often account for apparent nonconformity in sexual behavior. Recent trends suggest a shift away from double standards to a single standard,

[33] See Chap. 7.

from an absolute to a graded standard, and toward a closer identification between sex and intimacy. The variety of standards and meanings probably accounts for the failure of empirical investigation to link specific premarital and postmarital sexual practices with marital adjustment. Sex, love, and marriage can be regarded as three systems having different dynamics, whose inevitable interrelationships are handled by arranging them in a hierarchy of importance and by interpreting them as relatively close or separate. Sharp separation is probably possible only for a wealthy class or when the nuclear family is firmly subordinated to a stable matrilocal extended family. The pattern of closeness, with sex subordinated to love and love subordinated to marriage, maximizes the bond-intensification and conflict-conciliation power of sex and love, making marriage an intense relationship both in its gratifications and disruptions.

CHAPTER 14

SOCIALIZATION
INTERACTION PROCESS

The family is universally distinctive not only because it is built about the union of male and female but also because it is organized to combine children with adults. The combination necessarily involves unequal authority, differing external roles, and grossly different perspectives from which to assign meaning to family interaction. But perhaps most far-reaching in its effect on family interaction is the view that the adult-child relationship should be primarily guided by a responsibility to socialize the child.

The family is not distinctive in the fact that socialization takes place. As we noted earlier, socialization is a residue of all interaction, and the majority of socialization probably takes place without intent by the socializer or awareness by the socializee. But the family is a place of deliberate socialization. Adults and sometimes older siblings self-consciously attempt to socialize the children; and the children throughout most of their lives in the family of orientation understand that it is socially expected that they should accept and cooperate with these socialization efforts.

The conception that socialization is a major preoccupation in family interaction gives a special cast to the institutionalized inequality among age groups. Socialization is a major justification for unequal authority. The adult must not shirk the assertion and exercise of authority, for failure to do so also means failure to carry out his socialization responsibility. The child is serving his own interest by respecting adult authority, because in the long run acceptance of socialization is necessary to his effectiveness in society.

The point that will be developed in this chapter is that when the members of a small group conceive their relationship as pervaded by a socialization goal a distinctive component is added to the role differentiation in the group, special bargaining considerations and resistances to acquiescence are added to decision-making process, and peculiar sources of conflict and conditions for harmony develop.

In the study of socialization, the search for simple correlations between parental practice and child personality sometimes diverts attention from the genuinely interactive character of the process. The parent does not simply repeat a set course of behavior toward the child but adjusts his technique on the basis of the child's response. If enduring socialization effects are the cumulative residue of a succession of interaction episodes, each episode is marked by mutual testing for the response of the other and may be followed by a period of reassessment. Much as there are a strategy of conflict and a strategy in discussion, there are strategies in socialization on the part of both socializer and socializee. And the tentative character of all interaction applies to the implementation of these strategies.

A final caution is necessary against popular tendencies to attribute all the misbehavior or laudable qualities of children to the efforts of their parents. Deliberate socialization is only a small part of all socialization, and many socializing influences are not under parental control. Even if it were possible for parents to control all socializing influences, no parent could have the omniscience to predict all interpretations that the child might place on his gestures. Hence the parent's control of socialization is always partial. Later we shall discuss some of the variables that affect the degree of control that the parent may be able to exercise.

Socializing Agents

Few groups allow initiates simply to pick up the ways of the group without some kind of formal instruction. Most groups assign a tutorial responsibility to someone and assign someone to watch the initiate during an apprenticeship period. The assistant patrol leader who is given special responsibility for the tenderfoot scout, the petty officer who keeps watch over the new recruit, the "big sister" to the new member of a girl's organization, are all *agents* of the group, performing the socializing function. Parents are similarly regarded as agents of the larger society and of groups such as church, nation, state, clan, or class, depending on the society in question. Parents are not the sole agents. Teachers, religious officials, and police are among other officially designated socializing agents. In addition there are others who take on themselves a socializing function not officially assigned them, like the maternal uncle who preempts some of the paternal responsibility. When the mother is felt to have married beneath her station, her brother often feels a responsibility to see that the son receives training appropriate to the mother's proper station. Still others are naïve socializing agents, like the elder sibling who passes on each bit of newly acquired wisdom to the younger sibling or the guest in the family who, by his very freedom from socializing responsibility, voices attitudes and exhibits manners that the parents seek to keep from their children.

Each interactor acts according to one or more *standpoints*. He has his own standpoint in mind; that is, he is guided by his own values, of which his identity is the apex. To the extent to which he is appropriately bonded to the other he also bears the other's standpoint in mind; that is, he is guided in part by an effort to promote what he believes to be the other's values. In addition to these two standpoints an agent by definition has still another. He assumes the standpoint of some third party for whom he is acting. A socializing agent assumes the standpoint of the group whose patterns he seeks to inculcate in the newcomer. Parents, as agents of socialization, are involved in promoting the values of the larger society and of church and state in the child. Hence the action perspective of a socializing agent is more complex than that of a person in ordinary interaction. He tests the gesture exchange on the basis of his own values; since there is usually some identification bond, he carries some conception of the socializee's values as a criterion; and as a responsible agent he is guided by the standpoint of the society. In the happy situation of agreement among the three standpoints, action is clear and easy, and the convergence of values enables the agent to act with assurance. But in the frequent situation of contradiction among standpoints, the spontaneity of the agent is greatly limited.

The agent's standpoint leads him to place special interpretations on the socializee's behavior. A small act of defiance or the use of slang that is cute to neighbors is a serious matter to the parent. The child who assumes a socializing responsibility toward a younger sibling no longer acts solely according to the meaning of the sibling's gestures for their sibling relationship.

In addition to a special standpoint, the socializing agent also has a special position. He is the person in the middle. He must act toward the socializee in ways not fully of his own choosing, justifying and interpreting to him demands he may not fully understand or endorse. He is also accountable to the larger group for the effectiveness of the socialization without being in a position to exercise total control over the environment and behavior of the socializee. His position has much in common with that of the bureaucrat or the factory foreman. It incorporates many of the same stresses and difficult decisions, and it leads to many of the same adjustive devices. His position means that his relationships with the socializee affect his relationships with the society, and his relationships with society are reflected in his relationships with the socializee.

Demands on the Agent. The task of the agent in relation to society is rendered easy or difficult on the basis of several variables. We speak of ease or difficulty in satisfying the larger society in the short range rather than the long range, since many of the more important consequences of socialization are not fully observable until many years have passed. The socializer must, however, achieve a satisfactory relationship in the short term.

The more narrowly prescribed the acceptable range of behavior in the socializee, the more demanding the task of the agent. In a society that gives equal approval to many kinds of personality, the agent's task is simplified.

The greater the belief in the malleability of personality, the more stringent the agent's task. In societies or groups among whom a child is thought to be born with good or bad blood or with a destiny under supernatural control, the task of the agent is minor. An extreme view, such as expounded by the psychologist John B. Watson, that with sufficient skill an agent can turn any child into any kind of adult, augments the responsibility placed on the parent to an unprecedented degree.[1] A child of modest intelligence or a problem child is then a direct reflection on the character and competence of the parent. Under opposite assumptions the parent is to be pitied for having a black sheep. Even the extreme action of disowning or disinheriting a child is likely to be acceptable, although any such expedient is the ultimate personal failure in the society that believes in malleability.

Clarity of Expectation. The ease of the socializing agent's task is a function of the clarity and consistency of society's expectations. A major complaint of parents in the United States today is that teachers, pediatricians, and other parents in the neighborhood all have different conceptions of child rearing. Masculine and feminine ideals conveyed by the mass media of communication are at odds with traditional middle-class ideals. Contradictory ideals of rugged individualist versus organization man, inner-directed versus other-directed man, pervade the society, so that it is difficult for the parent to follow an ideal that receives full approval, even within his own restricted circle of associates.

A special kind of inconsistency is the divergence between *exemplary type* and *favored type*. By exemplary type we mean the set of individual characteristics which is most generally held to be desirable, which serves as a guide to parents and teachers in their socializing activities, and which is supposed to be adopted as the ideal self by persons undergoing socialization. Exemplary types are communicated through fables, ceremonies such as school graduations and initiations, ritual codes such as the scout oath and law, socializing discussions of citizenship and character, popular tales of folk heroes, and reflected in popular approval and

---

[1] John B. Watson, *Behaviorism*, Norton, New York, 1930, p. 104.

disapproval of the fruits of socialization. The favored type is that set of individual characteristics which is most likely to facilitate the attainment of rewards most highly valued and recognized in a society.[2] In American society these are characteristics which facilitate rise to the top of the business, political, and entertainment worlds, among others. In a society notable for its logical coherency, the characteristics that facilitate success (favored type) would be the same characteristics presented to the socializing agent and to the socializee as ideals to be emulated. But in our own society we know that the correspondence is far from perfect. When we teach a child not to take advantage of those less fortunate than himself, we may be instilling attitudes that impede his rise to the top of the business or political world. When we teach him to regard sex as a sacred matter, we may be preventing the commercial exploitation of sex that is often an essential condition to a successful entertainment career. To the degree to which there is a discrepancy between exemplary type and favored type in a society, those agents who take their socialization responsibilities most seriously are made most acutely aware of the possible disadvantages to their socializees.

In modern societies there is not just one but several favored types, as there are also several exemplary types. The exemplary types are not clearly distinguished so that the agent can make a definitive choice, and they are not securely anchored to corresponding favored types. Accordingly, the parent's job is one that can have only vague and uncertain direction from society.

Folk and Authoritative Technique. Goals and techniques of socialization must be distinguished. The task of the agent is manageable to the degree to which the goals are supported by a well-recognized set of techniques to guide the agent. Knowing the goal of socialization, such as promoting respect for honesty, is no assurance that techniques can be followed which will accomplish the result or which will satisfy the group and the agent that the latter is following the best course available. One agent may proceed by keeping close watch and punishing every transgression; another may proceed by ignoring minor violations.

Socializing techniques are of two kinds: folk techniques are those which are popularly known and communicated, and authoritative techniques are those which are communicated from persons recognized in the society to have some special competence in the area of socialization. Folk techniques are ordinarily learned partly from parent to child in the family of orientation and partly from the advice and help of more experienced

---

[2] The concept of favored personality is discussed by Martindale in Don A. Martindale and Elio D. Monachesi, *Elements of Sociology*, Harper & Row, New York, 1951, pp. 321 ff., and is based on the pioneering work of Ruth Benedict.

adult relatives and friends in the family of procreation.[3] Several generations are required for the establishment and diffusion of a rather uniform body of folk techniques, so that the young parent receives similar advice from different relatives and friends, and boys and girls from different families see similar techniques in use in their families of orientation. The mixture of people from different cultural heritages, radical changes in social structure that make old techniques conspicuously ineffectual, and the introduction of authoritative techniques at variance with tradition work to destroy the accumulation of folk techniques and impede the development of a new body. Folk techniques are not necessarily perfectly effective in the traditional setting, although they must have been moderately successful in order to persist. But they provide consistent direction for the socializing agent and supply him with the assurance that, if the results are not as anticipated, the fault is not his.

In twentieth-century United States the place of folk techniques in socialization has been largely taken by authoritative techniques advocated by child-rearing and educational experts. Pediatrics has emerged as a medical specialty with an important side function of advising parents in child rearing. Clinical psychologists and psychiatrists advise parents with problems. Great efforts have been made to develop a science of education in universities. Meantime, newspaper columnists and church officials advise parents, usually with a blend of the traditional folk techniques and the current authoritative techniques. If the authoritative techniques were complete enough to serve as a comprehensive guide, if they were stable enough to inspire popular confidence, and if the socialization goals of the authorities corresponded well enough with those of the people they advise, such techniques might well fill the void left by the decimation of folk techniques. But authorities are notably unable to answer the detailed questions presented to them by conscientious parents except in generalities. The authorities themselves usually hold a more secular ideal than those they advise, so that children raised according to their dictates are likely to disappoint their parents. And the instability of recommendations, as modified by each new intellectual movement, has been such as to incite popular disillusionment over the expert advice.

In an interesting study Celia Stendler examined all the articles on child rearing that appeared in the first year of each decade since 1890 in the *Ladies Home Journal, Woman's Home Companion,* and *Good Housekeeping.*[4] The number of articles ranged from 49 to 78 per decade. In the early years the major stress was on creating moral character, the idea of

[3] Robert E. L. Faris, *Social Disorganization,* Ronald, New York, 1955, pp. 9–11.
[4] Celia B. Stendler, "Sixty Years of Child Training Practices," *Journal of Pediatrics,* 36: 122–136, January 1950.

a well-adjusted personality being unknown. Character was assumed to develop by imitation. A Christian influence in the home, implemented by lavishing affection on the child, was the principal requirement for parents. Feeding procedures were not stressed. The mother was placed on a romantic and sentimental pedestal. By 1910 the stress was still on moral character, but the means had changed radically from love to a pattern of regimentation and sternness. Strict discipline, meaning punishment, and tight scheduling of the child's activities were demanded. By 1920 and 1930 the emphasis on moral character had passed, the emphasis on strict scheduling continued for a new reason, and proper nutrition became a keystone in child rearing. Behavioristic psychology was the dominant theory, and conditioning was the central mechanism of personality formation. Scheduling and the impersonal relationship between parent and child were necessary to ensure proper conditioning and prevent unintended conditioning. By 1940 behaviorism had been rejected, the mental-hygiene approach to personality development was uppermost, and psychoanalysis was being heard. Permissive, self-regulatory practices were advocated, parents were to ignore unpleasant by-products of stages in development, and mothering to create a secure individual was stressed.

From one point of view the foregoing summary suggests the swing of fashion from one extreme to another and back again (Figure 7). But in spite of the emphasis on mothering, the admonitions of the forties are different from those of 1890. Child rearing is now grounded in a thoroughly secular rather than religious ideal. Stendler suggests also that throughout

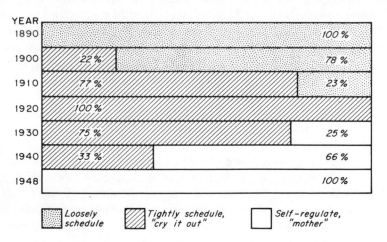

Figure 7.   **Infant disciplines recommended in three women's magazines.** (Adapted from Celia B. Stendler, "Sixty Years of Child Training Practices," *Journal of Pediatrics,* 36:126, January 1950.)

the period studied there was a progression in the direction of looking for the causes of the child's behavior in each case before making specific recommendations. From one standpoint this means that a more discriminating approach, taking greater account of individual differences, is urged. From another standpoint it means that the ordinary parent gets less specific direction and is more often thrown back on his own uneducated judgment when he appeals to an expert on child rearing.

Community Support. Since the agent cannot hope to control the entire range of socializing experiences, his task is facilitated to the degree to which other socializing experiences are consistent with the aims of the agent. This variable, in turn, is largely a function of the consistency of socialization ideals throughout the society. But two aspects are independent. First, in different societies and groups there are different conceptions of the degree to which the parent should have exclusive direction of the child and different conceptions of the propriety of an outsider's correcting or teaching a child. In some societies any adult or older child who sees a younger one misbehaving corrects him, applying discipline if necessary, and reports his misbehavior to the parent. Under such conditions the child has no sharply increased freedom when away from parental surveillance, and the parent's control is extended through the collaboration of the neighborhood and community. In societies, such as our own, where an adult who disciplined another's child might even be subject to lawsuit, where the child is not taught to accept direction and correction from others, and reporting a child's misbehavior to his parent is likely to be regarded as intruding into the privacy of the family, the parent's job is made more difficult.

Second, other socializing agents may defer to the parents, as principal socializers, or may take the position that their objective is to correct some of the faults of parental socialization. Contempt for parents has often been a part of extreme education movements, which viewed the school's job as nullifying the harm done by parents. Organized boys' groups in American society frequently take this position, not explicitly but by the shape of their programs. It is not uncommon for boys to be welcomed into camp with remarks such as "Your mothers have probably spoiled you, but you're going to learn to be men here." Boys' groups are regularly regarded as places where boys, and frequently the men who assist, can get away from the dominance of women, worrying less about cleanliness, intellectual and cultural matters, and gentleness. Scouts talking among themselves about their activities often express greatest delight over the opportunities to get away with things they could not do at home. The little league is a powerful point of reference that makes it impossible for parents to insist on gentility and politeness during an athletic event and renders parents inauthentic as the source of norms of sportsmanship. When other socializing agencies cultivate relationships of these kinds, they undercut the influence of the parents. For the child they create a coalition that can be used to combat parental influence and to disparage parental omniscience.

Total Role of Agent. The task of the socializing agent is facilitated to the degree to which the socializing activities are effectively integrated with other activities of the agent. In some primitive societies where the infant is strapped to the mother's back and taken with her to the fields where she works, and where socialization consists of having the child help at adult tasks as soon as he is able, there is little room for opposition between socialization activities and other tasks of the agent. But to the degree to which socialization becomes a specialized set of activities apart from the daily routine, the necessity for some organization arises. Some socializing schemes are more demanding of the agent than others. In a study by Robert O. Blood, Jr., permissive parents reported that more of their own activities were disrupted by their children and they experienced more difficulty in finding privacy for themselves than parents who followed more restrictive practices. However, permissive parents who also adhered to a developmental rather than traditional child-rearing philosophy generally felt that the sacrifices were worthwhile.[5]

Prestige of Socialization Activity. Finally, the clearer the prestige assigned to socializing activities, the easier the task. We are tempted to say that the task is eased by greater prestige. But the greater the prestige attached to socialization, the more the agent's identity depends on his performance of socialization responsibilities. When prestige is low and socialization can be freely delegated to nannys and older girls who serve as governesses and tutors, the socialization function has less impact on the parents' total identity than when these functions are important and are reserved to the parents. The balance of prestige and risk probably makes the amount of prestige less important than the clarity of prestige. When socialization activities are extolled at one moment and disparaged as mere baby sitting the next, the difficulties of organizing the socialization function effectively as a harmonious part of the agent's daily round of life are enhanced. As a consequence, parents who devote a great deal of time and effort to socialization activities are likely to envy the greater freedom and more interesting lives of other parents, and the latter imagine that the former are experiencing more real satisfactions out of life.

Agent Mechanisms. We may summarize the foregoing points by saying

---

[5] Robert O. Blood, Jr., "Consequences of Permissiveness for Parents of Young Children," *Marriage and Family Living*, 15:209–212. August 1953.

that society makes deliberate socialization easy or difficult, rewarding or frustrating. As an agent of society, the parent or other socializer carries on a relationship with the environing society at the same time that he is interacting with the socializee. Society either supports and facilitates the agent's task or complicates and impedes it. When the former situation exists, the socialization function is taken for granted as a part of the daily round of life and is a minimal threat to the identities of the agents and to the bonds of the family relationship. When the latter condition exists, mechanisms to relieve the strains are sure to be common.

One such tendency is ritualism, the tendency to adhere blindly to an arbitrary procedure, avoiding concern with its purposes or results.[6] Slavish adherence to outdated folk techniques or acceptance of a single authority as a guide to be followed without question are common adaptations by the parent. During the last few years in the United States there has been a vigorous resurgence of emphasis on discipline and authority in folk concern about child rearing. The emphasis has not been part of an integrated scheme of child rearing and hence is most probably a form of ritualism, a pseudo-return to earlier folk techniques. It is ritualism and a pseudo-return because only a segment of the traditional procedures has been plucked out of context. Without the total system for support it has little chance of being successful.

Sometimes independent but often an accompaniment of ritualism is a second device, the assertion of impotence. With the influence of television, the peer group, and the school, the parent can insist that exercise of any direction himself is hopeless. He can then turn to a castigation of evil influences in the community, blaming teachers and television for his problems.

A third device by which agents respond to a difficult relationship between themselves and the larger society is by a vigorous emphasis on family privacy and the maintenance of a false front before the outside world. Great emphasis is placed on not revealing details of family life to outsiders. Children are taught a sharp distinction between the perfect behavior required before outsiders and the daily mode of interaction. Visiting becomes a highly formal matter, and friends must not drop in before the front can be erected.

A fourth device is the devaluation of the socialization function itself. Complications of the socialization task make alternative ways of life that evade any such role more attractive. Many fathers have reacted to these complications by withdrawing entirely from the traditional male responsibilities in socialization, finding their time taken up with what they define

[6] See Robert K. Merton, *Social Theory and Social Structure*, Free Press, New York, 1957, pp. 149–153.

as more important work. Many mothers have assured themselves and any
who listen that child care is merely glorified housekeeping and hence not
worthy of their talents.

The Socialization Task

The parent or elder sibling or other agent performs his task by attempting to manipulate the interaction between himself and the socializee.
Under the simplest circumstances he objectively makes use of a repertoire
of interpersonal techniques as required by the circumstances and the
responses of the socializee. But inevitably he also reacts according to his
other relationships with the socializee, and the socializing efforts are re-
enforced or diverted as a consequence. We shall take up the simpler
interaction first.

The three broad procedures used by the agent are the creation, regulation, and interpretation of experiences. The relative preponderance of
these kinds of procedures depends on the degree to which the socializee's
life is lived within the circle that the agent can control. When control is
at a maximum as in the case of an infant who cannot leave the family
circle or a military recruit who is restricted to the training center, the
creation of experience predominates. When the control is lessened, as it
is with the child, the agent must depend more on selecting the child's
playmates, picking certain kinds of outside experiences for the child while
insulating him from others, and trying to regulate his experiences by
assisting in the leadership of youth organizations, keeping in touch with
teachers at school, and similar procedures. Finally, as control weakens
further and the parent is less able to manage outside experiences, he depends predominantly on supplying a basis for interpreting crucial kinds
of experience before the child encounters them and on offering him interpretations of experiences after they happen. Although this progression is
characteristic of induction into any group and is especially so for socialization of the child in the family, the three kinds of activity normally coexist at all stages.

For the socialization concerned with inculcating values and norms (as
distinct from teaching skills), the created experience is especially basic
and remains a point of reference for other socialization procedures. The
earliest created experiences are devised relationships between the agent
and the socializee in which the behavior of the agent is designed to bring
out the desired response in the other, either as reaction or acceptance of
the agent as model. The greatest difficulty with the created experience
lies in the demands imposed on the agent. The socializee does not discontinue learning just because the agent is no longer managing the situation from a socialization point of view. After the lesson is over, the agent

continues to be a model, and his behavior continues to evoke responses. The parent's white lies, lapses into poor English, naïvely expressed prejudices and injustices not only have their own effects but undercut the integrity of the contrived situation. Consequently, the relationship between the created situation and its effects on the socializee are likely to be greatest if the agent and socializee are isolated whenever deliberate socialization is not underway. Specialized agents concerned with values, such as teachers and ministers, ordinarily have a protective aura of mystery thrown about their private lives. The parent who is not in continuous contact with his children has an advantage in controlling effects of his own relationship with the children, although the children have intervening experiences over which he has little control. The agent in continuous contact probably has more effect on the socializee but is less able to control the kind of effect he has.

The difficulty with continuous contact stems from the fact that norms and values must first be presented in more absolute form than they are ultimately to be learned. Values and norms are qualified in use by numerous understood exceptions. Once the norm has been sufficiently accepted, the individual can begin to learn the situational limits to its application. But the pattern of exceptions is too complicated to be learned at first, and the general rule is often not apparent to the observer of behavior. The agent presents a set of rules in more absolute form than they are ordinarily practiced, and as a model he tries to exemplify them in perfect form himself. Hence his normal behavior must be held in abeyance while he engages in socialization.

This condition is augmented in societies, like our own, in which the agents often hope to establish a more perfect pattern of behavior than their own in the child. When a strong value is placed on upward mobility, parents seek to make their children more successful than they are themselves. A vital belief in human perfectibility makes each generation hope to obviate their own faults in their children. A considerable measure of guilt over personal inadequacies operates similarly. Under such conditions the socialization relationship can hardly proceed smoothly unless there is a good deal of institutional separation between parents and children to allow intervals of spontaneity.

Attempts to regulate outside socializing experiences affect the family structure deeply. Placement in a particular group or situation is easier than control of the child's attitude toward it. Exclusion may intensify the desire for an experience; reluctant exposure may distort the effect of the experience. But it may take the collaboration of the entire family to make an experience possible. All members may have to sacrifice in order to save the cost of private school or college for one child. The family schedule in the United States is frequently geared about driving children to and from the group meetings, music lessons, and special activities they are placed in.

The interpretation of experiences for the socializee depends most, among the three techniques, on the personal relationship between agent and child. When an individual looks to some person or group to legitimize the interpretations he places on experiences, we speak of his *reference group* or *reference individual*. The aftermath of a period during which his family has been the locus of key experiences and has had a controlling hand in selecting experiences outside the family is normally that the family becomes an important reference group. The parent then depends on referring back to lessons already learned in the family as a foundation for interpretations of current experience and exploits the child's bonds to the family as a source of pressures on the child to accept the parent's interpretations. The tighter the bonds to the family and the greater the prestige of the agent, the more likely it is that the effort will succeed.

Socialization Strategy. Each agent is guided in the use of these procedures by some strategy of socialization. Anselm Strauss has outlined some of the tactics that make up a strategy of what he calls coaching.[7] These are the prescription, the schedule, the challenge, the trial, and the accusation. Strauss uses the program of training for an athletic event as prototype, but the tactics are equally applicable to a wide range of socialization activities. The *prescription* consists of the standard lessons or exercises through which learning is to take place, and the *schedule* is a conception of just how much understanding can be expected at a given stage. The child who is expected not to steal at a particular age is nevertheless not expected to exhibit genuine self-sacrificing altruism until much older. Socialization is often held up by the risk involved in a new course of action and the comfort of the old way. The *challenge* is a device used to get the socializee to relinquish the less mature pattern and risk the new. The parent tries to convince the child that it takes nerve to stick by his principles, to dare him to try for better grades in school, to goad him into striving for leadership in his youth group. The *trial* occurs if the challenge is accepted, and the agent seeks to manipulate the trial so that it will be successful or that failure will be by so small a margin that the result is encouragement. *Accusations* are similar in their effect to the challenge but more drastic. Both invoke the self-image of the socializee in an attempt to involve it deeply enough to dislodge the individual from an established pattern of behavior. The challenge points to the unrealized potentiality, suggesting a self-conception superior to the self-image. Accu-

[7] Anselm L. Strauss, *Mirrors and Masks: The Search for Identity*, Free Press, New York, 1959, pp. 109–118.

sation is a disparagement of the self-image, with the self-conception implicated if correction is not made. Punishment is sometimes a way of dramatizing the accusation.

Reactions to Ineffectual Socialization. Not all socializing efforts are accepted as intended, and the behavior of the socializee is often a disappointment to the agent. Under such apparent failure the agent usually transforms the character of the socializing relationship. Probably the commonest transformation is to one of pure authoritarian coercion. The agent must be able to exercise control over the socializee's behavior in order to institute any scheme of experiences and regulate outside experiences. Normal socialization depends on the bonds that hold the child to the parent and the many structural advantages of the parent in maintaining domination. With control taken sufficiently for granted, the agent may turn his attention to strategy, noting each response and adjusting his own gestures accordingly. Because control is the precondition to socialization, failure turns the agent back to a preoccupation with control itself, to the assertion of authority backed up by coercion. Under stressful enough conditions effective coercion is accepted instead of more fundamental evidence of socialization as a measure of success. Parents are satisfied that the teacher must be doing their children some good if she maintains firm enough discipline in the classroom.

The problem with a relationship in which coercive authority looms large is that the coercion must be constantly maintained, and an adjustment of self-conceptions to the continuing character of the relationship is induced. Either the socializee becomes dependent on the coercion to move him and is incapable of initiative, or he is rebellious, taking any relaxation of coercion as a signal to defy the aims of the agent. The effectiveness of more subtle techniques, such as unobtrusive example, quiet suggestion, modest reward, encouragement, constructive intervention, and the like, becomes severely limited, since each is interpreted principally as a relaxation of coercion.

Socializing techniques may be classified as regular techniques and emergency devices. Accusations, punishments, and the use of negative examples are often emergency devices used only on exceptional occasions. Continued anxiety about the effectiveness of socialization leads to an inordinate dependence on such emergency devices. But such techniques, like sheer coercion, transform the relationship between parent and child. Such transformations are common when a family moves into a community or neighborhood where other socializing influences run counter to their own. Immigrants are likely to come to depend inordinately on such tactics as teaching the child to be suspicious of the morals and motives of all outsiders or teaching them the values of asceticism. In an environment in which the prohibited pleasures were not presented to the child it would seldom be necessary to make a virtue of asceticism. And in the homogeneous home community there would be little occasion to promote suspicion of persons in daily interaction with the socializee. Neighbors in the host culture are certain, however, to conclude that these techniques are the family's standard approach to socialization.

Involving other agents, either by forming coalitions or by shifting responsibility, is another common response. When coalitions are formed with other agents, the consequence may be to extend the alienation of the child. A large proportion of the reports of juvenile delinquency are made to the police by the parents who seek police assistance in their own ineffectual efforts.[8]

A final response is to develop an image of the child as unsocializable. "Born with a stubborn streak," "made of bad stuff," and other such folk expressions are applied.

Socialization in the Total Relationship

Socialization is only one of the relationships between agent and socializee when socialization takes place within the family. The values guiding parental response at any moment are likely to be partly those germane to socialization and partly those reflecting other bonds. But on different occasions the socialization values prevail or other values prevail. The general question is what determines the relative precedence of socialization values or nonsocialization values in the relations between a recognized agent and his socializee.

In a society in which socialization is closely integrated into the total relationship and there is a minimal discontinuity between the social worlds of adult and child, the problem seldom arises. Socialization consists of the agent going about his regular tasks, the child learning by apprenticeship. The boy learns an occupation by assisting his father. He learns the character of authority in the society, the system of stratification, and the norms regulating daily life through participation. The agent, then, engages in socializing activities as a by-product of other activities rather than as a special, separate kind of activity. The degree to which socialization activities are likely to be diverted by the preeminence of other values in the relationship between agent and socializee is a function of the discreteness of socializing techniques from other aspects of family routine. The discreteness in turn is largely a function of the discontinuity between child and adult worlds—the degree to which the activities of children are different in kind and socially separate from the activities of adults.

[8] Edwin H. Sutherland and Donald R. Cressey, *Principles of Criminology*, Lippincott, Philadelphia, 1960, p. 178.

Socializing activities are often diverted, first, by the normal tendency for any relationship to fall into an easily repeated pattern that can be followed with each successive episode, without the strain of innovating interpretations or interpersonal techniques. If the agent is to observe the progress of his socializing endeavors and alter his techniques as necessary, he has to be able periodically to disrupt the established pattern and inject novelty. This means that he has to be prepared to adjust his image of the socializee and disrupt interaction sufficiently so that his gestures force a reconceptualization of self and other on the socializee. But interactive innovation introduces risk, the abandonment of familiar reactions in order to provoke unknown responses. The new responses may be even more unfavorable to the socialization endeavor than the old. They may also disturb other aspects of the family relationship. Parents often despair of the fact that they repeat the same instructions, cautions, and corrections year after year to the child without notable effect. Sears, Maccoby, and Levin report, in their study of child rearing by Boston mothers, that when mothers handled problem behavior principally by punishment, the problem behavior did not usually go away.[9] Punishment for aggressiveness, dependency, or bed wetting was followed by persistence of the problem. In these cases parent and child had apparently fallen into a relationship that the mother was unable to disrupt. The repeated punishment had come to fit into the established self-other images of the child, serving merely to reinforce the relationship of which the problem behavior was a part.

In the short run, socialization activities are diverted by the competition of other activities and the interference of identity relations. Identity relations may take precedence when the requirements of socialization run counter to a close response bond or identification bond. A father cannot bring himself to disturb the gratifying response relationship with a loving daughter to correct her on occasion. A mother cannot admit the faults of her son in order to deal with them, because the identification bond between them implicates her in his mistakes. Identity relations may take precedence when the socialization activities place the child in a relationship with the parent that is grossly inconsistent with the latter's self-conception. A mother finds herself in the subservient role of maid to her children when she attempts to avoid demanding more neatness of them than they are capable of learning at an early age, consequently spending large portions of her time cleaning up after them. Or a father finds that dinner comes at unpredictable times, determined fortuitously by the children's scheduled group activities, after-school sports, and music lessons. Indeed,

[9] Robert R. Sears, Eleanor E. Maccoby, and Harry Levin, *Patterns of Child Rearing*, Harper & Row, New York, 1957, pp. 484–486.

subordination to the socializee is a frequent by-product of certain schemes of child rearing. The delegation of a considerable degree of socialization responsibility to outside agents on a group basis necessarily causes inflexible schedules to which individual families must adjust. The socializing groups become coalitions with the child against the parent, radically disturbing the standard domination relationships between parent and child.

A method of socialization in which the agent manipulates the interpersonal relationship without the use of authority or coercion normally has some by-products of subordination for the agent. Over a period of time the agent is the one who is required to exercise greater control over his impulses and to make the major adjustments to the other. When a relationship of this kind is institutionally circumscribed in time, as is the relationship between clinical psychologist and patient, the effects are neutralized. But when it is a pervasive element of an intimate and unbroken relationship, its effects are difficult to counter. Willard Waller called attention to the fact that the marital partner who tries to save a disturbed relationship by the use of insight eventually discovers himself subordinated to the other.[10] This is only one instance of the broader principle covering all socialization relationships not clearly circumscribed institutionally.

Diversion of the socialization relationship into conflict is a final characteristic form of change. The various entrees into conflict discussed in Chapter 7 are applicable here. Failure of the child to coordinate his behavior with the adult's blocks the decision-making aspects of the relationship. Resistance on the part of the child threatens the adult's self-conception to the degree to which being able to carry out the socialization task effectively is a component of the latter's identity. Evidence of superior learning in which the student surpasses the teacher threatens the teacher's identity when it is not offset by an identification relationship that is sufficiently strong so that the teacher benefits accordingly. There is a time when a father must be able to gain satisfaction through identification from the fact that his son can beat him in many contests.

There is characteristically a change in the relationship between parent and child at some point at which the latter becomes fully a person to the parent. So long as the child is not accorded the full status of a person, he may be annoying, much as a pet can be annoying, and his failure to respond may threaten the parent's conception of his own competence. But there can be no complete counterposing of identities, such as occurs in full-scale jealousy or indignation toward an equal. It is usually sometime during late childhood or adolescence, depending on the relevant facets of the parent's identity, that the child becomes a full person, capable of counter-

---

[10] Willard Waller and Reuben Hill, *The Family: A Dynamic Interpretation*, Dryden, New York, 1951, pp. 312–316.

posing identities completely. On the positive side this is the point at which parent and child can begin to be companions and on the negative side, true contestants.

Socializee Response

The perspectives of two parties to interaction often differ, and this is frequently the case in socialization. The infant and very small child have no conception of socialization, and the older child and adult often react to socialization efforts without attending to their socialization aspects. From the standpoint of the recipient the interaction is simply conflict or decision making or harmony, and his reactions are made on that basis. Since there is constant discovery and reassessment in all responses, socialization goes on irrespective of attention. Many strategies in deliberate socialization presume a naïve socializee who does not complicate the process by attempting to guess and parry the objectives of the agent. Even outright rejection of the agent in a particular situation may be a desired response. For example, a parent may attempt to break an excessive dependence by establishing a conflict relationship in which the child must reject parental assistance as damaging to his own identity. If the child understands sufficiently the socialization aim of the parent, he can continue to solicit parental help, bolstering his own identity at the expense of the parent's by thus outwitting and taking advantage of him.

But the family is a continuous relationship, and family socialization is comprehensive. Hence cumulative conflict arising out of responses to socialization efforts must be avoided. Chronic conflict that leads to systematic resistance against all recognized socialization efforts is likewise a danger when certain tactics are used. The intimate and repetitive character of family interaction means that most continued deliberate socialization strategies come to be recognized by the socializee and hence require his acceptance as a condition for success.

Confrontation. An important event for socialization process is the confrontation episode in which the socializee confronts the agent with the latter's concealed socialization objective. The socializee confronts the agent by challenging the tactics he is using ("Quit nagging me!" "Stop shoving me around!" "Stop being so indirect: come right out and say it;"); the specific socialization objective imputed to the agent ("You aren't going to get me to like opera no matter how you try!"); or the agent's right to attempt socialization at all ("I didn't marry you in order to have you reform all my bad habits!"). Besides the obvious effect of blocking further unwanted socialization efforts, the confrontation may benefit the socializee in two ways. First, exposure of hidden purposes is a threat to the agent's identity. He is shown to have been dissimulating in a relationship governed by norms of openness and confidence, and he is shown to have been inept in unsuccessfully concealing his efforts. Unless the agent can effectively deny the socialization intent or insist that the effort has been open and the intent revealed from the start, his self-image takes an unfavorable turn that gives the socializee a conflict advantage. If the socializee is not inclined to convert the relationship into conflict, he is then in a position to use alter's socialization aim as a bargaining asset. He may translate the relationship into a simple decision-making episode and exact a return benefit in exchange for complying with the other's socialization objective.

Confrontation need not block continuation of the same socialization sequence if the socializee does not seriously object or if the agent is in a position to bring about unwilling compliance. The socializee may confront the agent merely to protect his own identity or to collect a small bargaining advantage without any intention to forestall the socialization process. Confrontation may even be a harmonizing technique when it is done so as to show that two people have so much in common that each can have no secrets from the other.

In all cases in which the socializee recognizes some superior competence or experience in the agent there is an element of shared purpose. The two elements of socialization are learning the nature of the social and natural order and developing adaptations to them. Although he may resist understandings that seem irrelevant to him and may become surfeited, the socializee ordinarily is receptive to knowledge that expands his potential control of his environment and opens up new avenues of satisfaction to him. Barring specific resistances, the socializee and agent are likely to share a common purpose with respect to the imparting of understandings. But the agent normally does not separate the understandings from the adaptation. He often imparts the understandings and slants them in order to support a particular kind of adaptation. He explains the mentality of kidnappers to the child in order to teach him to cope with the neighborhood by staying near home and not being friendly with strangers. The socializee, however, may be anxious to acquire understandings so as to work out adaptations of his own. There is, then, not the same basis for common purpose in case of adaptation as there is in conveying understandings. When resistances arise on the basis of the task interaction (rather than identity interaction), they are more likely to revolve about the acceptance of a directed mode of adaption than about the acceptance of understandings.

Identity Sources of Resistance. There are a number of sources of potential resistance to socialization efforts in the identity aspects of the relationship, however. First is the necessary subordination of the socializee to the agent, allowing the latter to direct his responses. A woman can accept instruction in how to drive an automobile from a man outside the family or advice on how to rear her children from a pediatrician, although she rejects the same directions from her husband. The dominance in the former instances is institutionally circumscribed, and the fact that she solicits the direction with the understanding that it will be discontinued whenever she chooses maintains her ultimate domination. But within the family she cannot assure that the domination she accepts will not extend to other activities, nor can she shut it off when she chooses.

George Homans reviews evidence from other than family relations to suggest that a person finds it more satisfying to interact either with someone of the same status as himself or with someone of widely different status than with someone of only slightly different status.[11] There is a partial parallel to the socialization relationship. When the superior status of the agent is marked, the acceptance of socialization by the socializee is no threat to his identity. Since their inequality is clear to all, the acceptance of socialization by the subordinate does not threaten to change anything. When there are only small differences, as there are between parent and adolescent or young adult, acceptance of socialization may seem to magnify the slight subordination appreciably and thus threaten the socializee's identity. The same principle suggests that there will be less resistance to the socialization efforts of a much older sibling than to a sibling who is only slightly older than the socializee.

A second source of identity resistance is the implication for the competence of the socializee. The socializee admits to inferior competence in some respect when he accepts direction. The threat to the identity is most serious when the competencies violate cultural role conceptions or when they challenge the personal integrity or adequacy of the individual. A boy is likely to find it difficult to accept instruction in auto mechanics from his sister. An adult can accept instruction in a neutral skill from his spouse more readily than he can accept moral edification or assistance in acquiring socially mature attitudes. But any socialization effort invites resistance when the agent attempts to teach what the socializee already knows well. Minor skirmishes constantly arise between parent and child as the child tries to show the parent how much he knows before the parent offers him instruction, while the parent hastens to finish the instruction. "I know it" and "Who doesn't know that?" are among the common retorts by which children prevent their peers from gaining an identity advantage from a socialization effort. The socialization relationship has much of the same precariousness for the identity of the socializee that rivalry has for the identity of the loser. The same two rules that protect rivalry—avoid sensi-

[11] George C. Homans, *Social Behavior: Its Elementary Forms*, Harcourt, Brace & World, New York, 1961, pp. 316–335.

tive zones and don't rub in defeat—are equally relevant to socialization. The same consequence of deterioration into conflict or accommodation through discontinuing interaction ensues when these norms are violated or when the third rule—give the socializee a chance to show what he already knows—is contravened.

A third source of resistance is the necessity to accept interpersonal techniques that, in a nonsocializing relationship, would be an affront to the identity. Punishment is the most notable instance, but the trickery by which the teacher outmaneuvers the student, restriction of the right of serious challenge to the teacher, and baiting are among such tactics. Punishment is so severe a threat to the identity that children invariably develop strategies for coping with it. Where conflict has been cumulative in the socialization relationship, thwarting the punisher by impassivity in the face of punishment is common. Verbal or other gestures by which the punishment is defined as an act of lost self-control serve similarly. Shaming the punisher by overwhelming evidence of virtue or repentence and by going out of the way to be kind and affectionate toward the punisher are techniques more characteristic of chronic conflict. Retaliatory threats are often made. Under nearly all circumstances the socializee seeks to leave the presence of the punisher, escaping the situation in which his degradation has occurred. The necessity for a resistance tactic is heightened by the presence of an audience and especially of an uncommitted audience, such as his peers who might jeer or admire him, depending on his response.

A final source of resistance stems from the element of trust that is an essential component of the socialization relationship. As Strauss points out, the socializee places himself at the mercy of his tutor, whose understanding may be faulty or his techniques ineffectual.[12] But he also delivers his identity into the hands of his mentor, revealing weaknesses, the knowledge of which could be used as a weapon against him in the hands of an unscrupulous person. The condition under which a person freely takes this step is complete trust that the mentor will not make use of the knowledge outside the shared purposes of socialization. Suspicion that the trust has been violated provokes resistance. A child who overhears his mother relating one of his ineptitudes for the amusement of neighbors or whose mother uses the threat of revelation before an audience as a coercive device discovers that his trust has been violated.

Compliance and Acceptance. Leon Festinger has drawn attention to the difference between overt compliance and private acceptance of the values of a group.[13] Either may occur without the other. Overt resistance to

[12] Strauss, *op cit.*, pp. 114–115.
[13] "An Analysis of Compliant Behavior," in Muzafer Sherif and M. O. Wilson (eds), *Group Relations at the Crossroads*, Harper & Row, New York, 1953, pp. 232–256.

an instructional effort may be followed by its private acceptance. Even rebellious children usually acquire attitudes much more similar to their parents' than they are prepared to admit. Overt compliance or rejection is fundamentally a social maneuver rather than a clear indication of the private response that stabilizes after a reassessment period.

Conditions that determine whether the lesson will be privately accepted as the socializee believes the agent means it are both internal and external to the total relationship between agent and socializee. Acceptance of the socialization goal facilitates acceptance of the lesson, and the resistances we have discussed impede it. But in the total relationship, the preponderance of harmony over conflict and the strength of identification bond favor private acceptance. Harmony makes uniformation gratifying, and there is no threat to the identity from taking attitudes or knowledge from the other.

Among the external variables affecting acceptance are the availability of alternatives, support by other socializing agents, and reality testing. In the absence of alternative prescriptions for behavior in a particular situation, the individual has no choice but to follow the available suggestion, although he may have resisted it strongly when it was presented. The effectiveness of socialization in many tradition-bound and authoritarian settings depends on shielding the child from all contradictory models and ideas, so that the child becomes a close copy of the parent in spite of a great deal of active rebellion and even continual hatred between parent and child. The peer group, the school, and other agencies may undercut or reinforce parental teaching. And with varied enough opportunity the child tries out alternatives, even those he has manifestly rejected, and learns something of their effectiveness for himself.

Summary

Organization and interaction in the family are distinctive because of the assumption that all aspects of the adult-child relationship must at all times be deliberately shaped to serve the aim of socializing the child. In socializing the child, the parent is an agent for the larger community and must necessarily bear in mind his own standpoint, the standpoint of the child, and the standpoint of the community—all of which may be different. As a responsible agent, a parent differs from the child and from other adults in the meanings he ascribes to the child's behavior. The socializing agent's task is facilitated when society's expectations are clear and consistent, when there is a well-established fund of folk techniques or a consistent and stable body of authoritative techniques, when the community supports the agents, when the socialization activities fit well with other aspects of the parent role, and when socialization activities are assigned high prestige in the community. Few of these conditions are approximated in American society, and parents respond to the difficulties of their role by using such devices as ritualism. assertion of impotence, an exaggerated emphasis on family privacy, and devaluation of the socialization function. The socialization task consists of creating experiences, regulating experiences, and interpreting experiences, with shifting emphasis from the first to the last from childhood to youth. A common socialization strategy includes prescriptions, schedules, challenges, trials, and accusations. Ineffectual socialization efforts lead the socializer to become preoccupied with sheer control and to shift from regular socializing techniques to emergency techniques that often destroy the normal harmony and love between parent and child. When socialization is not a simple by-product of other activities, it is often diverted by routinization, competition from other activities, interference from identity relations, and conversion of the socializing relationship into conflict.

When parent and child perspectives diverge, the child may respond with confrontation. Identity sources of resistance to socialization include subordination of the socializee, the implication of inferior competence, the necessity to accept interpersonal techniques that affront the identity, and the precariousness of trust. Although socialization efforts are often ineffective, private acceptance of the socialization message frequently occurs in conjunction with overt noncompliance.

CHAPTER 15

PARENTS AND CHILDREN:
STARTING THE
LIFE CYCLE

If we add to the distinctive characteristics of the family that it is organized to provide for sustained interaction between representatives of at least two generations, we introduce at once several themes that are crucial to understanding the pattern of interaction. First, it is sometimes observed that the family, as a primary group, is the place where one can be himself, a unique individual rather than an instance of a category of persons, such as student, carpenter, or minority-group member. This observation has an aspect of truth because of the relaxation of many kinds of front within the family. But in other respects the statement is less true than it is in groups that are more homogeneous in their composition. A peer group can be relatively undifferentiated. A group that is heterogeneous but segmental, such as a group of art lovers, can take minimal account of age and sex differences. But because the family must provide a comprehensive pattern that permits interaction to proceed smoothly between a mature and self-sufficient adult and a completely dependent child, the family evolves a pervasive and highly self-conscious differentiation between parent and offspring roles. The parent can never cease to be primarily the parent in the presence of his children without damaging his ability to play the role later, and the child cannot discontinue being the child. Thus just because the family is the one small group in society that is specifically organized to bring representatives of the two sexes and grossly different age groups into sustained interaction, it is also one of those groups in which it is least possible for the member to forget his role and be a unique and uncategorized individual.

Second, the generational difference sets the members apart sufficiently so that they are identified with discrete and nonoverlapping age groups outside the family. The child who discusses a recent family dispute with his neighborhood playmates receives a totally different perspective from that of his mother who discusses the event with other parents. The organization of the family about different generations means, therefore, that family decision making and family conflict are normally not only the bargaining and dispute of individuals but are society's principal field for contention and reconciliation between perspectives that have been evolved and rigidified into social norms within distinct generational peer groups.

Third, the age pattern in the family makes the socialization and custodial functions central and pervasive to family life. The extended discussion of socialization process in Chapter 14 makes it unnecessary to elaborate the significance of this characteristic here.

Fourth, interaction in the family includes not just sex and age as separate dimensions but all the age-sex combinations. Although not all positions are actually filled in every family, the minimum complement from which each developing family must be prepared to draw consists of eight distinct and noninterchangeable relationships: father-son, father-daughter, mother-son, mother-daughter, father-mother, son-daughter, son-son (brothers), and daughter-daughter (sisters). Larger groups have many more pair interactions than the family. In a school classroom there may be 35 teacher-student pair relationships, as well as many more student-student interactions, but the 35 separate teacher-student pairs are all individual variations of a common role relationship. Hence, although there are many more people in a classroom, the pattern of organization is much simpler. It is probably correct to say that there is no other widespread and important group in which the complexity of organization is so great in relation to number of members as in the family.

For the understanding of family process there is a fifth observation that may be even more important than any of the foregoing. The pervasive preoccupation of the family is with the continuous and relatively rapid change in the system of age relationships within the family. The parent-infant relationship soon changes to a parent-child relationship and this in turn to a parent-adolescent relationship. The typical father of an infant or young child is not yet securely established and is overwhelmingly future-oriented in his work. The typical father of an adolescent, on the other hand, will either have moved into a position of some responsibility and adopted an appropriate perspective, or he will have abandoned his future orientation with respect to his nonresponsible position. Changes in the mother's outlook in some respects shadow the husband's, but there are also differing attitudes toward glamor and incorporating motherhood as the major anchorage for her self-conception.

In a vital sense there is no such thing as learning from experience in family relations, because the conditions from which we learn quickly change and the lesson is no longer applicable. The interpersonal techniques that are effective for a parent dealing with a three-year-old child provoke resentment after he has reached school age and acquired an institutionalized peer group. The father who is a favored confidante for his daughter quickly ceases to be the suitable recipient as the daughter enters puberty. If absolute authority is established as the basis for interaction at a young age, it is challenged later. If, by contrast, the parent permits dissent and depends on his superior knowledge and powers of reasoning to convince the child, he enters a later period when he no longer holds these advantages over the child. The father's companionship so actively sought and appreciated by the six- or seven-year-old boy is an embarrassment and a bore to the fourteen-year-old.

The age changes also mean that family interaction is never oriented exclusively to the present but is rooted in a perspective of passing time. The efforts of the child in school and in the execution of responsibilities cannot be seen apart from the parents' orientation toward a future acceptance of fuller responsibility and more perfect performance in all realms. The child cannot see his relations with his parents apart from his past immaturities nor apart from requiring assurances that the freedom essential to maturity will be granted at the appropriate time. Parents in many respects continue to see the child as he was in the recent past rather than as he is, and yet in their anxiety lest he fail to mature on schedule they make demands on him in terms of what he will become.

If we recall the earlier discussion of self-conceptions and alter conceptions, distinguished from the images of self and other, the significance of this extended and moving time perspective is clear. Interactions are directed by self- and alter conceptions rather than by the passing images. Hence the real people with whom family members interact are not the people as they are at the moment but are constituted in varying degrees under varying circumstances of the people whom they have known in the past and whom they see projected into the future.[1]

Stages in Development

Before taking up the nature of interaction at various stages in the family cycle, four elements that run through all the stages merit separate consideration. First is the existence of prescribed age roles as part of culture. Second is the development of role-taking capacity and the associated developments in conceptions of rules and objects. Third is the sequence in sex-role identification. Fourth is the formation and reformation of the individual's more comprehensive identity.

Prescribed Age Roles. In each society, there is a roughly defined set of age categories that helps shape people's relations to one another. Persons expect different accomplishments and are prepared to accept different

[1] Erik Erikson, "Ego Development and Historical Change," *Psychological Issues*, 1(1): 22, 1959.

failings according to the age group. One society makes more and finer age distinctions than another. In some societies the boundaries are precisely defined, and there are elaborate rites of passage that carry the individual from one age category to the next.[2] By contrast Hollingshead has documented the vague and contradictory indications of the transition to adulthood in American society, resulting in uncertainty over the selection of an age role.[3] The age categories are differently evaluated in different societies, with consequent implications for the self-conceptions of persons placed in them. The high evaluation of age in traditional societies makes for different family interaction patterns from the high evaluation of youth in American society. The age categories probably make the groupings explicit that are demanded by a particular scheme of economic and social organization. But through being made explicit, they become a fact of social structure and have their own effect. For example, the idea of youthful irresponsibility leads to a practice of denying responsible positions to youth, regardless of individual differences.

Margaret Mead was responsible for a pioneering investigation into the cultural relativitiy of age roles.[4] By contrasting the development of girls in Samoa with patterns in the United States she showed that the normal storm and stress of adolescence was lacking in Samoa. Indeed, there was clearly no concept of adolescence in Samoa as we know it. Subsequently, Margaret Mead pursued the different conceptions of childhood further, comparing societies in which the child is regarded as merely a small adult with those in which the child is thought to be qualitatively different.[5] In the United States, where the latter conception prevails, there is less continuity in treatment and development from childhood to adulthood than under the former conception.

In a classical study Philippe Aries applied a similar kind of analysis to medieval European society:

> In medieval society the idea of childhood did not exist; this is not to suggest that children were neglected, forsaken or despised. The idea of childhood is not to be confused with affection for children: it corresponds to an awareness of the particular nature of childhood, that particular nature which distinguishes the child from the adult, even the young adult. In medieval society this awareness was lacking.[6]

[2] Arnold van Gennep, *The Rites of Passage*, Routledge, London, 1909.
[3] August B. Hollingshead, *Elmtown's Youth*, Wiley, New York, 1949, pp. 148–152.
[4] Margaret Mead, *Coming of Age in Samoa*, Morrow, New York, 1928.
[5] Margaret Mead, "Social Change and Cultural Surrogates," *Journal of Educational Sociology*, 14:92–110, October 1940.
[6] Philippe Ariès, *Centuries of Childhood: A Social History of Family Life*, trans. Robert Baldick, Knopf, New York, 1962, p. 128. Quoted by permission of the publisher.

There was no special transition by initiation or education from infancy to adulthood. As soon as the child was weaned, he assumed a place, although subordinate because of his limited capabilities, in adult society. Paintings depict the child with the features of an adult, merely smaller in size.

A revival of interest in education in the sixteenth and seventeenth centuries introduced the idea that a period of special preparation was necessary before the individual could assume his place as an adult. Childhood became the period set aside for this training. As the child was treated differently from the immature adult, he was expected to behave differently, and his nature was understood to be different.[7]

Of even more recent invention in western society is the idea of adolescence. Musgrove attributes the idea that a special stage of development intervenes between childhood and adulthood to Rousseau.[8] Adolescence was a period during which the movement toward maturity should be retarded. The age at which the rights and responsibilities of adulthood are assumed is delayed and the intervening period filled by schooling—at least for the more privileged segments in society. In recent years technical training has been increasingly relegated to adolescence, with the emphasis on liberal education for those classes which do not require technical skills. With respect to the skills and knowledge required for ordinary adult life, the adolescent appears to be fully equipped. It is principally the less tangible qualities of wisdom, judgment, experience, and responsibility that are cited to justify his denial of adult rights to vote, to purchase alcoholic beverages, to drive an automobile.

Although adolescence as a fully established stage of development began with the nineteenth century, the development of a nationwide youth culture as the leading aspect of this period followed the First World War. There are peer groups in childhood, but they are more or less discrete and situational groupings. But the youth culture consists of an organized yet constantly changing set of patterns, exemplified by recognized youth leaders and commanding the loyalty of individual peer groups in the same way that a nationalistic movement commands the loyalty of each component community. A group of this kind has the capability to establish and justify norms, supplying the adolescent with a set of rules and values that can be counterposed to the ethic acquired from the family.

Thus the developing member of the family is not merely an individual growing up. He is a member of a cohort, passing through a set of stages that may be unique to his society. He has always at least a double group

[7] *Ibid.*, pp. 329 ff., *et passim.*
[8] F. Musgrove, *Youth and the Social Order*, Indiana University Press, Bloomington, 1964, pp. 33 ff.

identity. He is not only a representative of his family; he is also a representative of some culturally recognized age group. As he grows older, the age group increasingly presumes the right to demand that he act as its representative in matters in which age-group perspectives and interests may differ.

Development of Empathy. The distinctively human kind of interaction depends on the capacity of ego to take the role of alter. Placing oneself in the position of the other and inferring attitudes, motives, and sentiments from that point of view makes the subtleties of human interaction possible. The self-conception is impossible apart from a developed awareness that one has a certain appearance in any situation from the point of view of others. Hence identity interaction, the distinctions between disagreement and conflict and between agreement and harmony, as well as decision making through bargaining or persuasion depend on role taking.

The infant is not born with role-taking capacity. Hence an essential feature of family life is the gradual readjustment of interaction as the child's role-taking capacity develops. Interaction with a person lacking role-taking capacity is a demanding experience if ego cares for alter's feelings and his well-being. As the child begins to acquire role-taking capacity, the constant strain on the parent of having to be the one to understand and manipulate the situation is relieved. At the same time the child begins to make empathic interpretations of parent behavior and to bargain and manipulate in return. Role-taking ability also leads to a general change in the manner in which concepts and rules are understood, reshaping thereby the character of the socialization enterprise.

The incompletely social behavior of infancy consists largely of conditioned responses and imitations. A partial step toward role taking is illustrated in the following behavior of an infant in his second year:

As we sat eating dinner we could hear a soft repetitive sound coming from the living room side of the bookcase that served as a room divider. Listening closely we could hear the deliberately spoken word "no," repeated over and over. When we peered quietly around the bookcase, we saw our son sitting on the floor, beside a pile of books. He was taking the books out of the bookcase, one at a time, keeping up the steady flow of "no's," as he did so.

Beginning with the simplest kind of role taking, which consists of anticipating the approval or disapproval of a specific alter to one's own behavior, there is elaboration into a more complex response. Ego learns to take the different roles of different alters in response to the same behavior, to formulate a role of a more generalized nature, and to associate roles with categories of people in types of situations. He learns also to respond to other aspects of the alter role than simply approval or disapproval by discovering the idea of motives. He learns first to assign the simple motives that correspond to the evaluation of the act. Mother gives him breakfast because she loves him; Skipper hits his dog because he hates and wants to hurt. Quite late in the process he learns to try out motives of other kinds in accounting for the behavior of persons about him.

The most general term to describe the infant's perspective before he learns to take the role of others is *egocentric*.[9] There is an evolution of many stages toward a more *sociocentric* perspective. This move does not necessarily mean altruism, although altruism is impossible without it. It simply means that the individual assigns meanings in interaction that take account of the varied perspectives of others, rather than acting naïvely as if his were the only point of view.

In the chapter on family roles we reviewed Piaget's thesis of development from a morality of constraint to one of cooperation. This evolution is made possible not only, as Piaget observes, by the shift from authoritarian to relatively equalitarian relationships but by the development of role-taking capability.[10] Absolute rules cannot take individual points of view into account. For example, the rule that the children help equally with the dishes takes no note of the fact that one child enjoys playing house in this way but another lives in mortal fear that some of his peers will see him doing kitchen chores and humiliate him. Rules grant no consideration to the fact that one child can complete his school homework and emerge with flying colors after an hour's work each evening, but another must struggle for three or four hours in order to maintain undistinguished accomplishments. Hence there is an inherent tension between a developed role-taking capacity and a system of rigid rules.

This tension is not ordinarily resolved in the easy manner of Piaget's schoolchildren with their innocuous games of marbles. Role taking is a process beset by many errors in perception and inference. Furthermore, the child may take the role of a sibling and fail to take the role of his parent when considering the rules regarding family chores. In the case of rules from the larger society that are merely transmitted within the family, no member of the family may have had sufficient experience with the relevant alters to engage in appropriate role taking.

Hence the transition from an egocentric to a sociocentric perspective can mean a serious questioning and ambivalence about rules without sufficient experience and sufficient protection against biasing identification to allow role taking to guide behavior effectively. The role-taking per-

[9] Jean Piaget, *The Language and Thought of the Child*, Harcourt, Brace & World, New York, 1926.
[10] Jean Piaget, *The Moral Judgment of the Child*, Harcourt, Brace & World, New York, 1932.

spective is frequently seen as the humane point of view, so that struggles with parents over their efforts at rule enforcement are viewed by the young as humanitarian efforts. Sociocentrism makes behavior more flexible and, ideally, more rational. But it also enhances the unpredictability and the scope for conflict-inducing differences in the conception of the rules. This development reaches its peak during adolescence and will be elaborated further in Chapter 16.

Sex-role Identity. The molding of characteristically male and female personalities is a continuing feature of child development and a constant preoccupation of parents and other socializing agents. The infant is relatively asexual, apart from the distinguishing clothes and toys by which parents identify him, and the subtle differences in tone of voice and general treatment accorded him on the basis of his sex.[11] Childhood is the period during which sex identities are strongly implanted, and boys and girls develop increasingly separate spheres of activity. During adolescence the relations between boys and girls come to be implanted with increasingly sexual meanings. Boys and girls begin to come together again, but now according to a pattern of interaction that ritualistically takes account of the newly acknowledged sexual meanings.

In late infancy and early childhood there are typically changing identifications and preferences toward the father and mother. The early responsiveness by infants to the mother is often supplanted by a period in which young children of both sexes prefer the father. The famous Freudian sequence culminating in the Oedipal crisis is one effort to describe an invariant sequence applicable to this period. Whether or not there is such uniformity at an early stage, Kagan has aptly summarized the findings from several studies in the following terms:

The child as young as four has dichotomized the world into male and female people and is concerned with boy-girl differences. By the time he is seven he is intensely committed to molding his behavior in concordance with cultural standards appropriate to his biological sex and he shows uneasiness, anxiety, and even anger when he is in danger of behaving in ways regarded as characteristic of the opposite sex.[12]

Because of the salience of the sex role, an early, strong, and appropriate sex identity, indicated by overt behavior and inner confidence, facilitates participation in the customary patterns of interaction at home, at school, and in the play group. It is easier for parents, peers, and others to act

[11] The putatively secret sexual meanings of infant and child behavior do not concern us here.

[12] Jerome Kagan, "Acquisition and Significance of Sex Typing and Sex Role Identity," in Martin L. Hoffman and Lois W. Hoffman (eds.), *Review of Child Development Research*, Russell Sage, New York, 1964, vol. 1, p. 162. Quoted by permission of the publisher.

toward the child when his behavior is clear and sex-appropriate. Even when the child is not subject to abuse and ridicule for his failings, it is made easier for him to act with forthrightness and assurance when the behavior of alters toward him is direct and uninhibited.

The developing sex identities demand many revisions in family life. The requirements for privacy increase toward adolescence. The early brother-sister companionship is broken in mid-childhood but can often be resumed after the transitions of early adolescence have been passed. The often intimate attraction between mother and son is commonly forced underground lest the implication of unmasculine dependence be drawn from their public association. The continued harmony of mother-son relationships depends on the mother's acceptance of this restriction on her public behavior or on the son's acceptance of a less masculine identity. There is no comparable taboo against father-daughter association in middle-class neighborhoods, but here the continued relationship depends on the father's transforming his role from playmate to consort with the onset of adolescence.

Identity Formation. The many developments from infancy to adolescence and adulthood converge in a manner that is focal to family interaction in the formation of the self-conception. The identity can be no more complex than the elaboration of the individual's capacity for role taking permits. The sex-role identity and the memory of successful transitions between adjacent age-role identities make up a major portion of the self-conception.

It has also been proposed that there are certain steps toward the formation of an adult identity that must be taken in a predetermined order. Erik Erikson has offered a set of components, each posing a crucial task at a particular stage of development.[13] During the first year of life the infant develops either a *basic trust* or mistrust towards his environment. Once this basic trust is established, individual experiences of disappointment and deception do not shake the fundamental confidence in self and others. But unless such trust is established, the individual cannot proceed to the more complex tasks of self-development and self-discovery.

In the second and third years the infant moves from trust toward *autonomy*, the sense of being able to exercise self-control. Too early and rigid efforts by parents to enforce self-control lead to humiliating failures and to a loss of pride that may become a lasting sense of doubt and shame. Only with the pride of autonomy can the child move, in his fourth and fifth years, toward the exercise of *initiative*. During this period he explores his environment more freely and begins to see himself in terms of what he

[13] Erik Erikson, *op. cit.*, pp. 18–166.

may become as an adult. At this stage the danger is that suppression of his explorations will lead to a pervasive sense of guilt that will hereafter block the confident ability to exercise initiative.

If the identity in the third stage revolves about what the child can imagine himself to be, the years of elementary school are those in which he must find his identity in learning to produce things. When this stage proceeds successfully, he emerges with a *sense of industry*. When the accomplishments demanded of him are beyond his capabilities or achievement is in other respects blocked, his self-conception takes on a pervasive sense of inferiority.

During adolescence the self-conception must be integrated into a firm and distinctive characterization. Erikson refers to the problem here as the choice between identity, with the foregoing implication, and identity diffusion. Identity diffusion is expressed in the popular adolescent complaint that "I don't know who I am."

The remaining stages apply to adulthood and mature age, describing the transitions that parents must make while their children pass through the first five stages. In early adulthood the individual either finds out how to establish a genuine *intimacy* with spouse and others, or he moves into a sort of isolation that makes him a perpetual stranger among those he knows and associates with. In full adulthood he either discovers a vital "interest in establishing and guiding the next generation"[14] or falls into stagnation. This stage contributes *generativity* to the self-conception. The final achievement in the self-conception is *integrity*, a realistic and constructive acceptance of the dignity of life as it has occurred, and the ability to recognize and play both leader and follower parts. The failure to gain integrity leads to despair.

Erikson's stages mix, to the point of confusion, a description of actual development and the construction of a democratic ideal. Neverthless, there is considerable logic and empirical support for the sequence, at least through adolescence. The stages describe the kind of self-conception implicitly assumed in the culturally defined age roles. In order to play the part of a child in home and neighborhood, the individual must have a basic trust and degree of autonomy. In order to behave as an adolescent and warrant the roles that parents and others seek to play in dealing with him, the individual must have attained a certain sense of initiative and industry. Hence these evolving features of the self-conception do appear to correspond to some of the important interaction patterns during succeeding stages in the family cycle.

[14] *Ibid.*, p. 97.

Interaction with the Infant

To the young married couple, introduction of an infant signals an entirely new kind of relationship and demands extensive revision of the husband-wife pattern of interaction. The mother-infant pair is pivotal, and it is the character of this novel pair interaction that demands accommodative changes in the husband-wife association and in the relationships with any other children in the family. If we first examine the mother-infant relationship, it will then be easier to describe the contingent adjustments.

The infant is bonded to the mother only instrumentally, and the attachment is not unique. Initially, one person who supplies the immediate gratifications related to feeding and physical comfort is as good as another. Although an infant may soon develop a crescive bond through growing accustomed to one way of being handled and cared for, so that he rejects care by other people, there is no evidence to indicate that severe personal adjustments are required when a change of "parents" takes place during infancy. Because the infant lacks role-taking capability, he cannot yet form identity bonds. Viewed processually, infancy is the period during which a transition from nonselective to selective bonds takes place, with the infant coming increasingly to recognize and prefer his own parents.

Similarly, the infant's behavior is strictly consummatory and exploratory at first, and the only meanings he can assign to the behavior of others is in these terms. There is no temporal orientation to deprive him of enjoyment during a time of satiation through fear that there will be no food when he becomes hungry in the future or to make him disregard momentary discomfort in anticipation of gratifications to come. The infant has no conception of motivation and no set of motivational categories in which to place the parent's actions. The period of infancy witnesses the first developments toward anchoring interaction in a time perspective. The older infant develops a sense of security or a pervasive anxiety as he begins to be concerned with future gratifications. This is the problem of trust that Erikson places first in development of the identity. The older infant learns to identify the behavior of the moment on the basis of what it presages rather than for itself. Although he is not yet able to grasp the idea of motives for action, he takes the first step in this direction by starting to identify his own behavior on the basis of positive and negative responses that it is likely to evoke.

The most distinctive characteristic of the parent-infant relationship is its nonmutuality. Although there are effective bonds in both directions, they are quite different in kind and they lead to a pattern of *congruency* based on *dissensus*. The bonds that tie mother to infant are varied and complex.

Moral and legal responsibility for the welfare of the infant is an omnipresent tie. To the inexperienced and fearful parent, it often leads to almost constant preoccupation with the infant, attention that is only briefly interrupted, and unwillingness to delegate responsibility to others for brief periods. Although the responsibility bond may be superfluous in many instances and becomes increasingly less essential as the infant takes on the more human characteristics that permit other bonds to grow in salience, it supplies the necessary condition for the mother to define her attentions and sacrifices for the infant as morally creditable. Accordingly, the principle of reciprocity comes into play, and the start of a relationship in which the mother views herself as creditor and the infant as debtor comes into being.

The foundation for the pattern of interaction that will prevail during the longer period of childhood is laid with the evolving nature of response bonds. As the infant responds with signs of contentedness to feeding, to being held, then to the more subtle gestures of the smile and the spoken word, and even to the mere presence of the parent, the bond is made more diversified and more subtle. The pervasiveness of this bond is expressed as a recurrent theme in parent-infant interaction, the parent acting toward the infant with the principal aim of evoking a response. The parent shakes a rattle and glows when the infant tries to focus his eyes on the object. Later she speaks to the infant, often distracting him from other preoccupations, in order to gain a rewarding response. If the response is negative, with crying or a tantrum, the parent typically cuddles or soothes the infant until a positive response is evoked.

The most important bond tying parent to infant is usually the investment in incomplete action. The birth of the infant is preceded by an extended period of pregnancy. With its many preparatory actions and rituals, even an unplanned pregnancy is normally translated into a vital act in process. Although enjoyment of the older infant as he is sometimes becomes intense enough to create ambivalence about his growth into childhood, the principal bond is usually toward the growing infant in terms of what he may become. Societies and socioeconomic strata differ in the extent to which the bond causes the parent to push the infant in his development. In American society the bond is cemented by each indication of maturation—sitting up, walking, talking—and by anticipation of the next step.

This orientation toward more developed stages means that parents characteristically interpret infant gestures in terms of a more advanced stage of development than the infant has reached. Indeed, along with the search for response, the dominant theme of parental reaction during this period is the attempt to discover meanings in the infant's gestures that correspond to the world of mature motivation. A reflex mouth motion becomes a smile, a hard vocalization becomes "daddy," complex desires and satisfactions are inferred from infant behavior. Processually this period is marked by parental assignment of meanings, which come gradually to be accepted by the infant as the appropriate meanings for his own gestures. By the organized anticipatory nature of parental responses, the infant's gestures come increasingly to assume the conventional relationship to situations and to antecedent and subsequent behavior.

The decision-making process takes on a peculiar character because of the lack of mutuality. Authority in the strict sense is lodged almost entirely with the parent. The parent is supposed to control the infant. At the same time the parent's duty to the infant is paramount. Duty is not to comply with infant demands, however, but to serve the infant's needs. The parent rather than the infant is granted the right to determine what serves the infant's interests under the customary rules of interaction. Thus the parent's interpretations of gestures are at the empathic and diagnostic level rather than at face value. The infant is not expected to understand or respect the parent's interests, and he is only expected progressively to understand and respect their expressed wishes to the extent to which the parent has taught him to do so. The discrepancy between vesting authority in the parent but organizing the relationship entirely about the infant's needs is translated into a viable relationship only by granting the parent discretion in identifying the needs. But this device is nullified when a parent interprets the infant's discomfort as a peremptory demand on her. When the parent is inexperienced and lacks the counsel of an experienced person and when a value of interpersonal mastery makes the unrestrained crying of the child a reflection on her personal maturity and competence, the infant's complaint is likely to become an imperative command. Under these circumstances the gross contradiction between authority and dominance becomes a source of strain. A strongly futuristic orientation mitigates the strain for a limited period. The constant observation and anticipation of development in the infant offsets the tension. The sense of virtue, supported by society's view of the mother as madonna, supplies an offsetting reward. But still the strain must often be relieved by translating submission in the parent-infant pair into dominance in another pair relationship, as we shall observe in greater detail below.

The concepts of conflict and harmony are hardly applicable to the infant-parent relationship, except as the parent attributes an intentional and personal character to the infant's behavior. The behavior of an infant is often demanding and exasperating, and it frequently provokes anger and sometimes despair. But the parent does not ordinarily attribute a mature identity to him. Consequently his behavior has a less intimately personal significance. An infant cannot so readily hurt the parent deeply as can a child. Although the parent may wish to hurt the infant physically in difficult moments, her anger is not likely to incorporate the desire to humiliate him or take him down a peg that is found in dealings with a child and sometimes becomes overwhelming in relationships with an adolescent.[15] Likewise, the parent plays a game of love, and the infant begins to learn the rules without understanding the nature of the game. Exhibiting the forms of love becomes the subtle interpersonal technique learned by the infant. Likewise it becomes the most effective interpersonal technique in those families in which tantrums and urgent insistence are not rewarded.

In depicting the roles of the mother and infant, it is important to recognize that the development of behavior with age is not linear in all respects. The infant makes peremptory demands on parents which he will not be able to continue in childhood but which he may again be able to make in adolescence. A particularly striking discontinuity in American culture is the systematic training of the infant in baby talk and in a pattern of contrivedly naïve expression. It is generally assumed that baby talk is the natural way in which infants and young children speak and consequently the language they are best able to understand. But baby talk is not a spontaneous infantile expression but rather a special dialect taught to infants by the adults and children who surround them. Baby talk serves as an essential role cue. The occasional infant who is addressed in the same manner as adults learns adult talk and a pose of self-assurance and equality that is threatening to both adults and children with whom he has occasion to interact. Baby talk is a mode of address that indicates to the auditor that it is neither to be taken seriously nor at face value. This message defines the nature of the role of the infant and very young child, who are only to be taken seriously when their urgent physical wants are at stake. Humorous cartoons that picture the infant or small child as fully grasping the situation usually cast him in the role of a little monster with whom no one can cope. In a society that places attention to an infant's urgent needs above all other obligations, perhaps the only viable role is one that offsets potential tyranny by strongly institutionalizing a mode of interaction through which he is not normally taken seriously.

The most immediate and general effect of the infant-mother relationship is to impair the stable relationship between the mother and other family members. All other schedules must adjust to this pattern, and the wife can no longer be available strictly according to the husband's schedule. The implications of this development for the husband-wife bond depend on the nature of the bond between the father and infant, the conception

[15] These remarks must be qualified by calling attention to the substantial minority of exceptions, expressed in the currently serious problem of child beating.

of the paternal role, and the extent to which the wife resolves strain in her relationship with the infant through increasing dominance in relation to her husband.

When there is an intense polarization between male and female roles and a correspondingly great emphasis on masculinity, there is little basis for a close bond linking the father to the infant. Only in later childhood when the father and child can engage in collaborative tasks consistent with the masculine self-conception and when the child can achieve in fashions that enhance the father's self-image through identification does the bond take on some of the depth of the mother's bond to her offspring. Especially when the young adult is still in the process of establishing his own identity as a mature man is there a resistence to the sentimentality and subordination of an intimate parent relationship. Whenever problems of masculinity have become less important, the grandfather can often relate to the infant in a tender and unreserved manner that the father cannot.

When sex-role differentiation is less intense, the father can form many bonds with the infant parallel to those formed by the mother. Even when sex-role differentiation is great, the important anticipatory identification bond between the father and his male heir may overcome normal resistances to involvement in the woman's world.

In the latter instances, the common preoccupation of the mother and father with the infant supplies more than compensation for the husband's deprivation. The bond between the husband and wife is thereby intensified. But when the husband's bond to the infant is slight, the vulnerability of some of the husband-wife bonds is exposed. The weakening of bonds will normally have begun during pregnancy. There is a not uncommon pattern, sometimes called pregnancy desertion, in which the husband disappears soon after his wife becomes pregnant and remains away until the infant's habits have been regularized to the point that a fairly normal family schedule can be resumed.

We noted earlier the manner in which the inescapable scheduling demands often made on a man by his occupation are translated into a pattern of dominance within the family. In the same way, the urgent demands on the mother in the care of her infant can be translated into dominance and counterdominance in the family. Furthermore, the helplessness of the recently pregnant mother and her exhaustion from night feedings constitute a claim for greater solicitude on the part of the husband. Here is one of the rare circumstances under which an employer can be expected to abandon the priority normally placed on work demands. A mutuality of bondedness to the infant makes the scheduling adjustment consensual and consequently eliminates the implications for dominance in the marital relationship. Lack of mutuality leads to a disturbance in the usual dominance patterns unless the wife has been customarily ascendent.

When conflict has been endemic to the marriage, the infant-parent relationship supplies new means for carrying on the battle. The less insidious rivalry between the sexes finds an arena for contests to see who can gain maximum response from the infant. Full-fledged conflict can be played many ways. The failure of the infant to respond appropriately can be a wounding experience when witnessed by a hostile partner. The wife can magnify the urgency of infant demands on her enough so that the husband knows she is hurting him but not enough so that he can accuse her with impunity. The phenomenon of husbands who become jealous of the infant because they view him as a rival for the wife's attention has often been reported in clinical literature.

Sibling rivalry, a disguised form of conflict arising out of the older sibling's jealousy toward the younger, is widely noted in clinical literature. The pattern seems more likely to occur when the older sibling is a young child than when he is either adolescent or infant. The close dependence on the mother has already weakened by adolescence, and the dislocation is less intense. The lack of an identity and a repertoire of motives on the part of the infant makes it less likely that the dislocation will be experienced and interpreted in such a way as to feel a pervasive identity opposition with the new infant.

CHAPTER 16

PARENTS AND CHILDREN: PROGRESS IN THE LIFE CYCLE

Intergenerational relationships progress rapidly into early and late childhood, adolescence, and departure from the nuclear unit in maturity, leading to reestablishment of the marital dyad with which the family unit began.

Childhood

Bonding and Gesture Interpretation. During childhood there is a general shift in the prevailing kinds of family bonds, and there is a strong tendency toward differential bonding of pairs and other subgroups within the family, taking age and sex identities into account. Patterns vary widely among families, but overall the family bonding is frequently most intense during this period. Children are interested and disarmingly responsive, naïvely enthusiastic and compliant in family affairs. The steady maturation of the child is rapid and visible, and the mutual ties of parents to the child can serve to strengthen the marital bond. Children find parents useful and interesting, and their brief time perspective makes the parental rebuff a more transitory experience than later.

Task bonding of the child to the parent continues to be important throughout childhood. Although the growing child's dependence on his parents for survival and care is neither so urgent nor so irreplaceable as in infancy, the expanding and diversifying wants of the child multiply the points of dependence on parents enough to make up for his increasing ability to care for some elementary needs. Collaborative task bonds grow and are an important source of the spontaneous good feeling between the parent and child. Throughout much of childhood the adult still caters to the child, playing the child's games with him, choosing activities that fit the child's abilities and satisfy his interests. But some mutually enjoyable activities are engaged in with a spirit of genuine comradeship.

The task bonds are especially vulnerable to age changes. The child's interests shift, and the activity in which he has collaborated with the parent is no longer satisfying. Also, as the social world of the child expands, other children and even other adults become preferred partners for activities in which genuine parent-child comradeship was formerly felt. Involvement with the parent then becomes an impediment to the realization of a preferred companionship and is no longer a mutually effective bond. From the parent's catering to the child in early childhood the shift may be to the child's catering to the parent in late childhood and early adolescence.

Childhood is the period when identification bonds become central in importance. An elemental identification bond seems to develop almost automatically when people understand that they belong to the same group or stand in the same relationship to some other person or group. The apparently spontaneous identification of a preschool child with his infant sister is illustrated in the following account, prepared by the father:

My son was nearing three years of age and my daughter was two or three months old at the time of a routine visit to the pediatrician. Mother and father, with the infant daughter, were at the reception desk. A package containing a spare bottle and change of diapers had been left on a chair. Son was sitting on the chair next to it. A somewhat larger boy was attracted to the package, and started to pick it up. Son immediately showed signs of agitation and apparent fear. After a moment or two he acted suddenly, as if to break through his own fear of the larger boy. He jumped up, grabbed the package, and blurted out emotionally, "That's my sister's!" There were a few seconds of struggle in which son combined tears with aggressive determination, and the larger boy's advantage was offset by surprise and momentary indecisiveness. Then son wrested the packet free and assumed an aggressively defensive posture against any possible further attack. The larger boy looked for a moment in surprise and then rambled off to another part of the room. Father had looked back from the counter just in time to see the episode start, and decided not to interfere unless needed. Son's concentration on the boy and the packet was intense and unwavering, so that he never looked toward his parents for help, and, so far as I could judge, never knew he was being watched. Neither parent had ever suggested or expected that he should look after his sister's belongings. The response was entirely spontaneous.

That a more than ephemeral bond existed was indicated a few days later when the following incident occurred:

Mother was changing infant daughter's diaper in the bedroom at home. Daughter was being difficult to the point that Mother was driven to administer a resounding slap, that could be heard in the living room, fifteen feet away. Son, who was in the living room and to all appearances preoccupied with a game he was playing, visibly flinched at the sound of the slap. Tears came to his eyes, he jumped up and ran headlong through the hallway into the bedroom, and started slapping his mother angrily.

But the more complex identification bonding is made possible only when the individual has at least the beginnings of a self-conception and has sufficient understanding of the complexities of alter's behavior that he can see its implications for his self-conception. The socially based identification is always shaped by some audience. The child soon learns that for neighborhood purposes he is most importantly who his parents are. "Whose little girl are you?" is the standard opening question from adults. Which aspects of the parent's accomplishments or possessions are relevant and which irrelevant to identification depends on the child's understanding and his audience, both of which change with age. Because of the parent's visible superiority in so many areas of activity, the mere presence and availability of the parent serves the identification bond in early childhood. As the child grows older, however, mere presence is not enough, and more evidence of achievement or reputation is required. Superiority in white-collar and other symbol-manipulating fields is of little use for identification bonding until later childhood, when the child can begin to understand the aura that surrounds it.

Although task bonds between parents and child are normally a transitory phenomenon of childhood, the response bonds that predominate in infancy must usually either undergo a rather complete transformation so as to afford the foundation for enduring attachment or be eroded into ineffectuality by the end of childhood. As the child develops a varied repertory of behavior and as he grows in the capacity to understand and respond to more complex communications from his parents, the parent-child relationship often becomes a kind of mutual showing-off. Throughout a major portion of childhood the child hastens home to display each new skill or to brag of each new accomplishment. The parents, eager to see the child mature, respond with interest and encouragement. Reciprocally, the parent often finds in the child an appreciative audience for accomplishments that rate no special credit among his fellow adults. The mother's mediocre sewing skill, the father's average athletic prowess, and tales by either parent of effectively putting down troublesome business or neighborhood associates may impress the child.

The pattern in both directions here is the reciprocity of identification and response bonds. Because the child is tied through identification to the parent, he takes pride in parental accomplishments and responds approvingly. Because the parent is tied through identification to the child and evidence that the child is maturing redounds to the parent's credit, the parent responds approvingly to the child. This phenomenon of reciprocated identification-response bonding is one of the somewhat distinctive features of family organization, especially during the period of childhood. When the child begins to be labeled slow or a problem child in school, the parents' identification with the child is no longer a source of gratification. Hence their response to him is less enthusiastic, which in turn weakens the bond of the child to the parent by lessening his gratification from interacting with them. Or as the child grows older and discovers that his parent's accomplishments and community standing are commonplace, his identification bond to the parent is weakened. Consequently his response to the parent is less spontaneous, and the parent's gratification from interacting with him is accordingly lessened.

This kind of response bond is also vulnerable to translation of the relationship into a destructive rivalry. Seen against the brief time perspective of the child, his own achievements are magnified, and he is often mistakenly ready to try his muscle and his wits against the parent. When the parent regularly shows his full capability in such rivalry, the response to the child is undermined. The socializer role of the parent or elder sibling provides a legitimate vehicle through which a disguised competitive advantage can be realized. The child's writing can be praised and the occasion taken to demonstrate how it could be made even better. The guise of instruction then becomes a way for the parent to gain through rivalry with the child, to the detriment of the response bond.

The more potentially enduring form of response is found in the crescive bond of adjusted communication and response. The response here is less positive and directive; it is rather the response of listening and accepting. One person becomes a sounding board for the other. Normally this is a one-way relationship, in which the child is bound to the parent by the willingness of the parent to listen to the child's rehearsal of the day's events or his unresolved crises. Such a relationship may become more mutual, the parent sharing intimacies with the child in late childhood or adolescence. But the principal reciprocal bond is the parent's gratification over the willingness of the child to confide in him.

The principal obstacle to the formation of a strong crescive response bond is the dilemma of accepting correction. As socializer, the parent hears the child naïvely speak of his own discreditable behavior or express attitudes that are reprehensible. The parent then seeks to walk a tightrope between two extreme dangers. By making no judgments and suggesting no changes the parent encourages maximum communication from the child but allows his socializing responsibilities to go by default. By passing judgment in every relevant instance, the parent gradually discourages the child from relating his experiences and feelings, lessening the parent's knowledge of the child and undermining the basis for a response bond. When the parent is able to balance occasional correction against a general response of acceptance, the response bond can develop without damage to other bonding that depends on the parent's continuing performance of the socializer role.

There is a further vulnerability in response bonding, when the relationship is not mutual or sufficiently reciprocated by identification. We mentioned in an earlier chapter that a counsellor-counsellee relationship becomes oppressive to the former when the circumstances of the role relationship are not carefully bounded. Because of the unequal maturity of parent and child, much more is demanded of the parent than of the child in selecting a response that will not be misunderstood. If the parent continues to govern his response by insight into the effect of his remarks on the child, the relationship becomes unpleasant for the parent in at least two ways. First, the relationship loses all spontaneity with time. Without spontaneity there is also no simple pleasure; only the sense of moral reward at having done the proper thing or the sense of accomplishment in having provoked a predictable response remains. Second, increasingly it becomes clear that the child calls the tune—that in spite of the formal relationship of authority the child dominates and the parent adapts.

Childhood is the period when bonds become qualitatively and often quantitatively different according to sex as well as age. Task bonds are generally more likely to involve the mother than the father in contemporary society, because the child's world and mother's world overlap more than either does with the vocational world. The preponderant association of the mother with chores and routines, however, sometimes means that the father comes to be associated with play. In families in which the father eschews the disciplinary role and his entry into the home signals game time, there is commonly a period during early childhood when the children feel more warmly and spontaneously drawn toward the father than toward the mother. Subsequently, however, as sex-typed activity increasingly takes the place of the less differentiated play in early childhood, task bonds tend to link the child to the parent of the same sex, if they operate at all.

The reader will recall that the solidification of the kind of mutual task bonds that create a sense of comradeship depends on the presence of common goals and the development of a decision-making pattern that minimizes the obstacles to collaborative activity. The chances of such comradeship between the mother and daughter are greatest when the daughter forms a somewhat traditional self-conception. The common interest in domestic activities permits a collaboration that can continue even into adulthood, so long as the daughter's self-conception does not move toward a repudiation of traditional feminine activity. Effective bonding is especially vulnerable to nonadaptive division of labor.

Father-son collaboration in modern society follows a more complex and uncertain course. Except for the occasional householder whose home craftsmanship and landscape management become the means of personal creativeness, the work that is crucial to the male identity is usually removed from the home. Hence serious task collaboration between the father and son is likely to be restricted to home chores, often under direction and after urging from the mother. Hence collaboration does not revolve about highly valued mutual goals and is not likely to produce a strong bond. Collaboration in play is made possible where there is a strong mutual interest in sports. Often the play collaboration is transformed into a socialization task, accepted enthusiastically by the boy in early and middle childhood, but with less and less relevance in later childhood. Continuing companionship is often a frustrated ideal in the modern family.

Identification and response bonds have peculiarly different relationships to sex. Identification bonds generally develop most readily between the parent and child of the same sex, with certain exceptions we shall mention below. Response bonds, on the other hand, are facilitated between the parent and child of the opposite sex. Because identification bonds depend on alter's exemplification of valued features in ego's self-conception, identification with the father's manliness can be a special source of attraction to a son and identification with the mother's mature femininity to a girl. Later childhood sees the beginning of crucial transitions. In the case of girls, the youthful nature of the feminine ideal threatens a weakening of identification except when the mother has retained feminine attractiveness and poise. With boys, the father's occupational standing is the more crucial consideration as adolescence approaches.

Although identification bonds lead to admiration, they often impair easy and warm response. When identification is with a real person and one whom ego sees in his unguarded moments, there is a constant danger that alter will fall short of the manliness or femininity or other valued quality that is crucial to the relationship. Hence there is a degree of uneasiness or anxiousness and a tendency to attempt to direct alter's behavior. Although the mother admires her daughter's developing femininity, she is anxious lest the earlier tomboy attributes reassert themselves in late childhood. Even as she compliments her daughter, it is difficult not to offer a suggestion concerning how she might be still more of a young woman. The son who admires his father's position of community respect is nevertheless anxious, by later childhood, lest his father not keep up the proper appearance.

Because the father and daughter and the mother and son are less involved in identification, they are less troubled by this kind of uneasiness.

In each cross-sex pair, the members' own self-images are less implicated by virtue of what the other does. The parent can relax from his socializer role more easily with the opposite-sex child. Except when the subject matter is the private province of one sex, such as problems of menstruation, the child may find it easier to confide in the opposite-sex parent. When these cross-sex relationships develop during childhood as a welcome contrast to the more contrived and often rivalrous relationships between same-sex parent and child, the resulting bond is relatively invulnerable to the passage into adolescence and even into adulthood.

This sex differentiation in bonding is complicated by one further principle. Whenever the male is recognized as the crucial determiner of family status, there tends to be some nonmutual identification bonding from any female to any male. Hence the daughter's relationship to her father may be more of a mixture of tenderness and admiration than his to her. The apparent nature of the relationship may change from moment to moment as one or the other bond becomes relevant in the situation. In a sense the daughter's tie to the father is likely to be more complex and apparently changeable than the father's tie to his daughter.

It is in the mother's tie to her son that this dual nature is commonly and consequentially revealed. The literature of pathology is filled with illustrations of maternal behavior toward a son involving an unstable alternation between identification, with its accompanying pride and intense pressures toward achievement, and the entirely accepting and uncritical response.

The bonds between siblings are quite variable and, of all bonds within the family, subject to the most radical apparent transformations from moment to moment. Fundamentally, siblings are likely to form strong task bonds because of their common interests in childish matters. The apparent changes in bonding reflect the fact that task bonds are especially vulnerable to new opportunities. Hence siblings are close or distant in childhood depending on the presence or absence of other children. The identification-response bonding pattern is especially characteristic of relations between older and younger sibling. The younger child gains through identification with the older sibling's greater prowess. In addition, the older child is sometimes a source of prestige-giving association with older children outside the family and of secret information that parents are unwilling to reveal to the younger child. The older sibling is often a source of sex education for the younger. Although public association with the younger sibling can be embarassing and the younger child's immaturity makes him a poor collaborator in the older child's interests, it is difficult for the older child not to find some gratification in the younger sibling's naïve admiration. Once the younger sibling has reached an age when he can be depended on to keep a secret, he is also a sympathetic confidante for frustrations and achievements which the older sibling hesitates to reveal to his parents or which seem too unimportant to evoke much reaction from them.

When sex differences are added to age differences in sibling bonding, considerations become immensely complex. But it is not unlikely that the younger daughter-older son pair may produce the deepest and most invulnerable bonding over time. Initially, such a relationship is even more troubling to the boy than a similar relationship with a younger male sibling, because of the embarrassment of being seen with a little sister in tow. But mitigation of the rivalry found between same sex siblings and the reinforcing effect of older age and male sex in provoking sister's identification, with the resulting appreciative response, often permit this relationship to prevail in secret until the boy is old enough not to fear being seen with his little sister.

Decision Making. If there is no real group decision making involving the infant in the family, childhood represents the period of induction into family decision. The decision making, however, follows different patterns from those in the usual grouping of adults because of the following circumstances:

1. Throughout the period of childhood there is a shift from the initial role of *ward* toward the eventual role of *member* of the family.

2. The child is expected to participate actively in ever-broadening spheres of family decision making but always within a latitude ultimately supposed to be determined by the parents.

3. Decision making between the parent and child pits individuals with gross but progressively decreasing disparity in knowledge, understanding, and persuasive ability.

4. The two-headed nature of the family ensures that the child will discover the strategy of divide and conquer by fostering coalition with one parent to offset control by the other. Other coalitions are also facilitated by family composition.

5. Childhood is the period during which the individual learns to import into the family interpretations of events acquired in outside associations, a practice that had earlier been the exclusive province of parents.

A ward is sheltered and cared for by the family but does not participate in a broad range of family decisions and is not thought to make a reciprocal contribution to family well-being. Most matters on which the family must make a decision are throught not to be his province; the ward should not expect to be consulted, and if consulted, he should appreciate this extra consideration. To a considerable degree the role of ward continues throughout childhood. Children are likely not to be consulted about the purchase of an automobile, changing residence, family budgeting, choice of church membership, family vacations, and other matters that affect the family as a whole. Because the child generally raises questions about many of these family areas that are not his province and makes suggestions and states preferences, he learns to distinguish between being taken seriously and not. Parents mock seriousness, pat the child on the head, or laugh patronizingly. If he insists on being taken seriously, parents see him as invading their privacy and deal accordingly.

As the child becomes older, he engages in activities and plans of longer duration that are more deeply embedded in settings outside the family. Accordingly, he is more concerned with broad family decisions. Unless the family has already inducted him into the broader spheres, there is a recurrent interaction pattern in which the child attempts to participate in decisions that the parents have viewed as their own. Through a series of incidents, interspersed with rebuffs, the limits of the child's involvement are pushed back. The shifting position of these limits means that accommodative decisions are made by assent without firm commitment, and are constantly up for renegotiation.

Another characteristic difference between ward and member roles has to do with initiative. A group member is guided by the group's aims and interests, so that he acts on his own initiative when he sees that they are in some way at stake. The ward supports the group also, but he does so in response to direction from a member or leader of the group, since the general aims of the group are not his concern. The mother and father, as they walk about the home and property, typically pull an occasional weed, pick up stray paper, and generally do minor chores they see require doing. When the ward role is effectively implemented, the child performs chores willingly on direction but is not sensitized to see things that need to be done when they are not pointed out to him. In the small child this is the expected state of things. But characteristically the parents expect increasing acceptance of the responsibilities of membership more rapidly than they abandon the wardship conception of the child's right to participate in decisions. The result is a lack of role consensus that means accommodative rather than consensual decisions and an assessment of demands made on each other such as to provoke some feeling of injustice on both sides.

The mixed-authority situation in which the child is heard and his views increasingly taken into account, but with the latitude ultimately controlled by his opposite numbers in the decision-making interaction, reinforces the tendencies derived from wardship. In order to participate in this kind of arrangement the child must develop a self-conception that acknowledges his limited competency but incorporates sufficient orientation to the future so that he is not rendered incompetent to assume expanding participation.

The branching of roles during this stage can be in either of two other directions. First, the self-conception and the relationship to authority can prevent the development of any view of decision making as a process that can take place on the principle of mutuality. All decisions are viewed as unilateral, and the child learns such interpersonal techniques as supplication, wheedling, annoying, or merely overly good behavior in order to gain concessions. Second, the language of democratic decision making may be accepted to the extent that ultimate parental control is challenged as illegitimate. In this situation all decision making is fraught with high conflict potential.

The disparity in knowledge between the parent and child means that until late childhood there is little chance of the child's besting the parent in an argument on the basis of persuasion, except when the child is able to supply information from his own realm toward consensual decision. Parents may deal with the discrepancy by indulging the child—by granting concessions as if the child's arguments were valid—from time to time. Through discriminating application of this procedure, the child can be inducted gradually into decision making as his understanding and persuasive skills become better. When this procedure is not applied effectively, the child's mode of participation must increasingly become bargaining and coercion. Coercion is principally possible through the threat of embarrassment before outsiders or of carrying tales about one parent to the other or of an older sibling to the parent. But bargaining is a more generally applicable procedure.

On the basis of coalition theory, the parent-child relationship supplies an almost prototypical situation for the generation of coalitions. Although laboratory study has indicated that coalitions do not emerge with the same apparent strength and predictability that general theory leads the investigator to anticipate,[1] the constant use of coalitions is so evident to casual observation of most families in their normal settings that the laboratory findings must be treated with some discount.

There is, first of all, a tremendous gulf in power between parent and child, such that the child can seldom expect to win except when the parents are willing or when outsiders intervene. Second, the presence of two parents, each of whom may be approached directly and each of whom usually has much greater power than a child, facilitates the child's effort to create a coalition with one parent against the other. Absence of either of these conditions makes coalitions an ineffectual strategy. In a highly traditional family situation in which children can only approach the father through the mother, coalitions are inhibited. And relationships in which either the mother or the father immediately concedes to the dominant par-

[1] Fred L. Strodtbeck, "The Family as a Three-person Group," *American Sociological Review*, 19:23–29, February 1954.

ent in case of a confrontation render coalitions useless. When the norm that sentiment governs family relationships is strongly held, the explicit use of coalitions is unacceptable. And there is a widely accepted norm prescribing a stable husband-wife alliance as a defense against parent-child coalitions that either impair the socialization function of the family or threaten the marital bond. That parents should back each other up, that they should present a common front to the children, is one of the commonest directives in practical guidebooks for parents. When these two norms are respected, coalitions are used in disguised form. When the child learns to direct his request first to the parent who is more likely to be sympathetic, and wins assent, the parental alliance works in his favor rather than against him. A boy seeking to be excused from chores to attend an athletic event can ask his father and even suggest that they both go; when he claims exemption from chores because of illness, he may ask his mother first.

The formation of coalitions with siblings against a parent becomes feasible in later childhood, as the combined power of two or more children becomes great enough to offset the power of a single parent. But two other circumstances make it probable that sibling coalitions will be used. We have already observed that the response bond inhibits the exercise of full parental power. When the children form a coalition, the parent is doubly threatened by the impairment of response from both or all the children. But in addition, coalitions among children can be effective when they use the indirect tactic of controlling information. In the early period of childhood, when time perspectives are short, coalitions are unstable and are easily undermined by reasonably persistent or skillful parents. As the children acquire a longer time perspective, they move in the direction either of more calculating and cautious use of coalitions or of more stable alliances in which subgroup bonds prevent betrayal and exploitation of the coalition.

The child's play and school associations with his peers give him an external vantage point from which to see and participate in family decisions. As children shift from infantile parallel play toward more or less collaborative activity with one another, their most structured play consists of reenacting the characteristic roles from the real world as they see them. Children replay the standard situations in the home, each child assuming one or more of the parts. But the replaying of events necessarily leads to reinterpretation, which then affects the child's participation in the next real incident. Reinterpretation occurs because the child plays a role other than his own real-life part and must necessarily supply the attitude and simulate the motivation presumed to lie behind the behavior. Furthermore, the play requires that several children work out an acceptable common version of how such incidents take place to supplant the several individual versions they bring from their own family experiences. The result is a group product, with group sanction, but not quite the same as the version that comes out of the family group. The play-group scripts and meanings are then tried out in family interaction, leading either to illumination of events, modification of the family sequence, or repudiation of the child-group pattern.

As the child group advances from mere play acting to an arena for trading secrets, reporting triumphs and frustrations, and disseminating strategies, it becomes a positive influence on family decisions. Not only does the child enter the decision process with independent interpretations and expectations that have the peer-group stamp of authenticity, but the peer-group experience leads to the reopening of decisions that other members of the family thought were closed. When the child uses his peer group for the recapitulation of family events, other children use the occasion to brag about what they would have done. The game of rivalry, which is a principal theme in unregulated child-group interaction, is played as each child attempts to outdo the others with fantasy claims. One common effect is to encourage the child to return to the family with new arguments and new determination. Thus the balance in decision making is upset, as the child's assent is often not commitment.

Perhaps the most important effect of the child group is to supply a new dimension to the child's identity. Throughout the period of childhood he becomes less and less simply an individual and a representative of a family group. He becomes increasingly a representative of the age group. As a member of a child group with common interests that set members somewhat apart from other people, the child must increasingly act so as to protect and foster the group interest, although it may not correspond with his apparent individual interest of the moment. In the same way that an employer must contend with a class-conscious worker, the parent begins to encounter the age-conscious child in the family.

Acceptance of a group identity is both a form of imprisonment and a source of power for the child. Any group identity limits the scope of the individual's discretion and requires that he subordinate his personal judgment to the group's view of its interest. The child must now do child things and must forego behavior that betrays child interests. He must no longer admit a preference for the sometimes less competitive and more relaxing company of certain adults. At the same time, the group identity becomes a source of rights. As group identity matures in later childhood, the child can demand those rights which properly belong to children. He enters the arena of family decision making as the representative of a legitimate group rather than a lone individual. Thus he has a growing base from which to challenge the authority that the parent gains as a representative of the adult community.

Systems of Interaction. In a general sense childhood is the period during which there is a series of transitions by which activities and relationships that were simply play turn into matters of serious consequence. These transitions are especially related to the child's lengthening time perspective and developing self-conception and to the increasingly real consequences of the child's actions for himself and others. Goffman likens the mental hospital to the younger child's situation in the family:[2]

Here, incumbents have sufficiently little face to allow of their being scolded by senior staff and twitted by nurses, in that important arrangement by which children and others in training are permitted to pay for their mistakes in cash on the spot, thereby avoiding certain kinds of liens on their future.

Laughing at the child's poor English and sending him to bed without supper for hitting another child are replaced by concern lest these become fixed modes of behavior.

In preparation for adolescence, the solidification of a system of parent-child roles in which the child is taken seriously in the family is a crucial development. When this occurs, an underlying harmony is possible. Otherwise the parents take the child seriously only in his threatening and disruptive behavior, establishing a pervasive opposition between the parent and child identities. Latent conflict is then a continuous state.

A second pervasive role patterning is the polarization of parent-child relationships in the direction of consensus and accommodations that are made without reserving commitment or into bargaining and coercion. When every decision becomes a chance to gain an advantage that may be useful the next time, the stage is set for a full break during adolescence.

Finally, there develops in childhood a general perspective on the relationship between age-group identity and family identity. If the age-group identity can only be assumed and the age role played at the expense of the family identity, the child is forced into a difficult choice. He may retreat into the family during childhood. But if he does, the break from the family when he opts for the peer group in adolescence will be intensely disruptive. Those who stay with the family will be cut off from peer-group experience. Those who choose age-group identity while still in childhood will have reduced the family relationship to symbiosis and conflict by the onset of adolescence.

Adolescence

If childhood is the period during which the child's principal arena is the family while the outside world increasingly contests with the family for his time and loyalty, adolescence is the period in which the outside world

[2] Erving Goffman, *Encounters*, Bobbs-Merrill, Indianapolis, 1961, p. 140.

becomes the crucial locus for his identity and the family strives to retain a portion of his loyalty and time. (1) The shifting and uncertainty regarding the extent and nature of family bonds thus become a central theme shaping interaction. (2) The youth's preoccupation with the outside world and the shared sense of an imminent end to the family-household-unit pattern of life mean a reanchoring of the youthful self-conception and a tendency to see the present as if the future had already arrived. (3) Society still holds parents responsible for the conduct of youth and demands responsibility for socialization, although this youthful self-conception and the increasing activity beyond the direct surveillance of the family make continuation of a comprehensive pattern of child socialization impossible. We shall take up these three developments in order. First we should observe that there are often distinctive features to the parental situation that contribute to the course of decision making and the patterning into conflict or harmony between adolescent and parent.

The Parental Identity. Development does not stop with the attainment of adulthood, and there is commonly a readjustment in adult self-conceptions during the forties and early fifties. Adolescents typically have parents in this age range. Consequently, parental identity problems loom large just at the time when society seems to demand that the problems of youth receive first attention.

For the majority of families children are in the home during the least problematic period for parental self-conceptions. In occupations where a peak is reached early and present rather than future orientation prevails, the first twenty years of adulthood witness maximum productivity and earning and maximum fulfillment of masculinity. Wives can still recreate youthful glamor on occasion, while finding basic fulfillment through motherhood. Semiskilled and skilled workers are likely to follow this pattern. In career-oriented occupations that peak later, the frustrations of early low income are mitigated by future orientation. An irrepressible optimism regarding eventual social and economic achievement, reinforced by occasional advances up the bureaucratic ladder or expansions of business, makes frustrations of the moment tolerable.

But sometime during the forties or early fifties, both patterns are likely to undergo change. The present-oriented life begins to experience decline. The man's speed and physical endurance lessen, and he may begin to have greater difficulty in maintaining steady employment. The woman's sexual attractiveness demands ever more artificial enhancement, and menopause often comes as a drastic signal of approaching old age. Irritability and sensitivity to criticism often increase, just at the period when parents are forced to contend with the hypercritical attitude of adolescence. The self-conceptions of both the mother and father become precarious just at the time when youth can no longer take their own identities for granted but become increasingly preoccupied with the self-conception. Thus the roots for the heightened proportion of identity-oriented interaction between adolescents and their parents are often found in the adult stage of life as well as in the problems of adolescence.

In families whose lives are geared to an occupational career the late forties and early fifties are equally critical. Perhaps for most men, the peak of advancement is reached, or the rate of advancement is slowing down substantially. People who have not moved from the administrative ladder to the executive ladder, from teaching to principalship, by this time will normally be passed over in the future as selection is made from the younger men. For the much smaller number who have moved onto the upper ladders, there are new and more demanding standards of success, coupled with reevaluations of the merit of their life goals. Now is the time when almost reaching the top comes increasingly to signal failure. The excitement and novelty of the work have often gone, the technical superiority of the younger men is apparent, and the individual has invested so much and reached such a level that he can no longer consider changing his course. He has passed the point of no return.[3] Just at the time when the adolescent is questioning the goals that society offers him and seeks guidance and assurance in making crucial choices and commitments, his parents have typically reached the stage of reassessment, doubt, and sometimes despair regarding the goals that have shaped their lives in the two to three decades since they made their own adolescent choices. Again, it is a rare adolescent whose preoccupation with himself enables him to appreciate that his parents have problems of this kind. Likewise, society grants little recognition to these problems. The adolescent's plea for sympathy and understanding is legitimized; the adult dares not plead for similar understanding, lest his plea destroy whatever remnant of respect continues to hold his offspring to him and lest the community write him off as a failure .

Bonding. A simple interpretation of what happens at adolescence is that the adolescent's bonding to his parents weakens but no reduction of similar magnitude occurs in case of the parents' ties to the youth. The result is a tendency for much of the interaction to become a vehicle through which the parent strives to keep the adolescent within the family circle and the adolescent attempts to put off some of the remaining bonds. The balance of power in decision making shifts in favor of youth, in accordance with the principle of less interest.

Although we shall have to add complicating refinements and alternative developments, the foregoing observation presents in capsule form the most

[3]John B. Marquand, *Point of No Return*, Little, Brown, Boston, 1949.

generally applicable transformation of bonding at this period. Task bonds are lessened, because much of the youth's activities are now centered outside the family. Other youth are preferred companions and collaborators, and parents are less likely to have the superior knowledge or skill that is relevant to youthful activities. There is, however, no necessary decline in the desire for companionship and response on the part of parents.

Similarly identification bonds usually become less important for youth. Youthful ambition typically outstrips parental accomplishment, so that identification supplies no prestige gain. A transformation has been occurring in the peer society, so that it is less and less organized according to social origins and more and more organized according to apparent destinations. A stratification by origin links the child to the parent. But stratification by destination drives a wedge between the youth and his parent. He is now what he is making of himself, not what his parents are.

For the parents, on the other hand, identification may be as important and sometimes even more important at this stage. The abundant inconvenience and sacrifice of earlier years have been justified by anticipation of the day when the children will become young men and women. Furthermore, as the future orientation of the parents' own achievements begins to recede, the importance of identification with the accomplishments of their offspring becomes greater.

The potential gains to the youth from response may not be reduced, but the conduciveness of family interaction to providing suitable response is frequently impaired by the obstacles to decision making and the prevalence of conflict.

If this were the entire story, there could be little other than youth-dictated interaction or withdrawal from the family. The adolescent remains dependent on the family because the expanded period of education keeps him dependent on parents for financial support and because his legal status as a minor makes him dependent on parental sponsorship in many basic realms of activity. Because this symbiotic dependence on the family is relatively invulnerable for most adolescents, the question is not one of severing family ties but of the range of matters with which family interaction is concerned. The narrow bonding of the youth dictates a minimal kind of interaction, devoid of confidences and surveillance over behavior. The more diversified and social bonding of the parent calls for a more intimate and concerned relationship.

The slackening of identification and response bonding is seldom steady but often exhibits erratic resurgences of dependency because of the instability of the adolescent identity and the general insensitivity of the peer group to the individual personalities of its members. The family, if suitably organized, becomes a place of retreat from the constant demands for demonstrated achievement. In spite of its apparent affability, the peer group is marked by intense rivalry and demands thick skins of its members. Exchanging friendly insults and discounting the other's achievements are often main tactics of interpersonal exchange. To express naïve and unqualified admiration for a peer or to reveal elementary sentiments of affection runs against the norms of the group and invites ridicule. The average adolescent is not sufficiently adjusted to this pattern of treatment to escape hurt from every barb. When the response bond in the family has undergone the transformation from childhood response to an easy but supportive set of relationships, the adolescent finds relief and reassurance in the opportunity to interact exclusively within the family circle from time to time.

Families vary, therefore, from an active and important response bond to complete erosion of the response bond between the adolescent and parents. The pattern will have been largely set by the character of the transition in the response bond during late childhood.

The pattern of differential bonding by sex continues into adolescence, again tending to polarize according to the direction established in childhood. When rivalry has developed as the major theme in same-sex interaction, adolescence heightens this tendency, nullifying response bonds that might otherwise be important. Cross-sex bonds are vulnerable at this stage to jealousy. A crucial determinant of the persistence or weakening of these response bonds is the manner in which the parent can accept the adolescent's dating relationships.

There is also often a general difference in the bonding of the father and mother to the adolescent. The man's role outside the home often makes it easier for him to accept the loss of attention and interest from his offspring. As youth take less initiative in pursuing the father's association and offer less rewarding response to his advances, the father can make compensatory shifts. The result is a common phenomenon in which the imbalance of interest is once again reversed, and the adolescent finds his father unavailable or unprepared for the occasional resurgence of identification and search for response. By adjusting too readily to adolescent independence and withdrawal, the father frequently leaves the youth without wanted support.

The mother, on the other hand, is less likely to be able to move her attention to a different arena. Hence it is she who attempts to restore the earlier bonds and becomes victim of the less interest dominance by her offspring.

Adolescent Self-conception. Seldom in any interaction do ego's conception of alter and alter's conception of himself correspond precisely. When alter is a child, such discrepancies are frequent, but they are not usually completely disruptive of interaction, for two reasons. First, the imbalance of power and interpersonal skill favors the parent sufficiently so that interaction must usually be conducted on the basis of the parent's conceptions. Second, the child's self-conception is not yet strongly enough formed to withstand at least momentary revision or doubt in such interaction. But adolescence is the period when the discrepancy between the youthful self-conception and the adult's conception of the adolescent becomes a dominant theme of interaction.

The adolescent self-conception typically centers on future achievement, which is displaced in time into the present. The adolescent characteristically thinks of himself as already in large part what he is to become. He demands that others interact with him on the assumption that he has already achieved the wisdom, the responsibility, and the versatility that represent his personal goal. The discounting or distorting of the self-image in order to protect the future-anchored self-conception is at its maximum during this period. Parents likewise see the youth in terms of his future potential and often urge him to act accordingly. But unlike youth, parents do not merge the future into the present in their conception of the adolescent. The bias instead is in the opposite direction, the accumulated memory of past images dominating the parent's anticipations regarding behavior in the immediate present. As a consequence, the parent deals with the adolescent as he has been but not quite as he now is. The adolescent expects others to treat him as he is becoming but has not yet become. Each is dealing with what he believes is the real or actual person, and each is likely to find the gestures of the other noncongruent.

Youth's vigorous discounting of the momentary image and his insistence on playing the part that goes with his self-conception become arrogance and lack of realistic self-understanding to the parent. Congruency in the gesture exchange between the parents and youth is then attainable only by the development of a complementary set of alter conceptions. By seeing the youth as cocky and lacking in self-understanding, the parent is prepared for the kind of gestures the youth uses. By seeing parents as unperceptive and even jealous of his maturity, the adolescent is prepared for his parents' responses. The resulting congruence without consensus supplies the framework within which a repeatable pattern of interaction can emerge.

Viewed as a discrepancy in time orientation, the misunderstandings are easy to understand and might readily be interpreted to the interactors. But involving the identities of the participants, they are given normative interpretations. As a moral issue, the discrepancy becomes a problem of trust. No one ordinarily demands that his friends or associates render him unlimited trust. He commands trust normally by avoiding unreasonable demands for trust and by offering assurances and evidence to justify the trust. But much of the involvement of identities so as to produce chronic conflict between parent and adolescent revolves about the role implications of trust. The adolescent demands trust as a way of testing his parents. A major determinant of the degree to which chronic conflict prevails is whether a viable accommodation can be reached in the realm of trust. A relationship that takes account of continuing parental responsibilities for youthful behavior and youthful need for assurances of acceptance as a person and an adult can minimize the identity relevance of many disagreements of substance.

Deliberate Socialization. Throughout childhood the interaction of the parent and child has been shaped by a pervasive concern with socialization. Adolescence is the period in which the socializer-socializee roles are transformed, increasingly restricted and subordinated to other bases for interaction, and eventually abandoned, except during occasional interludes. If socialization were a simple linear activity, like learning to read, so that the socializer could gradually retreat from constant surveillance to periodic supervision to the ultimate stage of merely being available as counsellor when needed, the whole adjustment might be relatively smooth. Adolescence witnesses a good deal of unlearning that undercuts the impetus of earlier training and is a stage of entry into novel situations for which earlier learning does not provide the guidelines. Under hypothetically appropriate conditions, parents might be better qualified to handle socialization at this age than at any other, for the new situations are those of adulthood in which the parents are most recently experienced. But in American society, neither the parents nor the adolescents wish that the latter should follow exactly in the parents' footsteps. For youth, to accept, at this stage, a future world no better than that in which their parents live would be to concede failure. For parents, to allow their children to repeat all the mistakes they have made would be to renege in their prime socialization responsibilities.

Early socialization practices normally include, among others, two devices—concealment of the full facts and enforcement of absolute rules for behavior. These devices are necessitated because of the child's inexperience and inadequate judgment. For example, an adult crosses the street when he feels it is safe to do so; a small child is taught never to cross the street alone, because his judgment of the speed of approaching vehicles cannot be trusted. Likewise, most wisdom rests on actuarial principles: one increases his chance of illness by smoking or by not eating a balanced diet, but not everyone who does these things will experience the anticipated bad effects. The naïve egocentrism of the child makes it difficult for him to accept an ethic based on probabilities, since he tends to treat himself as one of the exceptions. Hence, parents present the consequences of disapproved actions as certainties rather than statistical probabilities.

A key to the readjustment of socialization relationships is found in the abandonment of concealment and absolute rules. It seems likely that the transition may not be disruptive to parent-youth relationships, and parents may continue to exercise socializing functions on occasion when they have gradually given up concealment and absolute rules during later childhood. But when these changes have not been made earlier, adolescence becomes a critical period in which the socializing role of the parent is reinterpreted by the youth, and a different kind of role pair established.

Characteristically the parent finds his authority as a socializer challenged by the adolescent. Unless the groundwork has been laid for a shift to a less authoritative and controlling role, the parent attempts to preserve his socializing position by further unsupportable assertions and bald insistence on conformity to absolute rules. The parent gets himself in deeper and deeper, as each response tends to discredit further his claims as a socializer in the eyes of the adolescent and to make his viewpoint more precarious in skillful debate. Depending on how seriously the matters under recurrent debate are valued, interaction commonly assumes a pattern of bargaining or a role polarization between defender and attacker of values.

When bargaining has already become a pervasive theme in parent-child interaction, the resources of the adolescent peer group supply a rhetoric that has been well tested for its effectiveness in debating with adults. Practice in its use in the classroom, where several students can help one another in confronting a single teacher, provides experience and sharpened skills for the one-to-one or pair-group encounters in the family. We speak of rhetoric, because the tactics are used because they are effective in winning decisions, not because they are necessarily taken seriously by the users.

A few examples of these tactics can be offered. First, the adolescent challenges the adult to state the rule at issue in general form, For example, when corrected, he asks, "What did I do?" or "What's wrong with that?" Except in the strictly legal realm, society does not operate with precisely formulated rules having complete generality. Rules are normally somewhat fuzzy generalizations that evoke in the socialized individual the situations in which the rules are to apply. Hence, it is usually possible to show fallacy in any generally formulated rule. By rising to the youth's demand the parent makes himself vulnerable to defeat on the grounds that there is no valid rule at stake. A second tactic is similar and consists of asking "why?" or demanding justifications. Again, the ordinary individual must necessarily operate on the basis of rules he has come to accept as valid, sometimes for reasons that he once understood but has since forgotten and sometimes without full understanding. In either case, few parents can be expected to be so well-informed on the theory and data of ethics as to present a case that can withstand the pooled experience of the peer group. A third tactic is to assert the distinctiveness of the young generation and of current conditions, so as to render the experience and judgment of elders irrelevant. A fourth tactic is to attempt to cast the parent in the role of responsible representative for the older generation, which in turn is assigned total moral responsibility for evils in the contemporary society. Finally, the tactic that has normally already been extensively practiced in childhood is to challenge the right of the socializer to correct the youth so long as he is in some respects imperfect himself.

As interpersonal technique, these tactics are used without serious thought to their justification as communication, because they are effective. The fact that none of these devices withstands examination as forms of argument is not likely to be a matter of concern. In the immediate situation the parent typically has the experience of being put down by the youth, although retaining an inner conviction that he cannot formulate adequately to the effect that he is really right and the youth is wrong.

A sharper polarization into roles of defender of traditional values and attacker of values occurs when the issues are more seriously considered. It is from this kind of polarization that the ideologies of angry youthful protest and the image of the unregenerate parent are derived. As the parent allows himself to be placed more and more tenuously in the position of the sole influences between his son or daughter and their entry into a dangerous or evil way of life, he finds himself falling in desperation back into the presentation of absolute rules and the exaggeration of evidence and opinion. Soon he is hopelessly committed to the unqualified defense of rules about which he privately has reservations and to the assertion of authoritative knowledge in areas in which he never previously claimed special competence. Under the general mechanism of polarization discussed in the chapter on role theory, the adolescent is then able to attack values more strongly than his beliefs would warrant, because of their assured defense by the parent. Furthermore, the extreme defenses for values divert attention from the sounder bases for customary values, making an unqualified attack easier than otherwise.

When the socializing relationship is transformed in this manner, the roles are often reconstructed from the point of view of youth as those of suppression and righteous protest. The parent is cast as a representative of a corrupt status quo, protecting it against the threat of improvement. The youth is then a representative of his generation, nobly registering his protest and helping to open the way for the reconstruction of society. Once role conceptions are polarized along this axis, and while adult responses supply congruent gestures, a distinctive pattern of interpretation emerges. In ordinarily interaction there seems to be a general rule accepted, that each participant must take the general trend of the other's behavior into account and thus not overreact to a single offensive or erroneous action.

But under the ethic of conflict, the reasonable behavior of alter can be discounted as dissimulation, and the protestor can seize on the occasional action taken in anger or desperation as indicating the true character of the opponent and use it to the limit in retaliation. When buttressed on one side by a youthful protest group and on the other by a disgusted group of parents, the participants are hopelessly enmeshed in a pattern of interaction that makes almost any response congruent with each one's conception of the other. There can then be nothing but pervasive and continuous conflict, so long as bonds keep parent and youth together.

The nature of the bonds sometimes forestalls developments of this kind. If the bonds are loose enough by mid-adolescence, accommodation is often achieved by the maintenance of separate lives. Even while living at home, adolescents are often granted freedom from accountability and come and go without communications any deeper than those which are customary among casual acquaintances. In other instances, the differential bonding and different attitudes toward conventional values permit one parent to become the confidante and supporter of the youth's questioning of the other parent's values.

Harmony or Conflict. Popular and academic discussions stress the prevalence of tensions between adolescent and parents. The foregoing discussion indicates some deep-seated structural conditions that are conducive to impaired decision making, transformation of disagreement into conflict, and an erosion of bonds. The discussion also underlines some continuing bases for interdependence of which the response bond arising out of acceptance of the adolescent as a unique individual is probably most important. In spite of the disputes over behavior, the family is more likely than the peer group to continue to accept the adolescent as a member when he breaches important group rules. Some of the apparently greater responsiveness to peer-group demands than to family demands derives simply from the fact that the penalties for violating the former are more serious than for deviating from family demands. Although youthful participation in public protest activities is often interpreted as displaced rebellion against parents, the evidence from empirical studies indicates quite the opposite. Activists in organized student protest are drawn disproportionately from families in which parents were permissive, in which parent-youth relations are more positive than average, and in which parents are in sympathy with the protest activities of their offspring.

The variables that determine the direction taken by parent-youth relationships are somewhat different from the parent and the youth sides. From the parent side, a transformation and relaxation of bonds is perhaps most crucial. A lessening of the identification bond and the socialization-task bond frees the parent's identity from constant implication in the behavioral experimentation by the youth. A lessening and transformation of the response bond frees the parent from resentment as the youth increasingly finds his most gratifying interaction with other people.

From the side of youth, the variable is the extent to which he can avoid total absorption in the youth role and youth culture so as to retain the capacity to take the role of parents and to continue to see the norms and values of youth society in the relativistic terms he has learned to apply to adult rules. By its divorcement from the conduct of the larger society, youth culture is enabled to deal in a normative system consisting of absolute rights. In order to account for the failure of other groups to accept the doctrines of absolute rights and the superiority of youthful competence and judgment, youth culture advances unfavorable conceptions of adult competence and motivation. If youth culture is accepted completely by the youth, the disagreements over mutual expectations are translated into irreconcilable conflicts of principle in which the identities of each are at stake. If the individual can participate and yet maintain a somewhat detached perspective on youth culture, disagreement can be handled through normal decision-making procedures without juxtaposing identities.

Return to the Marital Dyad

Many circumstances conspire to prevent the departure of other family members from the home and the restoration of the husband-wife dyad with which married life started. In earlier generations the unmarried daughter might settle down permanently as her mother's companion. Today the extended periods of education often mean long years in which the near-adult or young adult maintains his base in the family home. Frequently one or more of the grandparents has reached a stage so that he can no longer live alone and is brought into the home of his offspring in place of the departed children, and many marital pairs are already broken by death.

When the family does become a dyad again, a somewhat new pattern of relationships must be developed. The system of relationships from the beginning of marriage cannot be restored, since the husband and wife have both changed too greatly. The relationships that evolved with children in the home will not work without change. Task bonds are threatened unless the parents can find gratifying collaborative activity that no longer involves the children. The identification and response bonds which held in common toward the children and which supplied indirect bonds between them are no longer a source of union. Decision making is sometimes impaired when the husband and wife have come to use a third person as a means of reaching group decisions.

At this stage wives are especially likely to undergo identity crises that complicate relations with the husband. The wife may turn to the husband for the response and companionship she received from the children. Although the result may be increased closeness, it may also mean excessive demands on the husband, recapitulating some of the consequences of the earlier attempts to enforce more interaction with the adolescent. The extreme to which adjustment difficulties for the wife may go is indicated by the concentration of cases of involutional melancholia among women between 45 and 55 years of age. Inability to find a new role to replace the child-rearing role leads to a drastic loss of self-esteem, sometimes resulting in mental disorder.[4]

As in other stages, however, to summarize changes at this period as an overall weakening or strengthening of bonds is an oversimplification. Drawing on the research of others and his own interviews with 49 postparental spouses, Deutscher observes,

. . . despite expectations based on both theory and clinical experience, when urban middle-class postparental couples describe their life, the hurdle does not appear to have been insurmountable and the adaptations are seldom pathological.[5]

The phenomenon is rather one of change, but even here the changes may be concentrated in a few roles rather than extended to all aspects of life. One empirical investigation will indicate the kind of findings that are likely to emerge in this respect.

Sussman interviewed one or both members of 57 white married couples between the ages of 45 and 60, whose last living child had married during the preceding year, in order to identify role shifts at the postparental stage. Half or more of the couples reported changes since the last child left home in roles of parent, spouse, user of leisure time, and church member. Couples reported spending more time together and doing more things together, although these readjustments had already been made in cases when children had been away at college. There was frequently an increase in church activity. On the other hand, few couples reported changes in roles of worker, sibling, child of aging parents, aunt or uncle, club or association member, citizen, or friend. Changes were contingent on the extent to which association with offspring was maintained and were most frequent at higher socioeconomic levels.[6]

---

[4] Arnold M. Rose, "A Social-psychological Theory of Neurosis," in Arnold Rose (ed.), *Human Behavior and Social Processes*, Houghton Mifflin, Boston, 1962, pp. 544 ff.; see also Pauline B. Bart, *Depression in Middle-Aged Women: Some Sociocultural Factors*, unpublished doctoral dissertation, University of California, Los Angeles, 1967.

[5] Irwin Deutscher, "Socialization for Postparental Life," in Arnold Rose (ed.), *op cit.*, p. 509.

[6] Marvin B. Sussman, "Intergenerational Family Relationships and Social Role Changes in Middle Age," *Journal of Gerentology*, 15:71–75, January 1960.

Insofar as there have been tasks in whose collaboration the husband and wife could cement a firm bond, absence of interference and competition for time from the children reopens the way to bonding. If coalitions involving the children have impeded decision making or transformed decision processes into conflict, this source of derailment is removed. Lopata has shown from a study of 1000 housewives that many see themselves as constantly rushed during the child-rearing period and look forward to the stage when they will have time for themselves.[7]

The former theme is echoed with a more general reference in Deutscher's conclusion from his own sample of married couples:

This phase of the family cycle is seen by the majority of middle-aged spouses as a time of new freedoms: freedom from the economic responsibilities of children; freedom to be mobile (geographically); freedom from housework and other chores. And, finally, freedom to be one's self for the first time since the children came along. No longer do the parents need to live the self-consciously restricted existence of models for their own children: "We just take life easy now that the children are grown. We even serve dinner right from the stove when we're alone. It's hotter that way, but you just couldn't let down like that when your children are still at home."[8]

In most instances interlocking roles, adjusted communication and response, and symbiotic interdependence provide such firm bonds by this time that the relationship weathers whatever readjustments must be made. The important differences here, however, are between the stabilization of roles into a pattern of dead-level interaction, or even the assimilation of chronic conflict as a regular element of interaction, or into a vitally harmonious exchange. The latter outcome seems to depend particularly on the predominance of response bonds and of task bonds involving collaboration in activities that are intrinsically rather than extrinsically gratifying to the husband and wife.

Summary of Chapters 15 and 16

The fact that the family is organized to provide for sustained interaction between representatives of at least two generations has several consequences, foremost among which is the rooting of family interaction in a perspective of passing time. Each stage in the parent-child cycle involves a distinctive set of prescribed age roles, changes in empathic ability, a revised sex-role identity, and a new stage in identity formation. These changes apply to the adults as well as to the children.

The parent-infant relationship is peculiarly nonmutual, vesting authority in the parent but organizing the relationship exclusively about the in-

---

[7] Helena Znaniecki Lopata, "The Life Cycle of the Social Role of Housewife," *Sociology and Social Research*, 51:5–22, October 1966.
[8] Deutscher, *op. cit.*, p. 523. Quoted by permission of the publisher.

fant's supposed needs. Because the parent does not ascribe a mature identity to the infant, conflict in the strict sense does not occur. Infants are trained to use baby talk and infantile manners that indicate that their ordinary gestures are not to be taken seriously, thus offsetting the tyranny that might result from the urgent priority assigned to an infant's needs. The infant-mother relationship disturbs all other stable relationships in the family. When sex roles in the family are polarized, husband-wife bonds are likely to be weakened by the mother-infant relationship.

The parent-child relationship is often the most mutually bonded of intergenerational relationships, with task bonds in full force and identity bonds developing to full effectiveness in late childhood. The future of the parent-child relationship depends on the development of reciprocated identification-response bonding and the emergence of an adjusted communication and response bond during this stage. These bonds are threatened especially when the dilemma of accepting correction from the parent is not resolved and when the nonmutual features of the relationship destroy spontaneity. Differential bonding according to sex evolves during childhood, both between the parent and child and between siblings. The child is inducted into family decision making as his position shifts from ward to member and as he learns to use coalitions against the unequal power of parents, and he imports into the family interpretations of events acquired in outside associations. Involvement in the child group supplies a new dimension to the child's identity and affords a growing base from which to challenge the authority of parents. Childhood is the period during which activities that began as simply play turn into matters of serious consequence. The prevalence of either harmony or chronic and cumulative conflict in adolescence is partially predetermined during childhood by the extent to which a family role structure is developed in which the child is taken seriously, decisions are made by consensus or by accommodations in which commitment is not withheld, and age-group identities and family identities are reconciled.

During adolescence the outside world becomes the crucial locus of identity, and the family strives to retain a portion of the adolescent's loyalty and time. Adolescence often corresponds to a crucial period of identity crises for the middle-aged parents that greatly complicates their efforts to deal with the adolescent's more socially acknowledged problems. The adolescent's bonding to his parents weakens drastically, without a corresponding reduction in the parents' ties to the adolescent, resulting in a drastic shift of power in decision making in favor of the latter. Financial dependency during extended education generally prevents a complete break, and if response relationships are positive, the family becomes a haven for periodic retreat from the rivalry and tension of the adolescent peer group. The youth's tendency to adopt as his self-conception the person he hopes to become and the parent's tendency to see him still in his childhood image create one of the crucial causes of chronic conflict, which is often fought over the issue of trust. Especially critical are the readjustments in the socialization relationship with continuation of socialization on a limited scale dependent on parents' abandoning the concealment and absolute rules that are a prominent feature of childhood socialization. With support from the peer group, adolescents develop a high level of skill in bargaining, using a sophisticated rhetoric with which few adults can cope. Polarization into roles of defender and attacker of traditional values reaches a peak. Transformation and relaxation of some of the parent's bonds to the child and resistance by the youth against total absorption into youth culture make a combination that facilitates a continuing parent-child relationship beyond adolescence.

After children have left the family circle, a new mode of relationship must be developed between the husband and wife that is unlike the pattern at the start of the marriage. If new collaborative activity that does not involve the children can be developed and if the wife is able to find activities to take the place of her earlier preoccupation with the children, many couples are able to establish a new harmony based on the increased freedom, resources, and privacy of middle age with children no longer in the home.

Transition

The unique composition of the family determines the kinds of individual characteristics and social influences on individuals that are imported into the family. But the community at large is typically divided into units within units, and the family as a unit is also a component of some of the larger units into which the community is divided. Just as the individual is profoundly affected by being a unit within the family, so the family is profoundly shaped by being a unit within some larger organizational unit of society. The two such larger units that most extensively influence the patterns of family organization are kinship groupings and socioeconomic classes. Each nuclear family unit is one building block in the complex edifice of kinship. Socioeconomic classes or strata take family units rather than individuals as their natural units. The effects on families of being the units out of which kinship groupings and social strata are composed is the subject of Part 5.

PART 5

THE FAMILY IN THE COMMUNITY

CHAPTER 17

KINSHIP AND FAMILY INTERACTION

In examining the effects of kinship on family interaction processes, we shall first describe the conjugal family system as it prevails in the United States, next explore the effects of the functions and structure of kin groupings on nuclear family processes, then take up the peculiar relationship of the grandparents to the family unit, and finally consider the surprisingly impervious character of sibling bonds in adulthood.

The Conjugal Family in Modern Society

Ralph Linton supplied an early statement of the difference between a *conjugal* and a *consanguine* principle in kinship organization, with the United States sharply exemplifying the former:

A society may capitalize the sexual attraction between adults and do all it can to give permanence to mated relationships, or it may capitalize the associations formed on an asexual basis during childhood, reinforcing them and continuing them into adult life. Such asexual associations are most readily established between individuals brought up in the same functional family unit, i.e., real or socially designated brothers and sisters. In other words, the association of adults which is the necessary nucleus of any family as a functional unit may be based on either a conjugal or a consanguine relationship. . . .

In societies organized upon the conjugal basis we can picture the authentic functional family as consisting of a nucleus of spouses and their offspring surrounded by a fringe of relatives. In those organized on a consanguine basis we can picture the authentic family as a nucleus of blood relatives surrounded by a fringe of spouses.[1]

Recent usage often employs the more radical term *nuclear family* to identify the favored American unit. The concept of a nuclear family lays greater stress on the boundaries that separate husband, wife, and their children from all other kin. Under extreme versions of this conception, the marital pair prefer to establish their new household a long distance removed from their parents so as to ensure independence. Kinsmen are

[1] Ralph Linton, *The Study of Man*, Appleton-Century-Crofts, New York, 1936, p. 159. Quoted by permission of the publisher.

outsiders in the full sense, and other unrelated nuclear family units are preferred to kin as companions in joint family activities.

The Conjugal System. Patterns within the nuclear unit (mother, father, and children), including many that have been reviewed earlier in this book, often take the form they do because of the nature of relationships in the larger kin groupings. Many of the key features of American family behavior could not be sustained if the conjugal principle were undermined. Although it is often difficult for an investigator to distinguish between essential and accidental association, there is nevertheless a rather well-recognized pattern of family life identified with the conjugal system. William Goode has aptly summarized this pattern, while observing that the source is not strictly empirical observation. Rather,

. . . it is a *theoretical* construction, derived from intuition and observation, in which several crucial variables have been combined to form a hypothetical structural harmony. . . .

As a concept, the conjugal family is also an *ideal* in that when analysts refer to its spread they mean that an increasing number of people view some of its characteristics as *proper* and legitimate, no matter how reality may run counter to the ideal.[2]

Under the conjugal system the nuclear family is an autonomous unit that buttresses its independence and its defense against outsiders by the immediate establishment of an independent household. The family unit offers few services for the larger kin group and receives few services from them. There is relatively little surveillance of the conjugal unit by kinsmen, and the latter have few resources for exercising control over the conjugal group. The married couple tries, when circumstances permit, to maintain a certain impartiality between family lines. If contacts on both sides are kept to a minimum, the embarrassing demands to provide equal time may be avoided.

Although associations with the closest circle of relatives are often warm, they tend to become a form of mildly obligatory ritual whenever the family unit succeeds in building up a rich social life outside the kin group. When kinsmen must compete with friends for limited time, attention is often directed toward spacing visits with relatives as widely as possible without hurting their feelings. Good relatives are sensitive to this problem and try to avoid too frequent or close association with their kin so as not to wear out their welcome.

Any part that parents play in mate selection is at the sufferance of the

---

[2] William J. Goode, *World Revolution and Family Patterns*, Free Press, New York, 1963, p. 7. The following summary of the conjugal family as a theoretical construct relies closely on *ibid.*, pp. 7–10.

young person. Because marriage establishes an independent conjugal unit, it serves the interests of the young couple and not that of their parents or any group of kin. Marital selection is dictated by youthful attraction and youthful values rather than by the fruits of experience with marriage or the requirements of solidarity in a kinship organization. Similarly, family size is dictated by conjugal-family values and conditions. Large families occur in situations such as frontier agriculture where the conjugal unit requires many hands; the small family prevails when freedom to enjoy the resources of an affluent society is enhanced by a short period of child-bearing and childrearing.

Perhaps no observation about the nuclear family appears so frequently in comparative study as the intensity with which emotion is invested in a small number of relationships. Anthropologists note that the dependence of the child on the goodwill of the mother or father promotes intense attachments, causes great anxiety over relations with the parent, and contributes toward a vital ambivalence in parent-child relations. In the ideal-extended-family system several adults share some of the parental responsibilities toward the child, and he can easily avoid the angry parent until the wrath dies down. Similarly, husband-wife relations are more crucial and more precarious. In the ideal extended family, relationships can be partially segmentalized within the family, so that there is less carry-over of sentiment from one activity to another. Thus unsatisfactory sexual relations are less likely to complicate household management, and unsatisfactory response relationships are less likely to contaminate socialization decisions. Finally, disruption of the family by divorce or death is a more traumatic experience that requires greater readjustment in the conjugal system. The removal of one adult from an extended family does not mean the end of the unit when several adults share responsibilities. Parental, economic, and response functions are fairly easily redistributed in the roles of the adults who remain in the family.

Perhaps the main value orientation of the conjugal system can be summed up by saying that the larger kin group is only recognized and justified insofar as it serves the interests of the conjugal unit. Under the contrasting system, the conjugal unit is justified and evaluated largely for its contribution to the larger kin group. Under the conjugal system as it has evolved in the United States, the reversal of value between extended and conjugal units seems to be merely a step toward a shift of focus from the family unit of any kind to the individual. The conjugal unit is more important than the larger kin group only because it is closer to the individual. The conjugal unit is increasingly judged by its services to individual members. One result is that high divorce rates are possible under either conjugal or extended-family systems but for different reasons. Divorce under the extended-family system is justified in order to restore harmony and efficiency to the family group; divorce in the conjugal system severs family ties in the interests of the individual.

How closely practice in American society corresponds to the ideal typical conjugal system is a question to be explored briefly here. But first it is appropriate to ask whether the conjugal system is naturally associated with one kind of society rather than another. The anthropological evidence regarding the variations in kinship systems by type of society is vast and beyond the scope of this discussion. But if we grant that American society exhibits a closer approximation to the conjugal system than most other societies we know about, the immediate question is why this should be so.

Conjugal System and Society. The two major kinds of explanation for the affinity between American society and the conjugal system are cultural and socioeconomic. The first holds that the conjugal system reflects a broad complex of values transmitted as part of the cultural heritage. The second holds that the organization of a society on an industrial base creates a set of conditions that undermine supports for an extended family system and make the conjugal system both more viable for the individual and more functional for the society. The two lines of explanation are not necessarily incompatible, but when combined, one kind of causation is typically regarded as more fundamental than the other.

David and Vera Mace have attempted to sketch a broad contrast between the conception of family organization in the Orient and in the Occident.[3] The Eastern pattern is the patriarchal family, with male dominance and an unchallenged conception of female inferiority, the extended family as the functioning unit, worship of ancestors, and a strictly defined hierarchy based on ascription rather than achievement. Prior to the modern era, a quite similar pattern also prevailed in the West, and its demise can be attributed to industrialization. But for present purposes, the manner in which family patterns are embedded in a larger cultural complex merits special attention.

The Maces describe culture elements of two kinds. First, there is a belief system about the difference between men and women that makes any other than a patriarchal family indefensible. And, second, there is an approach to the organization of society that is simply repeated in the organization of family life.

The inferior position of women rests on an ancient but persisting misconception of the nature of reproduction. The act of impregnation was seen by analogy to planting a seed. A seed requires soil if it is to grow, but the source of life is in the seed rather than the soil. The seed, not the

[3] David Mace and Vera Mace, *Marriage: East and West*, Doubleday, Garden City, N.Y., 1960.

soil, determines what kind of plant will grow; the quality of the soil can determine only whether the plant grows well or poorly. Similarly, man plants the seed of human life in the womb, where it is sustained and nourished and allowed to grow:

But the seed was the man's seed and the child was the man's child. It was his ongoing spirit, his continuing life.

To the Eastern mind, therefore, the difference between the man and the woman was a basic difference, a fundamental difference of function. The woman could never be as important as the man, any more than the soil could be as important as the seed. By her very nature she was secondary, auxiliary.[4]

The contemporary East and West are also seen as differing in their view of how to make society or any of its component groups operate effectively. The Western formula is to grant maximum freedom and self-determination to individuals. Thus the small family, in which no member holds uncontestable authority over others, is a way of maximizing the chance that the family functions harmoniously and to the benefit of its members. The Eastern view holds that hierarchy is essential to prevent chaos and disorder. The majority of people require direction and discipline from a few leaders. Accordingly, several conjugal units are formed into an extended family whose members accept leadership and chastisement from one or two authoritarian elders.[5]

In common with most Occidental scholars the Maces doubt that the cultural determinants of kinship can withstand the change in their economic base. Many Eastern writers are convinced that, although making radical adaptation to industrialization, Oriental family systems will take a different course from the Occidental because of the cultural tradition.

The view that industrialization is the specific circumstance leading to the conjugal family system has been given more weight by sociologists than the cultural hypothesis. Raymond Firth has concisely summarized the main reasons why industrial society is thought to make the conjugal system dominant:

Industrial employment alters the occupational structure, lessens the time spent together by family and kin members, attracts able-bodied men away from their natal homes, loosens the bonds of obligation and control in respect of their elders, gives them a personal cash income which is easily convertible to their own purposes. Able to induce their wives to follow them to their place of employment or to obtain wives away from their home and the conventional local ties, they can form family units of an independent character, and take the responsibility for the support of their own wives and children. Wage-earning opportuni-

[4] *Ibid.*, pp. 30–31. Quoted by permission of the publisher.
[5] *Ibid.*, pp. 52–53.

ties for women, too, may loosen still further the traditional large-scale kin unit bonds. On the other hand, the presentation of a novel, wide range of consumer's goods, including such immaterial goods as new types of recreation and education, offers inducement and occasion for expenditure of a man's and woman's income upon their own family rather than upon their elders and other kin.[6]

In addition to physical mobility, establishment of a money economy, and expanded opportunities in the realm of consumption, Goode enumerates several other important features of industrialization. Opportunities for upward mobility place members of the same kin group at different socioeconomic levels, where differing resources and styles of life make close interaction more difficult. The urban community that grows in response to industrialization develops its own organization to provide police protection, education, money for loans, and other services for which the individual under other circumstances would depend largely on his kin. Industrialization depends on technical efficiency in its functionaries to such a degree that it promotes a general value of achievement. If a man's worth lies in what he can do, his kin are less able either to help or hinder his advancement, and he may wish to prove himself without calling on them for help. Finally, industrialization vastly multiplies the specialization in jobs, reducing the likelihood that a man's kin are in the right position to secure a job for him.[7]

Plausible as the argument may be, the evidence is by no means conclusive that industrial organization could not be altered so as to facilitate a different kind of family structure. The Japanese factory system has been immensely effective as measured by the wealth of the people and its success in competition for international markets. Yet factories have been organized and run according to kinship principles, highest pay going to the elders, nepotism being accepted practice, and major business houses being operated as extended family concerns.[8] Writers who see the emergence of a third world consisting of today's developing nations, insist that neither the American and West European pattern nor the Soviet pattern of development is inevitable.[9] Although the new pattern of development has not been specified, there is a vital faith that it will not repeat the American experience.

[6] Raymond Firth, "Family and Kinship in Industrial Society," *The Sociological Review Monograph No. 8: The Development of Industrial Societies*, October 1964, pp. 74–75. Quoted by permission of the Editor.
[7] Goode, *op. cit.*, pp. 369–370.
[8] James Abegglen, *The Japanese Factory*, Free Press, New York, 1958; Peter F. Drucker, "Baffled Young Men of Japan," *Harper's*, 222:65 ff., January 1961.
[9] See Peter Worsley, *The Third World*, University of Chicago Press, Chicago, 1964; and Irving L. Horowitz, *Three Worlds of Development*, Oxford University Press, New York, 1966.

In a most careful and comprehensive examination of this question, Goode concludes that there is a worldwide shift toward the conjugal system, that industrialization is the major cause, but that a cultural factor must be recognized to account for the speed of family change. Just what specific features of industrialization are crucial is not clear, but that the general impact is to undermine extended forms of family organization gains support from examination of worldwide trends. Goode observes, however, that it is necessary to recognize the independent power of the conjugal ideology, once it is introduced along with industrialization:

Everywhere the ideology of the conjugal family is spreading, even though a majority does not accept it. It appeals to the disadvantaged, to the young, to women, and to the educated. It promises freedom and new alternatives as against the rigidities and controls of traditional systems. It is as effective as the appeal of freedom or land redistribution or an attack on the existing stratification system. It is radical, and is arousing support in many areas where the rate of industrialization is very slight.[10]

Significance of Kinship in the United States. How important is the kinship network to the conjugal family in the United States? Students of family life until recently were inclined to address themselves to the declining importance of kinship, without attempting to say how far this process had gone or how far it might ultimately go. Occasionally a sociologist like Folsom suggested that there were limits: modern man "would probably hate to give up all recognition of his uncles and his cousins and his aunts and the sometimes pleasant customs which go with these relationships, even if they are shown to be quite unnecessary."[11] W. I. Thomas' radical designation of primary-group phenomena in modern society as disfunctional survivals from an earlier pattern of social life gave positive impact to the view that kinship would eventually disappear.[12] But most treatments implied that kinship was of no importance by simply omitting it from the topics examined.

The explicit theory of urban life indicated a general transfer of function from kinship to other social forms. In one of the most widely read statements of this position Louis Wirth observed:

The bonds of kinship, of neighborliness, and the sentiments arising out of living together for generations under a common folk tradition are likely to be

---

[10] Goode, *op. cit.*, p. 369. Quoted by permission of the publisher.
[11] Joseph K. Folsom, *The Family and Democratic Society*, Wiley, New York, 1943, p. 176.
[12] William I. Thomas, "The Persistence of Primary Group Norms in Present-day Society and Their Influence in Our Educational System," in Herbert S. Jennings et al., *Suggestions of Modern Science Concerning Education*, Macmillan, New York, 1917, pp. 159–197.

absent or, at best, relatively weak in an aggregate the members of which have such diverse origins and backgrounds. Under such circumstances competition and formal control mechanisms furnish the substitutes for the bonds of solidarity that are relied upon to hold a folk society together.[13]

In satisfying the needs of the individual, voluntary associations are modern urban society's invention to take the place of kin groups:

Being reduced to a stage of virtual impotence as an individual, the urbanite is bound to exert himself by joining with others of similar interest into organized groups to obtain his ends. This results in the enormous multiplication of voluntary organizations directed toward as great a variety of objectives as there are human needs and interests.[14]

By carrying the logic one step further it might be inferred that there is an inverse relationship between participation in kinship relations and in voluntary associations, with the most urbane populations finding no need for kinship at all.

Sparked by the work of Marvin Sussman,[15] an abundance of evidence has recently been assembled to show that kinship remains a factor in the lives of most American families at all socioeconomic levels and that relations among kin have more than token significance. Hence the idea of an isolated nuclear family as the typical American configuration is no longer defensible. Relations of sentiment, obligation, and support with the larger circle of kin cannot be overlooked as factors shaping interaction within the conjugal unit.

The hypothesis that voluntary associations in some respects replace kinship may be correct from the point of view of society but does not seem to apply to individuals. Those segments of the population who participate most extensively in voluntary associations may also be those who maintain active ties with kin, and those who isolate themselves altogether from their kinsmen also decline to join voluntary associations.[16]

Investigations of different populations in different parts of the United States have shown with amazing consistency that most people maintain some active contacts with their kin and that these relationships are not limited to parent and child; for example, Litvak generalizes from independent studies in Buffalo, Detroit, and Los Angeles that in large urban centers "almost 50 per cent of the middle class individuals saw relatives

[13] Louis Wirth, "Urbanism as a Way of Life," *American Journal of Sociology*, 44:11, July 1938. Quoted by permission of the University of Chicago Press.
[14] *Ibid.*, p. 22. Quoted by permission of the University of Chicago Press.
[15] Marvin B. Sussman, "The Help Pattern in the Middle Class Family," *American Sociological Review*, 18:22–28, February 1953, and several subsequent papers by Sussman.
[16] David L. Sills, "Voluntary Associations: Sociological Aspects," *International Encyclopedia of the Social Sciences*, 1968, vol. 16, p. 373.

once a week or more."[17] That these relationships are not necessarily superficial or expedient is documented by Bell and Boat's San Francisco finding
that approximately 90 percent of their sample named a kinsman as one
of their closest friends.[18] Studies in New Haven, Detroit, and Cleveland
indicate that the majority of families receive and give substantial assistance, both financial and in service, with kinsmen. Although the greatest
proportion of assistance involves the parent-child relationship, the amount
of help among other relatives is substantial, and the possibility of help is
even greater.[19]

The evidence on the bilateral nature of American kinship is likewise
not fully in keeping with the theory of a nuclear family system. Although
support for the bilateral principle is usually conveyed in explicit statements, the kinship ties are maintained principally by women, hence tend
to favor the maternal line. Schneider and Homans, in their analysis of the
terms of address used by 209 Harvard students in connection with their
kin, found that first names were more frequently used for relatives on the
mother's side than on the father's side.[20] First names often indicated a
closer and more personal relationship than the retention of formal kinship
terms of address. Robins and Tomanec report findings regarding closeness
of relationship for a haphazard sample of 140 informants. Closeness was
measured by a composite index including number of avenues used for
communication, performance of services, and fulfillment of kinship obligations. In the three major categories of grandparents, aunts and uncles,
and cousins, there were consistently more close relations in the maternal
compared with the paternal line of descent.[21] Schneider and Cottrell report
a further variation from bilaterality. Men are able to give more information
about father's family and women about mother's family. When informal
contacts are examined, men are impartial as respects their mothers' and
fathers' relatives, but women favor relatives of their mothers.[22]

[17] Eugene Litwak, "The Use of Extended Family Groups in the Achievement of Social
Goals: Some Policy Implications," Social Problems, 7:179, Winter 1960.
[18] Wendell Bell and Marion D. Boat, "Urban Neighborhoods and Informal Social Relations," American Journal of Sociology, 42:396, January 1957.
[19] Marvin B. Sussman and Lee G. Burchinal, "Parental Aid to Married Children: Implications for Family Functioning," Marriage and Family Living, 24:320–332, November
1962. For a comprehensive review of research findings indicating the prevalence of
kinship networks in American society, see Sussman and Burchinal, "Kin Family Networks: Unheralded Structure in Current Conceptualizations of Family Functioning,"
Marriage and Family Living, 24:231–240, August 1962.
[20] David M. Schneider and George C. Homans, "Kinship Terminology and the American Kinship System," American Anthropologist, 57:1199, December 1955.
[21] Lee N. Robins and Miroda Tomanec, "Closeness to Blood Relatives outside the Immediate Family," Marriage and Family Living, 24:340–346, November 1962.
[22] These are preliminary findings reported in private communication from David M.
Schneider. The refined analysis will appear in a forthcoming monograph by Schneider
and Calvert Cottrell.

The large body of accumulating evidence does not undermine the established generalizations about the declining importance of kinship compared with earlier historical periods. Nor does it undermine the general trend suggested by Burgess and Locke when they proposed that the family in Western society has been evolving away from the traditional extended family pattern into a system placing higher value on companionship than on kinship obligation.[23] But the evidence does indicate that kinship remains a significant context for the conjugal family unit and potentially an omnipresent influence on the bonding, decision making, conflict-harmony, and socialization within the smaller unit.

The Distinctive Nature of the Kin Group

For any small group to be a unit or subgroup within some larger grouping, even in a limited sense, is bound to have wide-ranging effects on the small group's inner processes and structure. But the specific nature of these effects depends on the character of the larger grouping. Two aspects of the kin grouping are especially important for our analysis. First, the functions, or the proper sphere of activity, of any larger grouping affects the manner in which it penetrates the boundaries of the component unit. Some aspects of family life are simply "none of the relatives' business!" Other aspects are very much their concern. Second, the nature of the internal organization of the larger grouping determines the manner in which its influence is brought to bear on the component group. The lines of communication and responsibility, the centralization or diffusion of authority, and the degree to which the grouping presents uniform boundaries and a unified image from the perspectives of its various members and subgroups are among the organizational characteristics that make important differences.

Functions of Kinship. The reassignment of functions from kinship to other agencies in society has not proceeded so much by the transfer of whole functions as by the transfer of major responsibility in the case of each function. Hence it is not easy to present a list of functions and say that they constitute the distinctive realm of kinship. Each function of kinship is extensively shared with other agencies in modern society. Leichter and Mitchell's list of five kinship functions can serve to illustrate this point.[24]

The *economic* function is radically eroded from the era in which an extended family might own the land and constitute the unit of production.

[23] Ernest W. Burgess and Harvey J. Locke, *The Family: From Institution to Companionship*, American Book, New York, 1954, pp. 18–31.
[24] Hope J. Leichter and William E. Mitchell, *Kinship and Casework*, Russell Sage, New York, 1967, pp. 22–24.

But property is still transmitted along kinship lines, and the nemesis of nepotism in government employment is often regarded as a virtue and an obligation in private business. The *assistance* function has to do with support in times of crisis or at times of unusual demand, as with the cost of education. Studies of large-scale disasters in American society document that kin expect and are expected to help in serious emergencies.[25] The *social-control* function has declined from the situation in which an individual's relationships with the larger community were almost entirely mediated through his kin group to the present situation in which intervention by kin is generally viewed uneasily. The *social-status* function has moved almost entirely from the larger kinship unit to the conjugal family, except in those instances when a family line has achieved such fame or notoriety that the individual is placed by the community in the larger category. Relatives still play a part in fostering upward mobility or in trying to repair downward mobility, as we shall have occasion to note more fully in Chapter 19. The *religious* function has likewise devolved more exclusively on the conjugal unit, although relatives often intervene to promote religious training for the young child, and major religious ceremonials still call for the active participation of kinsmen.

The foregoing list probably fits traditional kinship systems better than the contemporary pattern. Perhaps only the assistance function stands as one of the major terms in which people express their view of kinship. The body of research we have referred to indicates that people see the kin group as a resource body rather than a connection for permanent economic relations. There are exceptions, most notably in the father-son or brothers business partnership. More generally the kin are people one is anxious to help in need and who can be called on for help, ranging from babysitting to major financial assistance.

There is a second major function of contemporary kinship, omitted from the foregoing list. Contemporary research documents *companionship* as the ideal function of kinship. Intensive questioning of 15 adults between the ages of 50 and 80 in the Kansas City metropolitan area lead Cumming and Schneider to the following conclusion:

We found some reluctance among our respondents to discuss instrumental activities or mutual aid and an eagerness to discuss socio-emotional and ritual activities. In all 15 cases, initial questioning about financial aid among kinsmen elicited the belief that borrowing and lending among kindred was a mistake. Further questioning, however, revealed that such mutual aid had, in fact, taken place recently among 6 of the 15. Even exchange of service is discussed reluc-

[25] See Reuben Hill and Donald A. Hansen, "Families in Disaster," in George W. Baker and Dwight W. Chapman (eds.), *Man and Society in Disaster*, Basic Books, New York, 1962, esp. pp. 200–205.

tantly. Kinship appears to include friendliness, rites of passage, family reunions, and sociability, but ideally it does not include service or financial help, although this may, through bad fortune, be necessary.[26]

Any discussion of kinship function must be qualified by consideration of the general limits within which these functions are to be performed. Earlier we pointed out the importance of the privacy norm with respect to the family. Much of the freedom of expression and exemption from the consequence of one's errors that characterize the family are made possible by the maintenance of a privacy barrier against the outside world. One of the most important differences between contemporary family life and that of an earlier period lies in the placement of this barrier. Under a fully developed extended-family system the barrier surrounds the entire extended family but offers little protection for the separate units that form within the extended group. In modern society the barrier surrounds the nuclear unit and is only slightly more permeable to kinsmen than to other outsiders.

The tendency, therefore, is that the same kind of front is maintained in dealings with kin as with unrelated persons, and the diminution of front must follow the same course of trial and error.

In the case of the newly married, a front is initially erected against those who formerly belonged to the same nuclear unit. The offer of assistance then becomes a delicate matter. Even admission of knowledge that assistance is needed may imply that an improper invasion of privacy has taken place. And because kinship relationships are personal rather than impersonal, the acceptance of aid cannot occur without some more general adjustment in the total relationship. Help from an impersonal source may also be preferred, just because what the kinsmen learns when he penetrates the privacy barrier is likely to become common knowledge in the whole kinship network. In this situation a confusion in the meaning of gestures is most likely to occur. The new barrier seems to be a repudiation of former close relations. The proffer of unsolicited aid looks like willful invasion of the new family domain.

Even the meaning of the companionship function is confounded by the lingering element of obligation. During initial and occasional encounters there must be a lingering question over whether alter is friend to ego because of spontaneous enjoyment or because of dutifulness.

In summary, the two major functions of assistance and companionship are generally accepted in principle and in practice, but the manner in which they are to be carried out and the proper limits on their exercise

[26] Elaine Cumming and David M. Schneider, "Sibling Solidarity: A Property of American Kinship," *American Anthropologist*, 63:501, June 1961. Quoted by permission of the American Anthropological Association and the authors.

are not clearly defined in American culture. Because of the privacy barrier and because of the lack of clear definition, the implementation of these functions is, initially at least, a precarious matter. Behind the apparent uniformity of conception each family must develop a somewhat idiosyncratic pattern in the exercise and acceptance of kinship function.

Structure of the Kin Grouping. Part of the argument over the place of kinship in modern society derives from a misunderstanding about the organizational characteristics of the kin groupings. When sociologists in the first three decades of the twentieth century spoke of the decline of kinship and when Parsons later spoke of the dominance of the nuclear family, their observations conveyed two fairly distinct ideas. It has been customary to read their observations to mean a loss of contact between relatives who are not in the same conjugal unit and among members of the same nuclear unit after completion of its vital phase as a family of orientation. Evidence has been amassed to indicate the falsity of this view, showing that kinship relations remain latent and ready to be reactivated when the occasion is favorable and that the usual conjugal unit does maintain some active kinship relations most of the time.

These early observations, however, have more important reference to the declining functions of kinship and especially to the transformation of the organizational structure of kinship groups. Whatever may have happened to the frequency and stability of contacts among kin, the kin group is seldom an integrated and autonomous unit after the manner of the classic extended family and other kinship units. As a consequence the terms of the relationship between conjugal unit and kin have changed radically. Fundamentally, the kin group has no mechanism for acting as a unit without the voluntary cooperation of its affected members; it has neither a single dominant tradition nor an organizational principle for defining its leadership; and it has no group-based principle for defining membership uniformly from the vantage point of its component members and units.[27]

Two elemental principles of organization are present in any kinship system. First is the overlapping nature of nuclear units. Uncles and nephews belong to a common kinship grouping fundamentally because they are members of two distinct nuclear units having one member in common. The sister of the first is also the mother of the second. This organizing principle creates a congeries of interrelated units capable of almost infinite extension. The organizing and bounding principle is a

[27] Although the analysis does not correspond closely with the formulation by Talcott Parsons, many of the ideas in this section have been borrowed from his two seminal papers: "Age and Sex in the Social Structure of the United States," *American Sociological Review*, 7:604–616, October 1942; "The Social Structure of the Family," in Ruth N. Anshen (ed.), *The Family: Its Function and Destiny*, Harper & Row, New York, 1959, pp. 241–274.

distinction between relatives in nuclear units at various steps removed from ego. There are the one or two units to which he belongs directly. Next there are the units that share a member with ego's unit. Here fall the grandparent-grandchild, aunt or uncle-niece or nephew, sibling's spouse (in-law), and parent-in-law or son- or daughter-in-law relationships. Further removed are those who are linked through a nuclear unit that overlaps their two units. First cousins belong to nuclear groups that do not directly overlap but are tied by the sibling relationship between their respective parents. Similarly, the wife's or husband's brother- or sister-in-law is related in this manner, as are great grandparents and great grandchildren. Still more remote relationships are frequently identified.

Actual closeness does not correspond consistently with degrees of removal, for various reasons that need not be discussed at the moment. But insofar as this principle of organization is important, the arrangement of kin according to degrees of closeness is different for every member of the kin group except unmarried siblings. If the recognized kin group is bounded at any given number of steps removed from ego, no two persons except unmarried siblings have the same kin group.

The other universal organizing principle is that of lineage, which leads to a distinction being made between persons related through common ancestry (cognatic relatives) and persons linked through marriage (affinal relatives). The grandchild and the son-in-law are members of the same nuclear unit and are linked to ego through the daughter, who is also mother and wife respectively. But grandparent and grandchild are of the same lineage and therefore sometimes thought to have the more irrevocable bond of blood; father-in-law to son-in-law is formally more artificial and hence more revocable. Organization according to lineage means a grouping of ancestors and descendents of some specified individual into a common kin group. Any internal arrangement or bounding of kin groupings is different when lineage is the organizing principle from the arrangement according to degree of removal by nuclear unit.

It is plainly impossible for a group to act as such when the membership and hierarchy are different from the point of view of each member. When the kin group is assigned functions that require its actions as a unit, this is only possible when it is assigned a stable point of reference from which to determine membership, closeness, and leadership. One example of such a practice is the designation of the kin group as consisting of those nuclear units which belong to a restricted kind of lineage, such as by counting only the male line of descent and taking the oldest member of the line as the point of reference. By this and similar arrangements the true extended family is created, as a group whose membership is the same from the point of view of each member and can organize itself for group action. In order to maintain such a system, it is essential that one party at the time of marriage leave the kin group to which he has heretofore belonged and join his spouse's group.

Although lineage remains as a background theme in American kinship, there is no single principle of descent that is sufficiently more important than all others to make possible the formation of extended family units. There is sometimes confusion, because many old people do live with their adult children. But there is an essential difference here. Under an extended-family system the newly married pair come to live with the older couple; in contemporary United States the elderly couple typically join the household of the younger couple. The latter cut no other kinship ties in accepting the parents into their household.

When we speak of kin in the contemporary setting, we must therefore abandon the standard sociological concept of a group that acts and generates norms. Instead we must think of a reservoir of persons who can be classified as a grouping because of formal relationships with ego, whether they have significant formal relationships with one another or not. The most important sense of kinship is the reservoir of latent nuclear family units. A second sense is a reservoir of latent individual-to-individual relationships. And a third sense is a network that supplies the basis for a group that can be called on to act collectively under certain special circumstances. These three meanings merit further examination, beginning with the reservoir of latent units.

When a man or woman marries, one nuclear unit replaces another as the principal locus of his family life. His relationship with siblings and parents—the old nuclear family—now takes second place and may become almost totally latent. The most important and most frequent sense in which kinship affects the conjugal family unit is that the former nuclear family is partly or fully reactivated. In a crisis situation the middle-age woman becomes once again mother to her adult daughter, and either maternal or filial obligations take effect. Similarly, the brother-sister relationship for a time transcends or at least moderates the newer nuclear identities of adult family heads. In this respect, one of the most vital aspects of kinship is that the bonds of membership in a common nuclear unit are never completely dissipated when members leave to establish new units.

When the later stages of the old nuclear unit are marked by reasonable harmony and an effective decision-making pattern, the ease with which aid or companionship can be secured by reawakening the latent patterns supplies an excellent resource for the conjugal family unit. Family bonds are strengthened when interpersonal resources are enlarged through the joint family. Association of adult siblings with their families of procreation provides same-sex companionship for adults through the medium of family organization and enlarges the circle of peers at the younger generation through the association of cousins.

Reactivation of another nuclear pattern, however, inevitably demands readjustments in the organization of the principal conjugal unit. Patterns of dominance in any group are likely to be disturbed when an outsider who has an independent relationship with one of the members comes inside the circle of the group and interacts under the observation of other members. When the father's employer visits in the home, the father's deference to his employer may show him in a weaker role than the children otherwise see and encourage them to assert themselves. But there are at least three important protections against this kind of alteration taking effect. First, the involvement of outsiders within the family circle is usually transitory, so that the parent can resume control fairly quickly. Second, there is a special role of guest that tends to neutralize possible effects. The guest normally does not carry the full weight of his work relationship into the employee's household and treats his host with a respect not accorded in the work situation. Furthermore, all guests are treated with a generalized deference that blunts the significance of a particular relationship. Third, the guest does not ordinarily allow himself to become knowingly embroiled in the internal relationships of the family, because his main relationship with the family is segmental and concerns other topics for interaction.[28]

But these considerations play a less important part in mitigating the impact of kinship relations on family dominance. Relatives may be involved longer and repeatedly; the relative is less fully a guest either as members deal with him or as he deals with them. And finally, family affairs are the main concern of relatives. Consequently, the relative in the home often reenacts his part in the earlier conjugal unit and, in so doing, casts the member in a role that is not fully consistent with his role in the host conjugal unit.

The simplest relationship is that in which the dominance that prevailed in the earlier conjugal unit is exhibited. A dominant sibling or parent casts the father or mother in a subordinate or weak role for other family members to see. More complex relationships involve recasting the parent's role qualitatively. Brothers who had developed a role polarization in their family of orientation between the serious, responsible member and the lighthearted clown may unwittingly resume this mode of interaction when the latter is a guest in the former's household. By playing the clown part, the visiting relative highlights and exaggerates the serious or even dreary

---

[28] For an extended examination of the special roles of the guest in the family, see James H. S. Bossard and Eleanor S. Boll, *The Sociology of Child Development*, Harper & Row, New York, 1960, pp. 158–181.

mien of the other, a characteristic which his children may not have fully realized and which they may find unattractive.

On the other hand, a deferential relative or one who plays a less attractive role vis-à-vis the parent enhances the latter's position.

When patterns from the earlier nuclear unit transcend those based on the current unit, they create a division between insider and outsider within the conjugal unit. Undoubtedly much of the basis for hostility toward in-laws in popular humor arises from the threat they pose to the adult member of the conjugal unit who is related by marriage rather than blood. When the brother-sister relationship is strongly reinstated, the sister's husband is in danger of finding himself confronting a coalition in decision-making matters and becoming the guest in his own home. Similarly, reinstatement of the latent mother-son relationship without severe modification leaves the wife in a minority position and threatens to displace important aspects of the relationship with children from her to the grandmother.

If only the principle of overlapping nuclear units is in operation, the tendency is to treat all but the key persons as outsiders in the conjugal unit. The grandmother and grandfather who seek simply to reclaim their son tend to draw him and his resources away from his wife and children. But more commonly the nuclear principle is supplemented by the principle of lineage. Thus the grandparents claim their son and his children as members of their own nuclear unit, leaving the mother as outsider, or the adult brother pre-empts much of the father role in dealing with his sister's children.

Kinship relationships between persons in the closest relationships accordingly usually involve some contest for relative preponderance between old and new nuclear units. The strong American norm against subordinating the conjugal unit to the older nuclear unit leaves two major alternative principles: to merge units into a small replica of the traditional extended family or to establish that the proper role of kin is that of guests in the home. The former adjustment sometimes occurs between units headed by adult siblings, when the crescive bonds among the adults erase the significance of blood versus in-law relationships. Similarly the ties between son-in-law and his wife's parents may become such as to erase the distinction between blood and affinal relationships. The grandparents may then assume special roles as extensions of the conjugal family.

Besides the individualistic value that supports the isolated conjugal unit, the principal obstacle to some kind or degree of merger between units is the threat to relations with the complementary nuclear family unit. The incorporation of one set of grandparents into a merged unit leaves out the other set of grandparents. The essential condition for establishment of an extended family system becomes applicable, that ties with one lineage must be cut or subordinated. Hence merged units are most viable when death, physical separation, lack of siblings, or minimal nuclear ties in one family line obviate the challenge to other ties.

The guest role is more nearly the prevalent conception of the proper relationship, at least in middle-class homes. As guests who are somewhat privileged with respect to the intimacies of family life, however, they are also obligated to help with family chores in a way that would be inappropriate for a guest. Although relatives who carry the privileges of the guest role too far are notorious figures in popular humor, the culture does not yet convey any clear prescriptions for relatives. Hence the range of adjustments is relatively idiosyncratic, from the mutually gratifying and supporting visit to the crisis of preparation for relatives whose visits are much more troublesome than those of ordinary guests.

We have spoken of three senses in which kinship is a significant context for the conjugal family and have discussed the most important sense—as a set of latent nuclear family patterns. In the second sense, as a reservoir for individual-to-individual relationships, kinship provides a supply of potential friendships that can be activated under appropriate circumstances. These relationships apply especially to kinship relationships further removed than those we have discussed. There is, for example, an assumed bond among cousins whenever they happen to cross one another's paths or when they need help, although they may have lived for years without communication. An uncle may fairly be expected to help a nephew secure employment or gain business contacts, although there has been little contact heretofore.

The formal kinship ties are often supplemented by crescive bonds growing out of interaction, especially in the closer relationships with cousins and uncles or aunts. But a distinctive feature of kinship in general is the assumption that individuals who have had no contacts and who have few common interests to provide the basis for the usual bonding process suddenly become intimates when the occasion presents itself. The kinship system provides for instant friendship. The man or woman who visits a distinct place is supposed to look up his relatives there, and they expect to treat him as both honored guest and intimate in the family. The kinship sentiment is prevalent enough so that in a large share of these situations the encounters are anticipated with almost romantic warmth.

The attitude toward these potential kinship relationships is quite varied. The range is from persons who feel personally incomplete if they do not maintain close relationships with a wide group of relatives to those who fear and resist any extension of association from the immediate conjugal unit. But when those relationships are more than transitory, the ambiguity of guest versus family member requires that the special role be evolved with a minimum of cultural guidance.

Finally, a kin group may be activated as a unit under certain circumstances. Because of its membership characteristics and its lack of stabilized organization for action, it must be activated from the perspective of a focal individual or nuclear unit, with a choice of overlapping nuclear units or lineage as the organizing principle. The ceremonial occasions incident to birth, marriage, and death and the other rites of passage, such as christening and graduation, are culturally appropriate occasions for assembling the kin. Each of the ceremonial occasions takes the nuclear unit rather than a single individual as the focal point and consequently brings together nuclear units from both lineages. The assemblage of groups who have nothing in common except their mutual relationship to the focal nuclear unit symbolizes the unity of the latter group and their support of it. The marriage ceremony dramatizes that the new conjugal family embodies not only the private hopes of husband and wife but the expectations of a wide circle of kin and friends. Events in the life of the child provide occasions to celebrate the support of the two lineages united in him. Even the funeral symbolizes the solidarity of the former nuclear unit, since both lines are represented and express their condolence to the survivor in his bereavement.

To some extent these ceremonies as kin gatherings are vestigial. But they do reinforce the bonding of the family unit and stress group support of the socialization objectives of the parents toward the children. And they announce the availability of a group whose members can be called on and which might be activated for aid in misfortune or to celebrate great good fortune. But mostly they provide ritual substance to the romantic image of the conjugal family nestled in a vital and supporting body of kin.

The family reunion or family picnic typically calls up a somewhat different kin grouping. A single lineage usually forms the organizing principle here. Descendents from a single family line are called together, and the focal point is a nuclear unit that has become latent as the adult offspring formed their own families. These affairs are efforts to reanchor the disparate units of the present in the weakened unit of the past. Unless there are unusual advantages of prestige or material gain from identification with a particular family line, these events are prone to become a tissue of raw obligation. Children participate from duty to parents; the affinal adult participates out of obligation to his spouse; the spouse participates and brings the family from loyalty to her parent or aunt.

Like the family reunion, the crisis mobilization of kin depends largely on the activity of one or two relatives in calling the network into operation. Because of the absence of an action structure, the extent to which individuals find themselves supported by a compassionate kin group generally depends less on the goodwill of the kin as individuals and more on the presence of some effective catalysts who have the knack for getting the group into operation.

When the kin group mobilizes, then, it does so with reference to a nuclear unit rather than an individual, except when the individual is no longer in any active nuclear unit. The socially expected mode of operation is in the interest of the unity and success of the focal nuclear unit. But the presence of separate lineages makes kinship a keen instrument for involvement in family decision making and for the exaccerbation of family conflict. It is generally believed that such intervention creates commitment to irreconciled positions on the part of the members of the nuclear unit and makes the attainment of accommodative decisions without identity involvements and conflict more difficult.

Cumming and Schneider have called attention to one further principle of kinship organization that seems to have been imported into American kinship in conformity with a value that is prevalent in American society.[29] In the kinship systems which anthropologists normally identify in primitive societies and which historians report from more developed nations, the more durable bonds link generations by some principle of lineage. But Cumming and Schneider assemble contrasting evidence of collateral solidarity, linking kin of the same generation. Intensive interviews with 15 middle-aged and older adults showed the sibling bond to be next in strength after the parent-to-child bond and well ahead of the child-to-parent and spouse bonds, as measured by self-statements of closeness. Independent confirmation of collateral bonding is secured by determining the proportion of relatives in each category whose names are known to the informant. For example, the names of more than half of their cousins were known by all informants, but only about 70 percent could do as well with great-grandchildren, cousins of grandchildren, great grandparents, and great aunts and uncles. The formal relationships of cousins are no closer, but they involve persons in the same age groups. More restricted interviews with 220 adults between the ages of 50 and 80 confirmed the general importance of collateral relations.

The investigators point out that the generalized age grading of American society penetrates the kinship system and produces this collateral solidarity. In addition, the subjects describe kinship in terms of friendliness and sociability, with services and financial help deemphasized except in emergency. They conclude:

[29] Cumming and Schneider, *op. cit.*, pp. 498–507.

In a society in which industrialization demands a good deal of organic solidarity in the occupational world, but in which freedom of choice is highly valued, it is perhaps not surprising that the less demanding collateral bonds are emphasized, and that, within them, the mutual dependency of mutual aid is ideally absent, and sociability is predominant.[30]

These observations may be applied to our treatment of bonding. Generally identification bonds play a greater part in intergenerational relationships. Through carrying on the family line, descendants supply the opportunity for gain by identification; by providing a prestigeful origin, parents, grandparents, and ancestors generally may serve in this manner. The formal lines of responsibility as expressed in socialization and legally obligatory material support likewise follow the line from parent to child and later from child to parent. The bonds between collateral relatives, on the other hand, have more of the quality we suggested in the expression "instant friendship." Simple and dependable sociability is less confused by preoccupation with responsibility. In the earlier discussion of the nature of sentiment (see Chapter 10) we examined the peculiar mixture of obligation and spontaneity in the family and the manner in which love embodies obligation so as to give it the subjective character of spontaneity. Of these two components, obligation is somewhat more salient in the vertical organization of kinship and spontaneity in its collateral organization. The sentiment attaching to lineage is potentially the more intense, but because it may fail to generate sufficient spontaneity to mask the larger element of obligation, it is often more colored by ambivalence. Because the element of obligation is less and because the individual has less to lose through identification when a collateral's behavior and reputation are troublesome, specific relationships can be activated or remain latent according to desire. This difference will be important when we examine the impact of selected kinship relationships on the conjugal family in greater detail.

Grandparents and the Nuclear Unit

The most generally important kinship relationship affecting processes in the nuclear family unit is the continuing tie of parents to their adult children and the latter's offspring. In the absence of any consensual set of prescriptions, the nature of readjustment in nuclear family roles to accommodate the grandparents varies greatly from instance to instance. For example, a grandparent may preempt the role of a parent, leaving the latter with a less significant role to play, or may provide support so as to strengthen the role played by the parent. Likewise, the bonds between grandparent and parent or between grandparent and grandchild may

[30] *Ibid.*, p. 505. Quoted by permission of the American Anthropological Association and the authors.

compete with other bonds in the family, or they may operate in harmony so as to reinforce other bonds. The aim in this section will be to describe a few of the main contingencies that determine what effect grandparents have on family process.

Reciprocal Bonding. The foundation bonds between grandparents and the nuclear families of their children are the bonds developed during the final stages of interaction in the earlier conjugal family and those which have lasted through the transitions of adolescence. Hence there are highly variable and idiosyncratic ties which cannot be explained on the basis of characteristics of the grandparent situation but which nevertheless may play a most important part in determining how the roles are executed. Harmonious companionships, abject dependencies, deep antipathies continue or erode slowly, still coloring the new relationships. In describing unique features of the grandparent relationships, then, we are describing a superstructure that adjusts to a product of many years of prior interaction in a different kind of situation.

The conjugal-system norm, that nuclear bonds take precedence over all others, has a different meaning for the two generations. For the younger generation it means a gradual reduction in the earlier intense bonds to the family of orientation and their replacement with a new set of intense bonds to the family of procreation. Although there is a qualitative change in the character of the relationships and a new allocation that transfers the individual from the child role to the parent role, there is no net loss. In giving up one set of bonds, the individual becomes rebonded into a new set of relationships.

For the older generation there is no routine replacement. There is no fresh nuclear unit to provide anew the satisfaction they have relinquished. Consequently the ties are not relaxed so spontaneously, and there is considerable impetus to retain a closer bonding than the young adults desire. When only this aspect of the relationship is considered, there is a *less-interest* phenomenon operating to subordinate grandparents to their adult children. The imbalance is particularly likely to revolve about identification and response bonds, for both of which the young adults find increasing replacements in the new family unit.

Replacement of bonds also leads to a tendency to establish roles in the new family unit as a complete system, closed against the grandparents as supernumeraries. They tend to be closed in the same manner in which family relationships are closed against the gardener or housemaid, who have a household task but not a fully social part to play in the family. When the young parents have achieved a reasonable degree of personal independence and self-confidence, the transfer of ties leaves no particular need for the grandparents as a part of the core family structure. Hence their participation in the new family becomes somewhat artificial, so that the standard patterns of interaction are temporarily modified or set aside during the brief periods when grandparents are guests in the home.

Whether this less-interest relationship occurs depends on the independence and self-confidence of the young adults and also on whether the older couple find a unit to which they can transfer identity and response bonds. Sometimes the reactivation of latent conjugal family ties can serve to a degree in this manner. Sisters or brothers occasionally resume closer relationships, along with their spouses, at this stage in life. Other kinship relations or friendships can sometimes become the objects of intensified interest and satisfaction.

The conjugal ideal depicts the older couple as transfering response and identity gratifications in part from the children to each other. Identity bonds can be somewhat satisfied at a distance through the successes of the new family. But the older couple should have achieved sufficiently mature status so that they can take some pride in each other. The response bond is shifted principally to each other at a stage in life when the removal of other responsibilities gives them more time for each other and when the freedom from some of their financial burdens gives them the chance to satisfy some of their lifelong wishes.

There are notable instances in which an intensified response relationship and a companionship arising out of shared activity of a new kind work effectively. There is exhilaration from a newfound freedom to act on mutual impulse, not to have to reconcile the views of four or five persons in order to reach a family decision, even to indulge in sex at odd times without concern for probable invasions of the couple's privacy. But the evidence does not suggest that the conjugal ideal is easily achieved in most families. For example, among the fifteen persons between the ages of 50 and 80 interviewed intensively, Cumming and Schneider report that the spouse bond was little stressed as a source of satisfaction. The parent-child (but not child-parent) and the sibling bonds played a more important part than the spouse bond in these people's accounts of their own relationships.[31]

Although the advantage lies with the young adults so far as response gratifications are concerned, there is customarily some financial advantage in favor of the older generation at first. Once the young adults leave the household and assume responsibility for their own maintenance, expenses for the older generation drop sharply without a corresponding drop in

[31] *Ibid.*, pp. 502–505.

income. The younger generation, however, take on the costs of supporting a family and establishing an independent household at a time when their income is low.

If older parents are tied more strongly to their children, because there has been inadequate replacement of response and identification relationships, the young adults are tied to the older generation because of their needs for material assistance. From outright gifts or loans of money, to the much more common gifts in kind and to services, such as baby sitting, that save money, material aid from parents to adult children is commonplace. If such matters are viewed as bargaining, the older generation reciprocate for the valued gifts of occasional response and opportunity for identification gains by helping the young family materially.

For historical reasons public policy has been greatly concerned with material support for the aging by their adult children. But contemporary research overwhelmingly indicates that the American kinship system is more readily reconciled to material aid from parent to child than in the opposite direction. "Ideally, therefore, financial assistance should go from parents to children, not from children to parents: obligations to parents are met by giving, in turn, to one's own children."[32]

It is perhaps initially surprising that aid from grandparents can be so widespread, in the face of the insistence on maintaining nuclear independence. But several circumstances make it possible for gifts to pass unequally in this direction without implying dependency, although they cannot do so in the opposite direction without invidious meanings. First, gifts can often be proferred to the grandchildren rather than to the parents, so that they do not have the explicit meaning of contributions to the family economy. Thus clothes for the grandchildren, the gift of a trip to summer camp, and similar gifts relieve the parents of demands on their own resources. Yet because society recognizes the special relationship of affect between grandparents and grandchildren, they need not be interpreted in this fashion. There is no comparable way to redefine gifts from young adults to their parents. Second, gifts to the young family are viewed in a future perspective. The young family are on the way up; the gifts they receive now will not have to be repeated in later years and may even be repaid. The implication of failure in case of aid in the other direction is tragic; if the older adults are not self-sufficient by this age, their condition will become worse rather than better in the future. Third, gifts to the young family help them to live better rather than supplying absolute necesssities. Consequently the recipients can be grateful without being demeaned. Furthermore, the gifts in this direction are voluntary and do not impose so

[32] Leichter and Mitchell, *op. cit.*, p. 84.

one-sided a debt as compulsory gifts. The older person who accepts assistance from his offspring may be plagued by the fear that they help him because the law requires it or duty demands it and not because of their love for him. Finally, gifts from the older couple do not represent a competing demand against their other obligations. When young adults contribute to their parents, there is usually an agonizing sense of choice between helping the parents or providing the best for one's children.

Research indicates that a sensitiveness to the amenities of giving without creating embarrassment is not unusual among grandparents. Sussman and Burchinal found this in the case of 97 New Haven couples in relations with their 195 married children:

> After the initial financial gift at marriage few children received money regularly. Financial giving was limited to emergencies, for celebrations such as birthdays or anniversaries or for grandchildren. These patterns permit extension of aid yet prevent usurpation of provider roles in the newly formed child's family.[33]

It should be clear that in this peculiar reciprocity in which the young adults grant the elders a limited amount of response and an opportunity for occasional identity gains without seeking returns in like currency and in which the elders provide material subsidy while scrupulously trying to avoid asking for material reciprocation, there is a delicate balance. So long as the balance is maintained, relations with grandparents strengthen and supplement family roles, alleviate some potential crises, and facilitate family harmony. But imbalance in any direction can complicate decision making and set family identities in conflict-producing opposition. Gross dissatisfaction by the older generation tends to place their offspring in the position of their spokesman within the marital pair and create the presumption that the marital pair are at odds over accepting the older couple. Too great and open dependence on material aid from the older couple or their too great involvement in the response life of the family runs the danger of making outsiders of one or more members of the nuclear family. The maintenance of the delicate balance is, in turn, affected by the extent to which the older generation find substitute objects for response and identification gratifications and the material assets and prospects of both generations.

Socializing Role of the Grandparent. One of the more privileged and sacred relationships in American kinship is the grandparent-grandchild relationship. We have mentioned already that giving gifts to the grandchild is free of any demeaning implications, such as may accompany service to their parents. In a broader sense the entire relationship has the advantage of starting afresh in a way that the grandparent-parent relationship

[33] Sussman and Burchinal, "Parental Aid to Married Children," p. 321.

never can. The special relationship with grandchildren is one of the benefits that comes to the older person through disintegration of the extended family. As a responsible head of the extended family or as a resident member of the same household, the grandparent's relationship with the young child cannot be easily set apart from the whole conduct of family interaction. But as a privileged guest the grandparent can gear his relationship with less attention to the strains between parent and child or within the marital pair.

The point of balance that makes a viable and functional role of the grandparent's socializing activities varies greatly according to the unique family pattern. But imbalance in either direction may undermine the parent role and thereby affect the marital relationship. Just because the grandparent role is somewhat shielded from the whole family operation, it may include excessive indulgence of the children, thereby undermining family order and putting parents in the position of competing unfavorably for the children's affection. Young parents sometimes remark that it takes a day or two to get things back to normal in the home after a visit from grandparents, because the visit has been the occasion for license. The continuing concern of parents not to look bad in the eyes of their own parents may accentuate this tendency when they moderate their own discipline in order to avoid scenes with the children. The grandparent's desire to indulge the grandchildren may be enhanced by the memory of strains in relationships with his own children. By escaping the pervasive responsibilities of parental socialization the grandparent hopes to enjoy the grandchildren in a way that was impossible with his own children.

On the other hand, the search for a new identification bond and for a second chance to do better what he did imperfectly with his own children may lead the grandparent to concern himself so deeply with the behavior of the grandchildren that he infringes on the parental role. The likelihood that a grandparent will try to impose patterns at variance with the goals of the parents is enhanced by intergenerational shifts in standards. The precariousness of the grandmother's position when she claims the authority of superior experience in advising the young parents is indicated by the answer to a question used in Leichter and Mitchell's study of Jewish agency clients in New York:

. . . interviews indicate that frequently relatives give "a lot of advice even though it's not asked for"; kin feel it is their right and duty to offer child-rearing advice so that there is no need to seek advice. Nonetheless, most families indicated that if they were seeking advice they would turn to other sources. The most frequently checked source was books.[34]

[34] Leichter and Mitchell, *op. cit.*, pp. 118–119.

For two important reasons the grandparent is likely to expect too much and be disappointed in his relationship with the grandchildren. First, in the typical situation in which he is not resident in the household, the grandparent has neither the power nor the continuity of socializing contacts to play an effective part in shaping the grandchild as he wishes him to be. And second, the grandchild's reciprocal bondedness to the grandparent is transitory, typically beginning to wane as soon as the child reaches the age when he no longer enjoys being played with. Acceptance of the grandparent's attentions may continue because of gifts and out of an explicit moral obligation. If there are many grandchildren, the grandparent may replace each waning relationship with a new one, in the rare circumstance in which he fails to form deep attachments. But otherwise, for the grandparent who invests very heavily in the grandparent role there is likely to be a recapitulation of the same pains of increasingly unreciprocated bonding he has been through with his own children, but occurring sooner and marked by a greater sense of his own powerlessness.

The Assertion of Lineage. The four grandparents represent four lines of descent that converge on a nuclear family. More than other kin, each grandparent is the specific link to a line of descent. From time to time the grandparent becomes the agent through which the lineal principle of kinship organization is made salient. Insofar as members of the nuclear family think of themselves as a unit in the conveyance of a family tradition, it is the appropriate grandparent who gains in stature and influence by being the most authentic immediate exponent of the tradition.

The conjugal system readily accommodates the awareness of multiple lineages, but its mode of organization is threatened whenever one lineage is recognized over others. This is when the undifferentiated grandparent titles give way to the distinction between mother and mother-in-law. Enough was said earlier about the tensions between lineage and conjugal organizing principles so that elaboration is not required here. In brief, the effects include the strengthening of the bond between the child and one parent at the expense of the bond with the other parent, the establishment of an unbalanced decision-making relationship between the marital pair, and elimination of a viable role for grandparents from the opposite side of the family.

Several investigators report findings that indicate that the mother-daughter bond is the one most likely to persist most strongly. Women tend to be the most active carriers of kinship relations. In spite of the transmission of names through the male line, the wife's involvement with her own mother tends to make that the most important line. What, then, happens to the husband's mother? Leichter and Mitchell's data confirm the view that the greatest amount of interaction takes place with the wife's mother. But when they compare the frequency of conflict with kin, there is an interesting result (see Figure 8). When they count only conflicts that do not lead to conflict between the marital pair, wives most often mention conflicts with their own kin, and husbands most often report conflict with their own kin. This accords with the tendency for each to interact somewhat more with his own kin. But when conflicts that spill over into marital conflict are listed, both husbands and wives report the husband's kin much more frequently. One possible interpretation of this finding is that the husband's mother's efforts to regain equal involvement in her son's family are viewed as improper interference by the dominant alliance of wife and her mother. The son is then lead to take the side of his mother in a dispute with his wife.[35]

Obligation and Ambivalence. Many of the observations concerning the continuing relationship between the grandparent and the newer conjugal unit point toward the mixture of obligation with spontaneity and of explicitly instrumental motives with bonds of sentiment. This feature of kinship relations is not so much different in kind as in degree from relationships within the nuclear unit. As we observed in Chapter 10, a major function of the culturally based sentiments is to subsume obligation and instrumental considerations into a system of motivation experienced as spontaneous and intrinsically gratifying. The view that the family is formed and sustained from the purely personal liking of members for one another is a form of popular ideology and not to be dignified as a serious sociological hypothesis. The persistence of sentiment over the years is very largely dependent on the many facets of interdependence that are institutionalized through the common household and the tasks of family life.

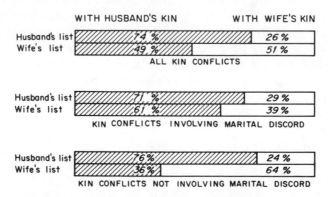

Figure 8. Kin named in conflict situation. (Adapted from Hope J. Leichter and William E. Mitchell, *Kinship and Casework*, Russell Sage, New York, 1967, p. 175.)

[35] *Ibid.*, pp. 174–181.

The intergenerational kinship relationship carries further the pattern that commonly develops between an older adolescent and his parents. The range and intensity of interaction decline, and the foci of interdependence become fewer. Hence there are fewer supports for family sentiment and a greater chance that the sense of sheer obligation and the feeling of instrumental dependency will become salient in all dealings. Whenever this condition prevails, the interactors are sensitized to identity considerations and tend to perceive identities in mutual opposition. This is the prototype situation for high conflict potential, although conflict may be suppressed because of obligation and instrumental considerations.

In the simplest of terms, love is supposed to continue unabated between all members of the nuclear unit and the grandparents, but the social-structural supports for love are weak, and the key response bonds in particular are incompletely reciprocated.

The commonplace of attending to grandparents because of mere duty or because of power or material goods is matched by grandparental grievance over failure by children and grandchildren to give them proper attention. Grandparents are likely to believe in more filial responsibility than their adult children, because standards have changed over time. Likewise, grandparents are unlikely to appreciate the extent to which the cultural shift toward child-centeredness has augmented the demands on young parents' time and money. The greater the degree to which grandparents are insulated from these cultural shifts and the less they are able to establish their own replacement for the earlier conjugal unit, the greater is the tendency toward an aggrieved sense of neglect.

Whenever normative elements become salient in this manner, the familiar tactic of manipulating morality is available for decision making and conflict. Hence there is a frequent pattern in which the grandparent attempts to wield control by making much of the years of sacrifice that went before. It may take the form of loud protestations or of suffering in silence conspicuously. The sensitivity to the sacrificing-mother syndrome and the ambivalence surrounding it are indicated in Leichter and Mitchell's report of their Jewish agency clients' reactions:

Almost half of the clients agreed that *"Parents are entitled to some return for all the sacrifices they have made for their children."* Some reacted strongly against this statement with the idea that assistance to parents was "not because the parents have sacrificed; you don't do it because your parents have sacrificed for you, because they gave birth to you, you do it because they are your parents." Or, as another client said, "The parents putting away money in the bank so they have 'my son, the doctor,' this isn't sacrifice for the child." Many reacted with strong negative feelings against the idea of a sacrificing mother. But even those who reacted against the notion of sacrifice still felt that parents should receive some direct return from their children, "just for the sake of common decency."[36]

The dangers of obligation divorced from sentiment probably contribute to what seems to be the most widely held view of the most satisfactory relationship between grandparents and their children. There should be a secure sense that the young adults are willing and even anxious to help their parents in case of need, but the need should not actually arise.

Collateral Relations: Brothers and Sisters

It was the discovery of the continuing importance of sibling and even cousin relationships, rather than three-generation ties, that posed a challenge to some forms of traditional sociological theory. The picture of a secular society in which each person sought out friends and associates on the basis of common interests or reciprocal usefulness, while rejecting all but the most insistent ties based on tradition, must surely be modified to accommodate the primary importance of siblings and their families and even cousins in voluntary social life.

In extreme cases the collateral bonds are developed to form an organized unit that suggests an embryonic counterpart to the extended family organized according to lineage. Several investigators have reported the existence of cousins' clubs, organized with officers, dues, regular meetings, and group tasks. These clubs may be most characteristic of second-generation immigrant groups. They preserve something of the traditional value placed on kinship by their foreign-born parents. At the same time, the club forms a sort of bulwark to protect the members against the pressures toward traditional patterns from their less acculturated parents.[37] Probably this form of kinship organization is a transitional phenomenon, and the more loosely structured visiting and mutual-aid relations between families linked through kinship are typical.

The concept of *mass society* provides a basis for understanding the importance of collateral kinship bonds. In contrast to the secular society in which all people belong to voluntary associations according to their several interests, voluntary associations are neither easily established or sustained, nor do they provide deep satisfactions for many people in mass society. Furthermore, they do not overcome the tendency for interpersonal relations to be segmentalized, so that interest-group "friends" tend to remain merely interest-group friends. In general, the abundance of quick and casual "friendships" does not easily lead to lasting and intimate friendships.

Building on an earlier nonsegmental sibling relationship or a childhood

---

[36] *Ibid.*, p. 84.
[37] *Ibid.*, p. 157.

cousin relationship may therefore be one of the easiest ways to establish an adult friendship. Furthermore, the member-by-member set of designated kin relationships facilitates involvement of whole families in these friendships. If the parents are brothers, the children are something special to one another as cousins, and the intergenerational linkages of uncle to nephew, aunt to niece, and others have their unique connotations. If the young daughter needs companionship on a family trip, it is less like bringing an outsider into the family if a young cousin is invited to come along.

With the last observation we point to the possibility that the use of kinship relations either for assistance or for friendship lessens the omnipresent anxieties in connection with the exposure and obligation of any new relationship. If a friend of the child, but not a relative, is invited on the trip, what may this mean for obligations to reciprocate, friendship between other members of the family, and exposure of the inner secrets of family life? If the child is a cousin, the assumption of an ongoing relationship obviates the requirement of direct reciprocation. The same kind of reason is frequently given for going to relatives rather than friends when financial or other aid is sought in an emergency. If people are unwilling to go to their relatives, they turn to impersonal agencies and not friends.

It has been easy for students imbued with the liberal American tradition to overlook the strains of an achievement-oriented society and fail to see the advantages of ascriptive relationships. When achievement pervades a society, it contaminates friendship, too. Friendships come more and more to be adjuncts to occupational progress. When a less successful man accepts the friendship of a more successful man, he is in danger in this kind of society of feeling a certain indebtedness to the other for having him as friend.

Kinship relationships do not altogether escape this same contamination. But there is something different about being friends just because you are brothers or cousins, which provides a little more defense against these difficulties than do some of the avenues to achieved friendship. There is something relaxing about a relationship in which you can never be much more than you are, because the others know too much about your past to forget it entirely.

Not only is the status of each party to the relationship ascribed; the bond, too, is ascribed. In a sense one must constantly work at maintaining an achieved relationship. If a visit is not reciprocated in a proper time, there is a suspicion that the friendship has cooled; reactivation of the friendship may then be a delicate matter. Again, kinship does not escape the same meanings, but the ascribed bond persists in some recognized form in case of neglect, and reactivating the association can be taken somewhat more easily in stride.

The advantages of ascriptive bonds have significance for the persistence of sibling ties compared with marital bonds. The marital relationship is achieved. It is understood to be achieved in the first place on the basis of interpersonal compatibility and response. Although marriage is generally viewed as being permanent, interpersonal compatibility of a comprehensive and intimate kind remains the central measure of satisfaction with the relationship. The research of Peter Pineo indicates that older couples are not necessarily dissatisfied that they find less exhilaration in each other's company than they did when younger.[38] But many people may still be unable to adjust the romantic ideal sufficiently. An ascriptive relationship does not evoke these same expectations. It is easier to play down the areas of lesser compatibility and find what is gratifying.

The nature of kinship also makes possible the development of a pattern of interdependence with separateness that is difficult in marriage. If siblings find satisfactions in certain shared activities, it is not essential that they go everywhere together or forever explain why the other is not present. Siblings may set up a common household without affronting each other if they plan to avoid the more intimate kinds of association. Especially in older age, many people find a less intimate and less demanding kind of association, such as commonly develops between siblings, a more satisfactory basis for social life than married life in it is traditional form.

Summary

The American nuclear family is a unit in a conjugal system, under which the larger kin groupings are recognized and justified only when they serve the interests of individual conjugal units. In a conjugal system the individual person is the ultimate value, and conjugal units take priority only because they are closer to the individual. On a worldwide basis the conjugal system appears to be a universal product of industrialization, although resistance offered by a well-elaborated consanguine family ideology slows down the change in many countries. Subordination of kin groups to the consanguine unit does not mean an end to mutual aid and friendship relationships among kin. In American society relationships with kin remain important for most families, membership in voluntary associations supplements rather than supplants participation in kin groupings, and formal bilateralism is belied in practice by the prevalence of somewhat more vital ties to the wife's relatives than to the husband's.

In American society, assistance and companionship are the two major functions of kin groups for the conjugal unit, although the privacy barrier and absence of clearly defined norms make implementation of the former

[38] Peter C. Pineo, "Disenchantment in the Later Years of Marriage," *Marriage and Family Living*, 23:3–11, February 1961.

function precarious. Because the kinship network for each individual (except siblings) is different, functioning kin groups are possible only when either of two organizing principles is recognized. The organizational principle of lineage, which underlies the formation of traditional extended family groupings, is displaced in American society by the principle of proximity based on overlapping nuclear family units. The kin must be understood not as a true sociological group but as a reservoir of latent nuclear units, latent individual-to-individual relationships, and the basis for a group that can be organized to act collectively in certain circumstances. Reactivation of a latent nuclear unit alters the bonds and decision-making structure within the functioning nuclear family and often injects lineage as a conflict-provoking source of cleavage. As a reservoir of individual-to-individual relationships the kinship system supplies instant friendships. Larger kin groupings are ritually mobilized in connection with key events in the nuclear units, symbolizing support for the bondedness of the latter. The intergenerational reservoir of kin is especially important for the assistance function and the intragenerational reservoir of kin for companionship.

When a new conjugal unit is formed, the young adults exchange the former close bonding to their parents for new bonds within the new family, but their parents have no new unit to replace the old. The result is often a struggle to determine the degree of involvement by grandparents in the new family unit. The grandparents' need for response is often met by the establishment of a special grandparent-grandchild relationship, and the new parents gratefully accept financial assistance that is discretely given. The grandparent role is a privileged one, sometimes supportive and sometimes disruptive of the grandchild's relationship with his parents, but its gratifications are fairly short-lived. As the range and intensity of interaction between grandparents and their adult children declines, there are fewer supports for family sentiment, and the sense of a relationship governed by obligation rather than spontaneity leads to ambivalence on both sides. In an achievement-oriented mass society, collateral kin associations, especially in older age, offer the advantages of an ascribed relationship and the possibility of an optimal combination of separateness with interdependence.

CHAPTER 18

SOCIAL STRATIFICATION
AND THE FAMILY

Social stratification is especially important for the family, because the family unit rather than the individual is the unit in the class system and all members are normally assigned the same class position. Social strata are ranked divisions in society. For the present purposes it will be sufficient to start with a rough division into four groupings. The (a) *upper middle* strata include the substantial professionals, major business entrepreneurs, executives, managers, successful agents and sales representatives, and related occupations. The (b) *lower middle* class and the (c) *stable working* class increasingly merge into an undivided continuum, to the extent that W. Lloyd Warner has suggested the term "common man" to designate both.[1] The distinction is often a matter of having one major attribute to set off a group from the laboring class. It may be *head* work rather than *hand* work, it may be the cleanliness of the work, the fact that skills are learned in school rather than on the job or an element of independence based on possession of a scarce skill or minor entrepreneurship.

Recent events have drawn increasing attention to the existence of many family units that do not fall into any of the regular socioeconomic strata, whose position does not incorporate any balanced set of rights and duties with respect to the larger system. The day laborer is hired only when his labor is needed and finds no segment of the system that feels any responsibility toward him beyond the payment of wages for occasional labor. The mother living on aid to dependent children is not involved in any reciprocation of rights and duties that would allow her aid payments to tie her into the larger system in the way that a salary does. These groups constitute the fourth stratum. They are disproportionately made up of minority racial and ethnic families and include a large segment of the "disreputable" and the criminal populations. They include the people whom Warner designated as a *lower lower* class to distinguish them from the poor but stable

---

[1] W. Lloyd Warner, *Democracy in Jonesville: A Study in Quality and Inequality*, Harper & Row, New York, 1949, pp. 22 ff.

upper lower class.[2] They include several of the groups to whom Michael Harrington has called our attention in his exposé of *The Other America*.[3] We call them the (d) *underclass*.

Each stratum is partially an ecological unit, partially a cultural unit, and partially a social unit. By an *ecological* unit is meant that the component families share a common set of resources and life chances, which are relatively impersonal in the manner in which they affect family life. Financial resources, security of employment, and the possibilities for lifetime planning are among the most important resources impersonally affecting family life. By a *cultural* unit is meant a grouping of people who to some degree impose a common way of life on one another. This is accomplished through espousal of particular values, advocacy of certain social norms, and the expression and demand for certain social sentiments. By a *social* unit is meant a collection of families whose relatively unsegmental interaction is principally with one another and who are more likely to establish and recognize unsegmental interpersonal ties within their social stratum than across stratum boundaries. As a consequence of these features of stratification, the typical family patterns in one stratum differ from those in another.

We begin the discussion by outlining certain aspects of the manner in which the nuclear family unit is fitted into the system as a whole and in which family functioning is affected by involvement in a *system* of social stratification. Next we shall examine the variations in family interaction patterns that reflect placement in different class positions. Chapter 19 deals with interclass marriages and the crucial questions of how the class-based family unit can foster intergenerational mobility and how it adjusts to the fact of intergenerational mobility.

The Family in the Stratification System

Involvement of the family in a system of stratification adds another framework from which meanings are attached to individual behavior and family processes. The behavior of the husband and wife in entertaining friends or acquaintances in their home is suffused with possibilities for consolidating, improving, or worsening the social standing of the family. Even if it is not seen in this manner by the husband and wife, it is surely so viewed by some of the invited and the uninvited. The deliberate socialization efforts directed toward children are interpreted by outsiders for what they signify regarding the class of the parents and the future class

[2] Warner and Paul S. Lunt, *The Social Life of a Modern Community*, Yale University Press, New Haven, Conn., 1941, pp. 81 ff.

[3] Michael Harrington, *The Other America: Poverty in the United States*, Macmillan, New York, 1963.

position for which they prepare the children. Implementation of class position becomes one of the general tasks of family operation and a standard for interpreting a wide range of behavior in the family.

Implementation of Class Position. At all levels in society a family tends to be evaluated according to its effectiveness in converting the resources and talents of its members into the highest appropriate position in the system of social stratification. This tendency is expressed through the manner in which the role performance of individual family members is evaluated. The artist who wins respect in his profession because he does not compromise his creativity for commercial gain is disparaged as a husband and father. Although he may be a good companion to his wife and children, he falls short on his most important obligation as a father, to exploit his talents so as to give his children the best possible start in life.

At each social level the manner in which the economic resources of the family are converted into economic consumption has important effects on their social standing. People are expected to live in a neighborhood befitting their resources, to dress appropriately, to drive a car in keeping with their situation. Gross discrepancies between level of consumption and level of resources reflect unfavorably on the family. The wife or children are blamed, or the household head is criticized for caring too little about his family. People are not surprised to see such families break up, since they suspect something is fundamentally wrong with the marriage to account for such strange behavior.

At the higher echelons in society, participation of the family as a unit in various community activities becomes a factor in converting economic standing into social class position. The wife who does not play social companion to her husband in corporation or professional life is downgraded as a wife and mother, regardless of how well she performs the home activities. The wife who participates effectively in neighborhood or community life so as to give the family an excellent reputation is thought to be a fine wife and mother, irrespective of other aspects of her role.

Downward mobility typically creates the suspicion of deficient family functioning. Even poor work performance by the husband is frequently blamed on trouble at home. A fine family is supposed to provide the motivation for the breadwinner to work hard at his job. Strain and conflict in family relationships or a spendthrift wife or children make it difficult for a man to devote himself to his work.

If one of the important tasks of the family unit is to convert the family's resources into appropriately high social standing, the obverse task is to bring the members into full and harmonious membership in the social stratum where they belong. Snobbish isolation reflects on the family as badly as failure to implement an adequate social standing. Similarly, family members are expected to accept membership in a common social stratum as the basis for their lives. The husband, wife, and each of the children may have somewhat separate spheres of activity, reflecting age and sex differences and culturally sanctioned alternatives, so long as all fall within the patterns and groupings of the same class.

Among the more specific tasks of family organization involved in the implementation of class position are three deserving special note. First, kin must be integrated and compartmentalized in relation to family position. The normal kinship network includes some diversity of class position because of vertical mobility within a generation or two. As the new nuclear unit moves toward establishing its class position, it encounters various problems. In bringing together two previously unrelated bodies of kin it has the responsibility for so regulating the relationships between them that class discrepancies among members do not become a serious problem. Within the wife's kin group, for example, the downwardly mobile uncle has already been assigned a unique position that allows him to participate but prevents him from exercising any direction over family affairs. But the patterns of accommodation by which he is accepted into the group while his influence is neutralized are not known to the husband's kin, who may inadvertently break down these accommodations by the manner in which they interact with him.

A second task in the implementation of class position is the development of an appropriate division of labor for both private and public situations. The division of responsibilites between husbands and wives is a popular topic for public banter at all levels in American society. Marked deviation from the stratum norms in this respect is quickly observed and interferes with normal social interchange. A working-class husband, for example, who shares too visibly in the domestic tasks assigned to the wife by the neighborhood threatens the division of responsibilities in other homes, where wives hold him up as an example to their husbands. Again, career mobility often demands some revision in these patterns, and flexibility of the entire family unit is an important consideration in determining whether career advancement can be translated satisfactorily into social mobility.

A third task is the exercise of appropriate control and socialization of children. Children extend the visibility of the family in the neighborhood and naïvely represent to outsiders many characteristics of the family. Conceptions of proper child behavior vary among the strata. There are differences in the extent to which children are allowed to roam freely about the neighborhood, the extent to which they are supposed to be kept under close supervision, the cleanliness and neatness of appearance expected, their mannerliness, and many other features. Through the agency of the children the class system forces the married pair to take notice of neighborhood meanings and standards.

Family Processes. The foregoing discussion indicates that placement in a system of stratification leads to the assignment of certain tasks to the family unit. Like any group tasks, these become bonds when family members combine forces to carry them out. A common concern with the implementation and improvement of class position and a division of labor to promote these ends become important bases for family interdependency. The relatively small amount of downward mobility in American society probably indicates in part how seriously families take these tasks and how effectively they perform them. The task of socializing and sponsoring the child into a station that is comparable to his parents' or slightly better is done so effectively that Bendix and Lipset can explain the rather modest rates of upward mobility on the basis that the sons and daughters of persons at higher levels are too well entrenched to be displaced.[4] The family undoubtedly also provides much of the motivation and responsibility to keep the adult fighting against downward career mobility. The classic case of the career downwardly mobile is unattached older men, although it would be hard at present to estimate accurately to what extent the downward mobility or the unattached status comes first.[5]

The extent to which stratification task bonds are a major force in maintaining family integrity varies according to the stake that family members have in the class system. Although individual families at each class level vary greatly in their preoccupation with stratification tasks, the stake tends to vary by stratum. As the stake varies in degree, the bonding power of stratification task bonds also varies. As the stake varies in kind, the nature of the activities that implement the bond vary. Among the underclass, there is generally little or no stake, and the whole collection of class-related incentives to family stability are at a minimum. Within the stable working class, the common-man class, and the upper middle class the stake is effective. It would be logical to assume that the stake is less as one moves down the ladder of stable strata, but this is not clearly the case. Since most people take as their reference groups and reference individuals those who are fairly close to them, people at all levels in the stable class system tend to be most aware of families a little better off and a little worse off than they. Differences in the quality of the stake and in relative concern with material display or respectability as criteria for distinguishing class positions will be considered in the next section.

---

[4] Seymour M. Lipset and Reinhard Bendix, *Social Mobility in Industrial Society,* University of California Press, Berkeley, 1959, esp. pp. 260 ff.
[5] Donald J. Bogue, *Skid Row in American Cities,* University of Chicago Community and Family Study Center, Chicago, 1963, pp. 315–354.

The most pervasive and immediate effect of the system of stratification on family decision making is to provide an important basis for differential dominance in the family. Because the implementation and advancement of class position are accepted as important family tasks, evidence of unequal contribution to the performance of these tasks affects dominance. A member who enhances family standing by his own achievements or by his association with persons of favored standing gains influence in family decision making thereby.

There are two kinds of role differentiation between the husband and wife that are common consequences of the involvement of the family with stratification. Because the husband is the chief income producer, except in the more emancipated working-class families, the woman's chance to establish her standing and protect her dominance rating in the family is greatest when she becomes a specialist in the art of implementing class position through consumption. By keeping informed about current fashions, by understanding the fine distinctions in taste taken as clues to class identity the wife can make a contribution to class position. If women are more preoccupied with symbols of status than men, it is because the enhancement of standing by occupational effort is less available to them and the role of class-discriminating consumption specialist constitutes the most viable and the most functional complement to the husband's role.

There is also a tendency toward role differentiation based on the fact that the range within which the wife can influence family class position is normally much less than that within which her husband can do so. One adjustment to this difference, as the wife seeks to render her role more viable and establish a basis for offsetting the unequal dominance of her husband, is to use the *irresponsible-critic* role. As we described this pattern in Chapter 9, the person who is practically unable to control family destiny becomes a regular critic of the person who does, reaping the benefit of being right whenever he is shown to be wrong. Because family standing depends mostly on the husband's occupational success, to which the wife can contribute very little, she suffers powerlessness in this crucial area of family life. The wife can then become a prod to her husband, constantly urging him to greater activity and ambition, criticizing him for his lack of initiative, effort, and daring. Thus undermining the husband's claims to role adequacy she weakens his voice in internal family affairs. And by constant reminder of how much more satisfactory the family position might be except for the limitations imposed on her as a woman, she builds up her own claim to dominance.

These two patterns of role differentiation in connection with family decision making are alternative adjustments to the woman's role brought about by anchorage of the family in the class system. They are not, of course, the only possible adjustments. But the former adjustment depends on both reasonably successful occupational performance by the husband and the possession of social skills by the wife. The second adjustment is more likely to be found when either or both of these conditions is lacking.

Although providing bonds, the class system also creates important issues for family conflict. Class membership is normally a salient aspect of individual identity. Hence family decisions and role behaviors that have implications for class position are especially prone to be transformed into conflict. When the family situation is further complicated by inclusion of members with somewhat different class backgrounds or current and future orientations, the stage is set for dissensus over the rules governing interaction. Thus another precipitant of conflict is present.

Finally, it is in the socialization process that the class implementation task finds its strongest expression. Parents, as we have observed (see Chapter 14), are agents of various groups in carrying out their socialization responsibilities. In an important sense they are agents of the class system, and the most crucial imprint they place on the child is his projection into one class or another as he approaches adulthood. The promotion of upward-mobility orientations in the child is so central to the American conception of socialization that we shall consider it separately in Chapter 19. But seldom are the parents of a child who skids downward in the class system viewed as having done a good job of childrearing, and seldom are parents of a child who moves up thought to have done a bad job.

The perspectives of parent and child typically differ with respect to just this aspect of socialization. Parents assign meaning to the child's behavior on the basis of its class signification. Taboo words, taboo gestures, taboo forms of amusement, taboo companions are typically those which signify inappropriate class liaison. Because of his more limited neighborhood perspective, the child cannot begin to understand what the context of stratification means for his future life. Hence the assignment of meaning by parents cannot fail to seem arbitrary, either to be accepted on authority, to be tolerated as a generation peculiarity, or to be resented and resisted. Here is a typical example of the kind of situation in which there may develop role polarization about responsibility for the promotion of a particular set of values (see Chapter 9). Because of the child's resistance and inability to understand the class meanings assigned to his behavior, the parents tend to devote rather more effort to promoting these meanings than their own concern with class would warrant. In marshaling his resistance to intensified parental preoccupation, the child plays a role expressing much more active denial of class consciousness than his associated tastes, ambition, and self-conception reflect.

Stratum Differences in Family Patterns

The most important effect of social stratification is not to undermine the family at one level and strengthen it at another, but to promote a different system of family roles as a consequence of the unique circumstances in each class setting. Roles are different because life situations in different strata make different arrangements functional and viable.[6]

Bonding. The relative importance of different kinds of family bonds appears to vary among social strata. Different bonds mean that different activities and different aspects of family life supply the satisfactions and points of vulnerability for the family unit. For clarity, we shall examine differences that apply to the marital relationship and suffuse the entire family group first, taking up bonding that involves the children later.

If we consider first the relatively impersonal group membership bonds, it is difficult to judge whether family membership and the married condition are more highly valued by one stratum than another. Rates of divorce and desertion are higher at the lower socioeconomic levels,[7] but these differences are probably adequately explained on the basis of the vulnerability of economic and other bonds at the lower-class levels. The median age at first marriage is older at higher socioeconomic levels,[8] but this difference probably reflects extended schooling, delayed economic independence, and parental pressure to achieve personal maturity before marrying rather than any lesser evaluation of marriage at the upper levels. There probably is, however, some difference in the implication of family life for men and women. Marriage in the lower strata is probably more often a way by which the girl can declare her independence and free herself from close surveillance by her parents. There are also fewer acceptable roles for the single young woman in the lower strata, so that marriage

[6] Several comprehensive comparisons among family patterns in different social strata have appeared in print and have been used liberally in preparing the present analysis. One of the first to make class differences a central concern for the sociology of family life was Ruth S. Cavan, in *The American Family*, Crowell, New York, 1953. A brief schematic summary by the present author appeared in Leonard Broom and Philip Selznick, *Sociology*, Harper & Row, New York, 1955, pp. 399–401. A more recent review and bibliography by Ruth Cavan appears in Harold T. Christensen (ed.), *Handbook of Marriage and the Family*, Rand McNally, Chicago, 1964, pp. 535–581. An interesting effort to state some of these differences in terms of Parsonian theory is found in Donald G. McKinley, *Social Class and Family Life*, Free Press, New York, 1964.
[7] William F. Ogburn, "Marital Separations," *American Journal of Sociology*, 49:316–323, January 1944; William J. Goode, "Marital Satisfaction and Instability: A Cross-cultural Class Analysis of Divorce Rates," *International Social Science Journal*, 14:507–526, October 1962.
[8] Paul C. Glick, *American Families*, Wiley, New York, 1957, pp. 115–122; Lee G. Burchinal, "Trends and Prospects for Young Marriages in the United States," *Journal of Marriage and the Family*, 27:243–254, May 1965.

becomes more important as a demonstration of virtue, normality, or personal attractiveness.

Tolerance of divorce and separation has become increasingly widespread at all levels. Broken families and unattached individuals are more in evidence at the lower levels. This fact undoubtedly relaxes the binding pressure of the mores regarding family solidarity. Another circumstance, however, intervenes at the lower middle-class level and to some extent the level of skilled craftsmen. Here are found people who are set apart subculturally from manual and menial service workers and yet lack the income and other resources to set themselves clearly apart from the hand workers by the neighborhoods where they live, the cars they drive, the vacations they take, and other visible evidence of social standing. In later life they may have more assets, but during their childrearing years they have little advantage. One of the responses to this situation is to place greater value on respectability. Joseph Kahl has presented the emphasis on respectability as the central feature of life for this stratum of American society.[9] For those who adopt this emphasis, the moral code against divorce and desertion becomes an especially strong marital bond. Hence it is likely that the mores form a more important part of the total set of bonds here than at either higher or lower socioeconomic levels.

Although the upper middle stratum affords more opportunities for the single woman to lead a full and respected life than at other levels, there is nevertheless a central core of upper middle-class community life that is open only to married couples. The problem is not so much one of formal exclusion—the divorcee or widow is invited to continue attending the church couples' club; it is rather that there is greater emphasis on social and civic participation by married pairs than individuals. By contrast, working-class social life is more extensively separated along sex lines, with the men together and the women together. The single man in a working-class neighborhood is not prevented from joining the married men at a local tavern or other gathering place; in the upper middle-class neighborhood he has difficulty finding a place where men congregate except with their wives. As a means of entry into routine neighborhood social life, marriage has special importance in upper middle-class circles.

The economic bond takes different forms at different levels. The traditional pattern in which the basic economic bond is the division of labor between producer and consumer applies to the upper and lower middle class and some portions of the working class. In a few upper middle-class marriages, the wife is economically independent, and the marriage rests almost entirely on other bonds. But in most instances the wife's earnings

[9] Joseph A. Kahl, *The American Class Structure*, Rinehart, New York, 1953, pp. 202–205.

are supplementary and insufficient for her to live at the level that her husband's earnings permit. Nevertheless, the economic bond operates to make life better for the husband and wife but is not entirely indispensable to either. In the manual stratum, more of the wives work, and many of them earn as much as their husbands. Many of those who do not work have neither skills nor work habits to enable them to be independent. In a substantial number of working-class and lower middle-class families the total financial dependency of the wife is an important marital bond. But for the large number of working-class families in which the wife's earning power equals her husband's, the bond is based on the savings that come from pooling resources and reducing overhead costs by maintaining a single household and from the insurance against total stoppage of income when one or the other is laid off from work for a period of time.

In the group that falls outside the stable system of stratification—the underclass—the traditional dependency is often reversed. Men who are relatively unemployable because of criminal records, lack of skills and education, ill health and personal handicaps, and personal attitudes toward the regimen of work often become dependent on the income of a woman either in formal marriage or some common-law marital relationship. Women are often able to secure menial work on a regular basis, leading to a rather different foundation for the marital relationship than prevails through most of society.

Among the crescive bonds, the binding power of incomplete actions is greatly affected by the time perspective in which the family lives. One of the recurrent observations about class differences deals with this variable. Members of the higher strata tend to organize their lives around longer time perspectives, undertaking plans that carry further into the future than persons of lower socioeconomic status. Living in the present or the immediate future distinguishes much working-class family life. There is less planning ahead for college education for the children and less of a tendency to live economically and save in order to buy a home in a better neighborhood after a few years. Hence there are fewer tangible contracts, investments, and mortgaged properties and fewer intangible hopes and plans that depend on the continued integrity of the family for their realization. In the work world, the typical working man's job contrasts with the profession or business career, with the developmental emphasis in the latter. As the middle-class wife identifies herself with the husband's career, sometimes helping in tangible ways, there is a temporal bond between them that is not available to the working-class pair.

Interlocking roles develop in every relationship. But this kind of growing dependency becomes especially important when opportunities and associations outside the family are limited. This kind of dependency, fairly devoid of joy and other strong positive feelings, is a frequent product of the rather restricted and routinized pattern of working-class and lower middle-class life.

Adjusted communication and response bonds of an intense kind are facilitated where there is an experience of intimacy and shared enthusiasm and disappointment. This kind of crescive bond is facilitated by the emphasis on intimacy and sharing experience found most explicitly in upper middle-class family life. In general the response bonds play a greater part in all relationships in middle-class families. Husband-wife, parent-child, and sibling relationships tend to be judged favorably when they are marked by personal response. It is sometimes believed that the very demand for response, coupled with the strains of involvement in long-range actions that are seldom finished, tends to destroy spontaneity. The response then becomes a sort of empty ritual behavior, contrasted with the more spontaneous and eruptive expressions of affection and anger in working-class homes. This is probably an unjustified belief, based on the superficial and romantic view that middle-class people sometimes have of working-class life, although careful research will be required to ascertain the true situation.

A factor in both the cohesiveness and decision-making patterns of the family is the degree to which an extended family or vital kinship network is in operation to support and control the nuclear unit and to augment the responsibility bond by involving more people in the consequences of family breakup. The traditional view in American sociology has been that in the middle classes, and especially the upper middle class, the isolated nuclear family is the rule, with ties to the kinship network severed because of heightened individualism and the constant orientation to spatial and social mobility required for success in middle-class occupations. In the small upper class, where surplus wealth, family name, and vast property holdings remain the rule, the extended family remains at its strongest. In the stable working class the extended family is preserved as part of the indispensable mutual aid and insurance system required to cope with the exigencies of life without economic surplus. With less concern for vertical mobility and a common tendency for brothers or sisters or even cousins to move their families together from one community to another so as to retain and reinforce the ties of the extended family, much of working-class life is thought to be firmly anchored and sometimes even restricted within the kin network. Among the underclass there may be a significant grandmother element, especially in fatherless families, or an occasional freeloading brother-in-law. But generally the kinship network as a whole is weak and performs no important support or control function for the nuclear family at this level. Only the mother-daughter tie persists in a substantial proportion of instances to provide the only dependable foundation for the next generation's nuclear family.

Recent discussions and evidence have challenged parts of this picture, however. The lack of generally effective kinship networks among the underclass and the predominance of extended families among the upper class remain relatively unchallenged, but there are reevaluations of the middle-class and working-class patterns. Recent research shows far more continuing kin relationships and far more support in emergencies among middle-class families than anticipated and far more isolated nuclear units among the stable working class.[10] William Goode has offered a tentative conclusion on the basis of worldwide data, negating the association of isolated nuclear units with middle-class status:

Whatever the complexities of the data when we finally know them, it is at least empirically obvious that the truncated or nuclear family—often without a male head—is more common towards the *bottom* of the social pyramid than toward the *top*. This is most strikingly the situation in the Carribean nations, where at least one element in the high illegitimacy rates is the lack of extended family controls. Although the nuclear family is sometimes thought of as harmonious adaptation to the needs of the industrial system, it is actually found in the stratum where the individual's family has the least to gain from exchanges of rights and obligations with his own kin. By contrast, toward the upper strata, kin networks can be kept alive because each family within the network has *resources* with which to exchange with the others."[11]

The overestimation of extended families in the working class probably resulted from a long-standing confusion in studies of American stratification between those patterns which reflect the recent ethnic origins of many members in the lower strata and those patterns which relate to stratification by itself. The most conspicuous and most studied components of the American working class during the period before the Second World War were the homogenous immigrant communities of Italians, Poles, Irish, Russian and Polish Jews, and other settlers who brought with them a strong kinship tradition and whose kinship supports and controls in the

[10] Marvin B. Sussman, "The Help Pattern in the Middle Class Family," *American Sociological Review*, 18:22–27, February 1953, Morris Axelrod, "Urban Structure and Social Participation," *American Sociological Review*, 21:13–18, February 1956; Scott Greer, "Urbanism Reconsidered: A Comparative Study of Local Areas in a Metropolis, *American Sociological Review*, 21:19–24, February 1956; Wendell Bell and Marion D. Boat, "Urban Neighborhoods and Informal Social Relations," *American Journal of Sociology*, 62:391–398, January 1957; Marvin B. Sussman and Lee Burchinal, "Kin Family Network: Unheralded Structure in Current Conceptualizations of Family Functioning," *Marriage and Family Living*, 24:231–240, August 1962. See, however, Floyd Dotson, "Patterns of Voluntary Association among Urban Working-class Families, *American Sociological Review*, 16:687–693, October 1951.
[11] William J. Goode, *Family and Mobility*, A Report to the Institute of Life Insurance, 1964, p. 58.

United States were temporarily intensified because of their isolation in a strange society. Similar patterns of kinship domination over the nuclear family probably do not apply to the indigenous working class and will probably apply less and less consistently to the descendents of the immigrant generations.

At least one distinctive aspect of middle-class kinship patterns has also contributed to underestimating the importance of kinship. A vital kinship network has often been equated with occupancy of a common household, and the traditional concept of the extended family is viewed in this way. Approximation to the extended family pattern, with two or more nuclear units establishing a common household, is probably most likely to be found in working-class communities, where the financial saving and the limited radius of normal travel and communication make it an asset. But among the middle classes the maintenance of separate households is more often regarded as a precondition for the establishment of supportive and harmonious kin relationships, in which interpersonal response is unhampered by the necessary accommodations to common living arrangements. It has become increasingly clear that the strong norm against the common household does not preclude a strong sense of involvement in kinship.

Decision Making. Two contradictory themes have long coexisted in sociological discussions of decision-making differences between middle-class and working-class families. On the one hand, there have been analyses that point to the more equalitarian and democratic values of the middle classes, contrasted to more traditional and authoritarian viewpoints in working-class families. A wide range of studies, not only of family life but of political attitudes and attitudes toward civil liberties and issues of war and peace, confirm that there is more support for the resolution of disagreement by the exercise of naked authority or force and less patience with negotiated settlements or continued tolerance of divergent opinions among working-class people.[12] The emphasis on self-discovery and self-expression in children was for long almost a monopoly of middle-class families. On the other hand, Arnold Green and other writers have asserted that the typical middle-class home is oppressive and smothering, especially toward the children.[13] Neuroses have been traced to the lack of genuine freedom in the middle-class home, middle-class women have been pictured as the victims of a personally degrading dependency, and low rates of middle-class delinquency.have been attributed to tighter controls over children in these homes.

[12] Samuel A. Stouffer, *Communism, Conformity, and Civil Liberties,* Wiley, New York, 1955; Seymour M. Lipset, *Political Man,* Doubleday, New York, 1960.
[13] Arnold Green, "The Middle Class Male Child and Neurosis," *American Sociological Review,* 11:31–41, February 1946.

Empirical studies at our disposal generally support the former assumption and fail to confirm the latter. Indications of strain from the conditions of middle-class life or the supposedly smothering nature of family relationships seem harder to find in middle-class children and adults than among working-class people. And the search for disproportionate evidence of adolescent rebellion against their parents has been generally fruitless.[14] Nevertheless, the class differences here may be more complex than a simple choice between the foregoing alternative conclusions.

Working-class and middle-class attitudes toward authority incorporate different views of the legitimacy of authority and the means by which it should be implemented. The genuineness of authority in middle-class homes is measured by the spontaneity of compliance. If authority has to be backed up with coercion, punishment, or physical force, it is felt to be an unfavorable reflection on the person exercising authority. The measure of genuine and capable authority is found in the recognition and willing acceptance of authority by those under it. The use of openly coercive and punitive methods is more generally accepted as an integral feature of authority among working-class people.[15] In the more extreme cases the working-class father administers occasional punishments in the absence of serious wrongdoing as a way of reminding the child, and even his wife, of his authority; the middle-class parent is reassured that his authority is secure only when an extended period of time has elapsed in which neither threats nor punishment had to be used.

These observations do not apply exclusively to the father-child relationships but describe also the manner in which the mother conceives of authority over the children and the husband's understanding of whatever authority he believes he holds over his wife. From the middle-class point of view many working-class husbands deal with their wives in gross and impersonal ways. A tactic for the enforcement of authority over the wife, such as not speaking for several days or withholding household allowances, is not uncommon.

These differences in the conception and implementation of authority may mask a similarity in the extent to which authority is assumed and effectively exercised over both the wife and children. Yet there is also a more explicit value of equalitarianism in all the pair relationships in the middle-class family that discountenances the open admission of authoritarianism. The difficult question to answer is whether the explicit emphasis

---

[14] David Gottlieb and Charles Ramsey, *The American Adolescent,* Dorsey, Homewood, Ill., 1964, pp. 80–94; Glen H. Elder, "Parental Power Legitimation and its Effect on the Adolescent," *Sociometry,* 26:50–65, March 1963.

[15] Robert R. Sears, Eleanor E. Maccoby, and Harry Levin, *Patterns of Child Rearing,* Harper & Row, New York, 1957, pp. 429–432.

on equalitarianism actually makes middle-class family relationships more equalitarian or whether it serves merely to undermine authority as a basis for dominance without supplying other procedures for reaching orderly decisions. The community holds parents as much or more responsible for the conduct of their children in middle-class families as in working-class neighborhoods. A wife whose obstinacy interferes with her husband's advancement in his career is not viewed charitably in middle-class circles. Perhaps the only reasonable conclusion at the present time is that, when there are two rather different ways of conceiving authority, it does not make very much sense to compare degrees of authority.

When we turn to the informal determinants of dominance, there are clearly some differences in the resources available for establishing dominance within different strata. In those working-class homes in which traditional peasant and rural beliefs in absolute male authority are not strong and the wife is able to work and her earning power equals her husband's, supports for husband dominance are at a minimum. With social activities extensively segregated along sex lines, the less-interest principal does not favor the male. Indeed, since the wife typically combines household skills with work skills, although her husband has only the latter, a certain amount of female dominance is facilitated.

Because of the instrumentally weak position of the husband from a bargaining point of view, there frequently develops a pattern marked by sporadic dominance followed by withdrawal, emphasis on freedom from responsibility rather than the ability to control and direct as evidence of masculine dominance, and the cultivation of incompetencies as evidence of superiority. Effective control and direction of the household is maintained by the women, except for the occasional disruptions caused by the husband's demands. The woman learns from the local women's subculture and from personal experience that these peroidic demands can be accepted without impairment of her effective and continuing control. Not being able to do feminine things becomes the husband's substitute for wielding real power over his wife and children. And freedom to come and go as he pleases, to accept responsibilities in the home only when it pleases him to do so, and never on a routine and accountable basis, is the preferred form of substitute dominance.

There may be something of a continuum from the ethnic peasant and rural kind of working-class family to the underclass, with the proletarian family falling between. Where ethnic peasant or rural patterns still govern family life, the wife's belief in male superiority inhibits her self-assertion, and she may never find a satisfactory work life outside the home. Hence, a combination of male dominance and male irresponsibility is possible. Among the underclass, men are almost without leverage to overcome entirely feminine domination, except as they can supply deeply needed personal response and validate the feminine value of sexual attractiveness. The proletarian family corresponds most nearly to the pattern of balance between the wife's greater control and the husband's greater freedom that we have described.

In the minority of middle-class families in which the wife has a profession or other career that matches her husband's and in which she has not irreparably damaged her career by withdrawing for an extended period of childbearing and childrearing there can be a genuine balance of bargaining resources between the husband and wife. Because incomes are not so close to the subsistence minimum, the husband's deficient household skills do not place him at a disadvantage. But in other middle-class homes the crucial importance of the husband's career, coupled with the centrality of economic success to the organization of life, gives the husband more of the bargaining assets. Although the scope of her life is much wider and the areas of freedom and equality are many, the ultimate submission of the middle-class wife to her husband may be greater than in the typical proletarian working-class family.

Children in the family reflect the general relationship between the parents. Evidence from several sources suggests that the father is likely to share socialization responsibilities with the mother more commonly in middle-class than working-class families.[16] The result is that father's direct control over children is more common in middle-class than working-class homes. In general, communication patterns in middle-class families are less frequently characterized by intermediaries who then acquire unofficial dominance because of their centrality. The father communicates directly with the children, rather than conferring indirectly through the mother. There is less tendency to communicate with younger children through the oldest child. The children are treated more equally, and the centrality of a single child is not marked. In working-class homes it is more common to establish the eldest child, or the eldest daughter, as the intermediary between the parents and children, with the result being a considerable degree of dominance by the one child.

Children in middle-class homes enter more fully into the decision-making process, especially in matters of general family concern. The freer use of physical punishment and the enforcement of inflexible and undiscussable rules give the appearance of greater control by working-class

[16] The class relationship may be less clear than this comment suggests. See Rachael A. Elder, "Traditional and Developmental Conceptions of Fatherhood," *Marriage and Family Living,* 11:98–101, Summer 1949; Annabelle B. Motz, "Conceptions of Marital Roles by Status Groups," *Marriage and Family Living,* 12:136, 162, Fall 1950. On the role separation at the poverty level, see Lee Rainwater, *And the Poor Get Children,* Quadrangle, Chicago, 1960, pp. 61–81.

parents over their children. Middle-class parents, however, receive more expert help in devising methods of controlling children through manipulation and are helped by the greater privacy and control over the child's environment that they command. Thus although middle-class children have more of a say in general family decisions, in matters of personal behavior they are probably subject to a closer yet less conspicuous control than working-class children.

As the children become older and approach adolescence, the class difference in instrumental bonds becomes more salient, with the result that subordination to parents continues longer for middle-class children. The requirement of parental help in acquiring higher education, in supplying financial backing for business ventures, and in personal sponsorship keeps the middle-class child under an ultimate control that is lacking to the working-class parent who is unable to provide services of this kind for his child.

Conflict. We have already called attention to the class difference in the acceptance of open conflict and physical violence in family relationships and noted that we cannot conclude that there is consequently any less conflict in middle-class families. The hint of a difference in the way conflict and harmony are experienced is gleaned from the responses of a nationwide sample of Americans to two questions regarding marital happiness. When asked if they ever felt inadequate in their marriages, only 33 percent of college-educated persons said they never felt inadequate, compared with 53 percent of the grade-school-educated persons. When asked to rate their marriages, however, 69 percent of college-educated subjects indicated they were very happy, compared with only 38 percent of grade-school-educated persons.[17] The middle class expressed more feelings of inadequacy in marriage and yet experienced more happiness in marriage. If the bonds of marriage in the middle classes are more intimate and involve more personal response and if there is greater investment of sentiment, then we should expect both conflict of the kind that leads the individual to question his own self-adequacy and, contrastingly, great joy in moments of vital harmony.

Descriptive and analytic studies of the conflict process in different class settings are almost altogether lacking. Hence no more than a brief set of speculative suggestions is justified. The initiation of conflict reflects those areas of interaction with which family members are most ego-involved and which family interaction is most likely to undermine. Since people in the higher strata are more deeply involved in the larger community and have their identities more firmly anchored in community standing, it is plausible

[17] Gerald Gurin, Joseph Veroff, and Sheila Field, *Americans View Their Mental Health,* Basic Books, New York, 1960, p. 105.

that disagreements in this area are more likely to be translated into conflict. At the lower levels, identities are anchored more firmly in interpersonal relations of restricted and situational scope, and conflicts are more likely to develop out of contests of will.[18] The greater concern over sexrole differentiation among working-class people means that challenges to sex identity are also a more common occasion for conflict among workingclass than middle-class people. Similarly, identification combined with the class emphasis on respectability means that deviations from moral and respectability norms by any family member are more fraught with conflict potential in lower middle-class and sometimes upper working-class families.

The tactics and strategy of conflict vary among the strata, with more sophisticated, better-guarded, and more disguised and subtle patterns prevailing at higher levels. A more elaborate set of rules distinguishing between proprieties and improprieties in the conduct of conflict causes more frequent suppression of potential conflict until a morally suitable occasion arises, more disguised attacks rather than open hostility, more manipulation of morality as a strategy of conflict, and more use of the private barb in the presence of outsiders as a means of protecting against retaliation.

The attitudes toward conflict and the many more ways in which the individual can expose himself to retaliation among the higher strata militate against the all-out sustained-conflict episode that is more common at lower levels. Instead, middle-class conflict is likely to consist of sporadic but connected attacks and exchanges separated by intervals of recessed conflict marked by preparation for the next exchange. The typically busy life of the upper middle-class person means that other matters of pressing importance often intervene during one of these recesses, so that the conflict is not continued. Hence interruption is an important source of accommodation in the conflict of middle-class families. This is as likely to be the case for parent-child conflict as for marital conflict, since the family recognizes the priority of outside demands on the child and often will not allow intrafamily matters to interfere with even the child's integration into his neighborhood play groups.

Deliberate accommodations vary among social strata. Among the lower strata the more passive forms of accommodation, namely, avoidance and submission, are much more common than at higher levels. It is common practice to walk away from a conflict, to leave the house and go next door or to the neighborhood tavern, in the case of the woman and man respectively. Or the conflict may be continued until one party effectively coerces

[18] Manford H. Kuhn, "Self-attitudes by Age, Sex, and Professional Training," *Sociological Quarterly*, 9:39–55, January 1960.

the other into submission. Deliberate accommodations are of a more active nature among the middle class, where the strategies of compromise and conciliation through bargaining with identities are more skillfully used. Although open bargaining in decision making is probably more widely practiced among the lower strata and regarded as in somewhat bad taste at higher levels, bargaining with identities as an accommodation technique is more distinctively middle class. The parent offers the child something; he praises him in some way so as to invite a softening of the child's attacks on him.

The linking of conflict episodes into chronic or cumulative patterns depends in part on time orientations. The greater here-and-now orientation of working strata suggests greater tolerance for chronic conflict and a lesser tendency to translate repeated conflict into a cumulative development. The stronger futuristic orientation of the higher strata suggests a greater tendency for successive conflict to be directional, either toward resolution and removal of the recurring conflict theme or toward cumulation with resulting erosion of family bonds. This conclusion appears not to accord with the evidence of greater family disorganization at lower socioeconomic levels. But the latter may be less a consequence of conflict patterns than of the weaker and less diversified set of bonds available to families in the lower strata compared with middle-class families.

Socialization. Much has already been said about the nature of the family relationships that shape the socialization experience in our review of bonding, dominance, and patterns of conflict. There are also differences in the manner in which parents conceive of the socialization endeavor, the extent of their responsibility in it, and the sources from which they seek help and guidance. If there is always a mixture between custodial and socializing emphases, the part played by socializing themes increases toward the upper middle stratum and the part played by custodial views increases toward the working classes. The view that the personality and the capabilities of the child can be shaped by conscientious and intelligent socialization activities is more widely and deeply held in the higher strata. The view that a child will grow up to be what he is destined to be and that parents can do relatively little to shape him in one way or another finds more support in working-class families. Hence the whole relationship with the child in middle-class families is governed by more deliberation, concern with possible long-range consequences of parental behavior, and suppression of parental impulse in dealing with the child. In the least socialization-oriented families it is understood that children may get into trouble, fall in with bad companions, become lazy because of insufficient prodding, and experience other exigencies of this kind. The working-class parent is typically concerned with keeping the child out of trouble and warding off laziness and often sees these as his primary tasks. Just because of this custodial emphasis, parental responsibilities toward the child tend to be defined negatively, as preventing and punishing. By contrast, middle-class childrearing exhibits much more encouragement, stimulation, and efforts to lure or prod the child into novel forms of behavior.[19] The preponderantly negative view of childrearing that is so prevalent among working-class families appears to smack of authoritarianism when seen through middle-class eyes. But the limited conception of childrearing as primarily a custodial responsibility and the lack of a conception that parents mold their children by their behavior leave the parent with principally negative and restrictive duties toward the child. This stratum difference does not preclude companionable activity between the parent and child, but playing and working together are less likely to be viewed as a phase of socialization in working-class neighborhoods. The negative character of childrearing also does not necessarily mean more friction and conflict between the parent and child. When asked about parental responsibilities, working-class children reply in much the same terms as their parents.[20] Although sporadic conflicts are a normal part of family life in response to many of the parental restrictions, a common understanding of the rules of parent-child relationships and the rather simple and unambiguous view of what parents are supposed to be doing lessen the probability that such episodes cumulate into full-scale confrontations.

Associated with these differences is the tendency for middle-class parents to look toward experts to guide their childrearing, but working-class parents rely more on folk wisdom and traditional formulas.[21] So long as external conditions do not change radically and thereby make traditional procedures entirely ineffectual, the advantages of a stable and consistent relationship attach to this approach. Furthermore, there is less difficulty in allowing grandparents and other kin and even neighbors to share in the childrearing responsibilities as needed. When the social setting changes radically, however, and the children are exposed to contradictory normative systems, the stage is set for a destructive and cumulative kind of parent-child conflict and rapid loss of parental control. The inflexibility of folk wisdom and the traditional approach is their greatest liability.

[19] Murray A. Straus, "Communication, Creativity, and Problem-solving Ability of Middle- and Working-class Families in Three Societies," *American Journal of Sociology*, 73:417–430, January 1968.

[20] Deborah I. Offenbacher, "Cultures in Conflict: Home and School as Seen through the Eyes of Lower-class Students," *The Urban Review*, 2:2–8, May 1968.

[21] Martha S. White, "Social Class, Child Rearing Practices, and Child Behavior," *American Sociological Review*, 22:704–712, December 1957.

This has been the pattern of second-generation disorganization and delinquency among peasant and working-class migrant families to the United States during the early part of the present century[22] and is reflected in the alarm of many working-class families during the transformations of the 1960s.

The view that parents can shape their children is also linked to an overwhelming middle-class tendency to project their own ambitions onto their children and attempt to relive their own lives through the children. There is a dynamic and persistent tension in typical middle-class childrearing between commitment to an explicit philosophy of encouraging independence and creative resourcefulness in the child and the tendency for the parent to realize his own ambitions through the child. Even when the latter tendencies are not oppressive by absolute standards, they are often made so by their incompatibility with the explicit values taught to the child. Taught to believe that their parents owe them discretionary freedom, they have more basis than working-class children to see parental efforts to shape them as a violation of the legitimate terms of parent-child relations.

Another difference between middle-class and working-class childrearing that has been noted frequently is the concern of working-class parents for behavior and the concern of middle-class parents for character or personality.[23] In oversimplified terms, motives for action are unimportant if the working-class child does the right things and stays out of trouble, but correct behavior in the middle-class child is less important in the short run than having the right motives. These perspectives relate to the exercise of discretion and probably parallel the kinds of tasks available at different locations of the occupational scale. Labor, menial service, and minor clerical tasks require that the worker follow directions and exercise minimal discretion. The consistency of his behavior from one situation to the next is not of great importance so long as he does what is demanded in the situation. Professional, entrepreneurial, and managerial tasks, however, require discretion in coping independently with novel situations as they arise. Since the exact behavior cannot be specified in advance, it is more important that the individual have the right values and broad understandings and capabilities. Middle-class people tend to believe more strongly than working-class people in a real inner self that is not necessarily revealed in every action. This inner self is more real and more important and

[22] See Pauline V. Young, *Pilgrims of Russiantown*, University of Chicago Press, Chicago, 1932; Robert E. Park and Herbert Miller, *Old World Traits Transplanted*, Harper & Row, New York, 1921.

[23] Melvin L. Kohn, "Social Class and Parental Values," *American Journal of Sociology*, 64:337–351, January 1959; Daniel R. Miller and Guy E. Swanson, *The Changing American Parent*, Wiley, New York, 1958, pp. 30–58.

is the primary concern of the middle-class parent in rearing his children. The learning required of the child in the middle class is consequently more complex and requires a richer communication between parent and child. And the possibilities that successful socialization may lead to innovations in behavior on the part of the child are greater.

The concern with visible behavior is frequently enhanced in working-class families by another circumstance. Josephine Klein points to the problem encountered by traditional working-class parents in England because of the heterogenity of many neighborhoods in which working-class people live. Middle-class neighborhoods are likely to be more homogeneous with respect to external standards of behavior, and such deviance as there is, is better concealed. In working-class neighborhoods the distinction between the "roughs" and the "respectables," living side by side, is frequently a central preoccupation of social life. Because of the family identity, clear manifestation that the child is one of the respectables takes on a great deal of importance. Occasional coarse behavior or minor delinquency can be handled in the middle-class neighborhood where socioeconomic attributes conspicuously set families apart from those beneath them. But without visible indicators to distinguish the respectable working class from others, every item of behavior that might be interpreted as a clue assumes disproportionate significance:

. . . certain forms of childish behavior are given particular attention because the child will be mis-classified as a rough if he engages in them: shouting, swearing and fighting are obvious examples at this level. Table manners and more refined speech forms would be preoccupations a little higher on the social scale.[24]

Although the puritanical theme among traditional British working-class people makes this distinction more salient there, a similar process can be found in American working-class and lower middle-class neighborhoods.

An important aspect of all socialization is sex typing, but the importance attached to ensuring sharply differentiated behavior is greater in working-class homes than in the typical middle-class home. Reviewing a large body of research, Jerome Kagan reports the following conclusions. The behavior of lower-class boys and girls is more strongly sex-typed than that of middle-class boys; that is, boys stick to masculine activities and girls to feminine activities. The class difference is especially marked for girls. Reporting their attitudes toward childrearing, lower-class mothers express more concern with encouraging sex typing than middle-class mothers. Both lower-class and middle-class boys tend to reject the effeminate boy, but only the lower-class boys link studiousness with effeminacy and reject

[24] Josephine Klein, *Samples from British Culture*, Routledge, London, 1965, vol. II, p. 632.

the studious boy. Both lower- and middle-class girls are willing to accept the studious girl, but only the middle-class girls reject an excessive interest in heterosexual relations.[25]

The preoccupation with sex typing in lower strata is somewhat anomalous in light of the disproportionately great part played in socialization by the mother at this level. By insisting on sex typing, the mother contributes to perpetuating the pattern of family life that already keeps her husband somewhat removed from the regular family routine. Perhaps the lack of a prestigeful father and the effective subordination of the father to the mother in all dealings with the children makes the demonstration of masculinity through undeviating sex-typed behavior more important. As with any insecure status, the assertion of the symbols of status takes on compensating importance.

For girls, the emphasis on sticking to feminine activities is probably a correlate of a traditional view of marriage as the only route to adult status for women. Sexual attractiveness and femininity then become as important in raising the working-class girl as ambition is for the middle-class boy.

Negro Families and the Culture of Poverty. The question of whether there are distinctive Negro family patterns in the United States has been brought into prominence recently because of a new application of Myrdal's vicious-circle interpretation of racial inequality. The argument is that the long-term consequence of poverty, lack of opportunity, and denial of personal dignity to the American Negro has been to erode the major bonds of family life. Raised in a setting of widespread family disorganization, without a father to assume essential parental tasks or to serve as role model to the child, many young Negroes are not socialized with the motivations and disciplines that are necessary to equip them to take advantage of whatever opportunities are available to them. Family disorganization adds to the other disadvantages of the Negro's position, serving to perpetuate his subjugation in spite of efforts to alter his external situation.

There is, of course, as much variation among Negro families as among white families, and the stable working- and middle-class Negro families parallel the patterns that prevail among white families of the same strata. But the U.S. Department of Labor report of March, 1965, which has come to be known as the Moynihan Report, called attention to a number of indices of exceptional deviation from conventional American family patterns among nonwhites in urban areas of the United States.[26] If we con-

---

[25] Martin Hoffman and Lois Hoffman (eds.), *Review of Child Development Research,* Russell Sage, New York, 1964, vol. I, pp. 142–153.
[26] U.S. Department of Labor, Office of Policy Planning and Research, *The Negro Family: The Case for National Action,* 1965; see also Jessie Bernard, *Marriage and Family among Negroes,* Prentice-Hall, Englewood Cliffs, N.J., 1966.

sider only women living in urban areas who have been married and whose husbands have not died, 22.9 percent of nonwhites fall in the divorced-or-husband-absent category, compared with 7.9 percent of whites. In the United States as a whole in 1963, 23.6 percent of all nonwhite births were illegitimate, compared with 3.1 percent of white births. Both of these rates have been steadily increasing since the Second World War. Thus the family organized about a female head with no functioning husband constitutes perhaps one-fifth to one-fourth of all urban Negro families.

Explanations for this pattern have been of three general kinds. The tradition of the matriarchy that evolved during slavery has been viewed as a part of contemporary Negro heritage. The pattern has been attributed directly to the effects of racial prejudice and discrimination on the performance of family roles. And the pattern has been identified as a part of a general culture of poverty, this form of family organization being an adaptation to the life circumstances of the underclass. Each of these explanations can be examined briefly.

E. Franklin Frazier called the attention of sociologists during the 1930s to the heritage of slavery and its effect on family life. Although there was great variation in the extent to which slave holders fostered or disregarded family ties among their slaves, often the mother-child bond was the only connection that was consistently respected. After freedom, the well-bonded unions remained. But for many former slaves,

. . . the loose ties that held men and women together in a nominal marriage relation during slavery broke easily during the crisis of emancipation. When this happened, the men cut themselves loose from all family ties and joined the great body of homeless men wandering about the country in search of work and new experience. Sometimes the women, chiefly those without children, followed the same course. But more often the woman with family ties, whether she had been without a husband during slavery or was deserted when freedom came, became responsible for the maintenance of the family group. Since often her sexual contacts continued to be of a more or less casual nature, she found herself, as in slavery, surrounded by children depending upon her for support and parental affection. Thus motherhood outside of institutional control was accepted by a large group of Negro women with an attitude of resignation as if it were nature's decree.[27]

Although acknowledging that a larger proportion of Negro families were under female authority in cities than in rural areas as late as 1930, Frazier believed that the move to the city would in the long run mean the absorp-

[27] E. Franklin Frazier, *The Negro Family in the United States,* University of Chicago Press, Chicago, 1939, pp. 106–107. Quoted by permission of the publisher.

tion of black workers into the proletariat and the end of the distinctively matriarchal form of family:

It appears that, as the Negro worker becomes an industrial worker, he assumes responsibility for the support of his family and acquires a new authority in family relations. Moreover, as the isolation of the black worker is gradually broken down, his ideals and patterns of family life approximate those of the great body of industrial workers.[28]

There is no satisfactory way to assess the importance of the matriarchal tradition as a factor in the present Negro family pattern. The failure of the lower stratum of Negroes to share proportionately in the economic advancements of the postwar period and the increasing isolation of poorer Negroes from intensive contact with whites has interrupted the assimilative process that Frazier envisaged. Under the stress of increasing unemployment, the Negro may have accepted the matriarchal adaptation more readily than would another group with no such tradition to fall back upon.

The second kind of explanation for the high rate of fatherless families assumes that race prejudice has a direct effect on the bonding process. Role and bond are closely interdependent. By playing the part of economic provider, the husband activates the task bond that draws other family members to him. By playing the role of man, a person of substance, power, and dignity, he activates the identification bonds. These two bonds are the most crucial ties that hold the wife and children to the husband, although many other ties develop on this foundation. The provider role we shall speak of later. But racial prejudice directly impairs the Negro man's ability to be someone worth identifying with. Because he absorbs the community's attitudes, he doubts his own worth, and his wife and children and neighbors share the low opinion of him. To speak seriously about public affairs as if his opinion mattered, to talk of his rights as if he had power to assert them, to hold up his head as if he could command personal respect by doing so—all these gestures are treated as pretenses, as ridiculous incongruities. It is this concern with claiming his personal worth and dignity as a man which Stokely Carmichael[29] and other advocates of black power repeatedly stress. They see the Negro as needing the self-respect that comes from having some real power and being able to command the respect of others.

It is a plausible hypothesis that identification bonds are always difficult to establish and highly vulnerable once established in the case of the poor. But race prejudice undermines the remnant of self-respect left to the poor

---

[28] *Ibid.*, p. 475. Quoted by permission of the publisher.
[29] Stokely Carmichael and Charles V. Hamilton, *Black Power: The Politics of Liberation in America*, Random House, New York, 1967.

man and augments a tendency found anywhere that the male is unable to play an effective breadwinner role. Unable to command respect, the adult male finds that interpersonal relations with his wife and children in the family setting are not viable.

Finally, the statistics of Negro family life have been attributed to the Negro's disproportionate location in the underclass, where they participate in the culture of poverty. In light of the high rate of unemployment and irregular employment among Negro males, and the increasing discrepancy between Negroes and whites in this respect, there is a prima facie case for interpreting Negro family patterns in this way.[30] Where the man has few resources for commanding the loyalty of family members, there is little incentive for him to take on the responsibilities of a husband and father. Where a husband's presence adds to the woman's work without relieving her of other responsibilities, there is little incentive other than a code of morality or respectability for the woman to add the formality of marriage to her sexual liaisons.

It is interesting to compare a Latin American pattern of family life found among peasants of the Cartegena area of Columbia. Formal marriage with legal and religious sanction is rare. Consensual unions, which resemble the common-law marriage recognized in some parts of the United States, and mother-centered households consisting of a woman, her younger children, and her grandchildren constitute most of the family units. Some indication of the magnitude of the situation is found in the fact that 60 percent of all births in the area were illegitimate in 1957. It is generally believed that the weight of responsibility in sanctioned marriages is too great for the ordinary male to handle. Hence women avoid formal marriage, because they feel that their men will leave them if formal marriage is contracted. And men resist formal marriage, because they do not want to compromise their masculine independence through submitting to control by a woman. The tradition of slavery and the culture of poverty are found here, and the fatherless family prevails, although the Latin culture and the peasant setting are in many ways quite different from urban United States.[31]

The question of greatest public concern regarding the fatherless family in the culture of poverty is the consequence of this arrangement for the socialization process. Insofar as delinquency, lack of disciplined work habits, and personal irresponsibility are disproportionately observed among

[30] The federal government program of aid to dependent children has also been given as an explanation for the absent fathers. Although this is a difficult argument to assess, contemporary evidence does not warrant the conclusion that these programs make more than a marginal contribution to the rates of father absence. See Bernard, *op. cit.*, p. 20.
[31] Celia Stopnicka Rosenthal, "Lower Class Family Organization on the Caribbean Coast of Colombia," *Pacific Sociological Review*, 3:12–17, Spring 1960.

the children of the underclass, it is difficult to say whether these result from the peculiar family organization or whether they are the pattern of learning appropriate to the life situation of the underprivileged. Perhaps these same lessons are learned in this kind of situation irrespective of famly structure and with or without a father to serve as role model. The discussion of achievement motivation in Chapter 19 suggests that father absence detracts from ambition in the child. But whether the presence of a subordinated and economically ineffectual father in the black-ghetto setting would produce any more ambition in the children than an absent father is yet to be ascertained.

THE FAMILY AND
UPWARD MOBILITY

Upward mobility in American society impinges on family life in so many ways that it warrants separate treatment. We shall examine first the situation in which marriage is between persons from different social strata, so that either the husband or wife is mobile through marriage. Then we shall explore at greater length those circumstances in which the family generates and must adjust to the mobility of children while the parents remain stationary.

Mobility Through Marriage

When marriage takes place between a man and woman from radically different socioeconomic levels or ethnic groups, they are likely to bring different understandings regarding the meanings of gestures and different conceptions of normal family roles. In addition, each brings a kinship network that is likely to center in his stratum of origin. Each kin network tends to reinforce the interpretations and role conceptions brought to the marriage and thus to resist the quick revision necessary to establish a satisfactory working relationship. The union of kin networks about the nuclear unit is less likely to be accomplished because of the socioeconomic differences, so that the disrupting effect of kinship is likely to outweigh its supportive effect.

But again the situation is more complex than this. For one thing, not all discrepant gesture interpretations are noncongruent. Particularly when the lives of the husband and wife are fairly segregated for large parts of the time and when association with the kin networks is minimized, the relationship may proceed with limited mutual understanding. Furthermore, some combinations of role conceptions simplify rather than complicate interaction. For example, among California Armenians, it has been an item of folk wisdom that the marriage of a second-generation Armenian girl to an "old American" man is a good marriage, but the reverse relationship is likely to fail. Both the old American and the Armenian cultures favor patriarchy over matriarchy, but the preference is much stronger and practice follows belief more closely among the Armenians. When the wife is Armenian, she is prepared to accept her husband's authority and indulge him to a greater degree than his background has led him to expect. At the same time, he is likely to be more considerate of his wife's wishes than she has been led to expect. The result is mutually gratifying deviation from role expectation. By contrast, the old American wife receives less consideration than she expects and the Armenian husband finds his wife unwilling to accept his authority in the unquestioning manner he has seen his mother and his aunts and cousins grant their husbands. Whether the folk wisdom in this instance actually describes things as they are would require a careful study of a number of instances of intermarriage, which is not available at present.

One study concerning religiously mixed marriages may supply evidence in support of this principle of folk wisdom, however. Judson Landis gathered information about their parents' marital status and religion from 4,108 students in his college classes. When he classified all the marriages by religious affiliation of husband and wife and computed rates of separation and divorce for each combination, the results in Figure 9 were obtained. In general, mixed marriages show a higher rate of dissolution than those between persons from similar religious backgrounds. Since religious affiliation in these broad categories is largely determined by ethnic background, with protestants coming from north and west Europe and catholics from south and east Europe, the findings probably indicate the fate of marriages between persons from quite dissimilar as compared with similar cultural backgrounds.

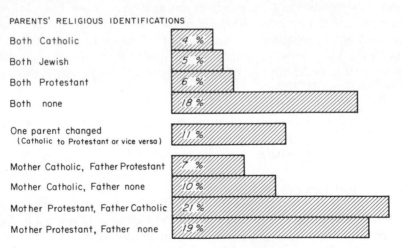

Figure 9. **Rate of divorce or separation by religious identification of husband and wife.** (Adapted from Judson T. Landis, "Marriages of Mixed and Non-mixed Religious Faith," *American Sociological Review,* 14:403, June 1949.)

The more interesting observation, however, comes from comparing Protestant husband–Catholic wife with Catholic husband–Protestant wife marriages. The dissolution rate of the former is probably no different from that of homogeneous Protestant marriages. But the dissolution rate of Catholic father–Protestant mother marriages is three times as great. Why this should be is a matter of speculation at the present time. And the manner of data collection leaves undetermined the kind of universe to which the sample applies. With these qualifications in mind, one may cautiously but plausibly interpret the data by noting relative degrees of patriarchalism. The Mediterranean and east European cultures generally grant more unqualified authority to the father than do the west and north European cultures. Hence the Protestant father–Catholic mother marriage is much like the more favorable old American father–Armenian mother union and appears to be as stable as a culturally homogeneous marriage.

Although interclass marriages represent minor deviations from the norm, the futuristic orientation of young adults in American society means that bonds can form as if husband and wife derived from the same backgrounds. Beauty and charm in a woman or talent and energy in a man are qualities that suggest upward mobility and nullify identification with the stratum of origin. As Goode has observed,

Women of social position may also exchange [their position] for *potential achievement*: that is, a talented young man may, even without much income, obtain a wife above him in the social scale, simply because his future is worth a good deal on the present marriage market.[1]

It is also likely that those who marry up or down are not typical members of their strata of origin, often already being mobile and having adopted systems of value in accord with their destinations. Hence, when we have adequate data on interclass marriages, we are not likely to find them set apart as a group from other marriages.

With respect to bonding and decision making, it is probably true that either a man or a woman has stronger bargaining power and benefits more strongly from the principle of less interest in relationships with a person of lower standing than with his stratum peers. But if the potential spouse has already concretely demonstrated upward mobility through educational, occupational, or financial success or through the establishment of significant social ties, this advantage evaporates. Once the marriage is completed and a separate household established, the general principles of relative contribution to family standing become more important than background by itself, just as in other families.

Although there is remarkably little research to confirm such findings as

[1] William J. Goode, *Family and Mobility*, pp. 36–37.

those of Landis just cited, it appears likely that subtle differences in the understanding of interaction rules and role conceptions may contribute to conflict in many such relationships. Even when anticipatory socialization has taken place prior to mobility, norms and values are often learned in a more rigid fashion outside the settings in which they are normally applied. When deep-seated conceptions of rights and duties have been internalized from different backgrounds, there is the basis for recurring experience of injustice and unfairness.

What happens in all the internal family relationships, and especially in the pattern of socialization adopted, is also affected by how close or separate are the ties to kinship networks. Where kin relationships are important, the advantage of the higher-stratum kin group is readily translated into a decision-making advantage for the spouse from that lineage and a tendency to oversee socialization efforts to make them correspond to the higher-stratum pattern. Intermarriage tends to affect the kinship ties differentially. Alice Rossi has observed that the normal tendency to have closer ties to the wife's kin than to the husband's is accentuated when the wife's background is higher than her husband's.[2] In a study of 799 residents of Greensboro, North Carolina, Bert Adams found that the character of kinship ties when one marriage partner had been mobile tended most generally to follow the pattern of their current position. The fact of mobility was less important than current placement in predicting the patterns of intergenerational ties and ties between adult siblings.[3]

Upward Mobility and Family Processes

Career mobility and mixed marriage require adjustments in family arrangements and internal structure until some kind of consolidation of the family unit into one class identity is achieved. But intergenerational mobility means the development of a divergent class orientation within an established family, leading eventually to a new nuclear family unit at a different level while the position of the original unit remains unchanged. Hence the key problems for the family are quite different. Instead of searching for a way to readjust family processes and roles so as to restore a unitary class anchorage, the family involved in intergenerational mobility must evolve a system of roles to foster and cope with two different class anchorages that become of greater rather than lesser significance during the course of the family life cycle.

The ease with which these adjustments can be made depends largely on the relationships between social strata that prevail in society at the

---

[2] Alice Rossi, personal communication.
[3] Bert Adams, "Occupational Position, Mobility, and the Kin of Orientation," *American Sociological Review*, 32:364–377, June 1967.

time. There are two ways in which the members of different strata view each other, which can be called *class consciousness* and *prestige identification*. The normal situation in any society is ambivalence, with both attitudes combined in the members' perspectives. But the mix is quite variable, and the preponderance of one or the other attitude is crucial for family adjustments to mobility.

Class consciousness means a highly developed ingroup-outgroup attitude. Members of outgroups (other strata) are viewed with resentment, contempt, suspicion, or fear, all tending toward hostility when any very active interclass relations are established. The class as ingroup demands first loyalty from its members, and any sign of identification with any other class is disloyalty and betrayal. The more highly developed and the more preponderant the class conscious attitudes of this kind, the more difficult for mobility orientations to originate and develop within the family, and the more disruptive the consequences of intergenerational mobility for the family.

Prestige identification means that within-class loyalties are subordinated to broader loyalties. Members of lower classes typically find personal gratification and support for these broad loyalties through identifying with conspicuous and successful members of higher classes. The sense of cross-class identity and the feeling of personal worth derived from this pattern of identification mute the potential hostility and suspicion. The more one can establish legitimate claims to identification with a person of high prestige, the more one's own prestige is enhanced. To have a relative, and especially a child, who is firmly established in a higher social stratum is then a source of prestige for other family members and even to a lesser degree for neighbors and friends. When prestige identification is prevalent, upward mobility has potentially positive consequences for family bonds, and its rewards supply the incentive for role adjustments.

It is not appropriate here to examine the circumstances that strengthen one of these tendencies at the expense of the other. It will become clear that the proponents of some of the conflicting theories regarding the family and intergenerational mobility differ because they have implicitly assumed that one or the other of these conditions prevailed. The weight of evidence regarding most components of the American class system rather clearly indicates that prestige identification outweighs class consciousness, and those theories which assume important areas of compatibility between family life and intergenerational mobility therefore correspond more frequently with observable facts. The opposing theories, however, also find support during periods of heightened class conflict and in those pockets of intensified class consciousness which coexist with the dominant emphases in American society.

We shall consider separately the two questions: how aspirations to mobility are generated and sustained within the family, and how family processes adjust to the presence of a mobility-oriented child within the family. The first is primarily a question regarding the socialization process, and the second emphasizes patterns of decision making and conflict, with implications for revisions in bonding.

In separating the two questions we must, however, avoid the error of a simplistic view of socialization as the one-time implanting of ambition in the individual. The upper middle-class son of a professional man who aspires to professional status himself has constant support for his aspirations from his family, school, and community organizations. If the ambition wavers, the support quickly turns into pressure and even coercion to keep him working toward the professional goal. Similarly it is unlikely that we can explain upward mobility on the basis of ambition implanted early and then pursued autonomously. It is much more plausible to suppose that upwardly mobile boys and girls find themselves in situations that reinforce and facilitate their goals and the pursuits necessary to the attainment of their goals over an extended period of time. Hence in order to account for upward mobility, we must look at the adjustments that the family makes to mobility in process as well as the implanting of the initial ambitions.

Socialization to Upward Mobility. The simplest way of explaining upward mobility aspirations can be labeled the *disjuncture* hypothesis. A family may publicly be located in one stratum because of family income or breadwinner's occupation, but members may, in important respects, identify with and follow patterns of family life taken from a higher or lower stratum. We refer to this condition as a disjuncture between family setting and private identity. If there is a disjuncture between the family and the class setting it is identified with, children in the family tend to aspire and receive family support for their aspirations in the direction of the family's private identity. In these instances the family is transmitting values and aspirations and teaching means for social ascent that are already part of the family repertoire, although at variance with neighborhood patterns.

In this hypothesis we are assuming the *conveyance of culture*, as described in Chapter 8. The assumption here is that the child learns the content of what is conveyed to him by the parents. What he learns is not some indirect or inadvertant consequence of the particular style of relationship that develops between parent and child but a direct internalization of values, attitudes, and behavior taught or exemplified by his parents. The parent-child relationship is such as to impede or facilitate the internalization of parental values but is not the source of the message.

A common form of disjuncture is created by downward mobility. A family with middle-class origins but located in the working class because of the breadwinner's limited occupational or educational achievement often holds tenaciously to middle-class values and self-conceptions. Defenses are erected against the working-class environment. Efforts are made to regulate the exposure of the child by selecting associates who share a more middle-class outlook than most people in the neighborhood. The child's experience with his working-class associates are invidiously interpreted for him from the perspective of middle-class values. The promotion of a middle-class standing for the child becomes part of the parents' effort to regain the higher status of their own families of orientation.

Not all such efforts are successful—perhaps only a minority succeed—but some mobility is undoubtedly induced in this way. In a British study of working-class boys who had been selected for upward mobility through the grammar schools, this pattern was especially prominent. As young men, these mobile people had a remarkably constricted view of the world, conservative, unsympathetic to the disadvantaged, self-isolating in many ways.[4] Very likely these attributes were a continuation of the defenses against the working-class neighborhoods in which they were raised and which they could not abandon once they had moved to middle-class settings.

A more complicated family situation is involved when a woman marries down and then seeks to promote in her son the success she misses in her husband. Such marriages often begin with the hope that the husband will be upwardly mobile in a short time. He will attend law school at night and make the transition from laborer to lawyer on completion. Mobility orientations are inculcated in the child in a manner similar to the preceding case, with the added element that a wedge is driven between father and son. The son must be taught not to accept his father as a role model. The father may be viewed with charity and pity but with only condescending respect for such workmanlike and humane virtues as he exhibits.

In a more general way it has often been supposed that the mother characteristically plays the key role in producing mobility. The father's efforts to do so may be self-defeating, like the aim of the teacher who says, "Do as I say, not as I do!" By disparaging his own accomplishments as suitable standards of success, the father undermines his force as a role model. But the mother, because she is not held responsible for the class placement of the family, can urge a higher standard of success without self-debasement. There is suggestive evidence that upwardly mobile boys

[4] Brian Jackson and Dennis Marsden, *Education and the Working Classes*, Routledge, London, 1962.

in American society tend to have closer ties to their mothers than fathers that is consistent with this view but also with other views we shall discuss later.[5]

When there is downward mobility of either kind, kin often play a didactic and supporting part. The mother's brother or father sometimes attempts to take the place of the boy's father and provides money for school and other experiences intended to encourage mobility. When the mother has married down, her family of orientation often reasserts itself, excluding her husband and attempting to integrate the son into their nuclear family rather than his own.

John Allingham has suggested a somewhat broader application of the disjuncture hypothesis to explain downward as well as upward mobility. He suggests a general principle of *class regression*:

The relationship observed is entitled class regression because the sons most likely to be upwardly mobile are sons of fathers who were downwardly mobile over their careers. Conversely, those most likely to be downwardly mobile are sons of fathers who have been upwardly mobile over their careers.[6]

There may also be instances of disjuncture that do not involve downward mobility but some lack of status crystallization instead.[7] Crystallization refers to a state of consistency among the elements that constitute a person's total position in society. Lack of crystallization means lack of a fully consistent class outlook and a basis for conveying discrepant values to the child. A study of 1,903 white Anglo high school seniors in Los Angeles suggests that mobility aspirations are associated with the presence of educational levels that are higher than necessary for the father's occupation. An ambition index was made up of occupational, educational, monetary, and entrepreneurial goals, with a parallel index for girls, including what they expected in their husbands. As summarized in Table 15, ambition level was significantly correlated with the father's education, father's occupation, and mother's education, with the father's education counting less than the other two. The crystallization hypothesis was tested by holding the father's occupation constant by the method of partial correlation. When this was done, both the father's and mother's education made small but significant additions to the prediction of both the sons' and daughters' ambitions.

These findings are also of interest because of what they suggest about

[5] William S. Bennett, Jr., "Class and Family Influences on Student Aspirations," *Social Forces*, 43:167, December 1964.
[6] John D. Allingham, "Class Regression: An Aspect of the Social Stratification Process," *American Sociological Review*, 32:442–449, June 1967; quotation from p. 442.
[7] Gerhard Lenski, "Status Crystallization: A Non-vertical Dimension of Social Status," *American Sociological Review*, 19:405–413, August 1954.

TABLE 15 CORRELATION OF FATHER'S AND MOTHER'S EDUCATION
WITH AMBITION*

Independent Variable and	Correlation with Ambition	
Variable Held Constant	Male	Female
Zero-order coefficients:		
Father's education	+.19	+.25
Mother's education	+.35	+.34
Father's occupation	+.30	+.36
Father's occupation held constant:		
Father's education	+.27	+.34
Mother's education	+.16	+.24
Father's occupation and education held constant:		
Mother's education	+.14	+.17

*Ambition was measured by a composite index. All coefficients are significant at the
.001 level by the *t* test.
SOURCE: Adapted from Ralph H. Turner, "Some Family Determinants of Ambition,"
Sociology and Social Research, 46:404, July, 1962.

the special influence of the mother in generating ambition. If the mother
played the disproprotionate part that many investigators assume, we
should expect to find a considerably larger coefficient of partial correlation
between the mother's education and the child's ambition than between the
father's education and the child's ambition, after the father's occupation
has been held constant. This is not the case, however. The evidence suggests rather that any disjuncture from the family's public placement,
whether located in the mother or the father, fosters ambitions at variance
from the family's established stratum. Cases of mothers who have married
down may be more common than cases of fathers who cannot find occupations to fit their educational attainment, but the impact of the latter
may be as great when it occurs.

A second broad hypothesis about the relationship of family functioning
to the development of upward-mobility orientations in the children may
be called the *default hypothesis*. Here the proposition is simply that the
ineffectuality of the family in socializing the child leaves the field open for
other influences to shape the child. Most of the neighborhood influences
at the lower levels of society are believed to operate against mobility
aspirations, so that the majority of children from weak families are not
upwardly mobile. But if the family normally operates to perpetuate its
own class identification, family default may permit a few individuals to

come under the influence of teachers, social-agency personnel, highly ambitious peers, or others whose influence fosters mobility.

The assumption in this hypothesis is again the conveyance-of-culture socialization mode. There is a further assumption that identification bonds are preeminent in the child's relationship to the father and therefore determine the kind of learning that can take place so long as these bonds retain their importance. The close ties of the child to his father are fostered by respect for his occupation and tend to reinforce that respect. Ambition is channeled into a wish to follow in father's footsteps, and mobility is impeded.

It is difficult to assign plausibility to these assumptions when they are applied to unskilled and menial labor, although certain positive values, such as independence, freedom to talk back to the boss, and not knuckling under to the system, are sometimes claimed for such work. The assumptions are more plausible when the father is a small entrepreneur or a craftsman who can lay claim to a set of traditional entrepreneurial and workmanship values in asserting the prestige of his occupation. Among the sample of twelfth grade high school boys in Los Angeles it was noteworthy that the greatest continuity between the father's occupation and the son's aspiration was found among sons of small businessmen, and the most consistent preference for a lifework in which one could be his own boss was found in the same group of students.[8] In these instances the close ties with the father are obstacles to mobility.

A variant of this hypothesis holds that upward mobility is inversely related to the strength of the extended family or kinship network. A strong and class-homogeneous kinship network may similarly lock the child into his class position. Weak kinship ties then provide more leeway for him to form other ties, some of which may foster mobility. In the study of urban Jewish kinship mentioned in Chapter 18, conflicts between the press toward mobility and kinship ties were frequently mentioned. Although the interviewees chose mobility even at the cost of impaired kinship ties, there was still widespread ambivalence.[9]

A third hypothesis involves the same assumption that strong family and neighborhood influences foster class continuity rather than mobility but sees unsatisfactory family relations exercising a definite push out of the parental stratum. According to the *escape* hypothesis, an intolerable state of maladjustment to his class environment drives the child to leave his unhappy setting. One of the ways to escape is by striving for upward

[8] Ralph H. Turner, *The Social Context of Ambition*, Chandler, San Francisco, 1964, p. 181.

[9] Hope J. Leichter and William E. Mitchell, *Kinship and Casework*, Russell Sage, New York, 1967, pp. 73–75.

mobility. According to this view the child who grows up with a satisfying family life and who establishes satisfactory relationships with his peers sets continuation in the same kind of neighborhood as his life goal and selects one of the occupations with which home and neighborhood have made him familiar. There is no incentive to strive in school work that is largely irrelevant to life at the familiar level, so that mediocre school records contribute to locking the child into his parental stratum.

The solidary family that is well integrated into a lower-stratum neighborhood can erect awesome barriers to mobility. Ambition is discountenanced as snobbery, as a display of being better than one's peers and family. The essential steps and means to mobility are discredited, with studiousness in school the most widespread example. In the name of working-class virtues the family makes demands on the child that are incompatible with devotion to self-advancing activities. Common examples are family chores that compete with assigned homework and the frequent expectation that a child will start contributing to family support by the age of eighteen or younger. In the presence of such obstacles only the grossly maladjusted youth could be so unresponsive to pressures and responsibilities as to persevere in his ambitions.

Although earlier evidence gave support for the finding that lower-class families see no point in mobility, there is considerable research support for the conclusion that working-class families today generally urge both upward mobility and attainment of a good school record on their children.[10] But there is also evidence that, even when mobility is accepted and promoted in lower-stratum homes, a self-defeating view of the nature and means to mobility is often conveyed. In the Los Angeles study a distinction was drawn between two patterns of mobility aspiration. One pattern revolved about an emphasis on education with fairly modest material goals and included traditional middle-class values of deferred gratification and self-reliance. The other stressed high material goals with minimal education and a kind of naked success drive. It is likely that persons fitting the first pattern have a better chance of succeeding in American society. But the second pattern was more prevalent among boys from working-class backgrounds.[11]

Finally, the positive value of mutual aid that pervades many working-class communities is opposed to the values of self-reliance and individualism that characterize middle-class life and seem to facilitate upward mobility. In his classic study of a slum neighborhood in Boston William F. Whyte drew a sharp contrast between two groups of youth. Doc's gang

[10] Deborah I. Offenbacher, "Cultures in Conflict: Home and School as Seen through the Eyes of Lower-class Students," *The Urban Review*, 2:2–8, May 1968.
[11] Turner, *op. cit.*, pp. 177–183.

was depicted as warm and cooperative but oriented toward the local neighborhood. Another group of boys were self-seeking, untrusted, and untrusting, and they were the climbers who were seeking a way out of the slum neighborhood.[12]

The view that maladjustment provides the motive force for mobility finds support in a study of 350 university students by Dynes, Clarke, and Dinitz. Students with high aspirations were disproportionately inclined to report that they felt rejection and favoritism from their parents, more often expressed little attachment to their parents, and less often stated that their childhood had been happy.[13] The evidence for the escape hypothesis, however, is not consistent. William Rushing found evidence to support what he calls the *deprivation-aspiration* hypothesis in the case of females in relation to their father but not for males or in relation to their mother.[14] A nationwide survey in the United States showed low achievement motivation (*n* Achievement) among men from homes broken by divorce, separation, or death of parents.[15] In the Los Angeles study three indicators of family stability were correlated positively but not significantly with level of ambition[16] With studies using different measures of ambition and adjustment in the family it is unclear whether these are genuinely contradictory findings or whether a refined statement of the hypothesis would be consistent with all the findings.

It should be observed that the escape hypothesis lends itself to either the *conveyance-of-culture* or the *reaction-to-frustration* view of the socialization process. Dynes, Clarke, and Dinitz derived their hypothesis from Freudian theory. Ambition may be seen as a sublimated expression of aggression, the acting out of rebellion against parents.

A fourth hypothesis stands in opposition to the three preceding ones, and especially to the latter two. We shall speak of the *consensus* hypothesis, since it rests on the fundamental assumption that the support for ambition and mobility are so widely diffused throughout the social structure that with proper care they can develop anywhere. The default and escape hypotheses derive naturally from the assumption that class con-

[12] William F. Whyte, *Street Corner Society,* University of Chicago Press, Chicago, 1955.
[13] Russell R. Dynes, Alfred C. Clarke, and Simon Dinitz, "Levels of Occupational Aspiration: Some Aspects of Family Experience as a Variable," *American Sociological Review,* 21:212–215, April 1956.
[14] William A. Rushing, "Adolescent-Parent Relationship and Mobility Aspirations," *Social Forces,* 43:157–166, December 1964.
[15] Reported in David C. McClelland, *The Achieving Society,* Van Nostrand, Princeton, N.J., 1961, p. 374.
[16] Ralph H. Turner, "Some Family Determinants of Ambition," *Sociology and Social Research,* 46:405–406, July 1962.

sciousness is the dominant pattern of interclass relationships. The disjuncture hypothesis fits the same assumption very well but is the easiest of the three to reconcile with a situation in which prestige identification is the dominant interclass pattern. But the consensus hypothesis is only plausible when class consciousness is minimal.

If the relationship among the strata is not primarily one of conflict, ambition for mobility and close ties with the father need not be incompatible. For the parent who shares a society-wide value placed on success but whose own success has been limited, the identification bond to his child becomes salient. By identifying with the child's progress toward a higher success than his own, the parent gains vicarious satisfaction of his own unrealized ambitions. Under these circumstances the tie to the child is not divisive but unifying for the family as a whole. It is the family as a unit that gains through identification with the mobile member.

Here we are assuming that socialization consists of the conveyance of family culture, recognizing that family members may believe strongly in values that they themselves have not achieved and may not even have adopted as personal goals. According to the assumption of value relevance a person may internalize a value strongly and use it in evaluating others without applying it as a goal for himself. His own experience has led him to see the value as unrealizable in his own situation or at the current stage in his career without lessening his conviction of the importance of the value. Although the data fall short of conclusiveness, there is suggestive evidence of such a mechanism among the boys in the Los Angeles study. Value items were worded differently in alternate questionnaire forms. A measure of personal goals was achieved by asking, "Which kind of person do you want to be?" Values in a more abstract sense were sought through the questions, "Which kind of person do you admire more?" Boys from middle- and working-class backgrounds who received the second form of the questionnaire showed equal admiration for the risk taker, the expert on serious topics, and the person who excells his friends. When the first questionnaire form was used, boys from working-class backgrounds less often endorsed these same values as goals for themselves than did middle-class boys.[17] Working-class fathers who shared a similar combination of attitudes could readily promote ambition in their sons in spite of their own limited achievements.

If the positive value of mobility is widespread, the family that functions effectively is better able than weak families to provide the support for upward mobility and to teach some of the attitudes that facilitate the

[17] Turner, *The Social Context of Ambition*, pp. 80–85.

achievement of mobility. Joseph Kahl identifies trust and the acceptance of deferred gratification as among the attitudes associated with socioeconomic achievement.[18] Both attitudes are more likely to be learned in a stable and harmonious family situation in which interpersonal relationships are dependable and warm. Self-confidence may be the key to converting a value that is abstractly held into a goal in one's own life. Positive relations in the family are generally thought to be conducive to self-confidence in the child.

On the basis of his own careful examination of socialization theories, Urie Bronfenbrenner concludes that such achievement behavior as leadership and responsibility in boys is facilitated by identification with the father. The development of girls is similarly promoted when instrumental and expressive interaction is principally with the mother. Strong identification with the same-sex parent is the key condition.[19] There is also evidence from kinship studies that kin sometimes cooperate to help with the education of a favored or promising child. In both instances the findings are those suggested by the consensus hypothesis. Strong identification with the parent of the same sex ensures the fullest internalization of cultural values appropriate to the respective sex roles.

There is also some evidence to suggest that ambition receives more support in the lower strata of society than is readily apparent on the surface. Findings from the Los Angeles study indicated that students with high ambitions and with good reputations as students were named disproportionately in response to the question, "Suppose you wanted to pick some people to be your *close friends* . . . " In the lower-stratum neighborhoods, however, this was not true of students identified as "wheels" or socially prominent individuals. A tentative conclusion was that the lower strata differ from the higher strata not in their admiration for success and mobility but in their attitude toward social climbing and social leadership as a means or accompaniment to mobility. The student who could learn to accept a certain amount of surface ridicule and who could avoid being identified as a social snob would have the support and respect of his peers in his pursuit of mobility.[20]

A final hypothesis is the *need-for-achievement* hypothesis. Except in case of the escape hypothesis we have consistently assumed that what the child learns is a cultural value of success or achievement or mobility. Differences in ambition reflect differences in exposure and internalization of the cul-

[18] Joseph A. Kahl, "Some Measurements of Achievement Orientation," *American Journal of Sociology*, 70:669–681, May 1965.
[19] Urie Bronfenbrenner, "Responsibility and Leadership in Adolescents," in Luigi Petrullo and Bernard M. Bass (eds.), *Leadership and Interpersonal Behavior*, Holt, New York, 1961, pp. 266–267.
[20] Turner, *The Social Context of Ambition*, pp. 122–124.

tural value. The family either directly conveys this cultural value or creates a favorable environment for conversion of the value into a personal goal of considerable force. Another approach looks for something in the interpersonal relationship of child to socializing agents that produces a strong need for achievement in the child. The search is for relationships that generate the achievement motive in the absence of any cultural value of achievement. Hence the socialization mechanism cannot be conveyance of culture but must be either *reaction to frustration and gratification* or *adaptation*. The best-known theory of this kind is that of David McClelland, who identifies a generalized achievement motive as the basis for success striving in all societies.

Since the achievement motive is a generalized motivation that can find expression in other accomplishments than pursuit of upward mobility, it is measured without reference to specific occupational or education goals. Projective procedures are generally used, and the frequency of achievement themes is ascertained. In making national comparisons, McClelland has used folktales as protocols. In comparing individuals, pictures from the Thematic Apperception Test are used and responses coded. An initial set of studies led McClelland to conclude that the need for achievement was promoted by a relationship in which parents expected early independent mastery of simple tasks, provided that there was no generalized restrictiveness, authoritarianism, or rejection of the child. The unique combination of demands that are difficult enough to constitute challenges without being totally unrealistic and the pattern of freeing the child from close and continual supervision in the performance of these tasks was judged essential for a highly developed achievement motive. Demands made either too early or too late are incompatible with a strong need for achievement. Further studies led McClelland to distinguish between achievement demands and caretaking demands. Caretaking tasks are those, such as bladder control and scheduled feeding, that serve principally to free the parents from much of the bother of childrearing. When these demands were made early, relative to achievement demands, the effect was to inhibit the development of the need for achievement. Early caretaking demands could also serve as an index of authoritarianism or rejection. Still another study indicated that both the mother and father of children with high need for achievement expressed more warmth and support for the child, while setting higher standards of excellence, in an experimental situation.[21]

The evidence regarding family structure is less clear, because different family patterns have different effects in different cultural settings. The

[21] McClelland, *op. cit.*, pp. 336–356.

development of a strong need for achievement appears to be inhibited by a very dominant or authoritarian father-son relationship, although mother authoritarianism does not impair the process. Absence of the father also works against strong need for achievement, perhaps because the result is likely to be too close and indulgent a relationship with the mother. Thus a family pattern in which the father is present as a respected family member but in which mother is definitely in charge of the children is most favorable to a developed need for achievement.[22]

The relationship of these projective measures to mobility ambitions is only incompletely charted at present. When the distinction between achievement demands and caretaking demands is introduced, there arises a question of whether we are identifying the spontaneous generation of achievement motive out of a particular childrearing relationship or the conveyance of an achievement value already supported by the parents. The pattern of family relationships may be a causal factor, whether direct or indirect in its effect, or it may be merely the form typically induced by conditions of middle-class life and of no independent consequence. Although the evidence has been accumulated from varied enough sources to lend unusual plausibility to the theory, the possibility that investigators may be indirectly tapping the simple conveyance of culture under favorable and unfavorable family conditions cannot be ruled out conclusively.

It would be foolhardy to offer conclusions regarding the family sources of mobility aspiration after this review of five broad hypotheses, except to make some general observations. First, we can probably be satisfied that mobility aspirations are extensively transmitted through culture conveyance. Whether there is also a peculiar pattern of family relations that can generate ambition autonomously is still to be ascertained. Second, ambitions are widely known enough and respected in American society so that theories relating mobility aspiration to stability and integrity of the family are probably more widely applicable than those attaching ambition to weakness of the family. Third, theories that appear mutually contradictory may each be correct but only under specifiable circumstances. The difference in the extent of class consciousness in different times and places makes one hypothesis applicable to one setting and the opposite applicable to another. Finally, we must repeat John Scanzoni's conclusion, drawn from a survey of prior research and an attempt to make a comparative test of alternative theories on the basis of his own data, that the findings are inconclusive with respect to the major available theories.[23]

Effects of Upward Mobility on the Family. The effects of having an

---

[22] *Ibid.*, pp. 373–376.
[23] John Scanzoni, "Inconclusiveness in Family Sources of Achievement," *Pacific Sociological Review*, 9:108–114, Fall 1966.

upwardly mobile member in the family differ according to which of the preceding hypotheses is applicable. Under any circumstance the development of distinct and subculturally different social universes between the mobile person and his family of orientation sets the terms under which continuing relationships are possible. A highly developed class consciousness in the community intensifies the difficulties in maintaining relationships, but a strong theme of prestige identification fosters certain continuing ties. Whether ambition is taught and supported within the family, or takes the form of rebellion against the family, or is unintended and neutrally regarded by the family has far-reaching significance for continuing family relationships. In examining possible effects on each of the major family processes, we must keep in mind that no single kind of consequence is likely to be generally applicable in all mobility situations..

During childhood and early adolescence of the mobile person the normal bonds of dependency on the family provide the stable substratum for parent-child relationships. But there is a gradual erosion of other bonds when mobility follows the default or escape hypothesis. The failure to establish response and identification bonds makes the relationship vulnerable to the inevitable end of dependency, and the separation of generations into distinct worlds without meaningful contact is to be expected.

When consensus in support of mobility or disjunction leads to support for the child's ambition, the short-term effect is to augment the bonds that link parent and child. Promotion of the child's education and ultimate social ascent becomes an important basis for collaborative activity, an investment in incomplete action. As the child achieves some successes in school and elsewhere, the identification bond of parent to child is intensified. Mobility efforts in turn make the child more dependent on a supportive family than otherwise. Transportation to organization meetings, such as boy scouts and YMCA, provision of suitable clothing, and many other kinds of family assistance increase the mobile child's dependency. Extended education also elongates the period of financial dependency. When support comes from kin outside the nuclear unit, the intensified bonding includes some of the kinship network.

If there is general support for the child's mobility within the family, the consequence should be a general strengthening of bonds between the husband and wife and other members. Both the collaborative task bond and the identification bond involve and reinforce the family as a unit. But differential bonding and the formation of coalitions that become lasting alliances may also occur. The favored eldest child in a family and community with a firmly accepted value of primogeniture serves as a generally unifying object. But without this value, the possibilities of coalition among less favored children are obvious.

Of special interest is the differential bonding that links mother to mobile son. When a downwardly mobile mother is the source of her son's mobility aspirations, this kind of alliance is unavoidable. But even with mutual support from the mother and father, the tendency to transfer some of the wife's emotional investments from her husband to her son is intensified whenever the son shows promise of achieving greater success in life than his father. The mother is also in the position to offer more direct support for the child in his efforts to advance himself and his dependency on her assistance is more immediate and apparent. Hence the hypothesis is offered that in families that support the son's mobility, regardless of the mutuality of the father and mother support, bonding is disproportionately intensified between the mother and mobile son.

Mobility of women is less well understood than that of men, and hence it is impossible to offer an equally plausible analysis. So long as the route for mobility is education, a similar kind of family sponsorship and bonding is possible. Otherwise there do not appear to be the same bases for predicting bonding patterns within the family.

If the normal family cycle means a progressive shift toward increasing influence by the child in family decision making, the shift is intensified by mobility in the short run when there is any support and respect for mobility in the family. School successes and anticipatory identification with prestigeful occupations provoke deference. As with all relationships in which an identification bond works chiefly in one direction, the principle of less interest increasingly favors the child over his parents. Countering this tendency might be the heightened dependency of the child, depending on how wholeheartedly family members accept the promotion of the child's ambitions as a family goal. A man working as a gardener, asked about his son who attended the state university, replied: "As long as I can afford it, it's alright for him to stay in school." In the presence of this kind of attitude, the child's extended dependency becomes a bargaining disadvantage in family decision making, a concession already made to him for which he must pay by conceding on other matters. But when the child's mobility is accepted as a family collaborative goal and when it becomes the basis for an identification bond, the social meaning of dependency is transformed. The mobile child gains, with each success, a progressively more privileged position in the family.

In spite of family support, mobility introduces some special sources of conflict into family relationships. The observation that mobility leads to psychological isolation in general was made by Pitrim Sorokin.[24] The development of a progressively widening gap of understanding between

[24] Pitirim A. Sorokin, *Social and Cultural Mobility*, Free Press, New York, 1959 (first published, 1927), pp. 522–523.

the mobile child and his family of orientation was documented early in a Belgian study.[25] The phenomena that lead specifically to conflict are primarily of two kinds: acquisition of different value systems and a different assessment of the balance of interpersonal credits and debits based on different role perspectives. If parents have no background in higher strata, school and other settings convey an unfamiliar value system to the child. The more individualistic middle-class values make the child seem ruthless and unhelpful to many working-class parents. The emphasis on sedentary, intellectual, and aesthetic pursuits conveys a lack of manliness. Such discrepancies in values mean that the parent and child use different standards in determining the interpersonal norms that regulate their interaction. As we noted in Chapter 7, it is this kind of disagreement over the rules of interaction which tends to bring identities into contention and translate disagreement into conflict.

Even when parents adhere to values of a higher class, some discrepancies are inevitable. Isolation from participation in the higher class means that parental values have not changed with the times and correspond increasingly with a system that is becoming obsolete in the higher class. Furthermore, values and norms always have a formal and a working aspect that are not the same. The working aspect consists of the general understandings about the kinds of compromises that are expected and the situations in which the values and norms are not to be applied literally. Isolation from the social milieu in which the values and norms are being applied means that parents come to identify the values and norms with an overly rigid, overly literalistic understanding of their formal aspect. The child's set of values is affected by absorption of some of the neighborhood value system and by induction into the higher strata with their contemporary version of the class values. Both exposures give the child value perspectives at odds with those of his parents. And the combination of value exposures makes for unstable value commitments, making the child unpredictable in family eyes and changeable in the interpersonal norms he recognizes as legitimate.

Even when there is consensus regarding the value of upward mobility and full family support is forthcoming, role perspectives are bound to differ in the extent to which the child is believed to be indebted to the family for the support they have given him and the sacrifices they have made. The parents' tendency to feel that they have gone far beyond the call of duty for the child does not square with the child's tendency to take parental support for granted as a part of normal responsibility toward the child. In this manner mobility is a prototypical conflict-inducing situation,

[25] Sylvain de Coster and Georges van der Elst, *Mobilité Sociale et Enseignement*, University of Brussels, Brussels, 1954, pp. 74–76.

but the pressures to avert open conflict and to maintain accommodations are also maximized on the one hand by the parents' identification bond to the child and on the other hand by the child's prolonged dependency on his parents.

Where kinship bonds are active and mobility is widespread, coalitions among the mobile children sometimes serve as a defense against the claims of indebtedness from parents. Leichter and Mitchell found that cousins' clubs were common among their Jewish subjects. Ostensibly the cousins' clubs gave expression to the strong ties of kinship. But in practice they served in large part as a union against the older generation to facilitate acculturation to the American scene.[26]

As the normal period for departure from the family of orientation arrives, the continuing relationships between the mobile person and his family are also affected. The lack of common experience because of their separate worlds increasingly undermines many of the interactive bonds. The collaborative task of promoting the child's mobility is largely finished and loses its efficacy. An important response bond may develop if the child is unsuccessful in translating his mobility into a satisfactory set of social relationships at the new level. But ordinarily the identification bond continues to make the relationship important for the parents, while the child's bonds to the parents tend to be eroded to a remaining responsibility bond. So long as the child is more successful than his parents, identification with his achievements can remain a powerful bond throughout the life of his parents or other kin.

The resulting pattern of rationed and dutiful association with his parents by the mobile child, never fully satisfying their desires for closer association, is only an intensified version of a pattern of intergenerational relationships frequently found in the absence of mobility. But the greater potential gain from identification with a person of higher social position exaccerbates the imbalance in dominance. The subordination of parents to their adult child is especially fostered by mobility. When the economic discrepancy is great, the subordination can be further emphasized by financial aid from the children.

The unequal dominance, the performance of obligations based on duty divorced from profound sentiments of personal attachment, the increasing sophistication of the upwardly mobile person would contribute to a high conflict potential if the parents and child were in close and continuous interaction. Typically, then, the situation is one of high conflict potential accommodated through avoidance.

Two role relationships in which the conflict potential can and often

---

[26] Leichter and Mitchell, *op. cit.,* pp. 156–159.

does find concrete expression are the in-law relationship and the grand-parent role. If the new spouse comes from the higher stratum, relationships with her or him can provide a focus for resentments. If, as we have indicated in Chapter 18, women are the principal carriers of kinship sentiments, the relationship between mother and the mobile son's wife should be the most conflict-prone tie. Not only does weakening of reciprocity in the more intense mother-son relationship accentuate maternal tendencies to be jealous of the daughter-in-law; a snobbishness attributed to the daughter-in-law can provide a ready explanation for the merely reluctant attention of the son to his parents.

The grandparent role can be a major opportunity to restore some of the balance of intergenerational ties. The grandparent-grandchild tie supplies a new bond, bringing the mobile person briefly back into a somewhat mutual relationship with his parents. But in many instances the grand-parent represents either the lower-stratum values that the mobile person despises or the more rigid and archaic set of middle-class values that looks askance on the newer sophistication of the middle classes. In either case the socializing impact of the grandparent on the grandchild may be feared by the mobiles and may become a new focus for conflict.

Summary of Chapters 18 and 19

Because families rather than individuals are the units of stratification, implementation of the appropriate class position becomes a family function and a basis for interpreting and evaluating family behavior. A common concern for class position becomes a family bond, leads to role differentiation according to how husband and wife respectively can contribute to maintenance of class position, supplies another dimension of identity-involvement leading to conflict, and contributes to role polarization between parents and children.

Among the many stratum differences in family bonds are the following: lower middle class emphasis on respectability, and limitation of a large social world in the upper middle class to married couples are incentives to marital persistence; economic bonds vary in kind, mutuality, and direction at different levels; the more futuristic orientation of the middle classes facilitates the crescive bond of incomplete action; interlocking roles become especially important in lower middle and working strata where activities and opportunities outside the family are more restricted; adjusted communication and response develop idiosyncratically at all levels, but are facilitated by upper middle class emphasis on intimacy; kinship support of family bonds is strong in ethnic groups at any level, but tends otherwise to be more effective at higher than at lower levels. Although middle classes are more explicitly equalitarian and look with less favor on overt coercion to implement authority, their families are generally under tighter control than working class families, especially with respect to children. The greater acceptability of open conflict in working class families may not indicate more actual conflict, though both conflict and harmonization can reach a more intense pitch in middle class families, tending toward cumulative rather than chronic patterns. Socialization in the working strata is more custodial and restrictive in emphasis, more concerned with visible behavior, and places greater emphasis on sex typing; while middle classes employ more planned socializing efforts and positive incentives, are more concerned with the child's inner self, and use children more as vehicles for the projection of incompletely satisfied parental ambitions. The high rate of mother-centered families among impoverished American Negroes has been explained on the basis of a matriarchal tradition born during slavery, the direct effects of racial discrimination, and the culture of poverty that characterizes much of the underclass.

Interclass marriage brings divergent meanings for the same gestures and different views of the rules governing family interaction, though some forms of noncongruancy facilitate harmony, and futuristic class perspectives mute the effect of class origins. The preponderance of prestige identification in American stratification makes for considerable compatibility between family life and intergenerational mobility, though reconciliation of the two is difficult in pockets and during periods of heightened class consciousness. Five theories are used to explain how upward mobility aspirations are generated and supported in the family: a *disjuncture* between private identity and objective class setting means that one or both parents socialize children according to the former rather than the latter; family *default* opens the way for crucial socialization by teachers and others who do not share the neighborhood class perspective; maladjustment to his class environment leads the child to seek *escape* to a different stratum; if community *consensus* on the value of ambition is strong enough, the family gains from the mobility of one of its members; an intense *need for achievement* may be produced by certain socializing procedures employed in a family where father is present and respected but mother is definitely in charge of the children. Family and community support for mobility probably mean a short-term strengthening of family bonds, though intensified bonding between mother and son is often observed. Upward mobility strengthens the child's position in family decision making, and his socialization to a different subculture contributes to the gap in understanding and interest between parent and adolescent. Relationships with kin may be difficult, especially with "in-laws" and grandparents representing divergent strata.

INDEX

INDEX